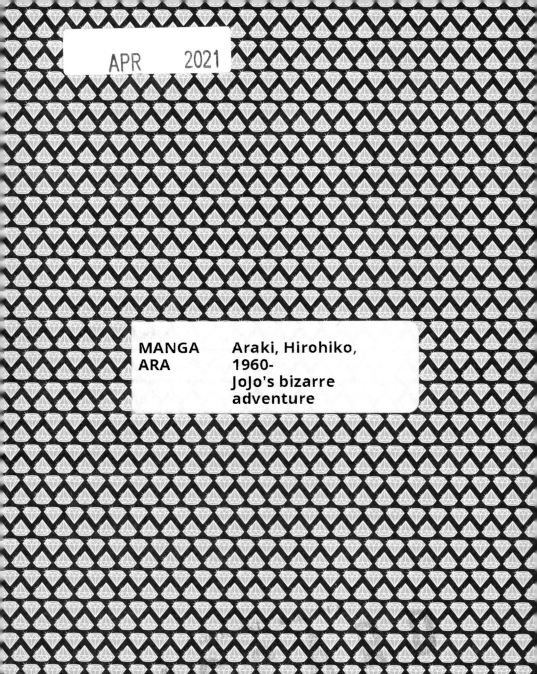

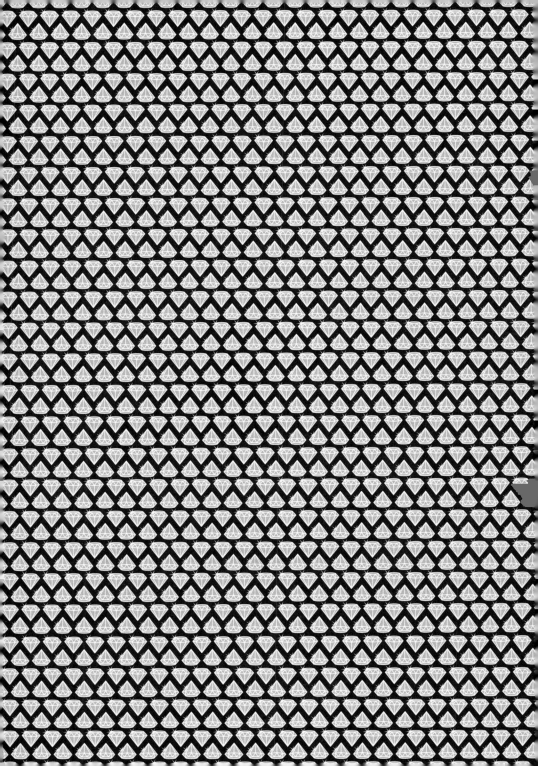

HIROHIKO ARAKI

JoJo's BIZARRE ADVENTURE

PART 4 ★ DIAMOND IS UNBREAKABLE

5

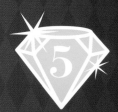

JoJo's
BIZARRE ADVENTURE

PART 4 ★ DIAMOND IS UNBREAKABLE

CONTENTS

CHAPTER 77

YOSHIKAGE KIRA WANTS TO LIVE QUIETLY, PART 1

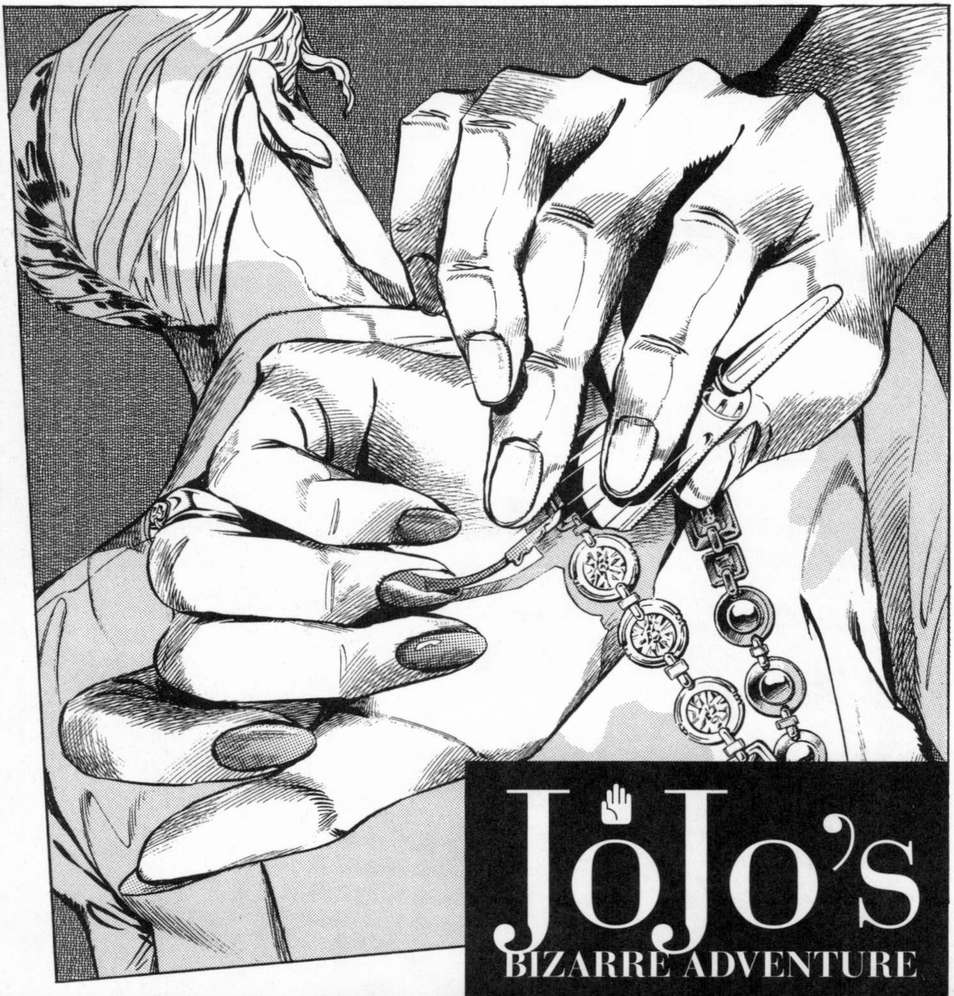
JoJo's
BIZARRE ADVENTURE

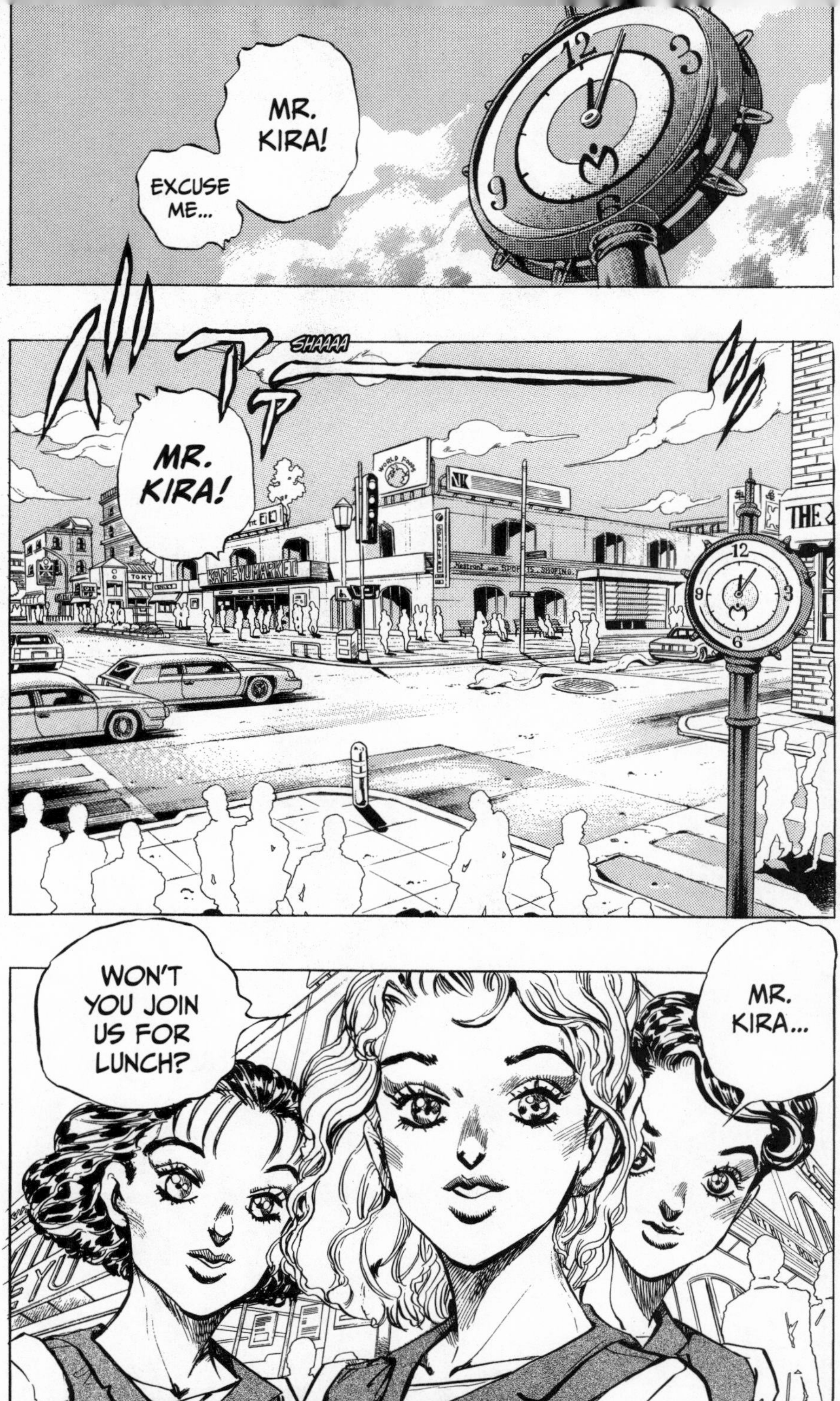
MR. KIRA!
EXCUSE ME...
SHAAAA
MR. KIRA!
MR. KIRA...
WON'T YOU JOIN US FOR LUNCH?

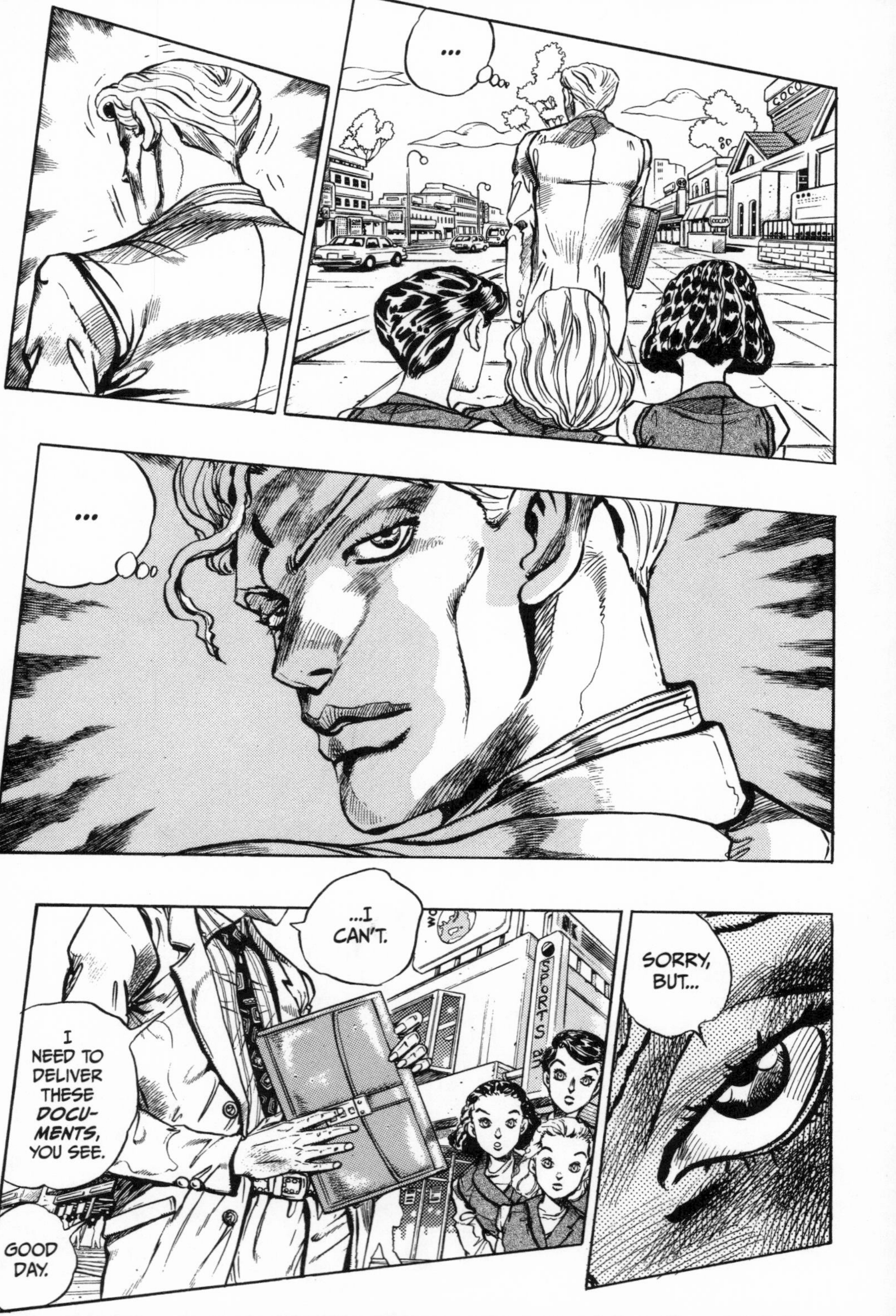
...
...
SORRY, BUT...
...I CAN'T.
I NEED TO DELIVER THESE *DOCUMENTS*, YOU SEE.
GOOD DAY.

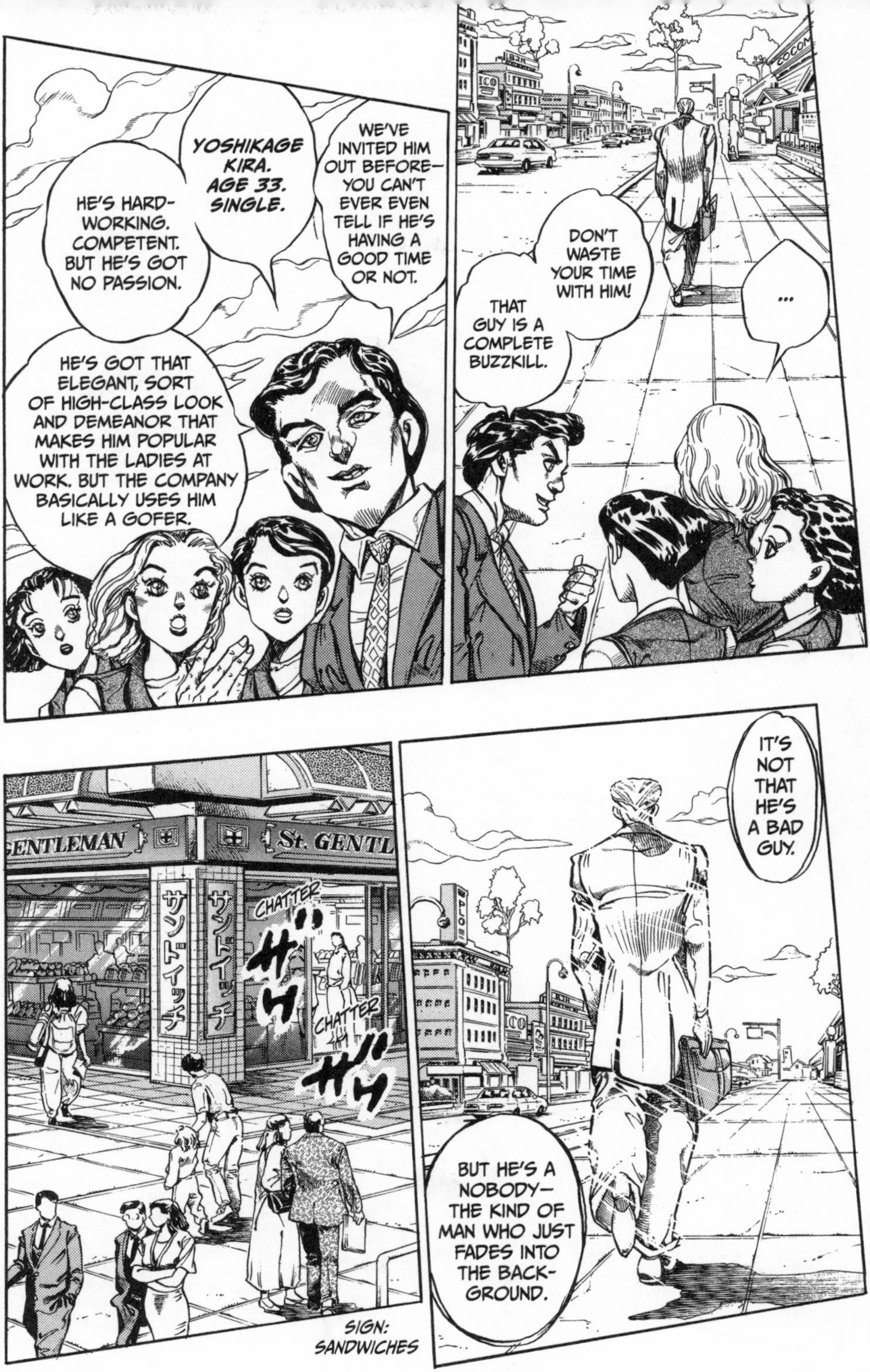
...
DON'T WASTE YOUR TIME WITH HIM!
THAT GUY IS A COMPLETE BUZZKILL.
WE'VE INVITED HIM OUT BEFORE—YOU CAN'T EVER EVEN TELL IF HE'S HAVING A GOOD TIME OR NOT.
YOSHIKAGE KIRA. AGE 33. SINGLE.
HE'S HARD-WORKING. COMPETENT. BUT HE'S GOT NO PASSION.
HE'S GOT THAT ELEGANT, SORT OF HIGH-CLASS LOOK AND DEMEANOR THAT MAKES HIM POPULAR WITH THE LADIES AT WORK. BUT THE COMPANY BASICALLY USES HIM LIKE A GOFER.
IT'S NOT THAT HE'S A BAD GUY.
BUT HE'S A NOBODY—THE KIND OF MAN WHO JUST FADES INTO THE BACK-GROUND.
ENTLEMAN
St. GENTL
サンドイッチ
サンドイッチ
CHATTER
ザワ
CHATTER
ザワ
SIGN: SANDWICHES

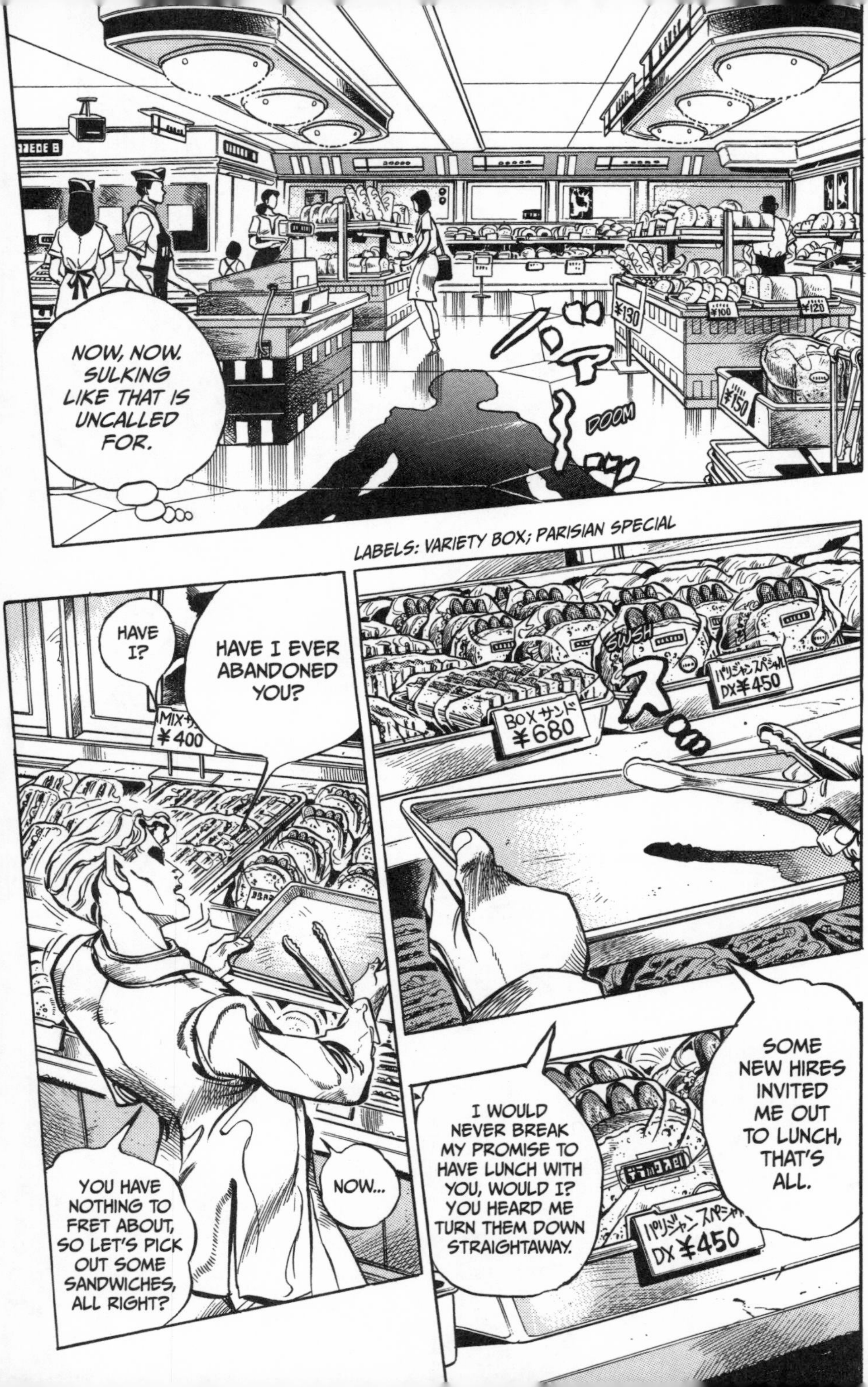
¥130
¥100
¥120
¥150
DOOM
NOW, NOW. SULKING LIKE THAT IS UNCALLED FOR.
LABELS: VARIETY BOX; PARISIAN SPECIAL
SWISH
パリジャンスペシャル DX ¥450
BOX サンド ¥680
SOME NEW HIRES INVITED ME OUT TO LUNCH, THAT'S ALL.
I WOULD NEVER BREAK MY PROMISE TO HAVE LUNCH WITH YOU, WOULD I? YOU HEARD ME TURN THEM DOWN STRAIGHTAWAY.
DX ¥450
HAVE I EVER ABANDONED YOU?
HAVE I?
¥400
NOW...
YOU HAVE NOTHING TO FRET ABOUT, SO LET'S PICK OUT SOME SANDWICHES, ALL RIGHT?

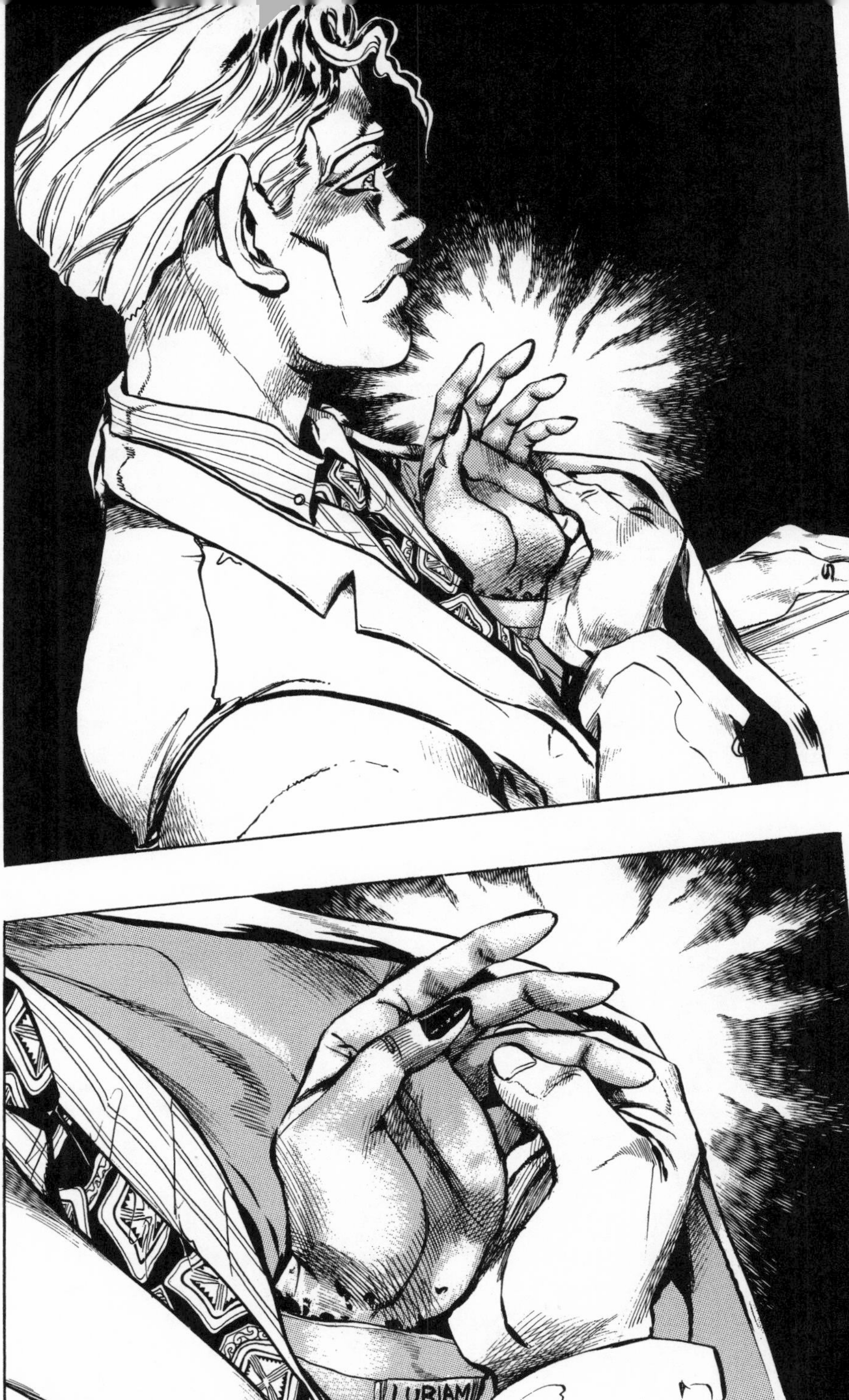
LUBIAM

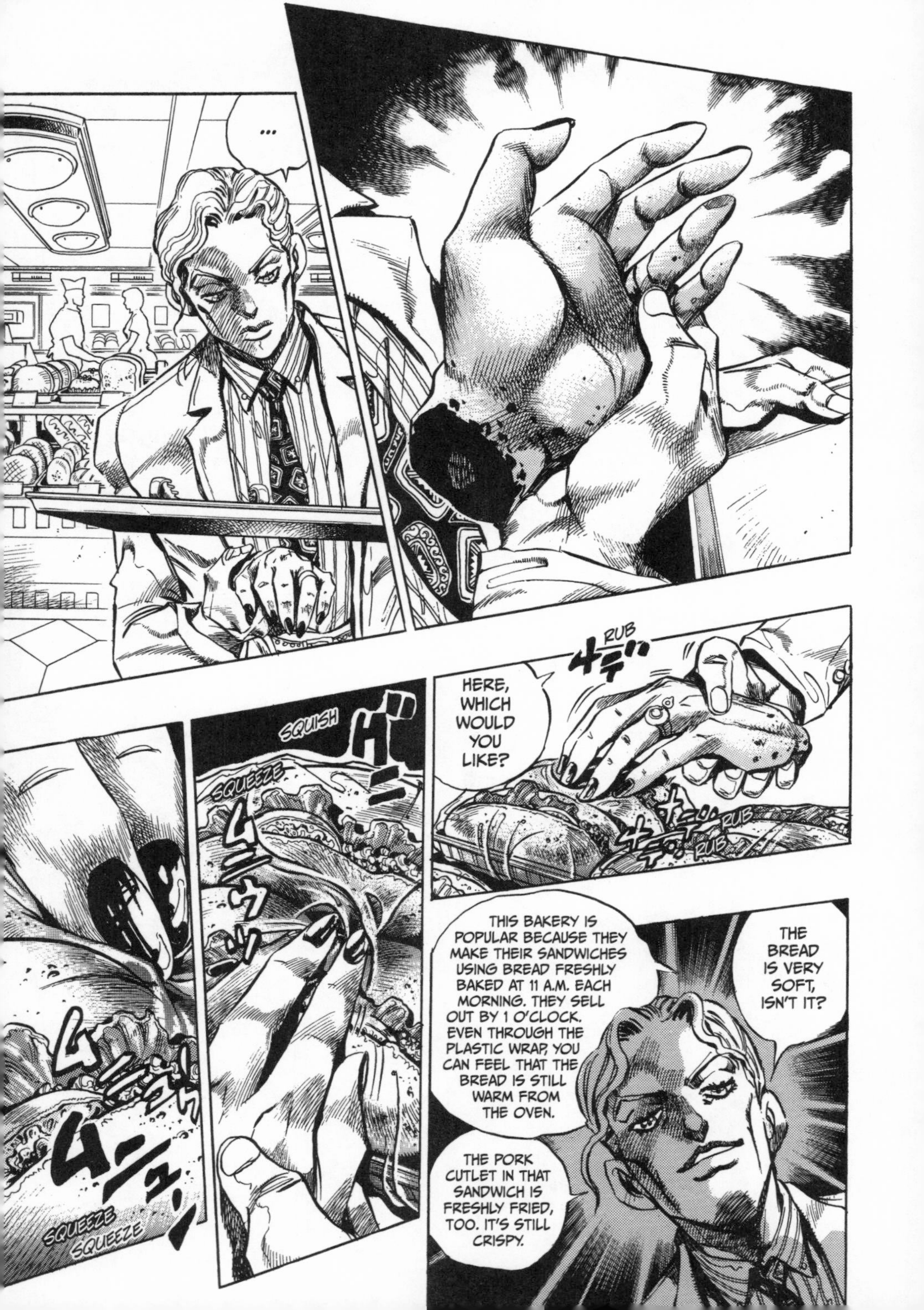
...
RUB
HERE, WHICH WOULD YOU LIKE?
RUB
RUB
THE BREAD IS VERY SOFT, ISN'T IT?
THIS BAKERY IS POPULAR BECAUSE THEY MAKE THEIR SANDWICHES USING BREAD FRESHLY BAKED AT 11 A.M. EACH MORNING. THEY SELL OUT BY 1 O'CLOCK. EVEN THROUGH THE PLASTIC WRAP, YOU CAN FEEL THAT THE BREAD IS STILL WARM FROM THE OVEN.
THE PORK CUTLET IN THAT SANDWICH IS FRESHLY FRIED, TOO. IT'S STILL CRISPY.
SQUISH
SQUEEZE
SQUEEZE
SQUEEZE

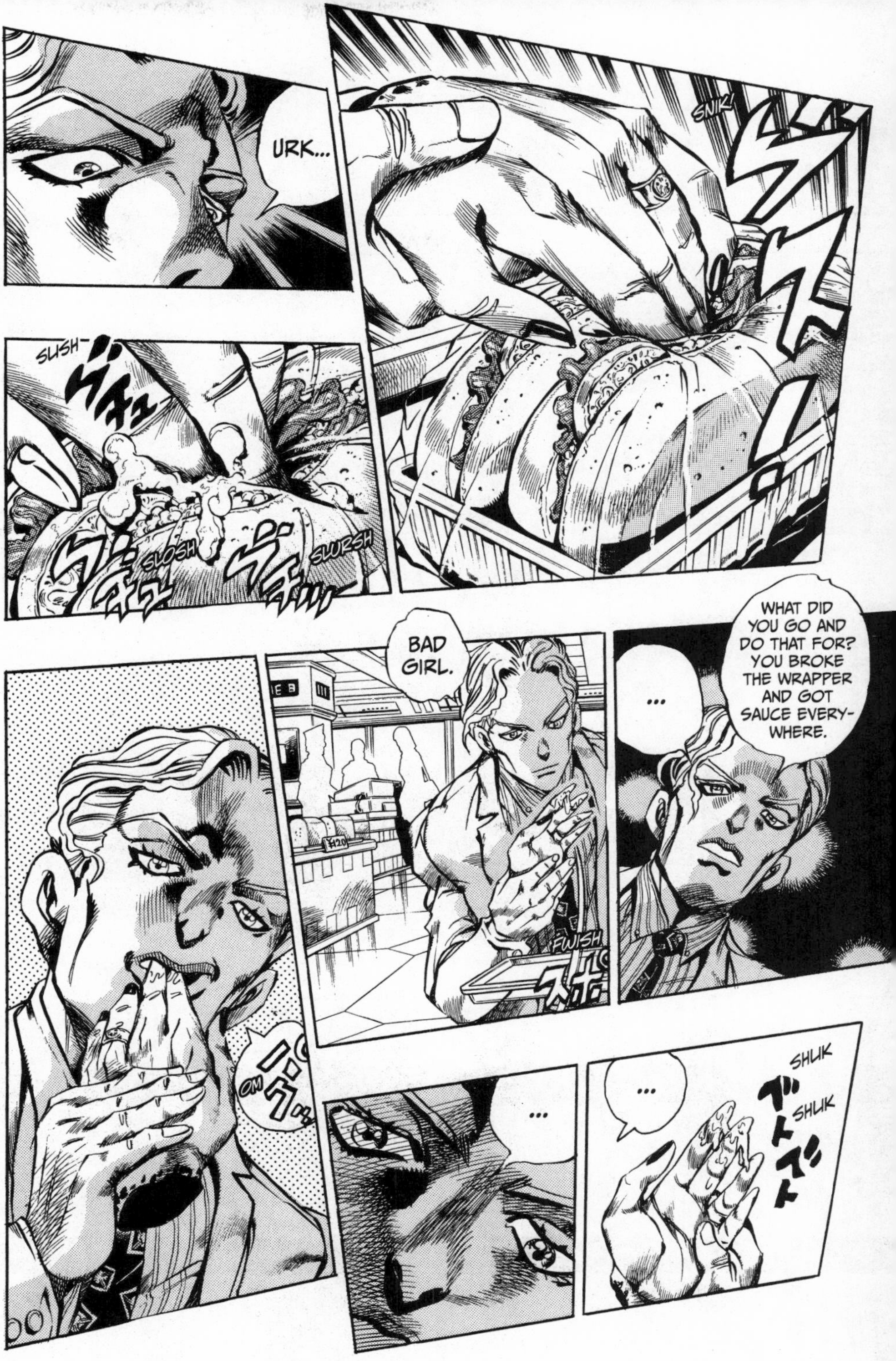

SNIK!
URK...
SUSH-
SLOSH
SLURSH
WHAT DID YOU GO AND DO THAT FOR? YOU BROKE THE WRAPPER AND GOT SAUCE EVERYWHERE.
...
BAD GIRL.
FWISH
SHUK
SHUK
...
...
OM

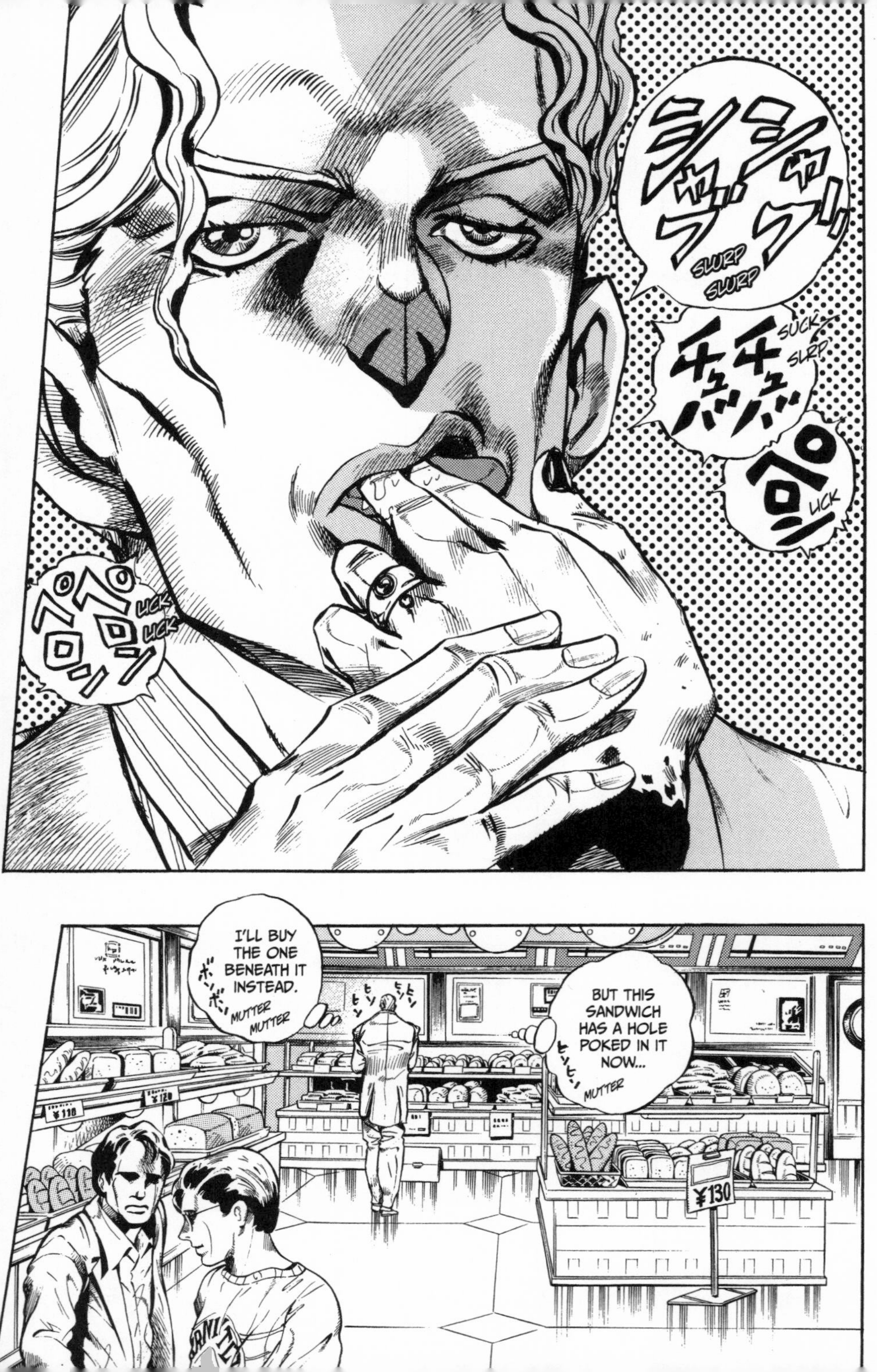
SLURP SLURP
SUCK SLRP
LICK
LICK LICK
BUT THIS SANDWICH HAS A HOLE POKED IN IT NOW...
MUTTER
¥130
I'LL BUY THE ONE BENEATH IT INSTEAD.
MUTTER MUTTER
¥120
¥110

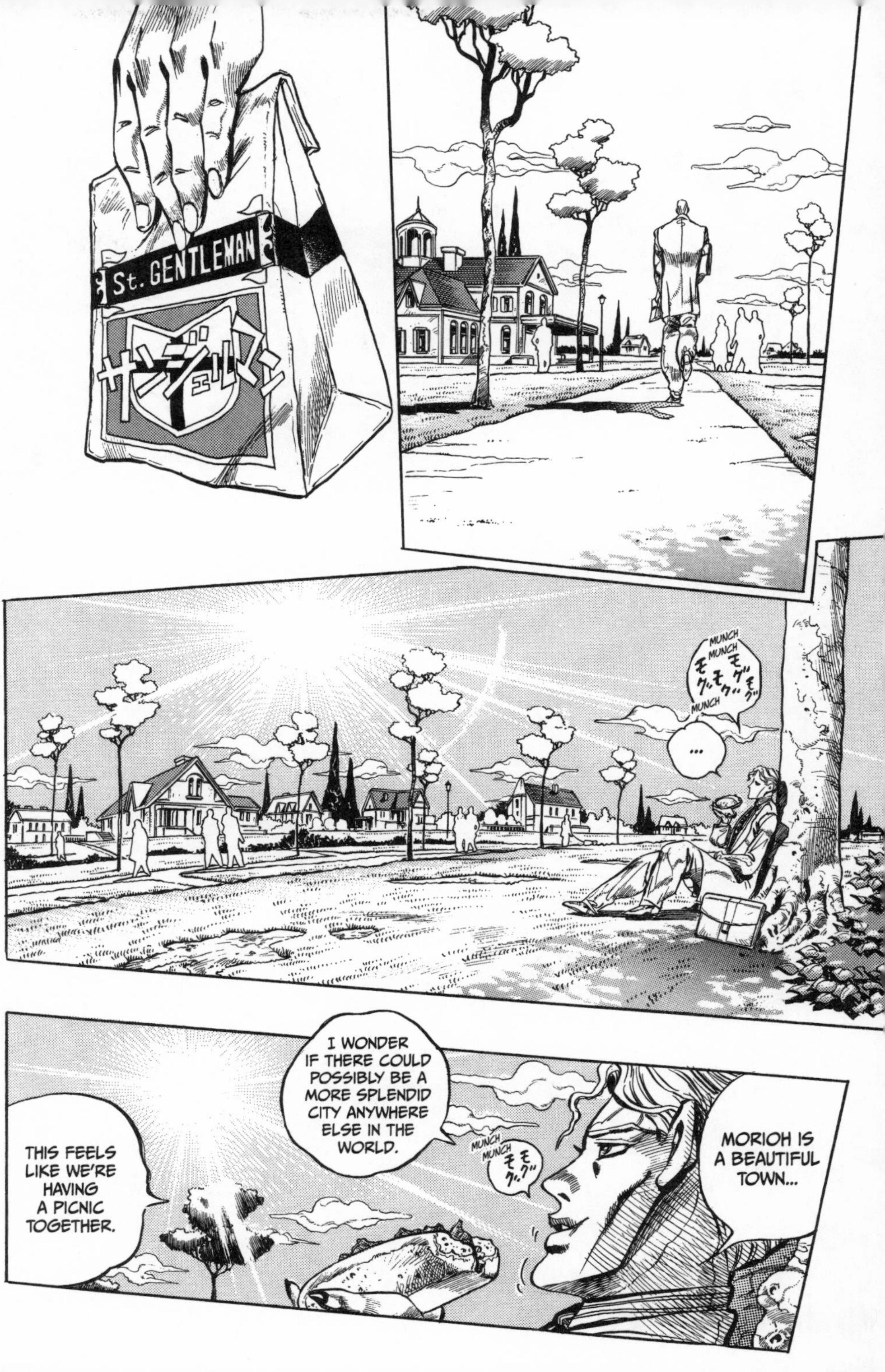
St. GENTLEMAN
サンジェルマン
MUNCH MUNCH MUNCH
モグモグモグ
...
MORIOH IS A BEAUTIFUL TOWN...
MUNCH MUNCH
モグ
I WONDER IF THERE COULD POSSIBLY BE A MORE SPLENDID CITY ANYWHERE ELSE IN THE WORLD.
THIS FEELS LIKE WE'RE HAVING A PICNIC TOGETHER.

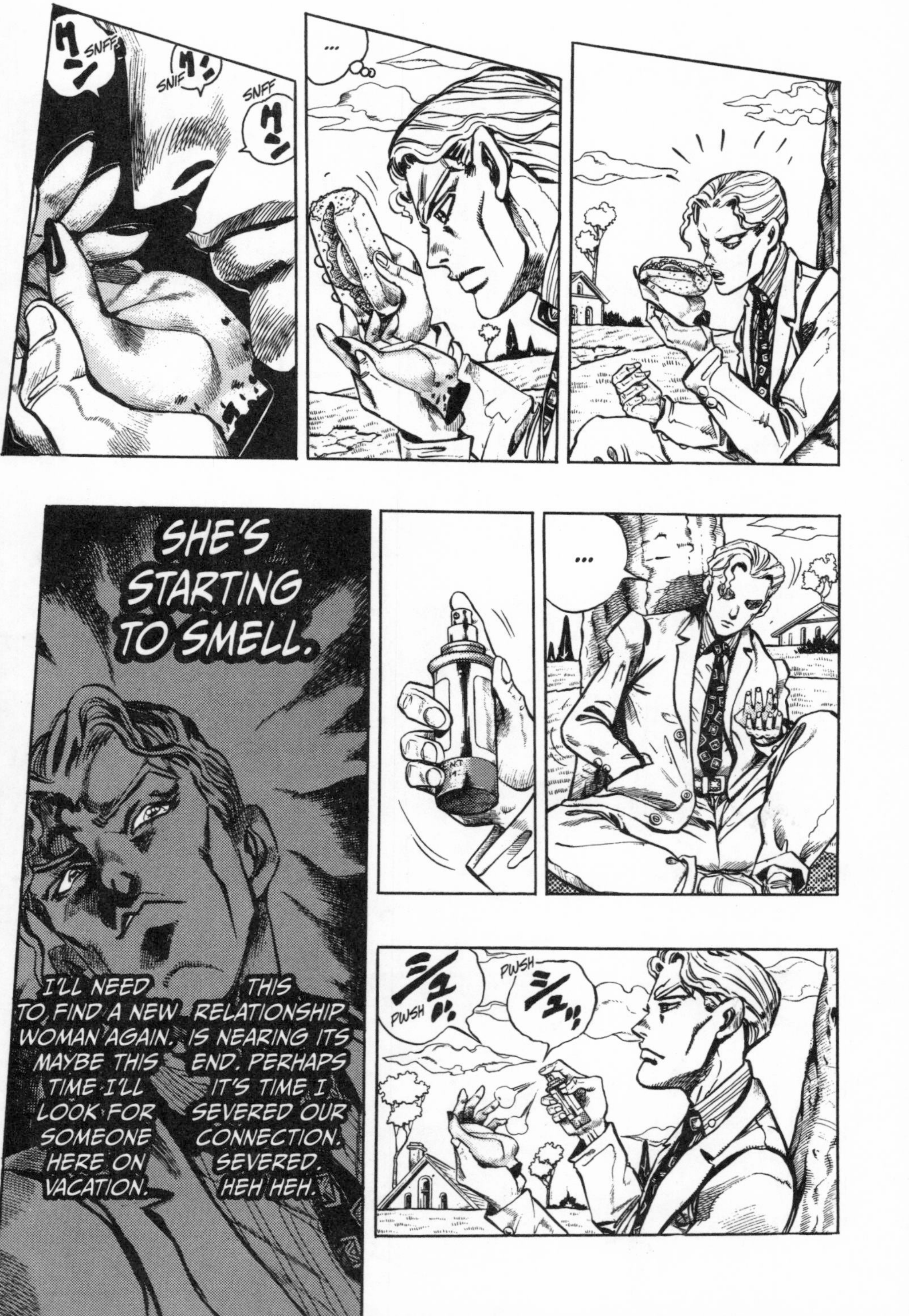
...
SNFF
SNIF
SNFF
...
PWSH
PWSH
SHE'S STARTING TO SMELL.
THIS RELATIONSHIP IS NEARING ITS END. PERHAPS IT'S TIME I SEVERED OUR CONNECTION. SEVERED. HEH HEH.
I'LL NEED TO FIND A NEW WOMAN AGAIN. MAYBE THIS TIME I'LL LOOK FOR SOMEONE HERE ON VACATION.

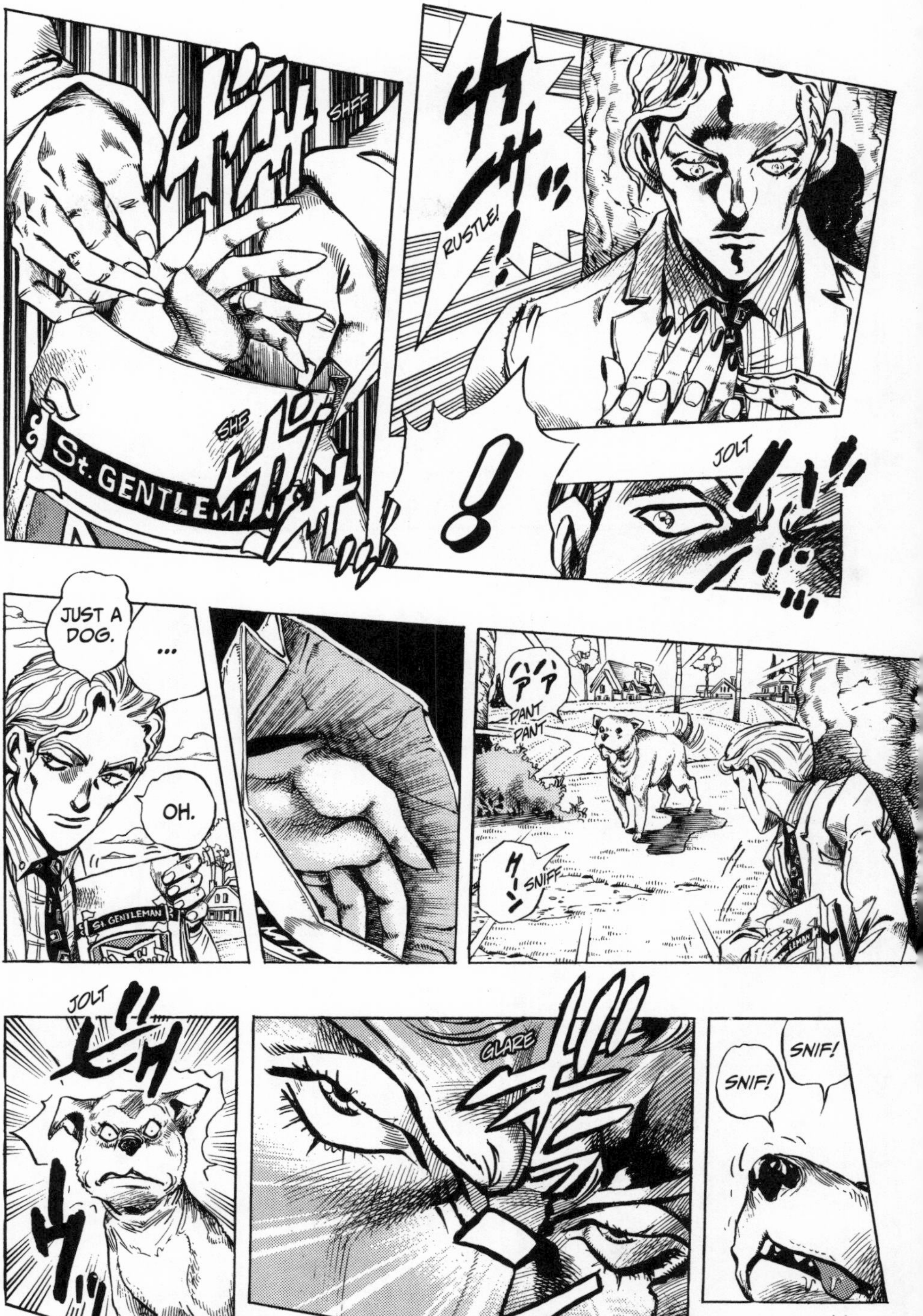
RUSTLE!
JOLT
SHFF
SHF
PANT PANT
SNIFF
JUST A DOG.
...
OH.
SNIF!
SNIF!
GLARE
JOLT

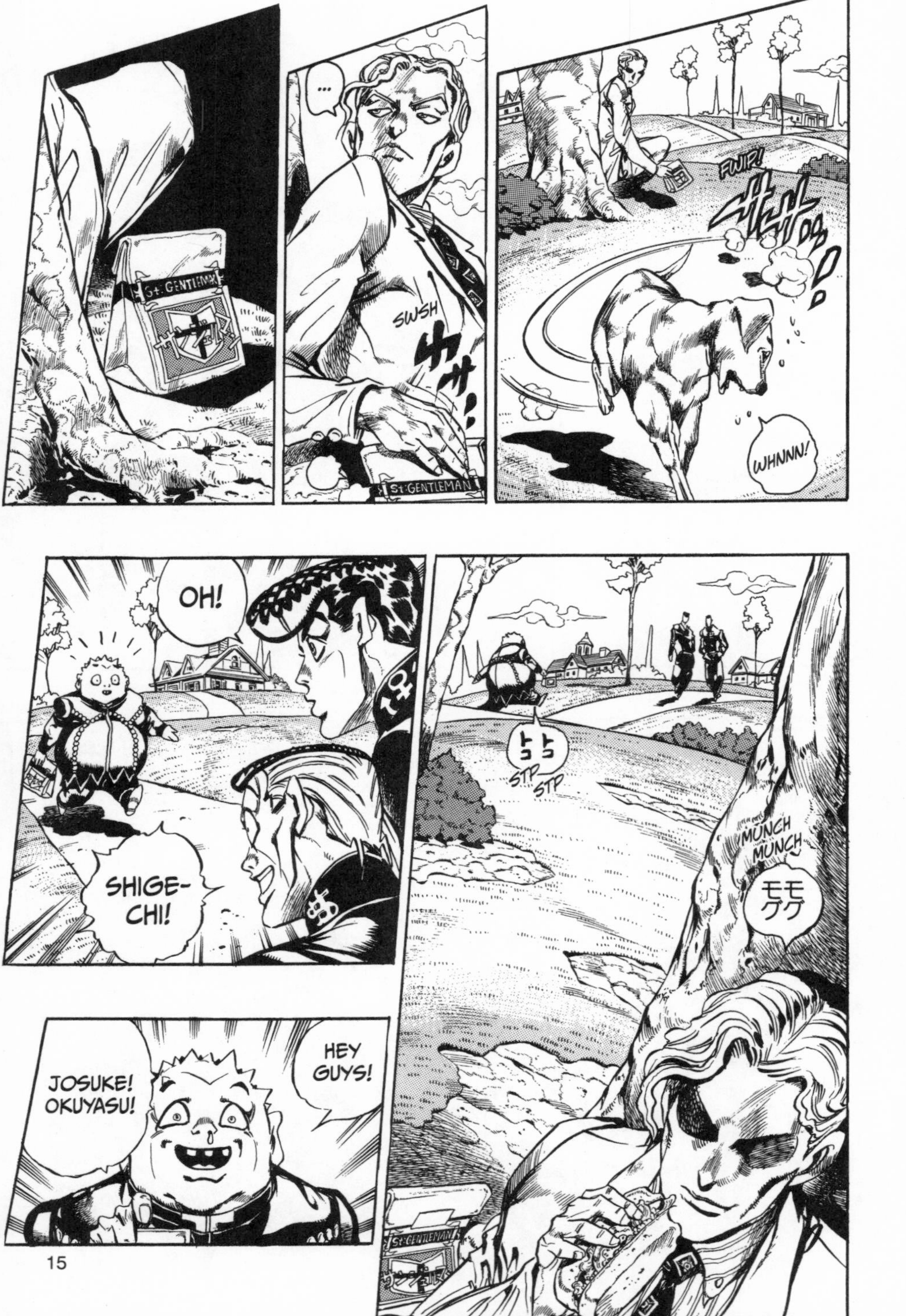
FWIP!
WHNNN!
...
SWSH
St. GENTLEMAN
St. GENTLEMAN
STP STP
MUNCH MUNCH
St. GENTLEMAN
OH!
SHIGE-CHI!
HEY GUYS!
JOSUKE! OKUYASU!

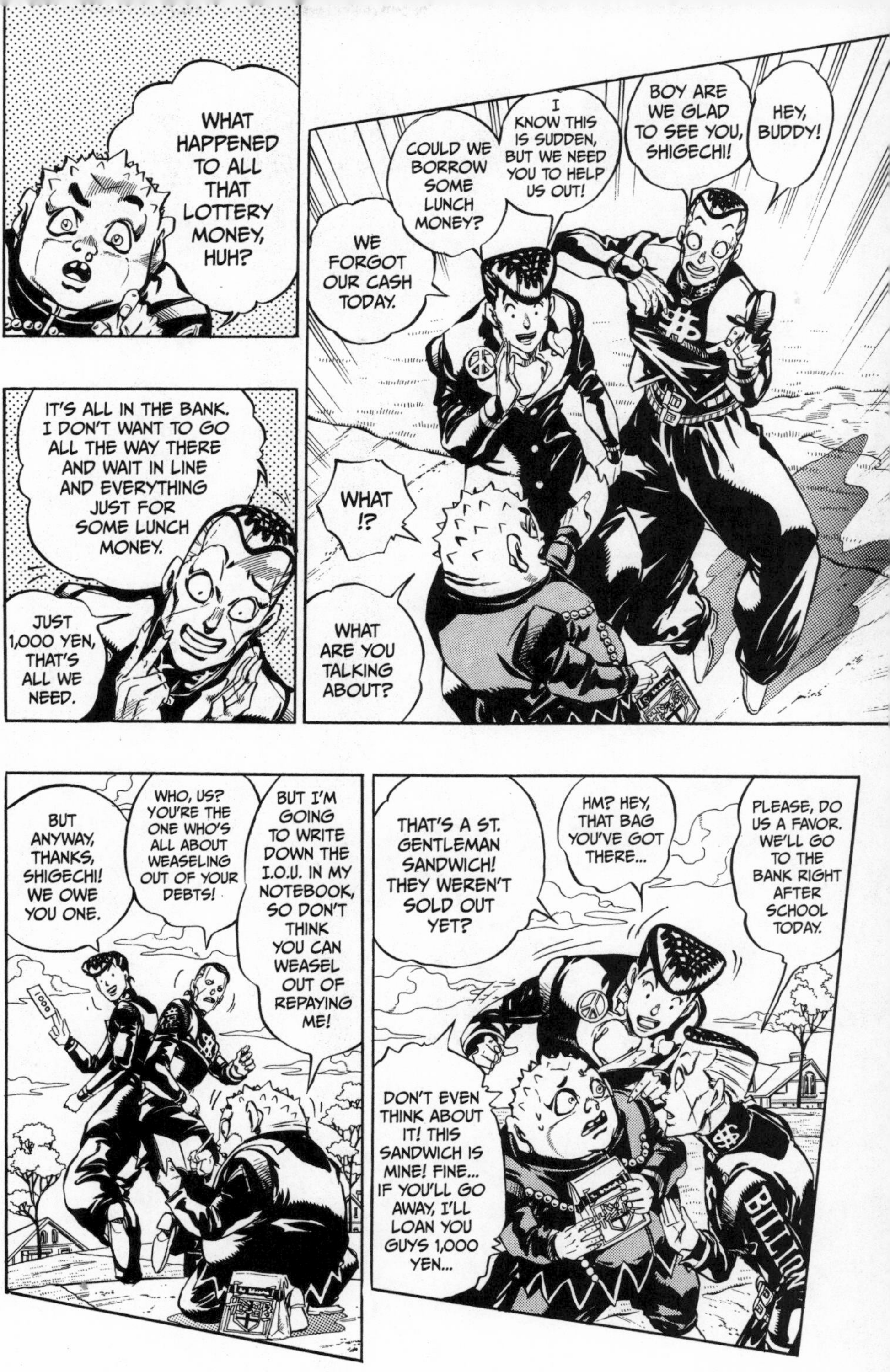
HEY, BUDDY!
BOY ARE WE GLAD TO SEE YOU, SHIGECHI!
I KNOW THIS IS SUDDEN, BUT WE NEED YOU TO HELP US OUT!
COULD WE BORROW SOME LUNCH MONEY?
WE FORGOT OUR CASH TODAY.
WHAT !?
WHAT ARE YOU TALKING ABOUT?
WHAT HAPPENED TO ALL THAT LOTTERY MONEY, HUH?
IT'S ALL IN THE BANK. I DON'T WANT TO GO ALL THE WAY THERE AND WAIT IN LINE AND EVERYTHING JUST FOR SOME LUNCH MONEY.
JUST 1,000 YEN, THAT'S ALL WE NEED.
PLEASE, DO US A FAVOR. WE'LL GO TO THE BANK RIGHT AFTER SCHOOL TODAY.
HM? HEY, THAT BAG YOU'VE GOT THERE...
THAT'S A ST. GENTLEMAN SANDWICH! THEY WEREN'T SOLD OUT YET?
DON'T EVEN THINK ABOUT IT! THIS SANDWICH IS MINE! FINE... IF YOU'LL GO AWAY, I'LL LOAN YOU GUYS 1,000 YEN...
BUT I'M GOING TO WRITE DOWN THE I.O.U. IN MY NOTEBOOK, SO DON'T THINK YOU CAN WEASEL OUT OF REPAYING ME!
WHO, US? YOU'RE THE ONE WHO'S ALL ABOUT WEASELING OUT OF YOUR DEBTS!
BUT ANYWAY, THANKS, SHIGECHI! WE OWE YOU ONE.
1000
BILLION

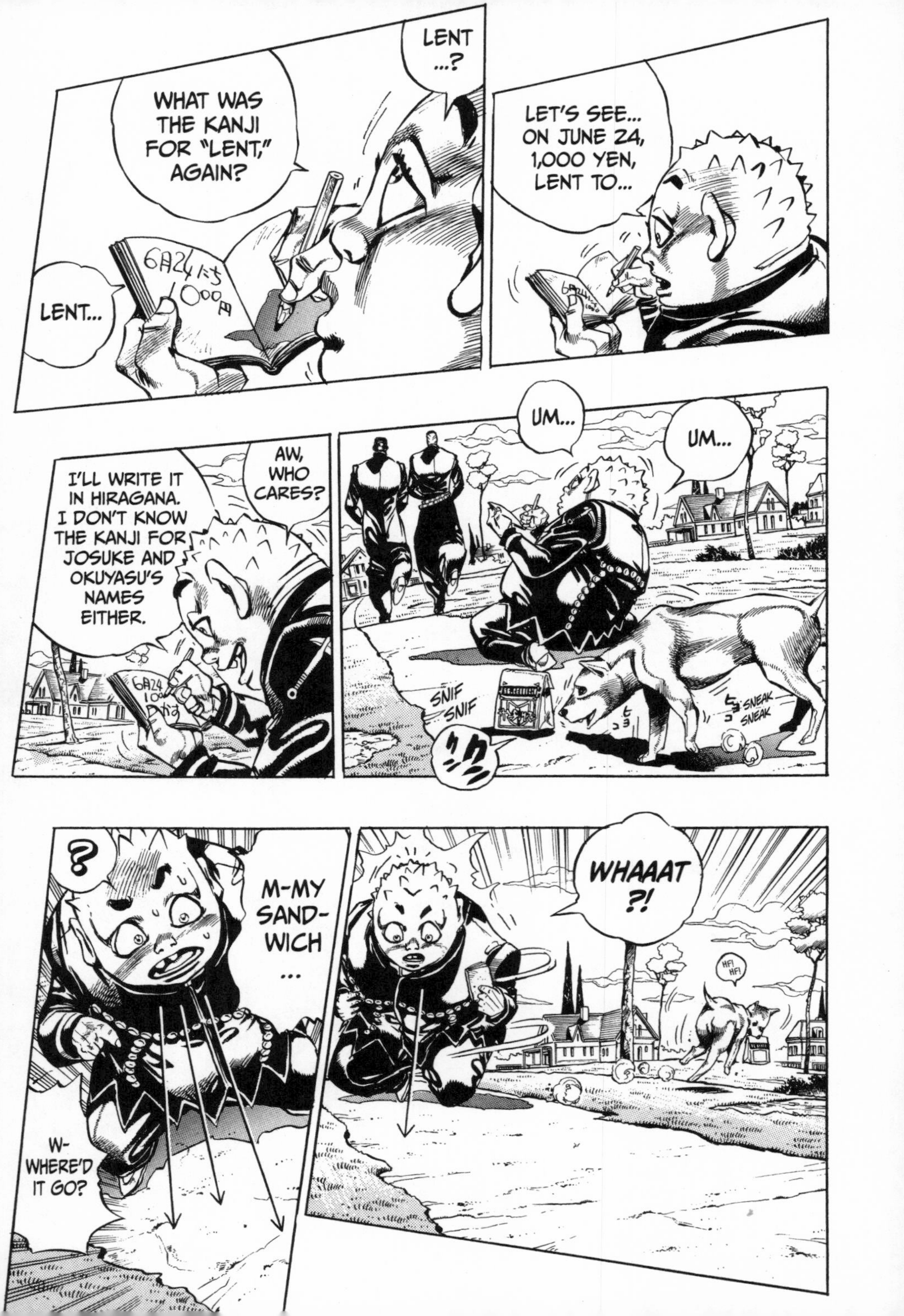
LET'S SEE... ON JUNE 24, 1,000 YEN, LENT TO...
LENT ...?
WHAT WAS THE KANJI FOR "LENT," AGAIN?
LENT...
UM...
UM...
SNIF SNIF
SNEAK SNEAK
AW, WHO CARES?
I'LL WRITE IT IN HIRAGANA. I DON'T KNOW THE KANJI FOR JOSUKE AND OKUYASU'S NAMES EITHER.
WHAAAT ?!
HF! HF!
?
M-MY SAND-WICH ...
W-WHERE'D IT GO?

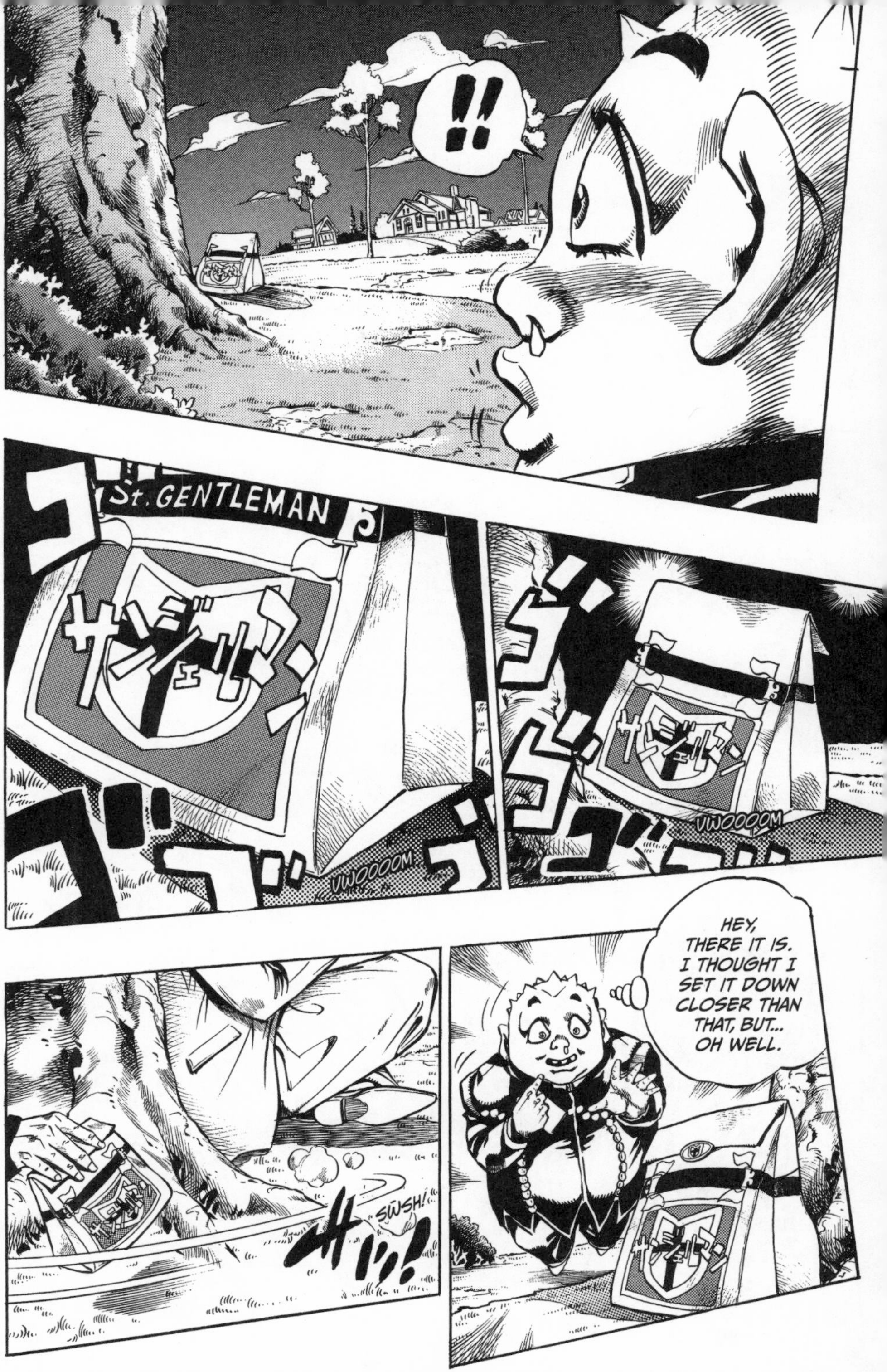
!!
UWOOOOM
St. GENTLEMAN 5
サンジェルマン
UWOOOOM
HEY, THERE IT IS. I THOUGHT I SET IT DOWN CLOSER THAN THAT, BUT... OH WELL.
SWSH!

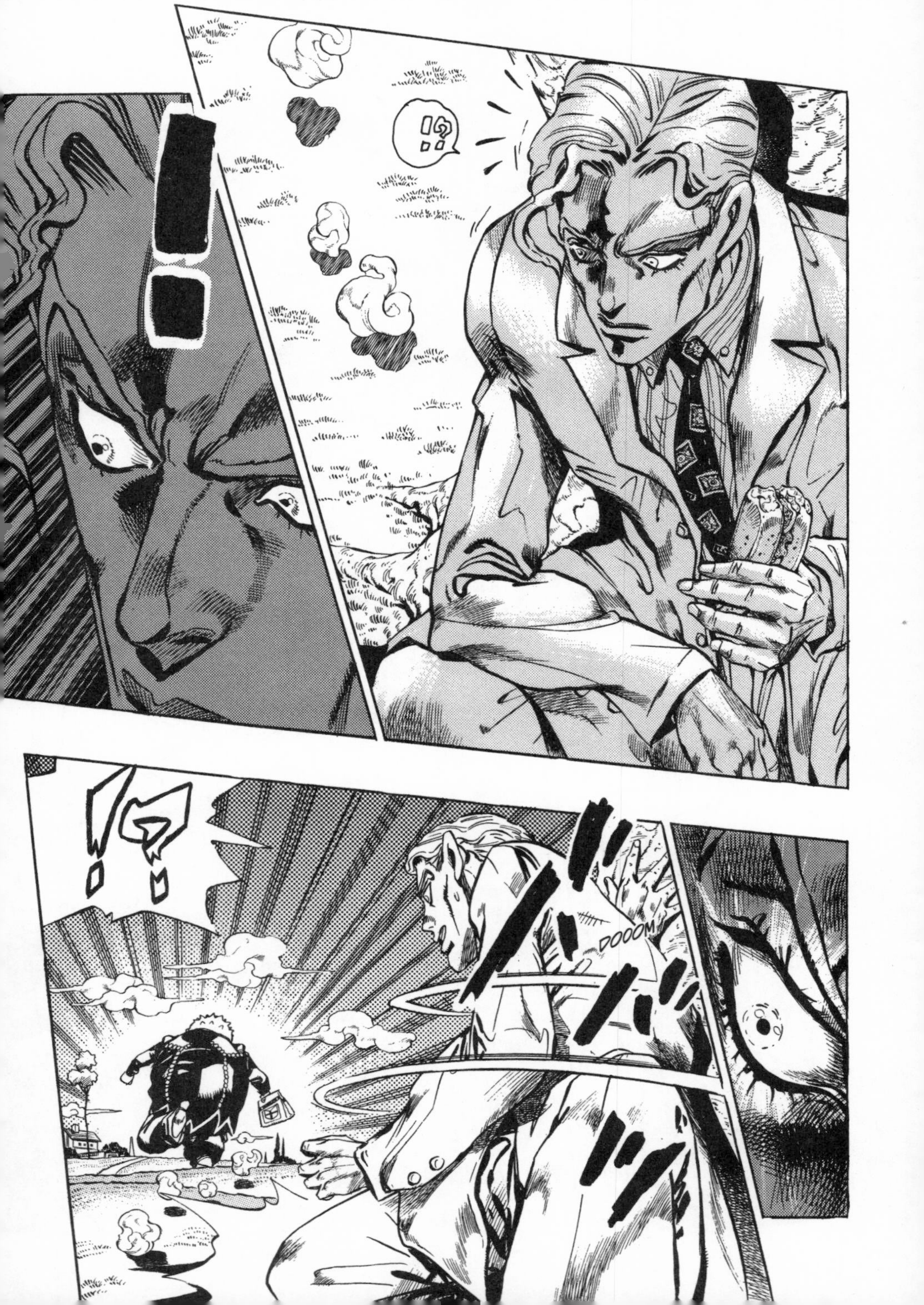

!?
DOOOM

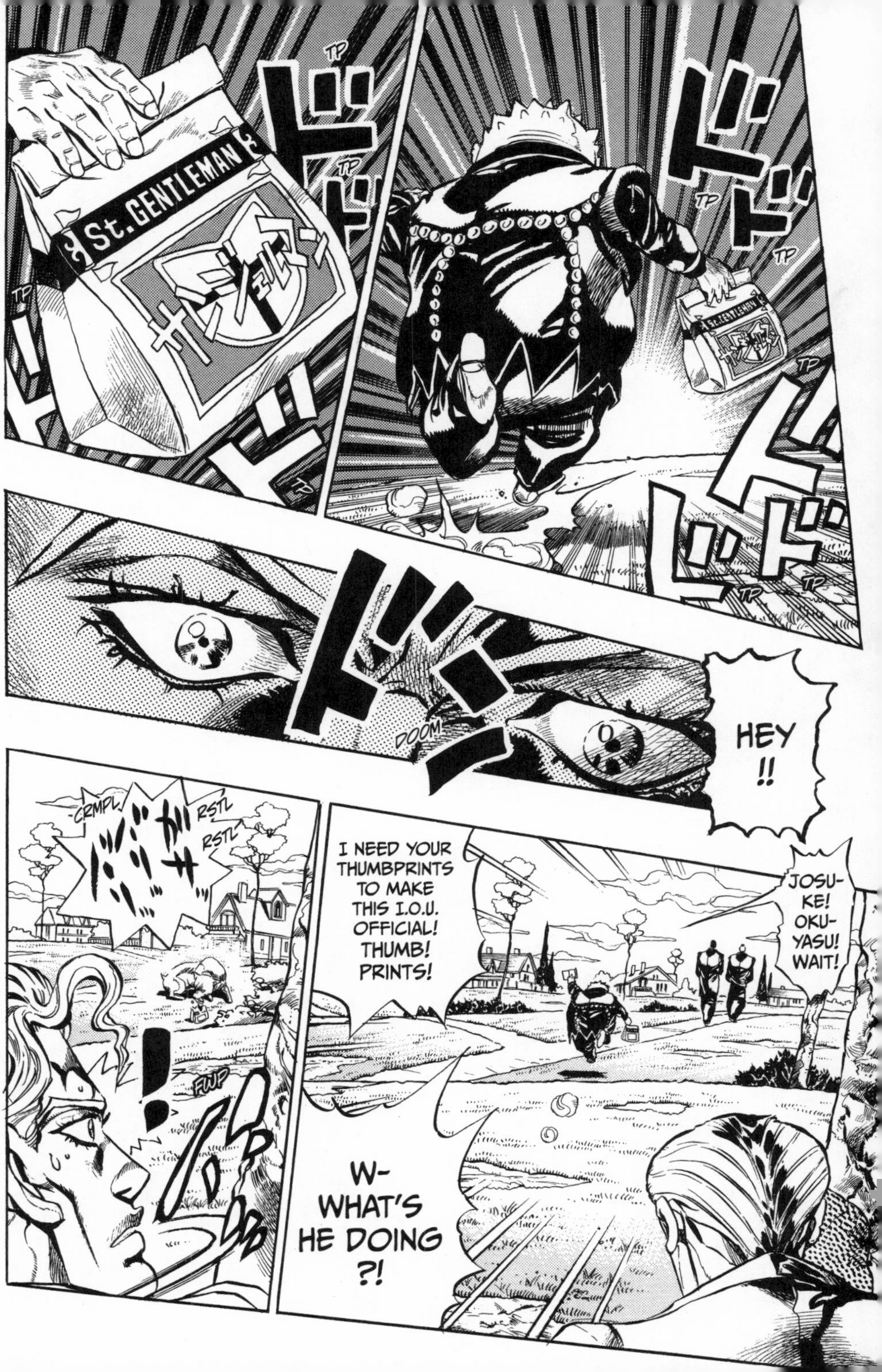
TP
TP
TP
TP
St. GENTLEMAN
TP
TP
TP
St. GENTLEMAN
TP
TP
TP
HEY !!
DOOM
JOSU-KE! OKU-YASU! WAIT!
I NEED YOUR THUMBPRINTS TO MAKE THIS I.O.U. OFFICIAL! THUMB! PRINTS!
CRMPL
RSTL
RSTL
FWUP
W- WHAT'S HE DOING ?!

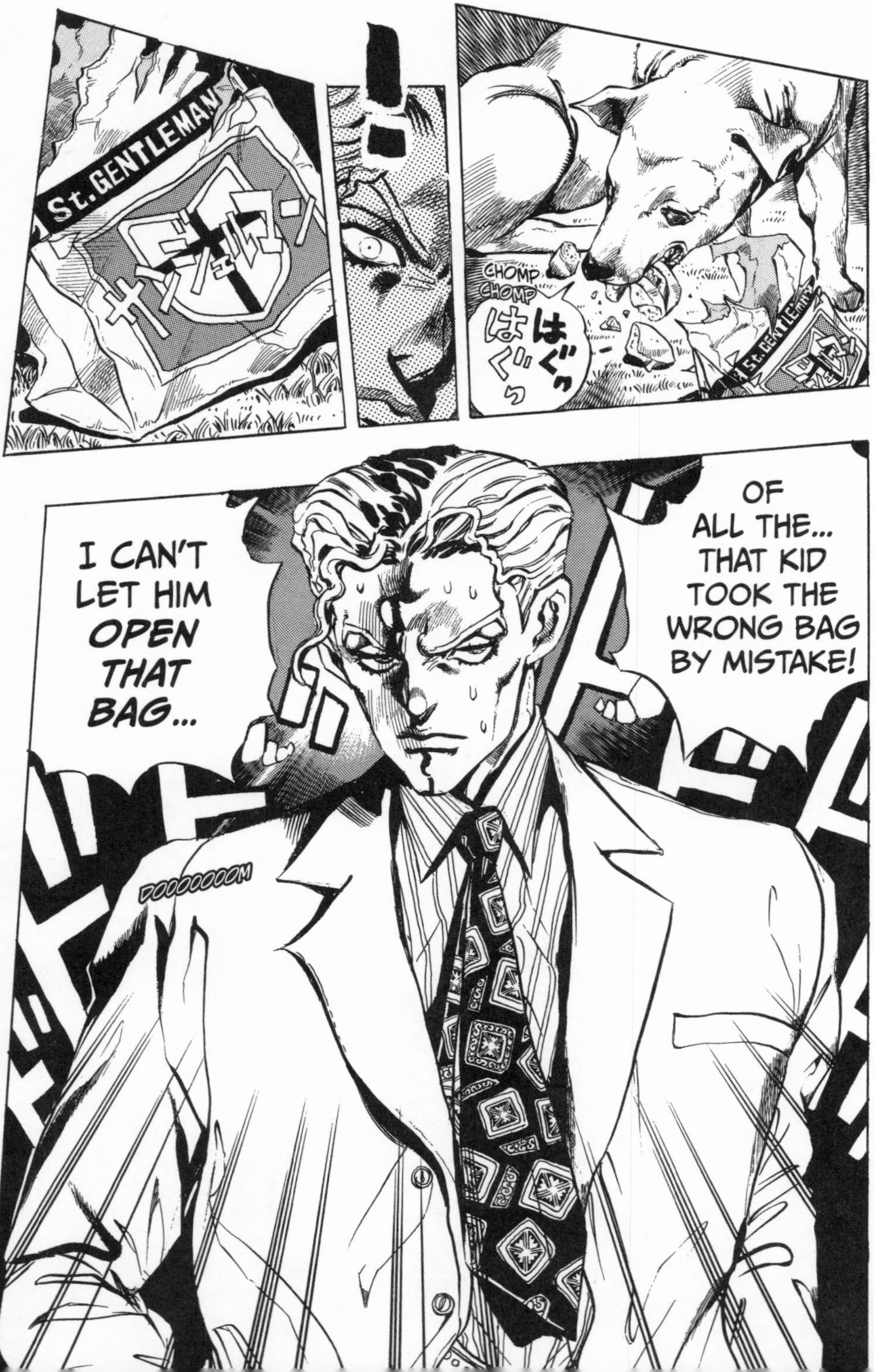
CHOMP CHOMP
はぐっ はぐっ
St. GENTLEMAN
St.GENTLEMAN
OF ALL THE... THAT KID TOOK THE WRONG BAG BY MISTAKE!
I CAN'T LET HIM OPEN THAT BAG...
DOOOOOOOOM

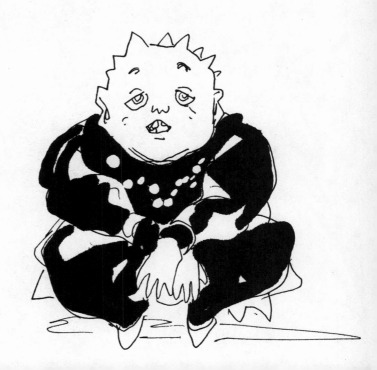

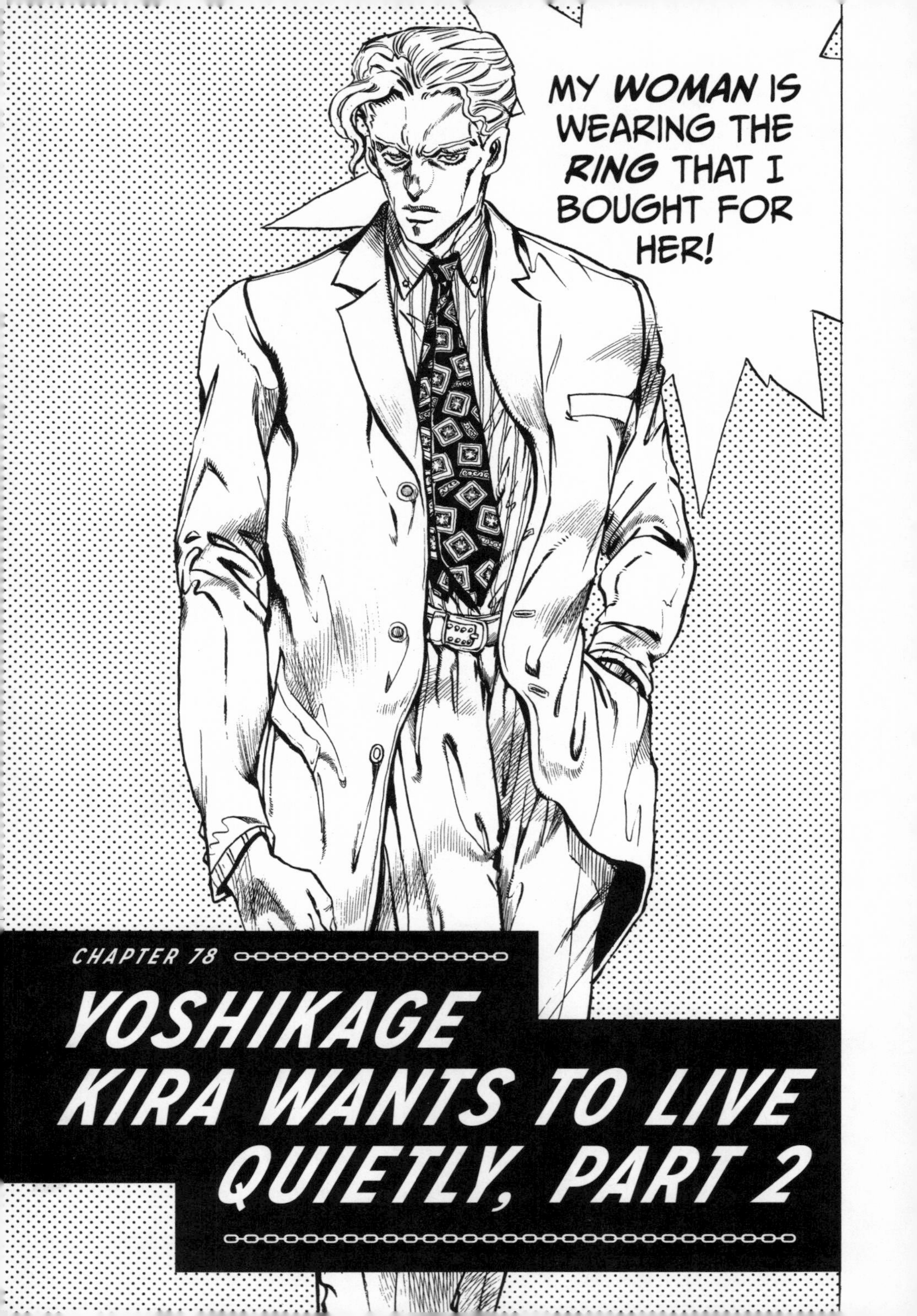
MY WOMAN IS WEARING THE RING THAT I BOUGHT FOR HER!

CHAPTER 78

YOSHIKAGE KIRA WANTS TO LIVE QUIETLY, PART 2

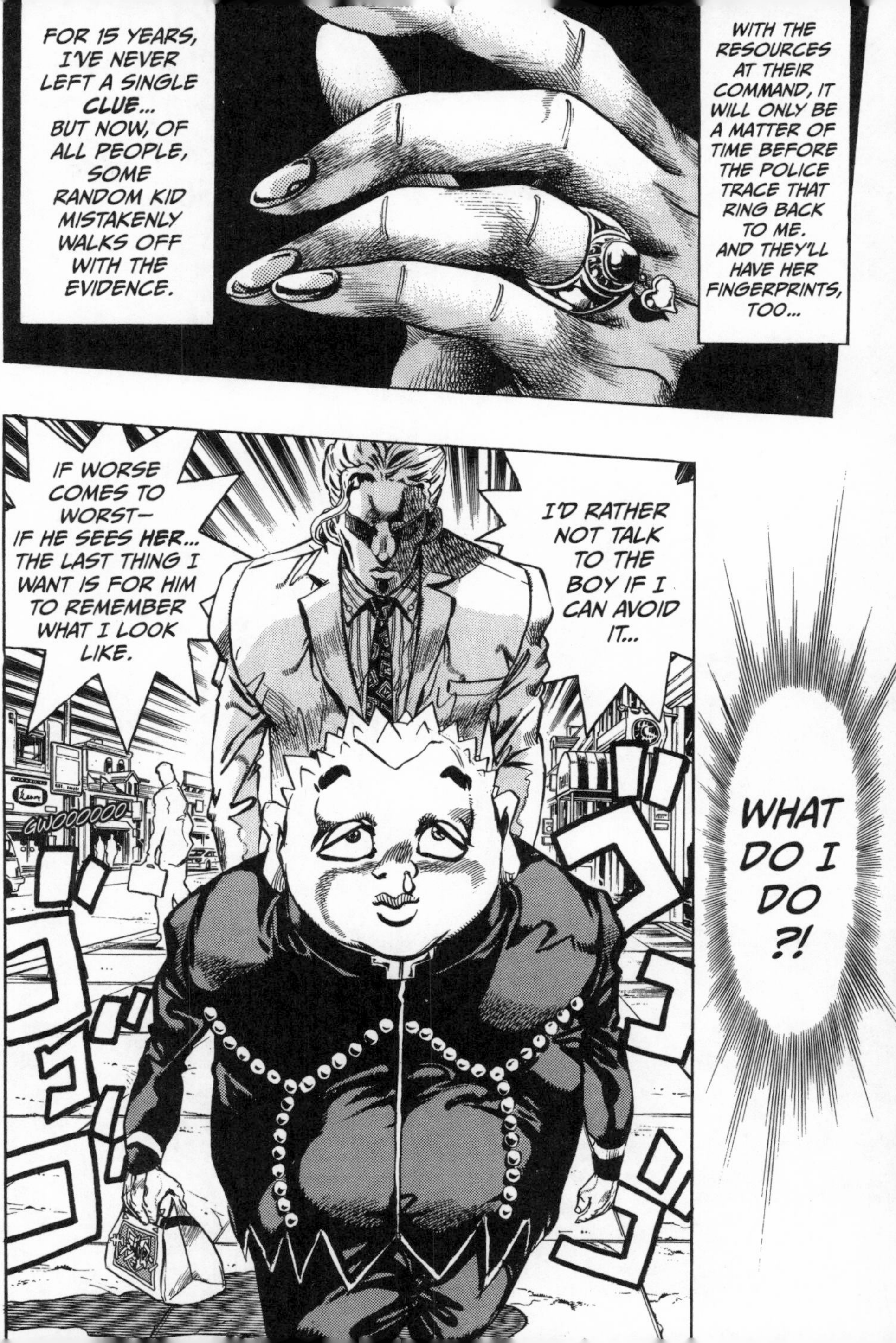
WITH THE RESOURCES AT THEIR COMMAND, IT WILL ONLY BE A MATTER OF TIME BEFORE THE POLICE TRACE THAT RING BACK TO ME. AND THEY'LL HAVE HER FINGERPRINTS, TOO...
FOR 15 YEARS, I'VE NEVER LEFT A SINGLE CLUE... BUT NOW, OF ALL PEOPLE, SOME RANDOM KID MISTAKENLY WALKS OFF WITH THE EVIDENCE.
WHAT DO I DO ?!
I'D RATHER NOT TALK TO THE BOY IF I CAN AVOID IT...
IF WORSE COMES TO WORST— IF HE SEES HER... THE LAST THING I WANT IS FOR HIM TO REMEMBER WHAT I LOOK LIKE.
GWOOOOOO

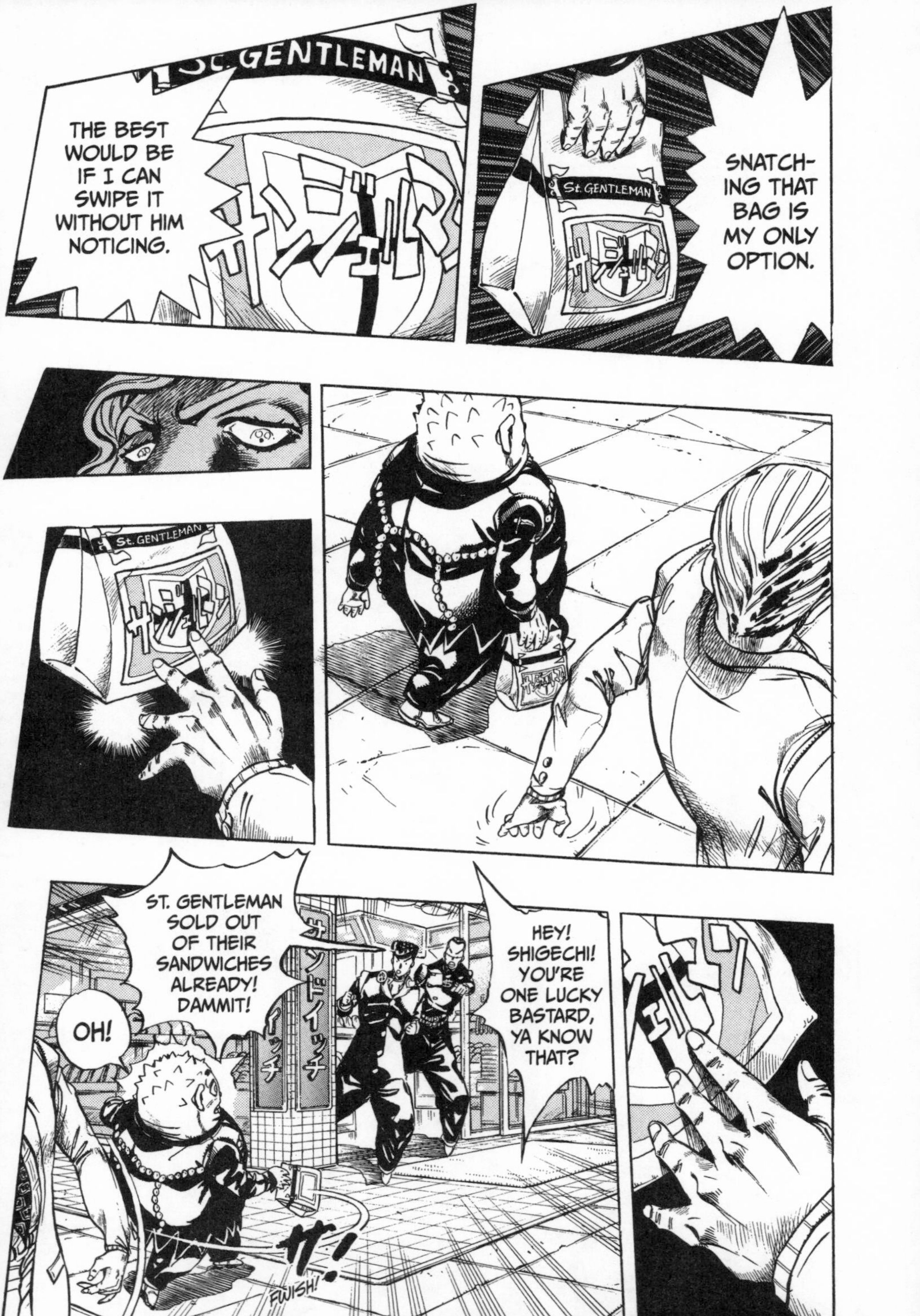
SNATCHING THAT BAG IS MY ONLY OPTION.
St. GENTLEMAN
THE BEST WOULD BE IF I CAN SWIPE IT WITHOUT HIM NOTICING.
St. GENTLEMAN
St. GENTLEMAN
HEY! SHIGECHI! YOU'RE ONE LUCKY BASTARD, YA KNOW THAT?
ST. GENTLEMAN SOLD OUT OF THEIR SANDWICHES ALREADY! DAMMIT!
サンドイッチ
OH!
ザッ!
FWISH!

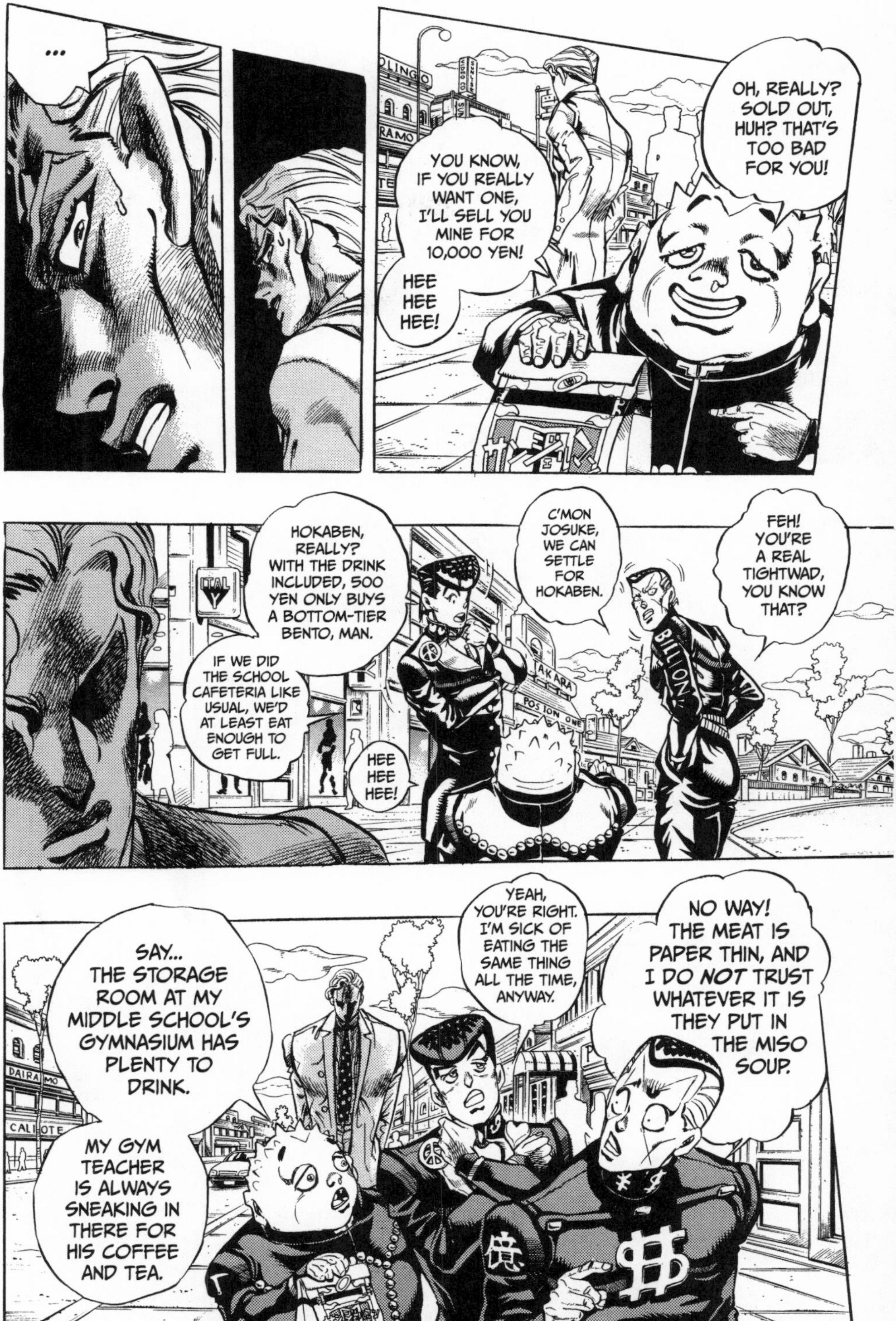
OH, REALLY? SOLD OUT, HUH? THAT'S TOO BAD FOR YOU!
YOU KNOW, IF YOU REALLY WANT ONE, I'LL SELL YOU MINE FOR 10,000 YEN!
HEE HEE HEE!
...
FEH! YOU'RE A REAL TIGHTWAD, YOU KNOW THAT?
C'MON JOSUKE, WE CAN SETTLE FOR HOKABEN.
HOKABEN, REALLY? WITH THE DRINK INCLUDED, 500 YEN ONLY BUYS A BOTTOM-TIER BENTO, MAN.
IF WE DID THE SCHOOL CAFETERIA LIKE USUAL, WE'D AT LEAST EAT ENOUGH TO GET FULL.
HEE HEE HEE!
NO WAY! THE MEAT IS PAPER THIN, AND I DO *NOT* TRUST WHATEVER IT IS THEY PUT IN THE MISO SOUP.
YEAH, YOU'RE RIGHT. I'M SICK OF EATING THE SAME THING ALL THE TIME, ANYWAY.
SAY... THE STORAGE ROOM AT MY MIDDLE SCHOOL'S GYMNASIUM HAS PLENTY TO DRINK.
MY GYM TEACHER IS ALWAYS SNEAKING IN THERE FOR HIS COFFEE AND TEA.

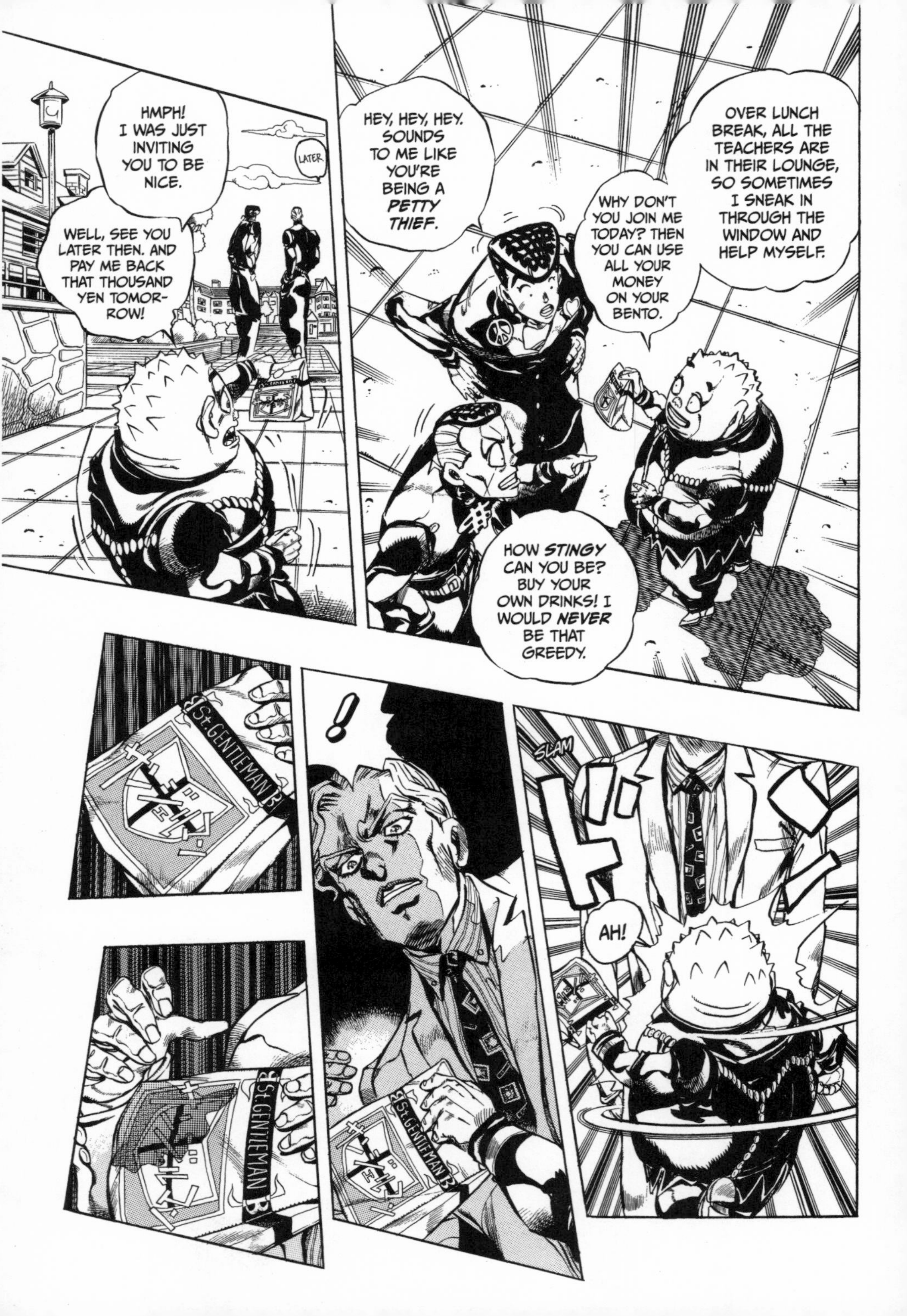
OVER LUNCH BREAK, ALL THE TEACHERS ARE IN THEIR LOUNGE, SO SOMETIMES I SNEAK IN THROUGH THE WINDOW AND HELP MYSELF.
WHY DON'T YOU JOIN ME TODAY? THEN YOU CAN USE ALL YOUR MONEY ON YOUR BENTO.
HEY, HEY, HEY. SOUNDS TO ME LIKE YOU'RE BEING A *PETTY THIEF*.
HOW *STINGY* CAN YOU BE? BUY YOUR OWN DRINKS! I WOULD *NEVER* BE THAT GREEDY.
LATER.
HMPH! I WAS JUST INVITING YOU TO BE NICE.
WELL, SEE YOU LATER THEN. AND PAY ME BACK THAT THOUSAND YEN TOMORROW!
SLAM
AH!
!
St. GENTLEMAN
St. GENTLEMAN
St. GENTLEMAN

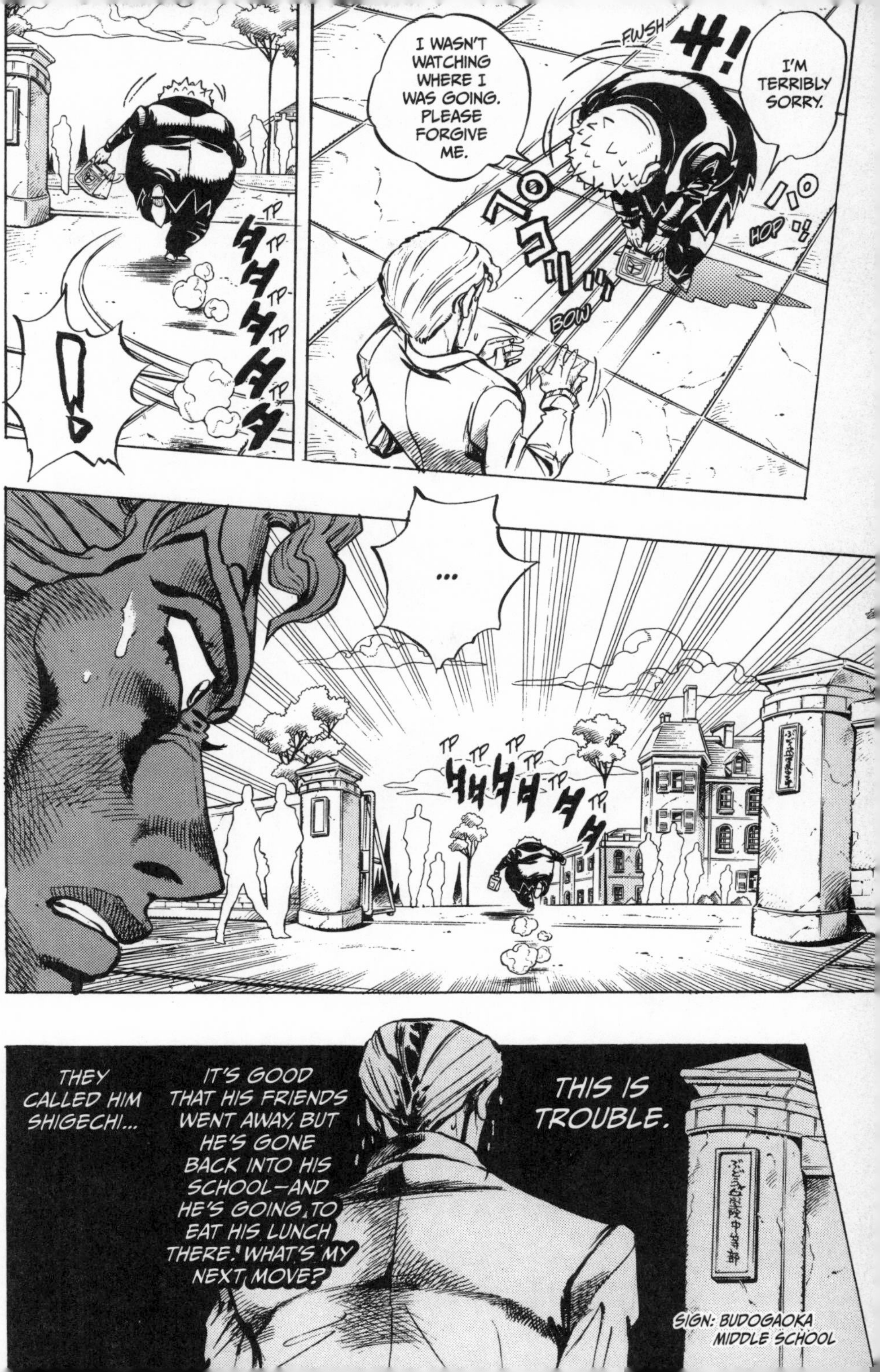

FWSH
I'M TERRIBLY SORRY.
I WASN'T WATCHING WHERE I WAS GOING. PLEASE FORGIVE ME.
HOP
BOW
TP
TP
TP
TP
TP
TP
...
TP
TP
TP
TP
TP
TP
THIS IS TROUBLE.
IT'S GOOD THAT HIS FRIENDS WENT AWAY, BUT HE'S GONE BACK INTO HIS SCHOOL—AND HE'S GOING TO EAT HIS LUNCH THERE. WHAT'S MY NEXT MOVE?
THEY CALLED HIM SHIGECHI...
SIGN: BUDOGAOKA MIDDLE SCHOOL

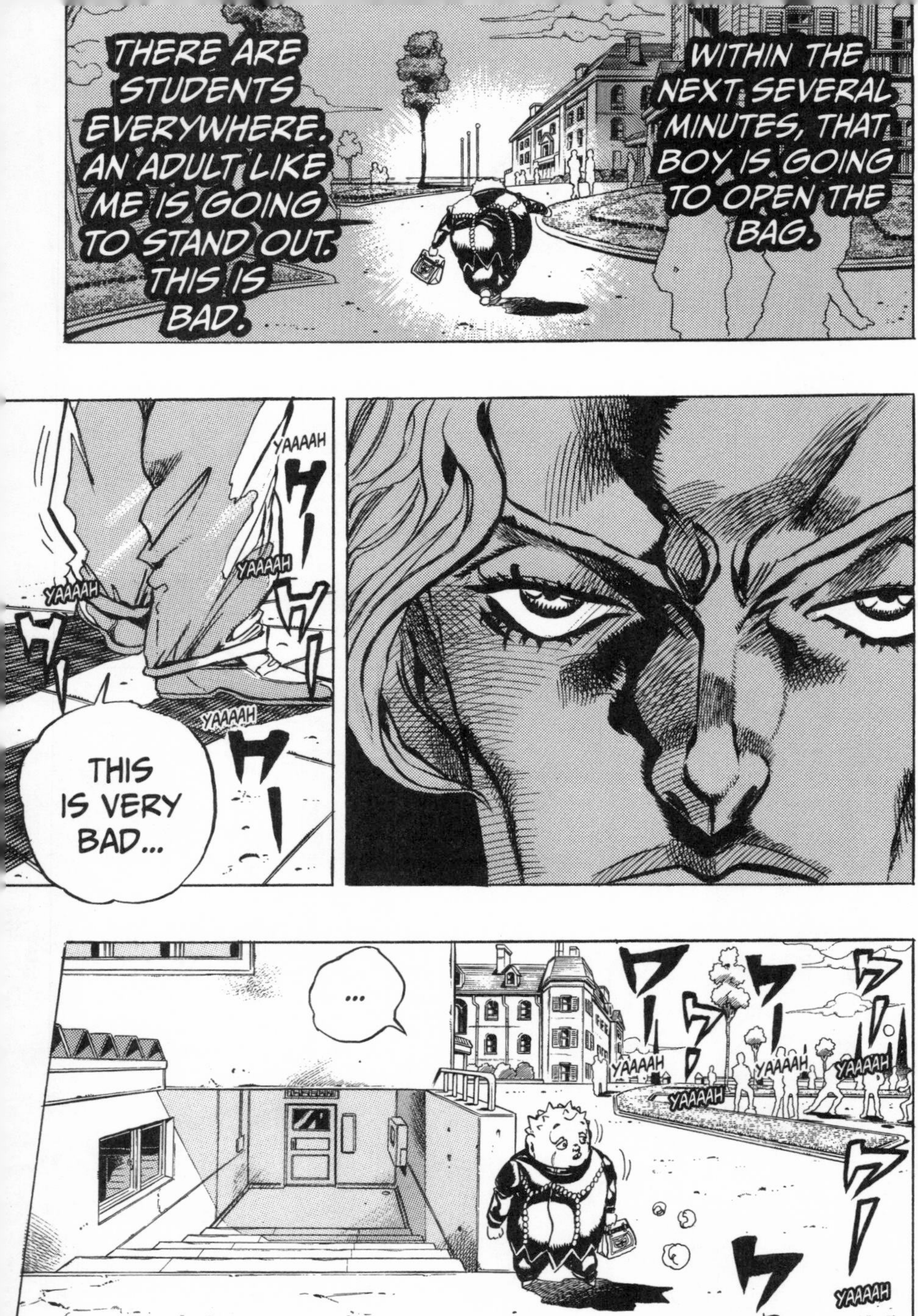
WITHIN THE NEXT SEVERAL MINUTES, THAT BOY IS GOING TO OPEN THE BAG.
THERE ARE STUDENTS EVERYWHERE. AN ADULT LIKE ME IS GOING TO STAND OUT. THIS IS BAD.
YAAAAH
YAAAAH
YAAAAH
YAAAAH
THIS IS VERY BAD...
YAAAAH
YAAAAH
YAAAAH
YAAAAH
...
YAAAAH
YAAAAH
YAAAAH

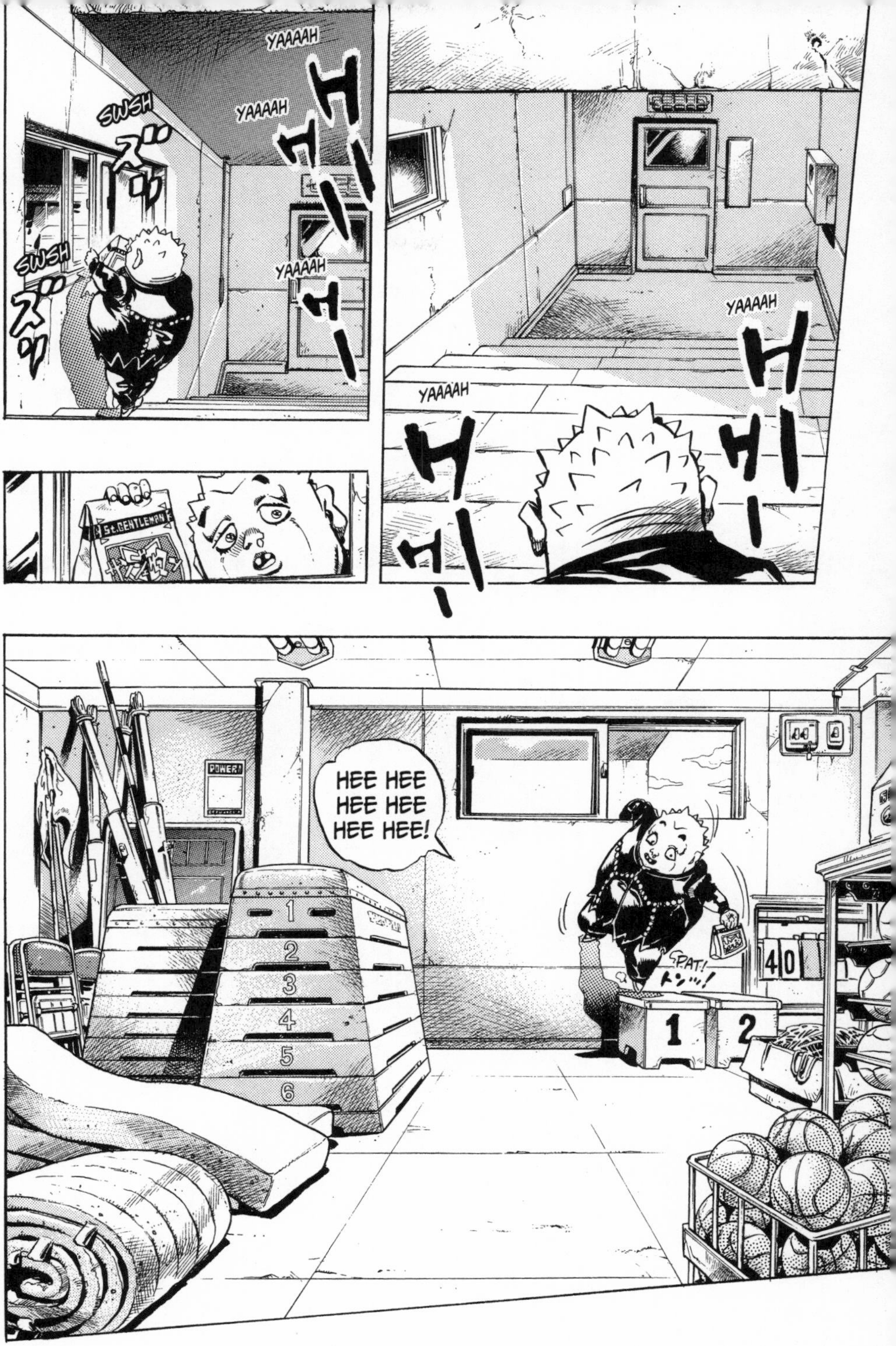
YAAAAH
YAAAAH
YAAAAH
SWSH
YAAAAH
SWSH
YAAAAH
St.GENTLEMAN
POWER!
HEE HEE HEE HEE HEE HEE!
PAT!
40

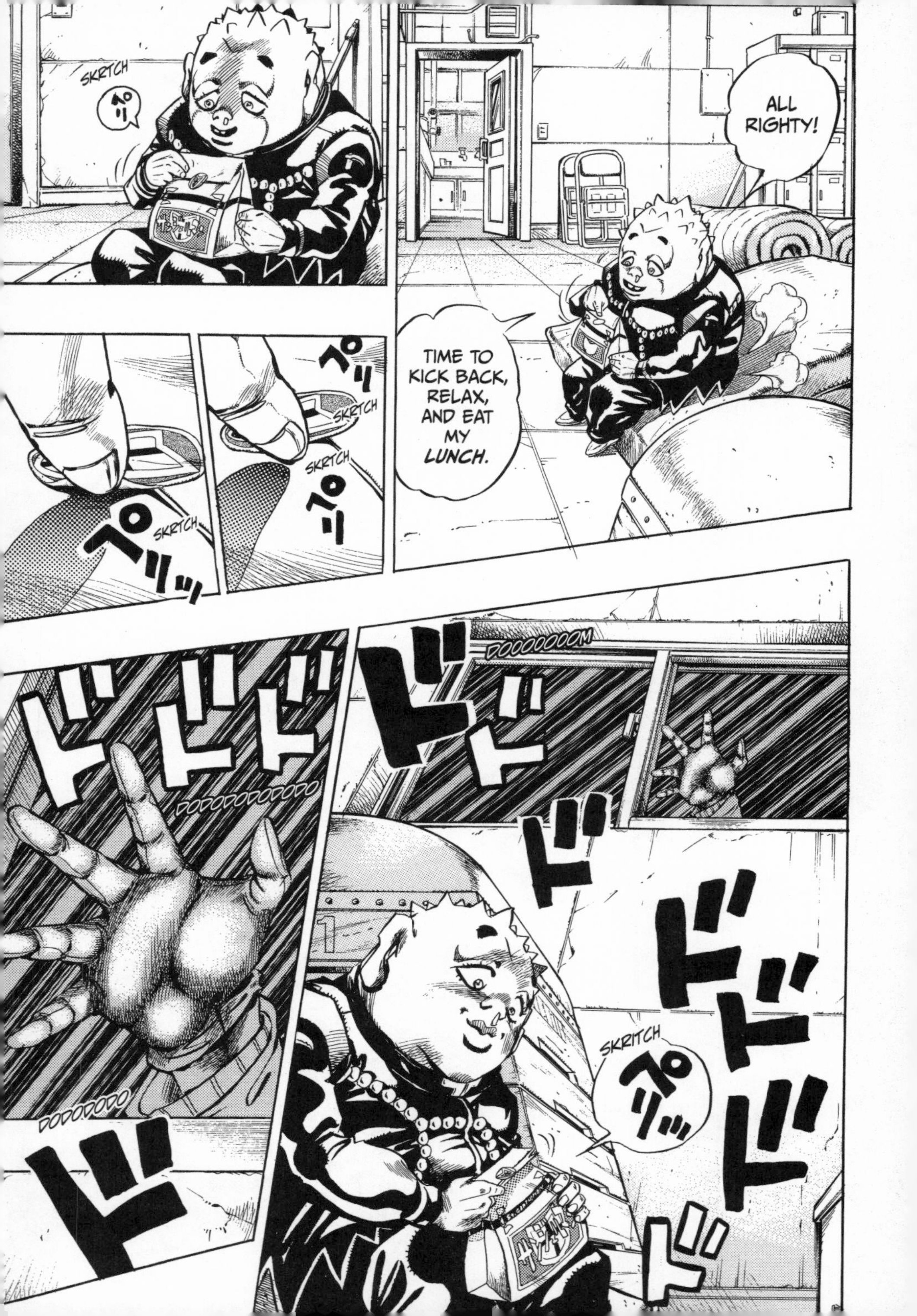
ALL RIGHTY!
TIME TO KICK BACK, RELAX, AND EAT MY LUNCH.
SKRTCH
ぺり
ペリ
SKRTCH
SKRTCH
ペリ
SKRTCH
ペリッ
DOOOOOOOM
SKRITCH
DODODODODODO
DODODODO

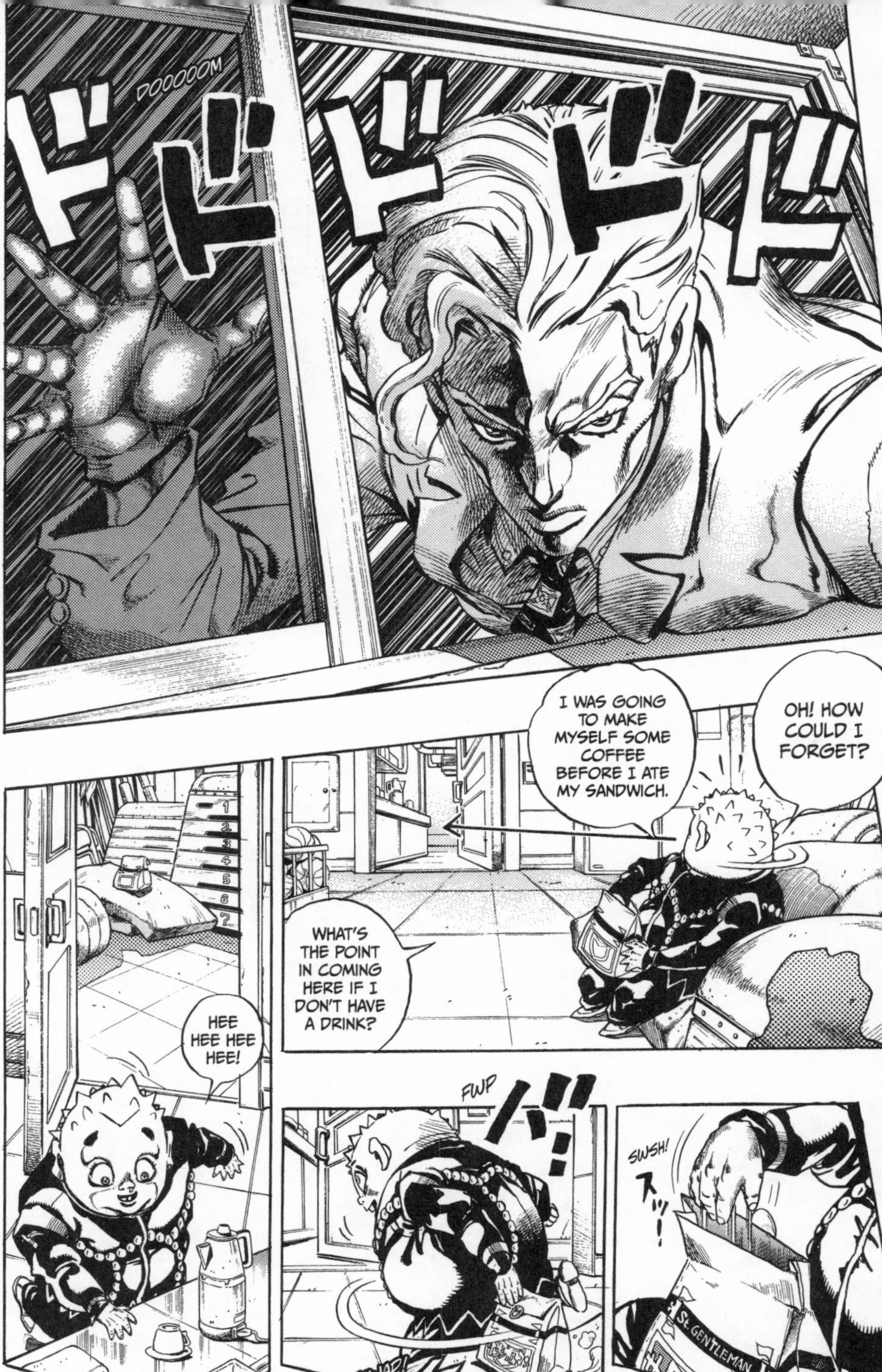

ドドドド
DOOOOOM
ドド
OH! HOW COULD I FORGET?
I WAS GOING TO MAKE MYSELF SOME COFFEE BEFORE I ATE MY SANDWICH.
WHAT'S THE POINT IN COMING HERE IF I DON'T HAVE A DRINK?
SWSH!
スッ
St. GENTLEMAN
FWP
バッ
THWAP!
スト!
HEE HEE HEE HEE!

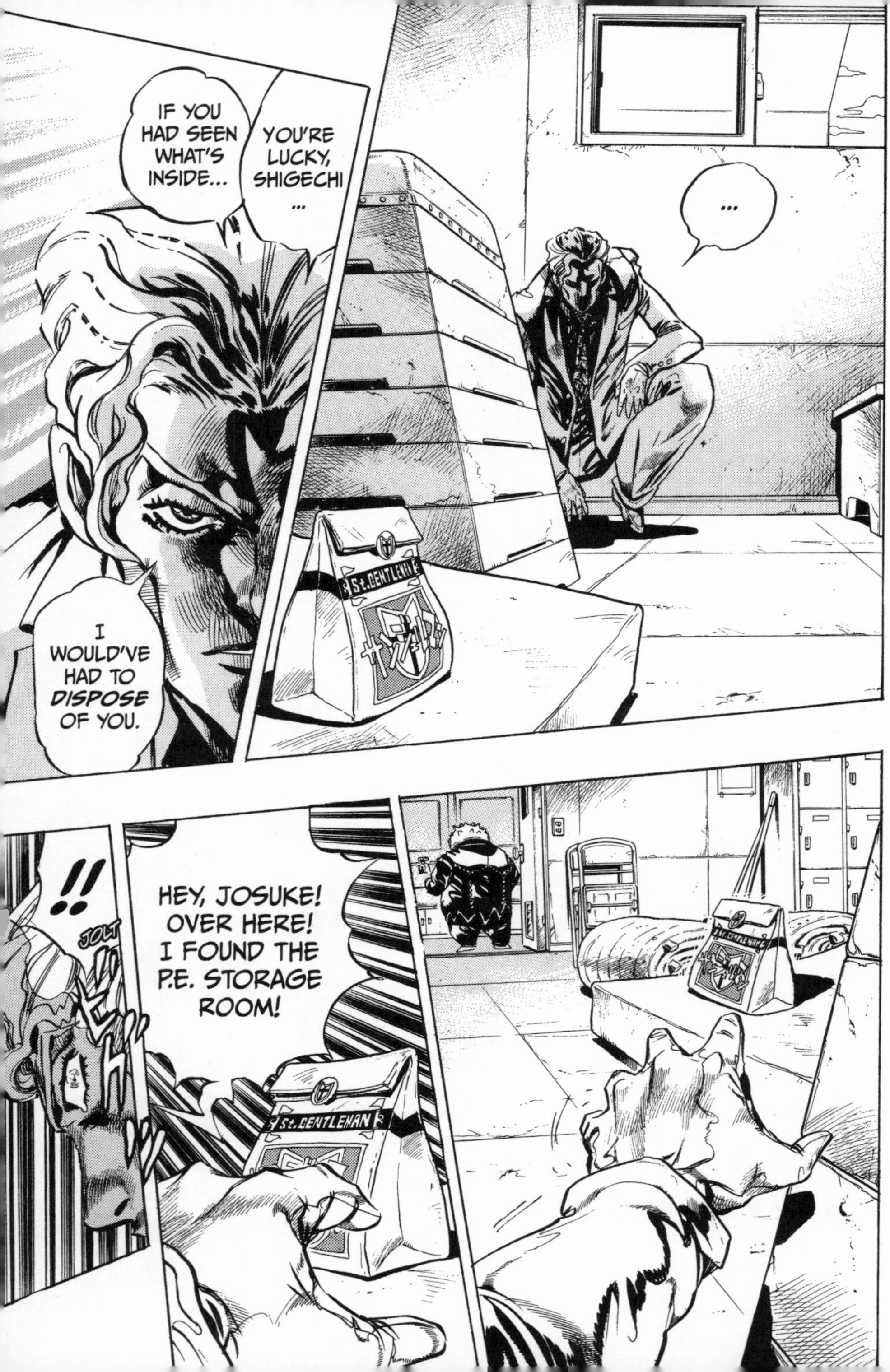
...
YOU'RE LUCKY, SHIGECHI...
IF YOU HAD SEEN WHAT'S INSIDE...
I WOULD'VE HAD TO *DISPOSE* OF YOU.
HEY, JOSUKE! OVER HERE! I FOUND THE P.E. STORAGE ROOM!
St. GENTLEMAN
!!
JOLT

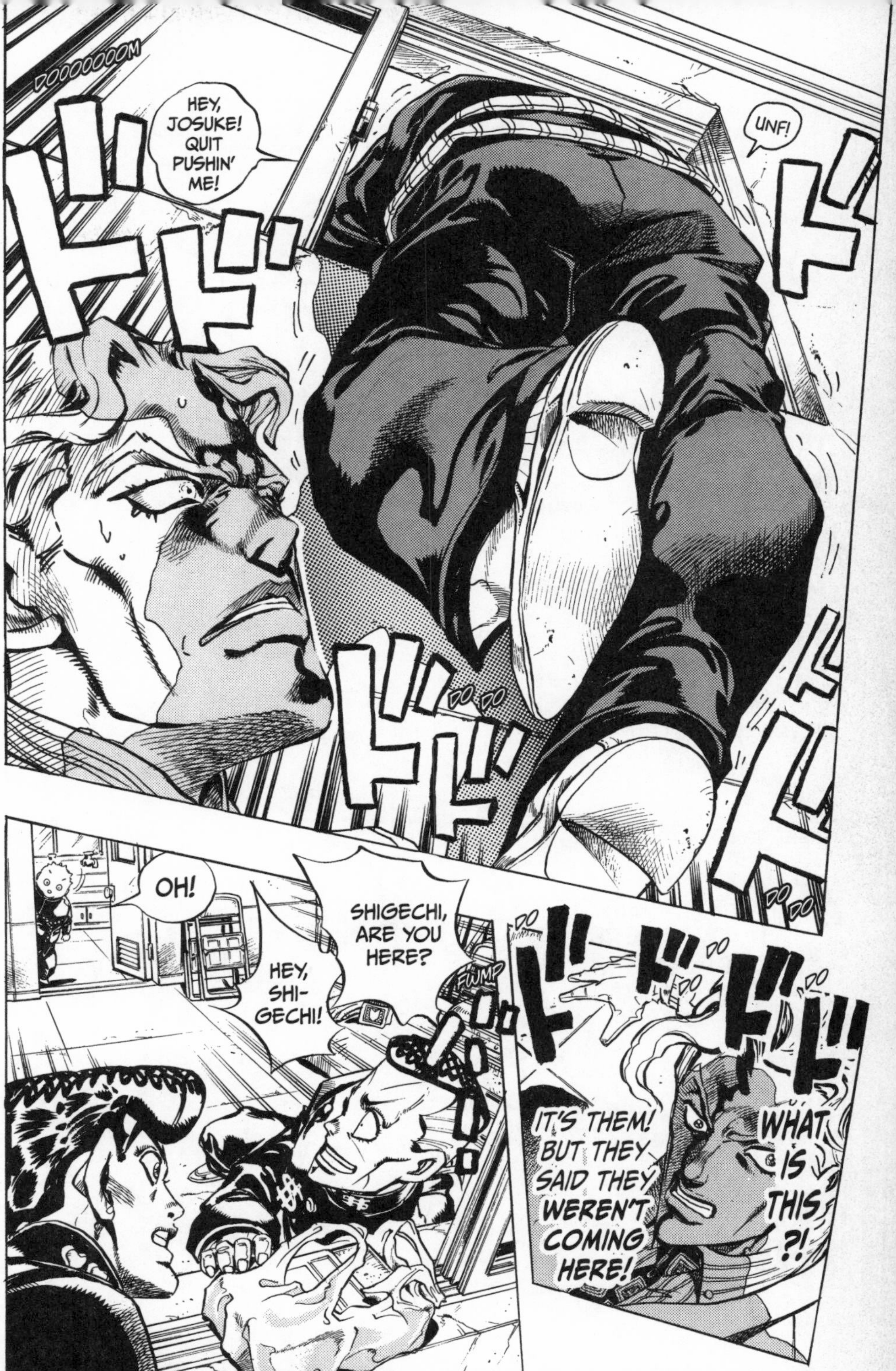
UNF!
HEY, JOSUKE! QUIT PUSHIN' ME!
DOOOOOOOM
DO DO
DO DO
DO
DO
DO
DO
WHAT IS THIS ?!
IT'S THEM! BUT THEY SAID THEY WEREN'T COMING HERE!
SHIGECHI, ARE YOU HERE?
FUMP
OH!
HEY, SHI-GECHI!

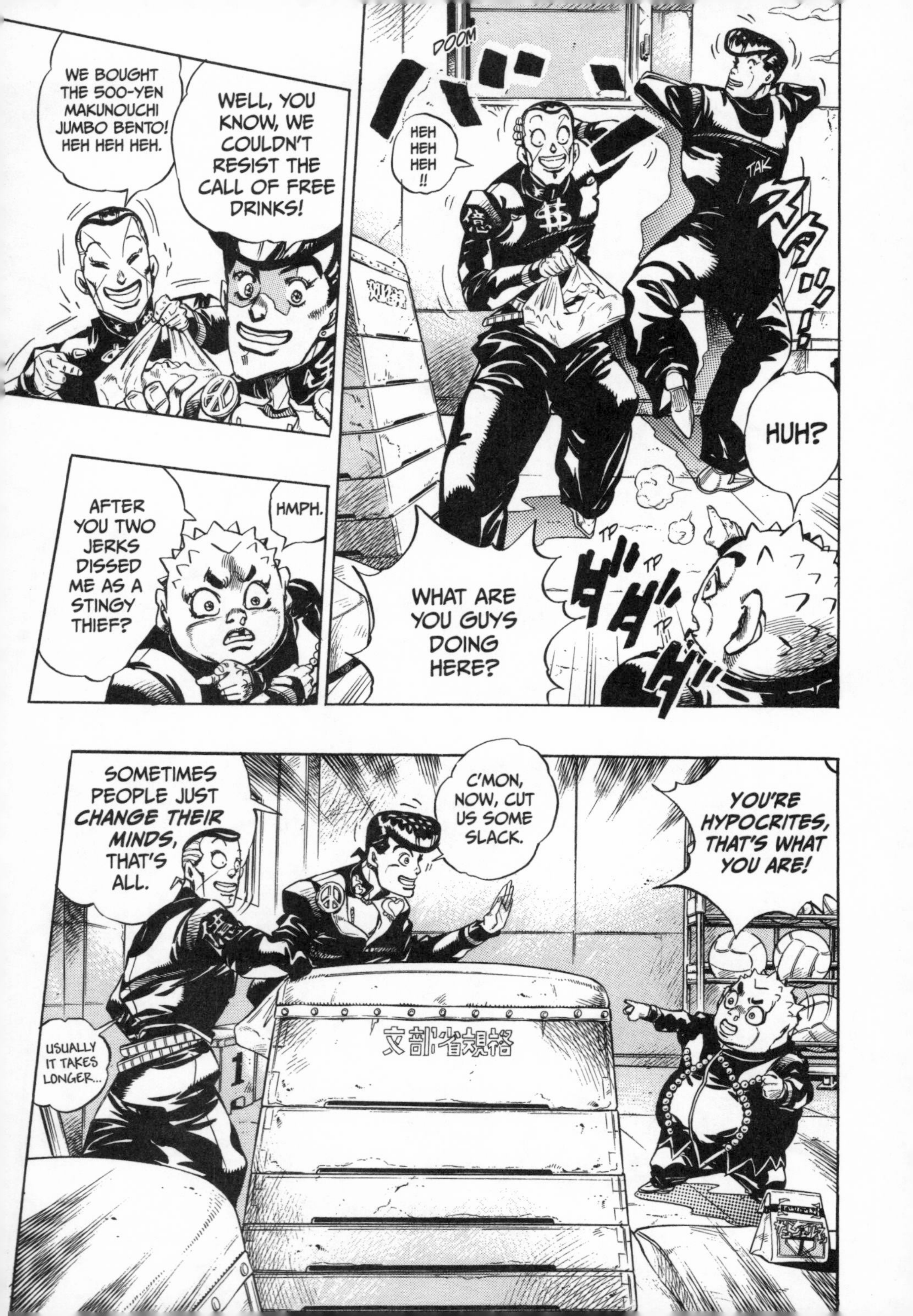
DOOM
HEH HEH HEH!!
TAK
HUH?
WHAT ARE YOU GUYS DOING HERE?
TP
TP
TP
WELL, YOU KNOW, WE COULDN'T RESIST THE CALL OF FREE DRINKS!
WE BOUGHT THE 500-YEN MAKUNOUCHI JUMBO BENTO! HEH HEH HEH.
HMPH.
AFTER YOU TWO JERKS DISSED ME AS A STINGY THIEF?
YOU'RE HYPOCRITES, THAT'S WHAT YOU ARE!
C'MON, NOW, CUT US SOME SLACK.
SOMETIMES PEOPLE JUST CHANGE THEIR MINDS, THAT'S ALL.
USUALLY IT TAKES LONGER...
文部省規格

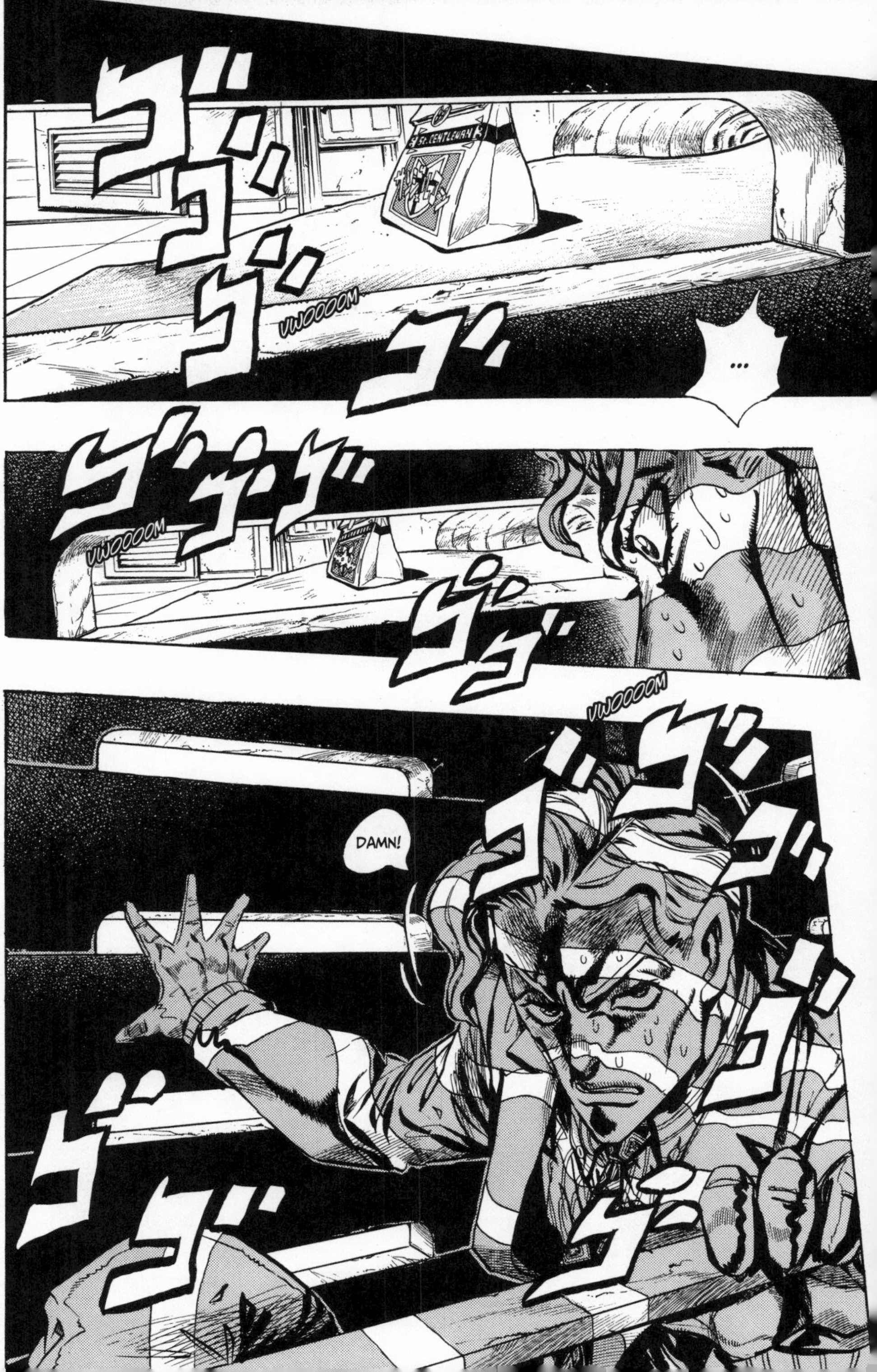
VWOOOOM
...
VWOOOOM
VWOOOOM
DAMN!

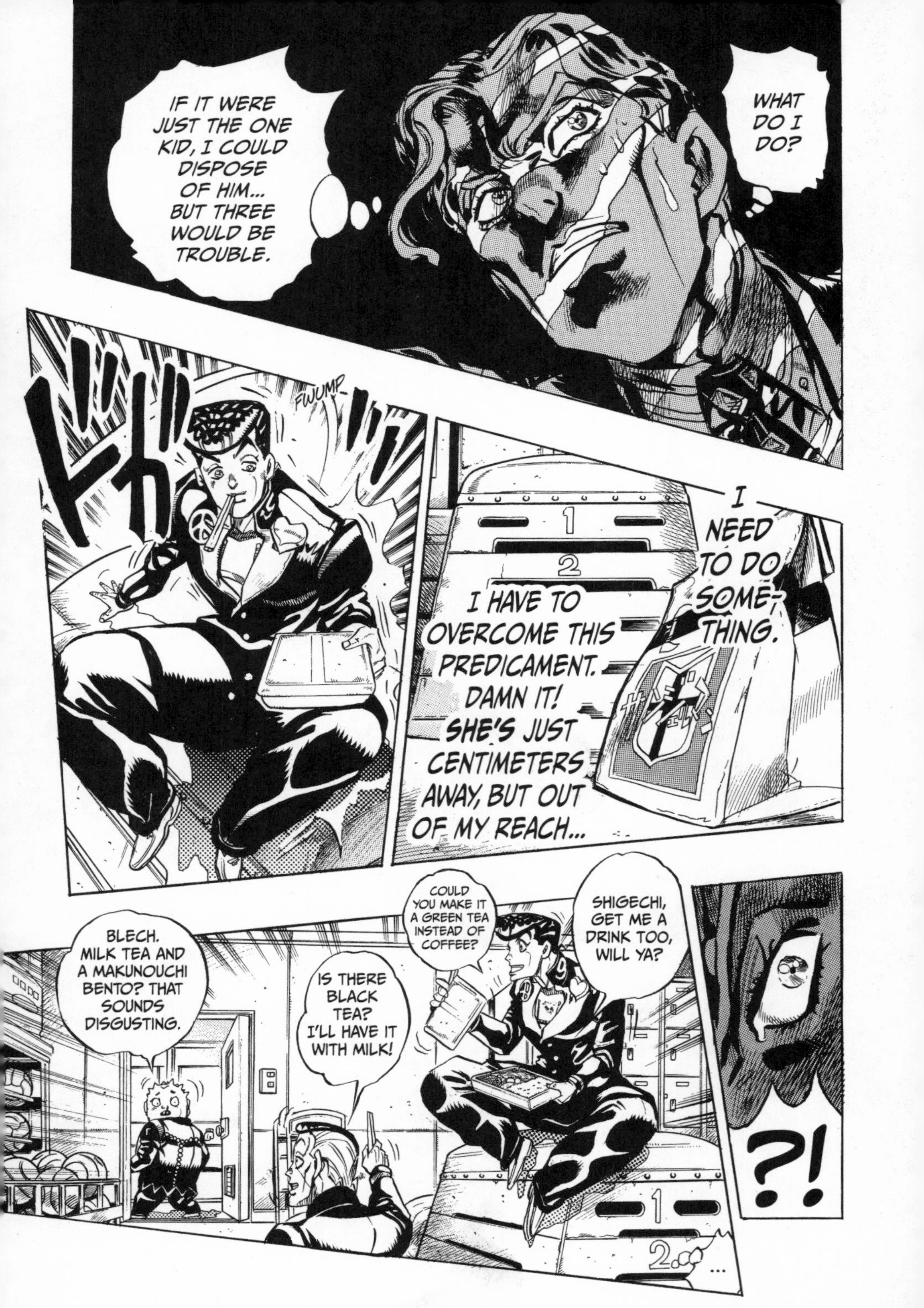
WHAT DO I DO?
IF IT WERE JUST THE ONE KID, I COULD DISPOSE OF HIM... BUT THREE WOULD BE TROUBLE.
I NEED TO DO SOME-THING.
I HAVE TO OVERCOME THIS PREDICAMENT. DAMN IT! SHE'S JUST CENTIMETERS AWAY, BUT OUT OF MY REACH...
FWUMP
?!
SHIGECHI, GET ME A DRINK TOO, WILL YA?
COULD YOU MAKE IT A GREEN TEA INSTEAD OF COFFEE?
IS THERE BLACK TEA? I'LL HAVE IT WITH MILK!
BLECH. MILK TEA AND A MAKUNOUCHI BENTO? THAT SOUNDS DISGUSTING.
...

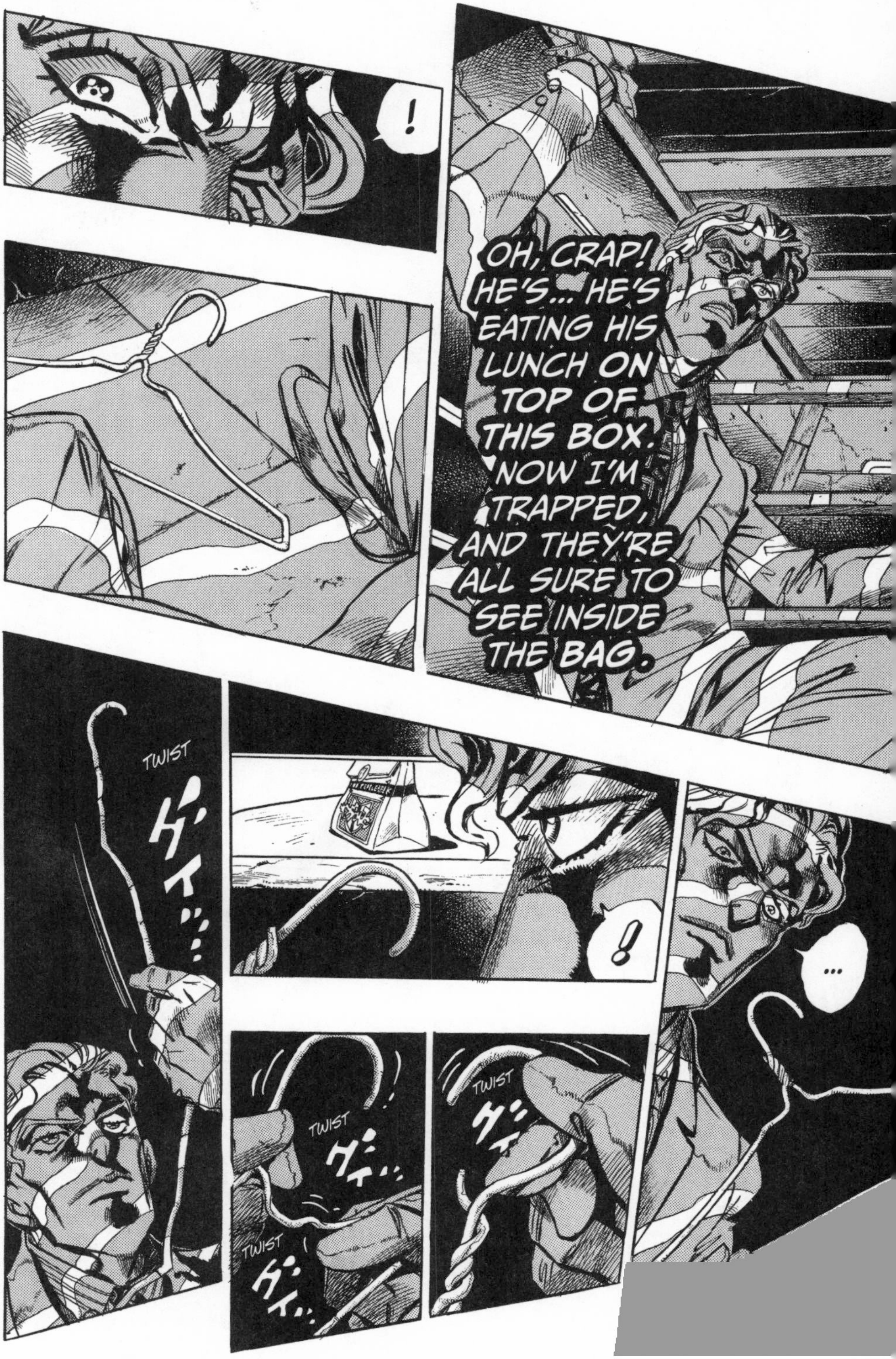
OH, CRAP! HE'S... HE'S EATING HIS LUNCH ON TOP OF THIS BOX. NOW I'M TRAPPED, AND THEY'RE ALL SURE TO SEE INSIDE THE BAG.
!
...
!
TWIST
グイ…
TWIST
グイ…
TWIST
グイ…
TWIST
グイ…

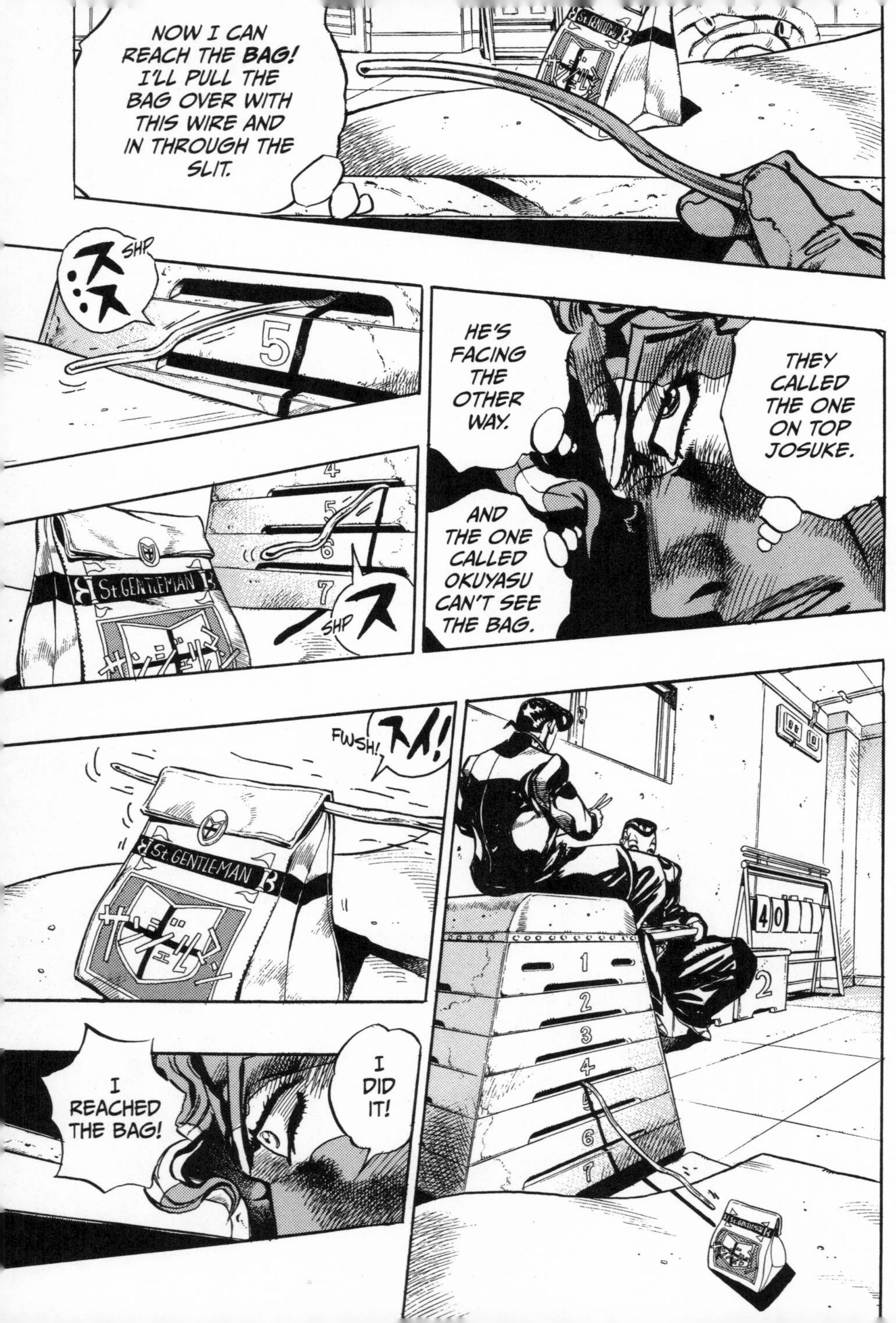
NOW I CAN REACH THE BAG! I'LL PULL THE BAG OVER WITH THIS WIRE AND IN THROUGH THE SLIT.
THEY CALLED THE ONE ON TOP JOSUKE.
HE'S FACING THE OTHER WAY.
AND THE ONE CALLED OKUYASU CAN'T SEE THE BAG.
スス
SHP
St. GENTLEMAN
ス
SHP
スイ!
FWSH!
St. GENTLEMAN
I DID IT!
I REACHED THE BAG!

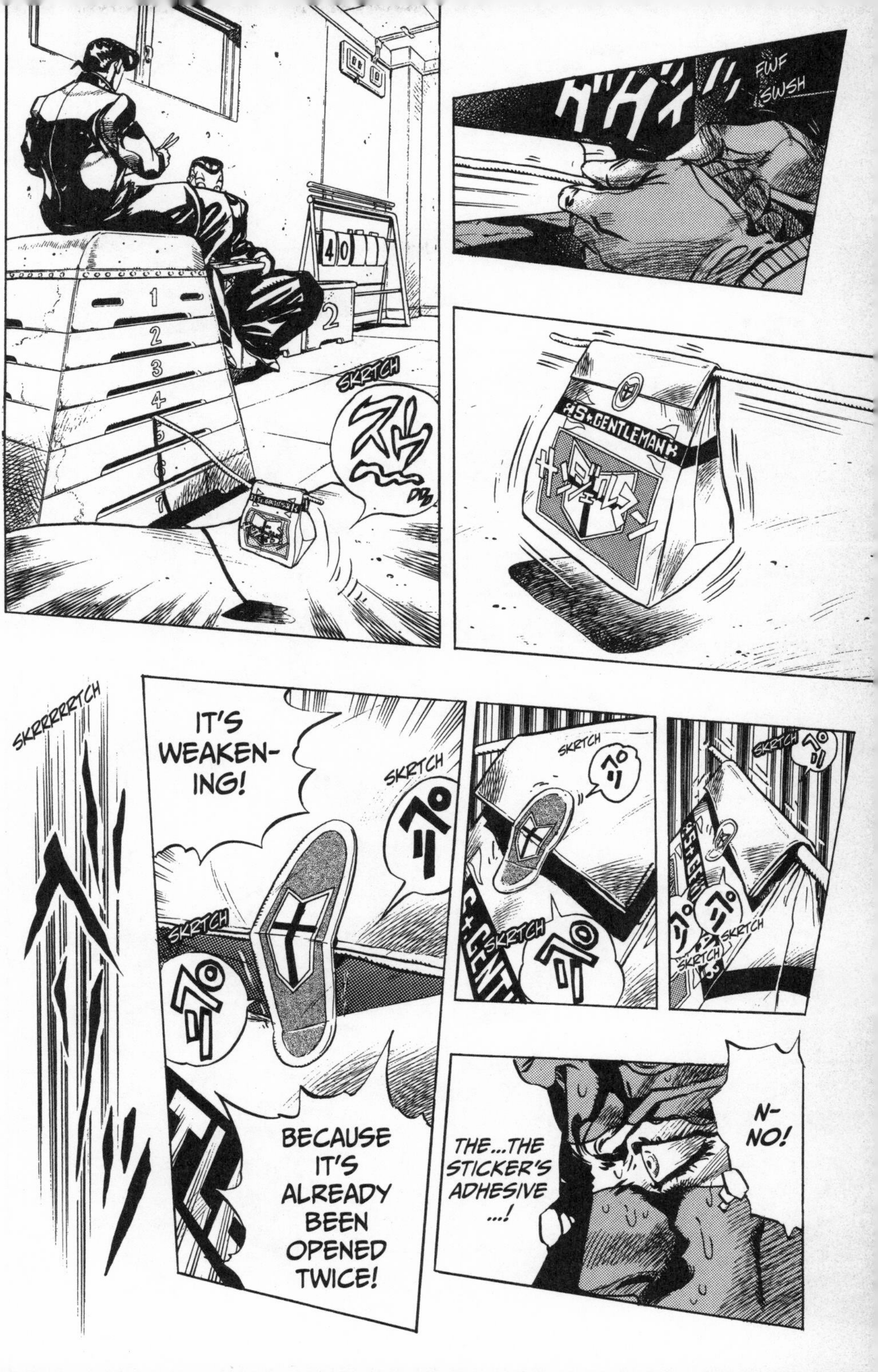
FWF
SWSH
SKRTCH
SKRTCH
SKRTCH
SKRTCH
SKRTCH
SKRTCH
N-NO!
THE...THE STICKER'S ADHESIVE ...!
IT'S WEAKENING!
SKRTCH
SKRTCH
BECAUSE IT'S ALREADY BEEN OPENED TWICE!
SKRRRRRTCH

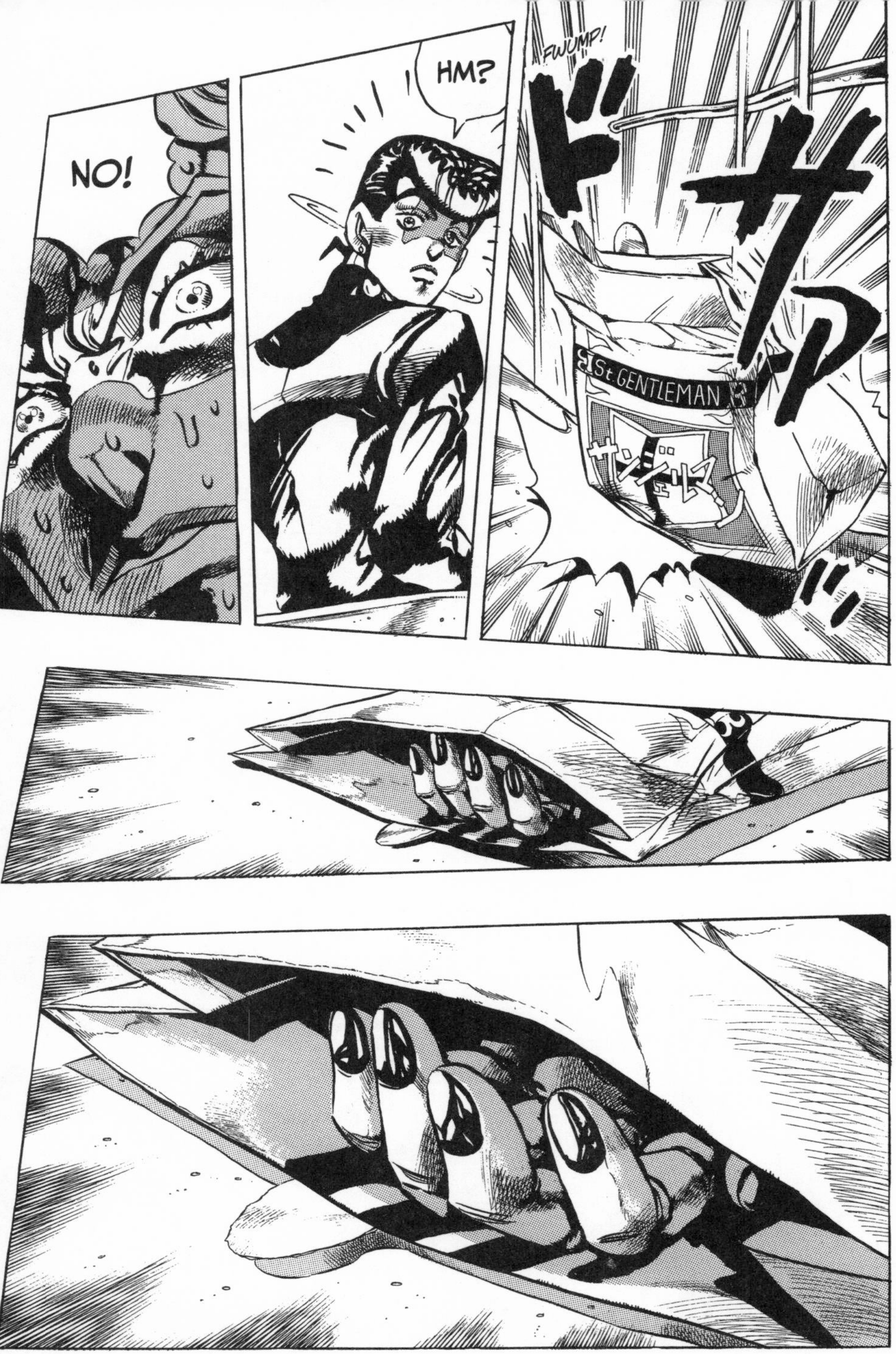
FWUMP!
ドサッ
St. GENTLEMAN
サンジェルマン
HM?
NO!

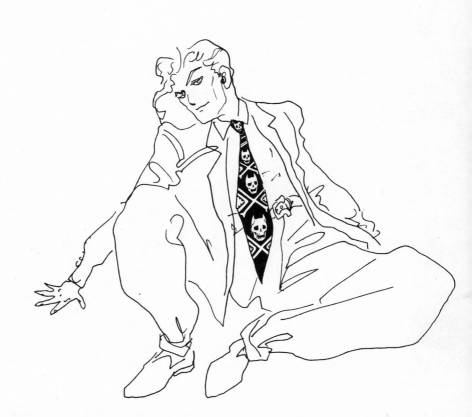

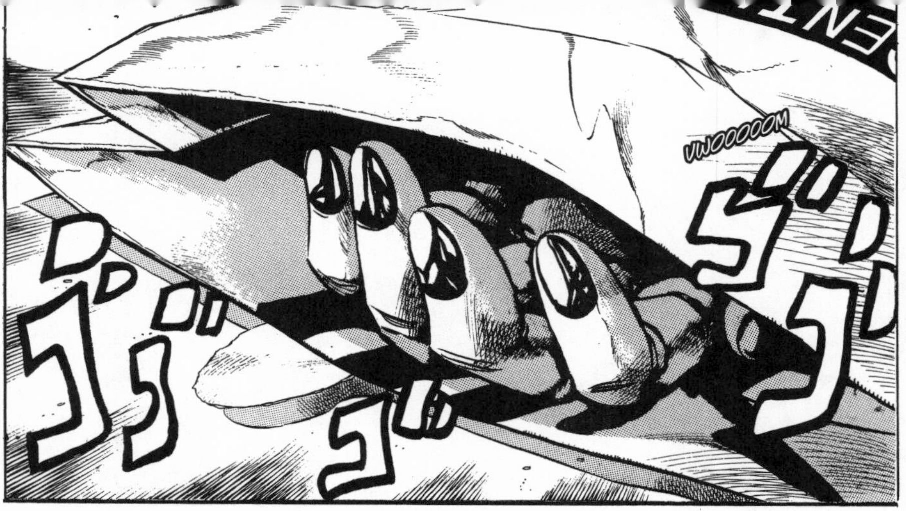
VWOOOOOM

CHAPTER 79

YOSHIKAGE KIRA WANTS TO LIVE QUIETLY, PART 3

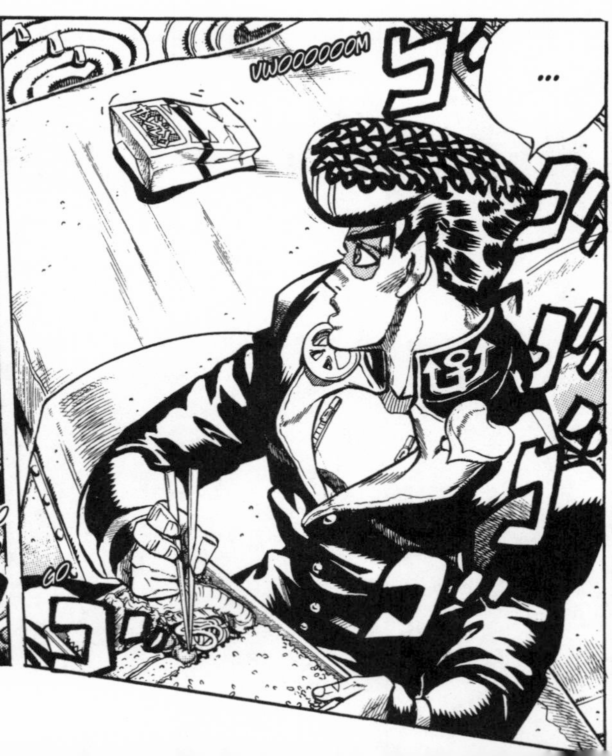
VWOOOOOOM
...
GO

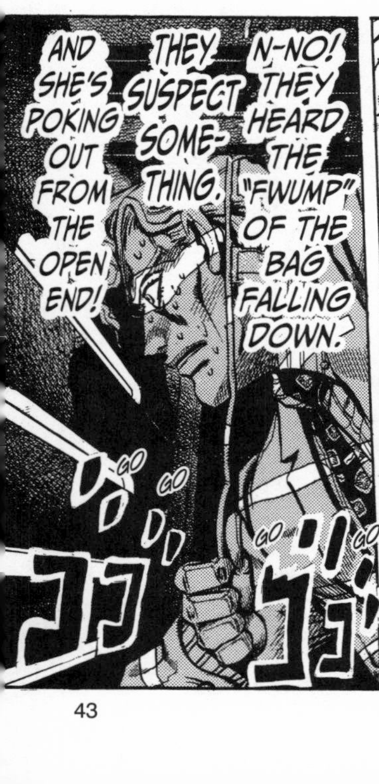
N-NO! THEY HEARD THE "FWUMP" OF THE BAG FALLING DOWN.
THEY SUSPECT SOME-THING.
AND SHE'S POKING OUT FROM THE OPEN END!
GO
GO
GO
GO

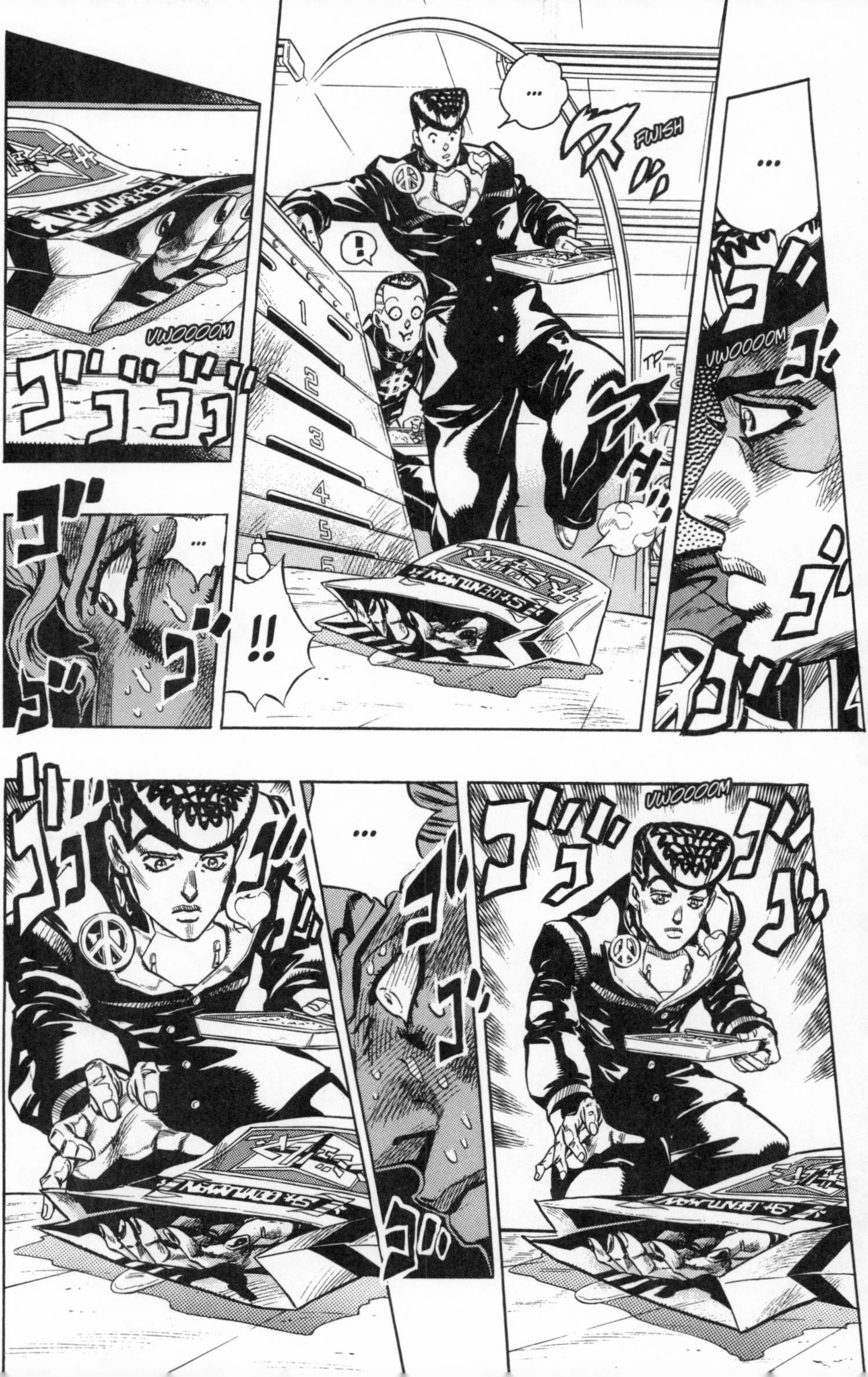
...
VWOOOOM
...
FWISH
!
TP
!!
VWOOOOM
...
VWOOOOM
...

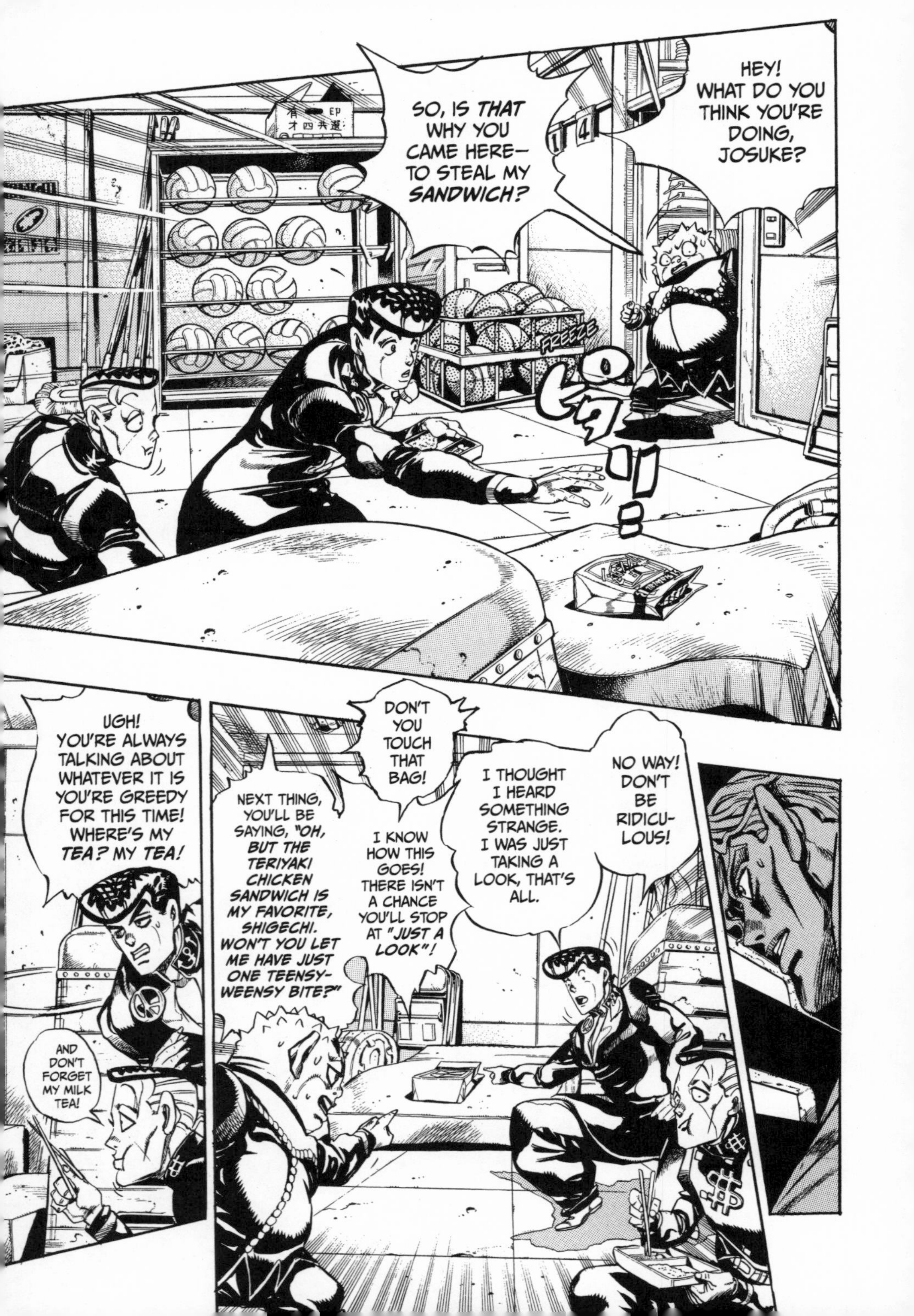
HEY! WHAT DO YOU THINK YOU'RE DOING, JOSUKE?
SO, IS THAT WHY YOU CAME HERE— TO STEAL MY SANDWICH?
FREEZE
NO WAY! DON'T BE RIDICU-LOUS!
I THOUGHT I HEARD SOMETHING STRANGE. I WAS JUST TAKING A LOOK, THAT'S ALL.
DON'T YOU TOUCH THAT BAG!
I KNOW HOW THIS GOES! THERE ISN'T A CHANCE YOU'LL STOP AT "JUST A LOOK"!
NEXT THING, YOU'LL BE SAYING, "OH, BUT THE TERIYAKI CHICKEN SANDWICH IS MY FAVORITE, SHIGECHI. WON'T YOU LET ME HAVE JUST ONE TEENSY-WEENSY BITE?"
UGH! YOU'RE ALWAYS TALKING ABOUT WHATEVER IT IS YOU'RE GREEDY FOR THIS TIME! WHERE'S MY TEA? MY TEA!
AND DON'T FORGET MY MILK TEA!

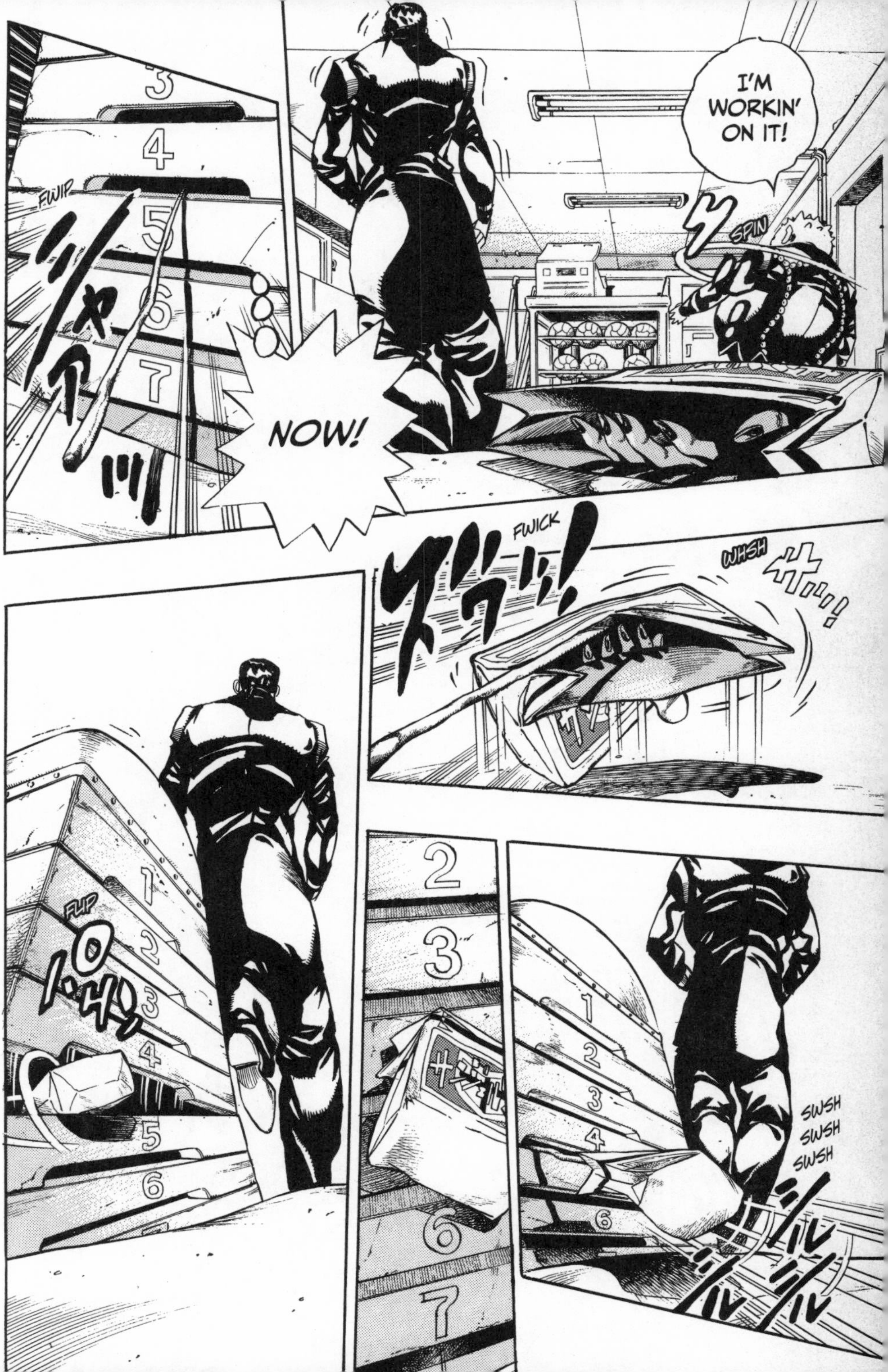
I'M WORKIN' ON IT!
SPIN
NOW!
FWIP
FWICK
WHSH
SWSH
SWSH
SWSH
FLIP

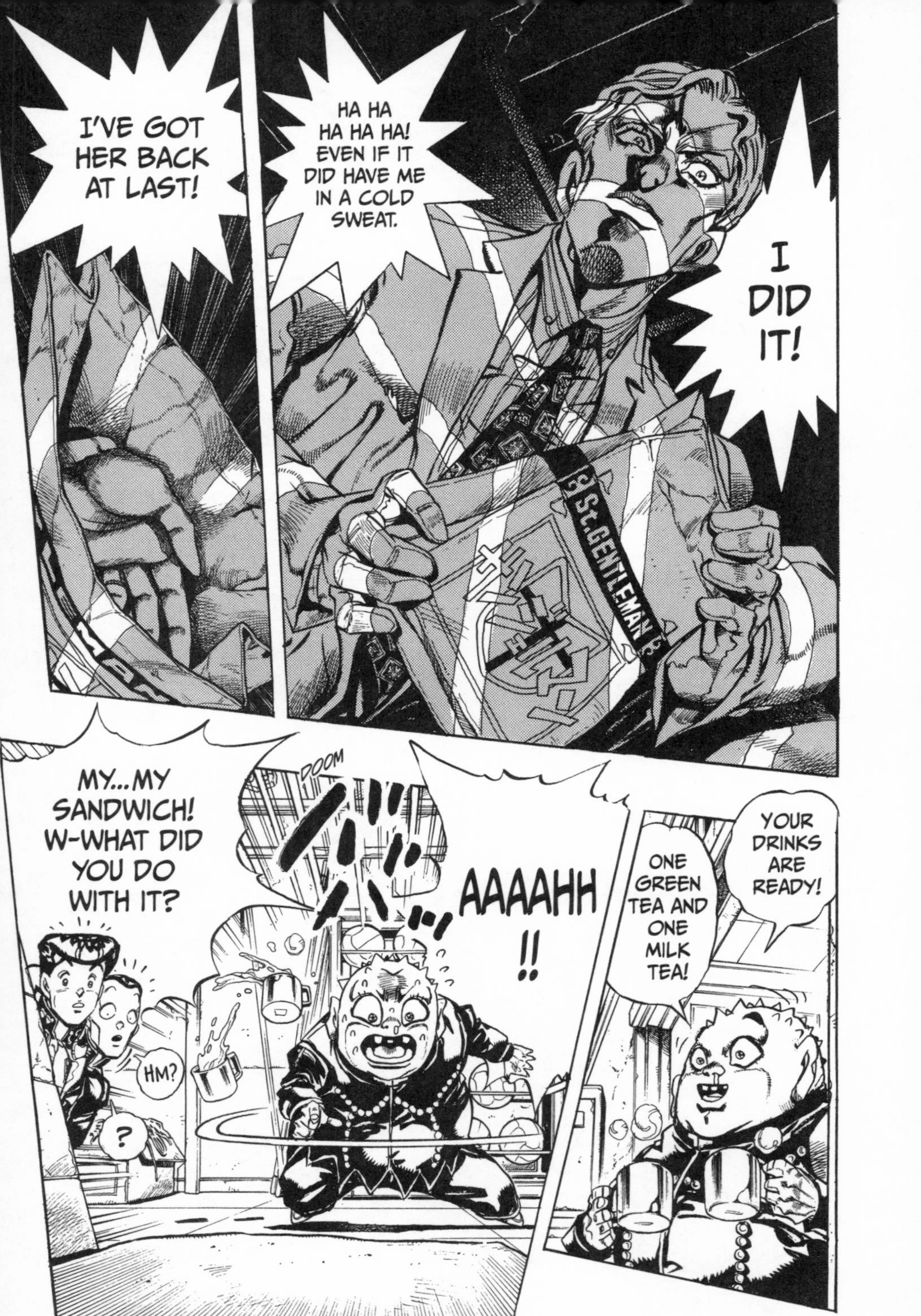
HA HA HA HA HA! EVEN IF IT DID HAVE ME IN A COLD SWEAT.
I DID IT!
St.GENTLEMAN
I'VE GOT HER BACK AT LAST!
YOUR DRINKS ARE READY!
ONE GREEN TEA AND ONE MILK TEA!
DOOM
AAAAHH !!
MY...MY SANDWICH! W-WHAT DID YOU DO WITH IT?
HM?
?

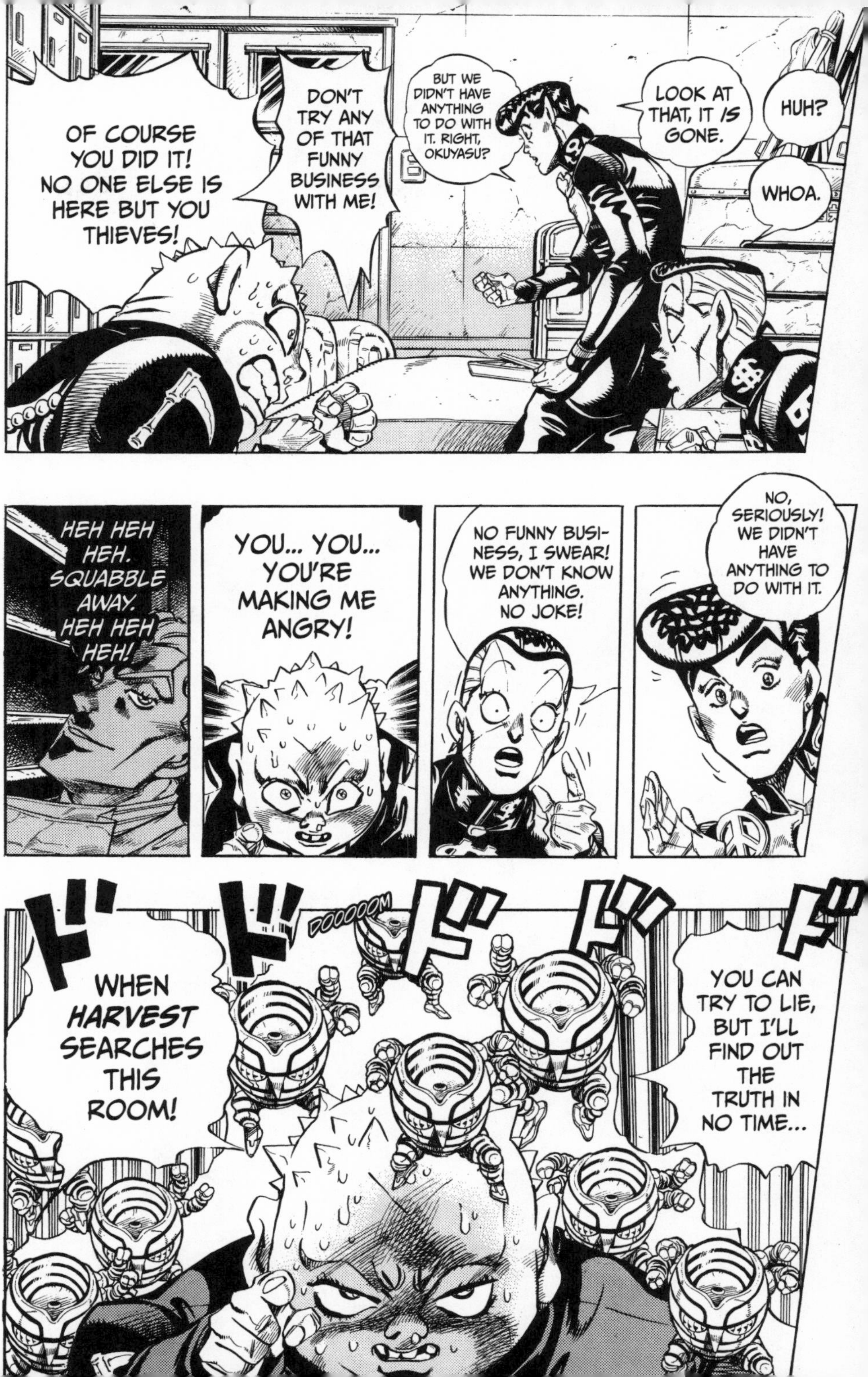
HUH?
WHOA.
LOOK AT THAT, IT *IS* GONE.
BUT WE DIDN'T HAVE ANYTHING TO DO WITH IT. RIGHT, OKUYASU?
DON'T TRY ANY OF THAT FUNNY BUSINESS WITH ME!
OF COURSE YOU DID IT! NO ONE ELSE IS HERE BUT YOU THIEVES!
NO, SERIOUSLY! WE DIDN'T HAVE ANYTHING TO DO WITH IT.
NO FUNNY BUSI-NESS, I SWEAR! WE DON'T KNOW ANYTHING. NO JOKE!
YOU... YOU... YOU'RE MAKING ME ANGRY!
HEH HEH HEH. SQUABBLE AWAY. HEH HEH HEH!
ドドドドド
DOOOOOOM
YOU CAN TRY TO LIE, BUT I'LL FIND OUT THE TRUTH IN NO TIME...
WHEN *HARVEST* SEARCHES THIS ROOM!

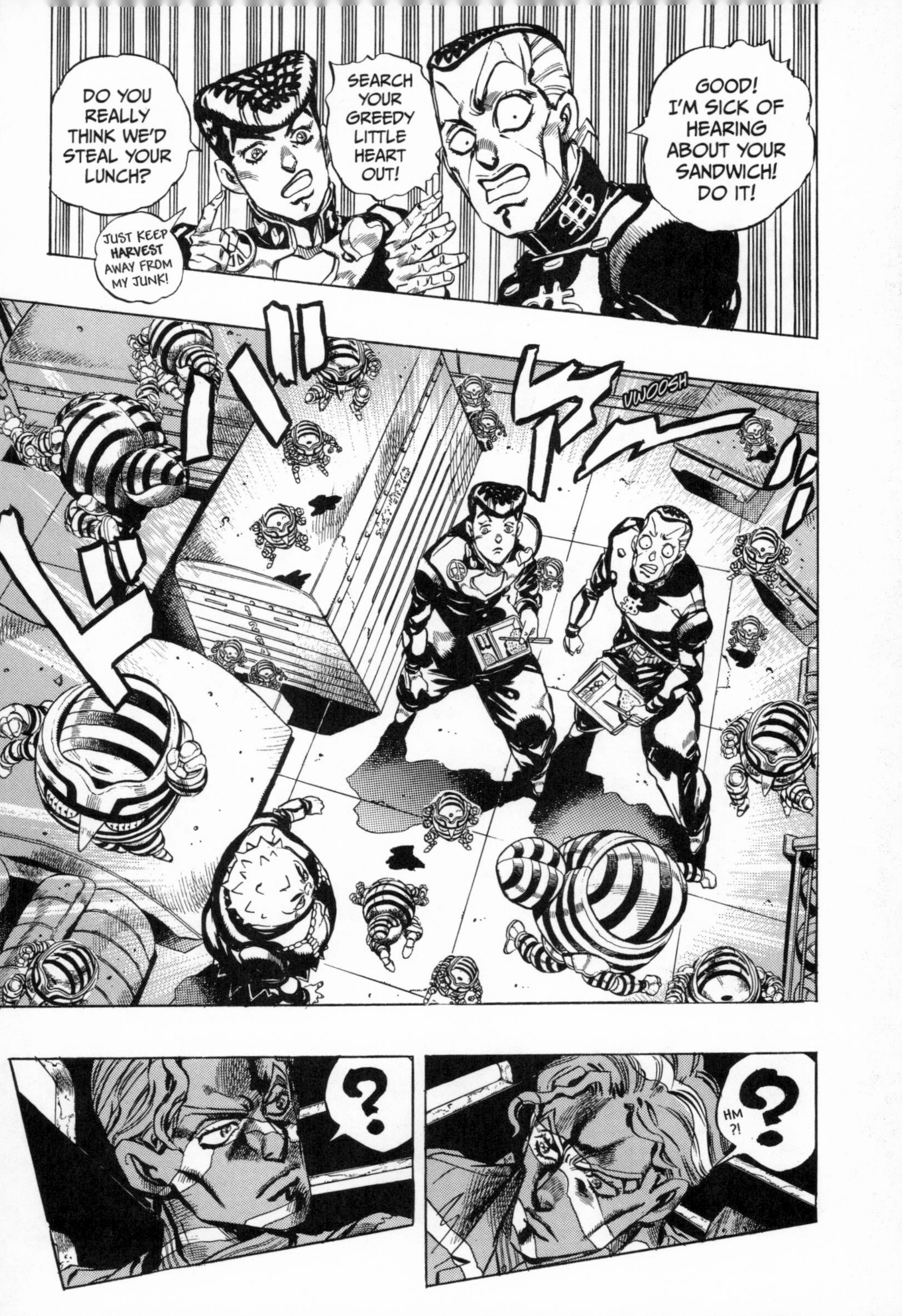
GOOD! I'M SICK OF HEARING ABOUT YOUR SANDWICH! DO IT!
SEARCH YOUR GREEDY LITTLE HEART OUT!
DO YOU REALLY THINK WE'D STEAL YOUR LUNCH?
JUST KEEP HARVEST AWAY FROM MY JUNK!
VWOOSH
?
HM ?!
?

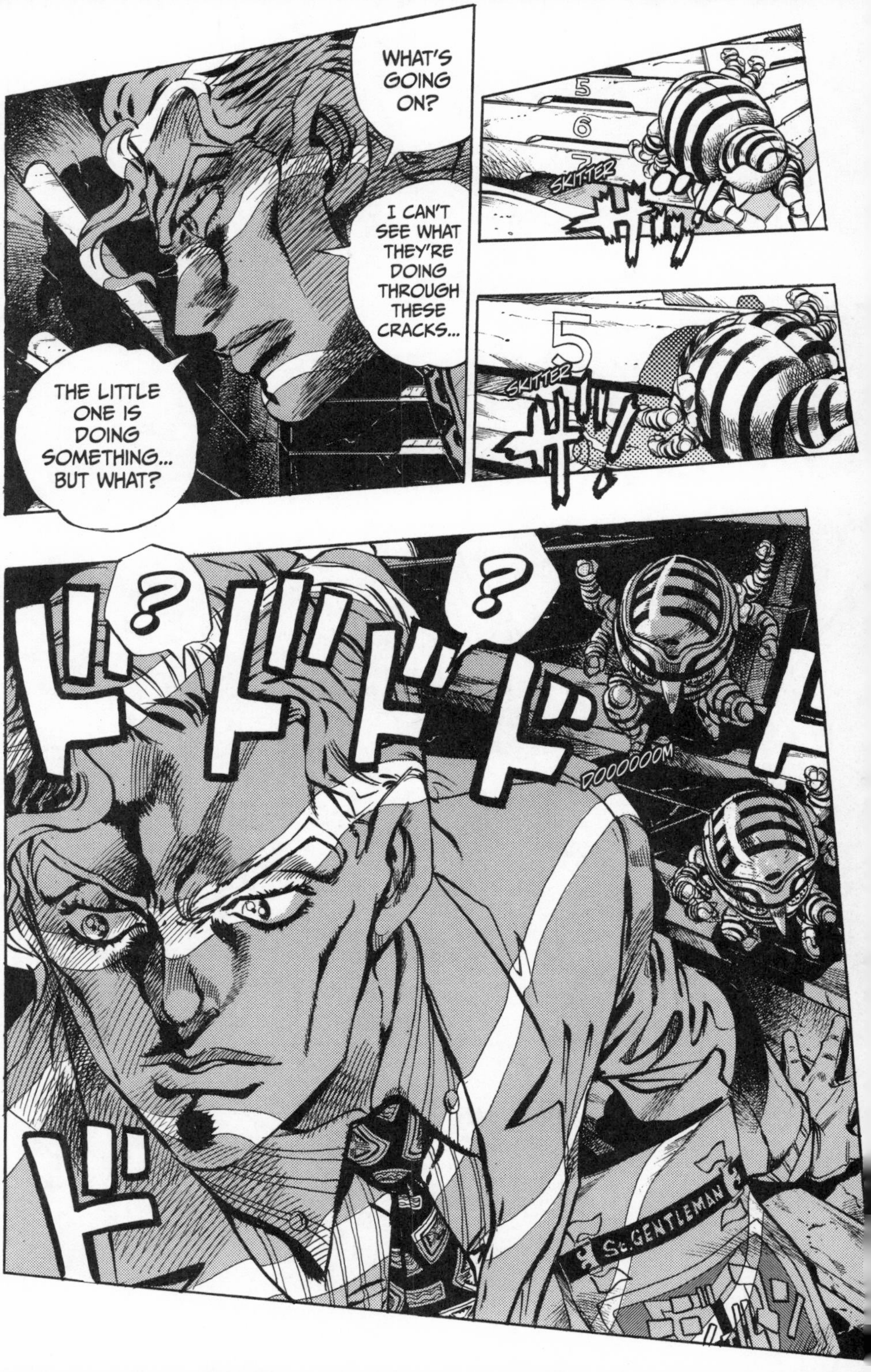
SKITTER
SKITTER
WHAT'S GOING ON?
I CAN'T SEE WHAT THEY'RE DOING THROUGH THESE CRACKS...
THE LITTLE ONE IS DOING SOMETHING... BUT WHAT?
?
?
DOOOOOOM
St. GENTLEMAN

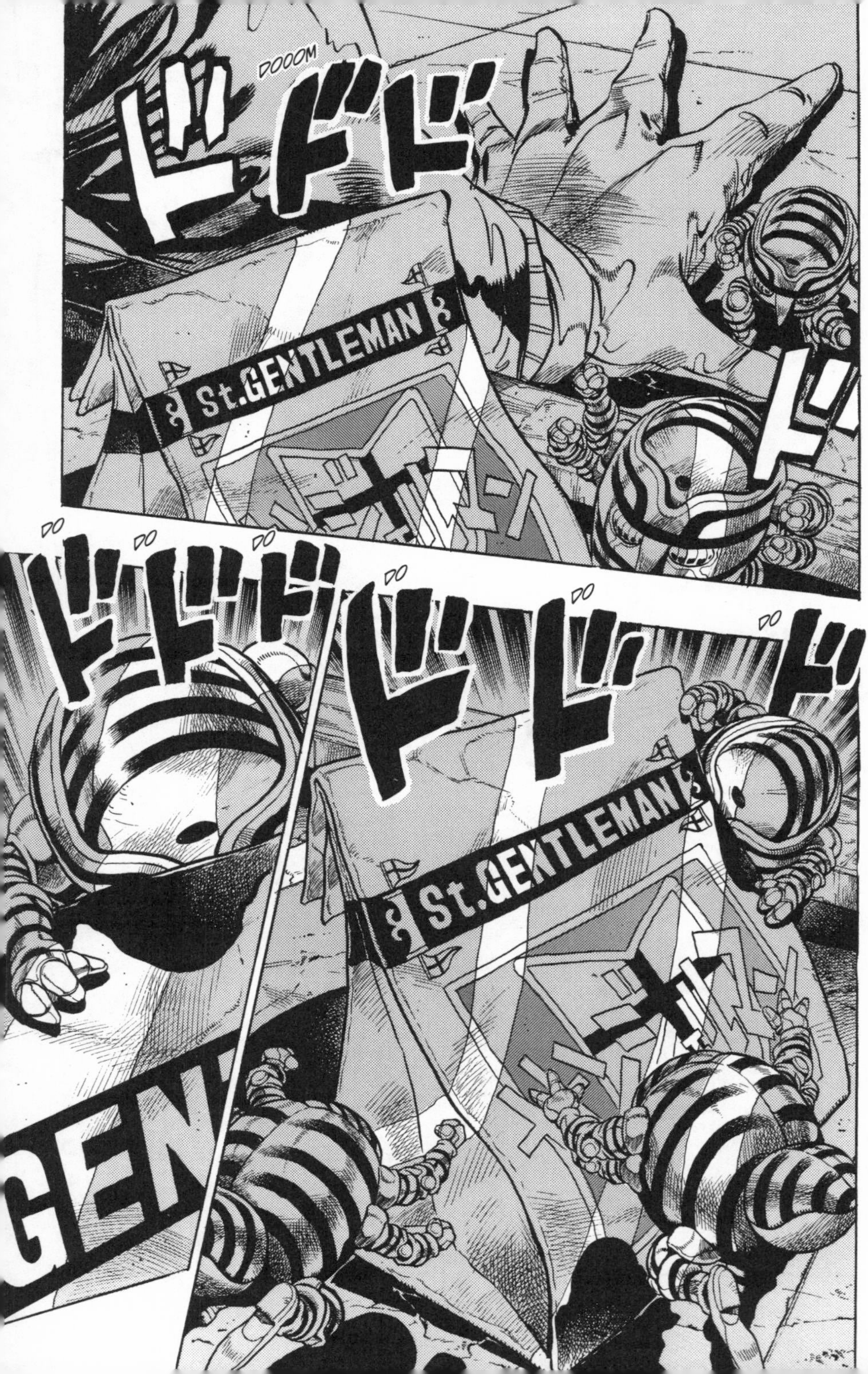
DOOOM
ドドド
St.GENTLEMAN
ド
DO
ドドド
DO
DO
St.GENTLEMAN
DO DO DO
ドドド
GEN

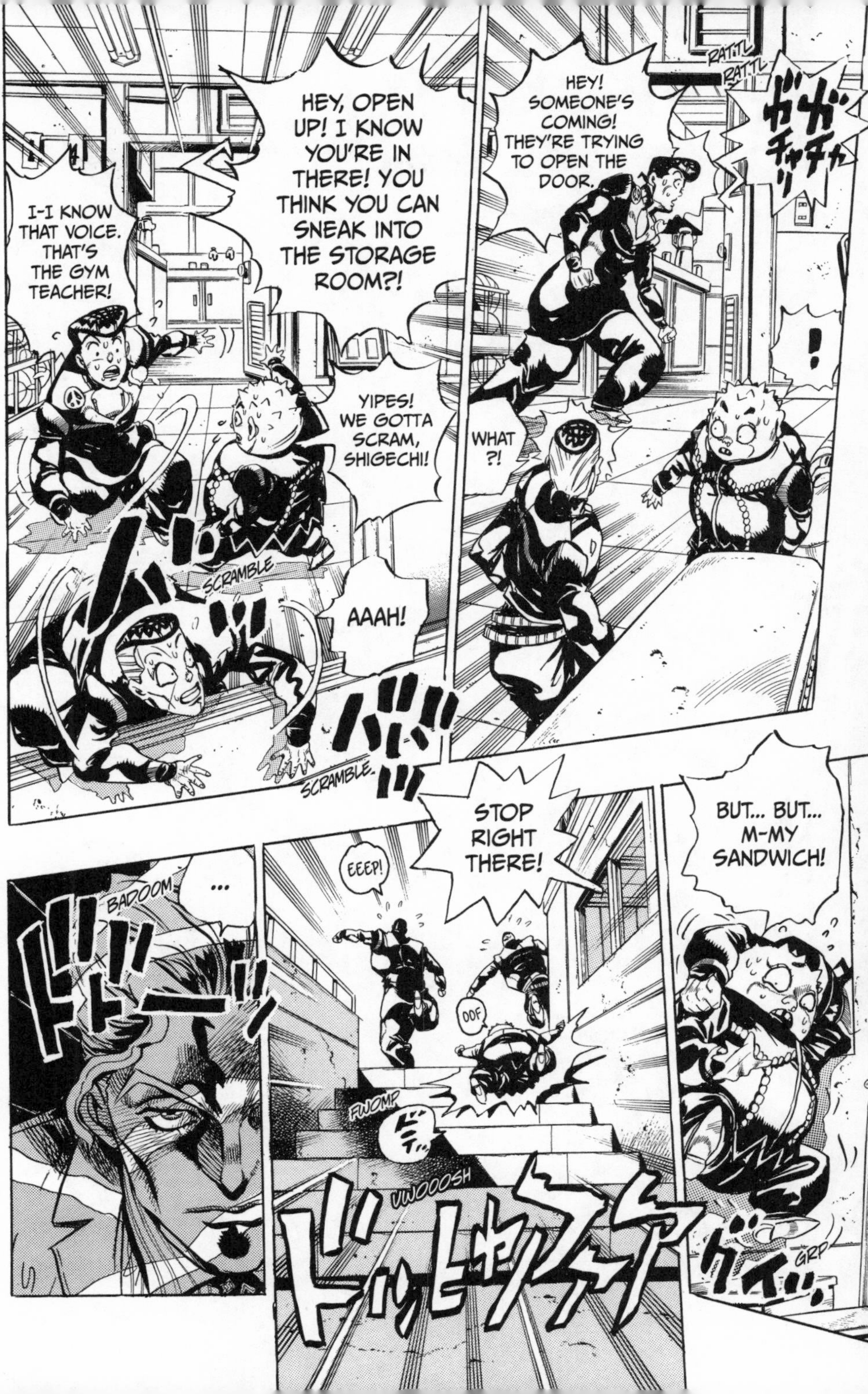
RATTL RATTL
HEY! SOMEONE'S COMING! THEY'RE TRYING TO OPEN THE DOOR.
!
WHAT ?!
HEY, OPEN UP! I KNOW YOU'RE IN THERE! YOU THINK YOU CAN SNEAK INTO THE STORAGE ROOM?!
I-I KNOW THAT VOICE. THAT'S THE GYM TEACHER!
YIPES! WE GOTTA SCRAM, SHIGECHI!
SCRAMBLE
AAAH!
SCRAMBLE
BUT... BUT... M-MY SANDWICH!
GRP
STOP RIGHT THERE!
EEEP!
OOF
FWOMP
UWOOOSH
BADOOM
...

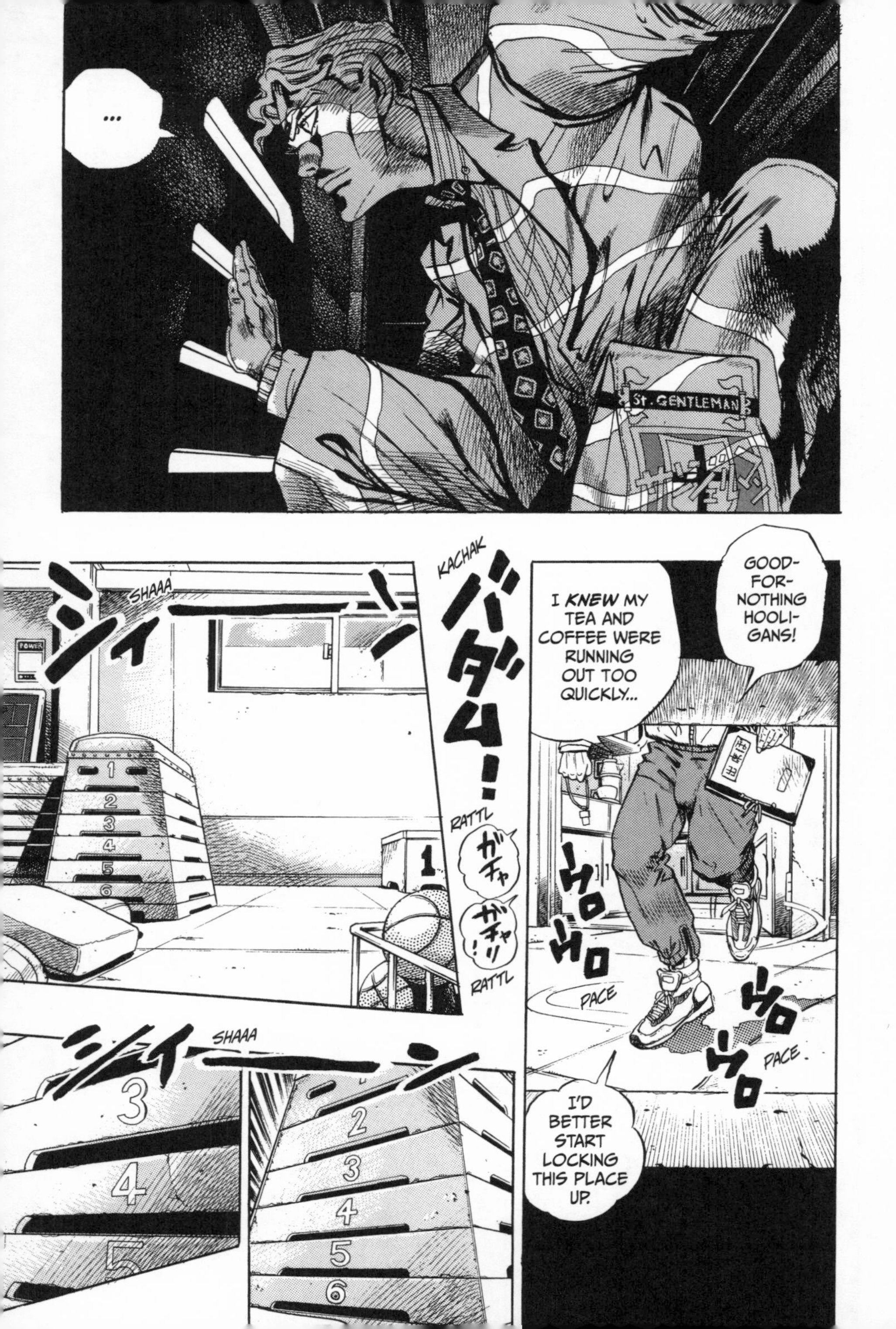
...
St. GENTLEMAN
GOOD-FOR-NOTHING HOOLIGANS!
I KNEW MY TEA AND COFFEE WERE RUNNING OUT TOO QUICKLY...
PACE
PACE
I'D BETTER START LOCKING THIS PLACE UP.
KACHAK
バダム!!
SHAAA
シィーーン
RATTL
ガチャ
ガチャリ!
RATTL
SHAAA
シィーーン

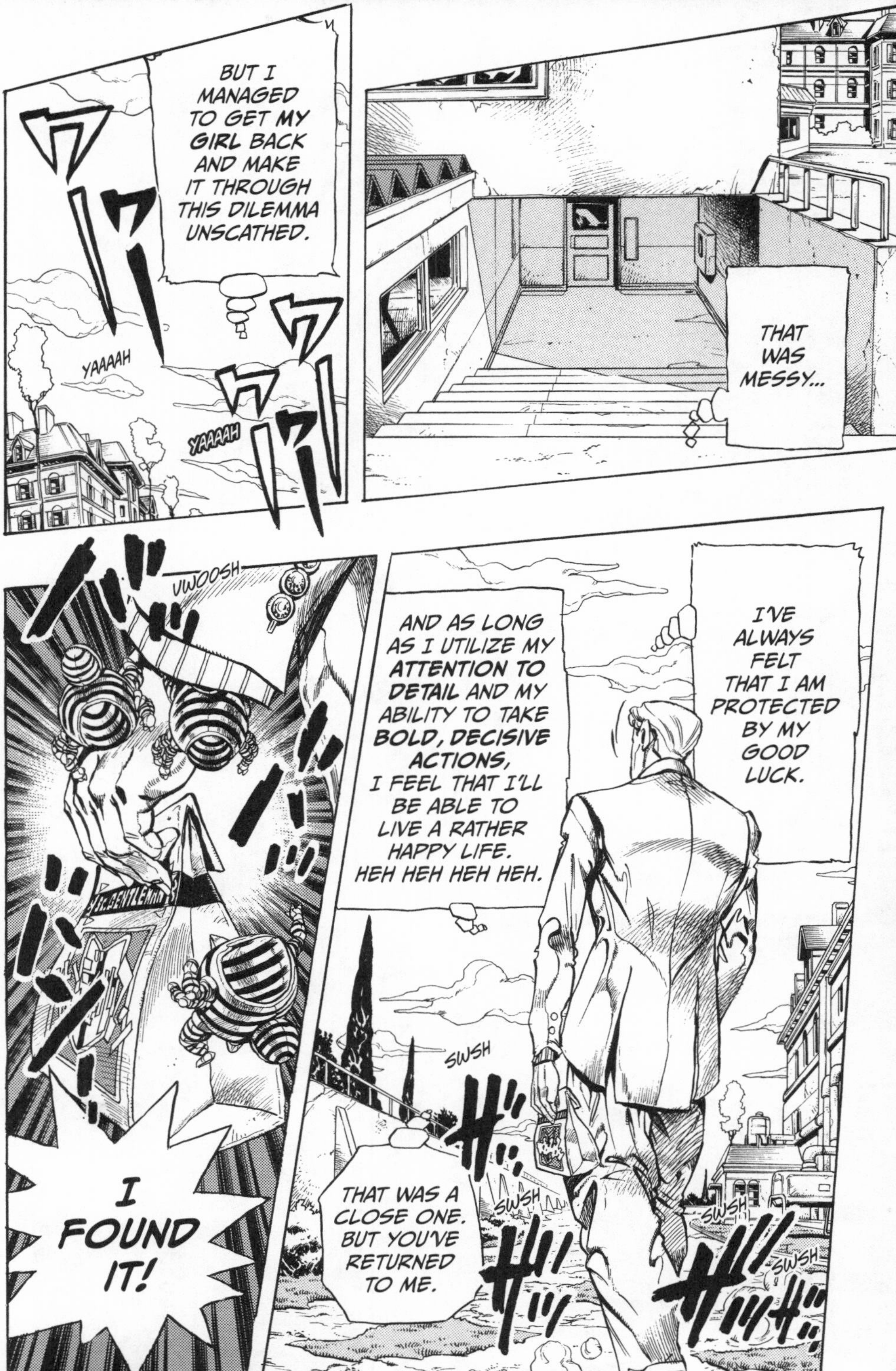
THAT WAS MESSY...
BUT I MANAGED TO GET MY GIRL BACK AND MAKE IT THROUGH THIS DILEMMA UNSCATHED.
YAAAAH
YAAAAH
I'VE ALWAYS FELT THAT I AM PROTECTED BY MY GOOD LUCK.
AND AS LONG AS I UTILIZE MY ATTENTION TO DETAIL AND MY ABILITY TO TAKE BOLD, DECISIVE ACTIONS, I FEEL THAT I'LL BE ABLE TO LIVE A RATHER HAPPY LIFE. HEH HEH HEH HEH.
SWSH
THAT WAS A CLOSE ONE. BUT YOU'VE RETURNED TO ME.
SWSH
SWSH
SWSH
VWOOSH
I FOUND IT!

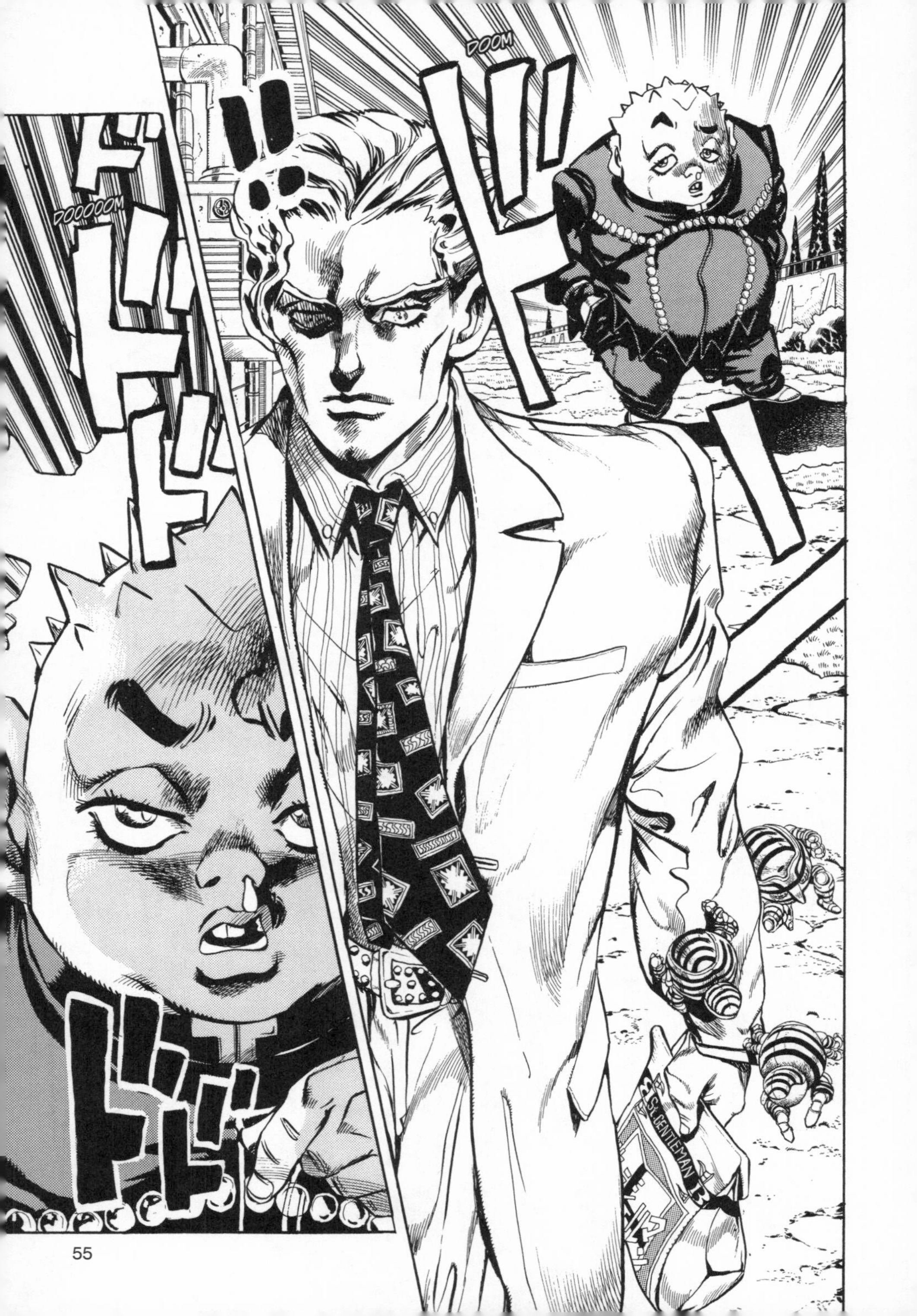
DOOM
St. GENTLEMAN
DOOOOOM

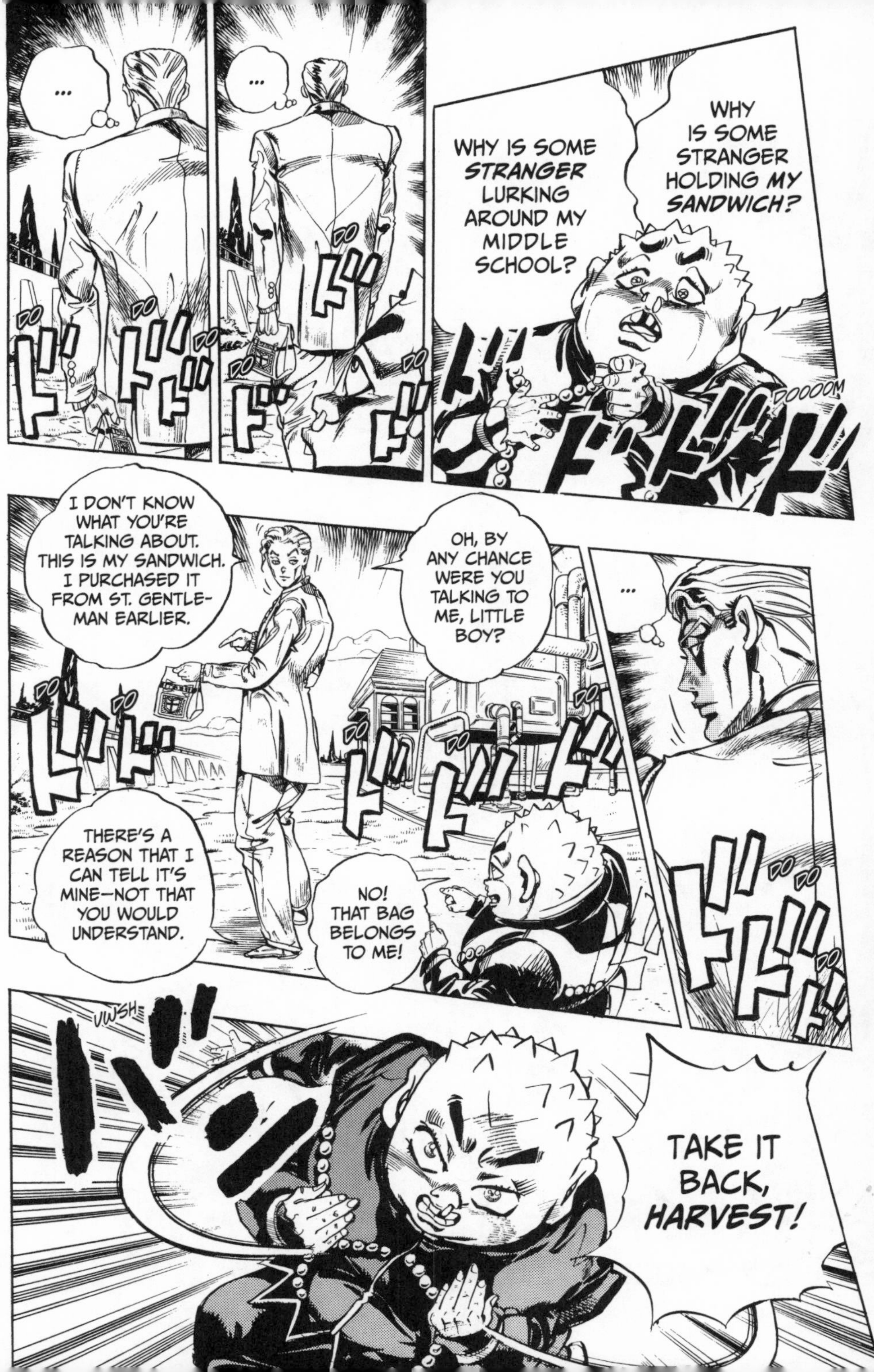
WHY IS SOME STRANGER HOLDING MY SANDWICH?
WHY IS SOME STRANGER LURKING AROUND MY MIDDLE SCHOOL?
DOOOOM
...
DO DO DO
...
DO DO DO
...
DO DO DO
OH, BY ANY CHANCE WERE YOU TALKING TO ME, LITTLE BOY?
I DON'T KNOW WHAT YOU'RE TALKING ABOUT. THIS IS MY SANDWICH. I PURCHASED IT FROM ST. GENTLEMAN EARLIER.
DO DO DO DO
NO! THAT BAG BELONGS TO ME!
THERE'S A REASON THAT I CAN TELL IT'S MINE—NOT THAT YOU WOULD UNDERSTAND.
TAKE IT BACK, HARVEST!
VWSH

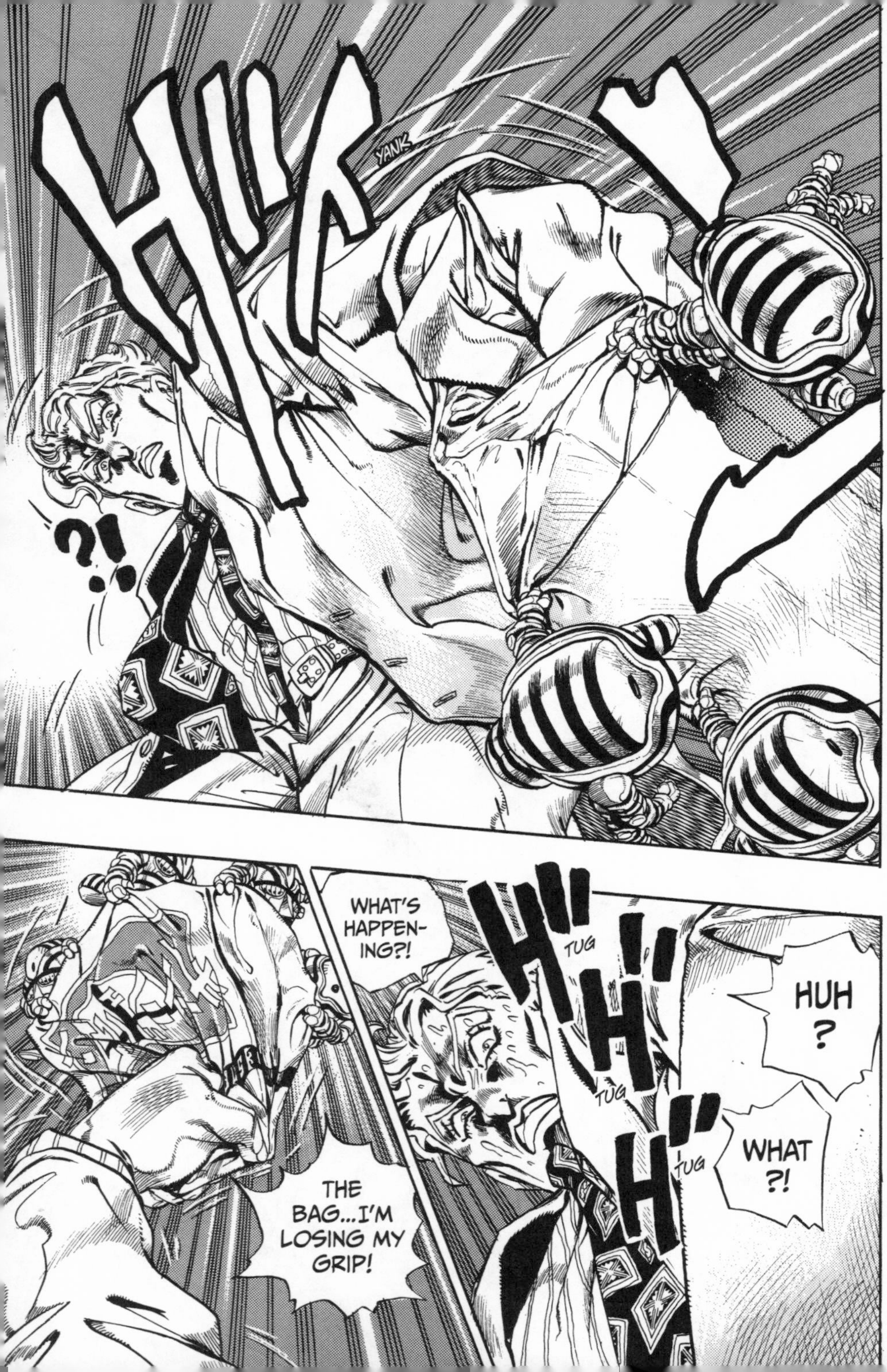
YANK
?!
HUH ?
WHAT ?!
WHAT'S HAPPEN-ING?!
TUG
TUG
TUG
THE BAG...I'M LOSING MY GRIP!

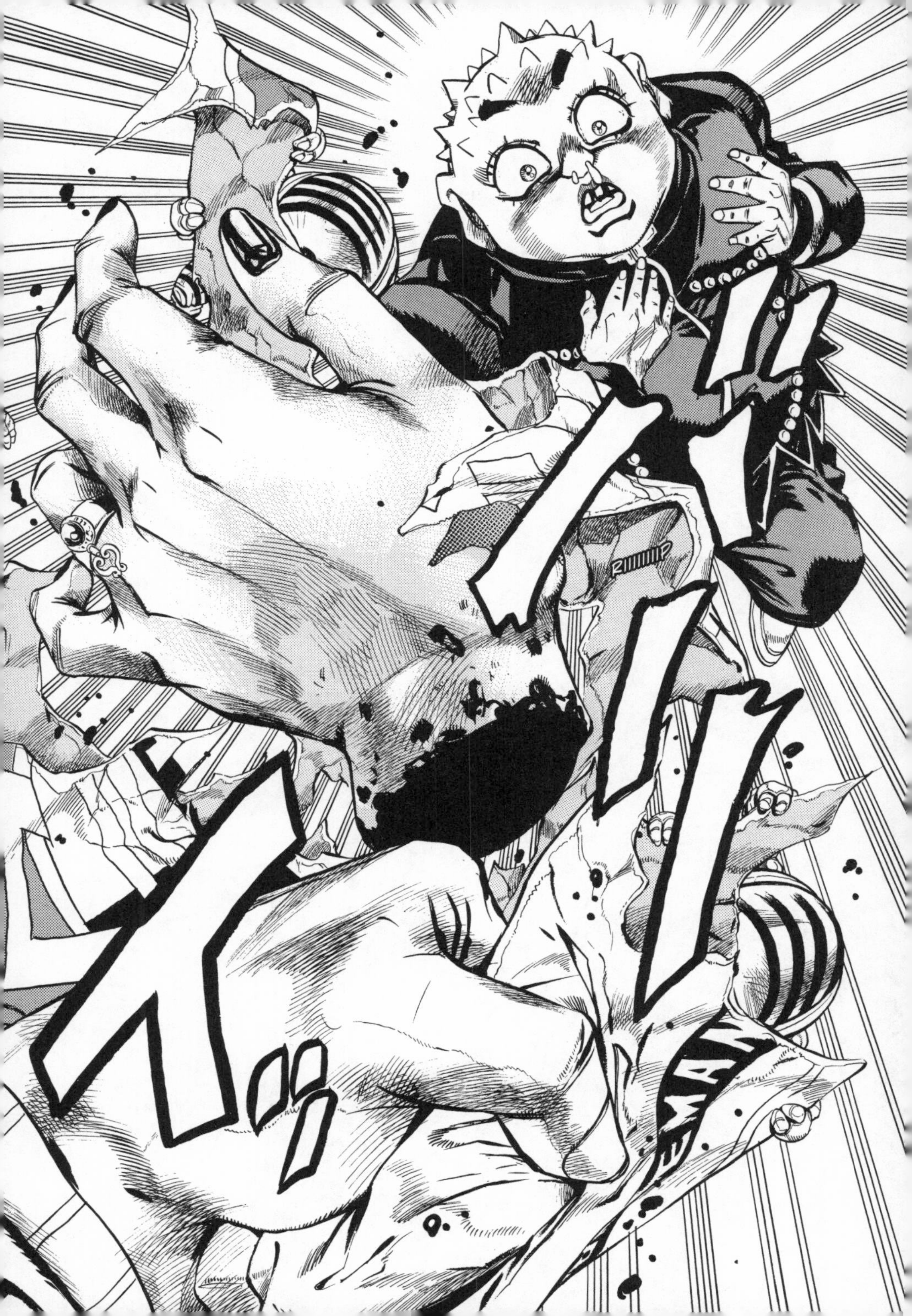
RIIIIIIIP

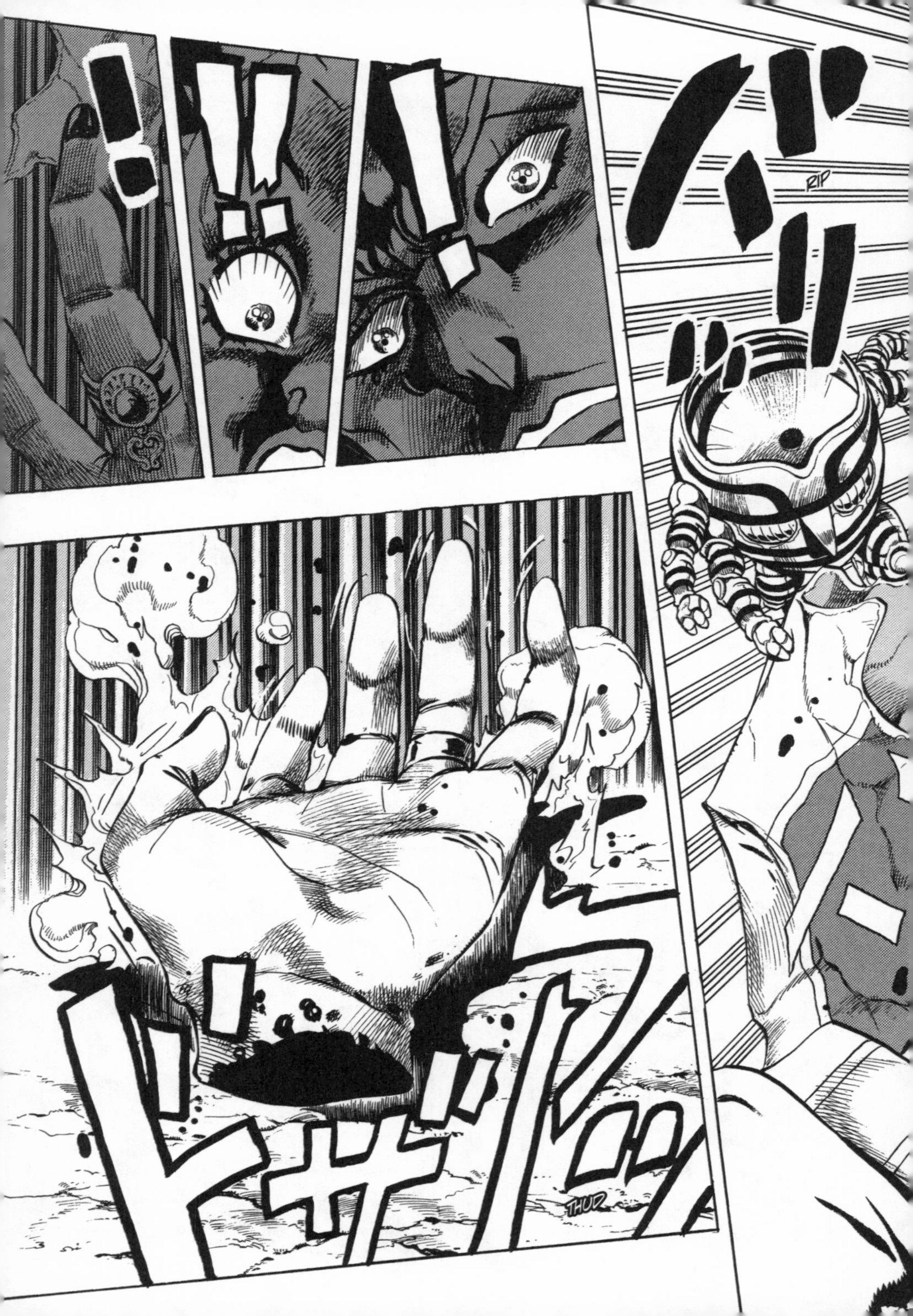
RIP
THUD

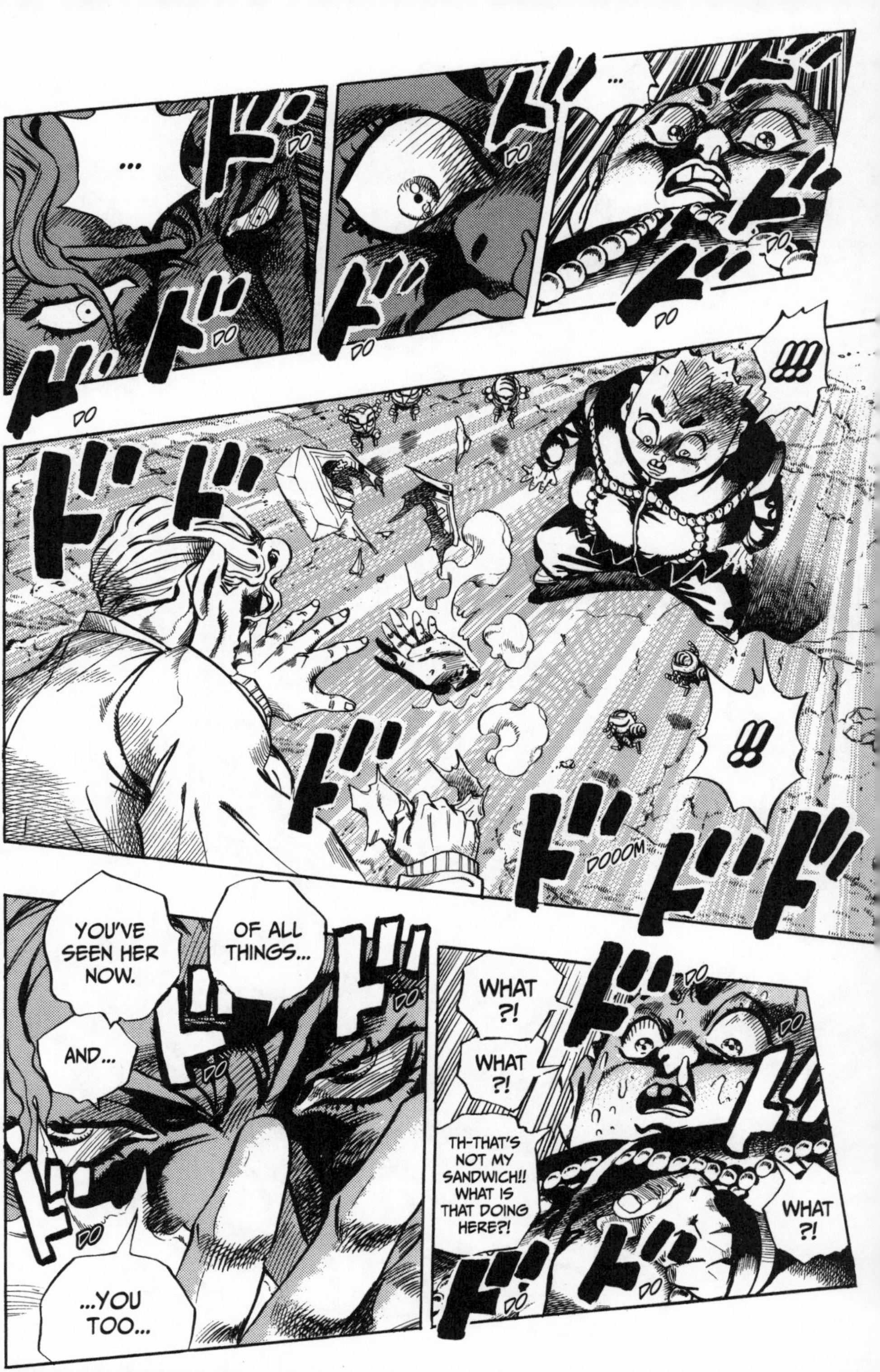
...
DO
DO
DO
DO
DO
...
DO
DO
!!!
!!
DOOOM
DO
DO
WHAT ?!
WHAT ?!
TH-THAT'S NOT MY SANDWICH!! WHAT IS THAT DOING HERE?!
WHAT ?!
DO
DO
OF ALL THINGS...
YOU'VE SEEN HER NOW.
DO
DO
AND...
DO
...YOU TOO...

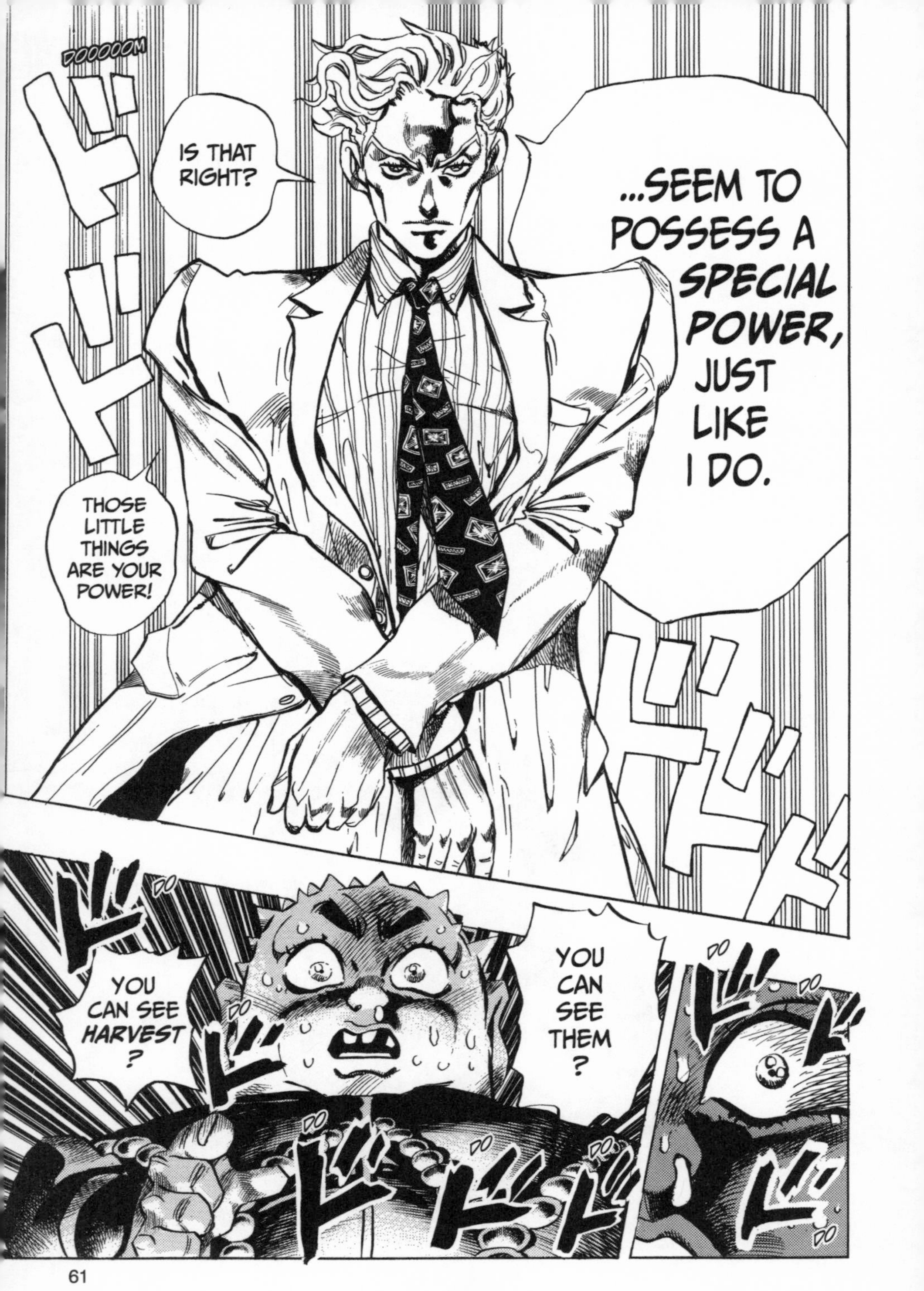
...SEEM TO POSSESS A SPECIAL POWER, JUST LIKE I DO.
IS THAT RIGHT?
DOOOOOM
THOSE LITTLE THINGS ARE YOUR POWER!
YOU CAN SEE THEM?
YOU CAN SEE HARVEST?

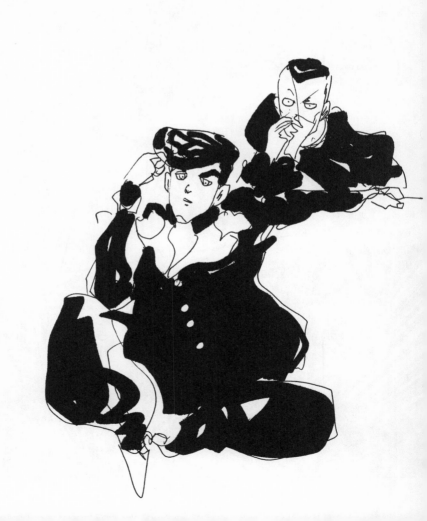

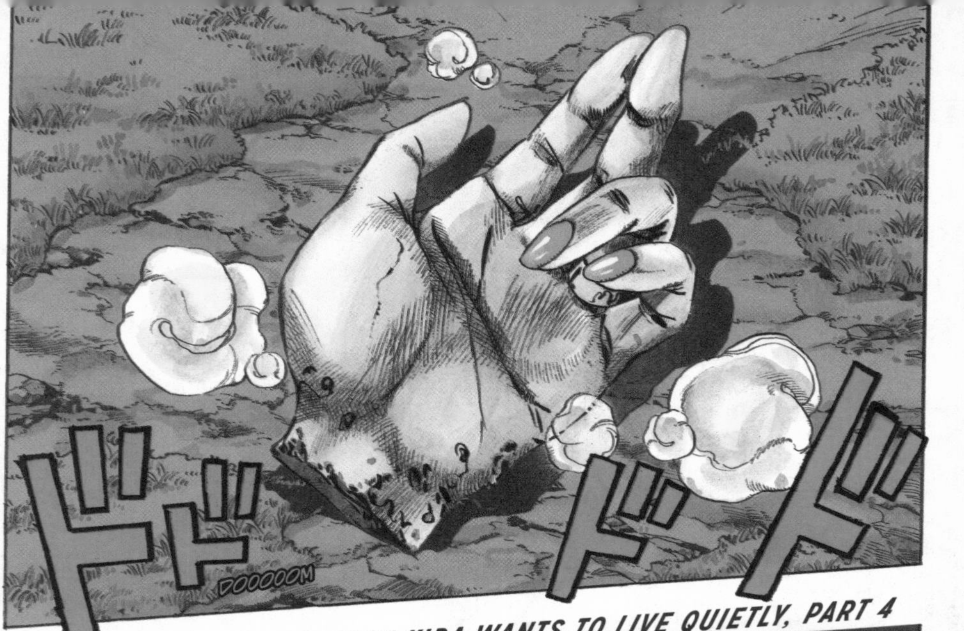
DOOOOOM

CHAPTER 80 ★ YOSHIKAGE KIRA WANTS TO LIVE QUIETLY, PART 4

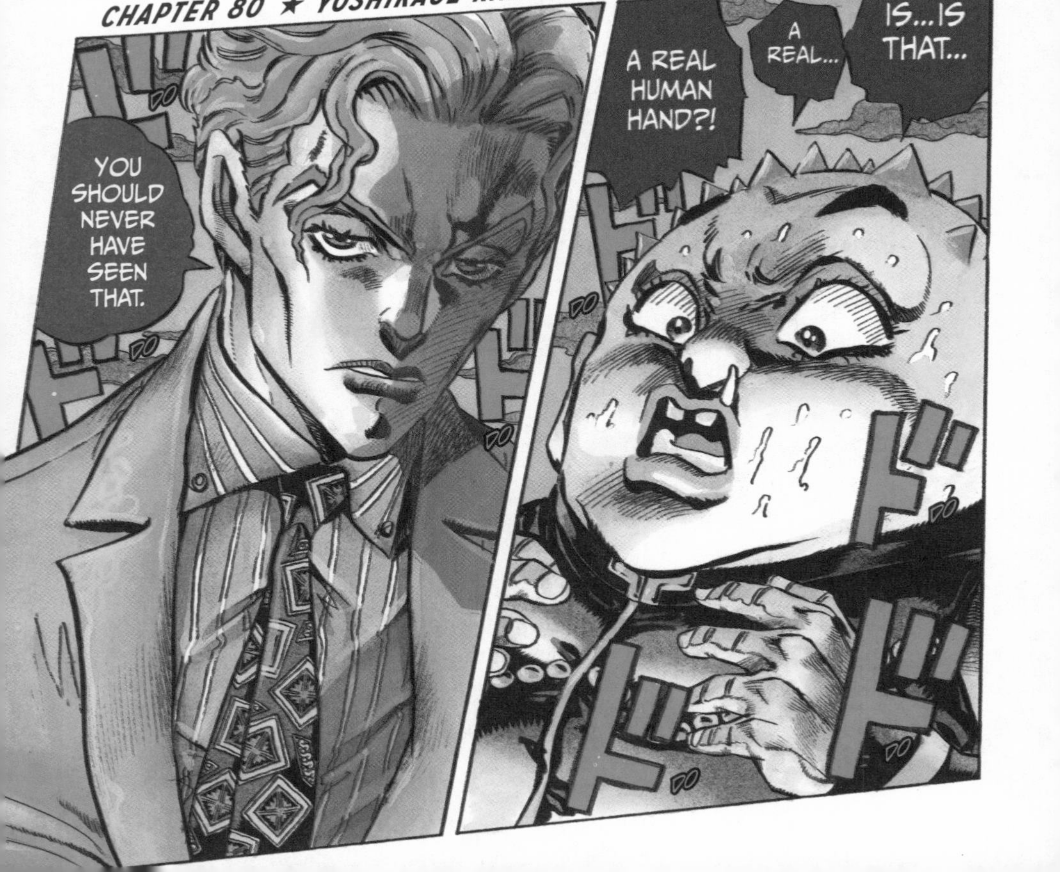
IS...IS THAT...
A REAL...
A REAL HUMAN HAND?!
DO
DO
DO
YOU SHOULD NEVER HAVE SEEN THAT.
DO
DO
DO

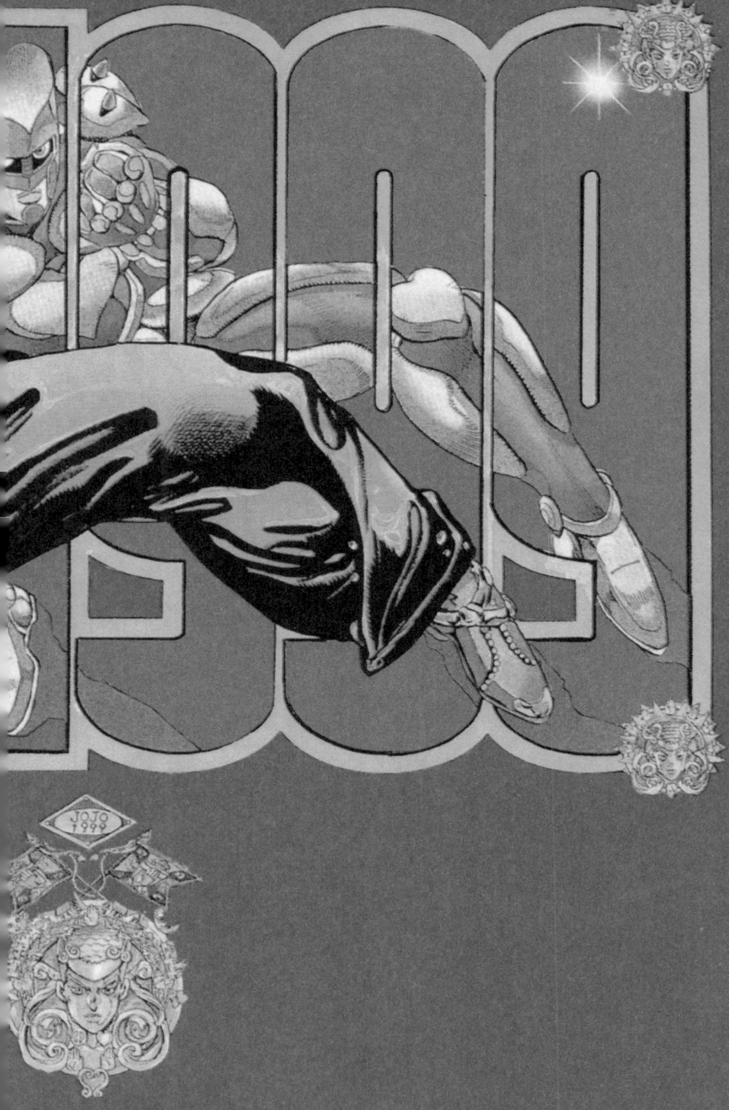
JOJO
1999

TO LIVE QUIETLY, PART 4

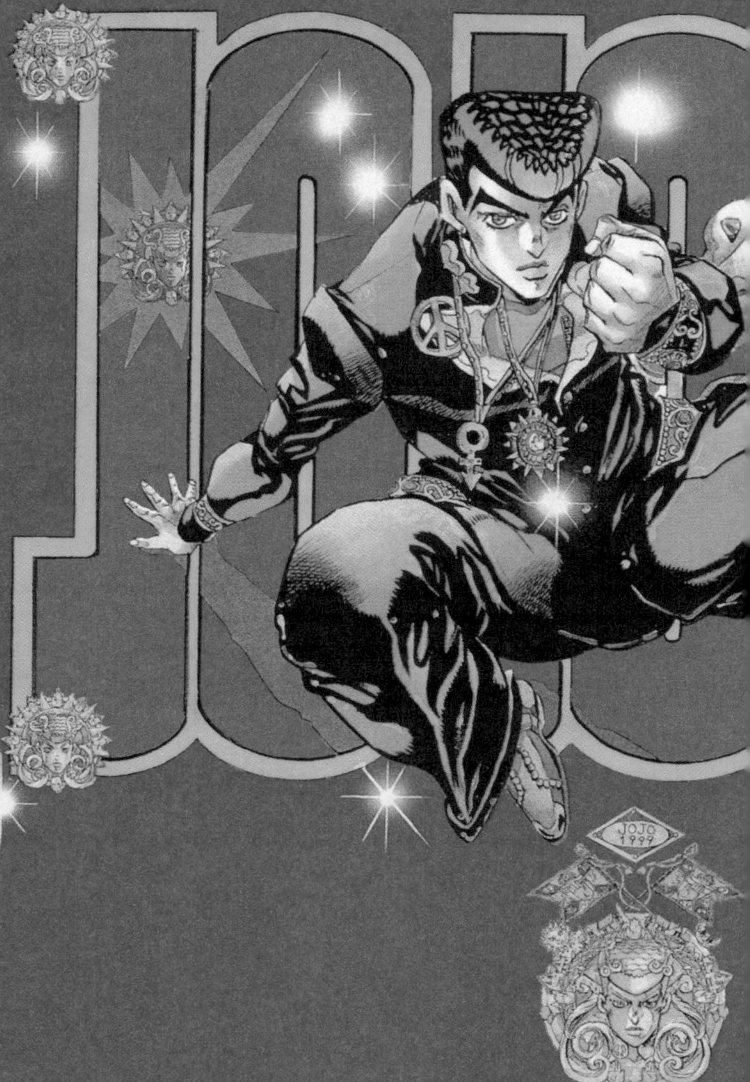
JOJO
1999

CHAPTER 80

YOSHIKAGE KIRA WANTS

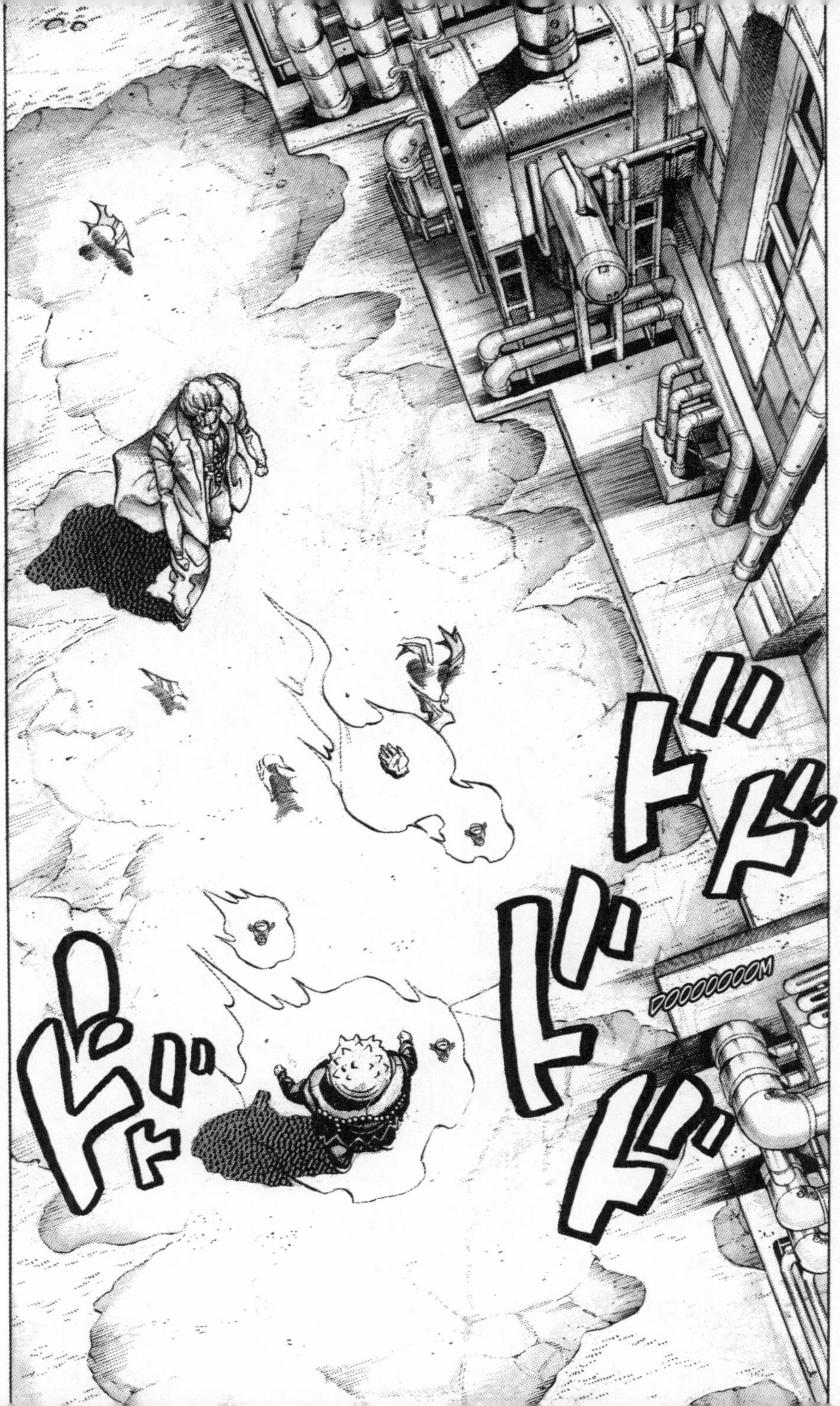
ドドドドド
ドド
DOOOOOOOOM

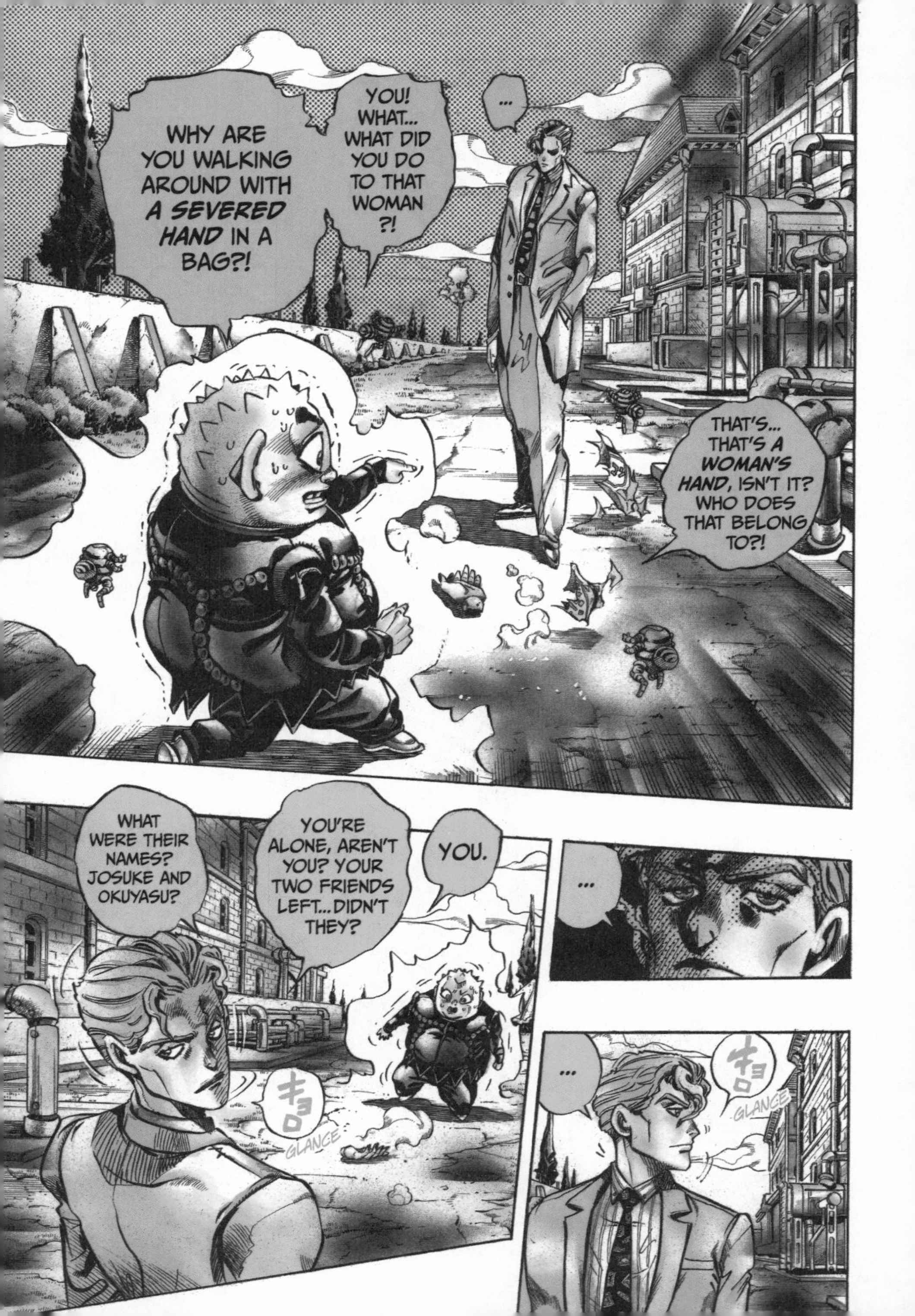
...
YOU! WHAT... WHAT DID YOU DO TO THAT WOMAN ?!
WHY ARE YOU WALKING AROUND WITH *A SEVERED HAND* IN A BAG?!
THAT'S... THAT'S A *WOMAN'S HAND*, ISN'T IT? WHO DOES THAT BELONG TO?!
...
...
キョロ
GLANCE
YOU.
YOU'RE ALONE, AREN'T YOU? YOUR TWO FRIENDS LEFT...DIDN'T THEY?
WHAT WERE THEIR NAMES? JOSUKE AND OKUYASU?
キョロ
GLANCE

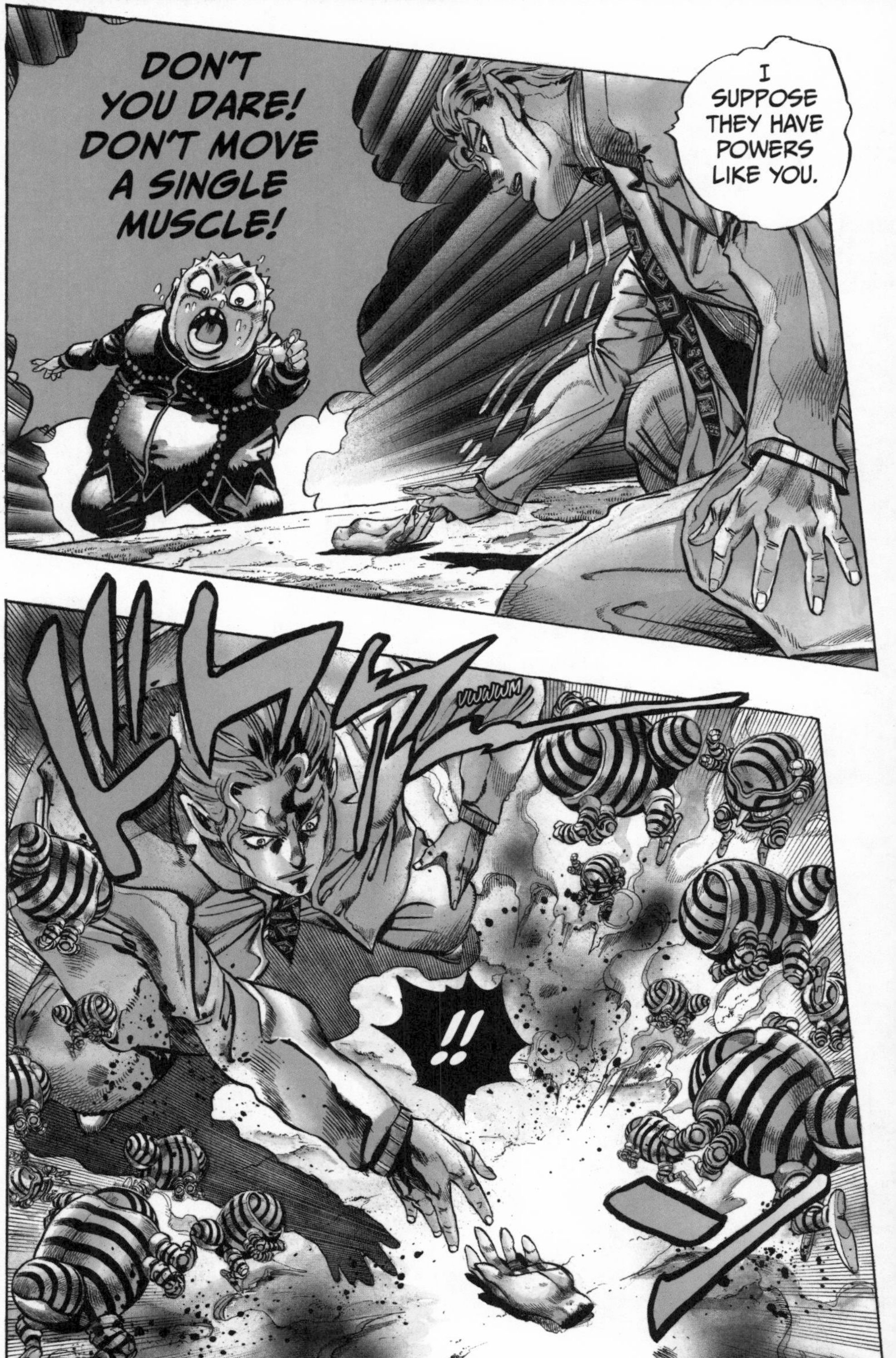
I SUPPOSE THEY HAVE POWERS LIKE YOU.
DON'T YOU DARE! DON'T MOVE A SINGLE MUSCLE!
VWWWM
!!

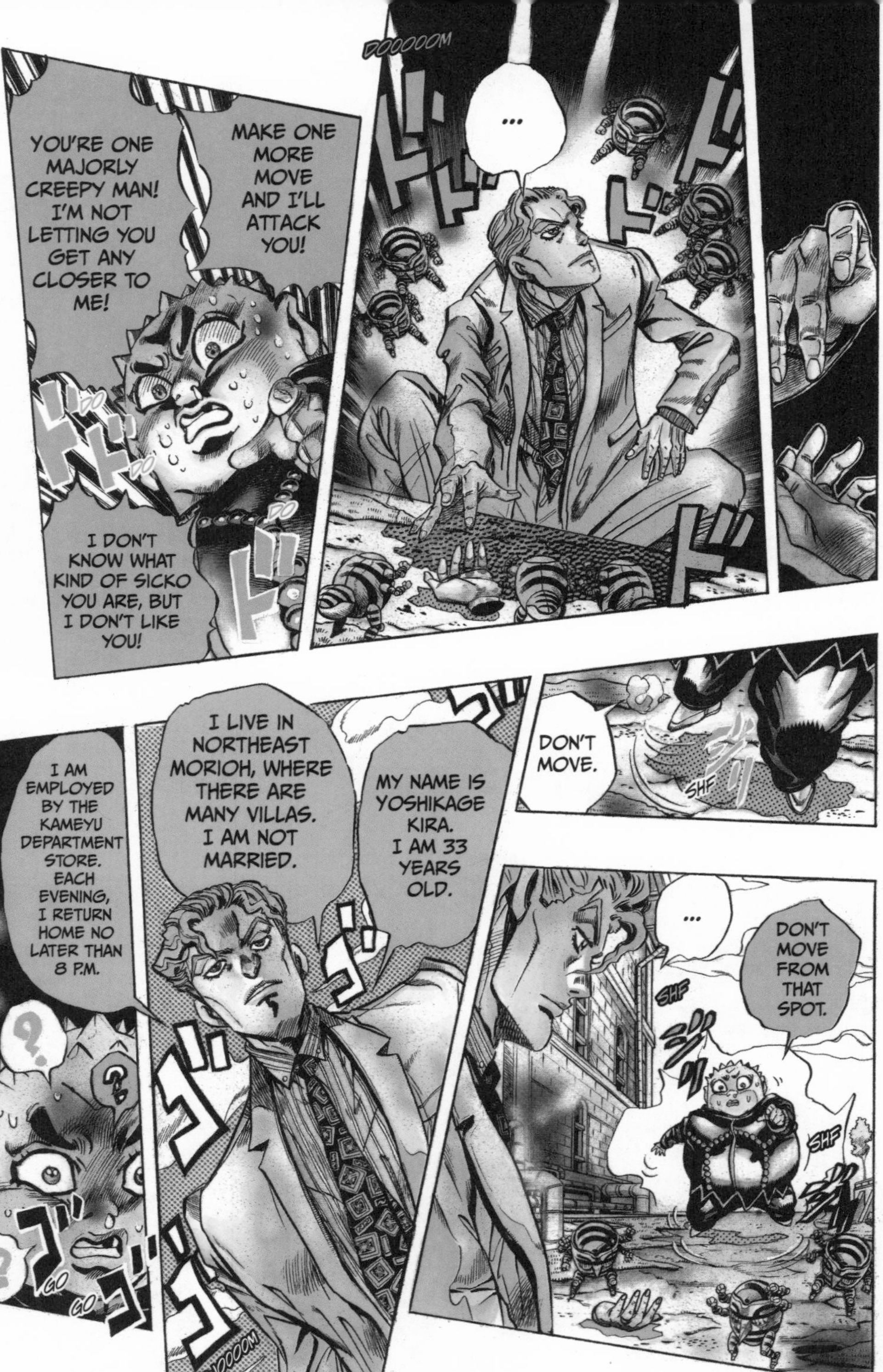
DOOOOOM
...
MAKE ONE MORE MOVE AND I'LL ATTACK YOU!
YOU'RE ONE MAJORLY CREEPY MAN! I'M NOT LETTING YOU GET ANY CLOSER TO ME!
DO
DO
DO
I DON'T KNOW WHAT KIND OF SICKO YOU ARE, BUT I DON'T LIKE YOU!
DON'T MOVE.
SHF
...
DON'T MOVE FROM THAT SPOT.
SHF
SHF
MY NAME IS YOSHIKAGE KIRA. I AM 33 YEARS OLD.
I LIVE IN NORTHEAST MORIOH, WHERE THERE ARE MANY VILLAS. I AM NOT MARRIED.
VWOOOOM
I AM EMPLOYED BY THE KAMEYU DEPARTMENT STORE. EACH EVENING, I RETURN HOME NO LATER THAN 8 P.M.
GO
GO

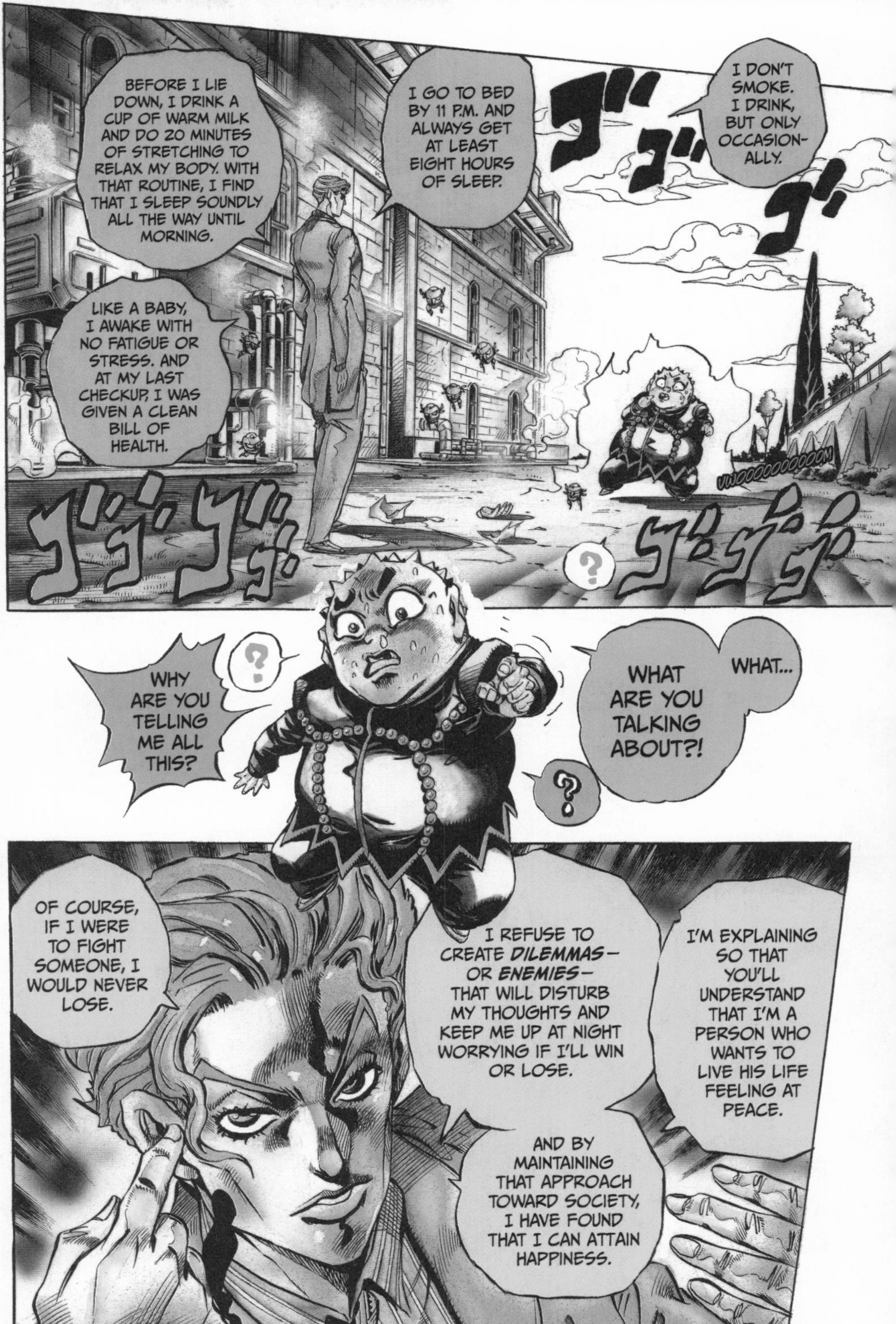
I DON'T SMOKE. I DRINK, BUT ONLY OCCASION-ALLY.
I GO TO BED BY 11 P.M. AND ALWAYS GET AT LEAST EIGHT HOURS OF SLEEP.
BEFORE I LIE DOWN, I DRINK A CUP OF WARM MILK AND DO 20 MINUTES OF STRETCHING TO RELAX MY BODY. WITH THAT ROUTINE, I FIND THAT I SLEEP SOUNDLY ALL THE WAY UNTIL MORNING.
LIKE A BABY, I AWAKE WITH NO FATIGUE OR STRESS. AND AT MY LAST CHECKUP, I WAS GIVEN A CLEAN BILL OF HEALTH.
VWOOOOOOOOOOM
?
WHAT...
WHAT ARE YOU TALKING ABOUT?!
?
?
WHY ARE YOU TELLING ME ALL THIS?
I'M EXPLAINING SO THAT YOU'LL UNDERSTAND THAT I'M A PERSON WHO WANTS TO LIVE HIS LIFE FEELING AT PEACE.
I REFUSE TO CREATE *DILEMMAS*— OR *ENEMIES*— THAT WILL DISTURB MY THOUGHTS AND KEEP ME UP AT NIGHT WORRYING IF I'LL WIN OR LOSE.
OF COURSE, IF I WERE TO FIGHT SOMEONE, I WOULD NEVER LOSE.
AND BY MAINTAINING THAT APPROACH TOWARD SOCIETY, I HAVE FOUND THAT I CAN ATTAIN HAPPINESS.

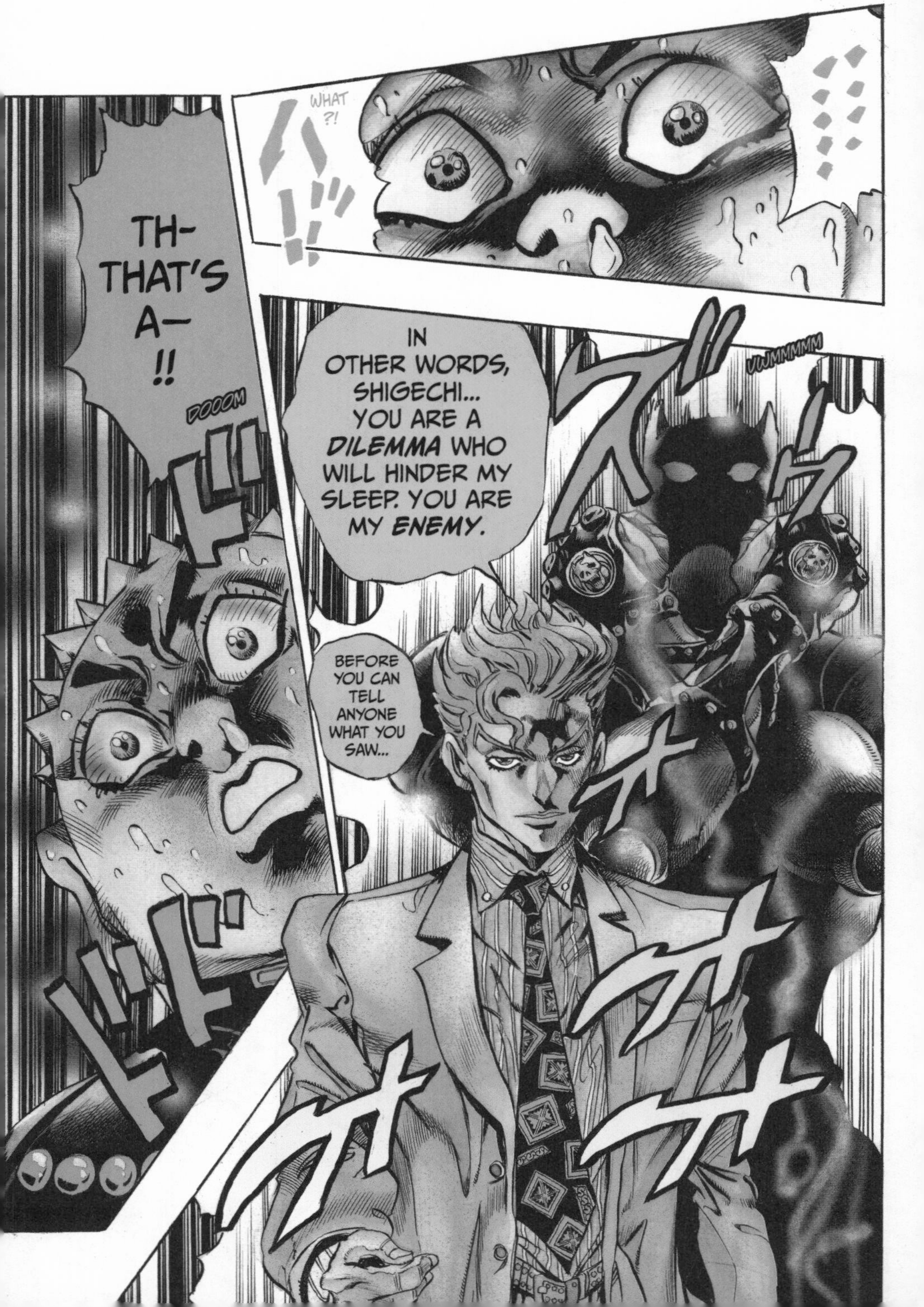
WHAT ?!
UWMMMMM
IN OTHER WORDS, SHIGECHI... YOU ARE A *DILEMMA* WHO WILL HINDER MY SLEEP. YOU ARE MY *ENEMY*.
BEFORE YOU CAN TELL ANYONE WHAT YOU SAW...
TH- THAT'S A— !!
DOOOM

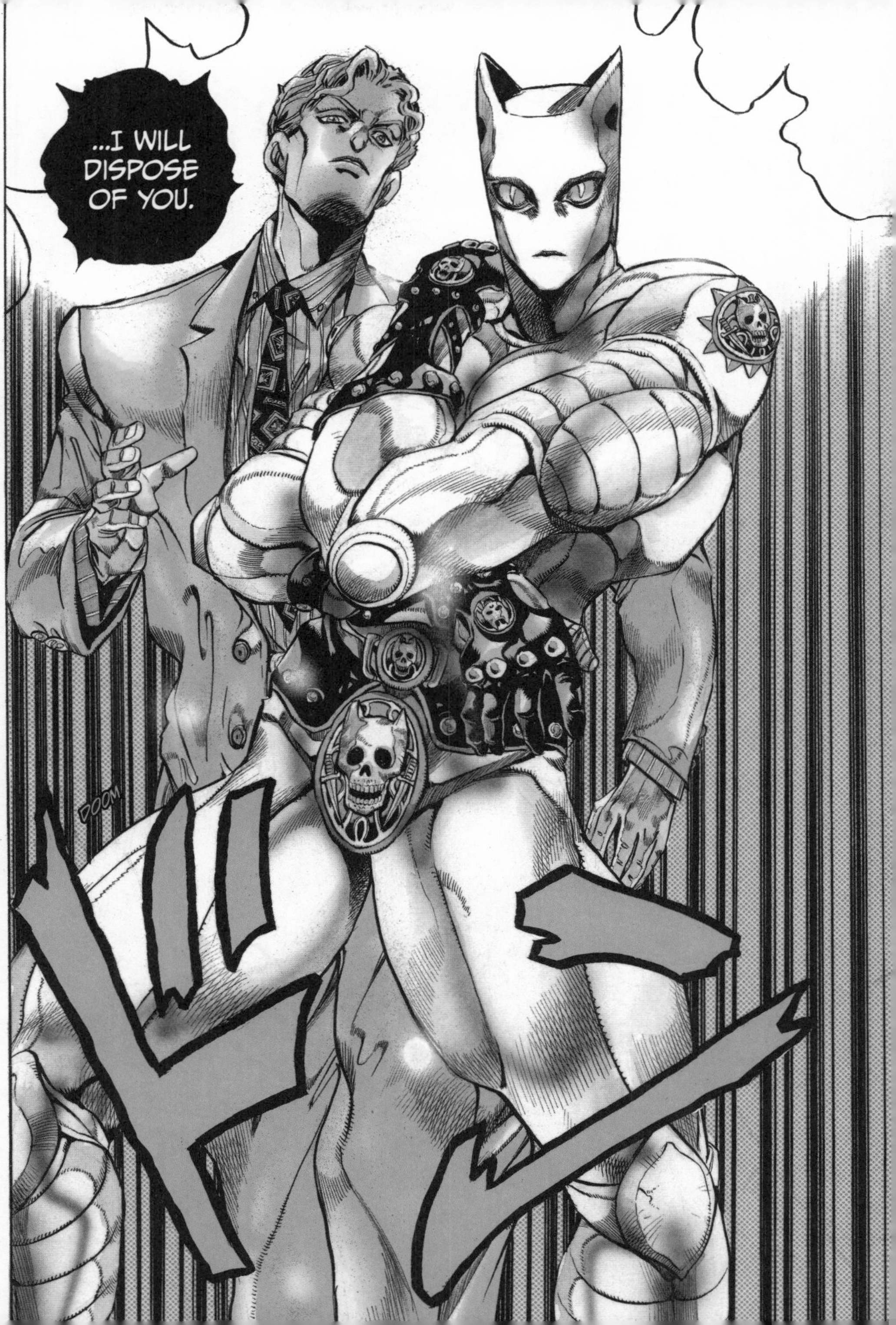
...I WILL DISPOSE OF YOU.
DOOM

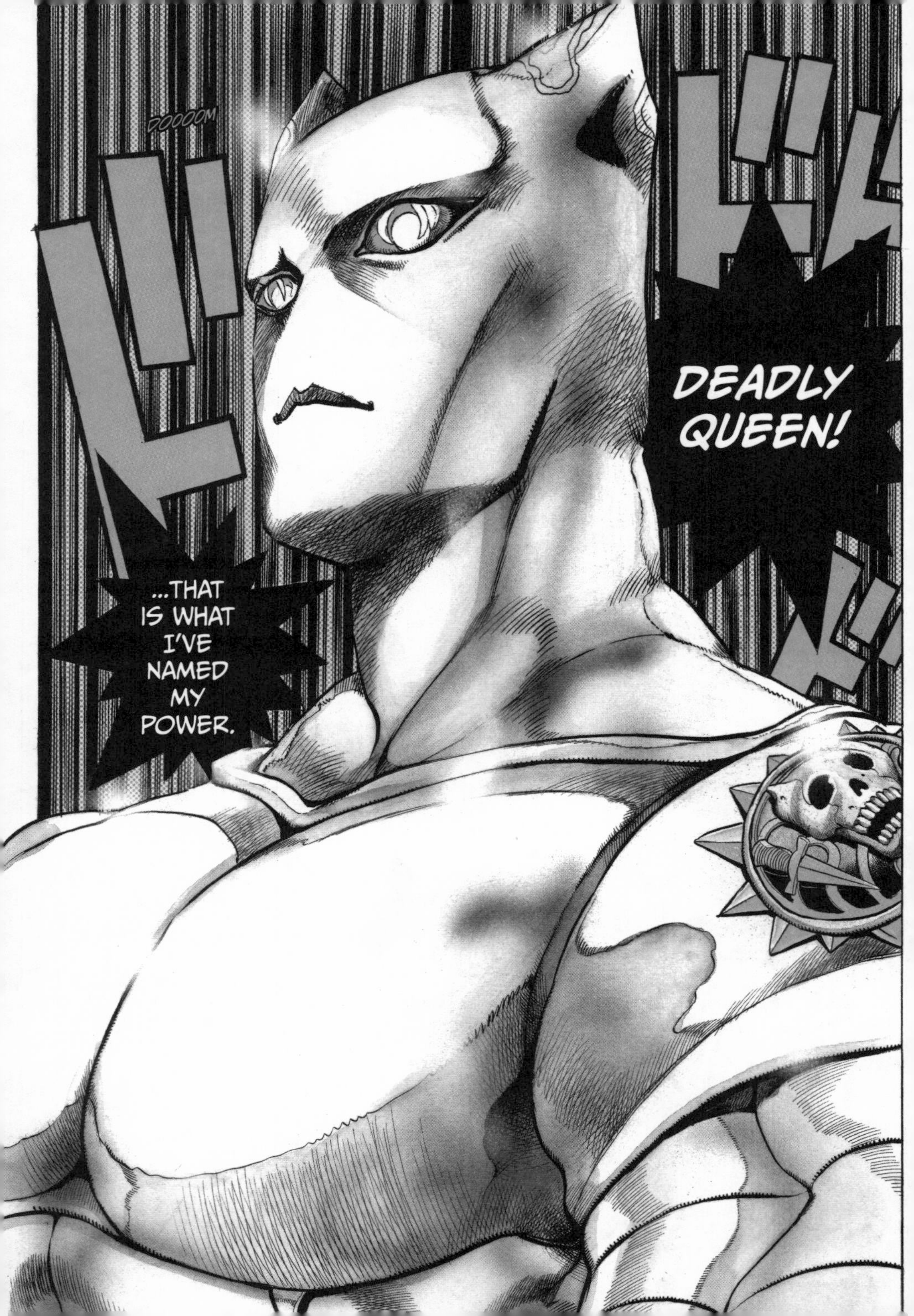
DOOOOM
DEADLY QUEEN!
...THAT IS WHAT I'VE NAMED MY POWER.

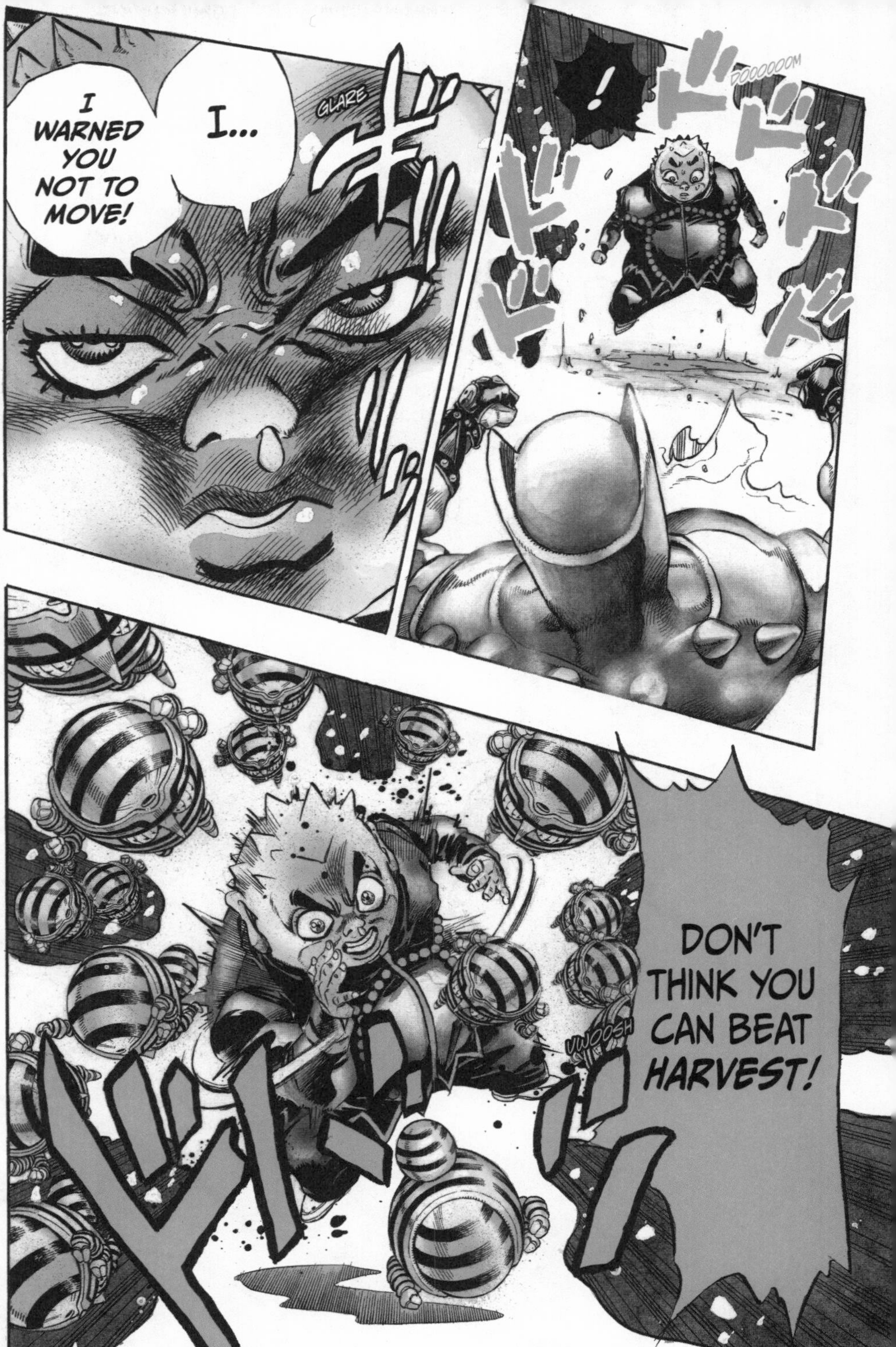
!
DOOOOOOM
I...
I WARNED YOU NOT TO MOVE!
GLARE
DON'T THINK YOU CAN BEAT HARVEST!
VWOOSH

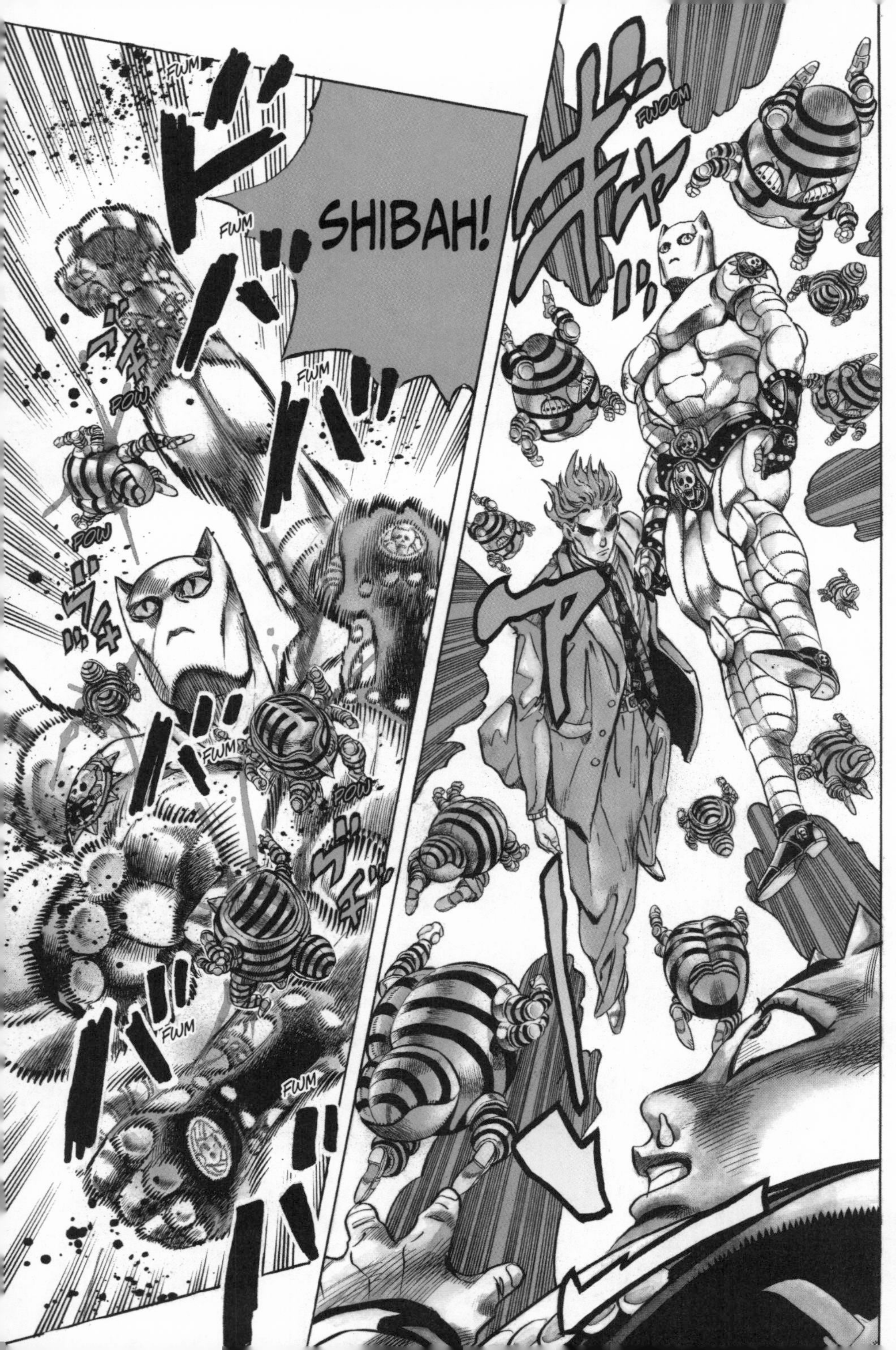

FWOOM
SHIBAH!
FWM
FWM
FWM
POW
POW
FWM
POW
FWM
FWM

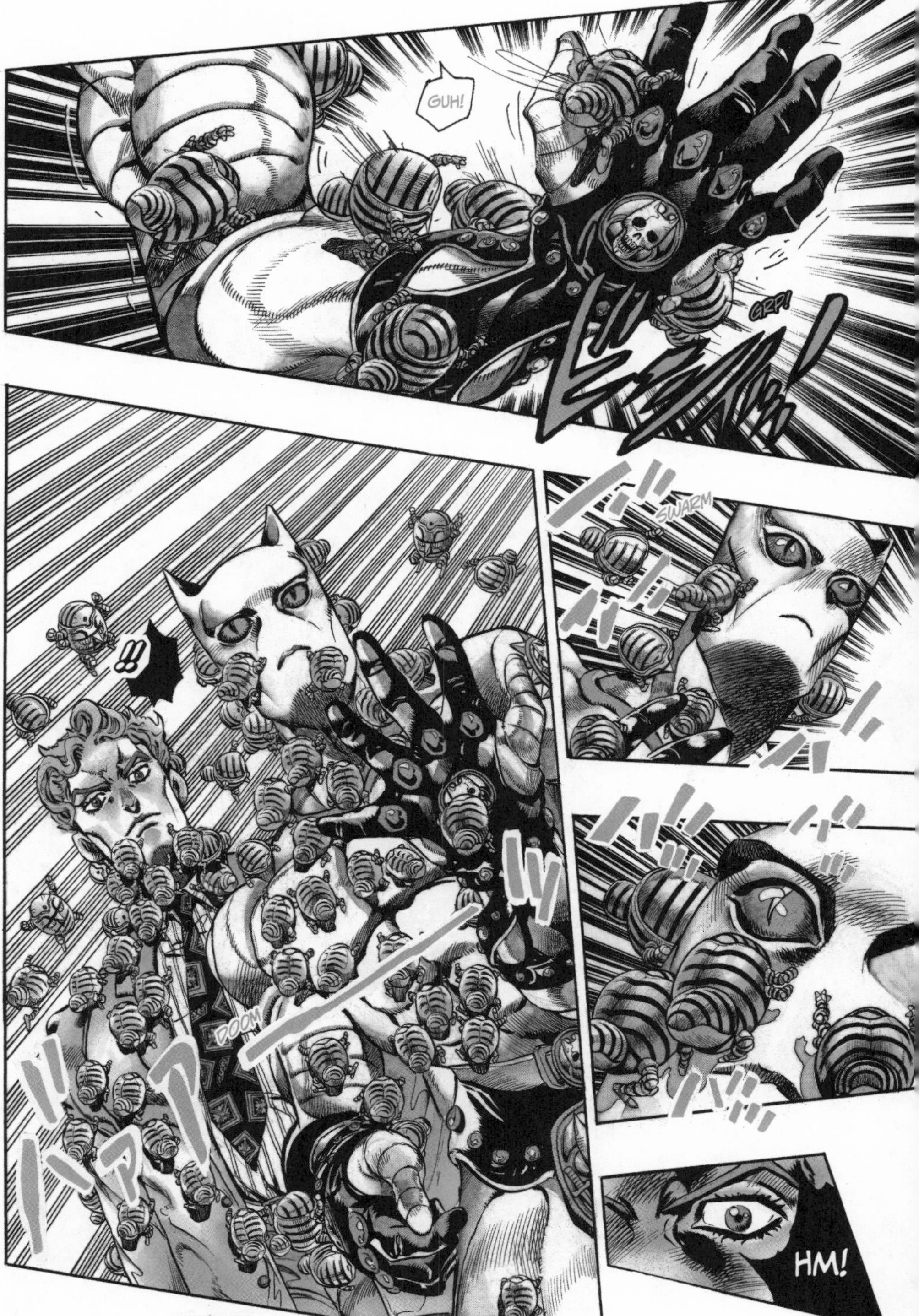
GUH!
GRP!
SWARM
HM!
!!
DOOM

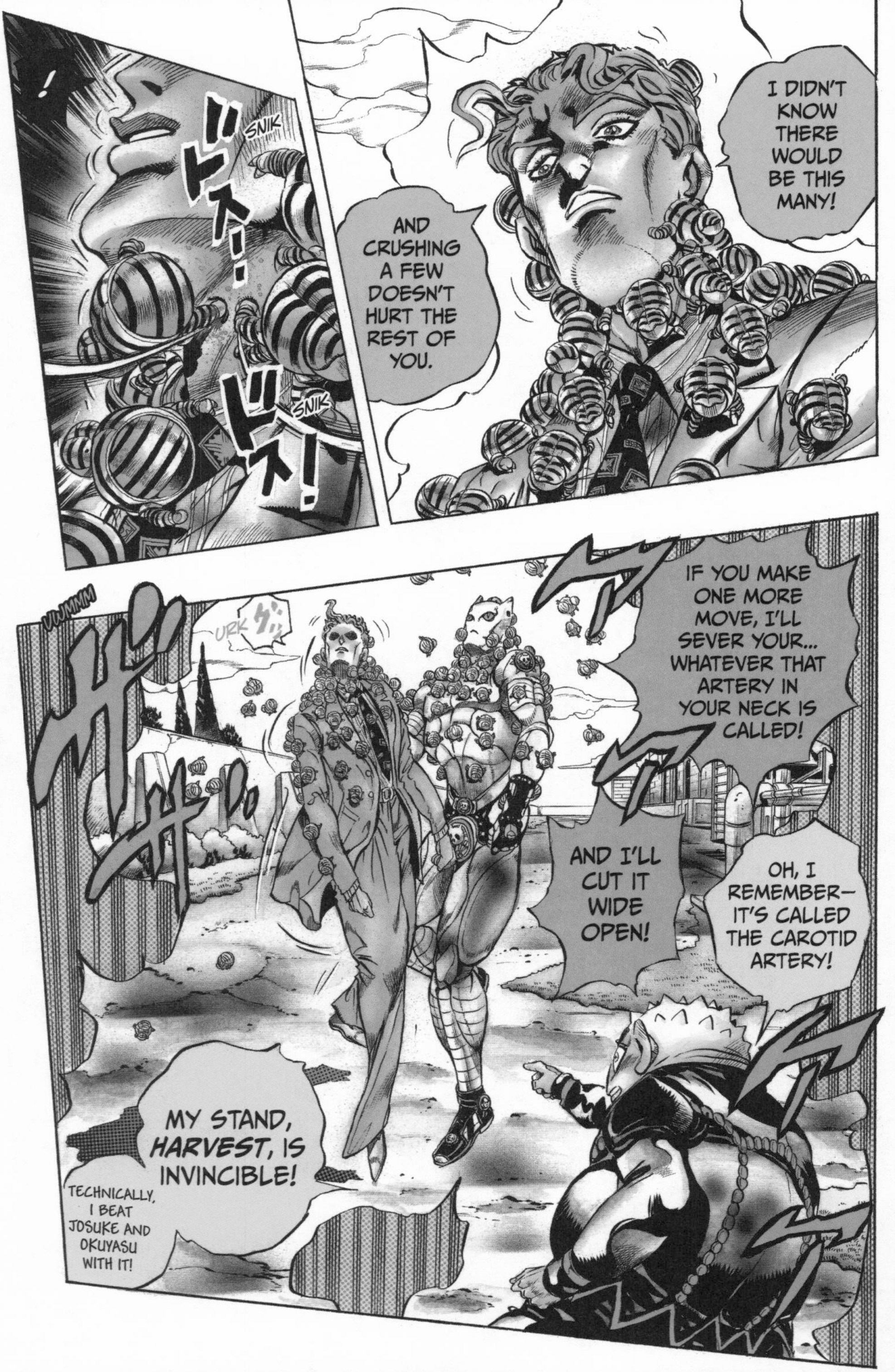
I DIDN'T KNOW THERE WOULD BE THIS MANY!
AND CRUSHING A FEW DOESN'T HURT THE REST OF YOU.
!
SNIK
SNIK
IF YOU MAKE ONE MORE MOVE, I'LL SEVER YOUR... WHATEVER THAT ARTERY IN YOUR NECK IS CALLED!
OH, I REMEMBER— IT'S CALLED THE CAROTID ARTERY!
AND I'LL CUT IT WIDE OPEN!
URK
VUUMMM
MY STAND, HARVEST, IS INVINCIBLE!
TECHNICALLY, I BEAT JOSUKE AND OKUYASU WITH IT!

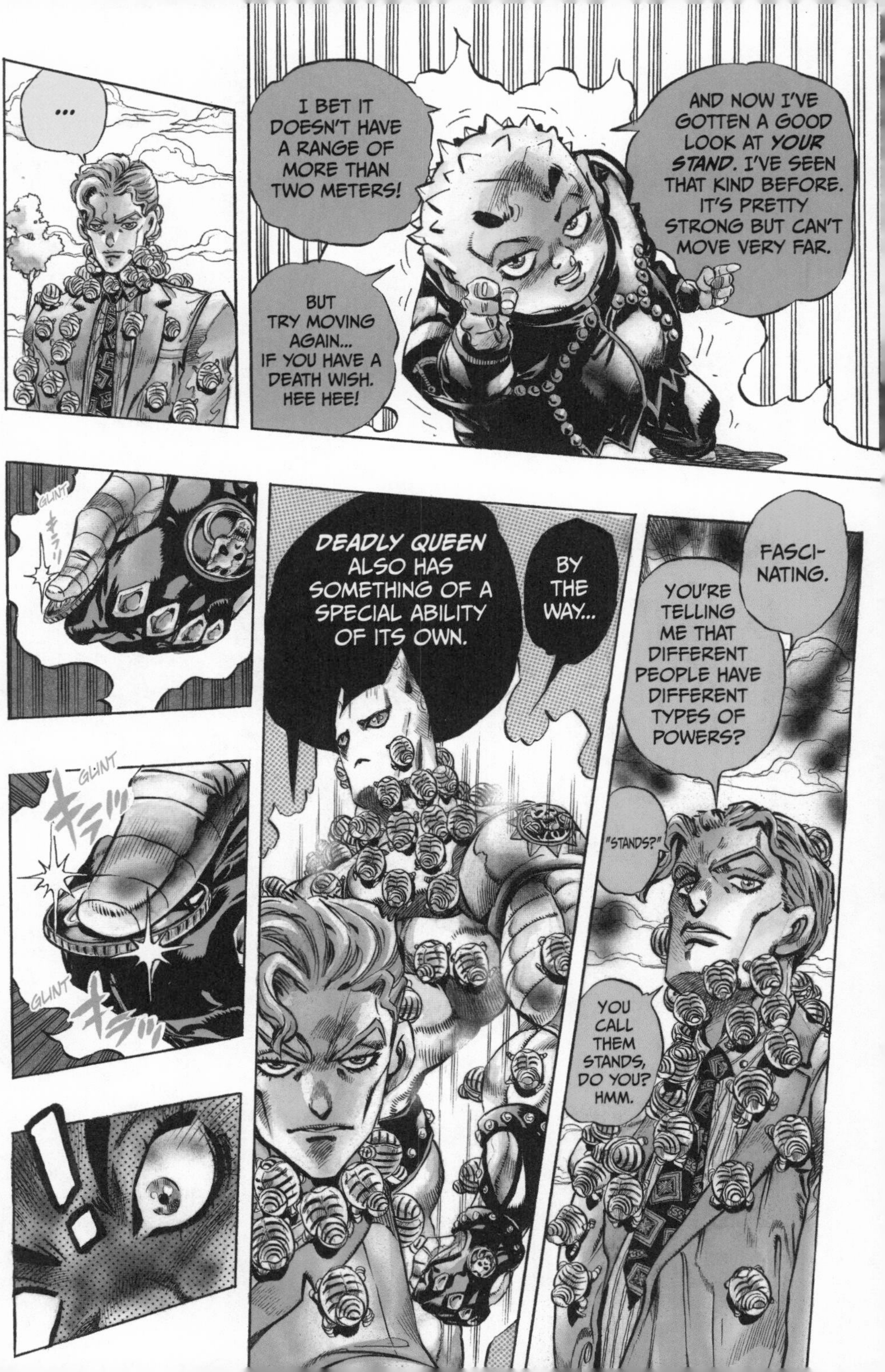
AND NOW I'VE GOTTEN A GOOD LOOK AT YOUR STAND. I'VE SEEN THAT KIND BEFORE. IT'S PRETTY STRONG BUT CAN'T MOVE VERY FAR.
I BET IT DOESN'T HAVE A RANGE OF MORE THAN TWO METERS!
BUT TRY MOVING AGAIN... IF YOU HAVE A DEATH WISH. HEE HEE!
...
FASCI-NATING.
YOU'RE TELLING ME THAT DIFFERENT PEOPLE HAVE DIFFERENT TYPES OF POWERS?
"STANDS?"
YOU CALL THEM STANDS, DO YOU? HMM.
BY THE WAY...
DEADLY QUEEN ALSO HAS SOMETHING OF A SPECIAL ABILITY OF ITS OWN.
GLINT
GLINT
GLINT
!

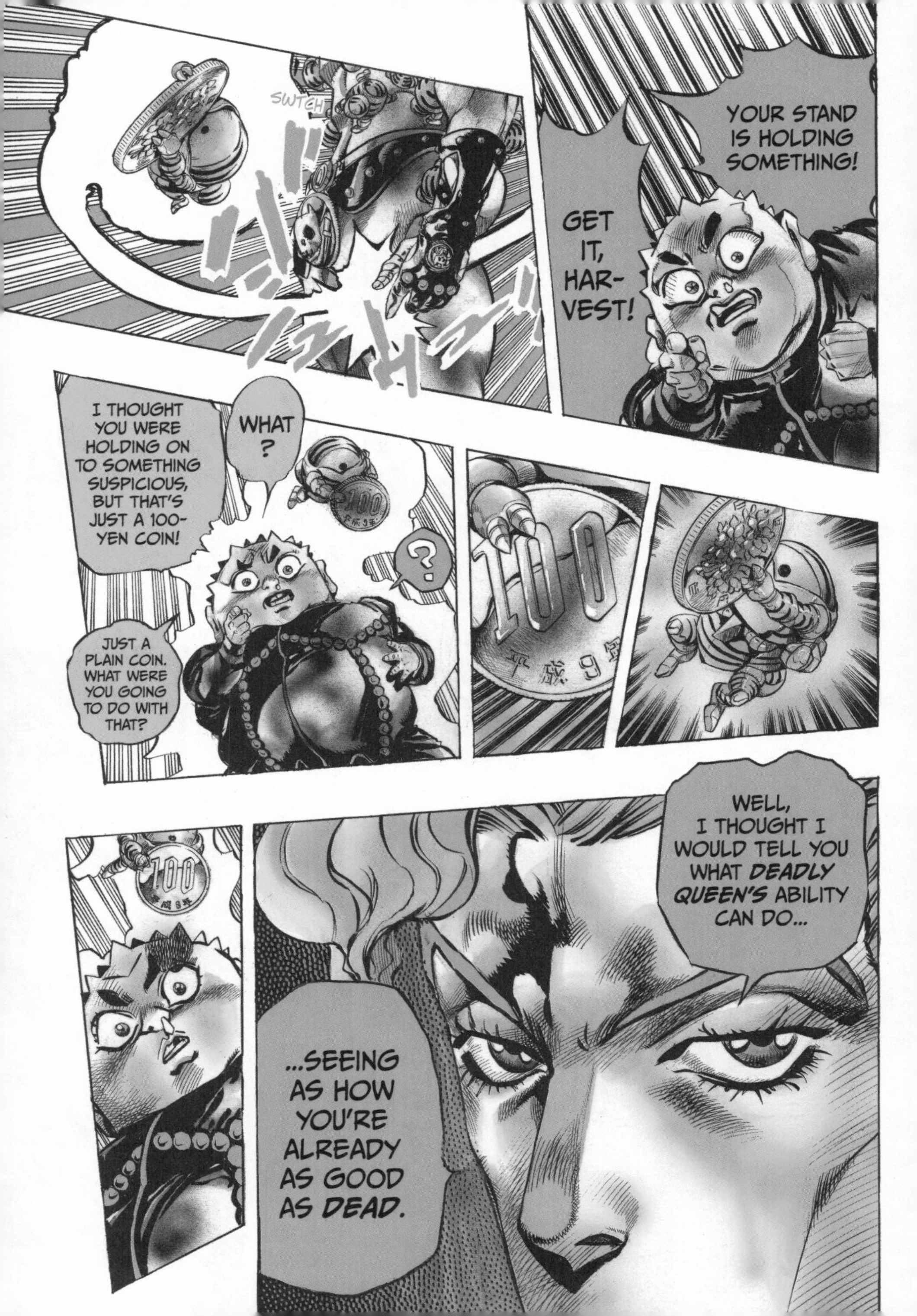
YOUR STAND IS HOLDING SOMETHING!
GET IT, HAR-VEST!
SWTCH
WHAT ?
I THOUGHT YOU WERE HOLDING ON TO SOMETHING SUSPICIOUS, BUT THAT'S JUST A 100-YEN COIN!
?
JUST A PLAIN COIN. WHAT WERE YOU GOING TO DO WITH THAT?
WELL, I THOUGHT I WOULD TELL YOU WHAT DEADLY QUEEN'S ABILITY CAN DO...
...SEEING AS HOW YOU'RE ALREADY AS GOOD AS DEAD.

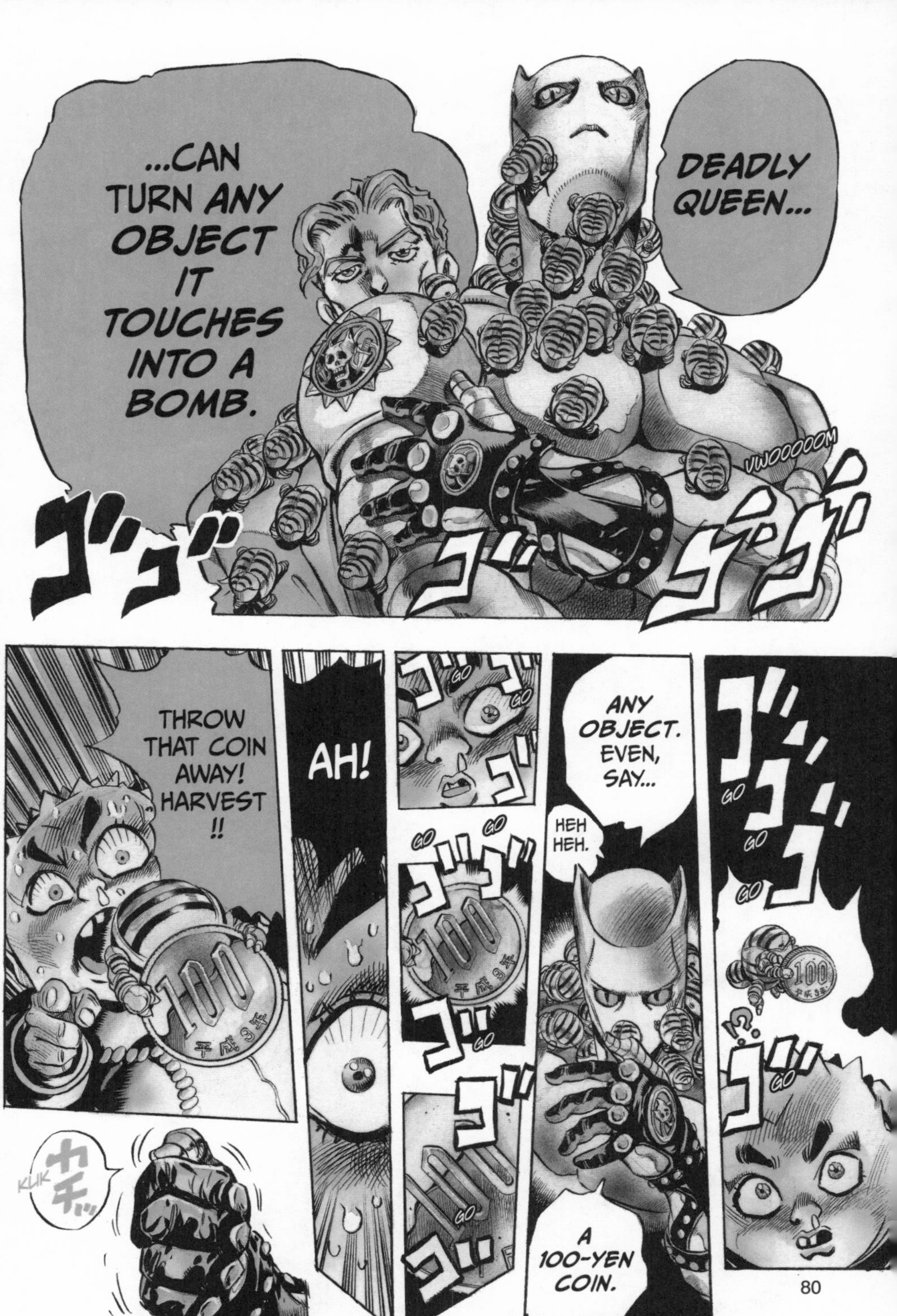
DEADLY QUEEN...
...CAN TURN ANY OBJECT IT TOUCHES INTO A BOMB.
VWOOOOOM
GO
GO
GO
GO
ANY OBJECT. EVEN, SAY...
HEH HEH.
A 100-YEN COIN.
GO
GO
GO
GO
GO
AH!
THROW THAT COIN AWAY! HARVEST !!
KLIK

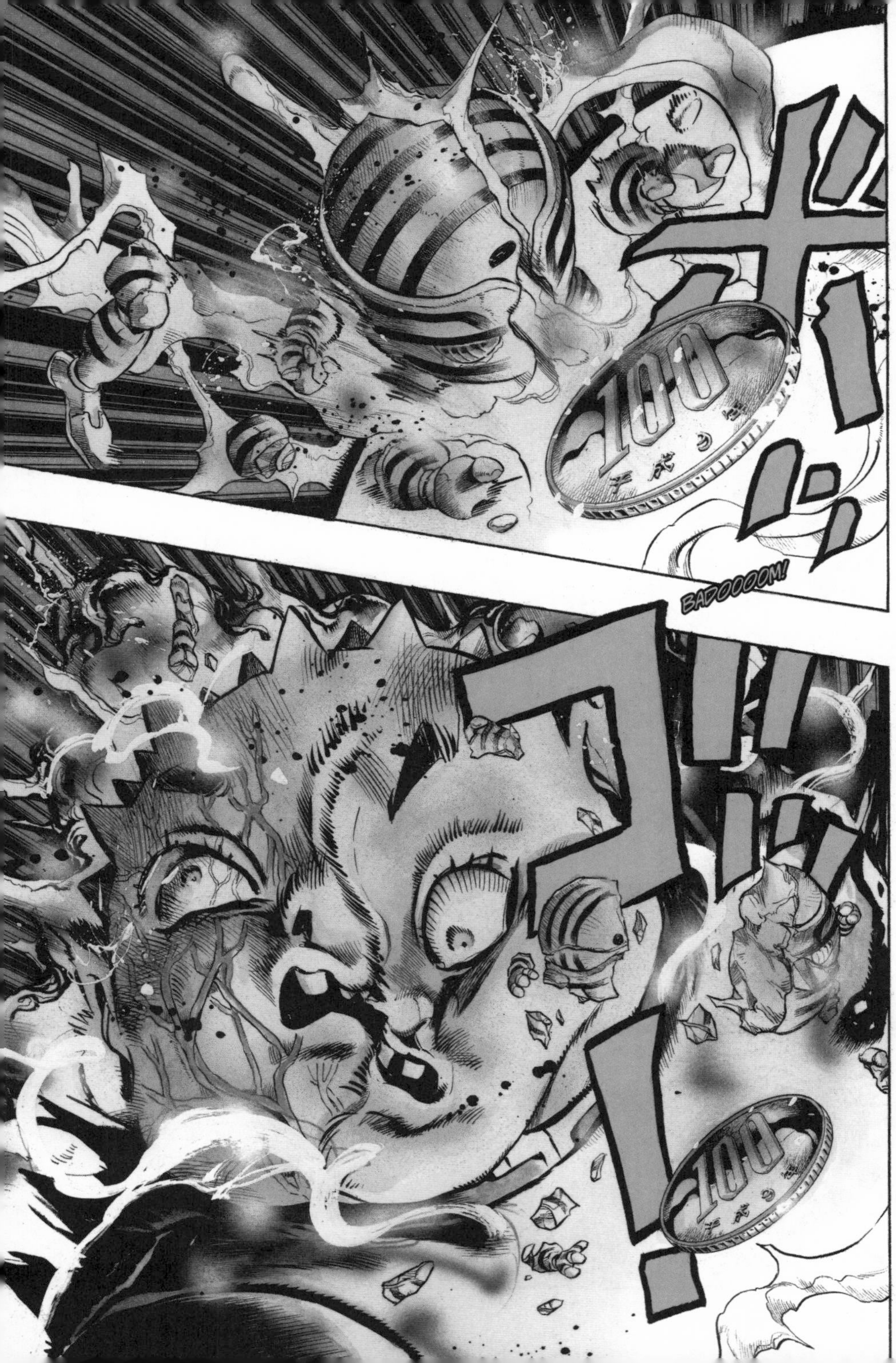
BADOOOOM!

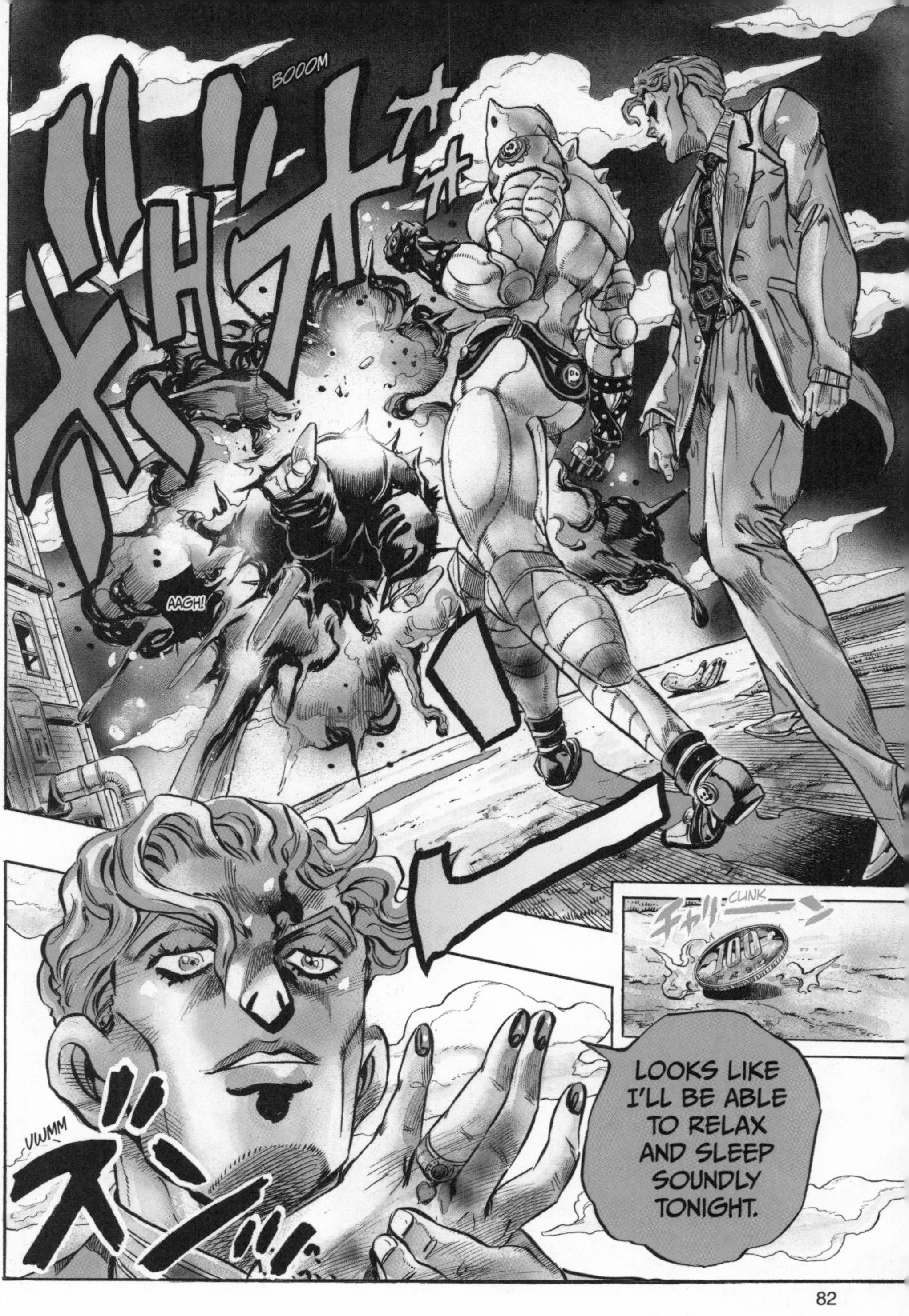
BOOOM
AAGH!
CLINK
LOOKS LIKE I'LL BE ABLE TO RELAX AND SLEEP SOUNDLY TONIGHT.
VWMM

CHAPTER 81

YOSHIKAGE KIRA WANTS TO LIVE QUIETLY, PART 5

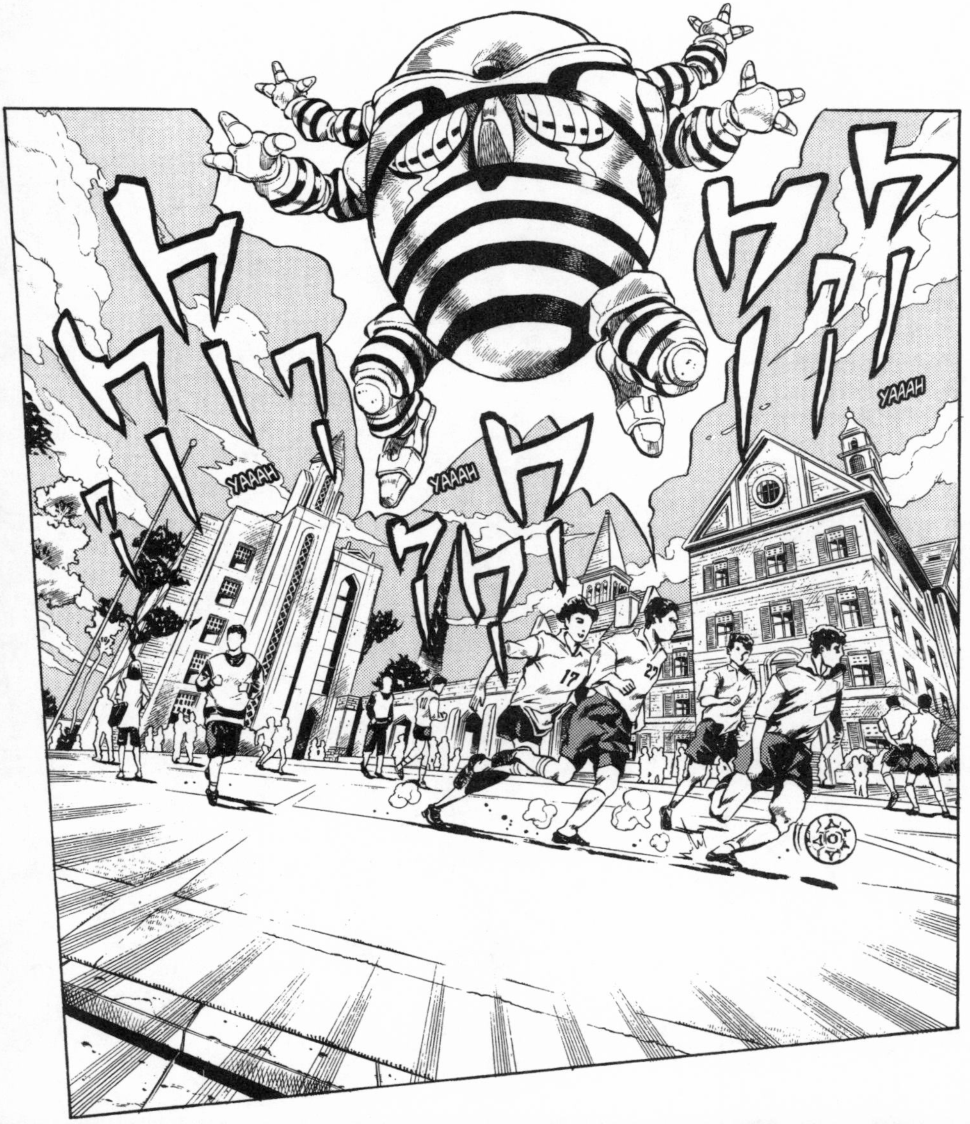
YAAAH
YAAAH
YAAAH

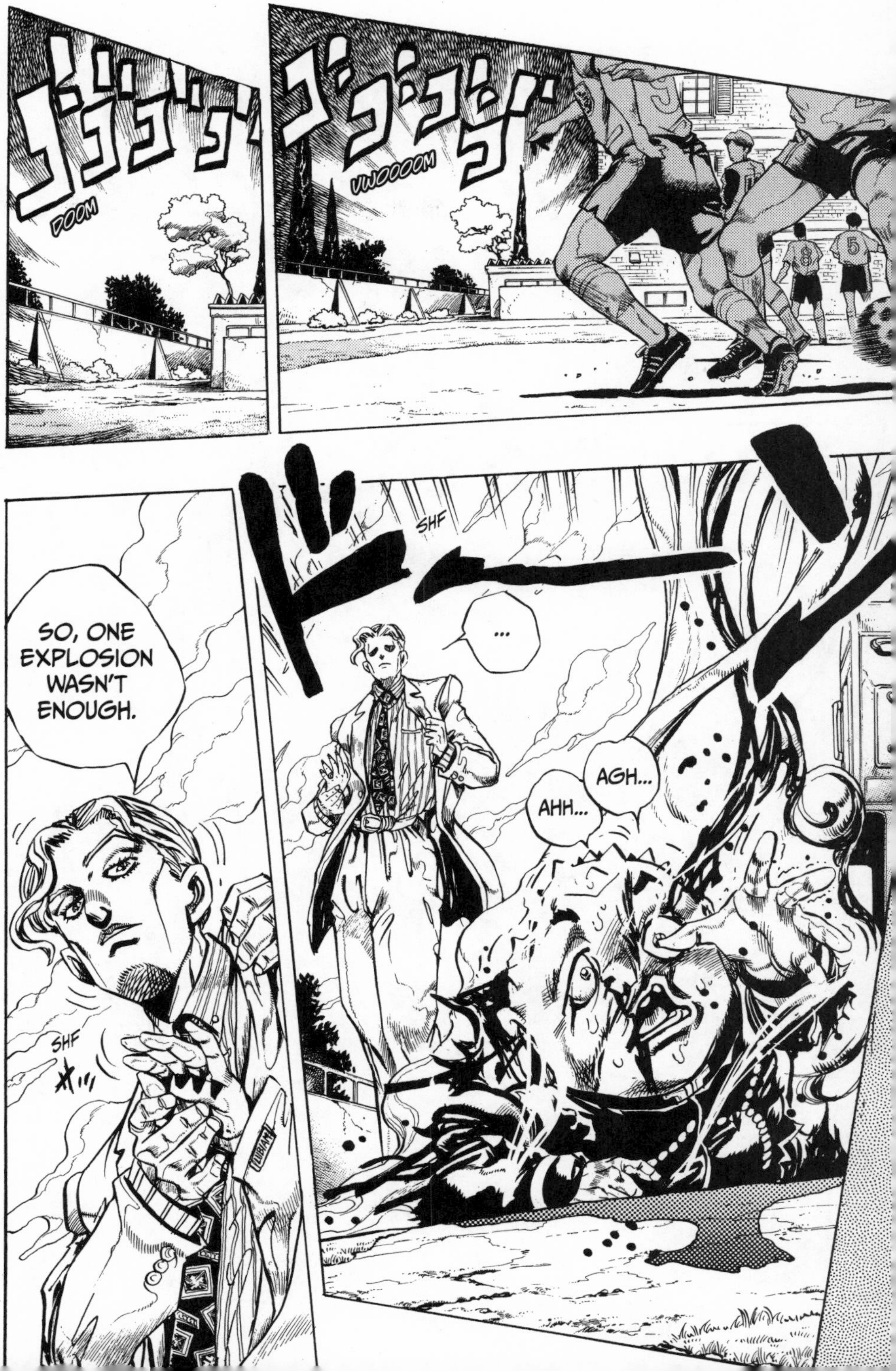
VWOOOOM
DOOM
ドーン
SHF
...
AGH...
AHH...
SO, ONE EXPLOSION WASN'T ENOUGH.
SHF

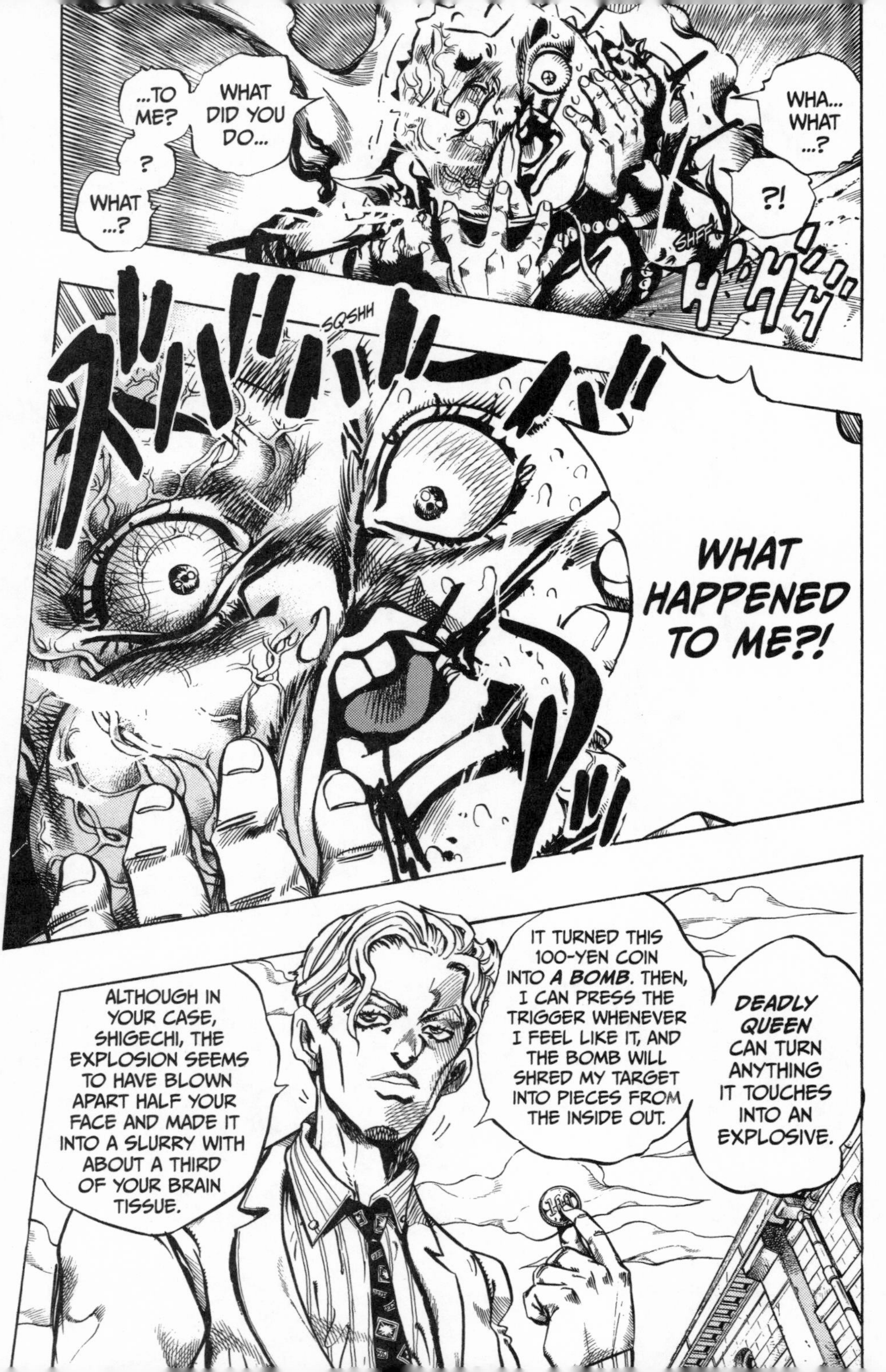

WHA... WHAT ...?
?!
SHFF
WHAT DID YOU DO...
...TO ME?
?
WHAT ...?
SQSHH
WHAT HAPPENED TO ME?!
DEADLY QUEEN CAN TURN ANYTHING IT TOUCHES INTO AN EXPLOSIVE.
IT TURNED THIS 100-YEN COIN INTO *A BOMB*. THEN, I CAN PRESS THE TRIGGER WHENEVER I FEEL LIKE IT, AND THE BOMB WILL SHRED MY TARGET INTO PIECES FROM THE INSIDE OUT.
ALTHOUGH IN YOUR CASE, SHIGECHI, THE EXPLOSION SEEMS TO HAVE BLOWN APART HALF YOUR FACE AND MADE IT INTO A SLURRY WITH ABOUT A THIRD OF YOUR BRAIN TISSUE.

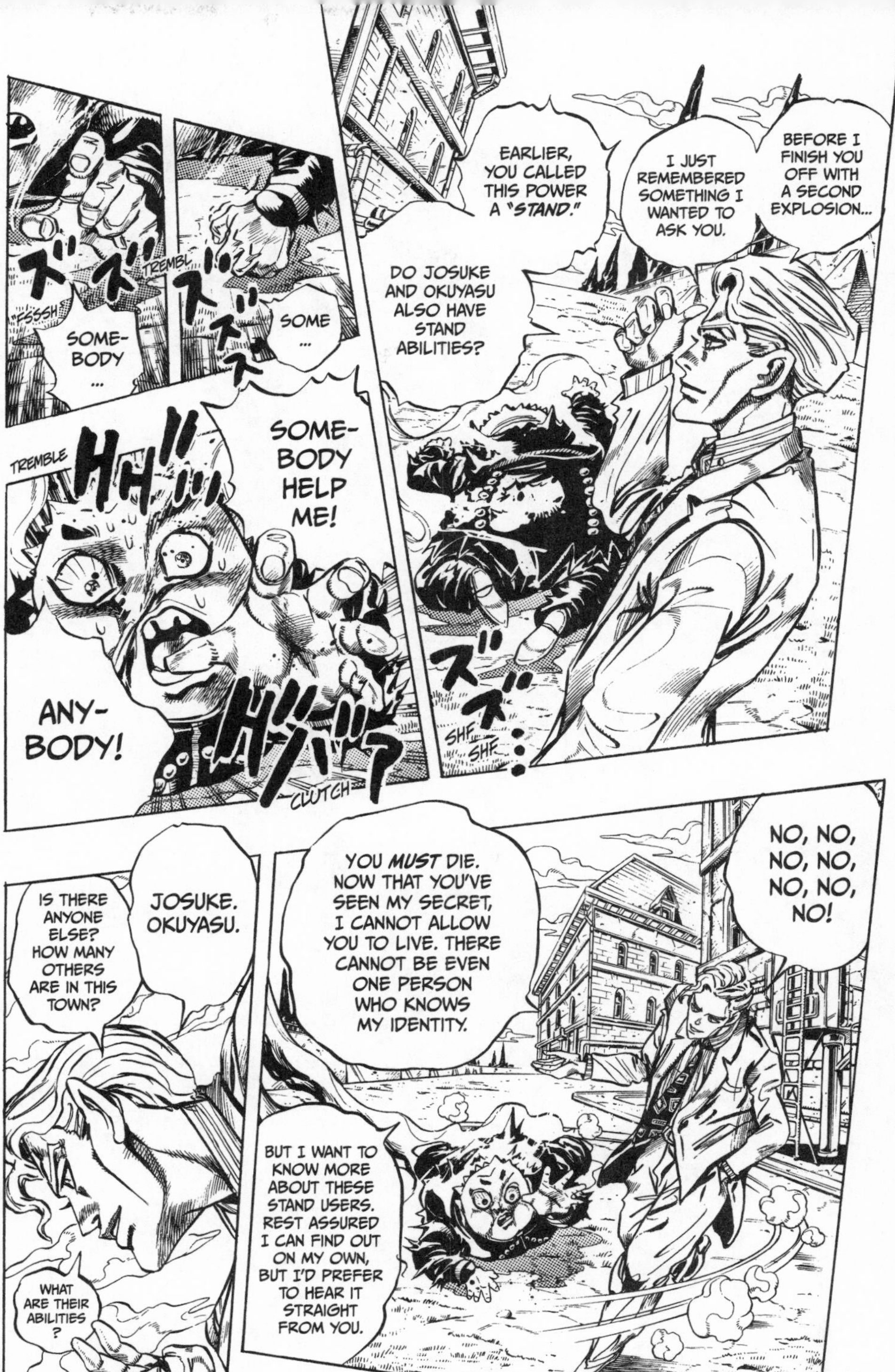
BEFORE I FINISH YOU OFF WITH A SECOND EXPLOSION...
I JUST REMEMBERED SOMETHING I WANTED TO ASK YOU.
EARLIER, YOU CALLED THIS POWER A "STAND."
DO JOSUKE AND OKUYASU ALSO HAVE STAND ABILITIES?
SHF SHF
TREMBL
SOME ...
FSSSH
SOME-BODY ...
SOME-BODY HELP ME!
TREMBLE
ANY-BODY!
CLUTCH
NO, NO, NO, NO, NO, NO, NO!
YOU MUST DIE. NOW THAT YOU'VE SEEN MY SECRET, I CANNOT ALLOW YOU TO LIVE. THERE CANNOT BE EVEN ONE PERSON WHO KNOWS MY IDENTITY.
BUT I WANT TO KNOW MORE ABOUT THESE STAND USERS. REST ASSURED I CAN FIND OUT ON MY OWN, BUT I'D PREFER TO HEAR IT STRAIGHT FROM YOU.
JOSUKE. OKUYASU.
IS THERE ANYONE ELSE? HOW MANY OTHERS ARE IN THIS TOWN?
WHAT ARE THEIR ABILITIES?

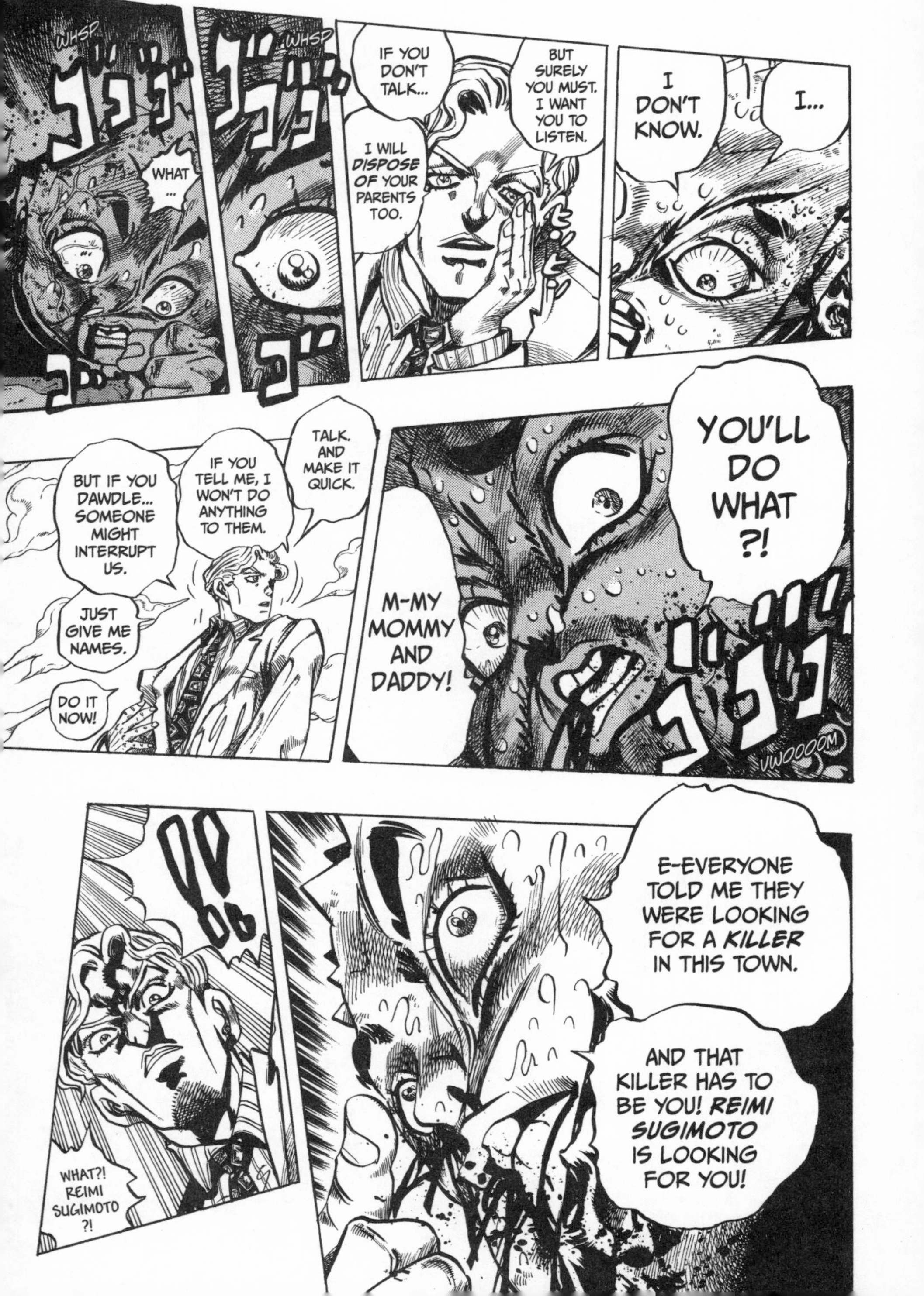
I...
I DON'T KNOW.
BUT SURELY YOU MUST. I WANT YOU TO LISTEN.
IF YOU DON'T TALK...
I WILL *DISPOSE* OF YOUR PARENTS TOO.
WHSP
WHSP
WHAT ...
YOU'LL DO WHAT ?!
M-MY MOMMY AND DADDY!
VWOOOOM
TALK. AND MAKE IT QUICK.
IF YOU TELL ME, I WON'T DO ANYTHING TO THEM.
BUT IF YOU DAWDLE... SOMEONE MIGHT INTERRUPT US.
JUST GIVE ME NAMES.
DO IT NOW!
E-EVERYONE TOLD ME THEY WERE LOOKING FOR A *KILLER* IN THIS TOWN.
AND THAT KILLER HAS TO BE YOU! *REIMI SUGIMOTO* IS LOOKING FOR YOU!
WHAT?! REIMI SUGIMOTO ?!

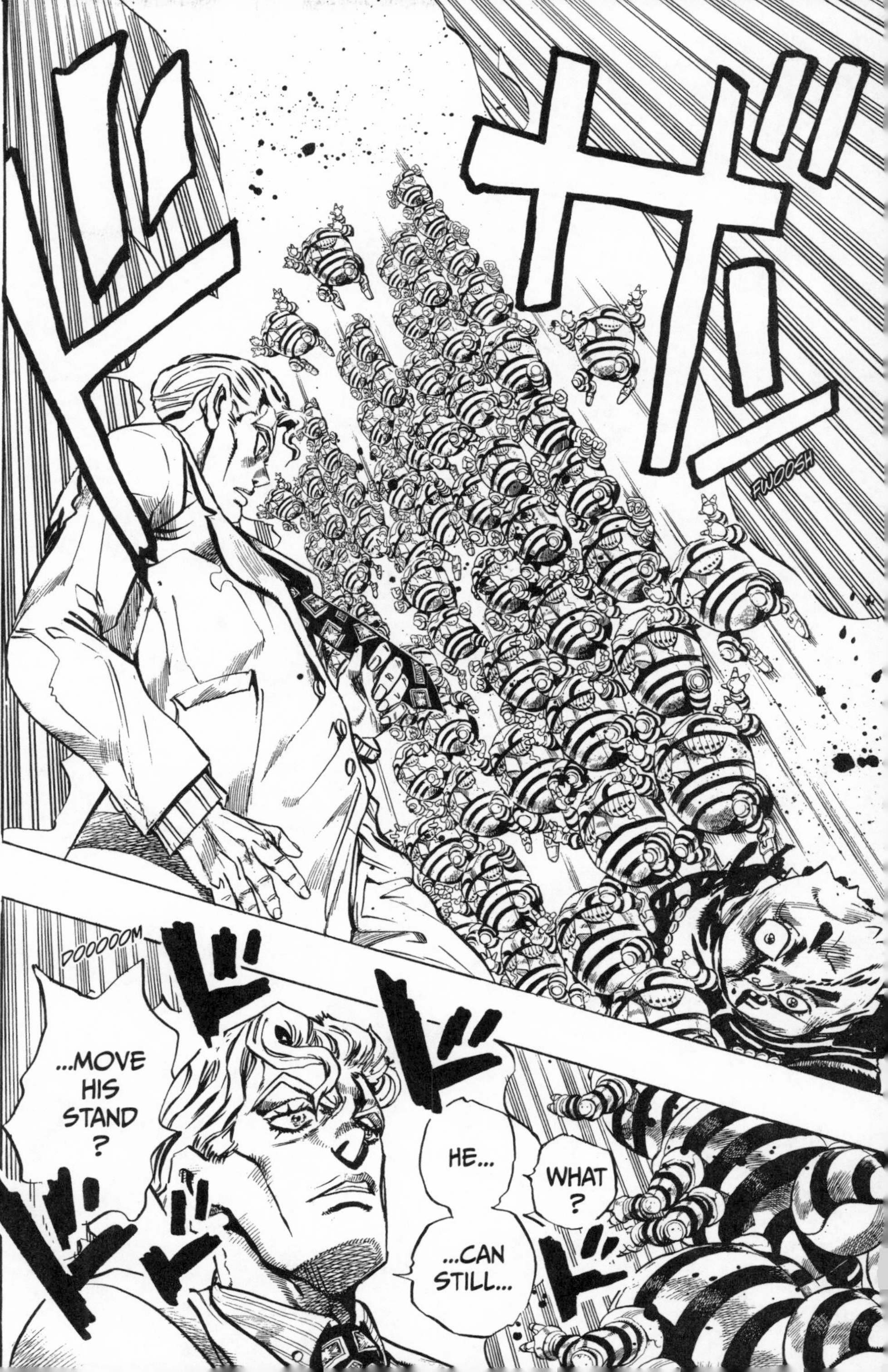
FWOOSH
DOOOOOM
WHAT?
HE...
...CAN STILL...
...MOVE HIS STAND?

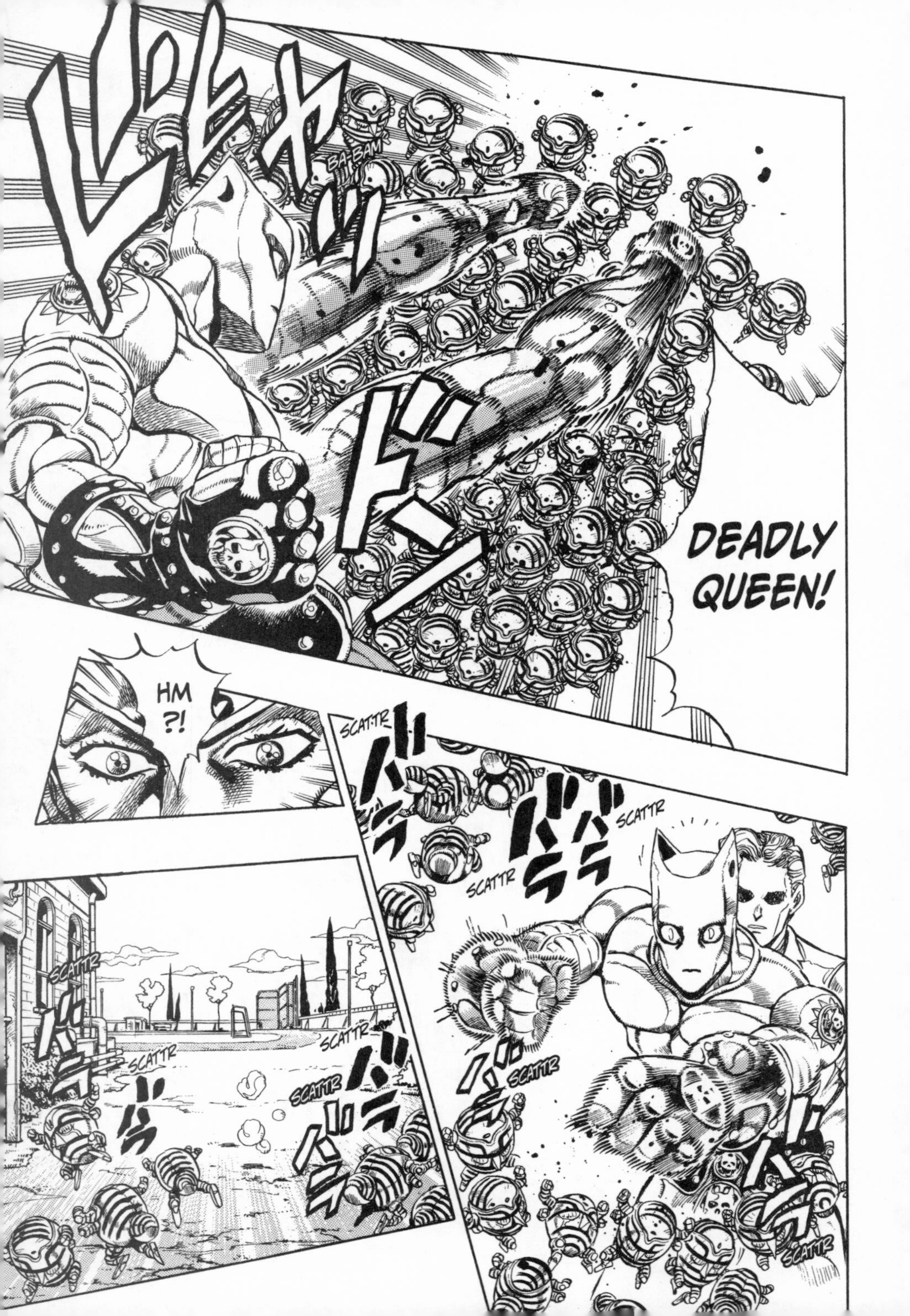
BA-BAM
DEADLY QUEEN!
SCATTR
SCATTR
SCATTR
SCATTR
SCATTR
HM ?!
SCATTR
SCATTR
SCATTR
SCATTR

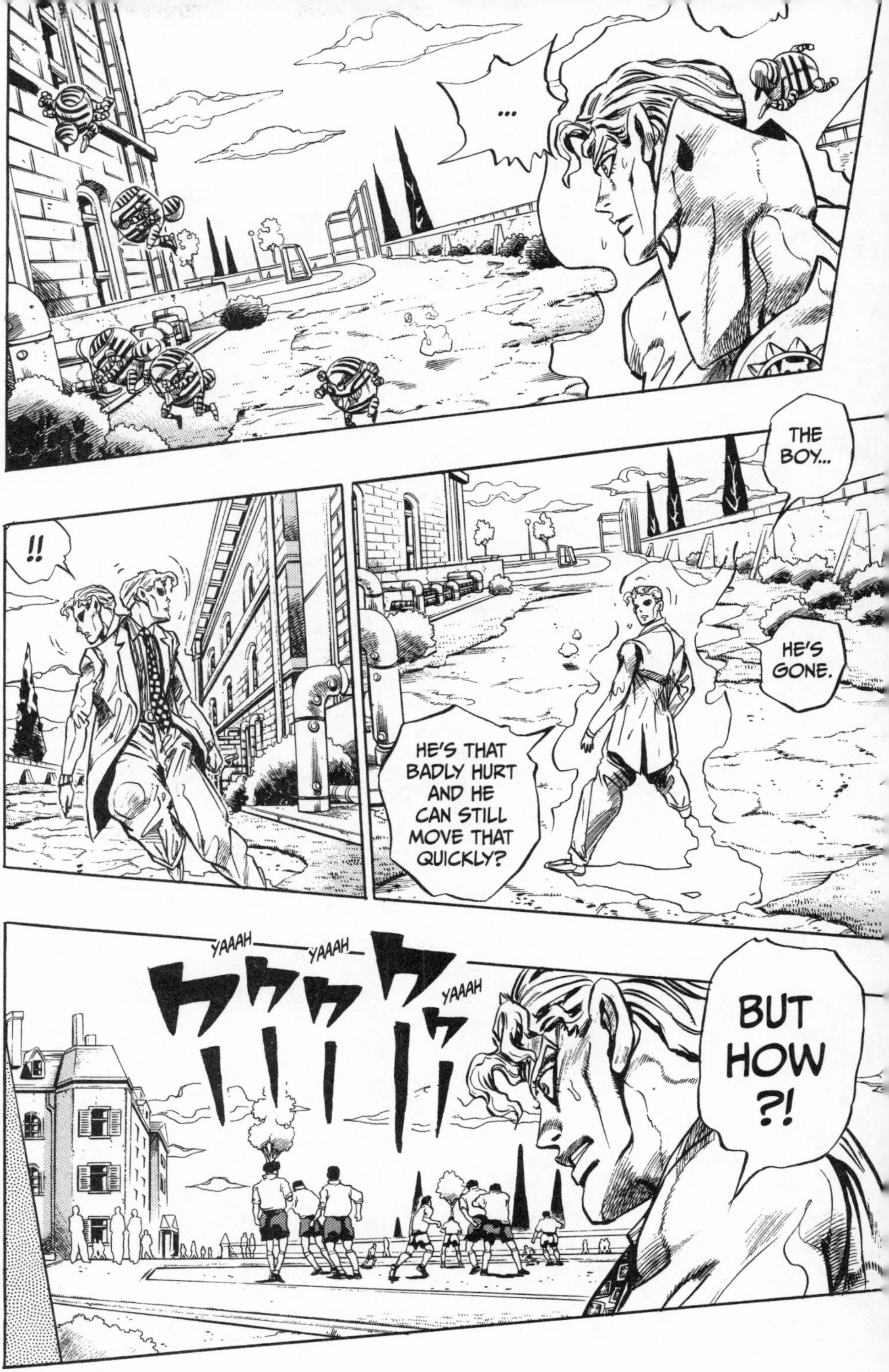
...
THE BOY...
HE'S GONE.
HE'S THAT BADLY HURT AND HE CAN STILL MOVE THAT QUICKLY?
!!
BUT HOW ?!
YAAAH
YAAAH
YAAAH

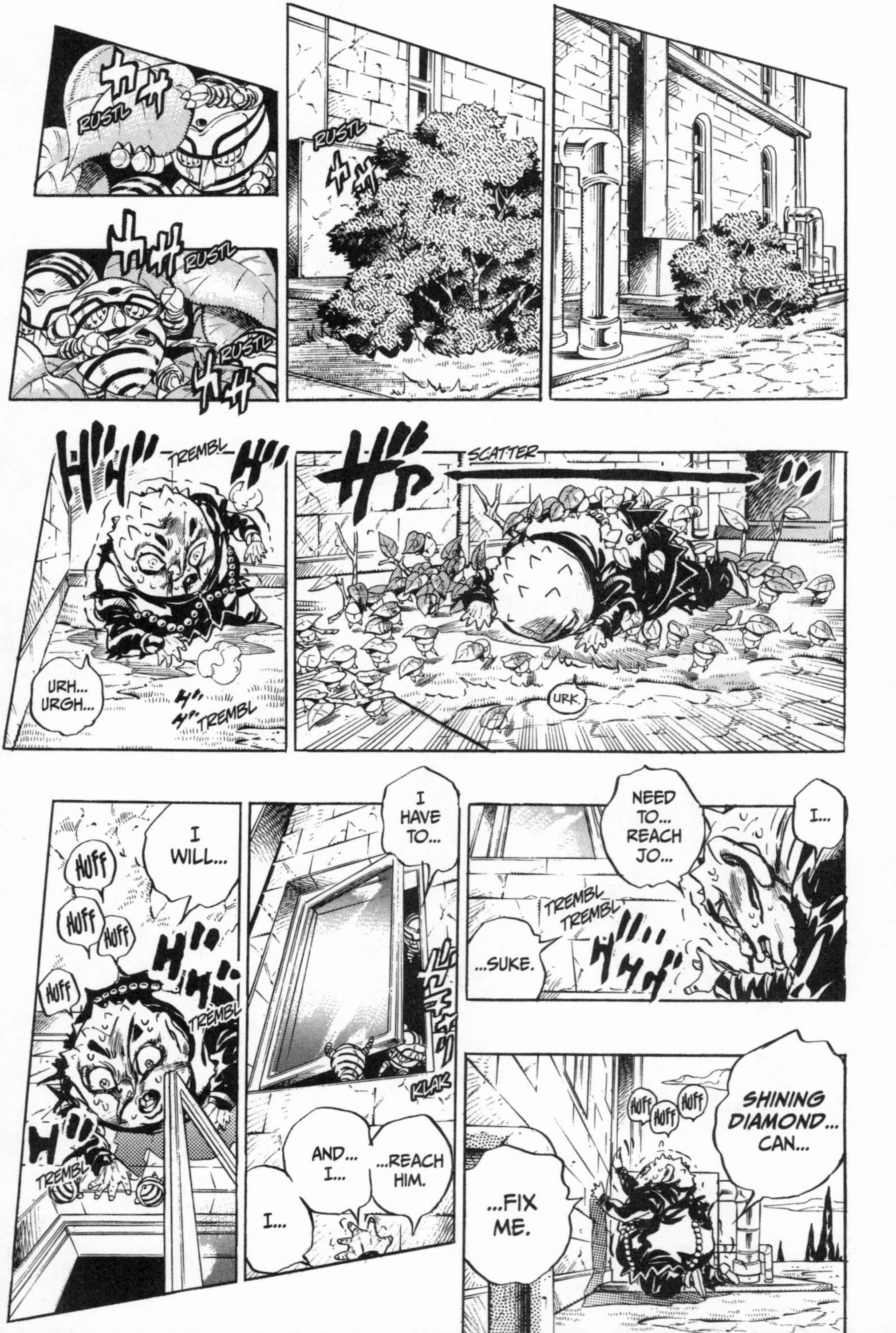
RUSTL
RUSTL
RUSTL
RUSTL
SCATTER
URK.
TREMBL
URH... URGH...
TREMBL
I...
NEED TO... REACH JO...
TREMBL TREMBL
...SUKE.
SHINING DIAMOND... CAN...
HUFF
HUFF
HUFF
...FIX ME.
I HAVE TO...
KLAK
...REACH HIM.
AND... I...
I...
I WILL...
HUFF
HUFF
HUFF
HUFF
TREMBL
TREMBL

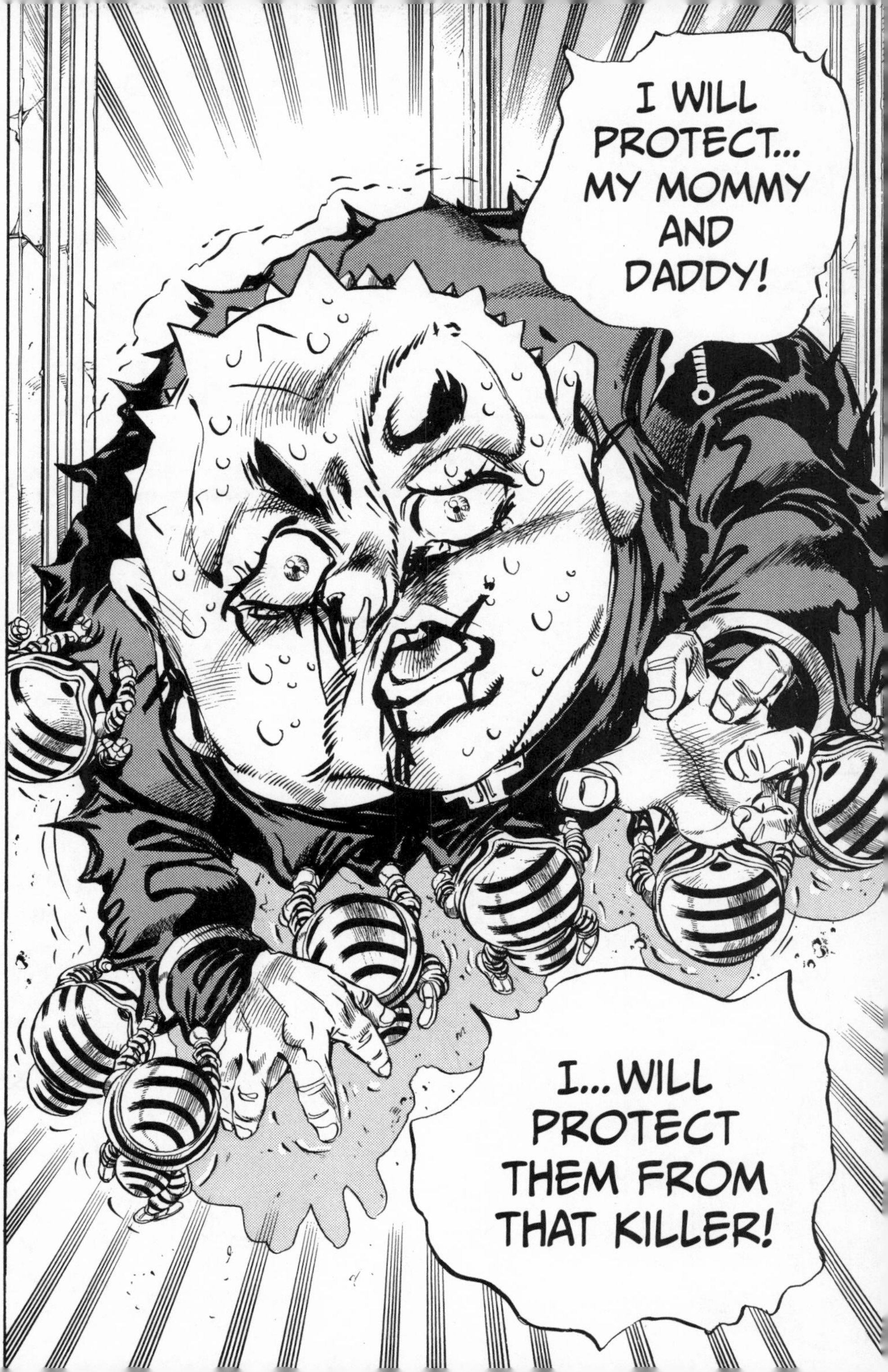
I WILL PROTECT... MY MOMMY AND DADDY!
I...WILL PROTECT THEM FROM THAT KILLER!

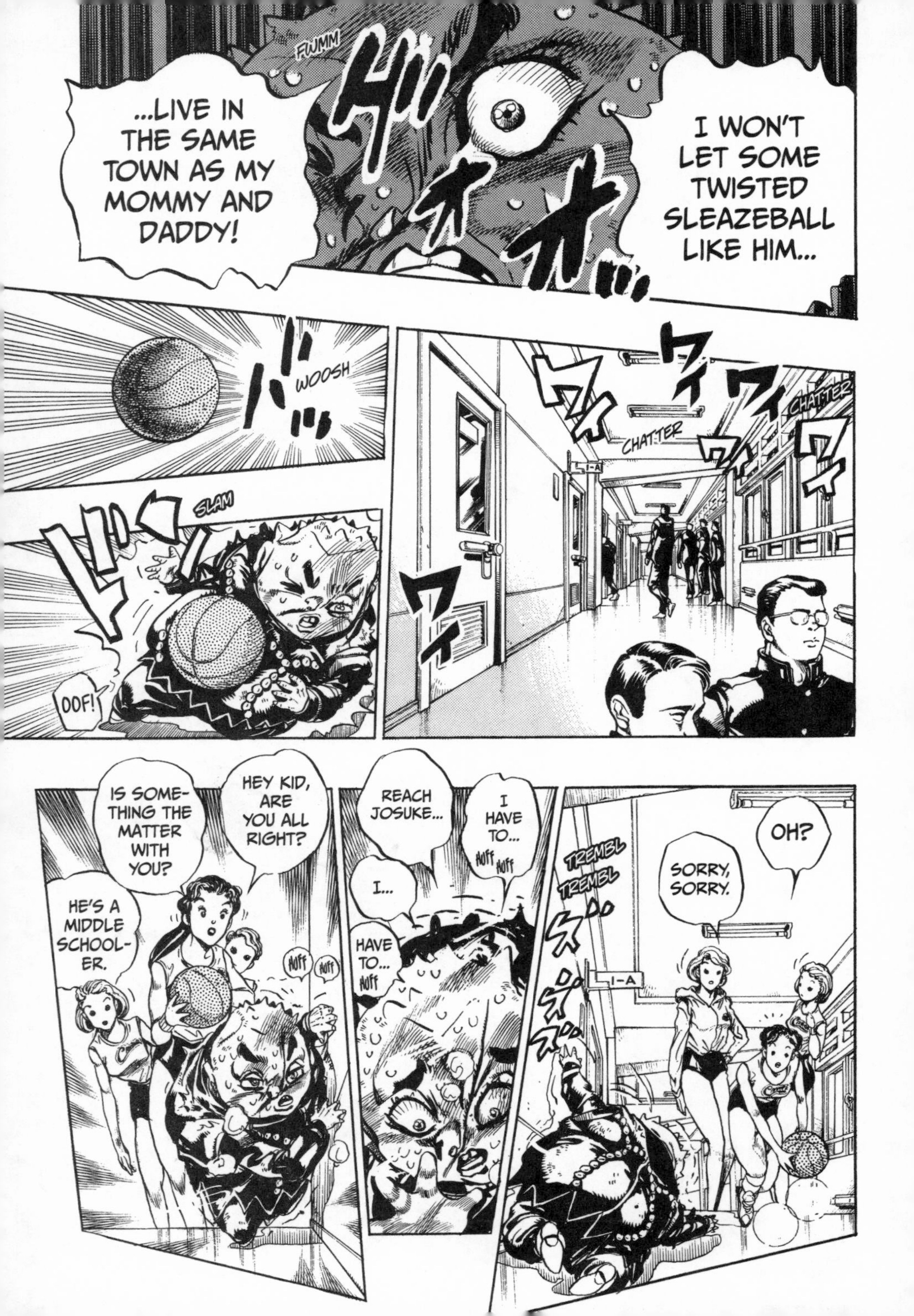
I WON'T LET SOME TWISTED SLEAZEBALL LIKE HIM...
FWUMM
...LIVE IN THE SAME TOWN AS MY MOMMY AND DADDY!
CHATTER
CHATTER
WOOSH
SLAM
OOF!
OH?
SORRY, SORRY.
TREMBL
TREMBL
I HAVE TO...
HUFF HUFF
REACH JOSUKE...
I...
HAVE TO...
HUFF
HEY KID, ARE YOU ALL RIGHT?
IS SOME-THING THE MATTER WITH YOU?
HE'S A MIDDLE SCHOOL-ER.
HUFF
HUFF

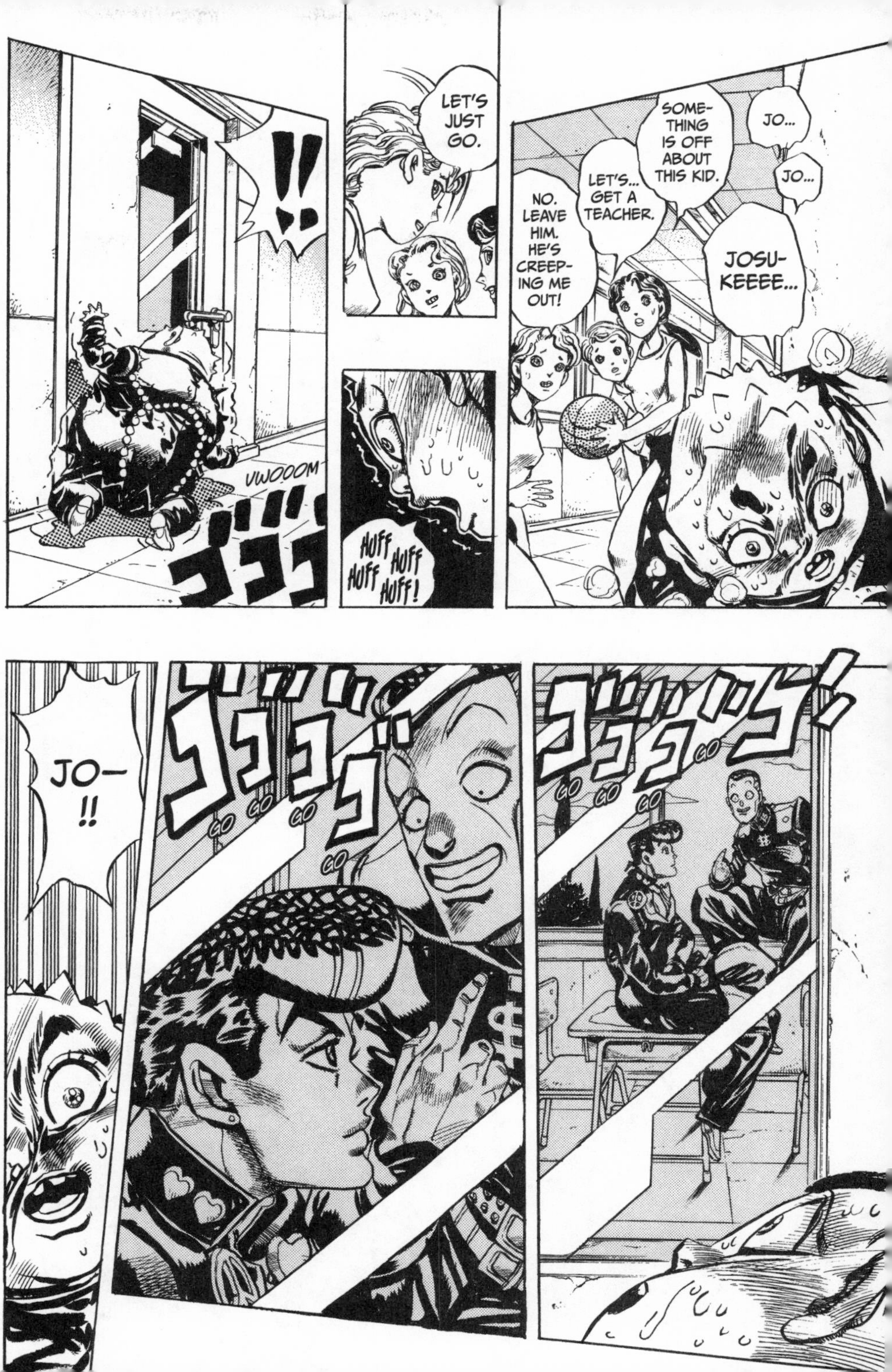
JO...
JO...
JOSU-KEEEE...
SOME-THING IS OFF ABOUT THIS KID.
LET'S... GET A TEACHER.
NO. LEAVE HIM. HE'S CREEP-ING ME OUT!
LET'S JUST GO.
HUFF HUFF HUFF HUFF HUFF!
!!
VWOOOM
GO GO GO
GO GO GO GO
JO—!!

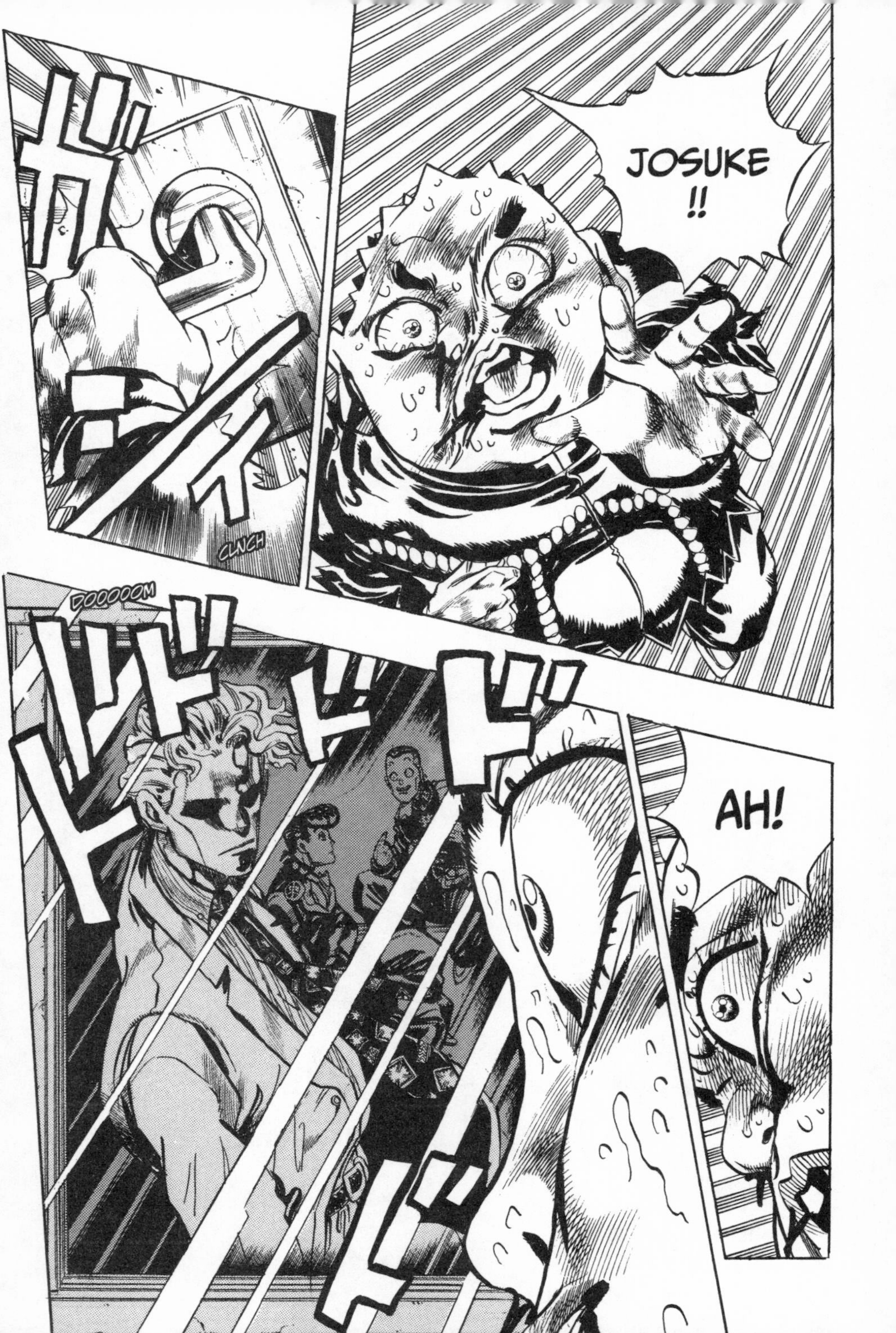
JOSUKE !!
CLNCH
AH!
DOOOOOM

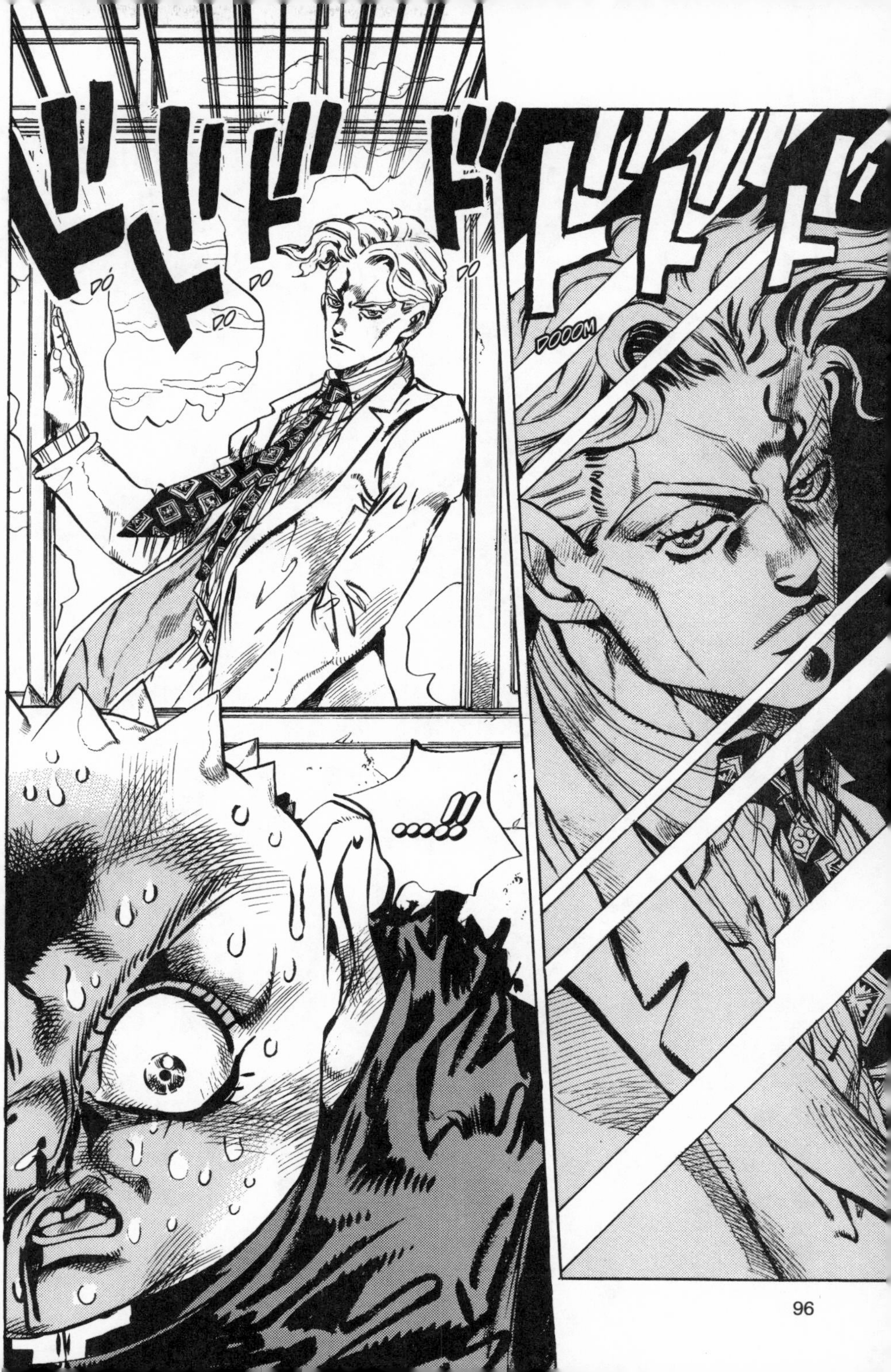
DOOOM
DO
DO
DO
DO
......!!

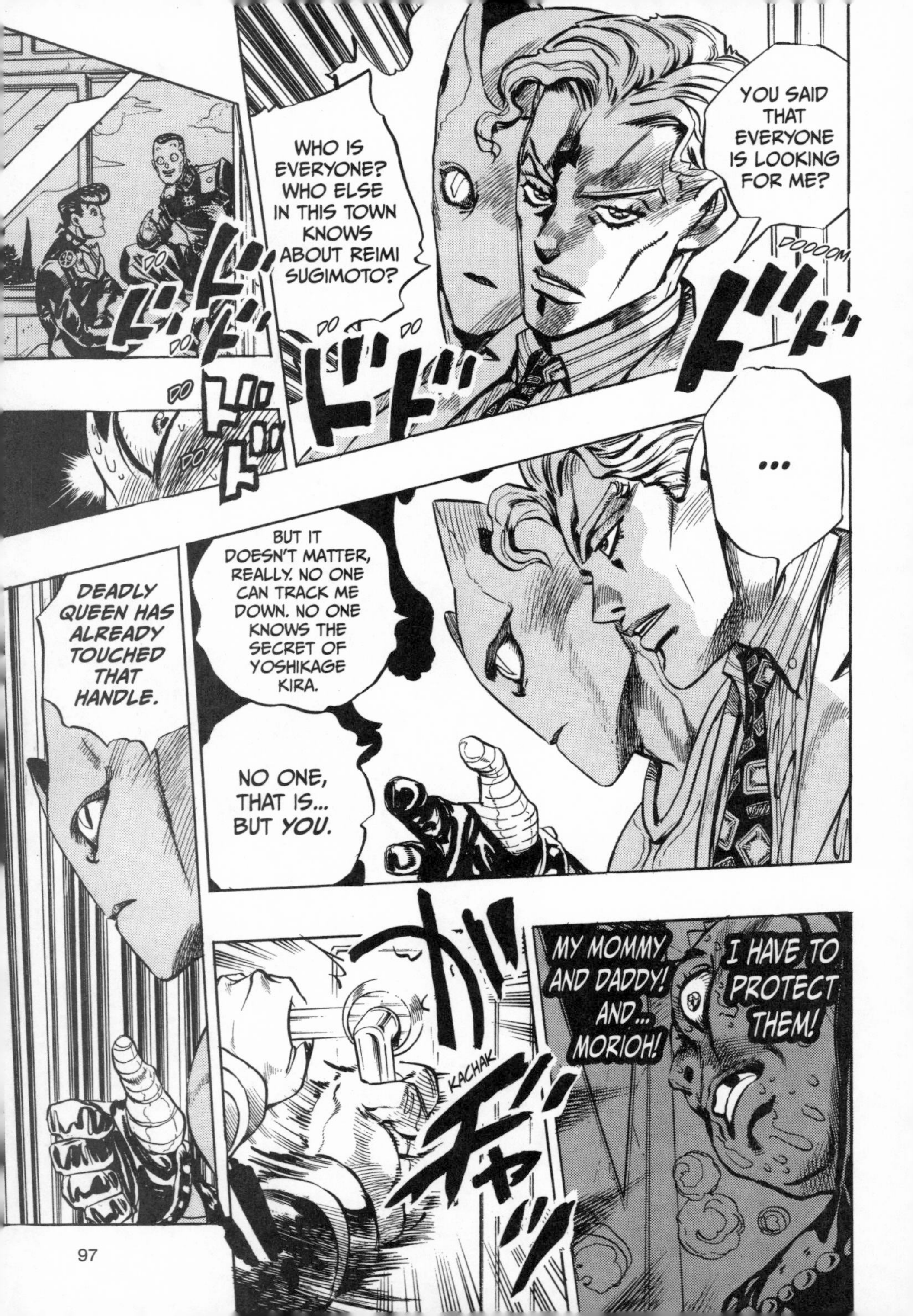
YOU SAID THAT EVERYONE IS LOOKING FOR ME?
WHO IS EVERYONE? WHO ELSE IN THIS TOWN KNOWS ABOUT REIMI SUGIMOTO?
DOOOOM
DO DO
DO DO DO DO
...
BUT IT DOESN'T MATTER, REALLY. NO ONE CAN TRACK ME DOWN. NO ONE KNOWS THE SECRET OF YOSHIKAGE KIRA.
NO ONE, THAT IS... BUT *YOU*.
DEADLY QUEEN HAS ALREADY TOUCHED THAT HANDLE.
I HAVE TO PROTECT THEM!
MY MOMMY AND DADDY! AND... MORIOH!
KACHAK

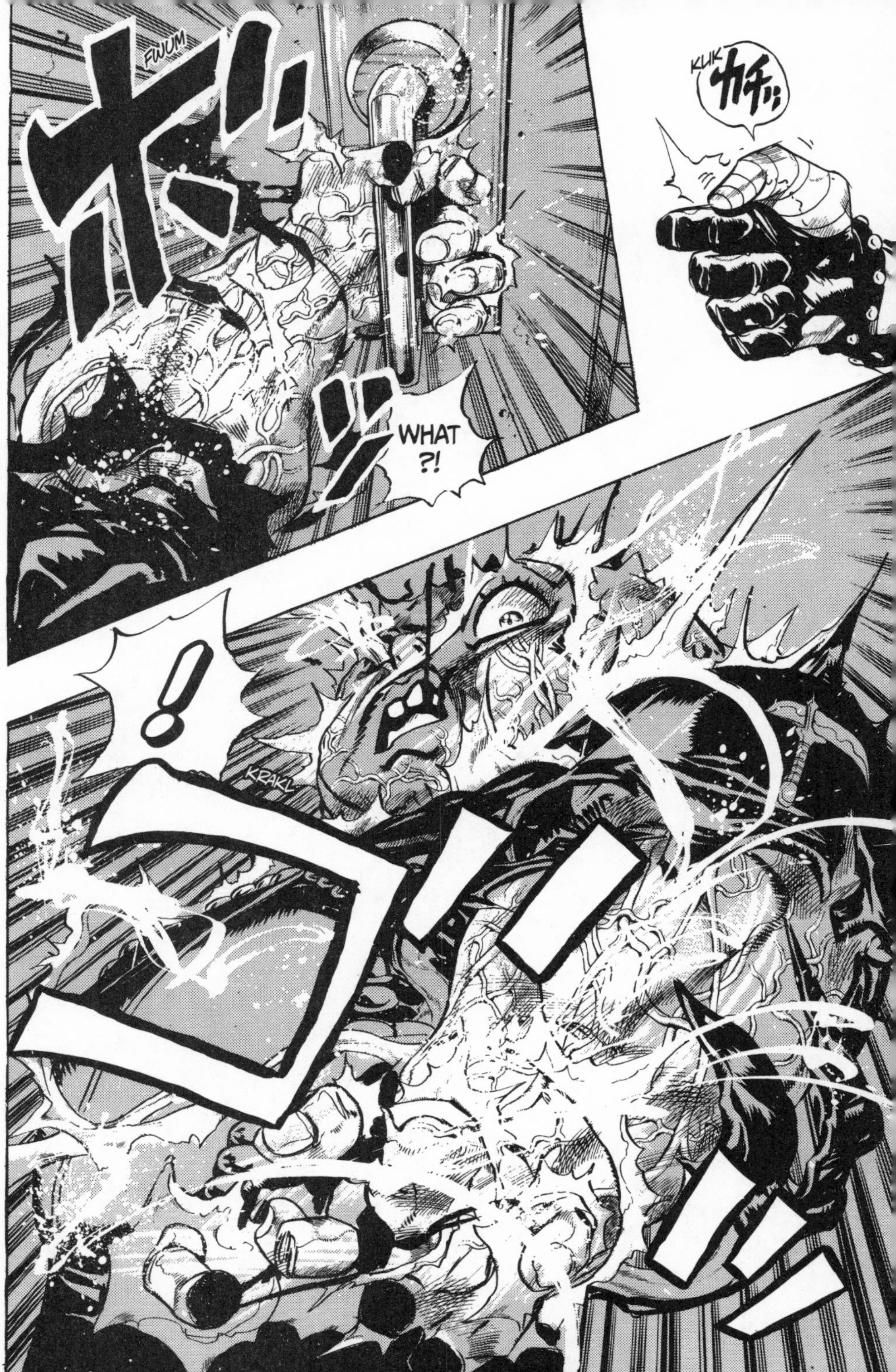
KUK
カチッ
FWUUM
WHAT ?!
!
KRAKL

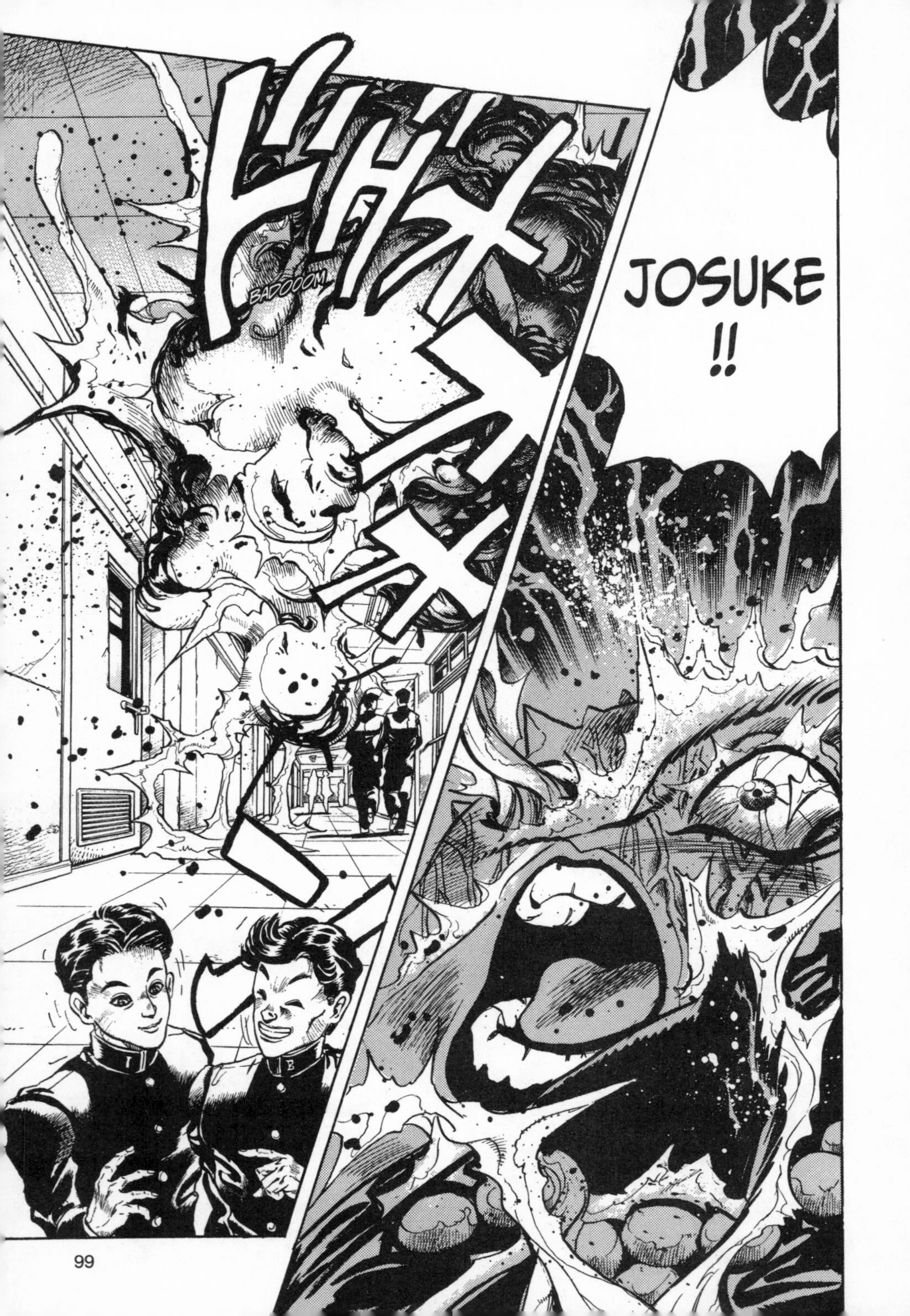
JOSUKE
!!
BADOOOM

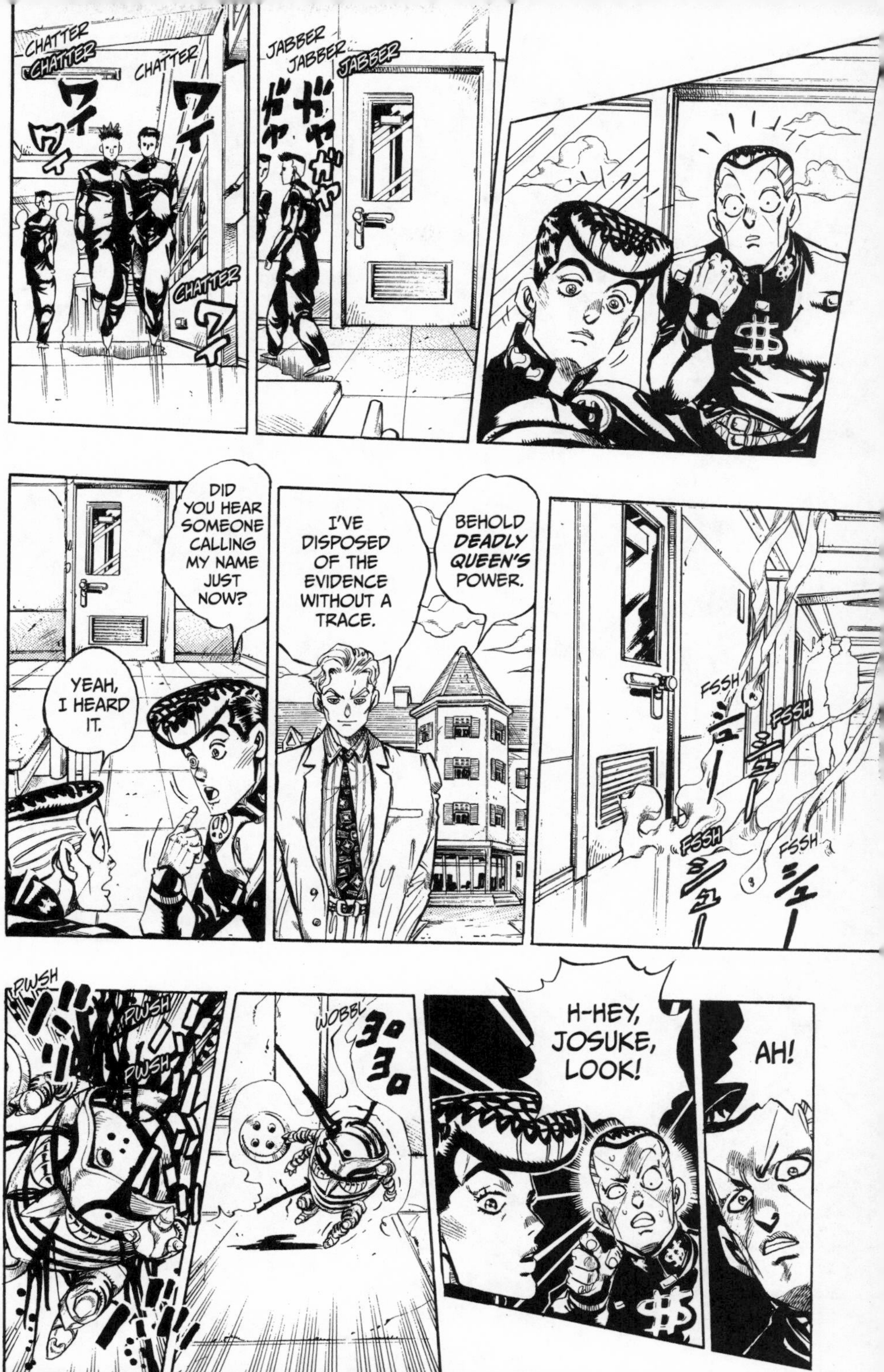
JABBER
JABBER
JABBER
CHATTER
CHATTER
CHATTER
CHATTER
BEHOLD DEADLY QUEEN'S POWER.
I'VE DISPOSED OF THE EVIDENCE WITHOUT A TRACE.
DID YOU HEAR SOMEONE CALLING MY NAME JUST NOW?
YEAH, I HEARD IT.
FSSH
FSSH
FSSH
FSSH
AH!
H-HEY, JOSUKE, LOOK!
WOBBL
PWSH
PWSH
PWSH

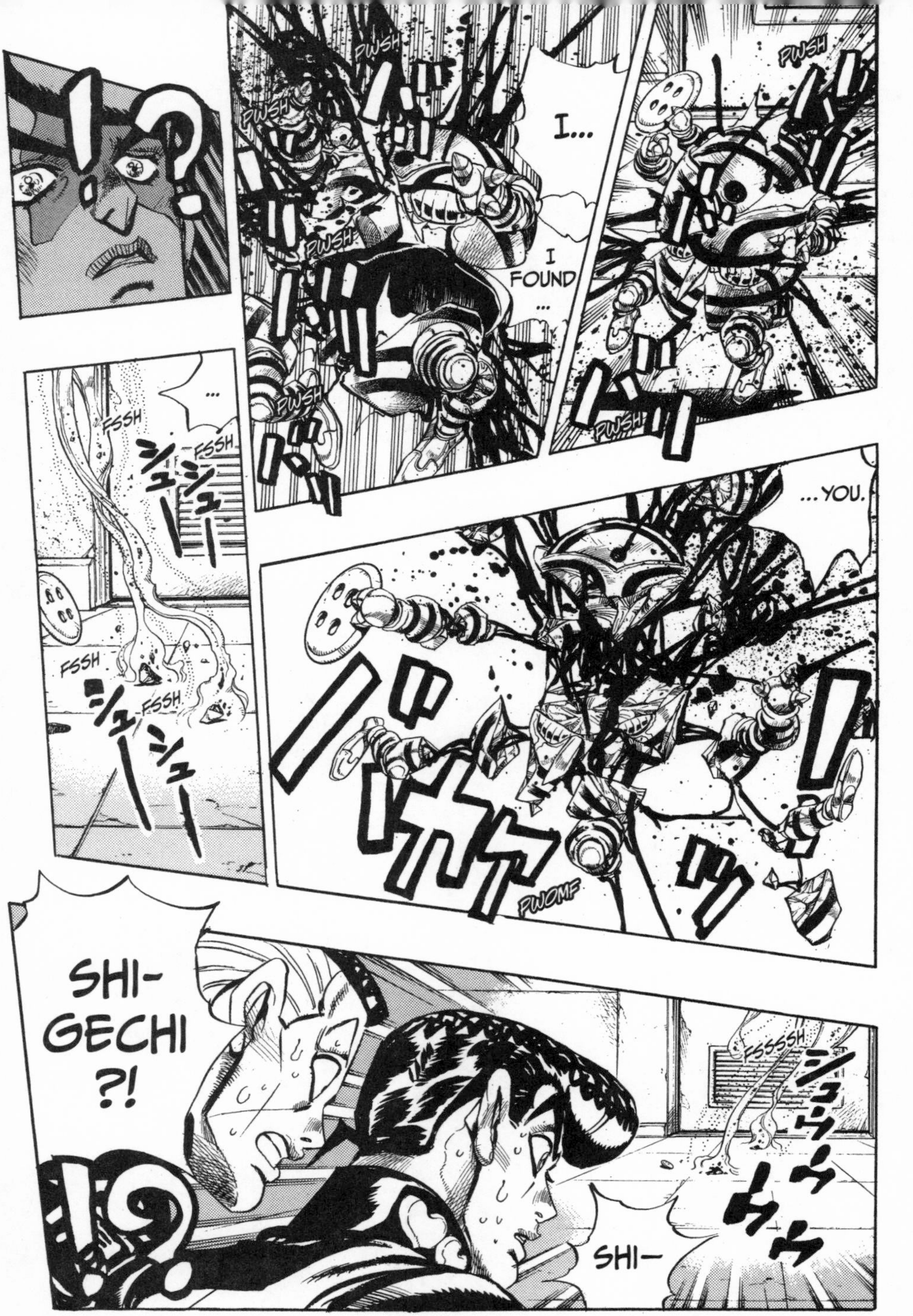
PWSH
PWSH
PWSH
PWSH
I...
I FOUND ...
PWSH
PWSH
...YOU.
PWOMF
...
FSSH
シュシュー
FSSH
FSSH
シュシュー
FSSH
FSSSSH
SHI–
SHI-GECHI?!

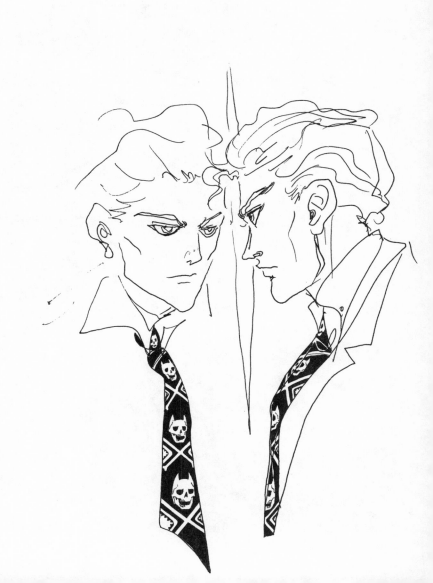

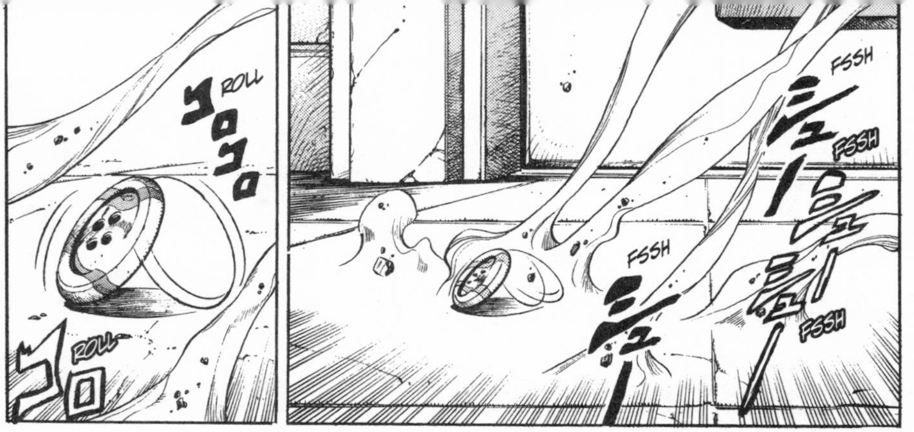
FSSH
FSSH
FSSH
FSSH
ROLL
ROLL

CHAPTER 82

THE PEOPLE OF MORIOH

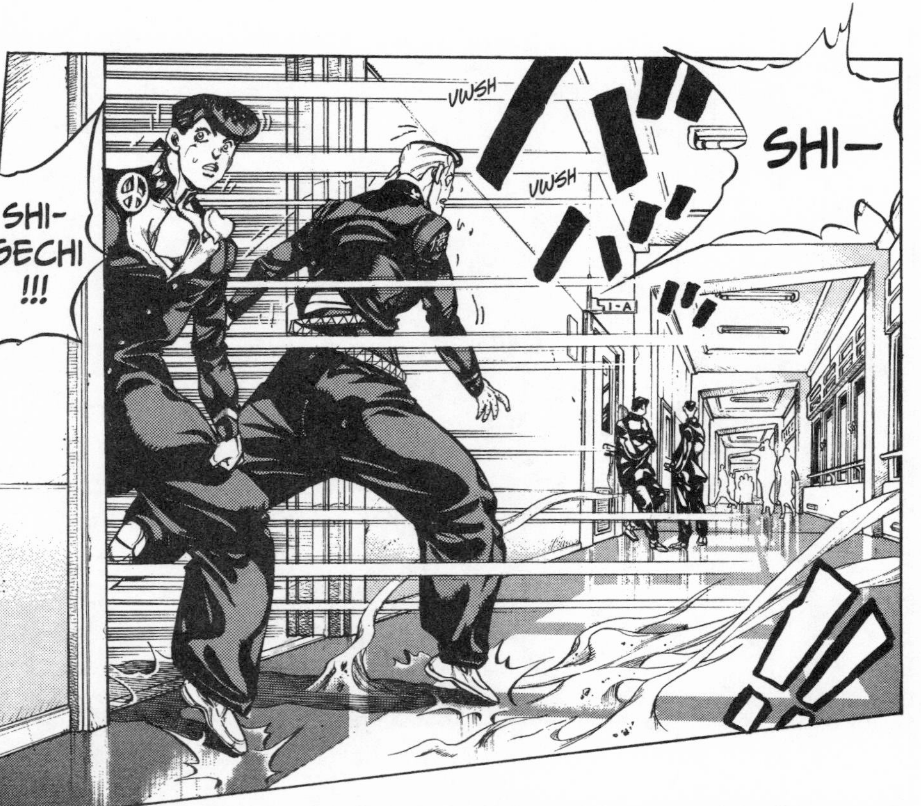
SHI—
VWSH
VWSH
SHI-GECHI!!!

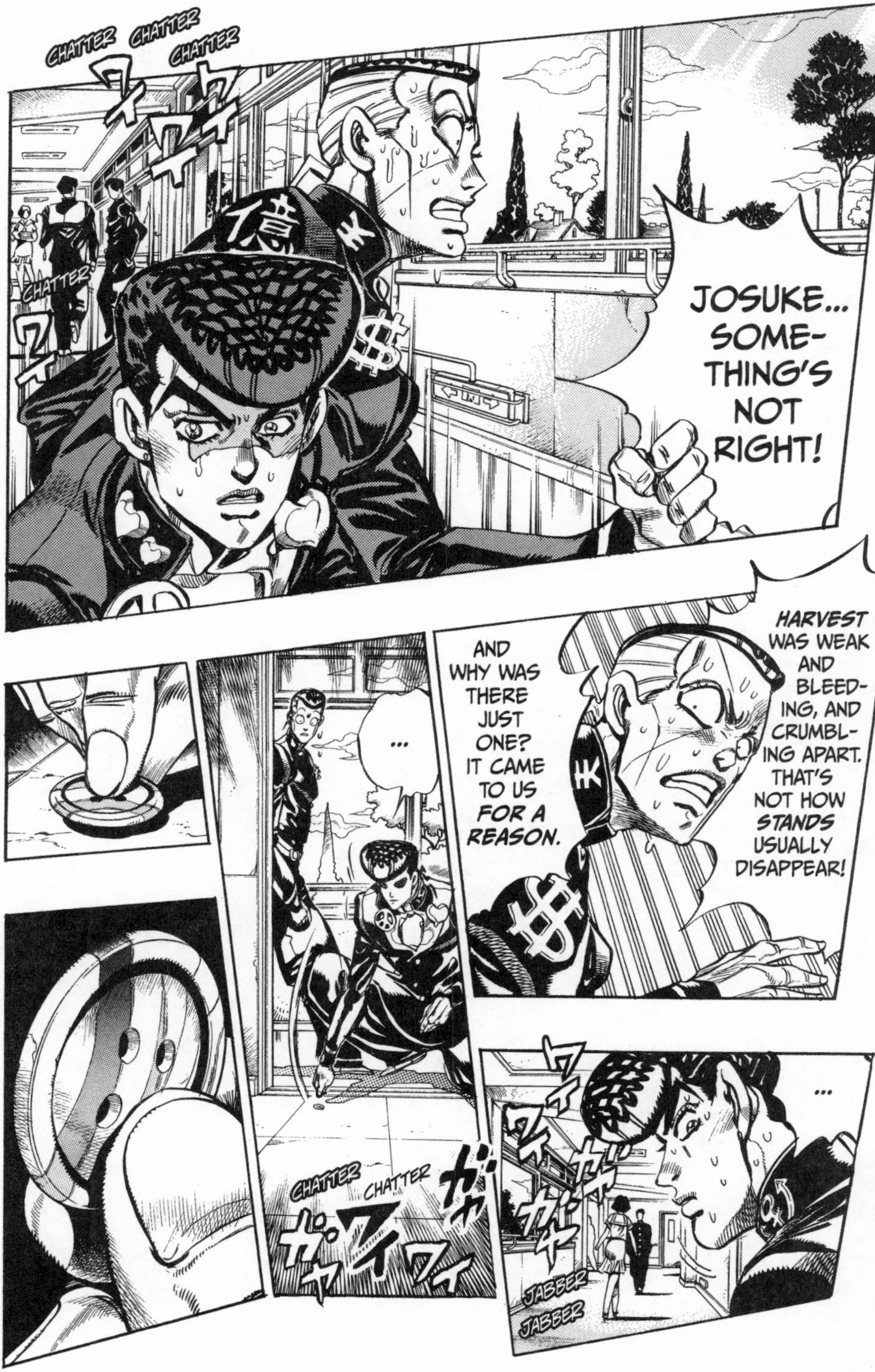
CHATTER CHATTER CHATTER
CHATTER
JOSUKE... SOMETHING'S NOT RIGHT!
HARVEST WAS WEAK AND BLEEDING, AND CRUMBLING APART. THAT'S NOT HOW STANDS USUALLY DISAPPEAR!
...
JABBER JABBER
AND WHY WAS THERE JUST ONE? IT CAME TO US FOR A REASON.
...
CHATTER CHATTER

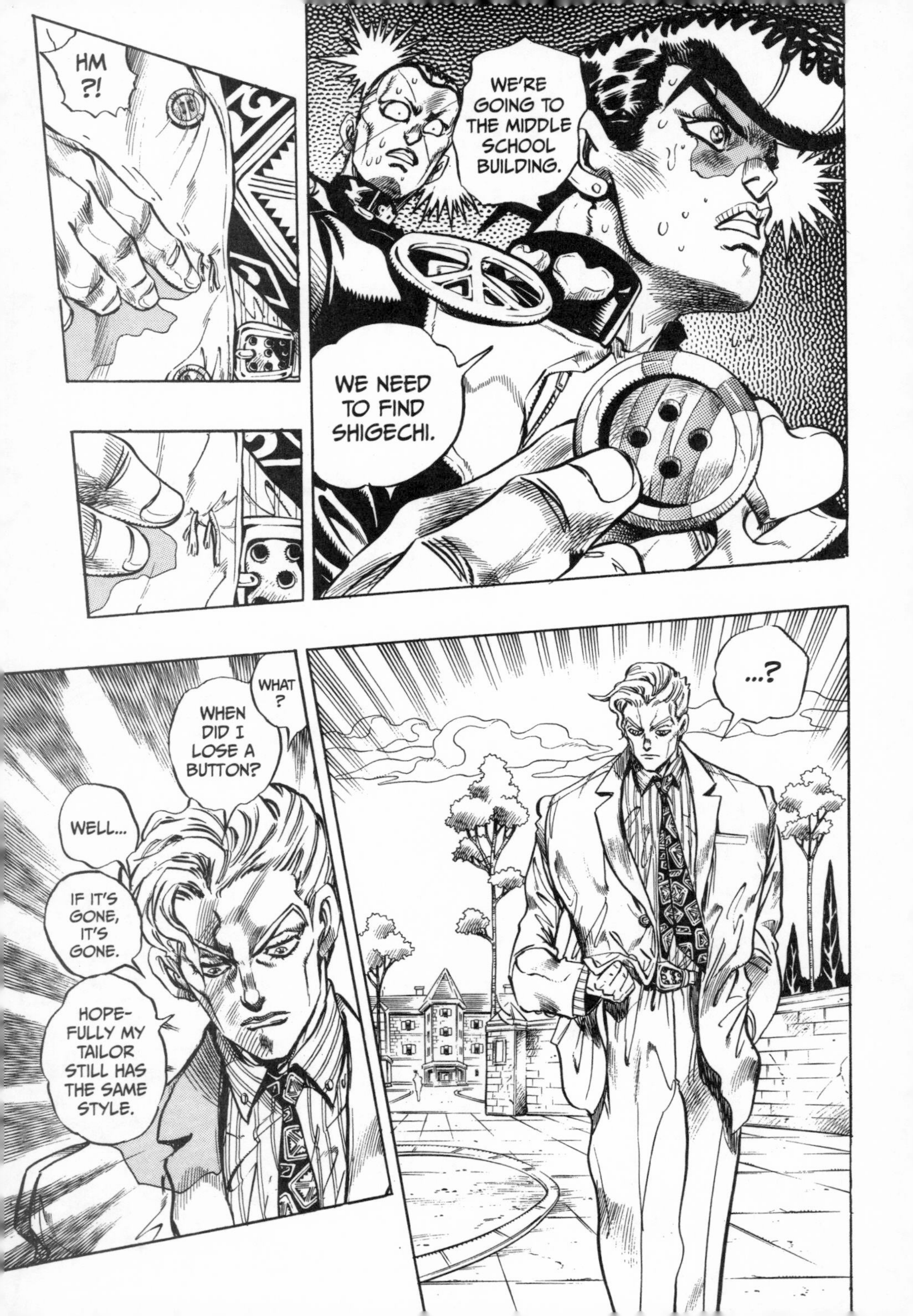
WE'RE GOING TO THE MIDDLE SCHOOL BUILDING.
WE NEED TO FIND SHIGECHI.
HM ?!
...?
WHAT ?
WHEN DID I LOSE A BUTTON?
WELL...
IF IT'S GONE, IT'S GONE.
HOPEFULLY MY TAILOR STILL HAS THE SAME STYLE.

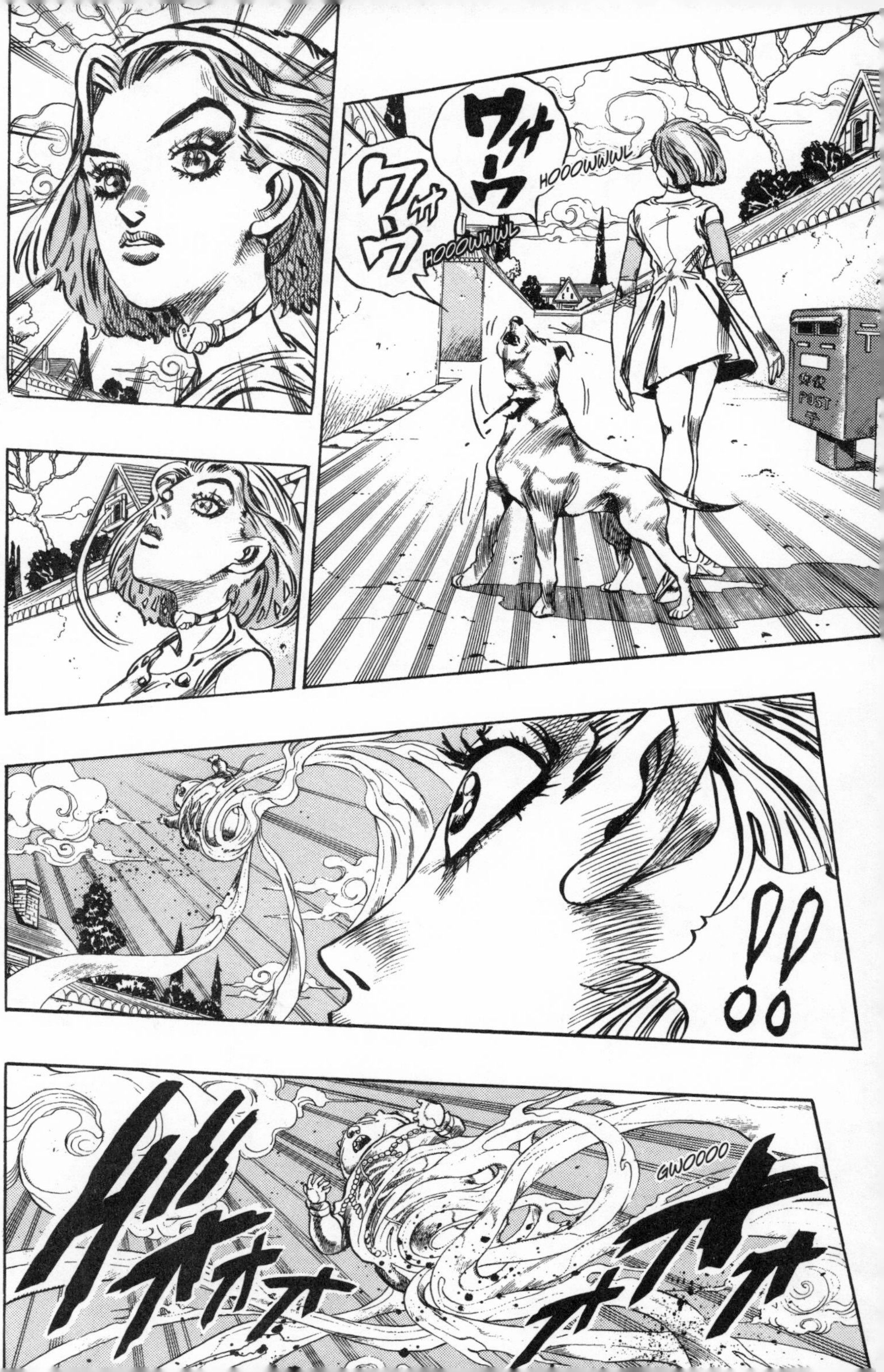

HOOOWWWL
HOOOWWWL
!!
GWOOOO

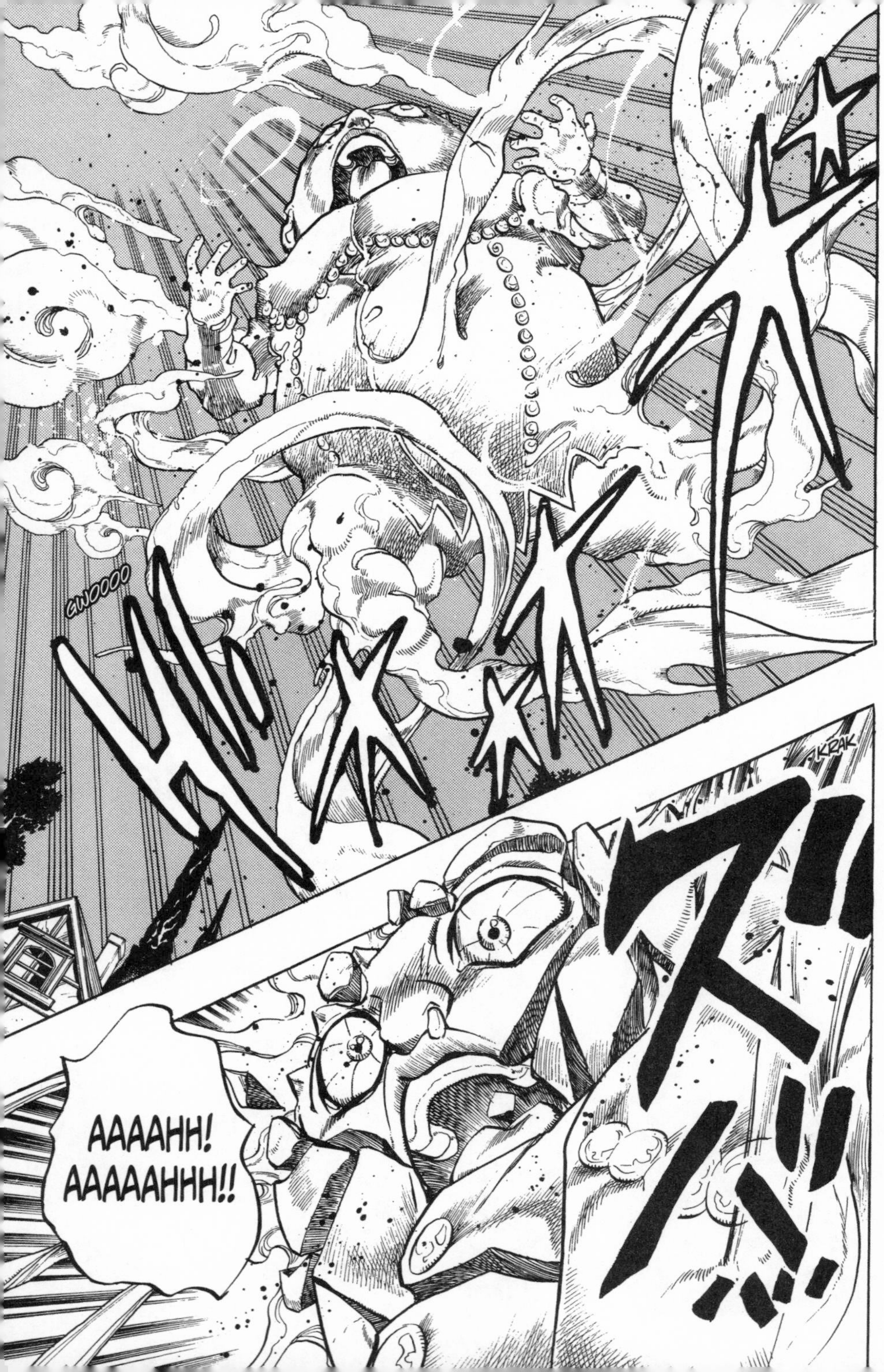
GWOOOO
KRAK
AAAAHH!
AAAAAHHH!!

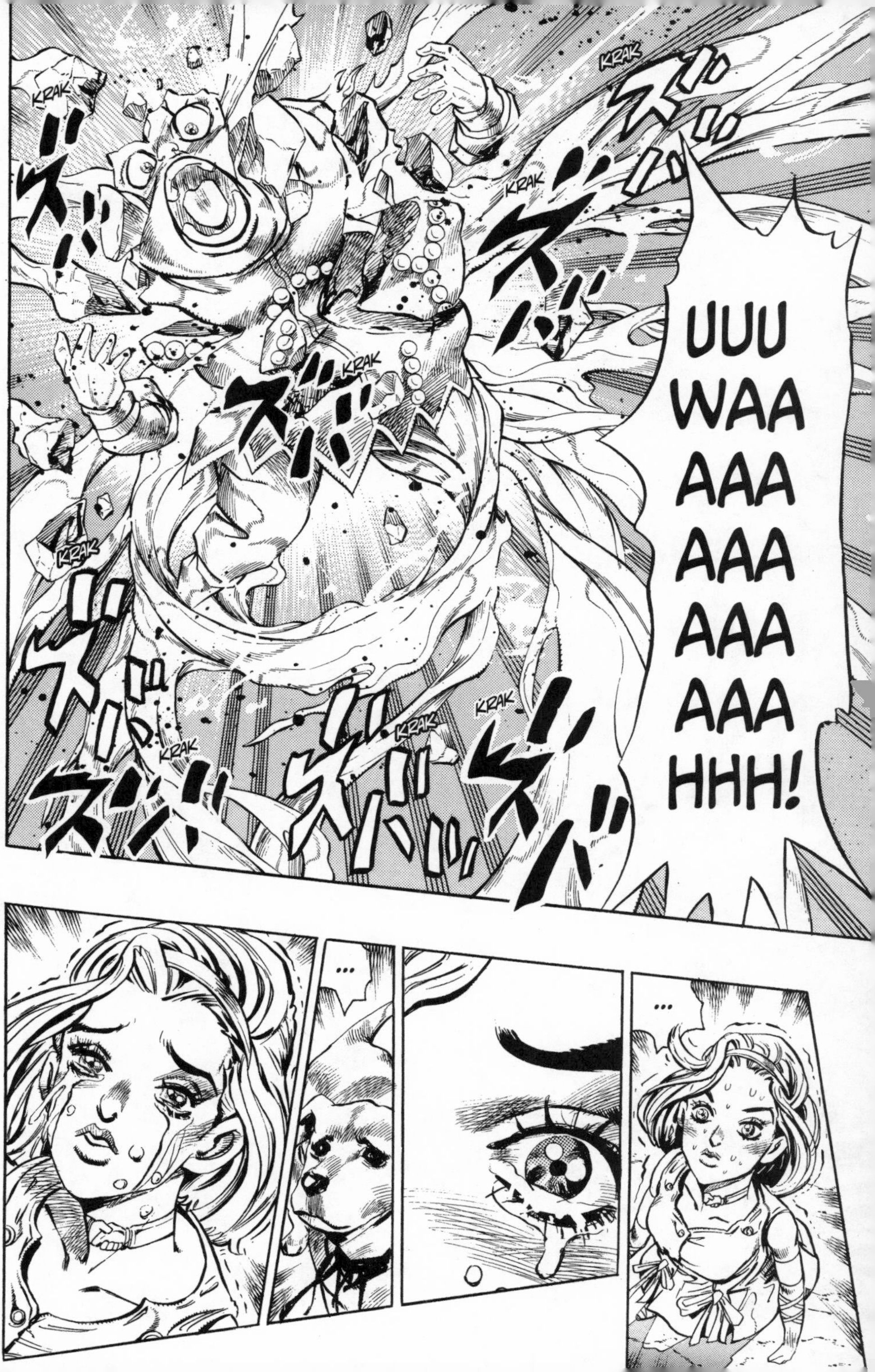
KRAK
UUUWAAAAAAAAAAAAAAAAAAAHHH!
KRAK
KRAK
KRAK
KRAK
KRAK
KRAK
KRAK
...
...

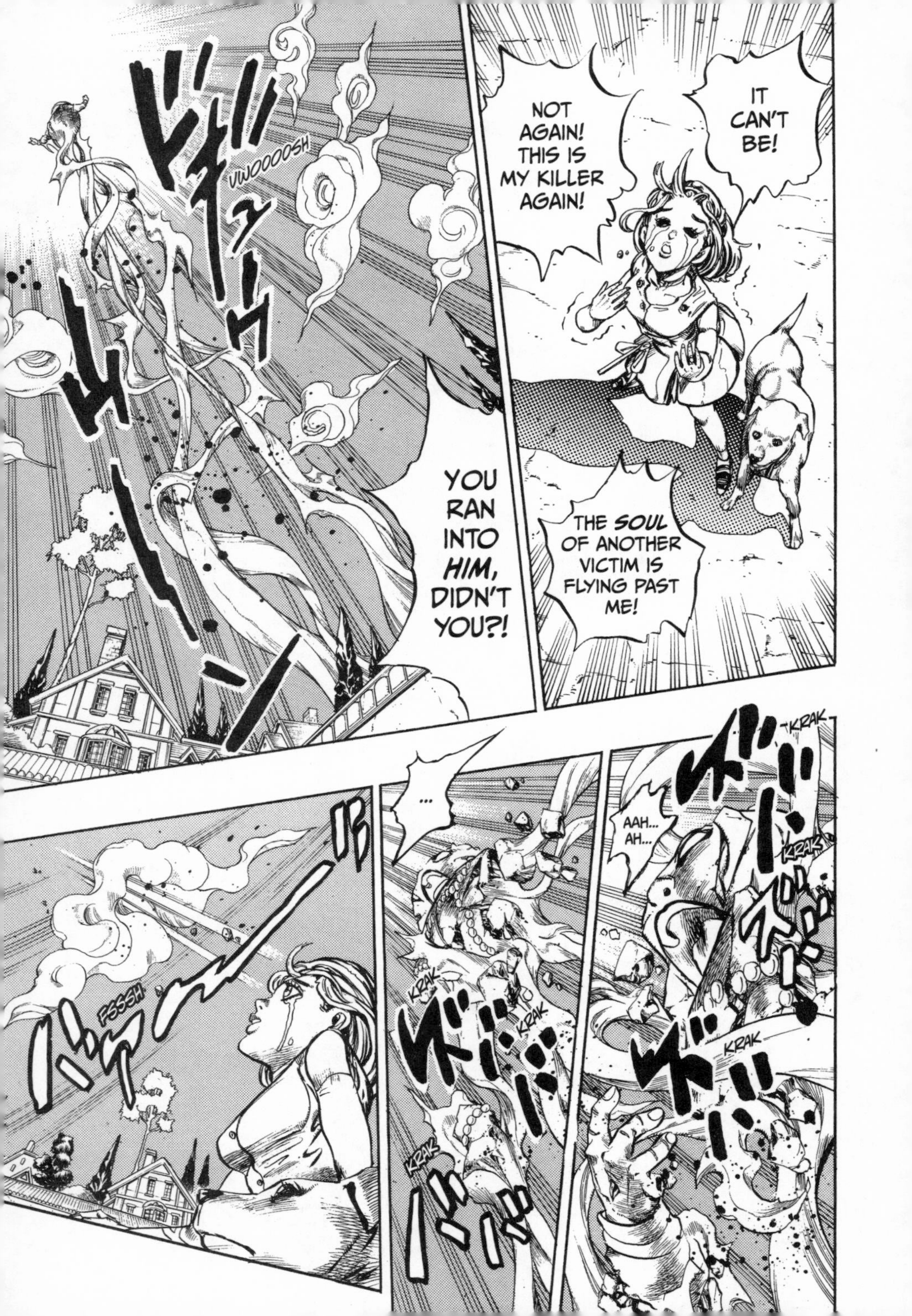
IT CAN'T BE!
NOT AGAIN! THIS IS MY KILLER AGAIN!
THE SOUL OF ANOTHER VICTIM IS FLYING PAST ME!
VWOOOOSH
YOU RAN INTO HIM, DIDN'T YOU?!
KRAK
AAH... AH...
KRAK
KRAK
...
KRAK
KRAK
KRAK
FSSSH

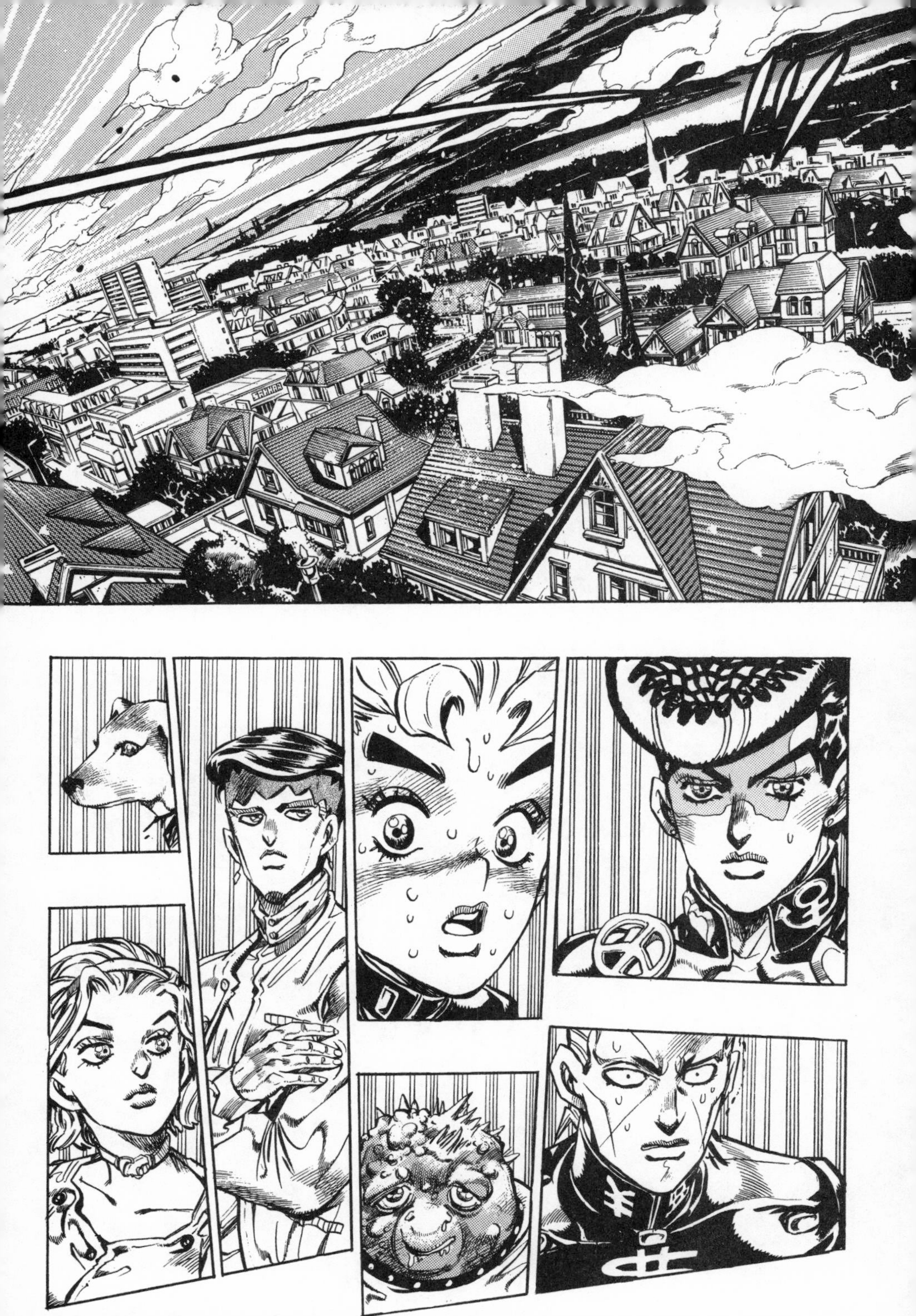

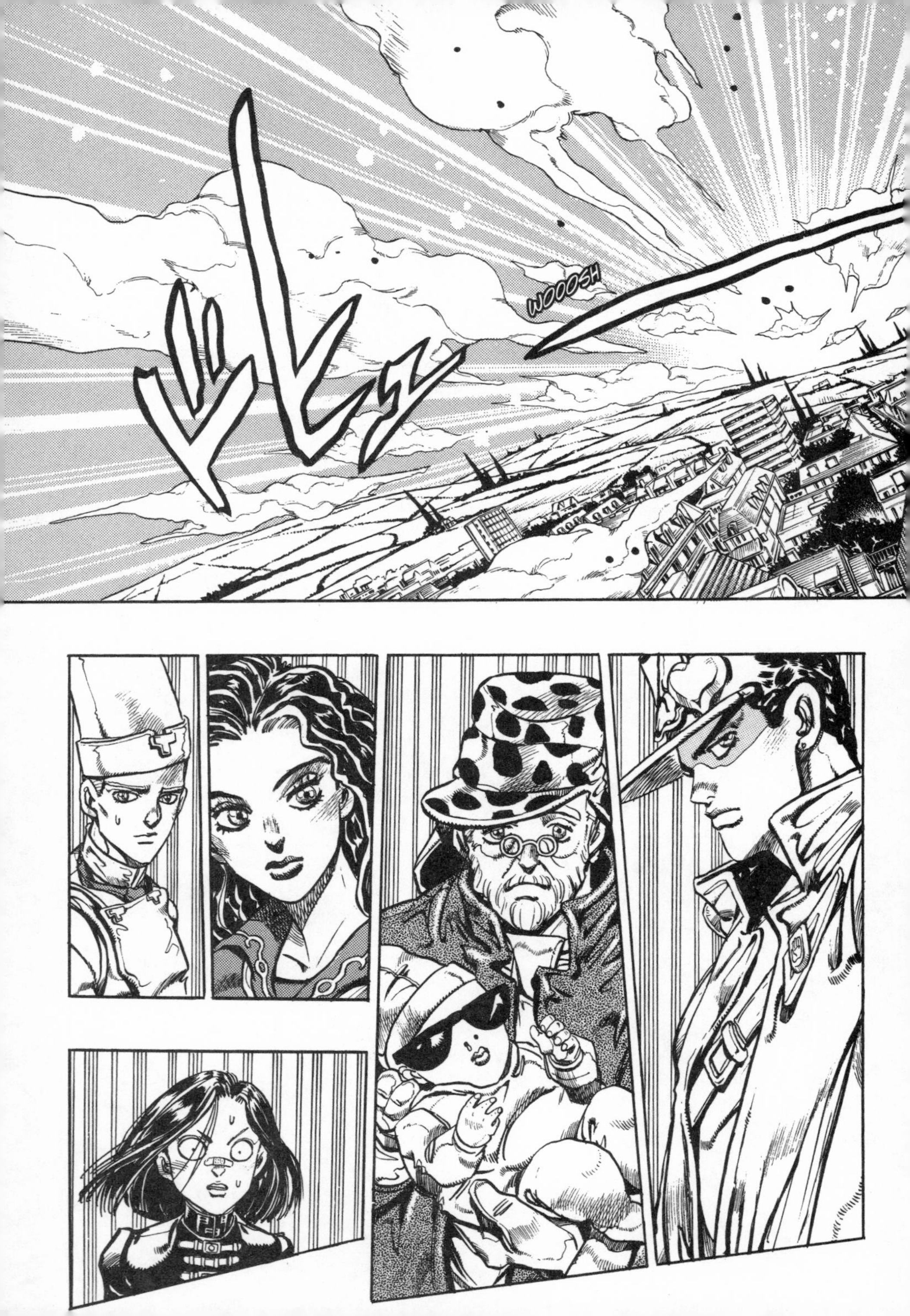
WOOOSH

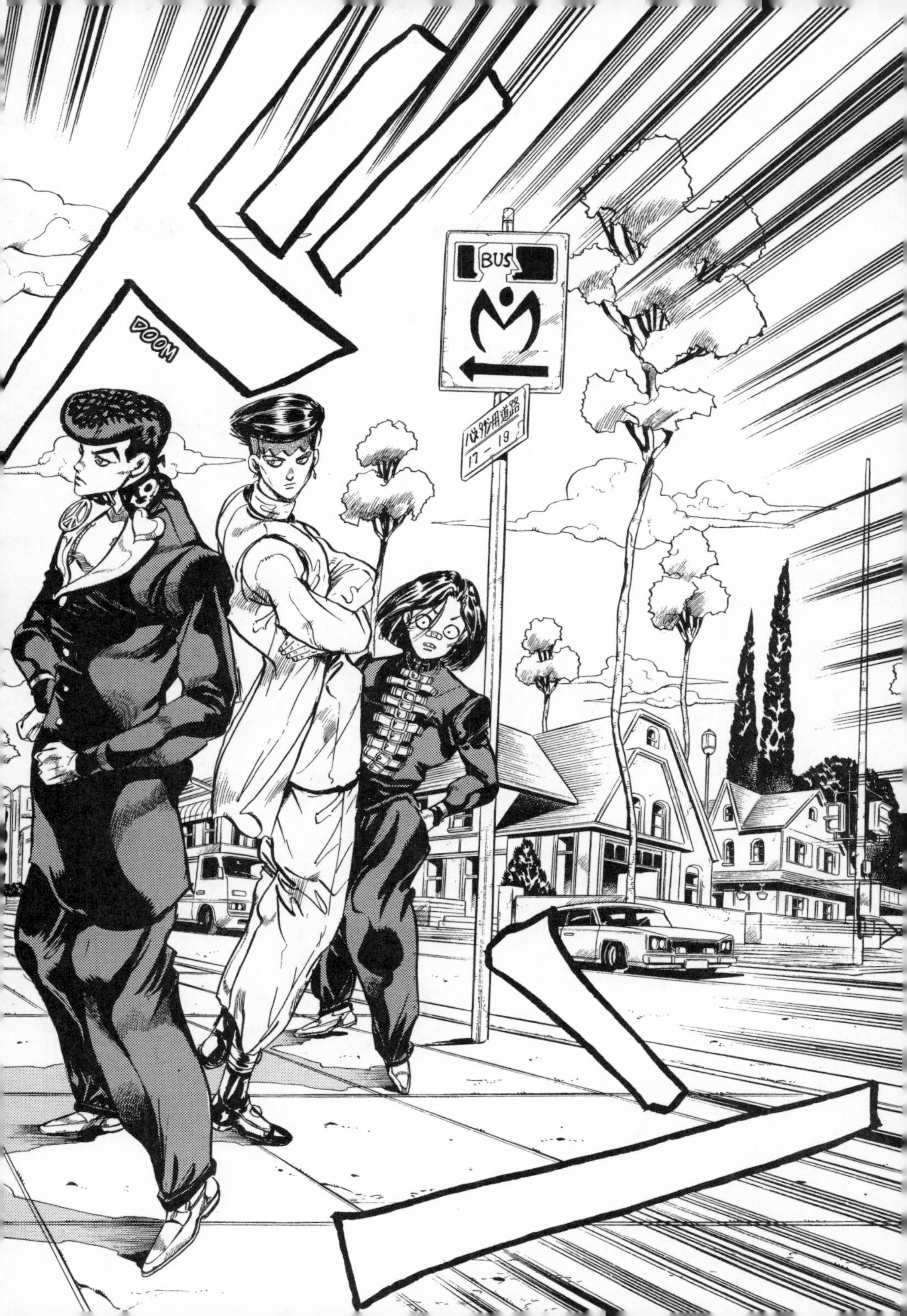
DOOM
BUS
17 – 19

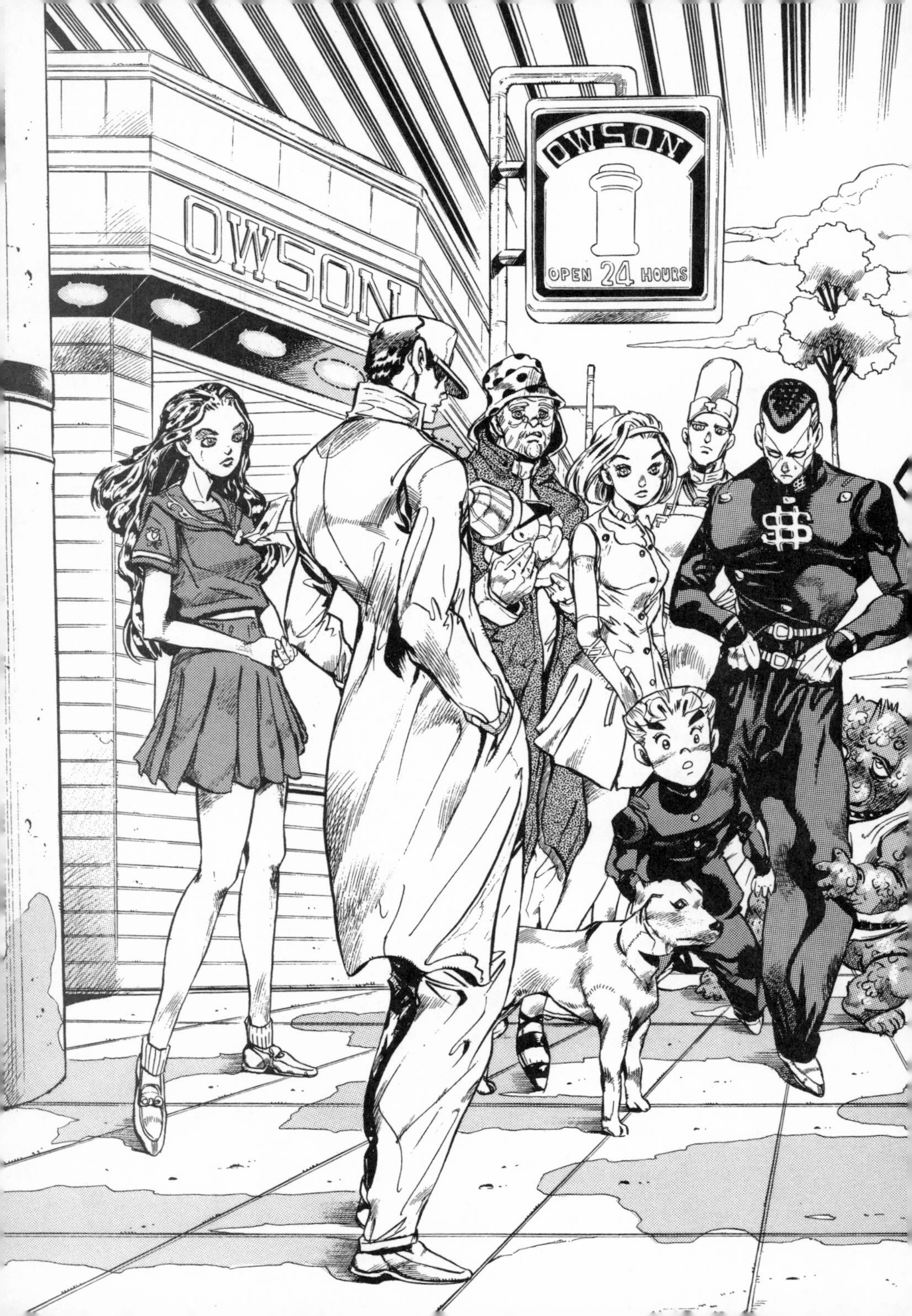
OWSON
OWSON
OPEN 24 HOURS

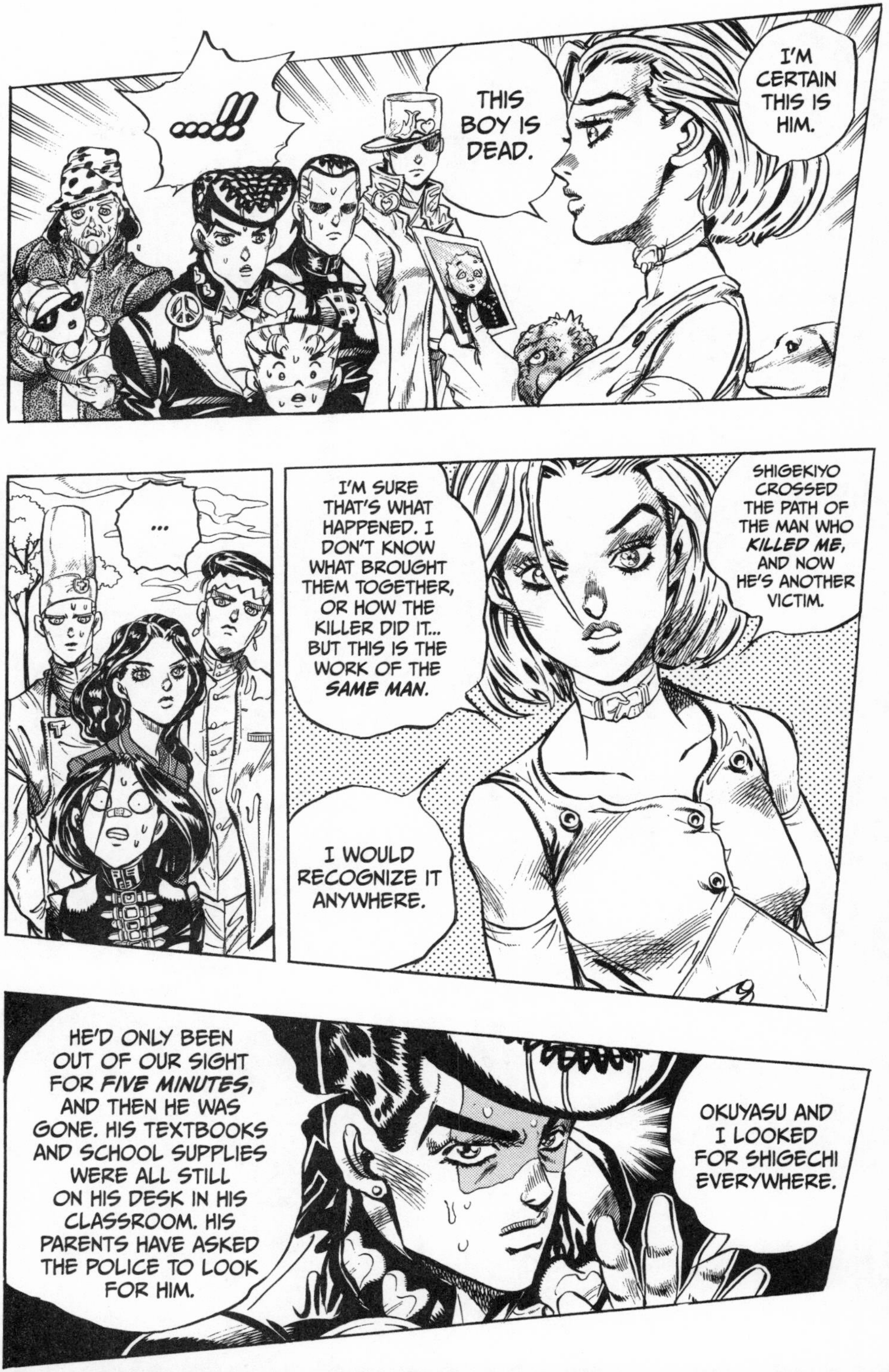
I'M CERTAIN THIS IS HIM.
THIS BOY IS DEAD.
...!!
SHIGEKIYO CROSSED THE PATH OF THE MAN WHO *KILLED ME*, AND NOW HE'S ANOTHER VICTIM.
I'M SURE THAT'S WHAT HAPPENED. I DON'T KNOW WHAT BROUGHT THEM TOGETHER, OR HOW THE KILLER DID IT... BUT THIS IS THE WORK OF THE *SAME MAN*.
I WOULD RECOGNIZE IT ANYWHERE.
...
OKUYASU AND I LOOKED FOR SHIGECHI EVERYWHERE.
HE'D ONLY BEEN OUT OF OUR SIGHT FOR *FIVE MINUTES*, AND THEN HE WAS GONE. HIS TEXTBOOKS AND SCHOOL SUPPLIES WERE ALL STILL ON HIS DESK IN HIS CLASSROOM. HIS PARENTS HAVE ASKED THE POLICE TO LOOK FOR HIM.

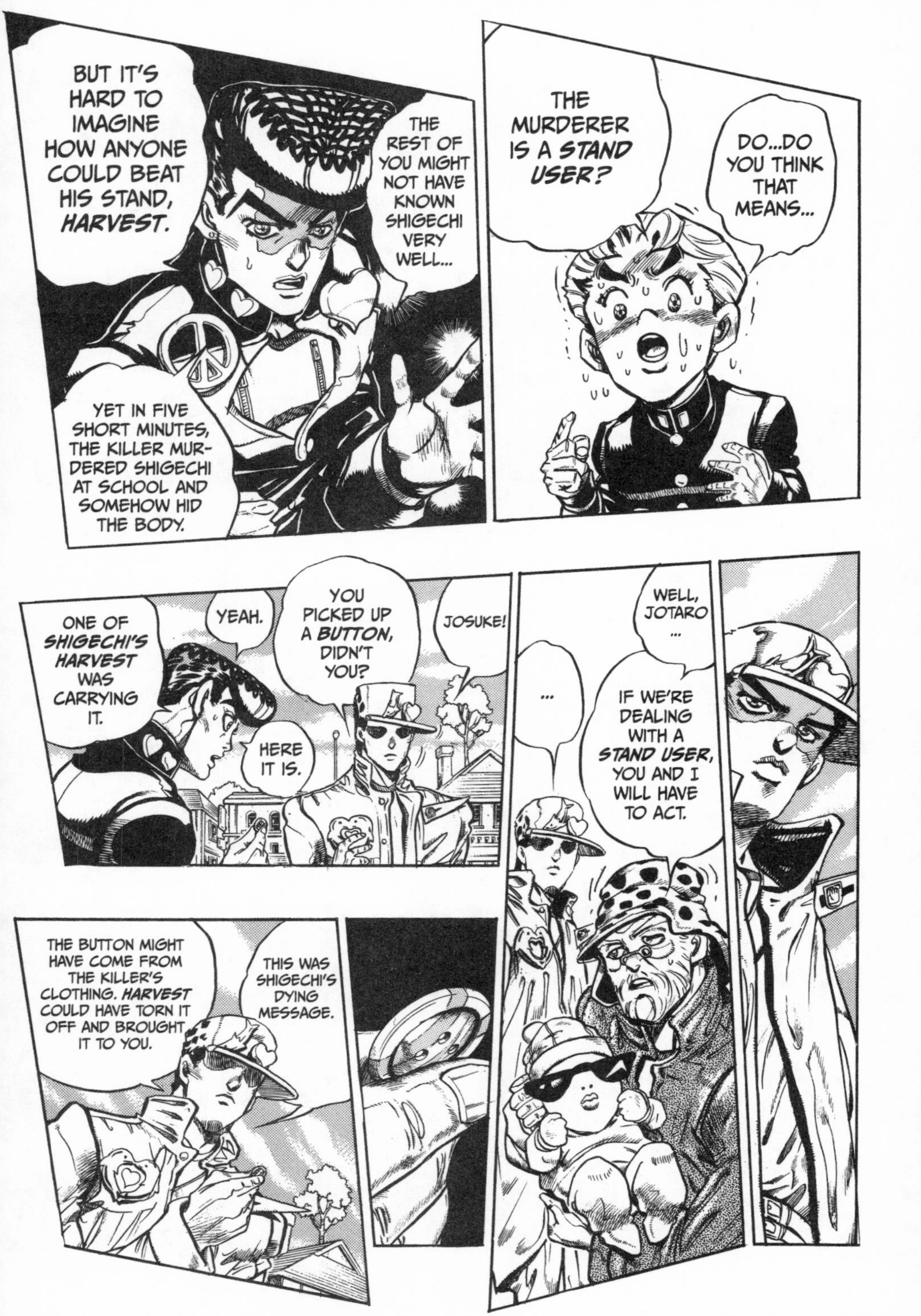
DO...DO YOU THINK THAT MEANS...
THE MURDERER IS A STAND USER?
THE REST OF YOU MIGHT NOT HAVE KNOWN SHIGECHI VERY WELL...
BUT IT'S HARD TO IMAGINE HOW ANYONE COULD BEAT HIS STAND, HARVEST.
YET IN FIVE SHORT MINUTES, THE KILLER MURDERED SHIGECHI AT SCHOOL AND SOMEHOW HID THE BODY.
WELL, JOTARO ...
IF WE'RE DEALING WITH A STAND USER, YOU AND I WILL HAVE TO ACT.
...
JOSUKE!
YOU PICKED UP A BUTTON, DIDN'T YOU?
YEAH.
ONE OF SHIGECHI'S HARVEST WAS CARRYING IT.
HERE IT IS.
THIS WAS SHIGECHI'S DYING MESSAGE.
THE BUTTON MIGHT HAVE COME FROM THE KILLER'S CLOTHING. HARVEST COULD HAVE TORN IT OFF AND BROUGHT IT TO YOU.

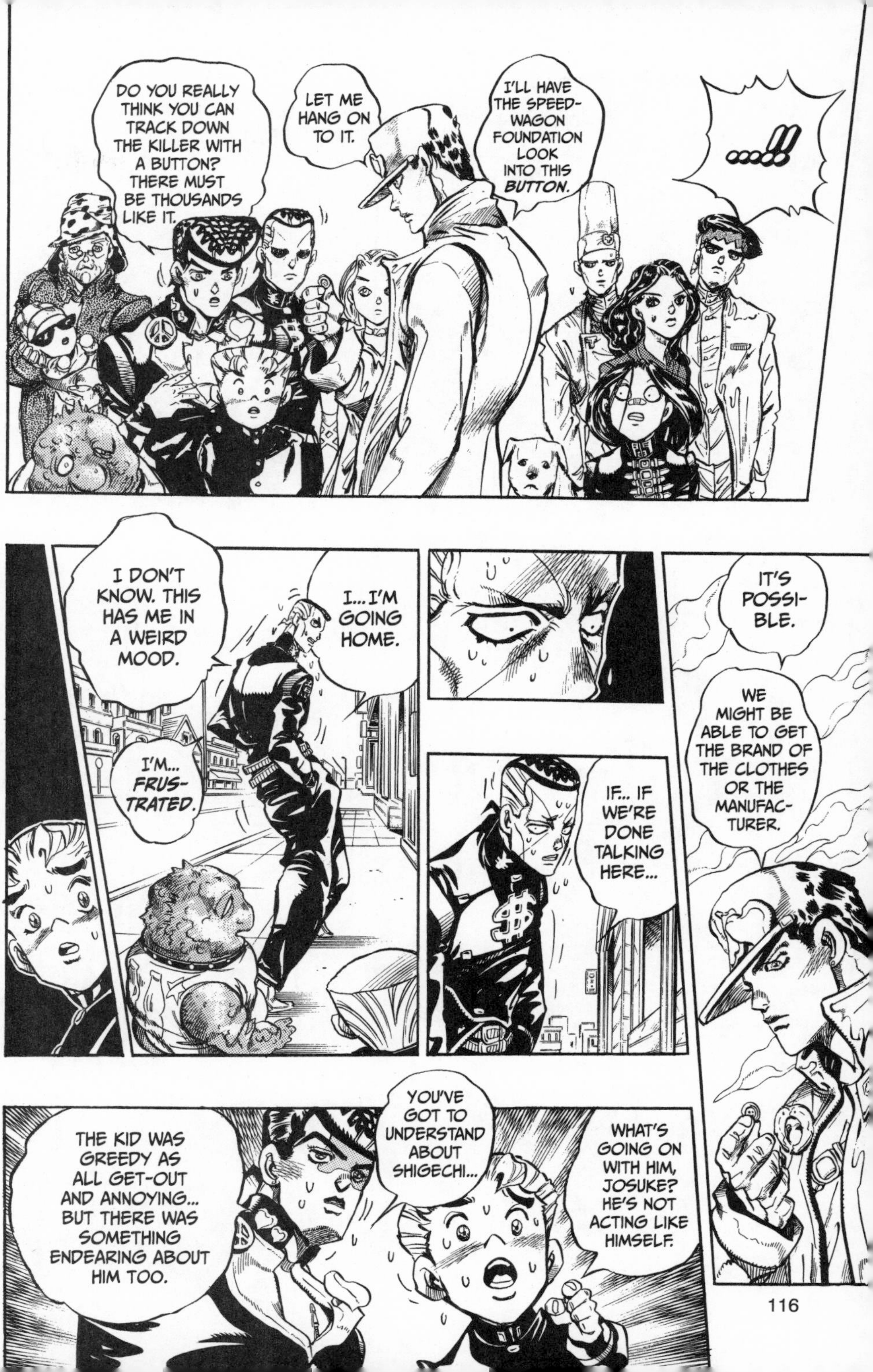
...!!
I'LL HAVE THE SPEED-WAGON FOUNDATION LOOK INTO THIS *BUTTON*.
LET ME HANG ON TO IT.
DO YOU REALLY THINK YOU CAN TRACK DOWN THE KILLER WITH A BUTTON? THERE MUST BE THOUSANDS LIKE IT.
IT'S POSSI-BLE.
WE MIGHT BE ABLE TO GET THE BRAND OF THE CLOTHES OR THE MANUFAC-TURER.
IF... IF WE'RE DONE TALKING HERE...
I...I'M GOING HOME.
I DON'T KNOW. THIS HAS ME IN A WEIRD MOOD.
I'M... *FRUS-TRATED*.
WHAT'S GOING ON WITH HIM, JOSUKE? HE'S NOT ACTING LIKE HIMSELF.
YOU'VE GOT TO UNDERSTAND ABOUT SHIGECHI...
THE KID WAS GREEDY AS ALL GET-OUT AND ANNOYING... BUT THERE WAS SOMETHING ENDEARING ABOUT HIM TOO.

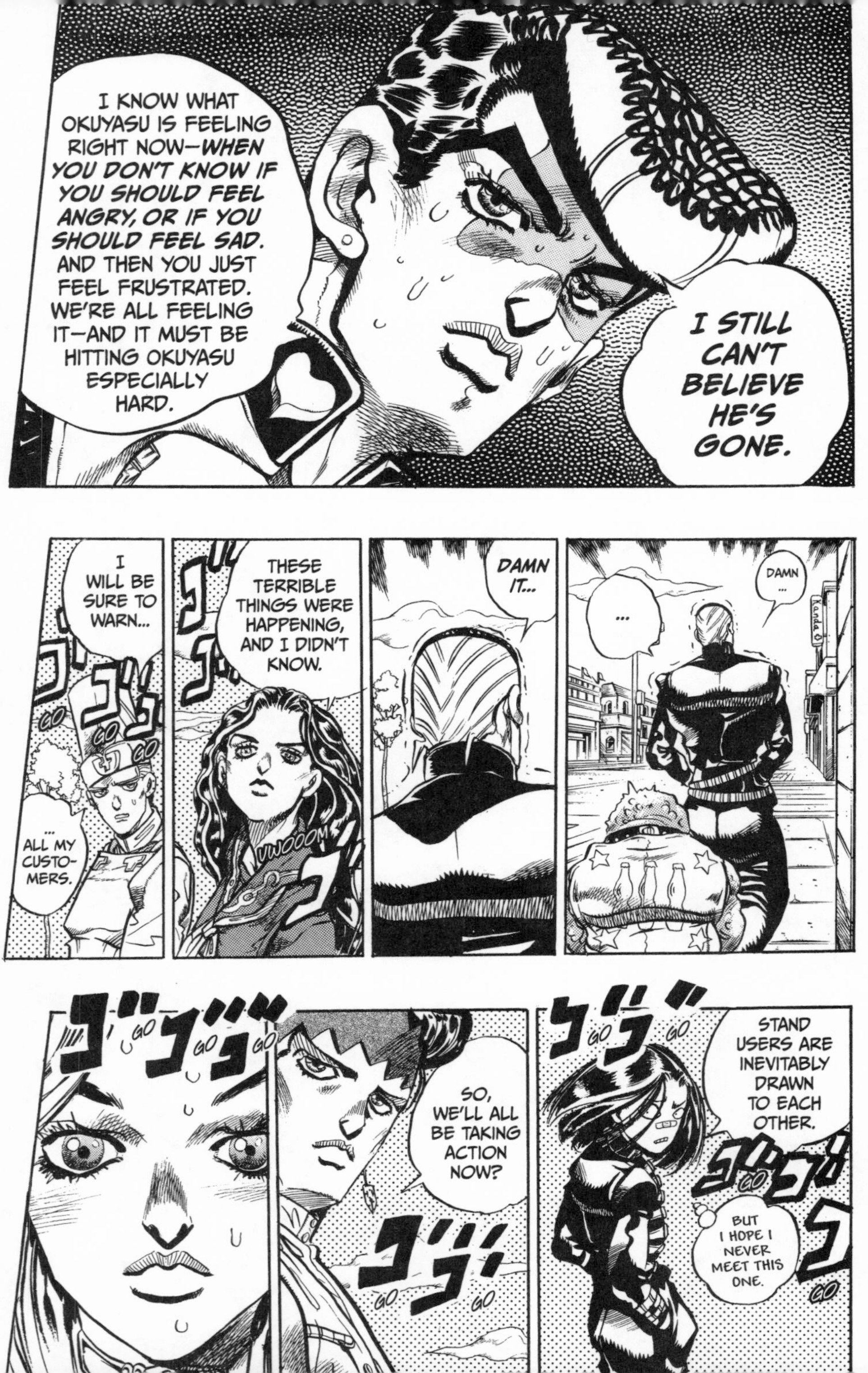

I STILL CAN'T BELIEVE HE'S GONE.
I KNOW WHAT OKUYASU IS FEELING RIGHT NOW—WHEN YOU DON'T KNOW IF YOU SHOULD FEEL ANGRY, OR IF YOU SHOULD FEEL SAD. AND THEN YOU JUST FEEL FRUSTRATED. WE'RE ALL FEELING IT—AND IT MUST BE HITTING OKUYASU ESPECIALLY HARD.
DAMN ...
...
DAMN IT...
THESE TERRIBLE THINGS WERE HAPPENING, AND I DIDN'T KNOW.
UWOOOM
I WILL BE SURE TO WARN...
... ALL MY CUSTOMERS.
GO GO GO
STAND USERS ARE INEVITABLY DRAWN TO EACH OTHER.
BUT I HOPE I NEVER MEET THIS ONE.
GO GO GO
SO, WE'LL ALL BE TAKING ACTION NOW?
GO GO
GO GO GO

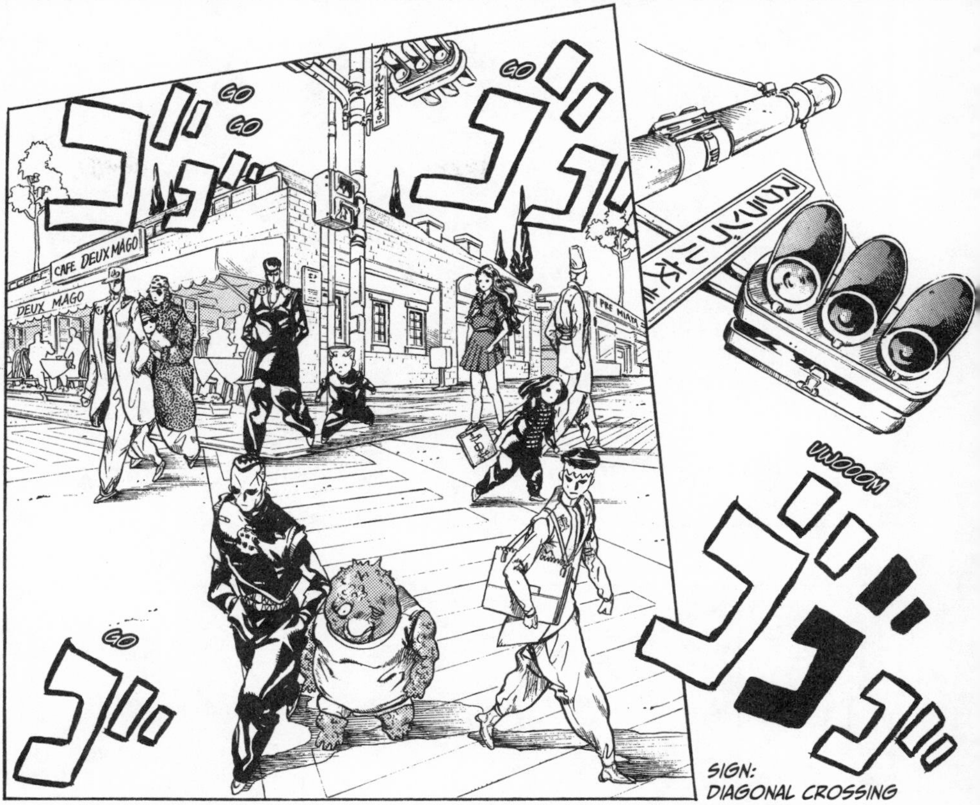
VWOOOM
SIGN:
DIAGONAL CROSSING
GO
GO GO
GO
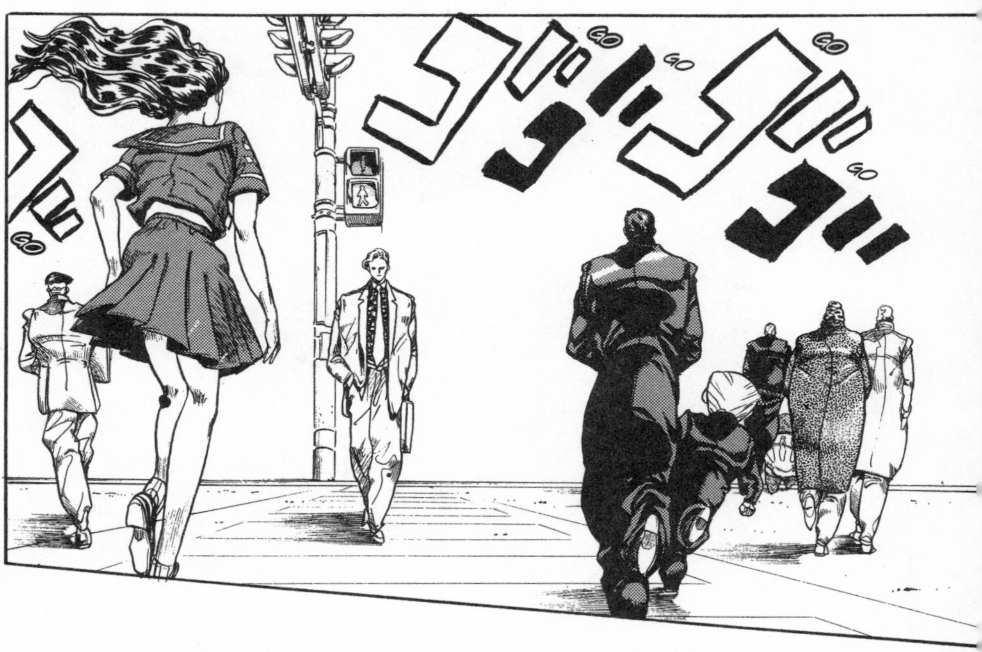
GO
GO
GO
GO
GO

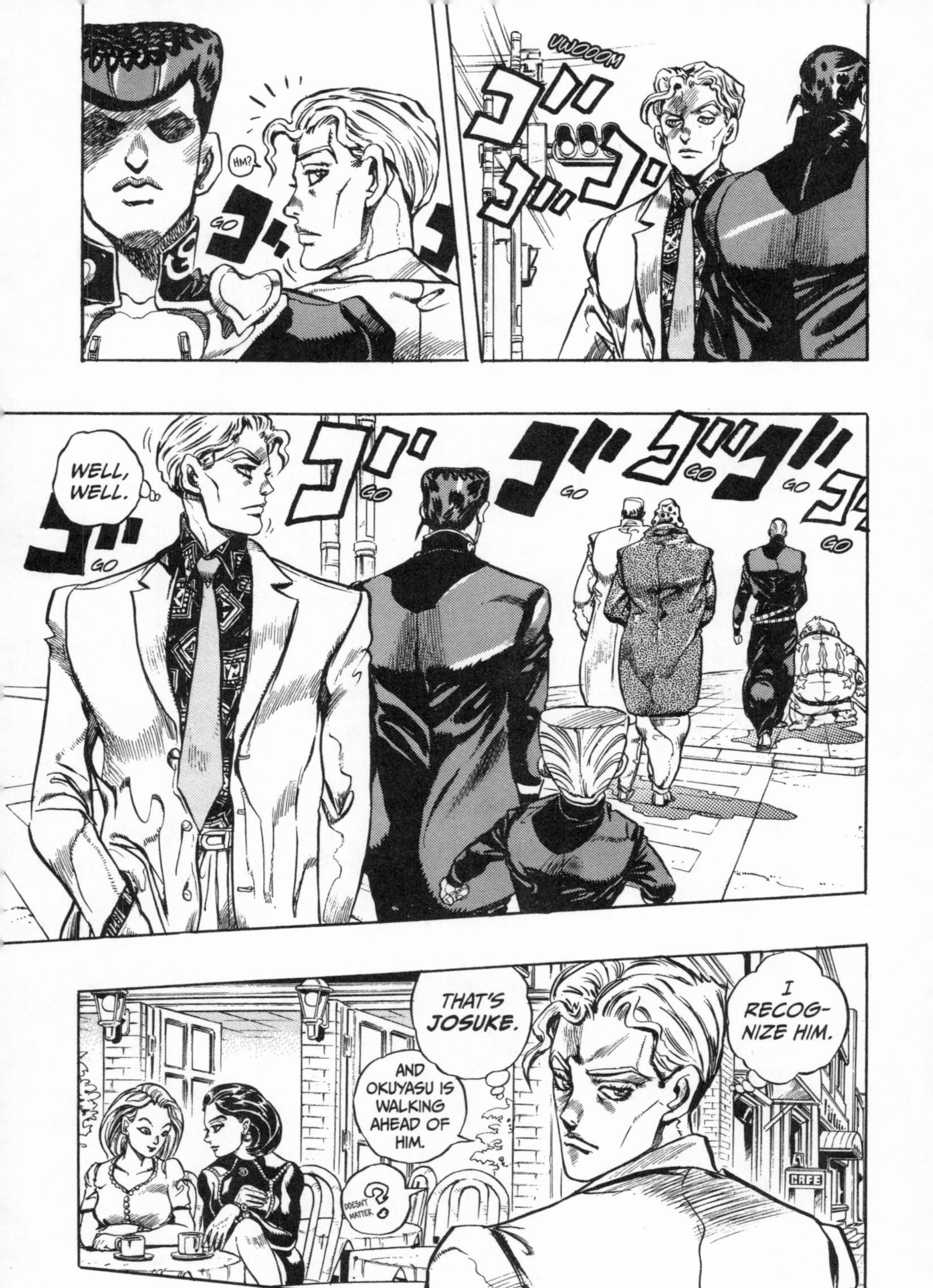
VWOOOM
HM?
GO
WELL, WELL.
GO
GO
GO
GO
GO
GO
I RECOGNIZE HIM.
THAT'S JOSUKE.
AND OKUYASU IS WALKING AHEAD OF HIM.
DOESN'T MATTER
CAFE

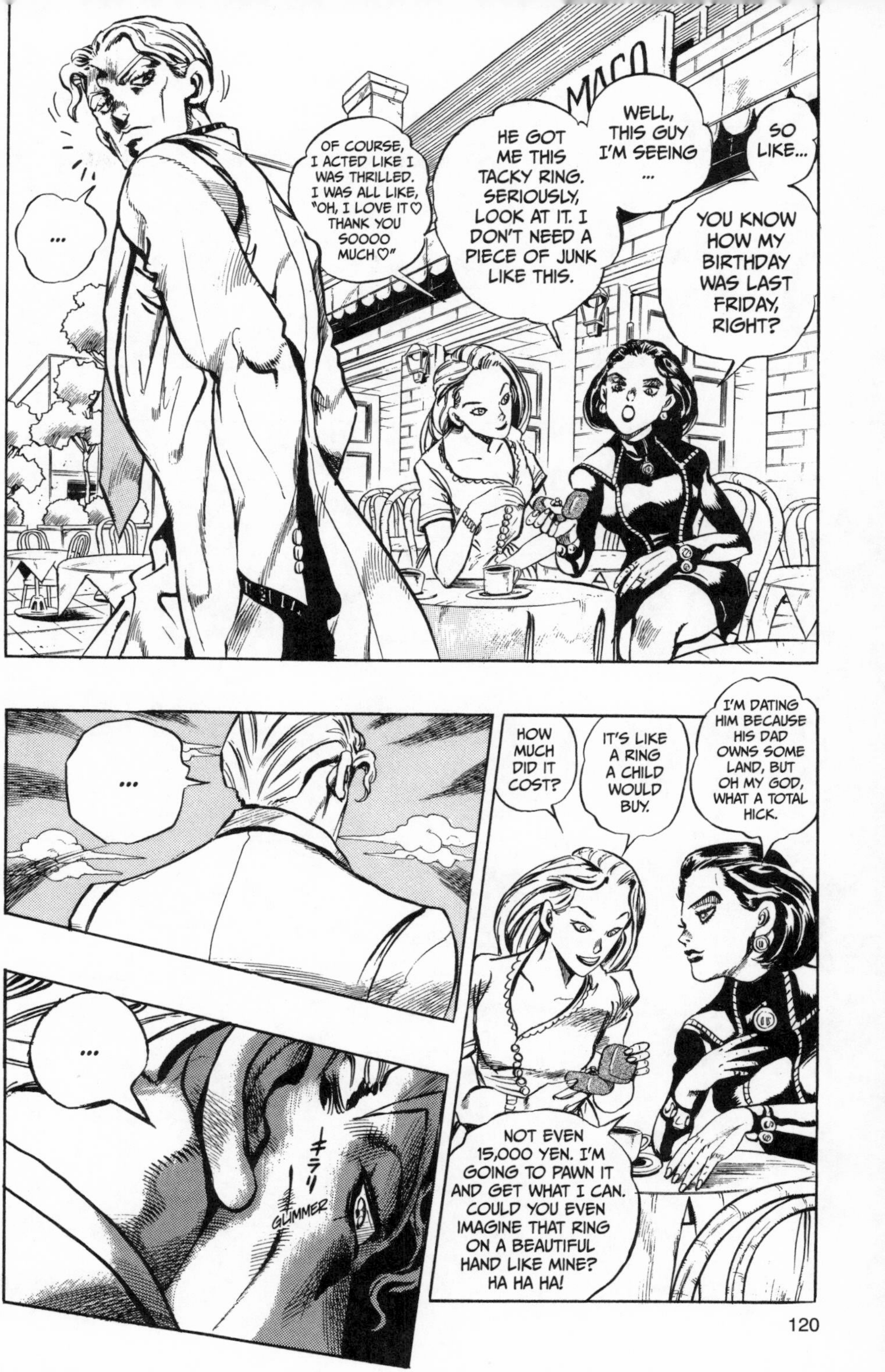
SO LIKE...
YOU KNOW HOW MY BIRTHDAY WAS LAST FRIDAY, RIGHT?
WELL, THIS GUY I'M SEEING ...
HE GOT ME THIS TACKY RING. SERIOUSLY, LOOK AT IT. I DON'T NEED A PIECE OF JUNK LIKE THIS.
OF COURSE, I ACTED LIKE I WAS THRILLED. I WAS ALL LIKE, "OH, I LOVE IT♡ THANK YOU SOOOO MUCH♡"
...
I'M DATING HIM BECAUSE HIS DAD OWNS SOME LAND, BUT OH MY GOD, WHAT A TOTAL HICK.
IT'S LIKE A RING A CHILD WOULD BUY.
HOW MUCH DID IT COST?
NOT EVEN 15,000 YEN. I'M GOING TO PAWN IT AND GET WHAT I CAN. COULD YOU EVEN IMAGINE THAT RING ON A BEAUTIFUL HAND LIKE MINE? HA HA HA!
...
...
キラリ
GLIMMER

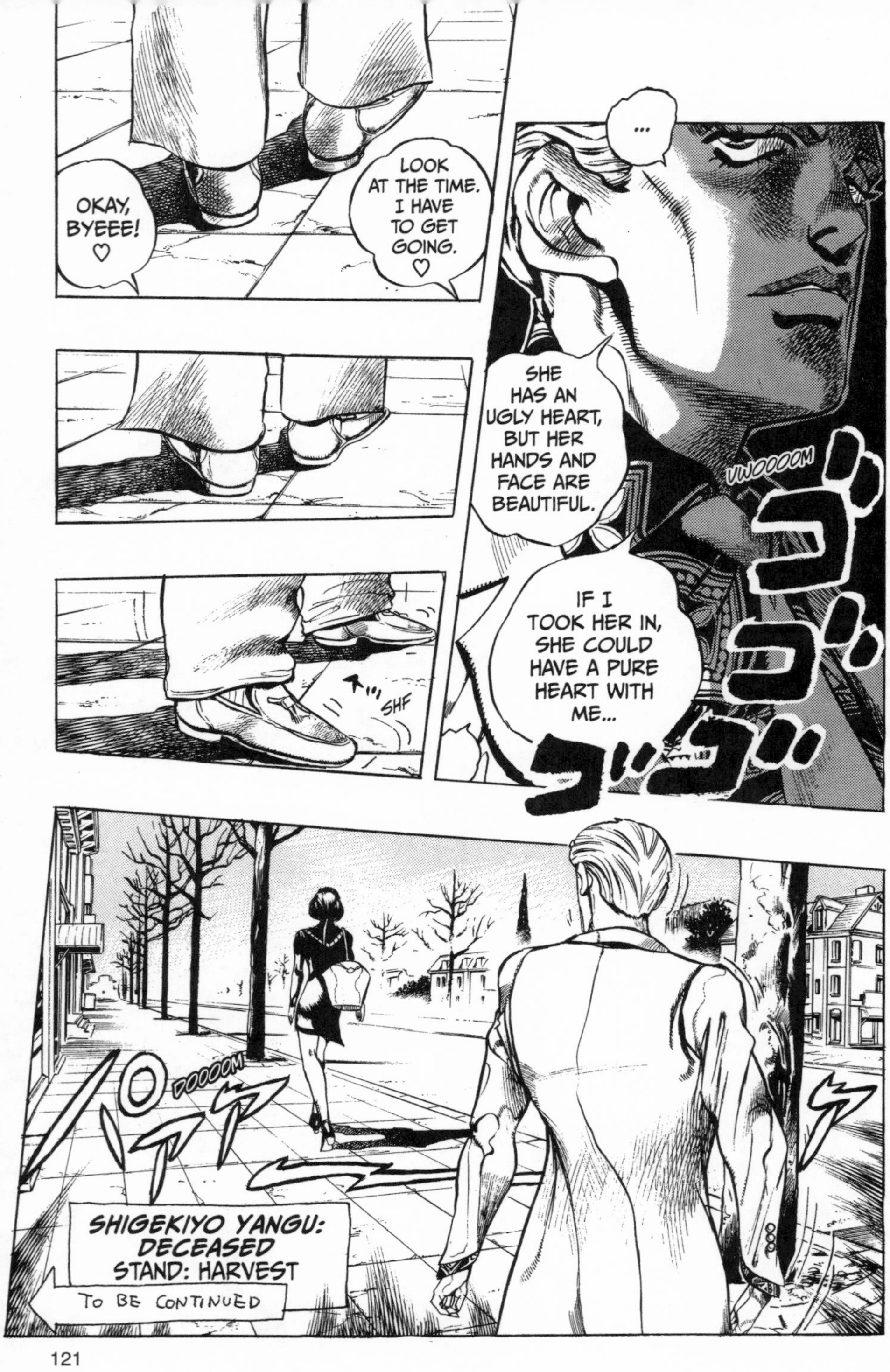
...
SHE HAS AN UGLY HEART, BUT HER HANDS AND FACE ARE BEAUTIFUL.
VWOOOOM
IF I TOOK HER IN, SHE COULD HAVE A PURE HEART WITH ME...
LOOK AT THE TIME. I HAVE TO GET GOING. ♡
OKAY, BYEEE! ♡
SHF
DOOOOM
SHIGEKIYO YANGU: DECEASED
STAND: HARVEST
TO BE CONTINUED

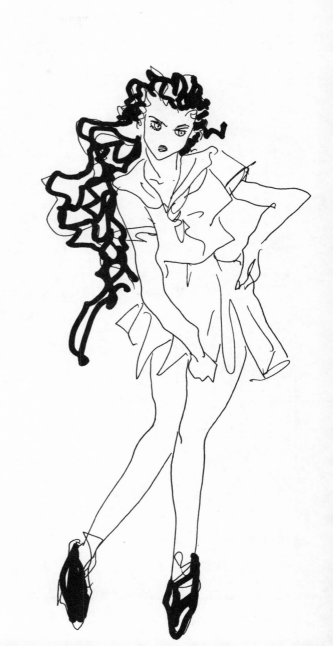

CHAPTER 83

YUKAKO YAMAGISHI DREAMS OF CINDERELLA, PART 1

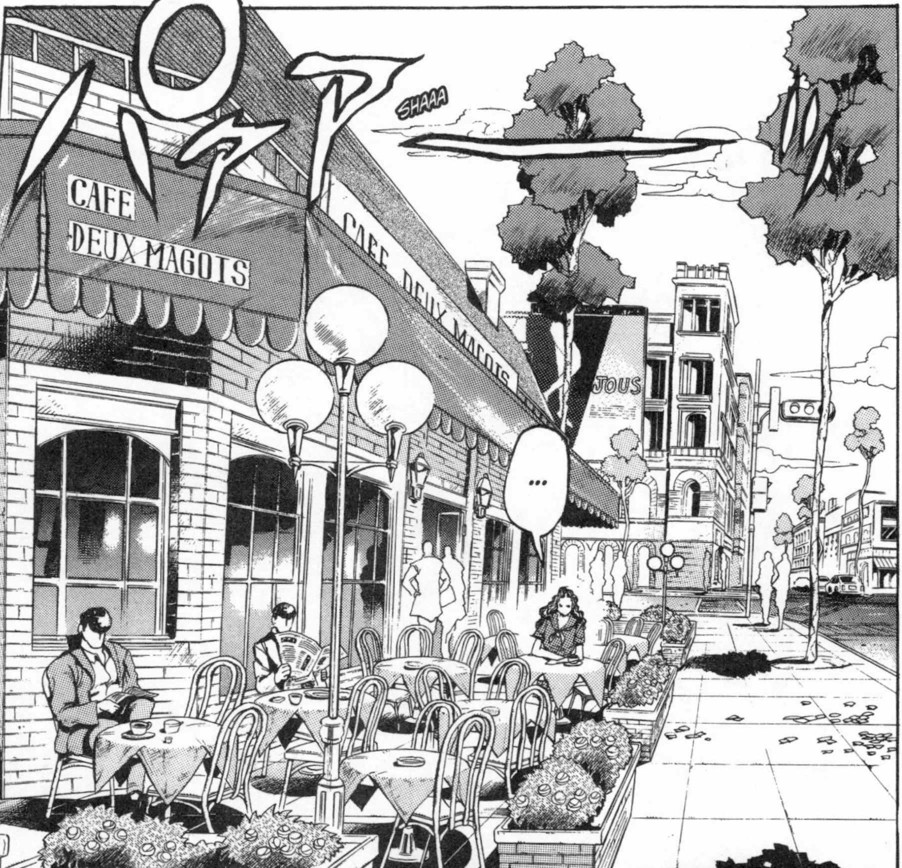
SHAAA
CAFE
DEUX MAGOTS
...

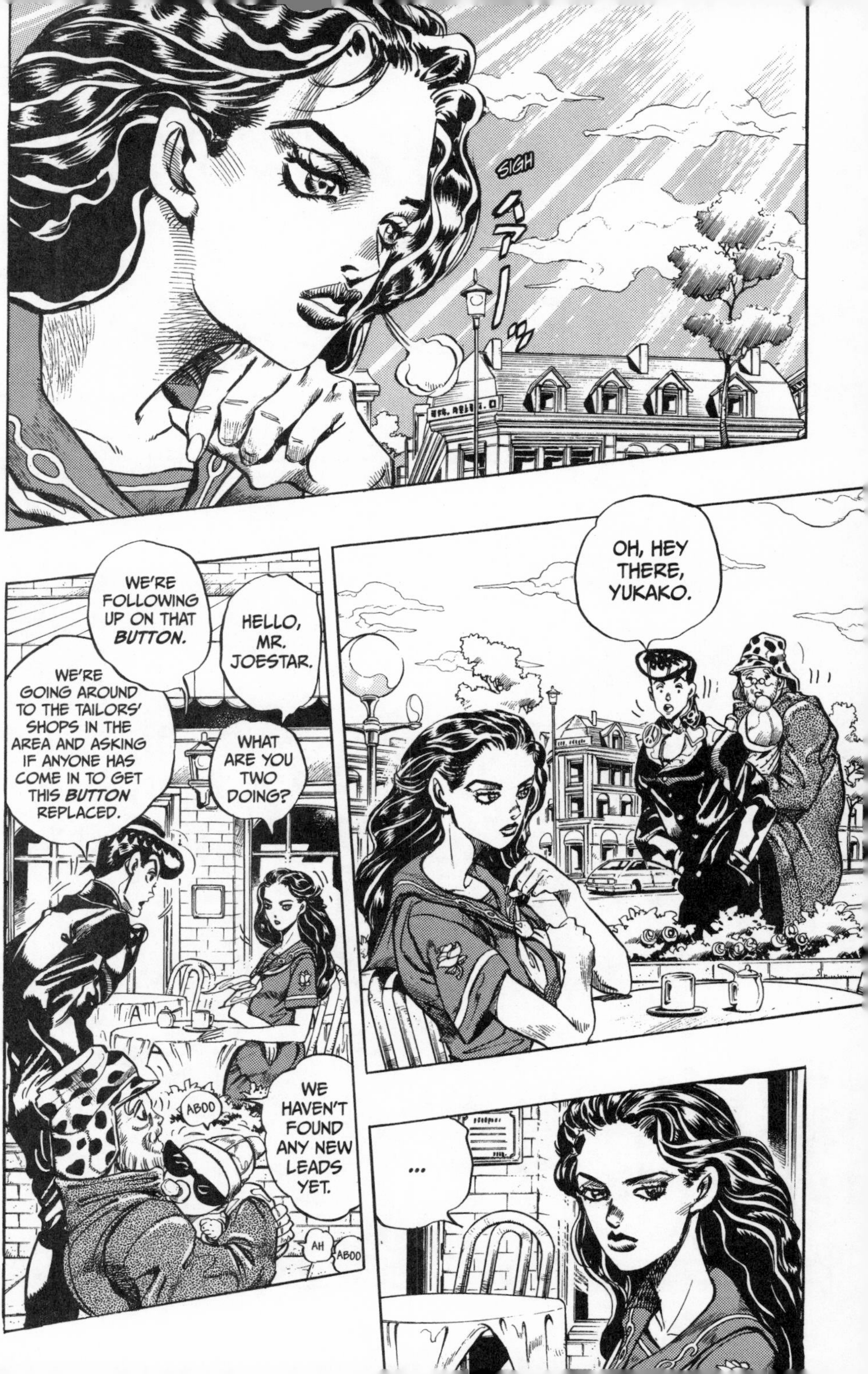
SIGH
OH, HEY THERE, YUKAKO.
HELLO, MR. JOESTAR.
WHAT ARE YOU TWO DOING?
WE'RE FOLLOWING UP ON THAT BUTTON.
WE'RE GOING AROUND TO THE TAILORS' SHOPS IN THE AREA AND ASKING IF ANYONE HAS COME IN TO GET THIS BUTTON REPLACED.
ABOO
WE HAVEN'T FOUND ANY NEW LEADS YET.
AH
ABOO
...

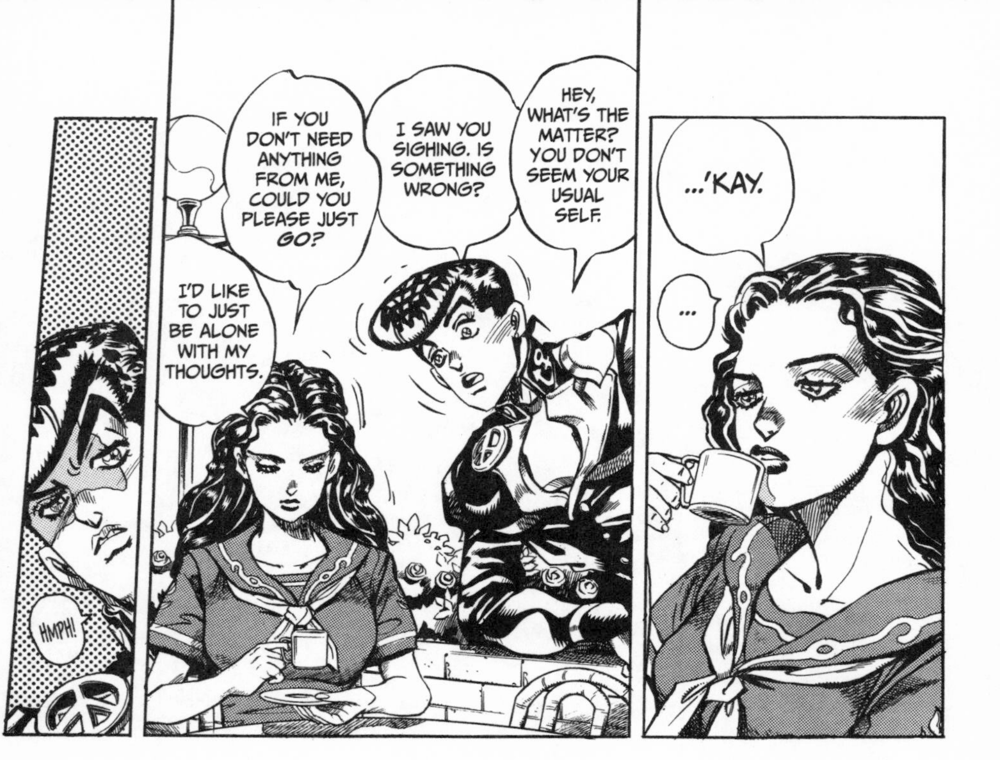
...'KAY.
...
HEY, WHAT'S THE MATTER? YOU DON'T SEEM YOUR USUAL SELF.
I SAW YOU SIGHING. IS SOMETHING WRONG?
IF YOU DON'T NEED ANYTHING FROM ME, COULD YOU PLEASE JUST *GO?*
I'D LIKE TO JUST BE ALONE WITH MY THOUGHTS.
HMPH!

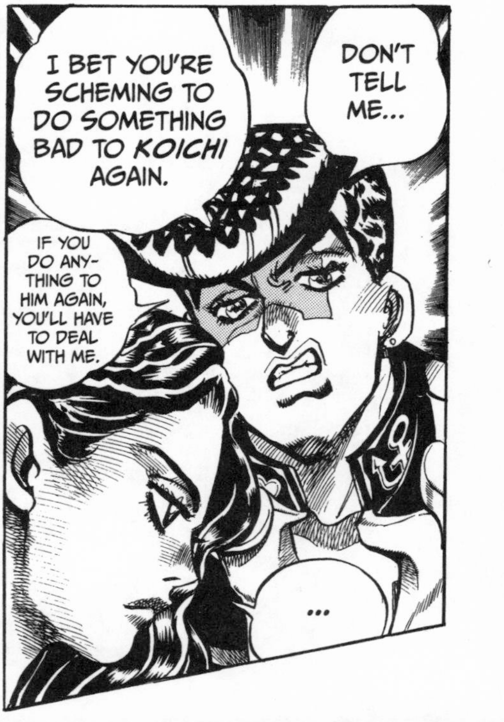
DON'T TELL ME...
I BET YOU'RE SCHEMING TO DO SOMETHING BAD TO *KOICHI* AGAIN.
IF YOU DO ANY-THING TO HIM AGAIN, YOU'LL HAVE TO DEAL WITH ME.
...

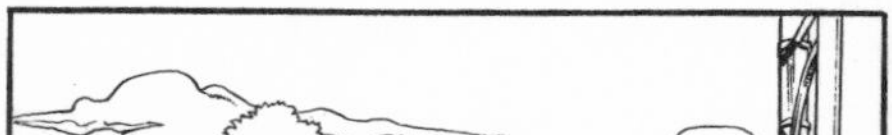
CAFE DEUX MAGOTS

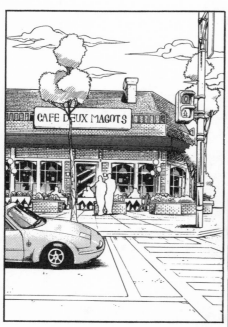

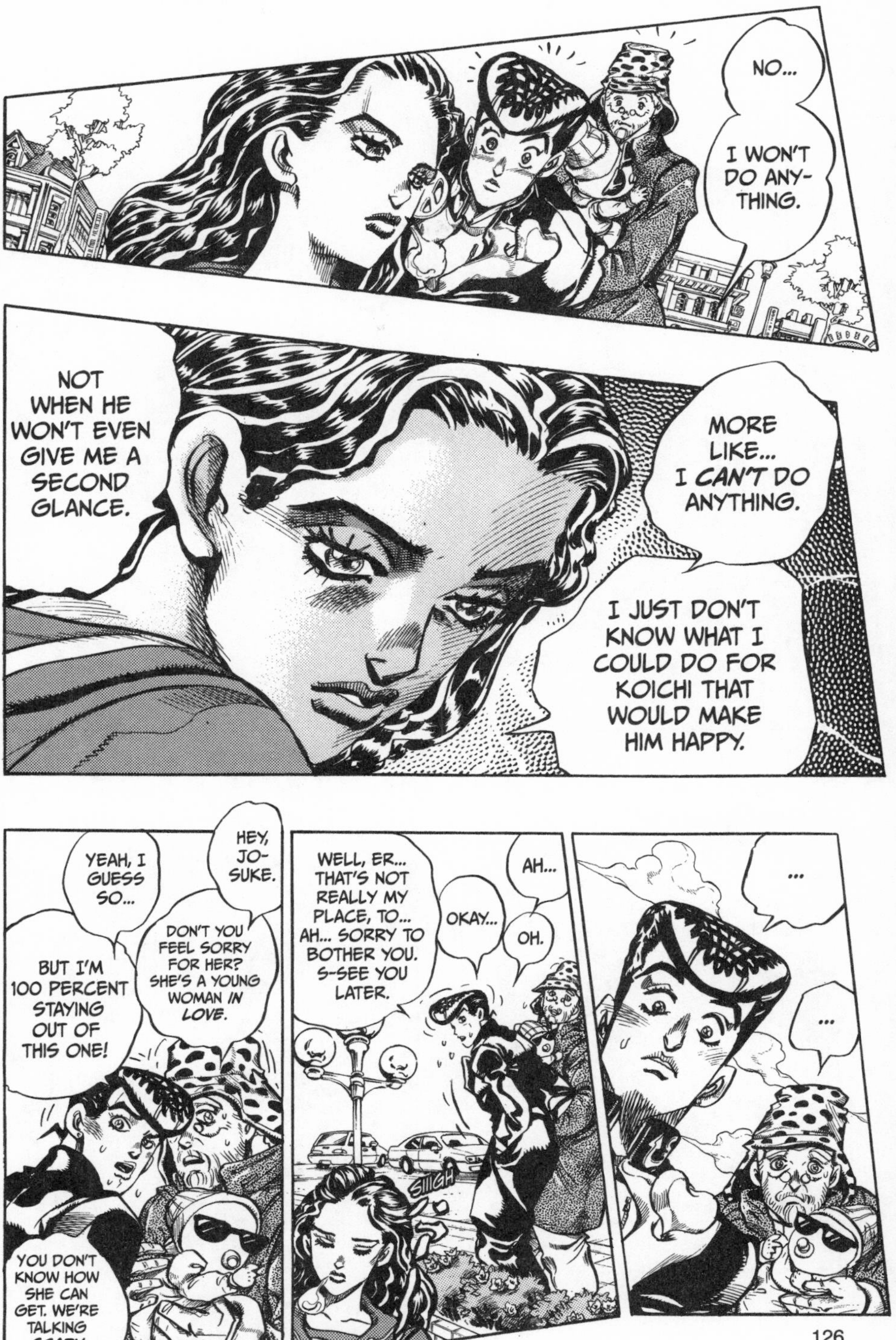
NO...
I WON'T DO ANYTHING.
MORE LIKE... I *CAN'T* DO ANYTHING.
I JUST DON'T KNOW WHAT I COULD DO FOR KOICHI THAT WOULD MAKE HIM HAPPY.
NOT WHEN HE WON'T EVEN GIVE ME A SECOND GLANCE.
...
...
AH...
WELL, ER... THAT'S NOT REALLY MY PLACE, TO... AH... SORRY TO BOTHER YOU. S-SEE YOU LATER.
OKAY...
OH.
SIIIGH
HEY, JO-SUKE.
YEAH, I GUESS SO...
DON'T YOU FEEL SORRY FOR HER? SHE'S A YOUNG WOMAN *IN LOVE*.
BUT I'M 100 PERCENT STAYING OUT OF THIS ONE!
YOU DON'T KNOW HOW SHE CAN GET. WE'RE TALKING *SCARY* CRAZY.

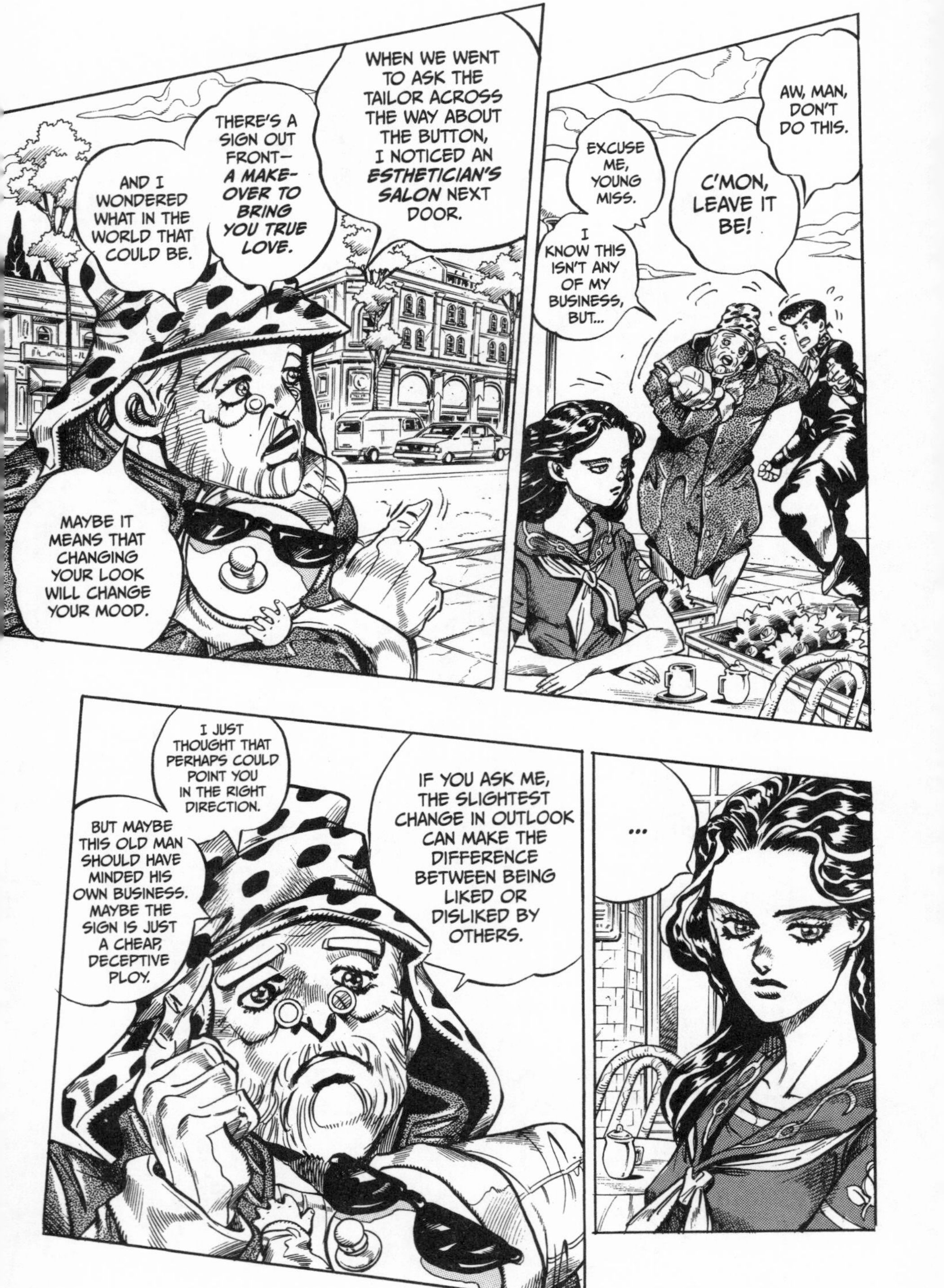
AW, MAN, DON'T DO THIS.
C'MON, LEAVE IT BE!
EXCUSE ME, YOUNG MISS.
I KNOW THIS ISN'T ANY OF MY BUSINESS, BUT...
WHEN WE WENT TO ASK THE TAILOR ACROSS THE WAY ABOUT THE BUTTON, I NOTICED AN *ESTHETICIAN'S SALON* NEXT DOOR.
THERE'S A SIGN OUT FRONT— *A MAKE-OVER TO BRING YOU TRUE LOVE.*
AND I WONDERED WHAT IN THE WORLD THAT COULD BE.
MAYBE IT MEANS THAT CHANGING YOUR LOOK WILL CHANGE YOUR MOOD.
...
IF YOU ASK ME, THE SLIGHTEST CHANGE IN OUTLOOK CAN MAKE THE DIFFERENCE BETWEEN BEING LIKED OR DISLIKED BY OTHERS.
I JUST THOUGHT THAT PERHAPS COULD POINT YOU IN THE RIGHT DIRECTION.
BUT MAYBE THIS OLD MAN SHOULD HAVE MINDED HIS OWN BUSINESS. MAYBE THE SIGN IS JUST A CHEAP, DECEPTIVE PLOY.

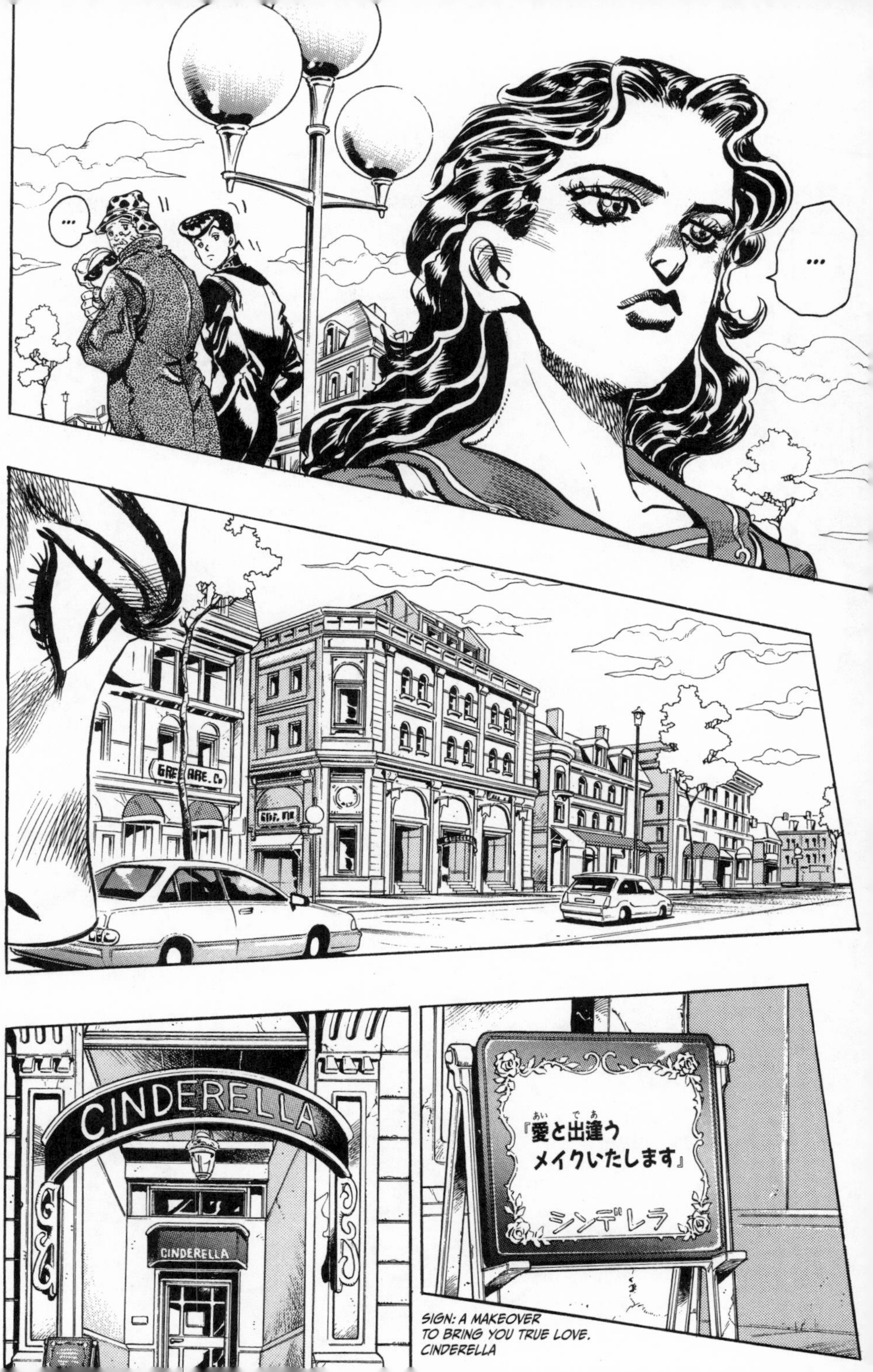
...
...
『愛と出逢う
メイクいたします』
シンデレラ
SIGN: A MAKEOVER
TO BRING YOU TRUE LOVE.
CINDERELLA
CINDERELLA
CINDERELLA

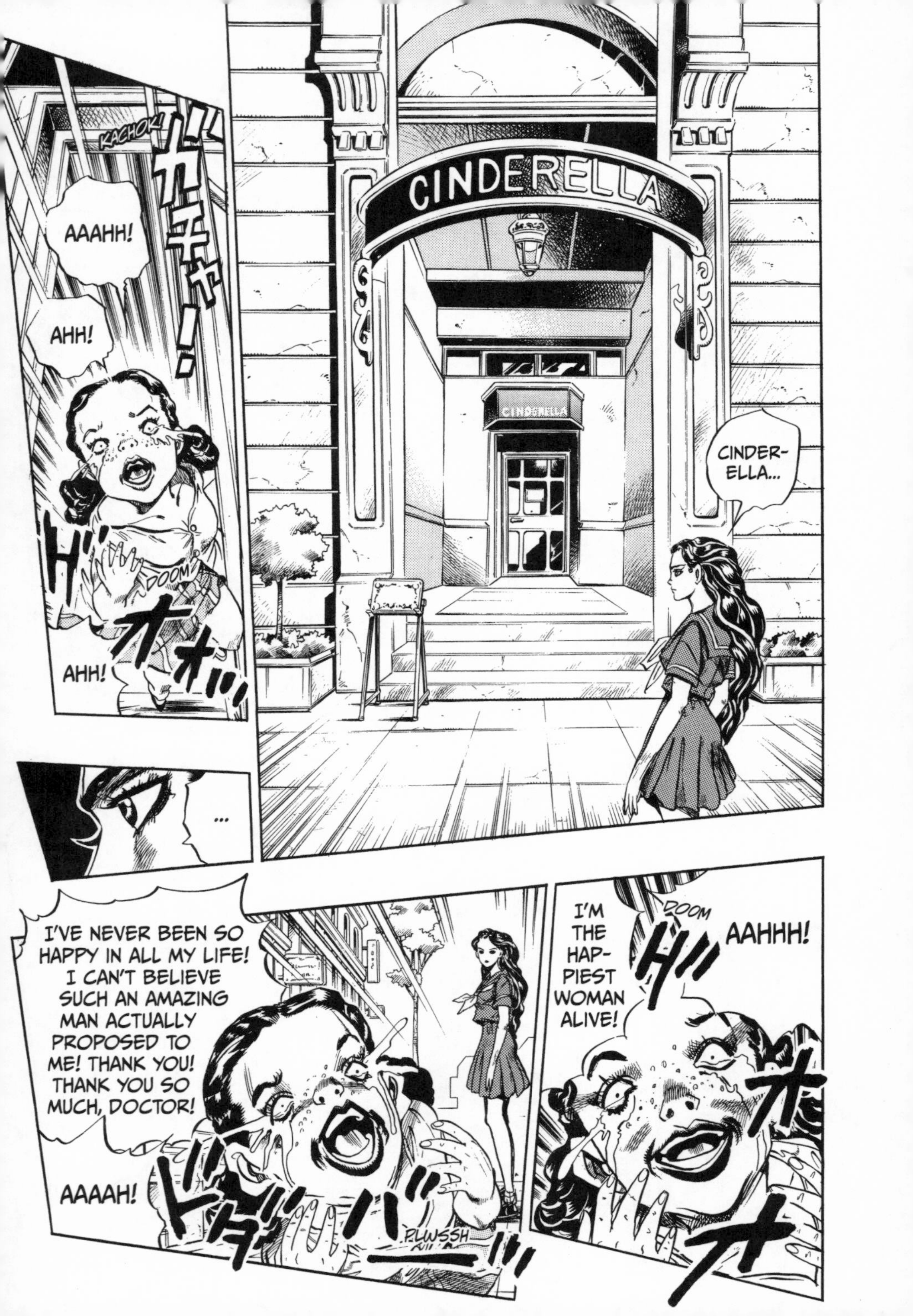
CINDERELLA
CINDERELLA
CINDER-ELLA...
KACHOK
AAAHH!
AHH!
DOOM
AHH!
...
I'M THE HAPPIEST WOMAN ALIVE!
DOOM
AAHHH!
I'VE NEVER BEEN SO HAPPY IN ALL MY LIFE! I CAN'T BELIEVE SUCH AN AMAZING MAN ACTUALLY PROPOSED TO ME! THANK YOU! THANK YOU SO MUCH, DOCTOR!
AAAAH!
PLWSSH

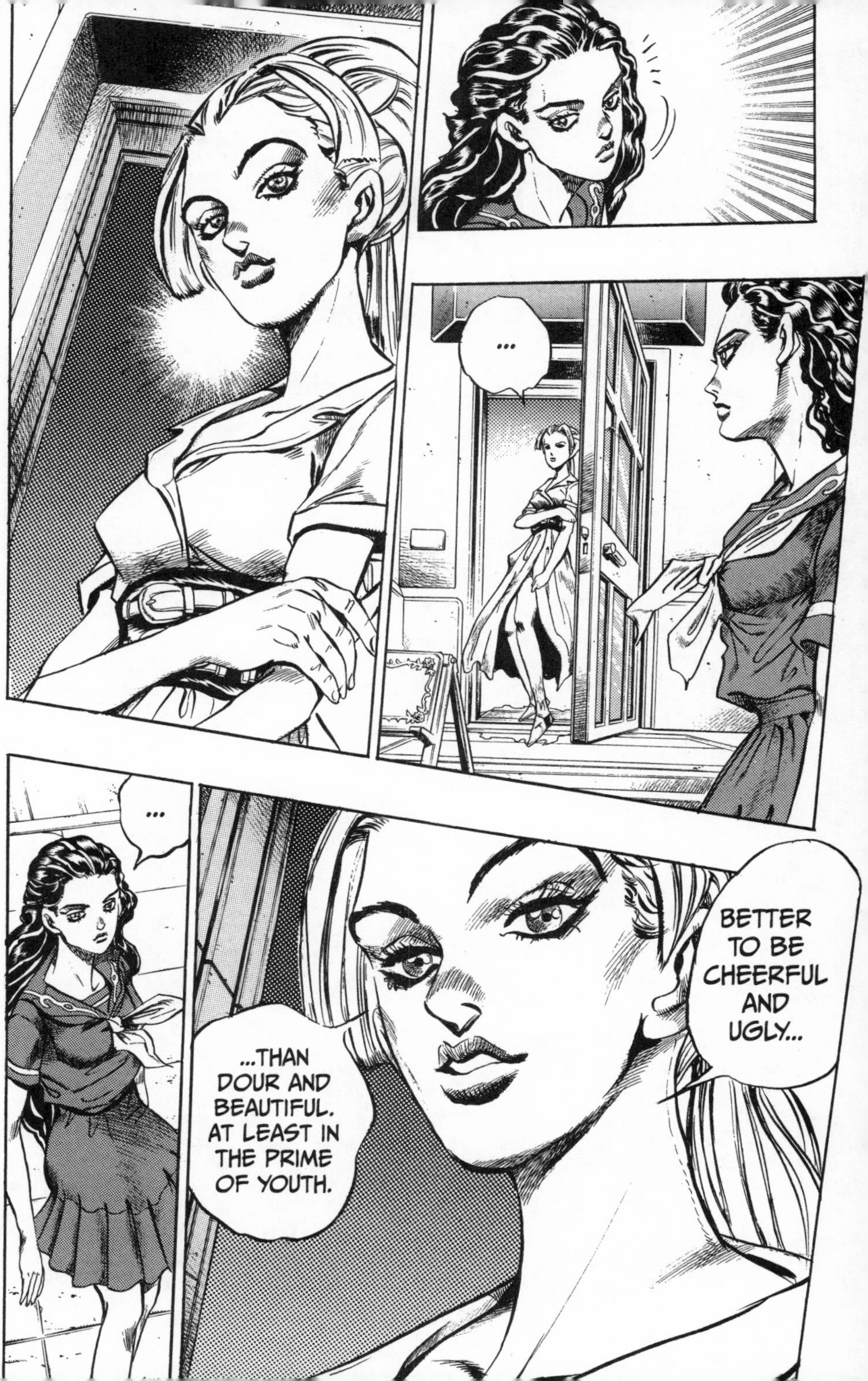
...
BETTER TO BE CHEERFUL AND UGLY...
...THAN DOUR AND BEAUTIFUL. AT LEAST IN THE PRIME OF YOUTH.
...

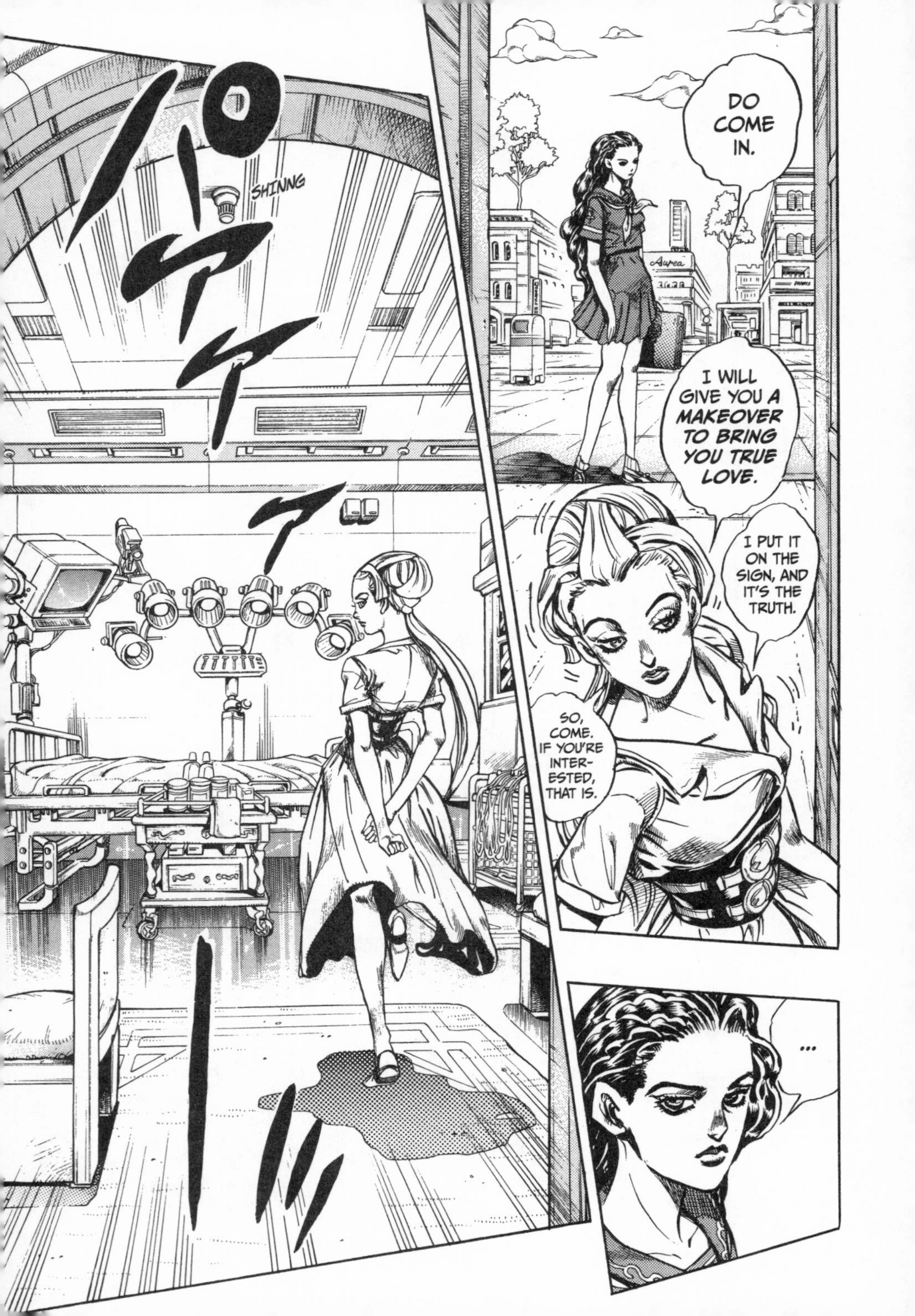
DO COME IN.
Aurea
I WILL GIVE YOU A MAKEOVER TO BRING YOU TRUE LOVE.
I PUT IT ON THE SIGN, AND IT'S THE TRUTH.
SO, COME. IF YOU'RE INTER-ESTED, THAT IS.
...
SHINNG

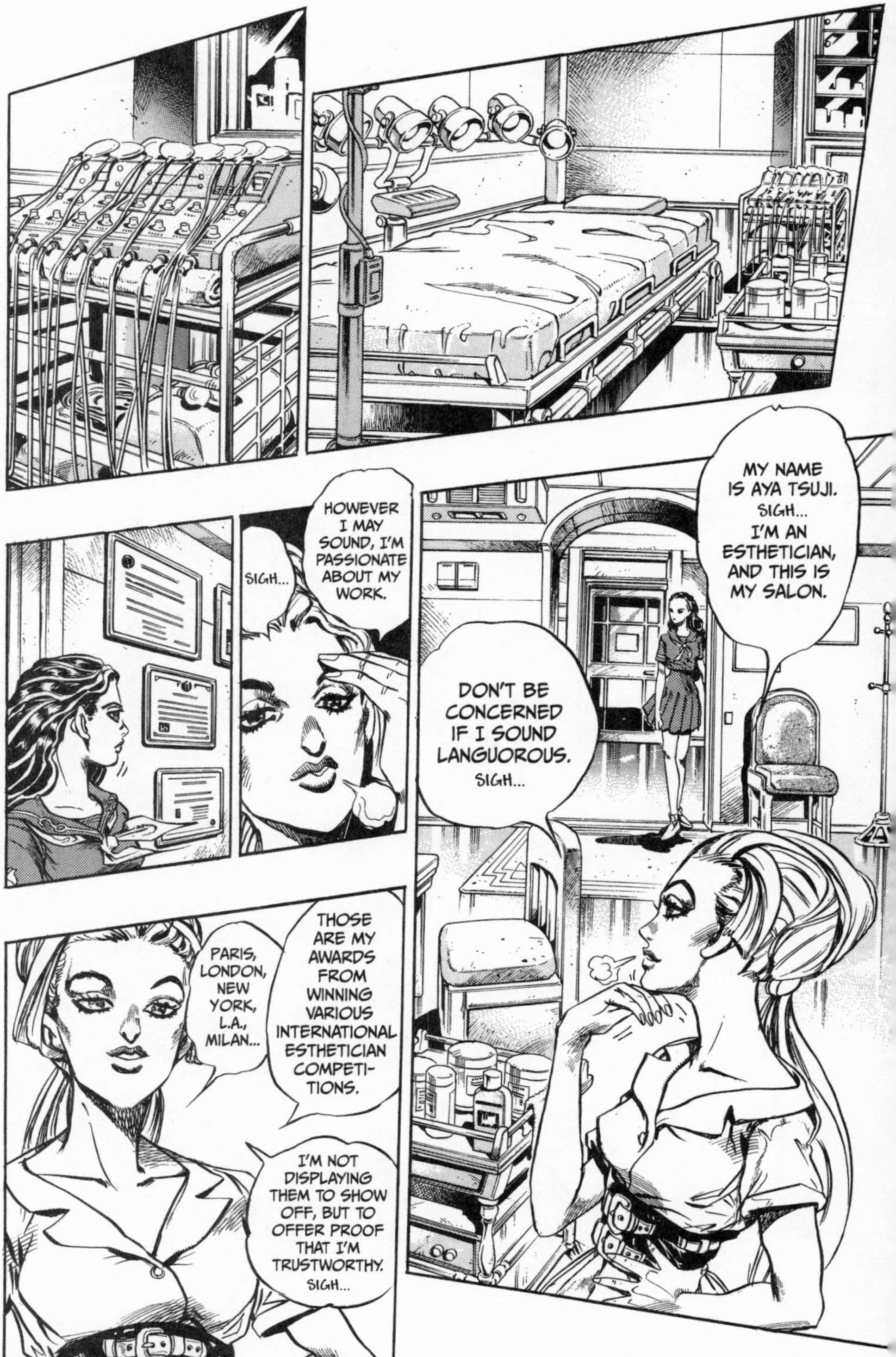
MY NAME IS AYA TSUJI. SIGH... I'M AN ESTHETICIAN, AND THIS IS MY SALON.
DON'T BE CONCERNED IF I SOUND LANGUOROUS. SIGH...
HOWEVER I MAY SOUND, I'M PASSIONATE ABOUT MY WORK.
SIGH...
THOSE ARE MY AWARDS FROM WINNING VARIOUS INTERNATIONAL ESTHETICIAN COMPETI-TIONS.
PARIS, LONDON, NEW YORK, L.A., MILAN...
I'M NOT DISPLAYING THEM TO SHOW OFF, BUT TO OFFER PROOF THAT I'M TRUSTWORTHY. SIGH...

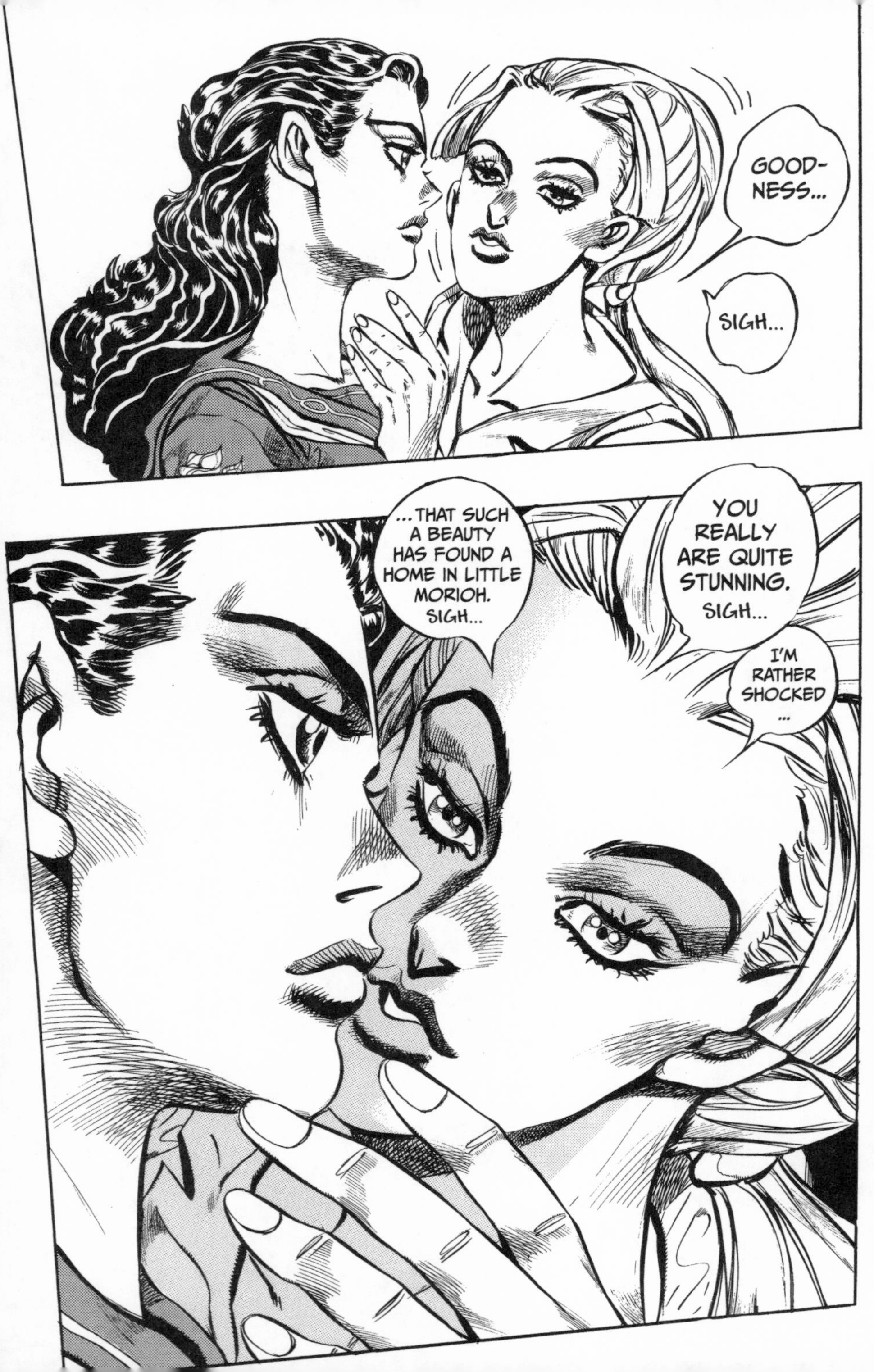
GOODNESS...
SIGH...
YOU REALLY ARE QUITE STUNNING. SIGH...
I'M RATHER SHOCKED ...
...THAT SUCH A BEAUTY HAS FOUND A HOME IN LITTLE MORIOH. SIGH...

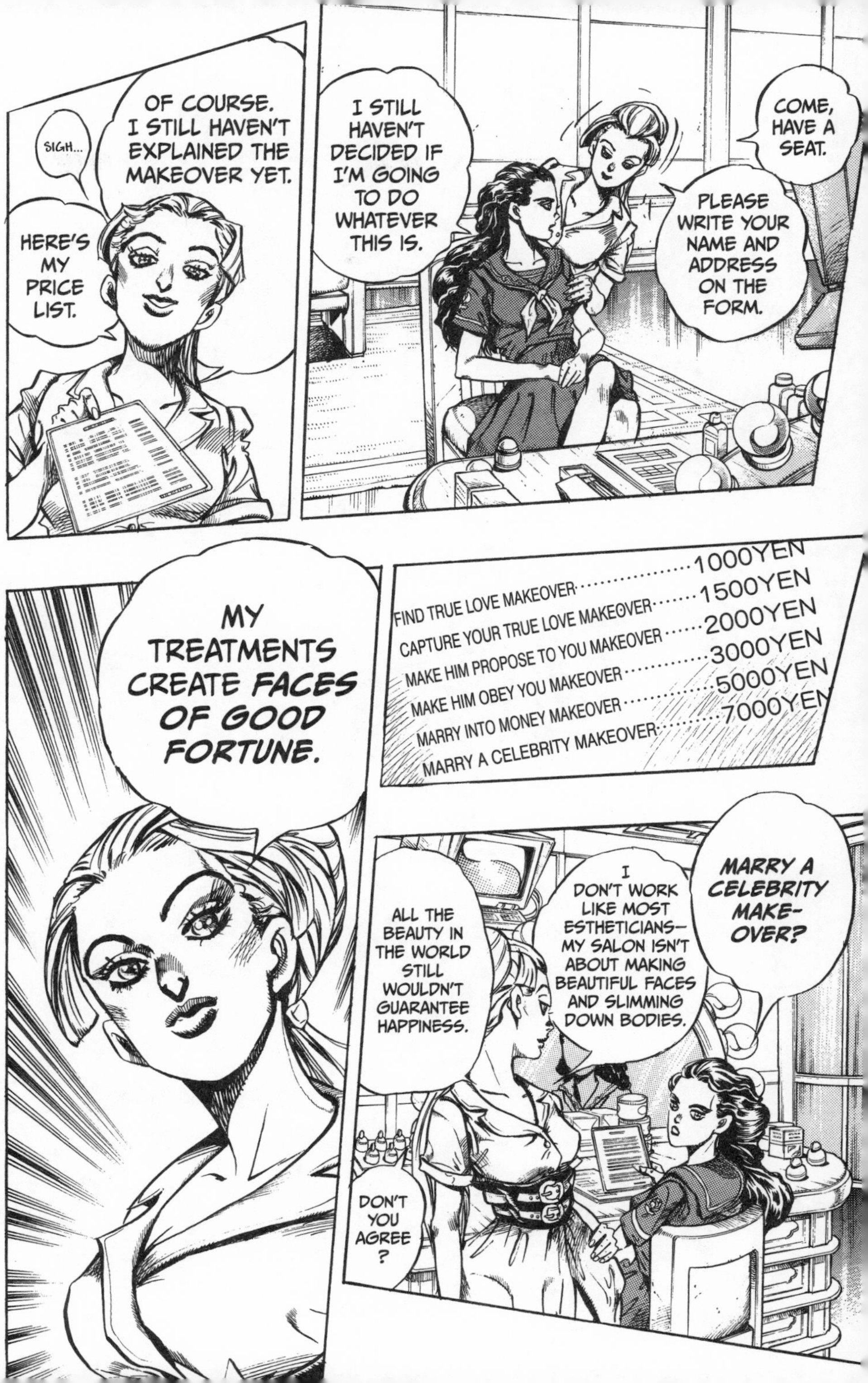
COME, HAVE A SEAT.
PLEASE WRITE YOUR NAME AND ADDRESS ON THE FORM.
I STILL HAVEN'T DECIDED IF I'M GOING TO DO WHATEVER THIS IS.
OF COURSE. I STILL HAVEN'T EXPLAINED THE MAKEOVER YET.
SIGH...
HERE'S MY PRICE LIST.
FIND TRUE LOVE MAKEOVER......1000YEN
CAPTURE YOUR TRUE LOVE MAKEOVER......1500YEN
MAKE HIM PROPOSE TO YOU MAKEOVER......2000YEN
MAKE HIM OBEY YOU MAKEOVER......3000YEN
MARRY INTO MONEY MAKEOVER......5000YEN
MARRY A CELEBRITY MAKEOVER......7000YEN
MARRY A CELEBRITY MAKE-OVER?
I DON'T WORK LIKE MOST ESTHETICIANS—MY SALON ISN'T ABOUT MAKING BEAUTIFUL FACES AND SLIMMING DOWN BODIES.
ALL THE BEAUTY IN THE WORLD STILL WOULDN'T GUARANTEE HAPPINESS.
DON'T YOU AGREE?
MY TREATMENTS CREATE FACES OF GOOD FORTUNE.

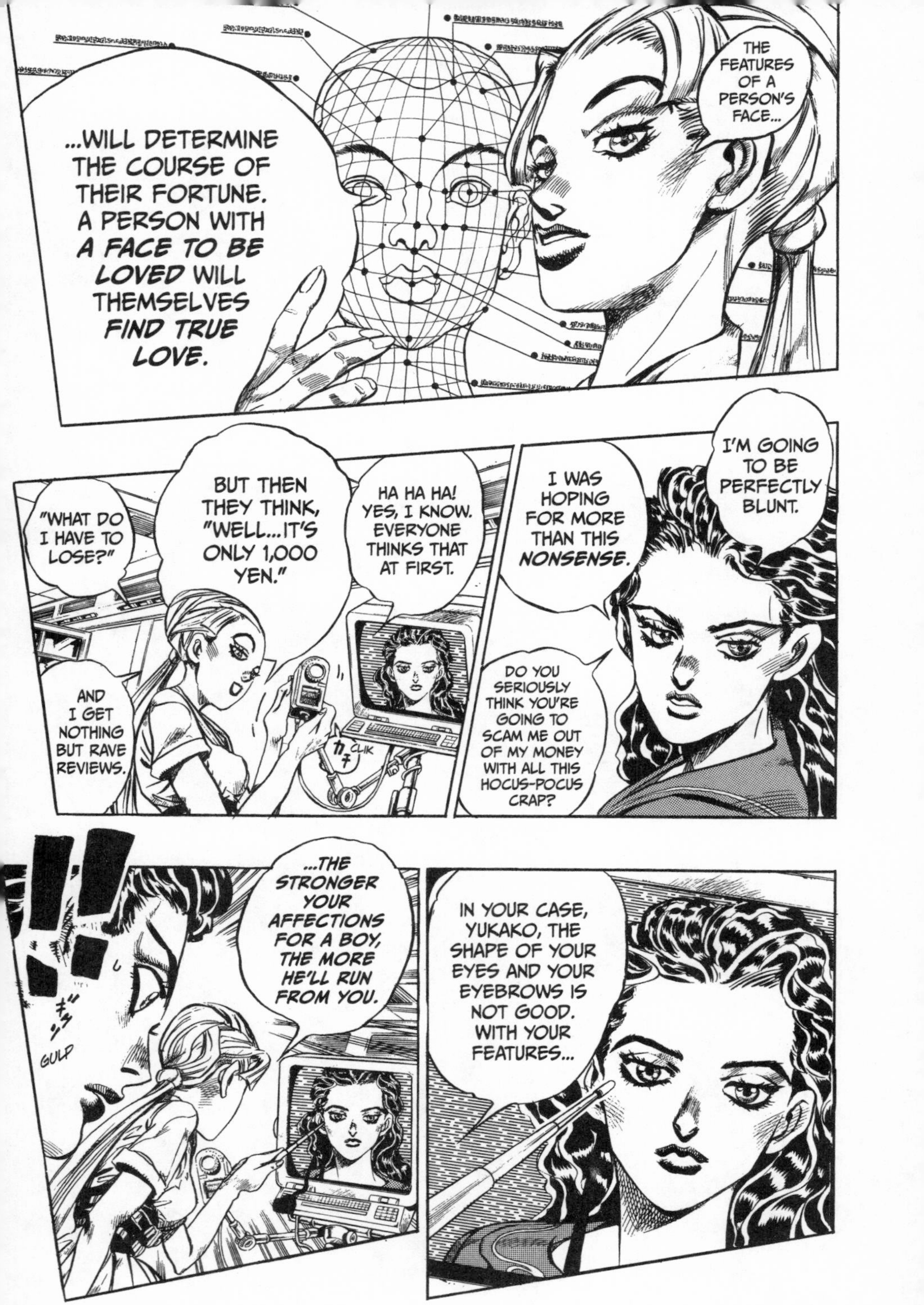
THE FEATURES OF A PERSON'S FACE...
...WILL DETERMINE THE COURSE OF THEIR FORTUNE. A PERSON WITH *A FACE TO BE LOVED* WILL THEMSELVES *FIND TRUE LOVE*.
I'M GOING TO BE PERFECTLY BLUNT.
I WAS HOPING FOR MORE THAN THIS *NONSENSE*.
DO YOU SERIOUSLY THINK YOU'RE GOING TO SCAM ME OUT OF MY MONEY WITH ALL THIS HOCUS-POCUS CRAP?
HA HA HA! YES, I KNOW. EVERYONE THINKS THAT AT FIRST.
BUT THEN THEY THINK, "WELL...IT'S ONLY 1,000 YEN."
"WHAT DO I HAVE TO LOSE?"
AND I GET NOTHING BUT RAVE REVIEWS.
カチ CLIK
IN YOUR CASE, YUKAKO, THE SHAPE OF YOUR EYES AND YOUR EYEBROWS IS NOT GOOD. WITH YOUR FEATURES...
...THE STRONGER YOUR AFFECTIONS FOR A BOY, THE MORE HE'LL RUN FROM YOU.
GULP

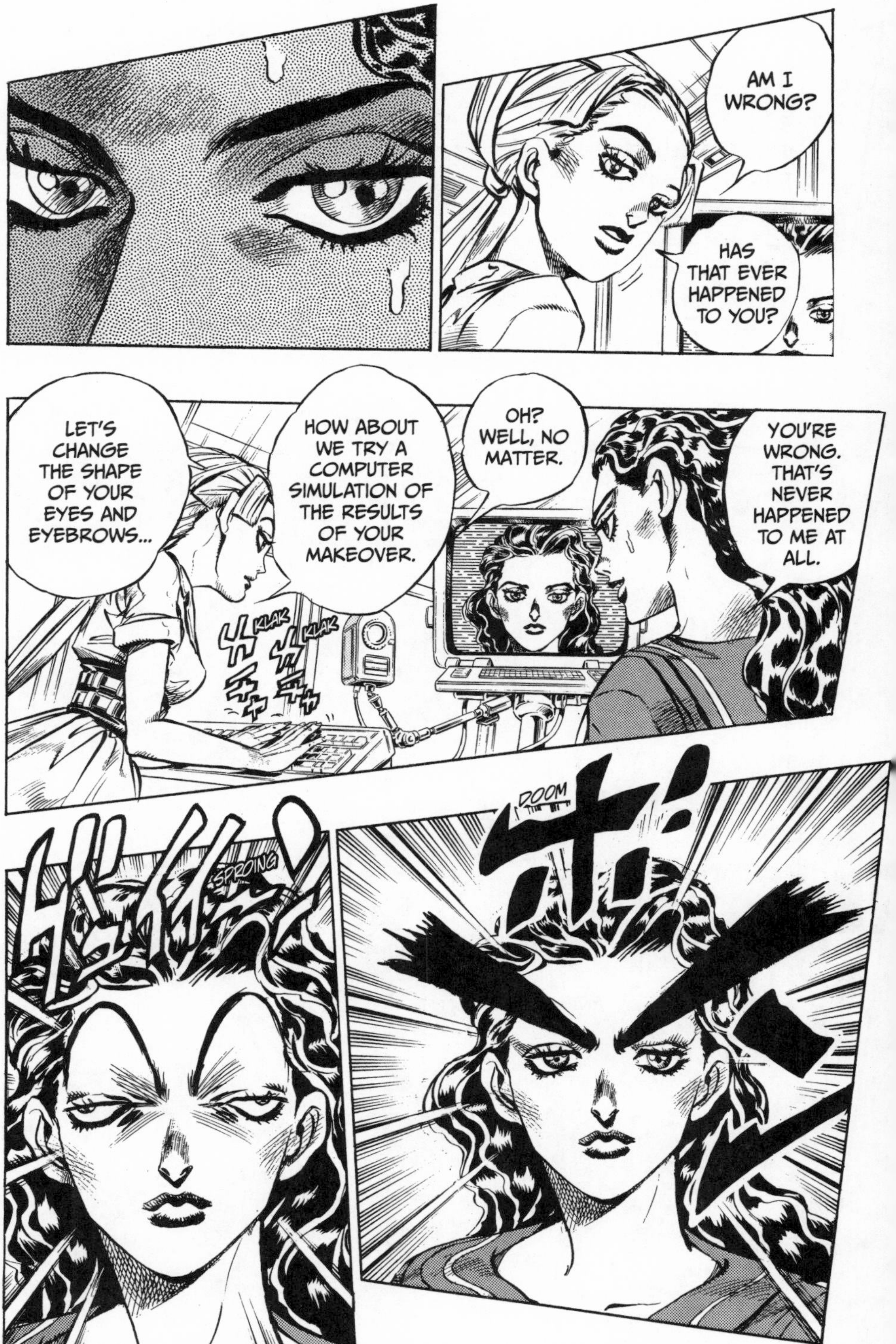
AM I WRONG?
HAS THAT EVER HAPPENED TO YOU?
YOU'RE WRONG. THAT'S NEVER HAPPENED TO ME AT ALL.
OH? WELL, NO MATTER.
HOW ABOUT WE TRY A COMPUTER SIMULATION OF THE RESULTS OF YOUR MAKEOVER.
LET'S CHANGE THE SHAPE OF YOUR EYES AND EYEBROWS...
KLAK
KLAK
DOOM
SPROING

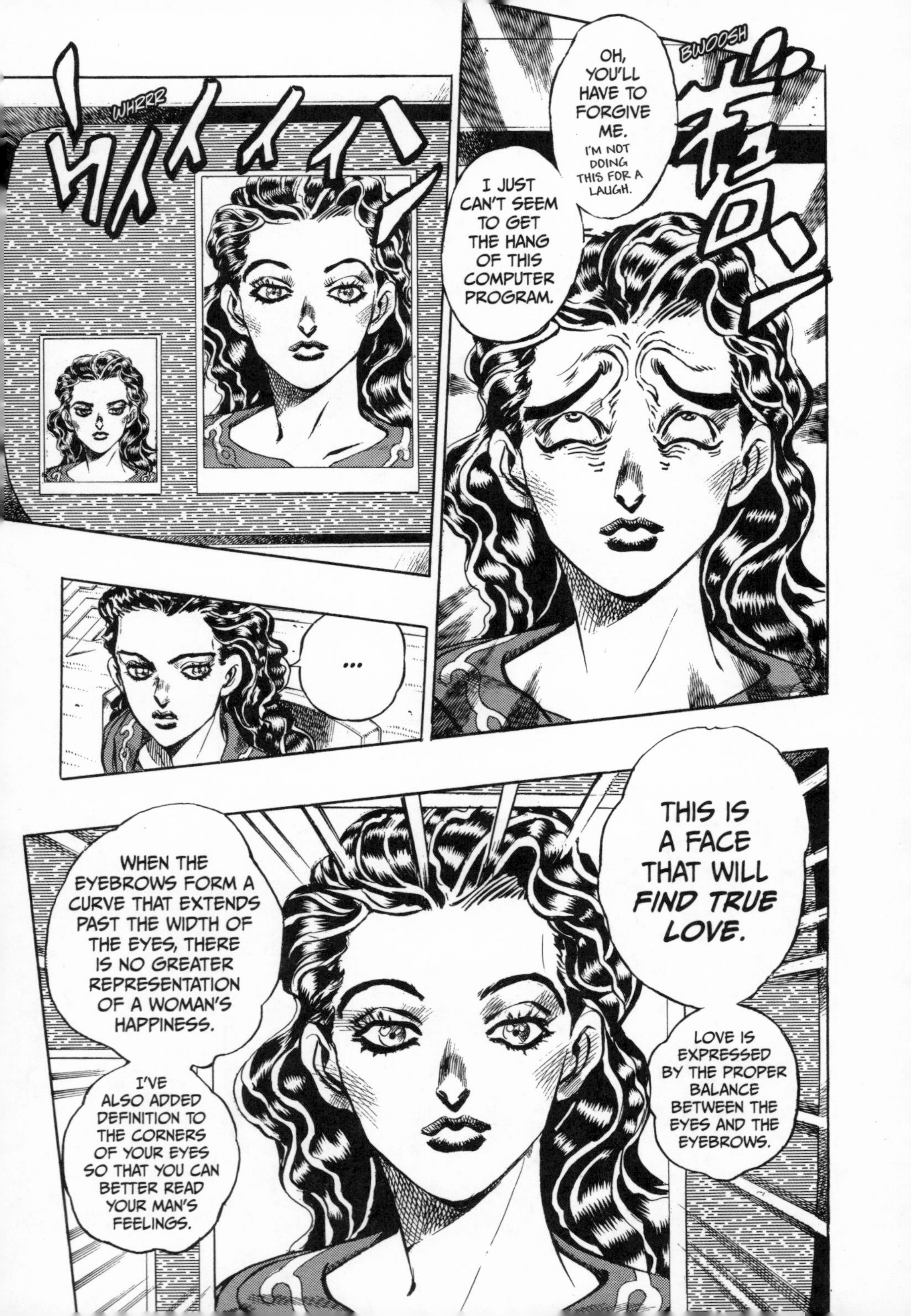
BWOOSH
OH, YOU'LL HAVE TO FORGIVE ME.
I'M NOT DOING THIS FOR A LAUGH.
I JUST CAN'T SEEM TO GET THE HANG OF THIS COMPUTER PROGRAM.
WHRRR
...
THIS IS A FACE THAT WILL *FIND TRUE LOVE.*
WHEN THE EYEBROWS FORM A CURVE THAT EXTENDS PAST THE WIDTH OF THE EYES, THERE IS NO GREATER REPRESENTATION OF A WOMAN'S HAPPINESS.
LOVE IS EXPRESSED BY THE PROPER BALANCE BETWEEN THE EYES AND THE EYEBROWS.
I'VE ALSO ADDED DEFINITION TO THE CORNERS OF YOUR EYES SO THAT YOU CAN BETTER READ YOUR MAN'S FEELINGS.

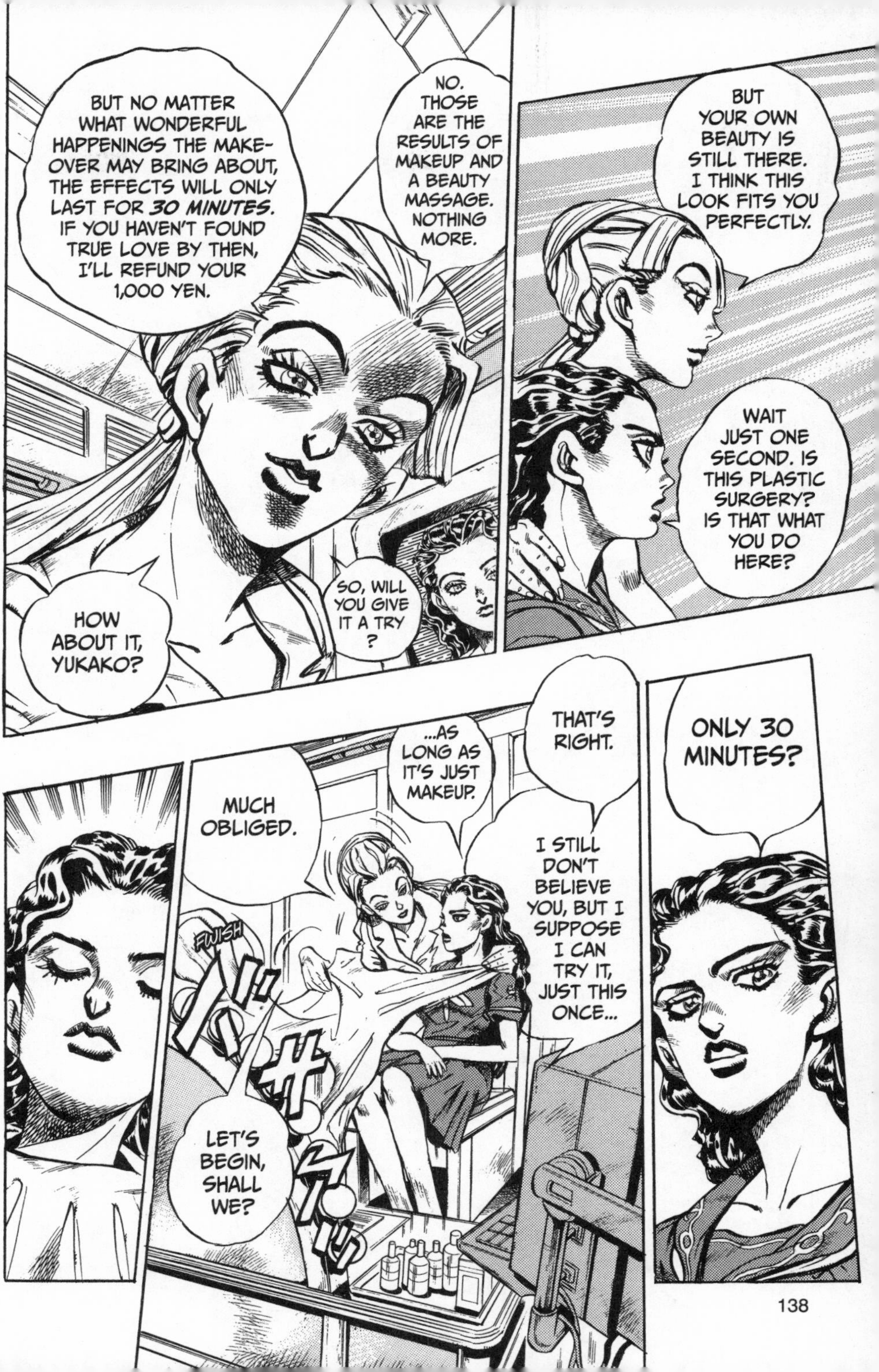
BUT YOUR OWN BEAUTY IS STILL THERE. I THINK THIS LOOK FITS YOU PERFECTLY.
WAIT JUST ONE SECOND. IS THIS PLASTIC SURGERY? IS THAT WHAT YOU DO HERE?
NO. THOSE ARE THE RESULTS OF MAKEUP AND A BEAUTY MASSAGE. NOTHING MORE.
BUT NO MATTER WHAT WONDERFUL HAPPENINGS THE MAKE-OVER MAY BRING ABOUT, THE EFFECTS WILL ONLY LAST FOR ***30 MINUTES***. IF YOU HAVEN'T FOUND TRUE LOVE BY THEN, I'LL REFUND YOUR 1,000 YEN.
SO, WILL YOU GIVE IT A TRY?
HOW ABOUT IT, YUKAKO?
ONLY 30 MINUTES?
THAT'S RIGHT.
I STILL DON'T BELIEVE YOU, BUT I SUPPOSE I CAN TRY IT, JUST THIS ONCE...
...AS LONG AS IT'S JUST MAKEUP.
MUCH OBLIGED.
FWISH
LET'S BEGIN, SHALL WE?

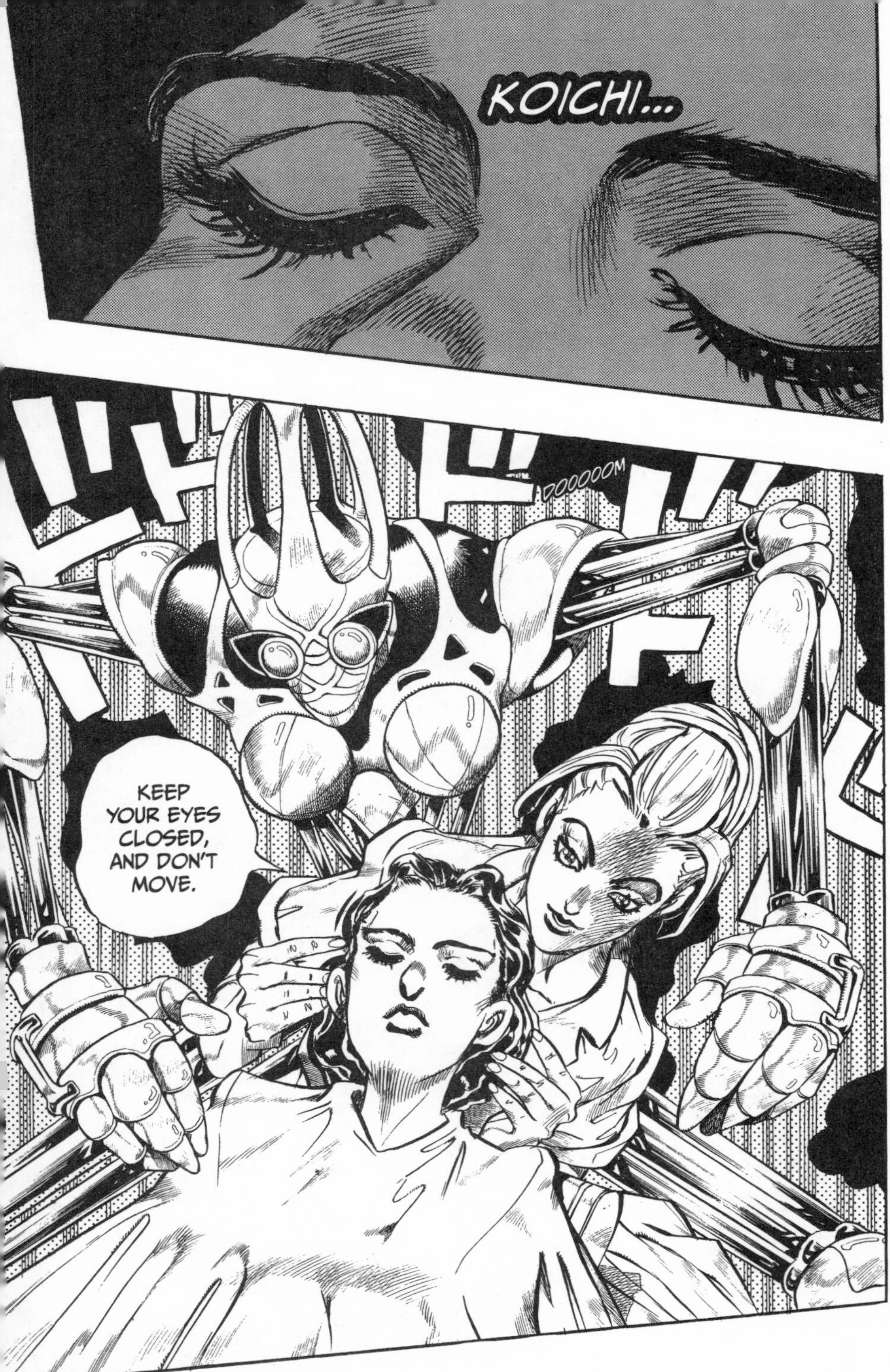
KOICHI...
DOOOOOOM
KEEP YOUR EYES CLOSED, AND DON'T MOVE.

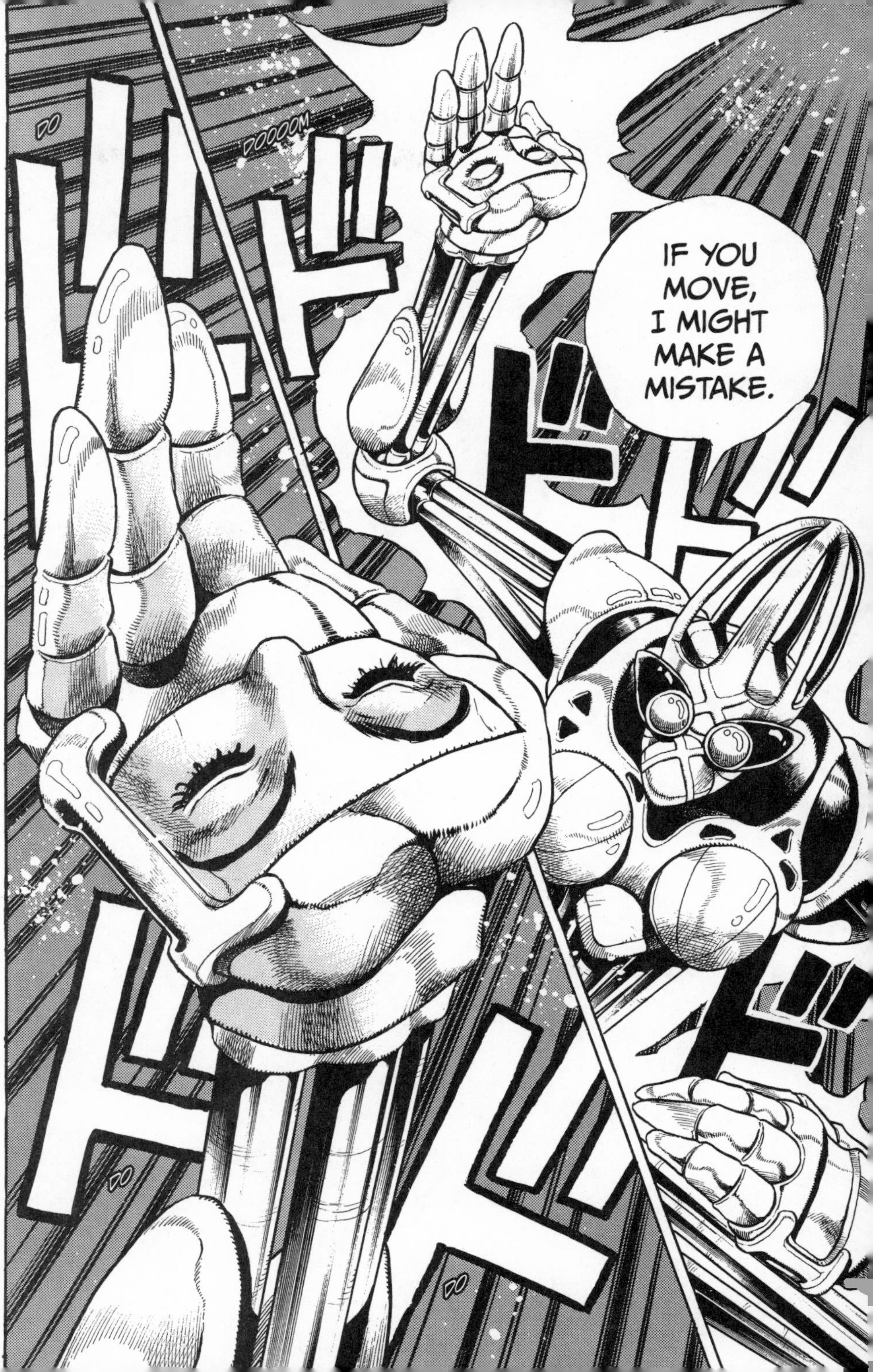
DO
DOOOOM
IF YOU MOVE, I MIGHT MAKE A MISTAKE.
DO
DO

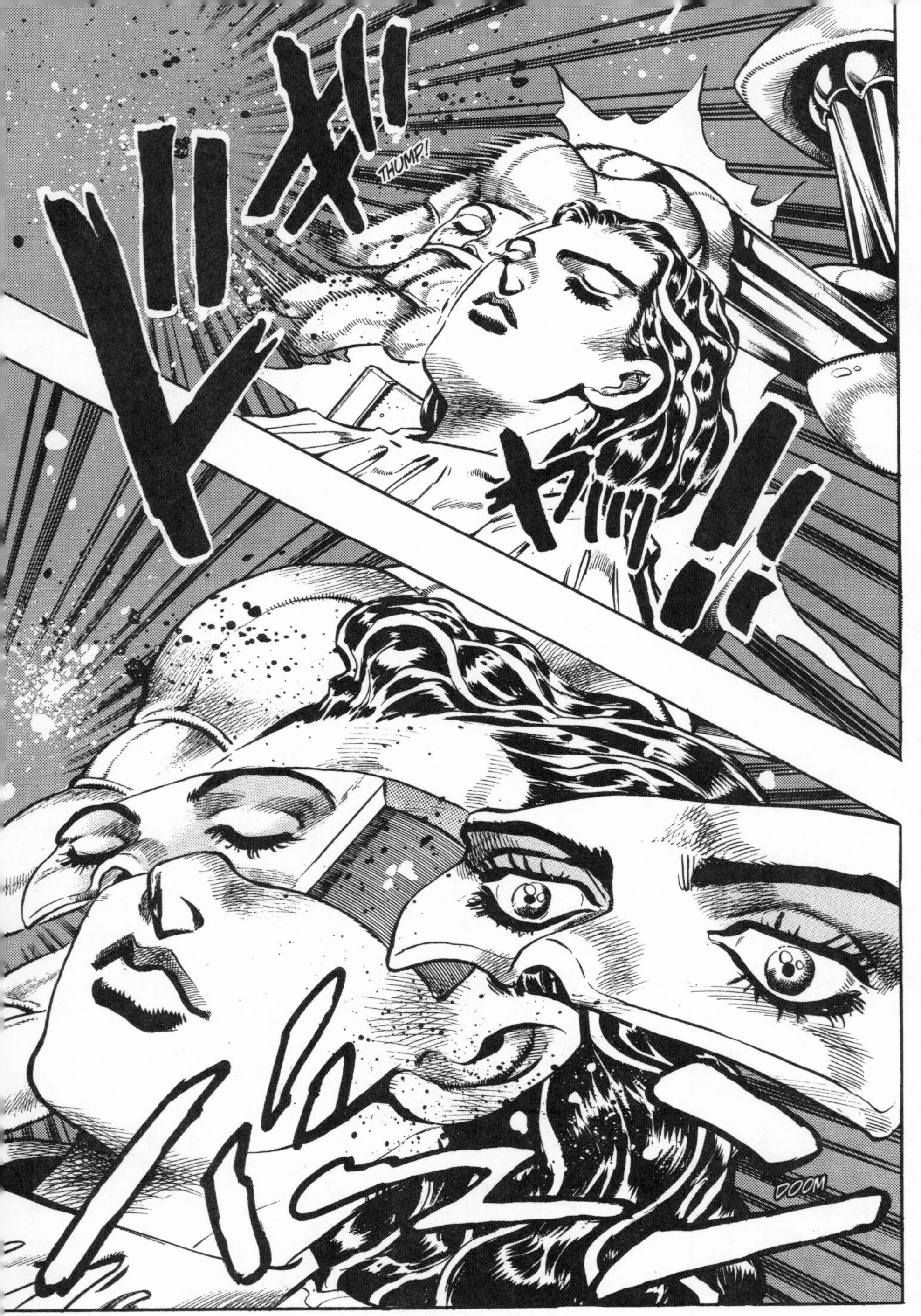
THUMP!
DOOM

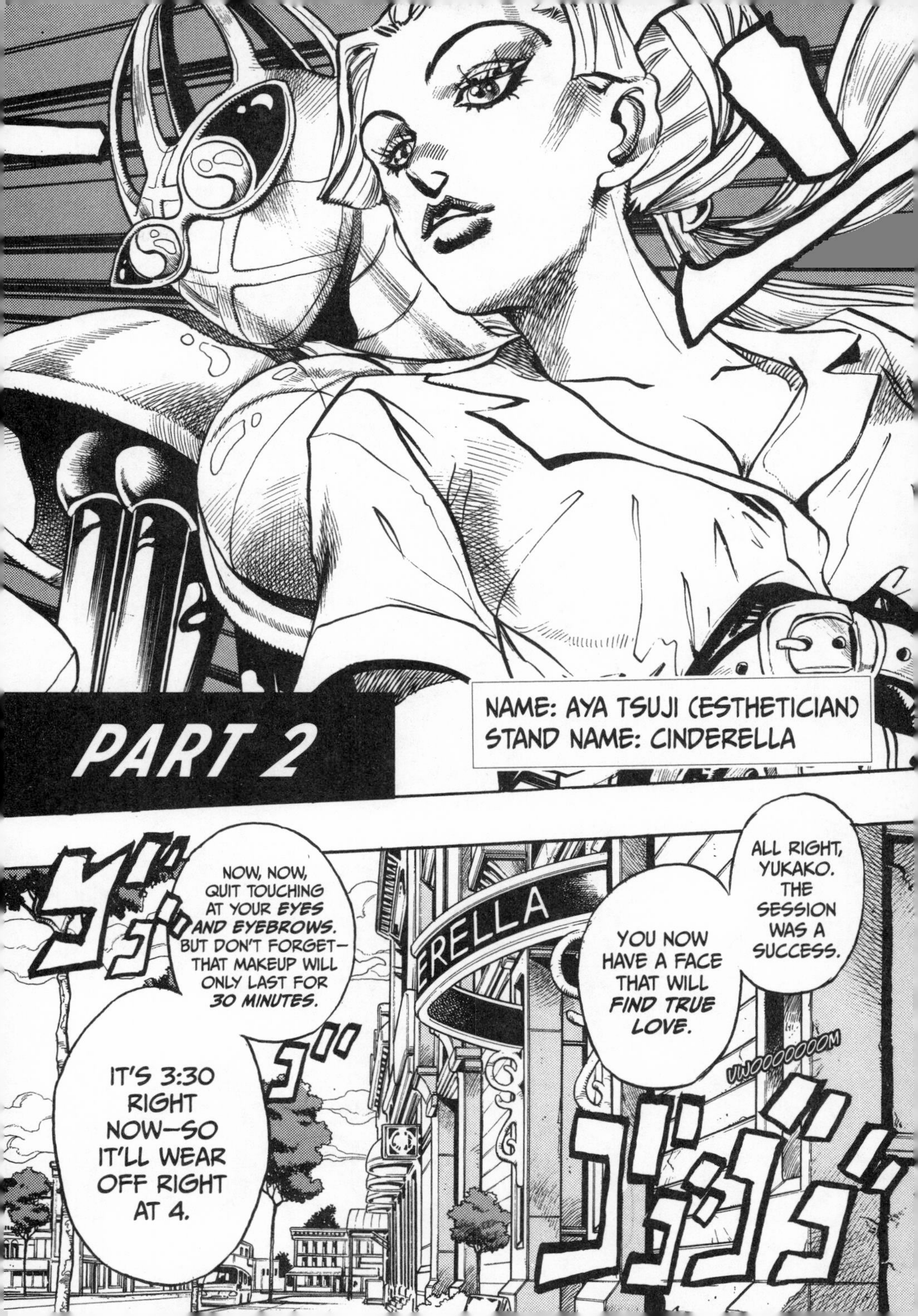
PART 2
NAME: AYA TSUJI (ESTHETICIAN)
STAND NAME: CINDERELLA
ALL RIGHT, YUKAKO. THE SESSION WAS A SUCCESS.
YOU NOW HAVE A FACE THAT WILL *FIND TRUE LOVE.*
VWOOOOOOOOM
NOW, NOW, QUIT TOUCHING AT YOUR *EYES AND EYEBROWS.* BUT DON'T FORGET— THAT MAKEUP WILL ONLY LAST FOR *30 MINUTES.*
IT'S 3:30 RIGHT NOW—SO IT'LL WEAR OFF RIGHT AT 4.

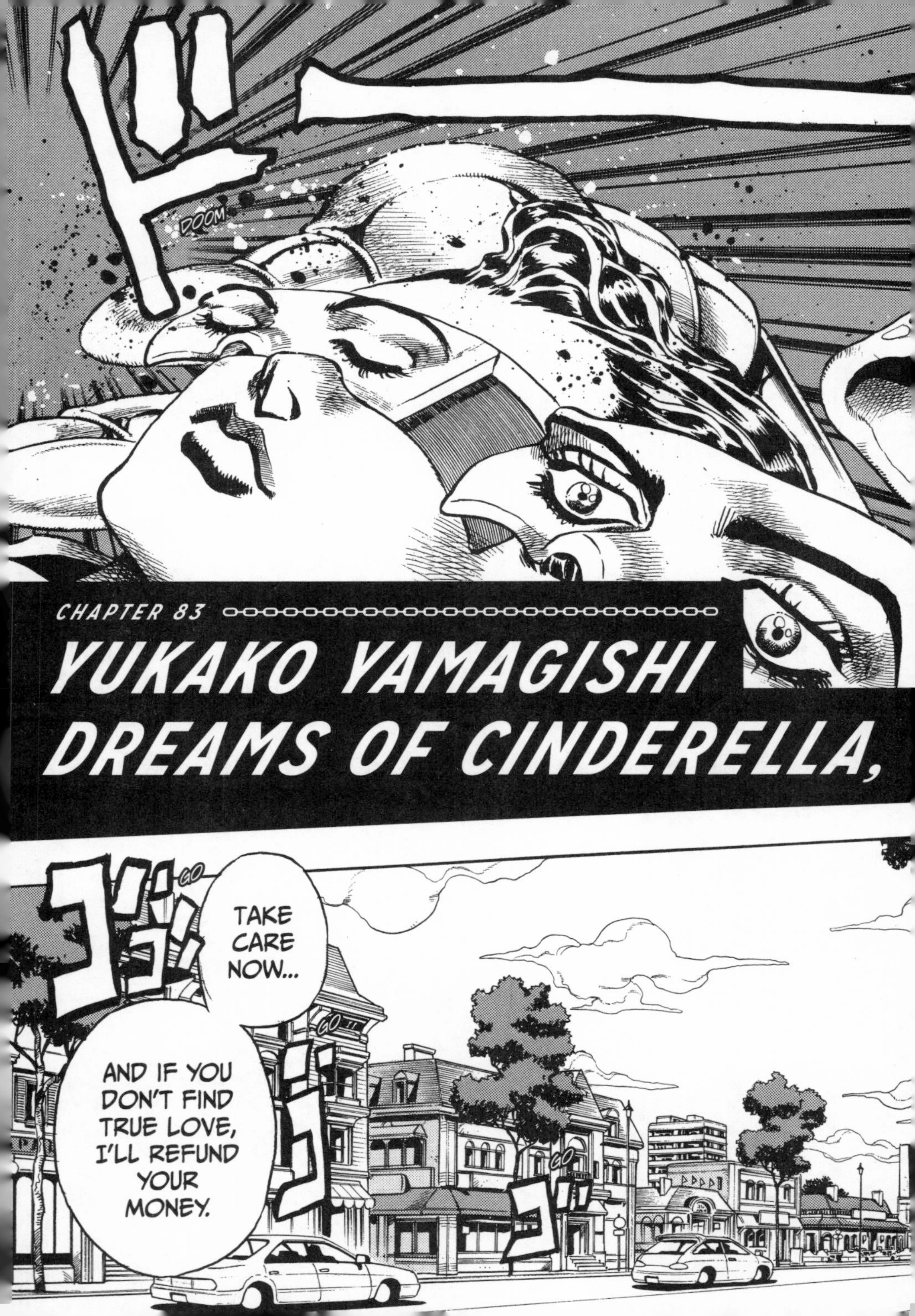
DOOM
CHAPTER 83
YUKAKO YAMAGISHI DREAMS OF CINDERELLA,
GO
GO
GO
TAKE CARE NOW...
AND IF YOU DON'T FIND TRUE LOVE, I'LL REFUND YOUR MONEY.

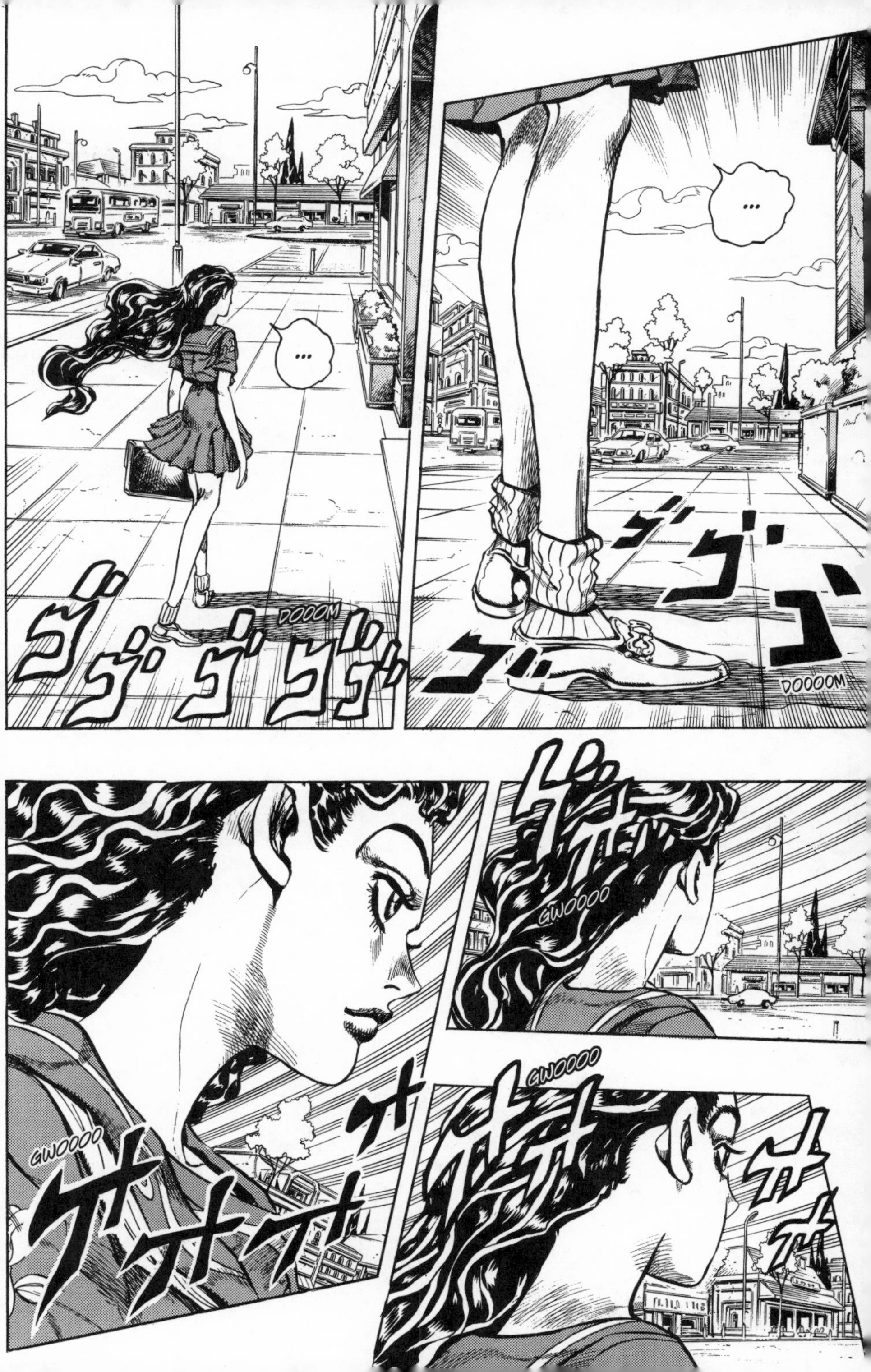

...
DOOOOM
...
DOOOM
GWOOOO
GWOOOO
GWOOOO

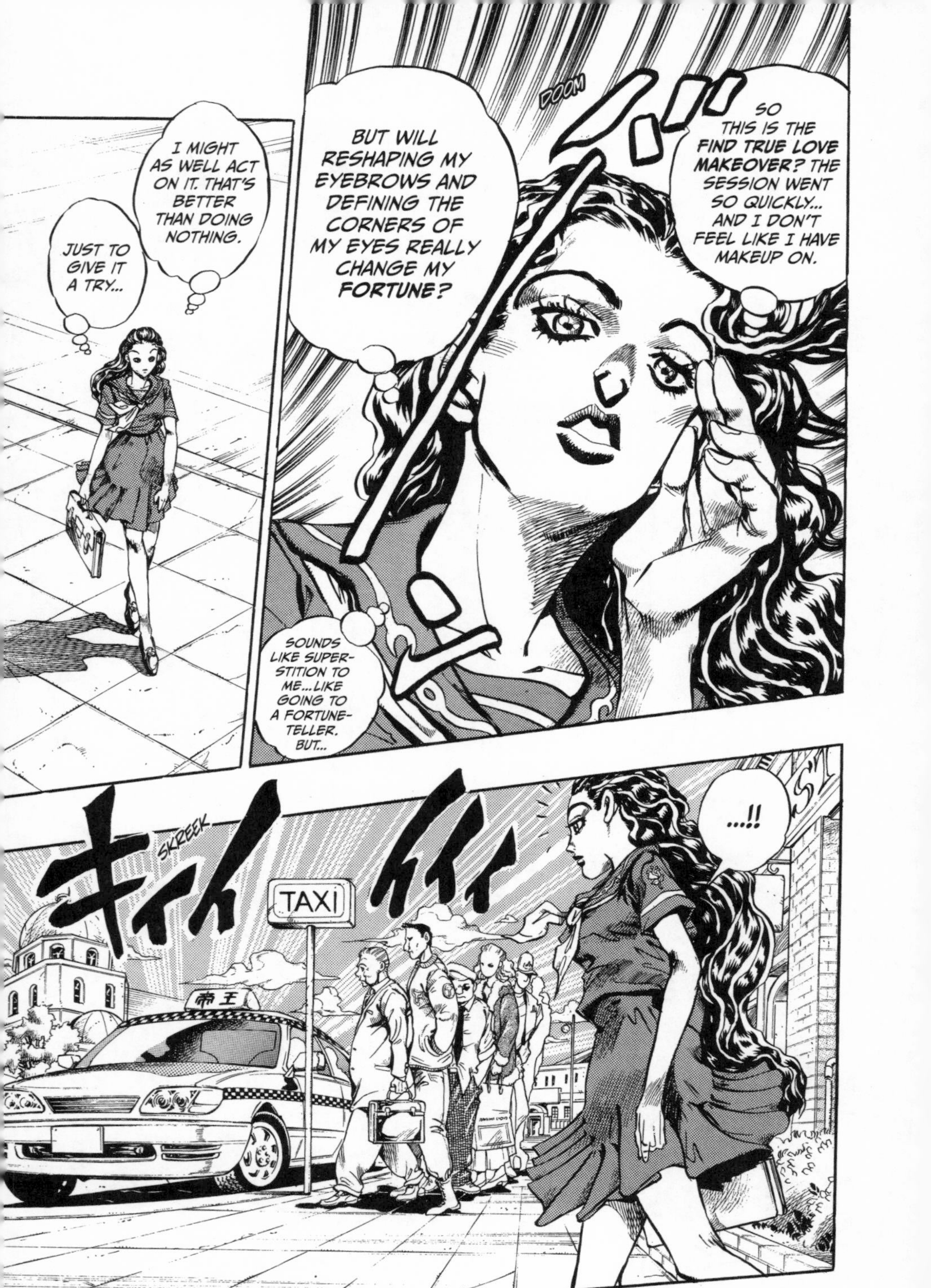
DOOM
SO THIS IS THE FIND TRUE LOVE MAKEOVER? THE SESSION WENT SO QUICKLY... AND I DON'T FEEL LIKE I HAVE MAKEUP ON.
BUT WILL RESHAPING MY EYEBROWS AND DEFINING THE CORNERS OF MY EYES REALLY CHANGE MY FORTUNE?
SOUNDS LIKE SUPER-STITION TO ME...LIKE GOING TO A FORTUNE-TELLER. BUT...
I MIGHT AS WELL ACT ON IT. THAT'S BETTER THAN DOING NOTHING.
JUST TO GIVE IT A TRY...
...!!
SKREEK
TAXI
帝王

TAXI'S SIGN: IMPERIAL

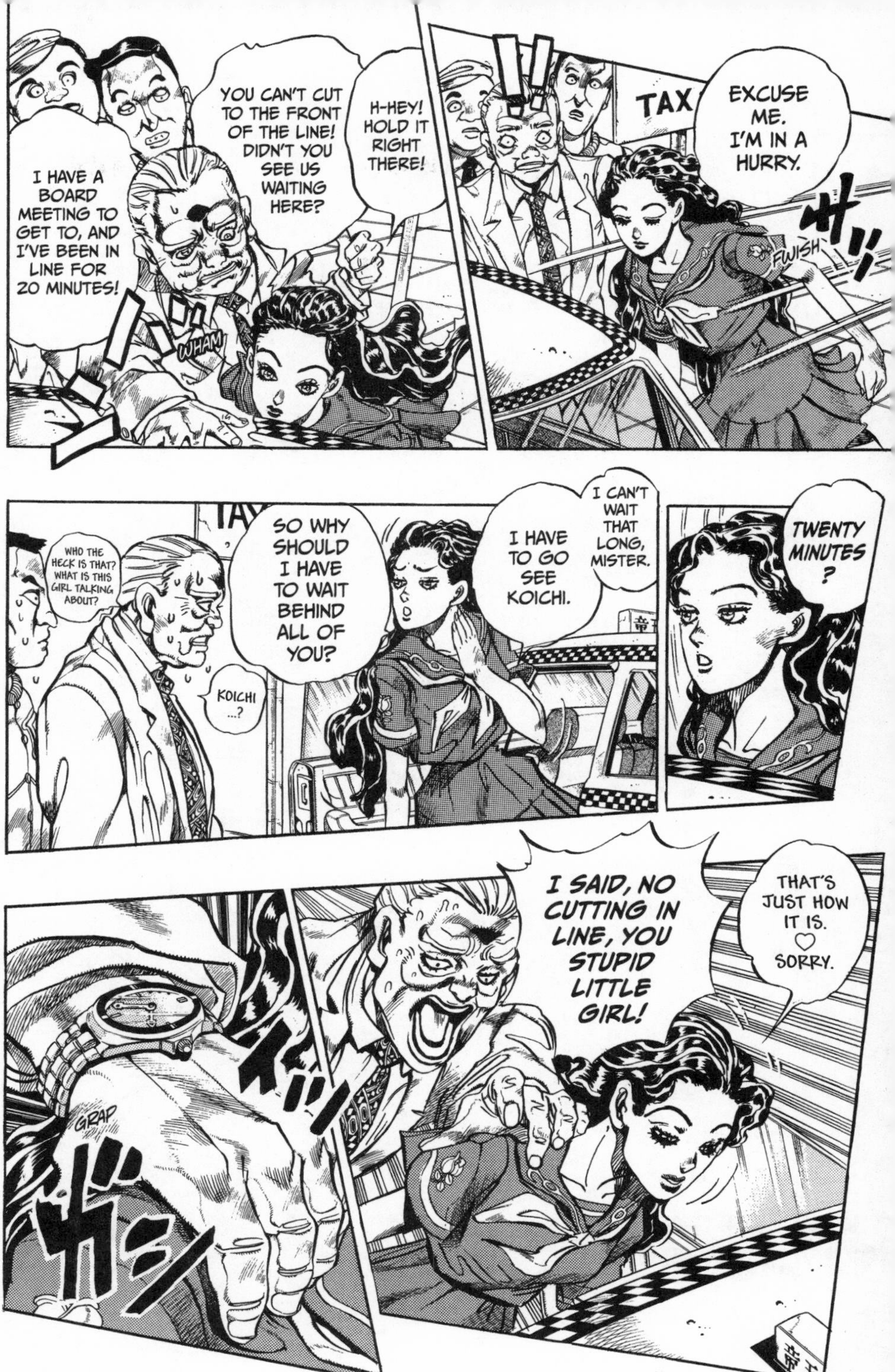
TAX
EXCUSE ME. I'M IN A HURRY.
FWISH
H-HEY! HOLD IT RIGHT THERE!
YOU CAN'T CUT TO THE FRONT OF THE LINE! DIDN'T YOU SEE US WAITING HERE?
I HAVE A BOARD MEETING TO GET TO, AND I'VE BEEN IN LINE FOR 20 MINUTES!
WHAM
TWENTY MINUTES?
I CAN'T WAIT THAT LONG, MISTER.
I HAVE TO GO SEE KOICHI.
SO WHY SHOULD I HAVE TO WAIT BEHIND ALL OF YOU?
WHO THE HECK IS THAT? WHAT IS THIS GIRL TALKING ABOUT?
KOICHI ...?
THAT'S JUST HOW IT IS. ♡ SORRY.
I SAID, NO CUTTING IN LINE, YOU STUPID LITTLE GIRL!
GRAP

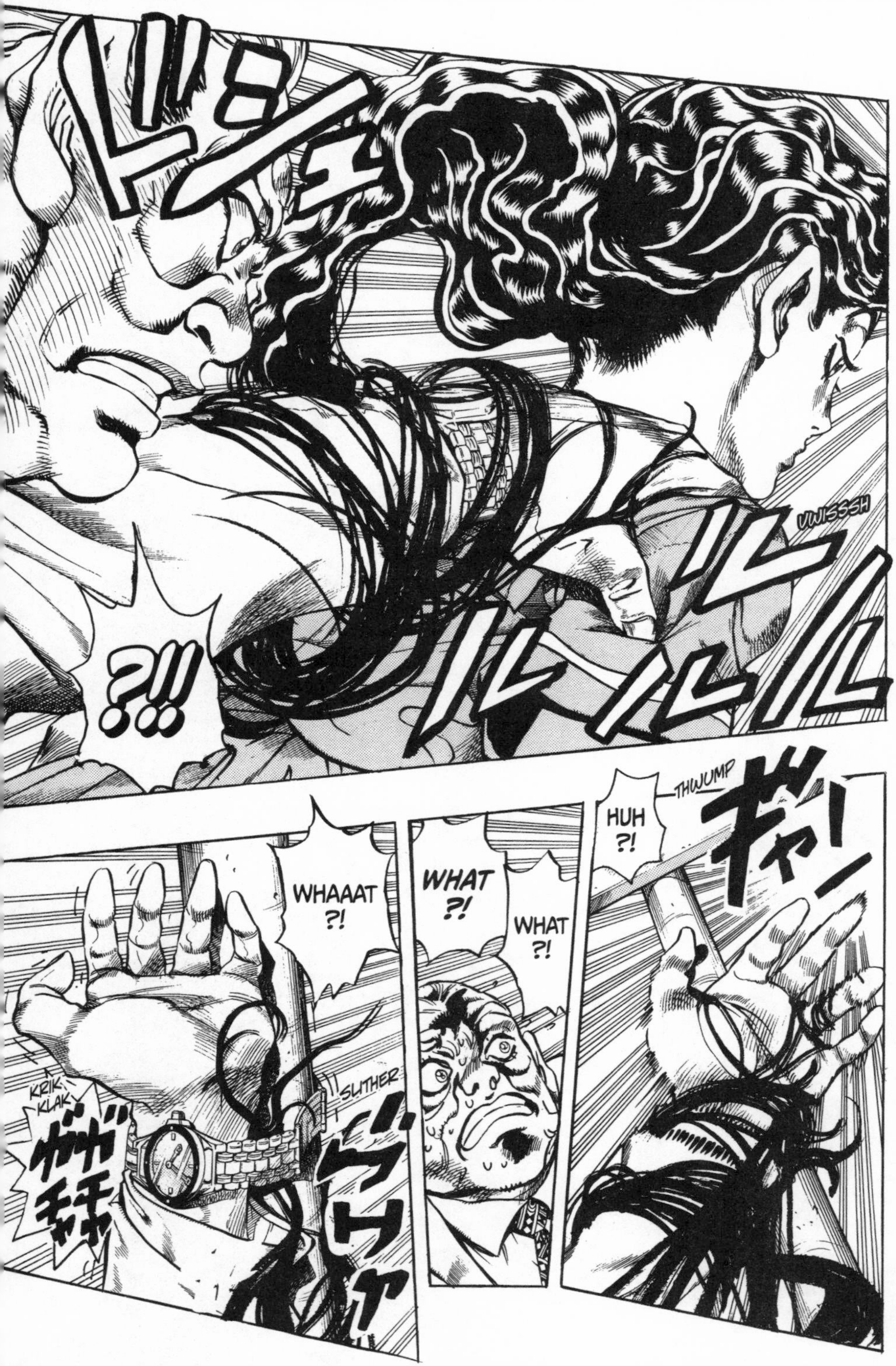
VWISSSH
?!!
THWUMP
HUH ?!
WHAT ?!
WHAT ?!
WHAAAT ?!
SLITHER
KRIK KLAK

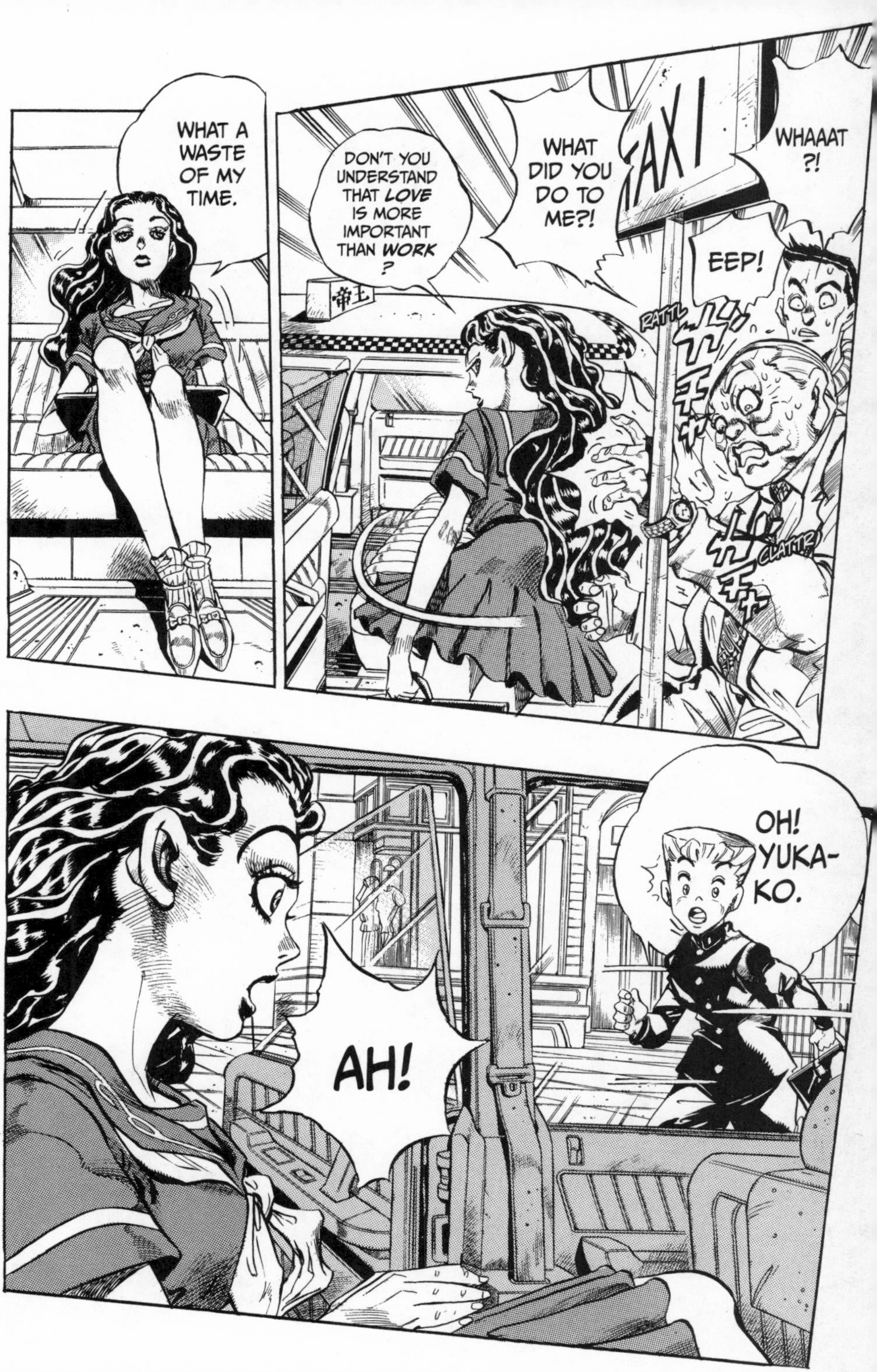
WHAAAT ?!
TAXI
WHAT DID YOU DO TO ME?!
EEP!
DON'T YOU UNDERSTAND THAT *LOVE* IS MORE IMPORTANT THAN *WORK* ?
帝王
RATTL
CLATTR
WHAT A WASTE OF MY TIME.
OH! YUKA-KO.
AH!

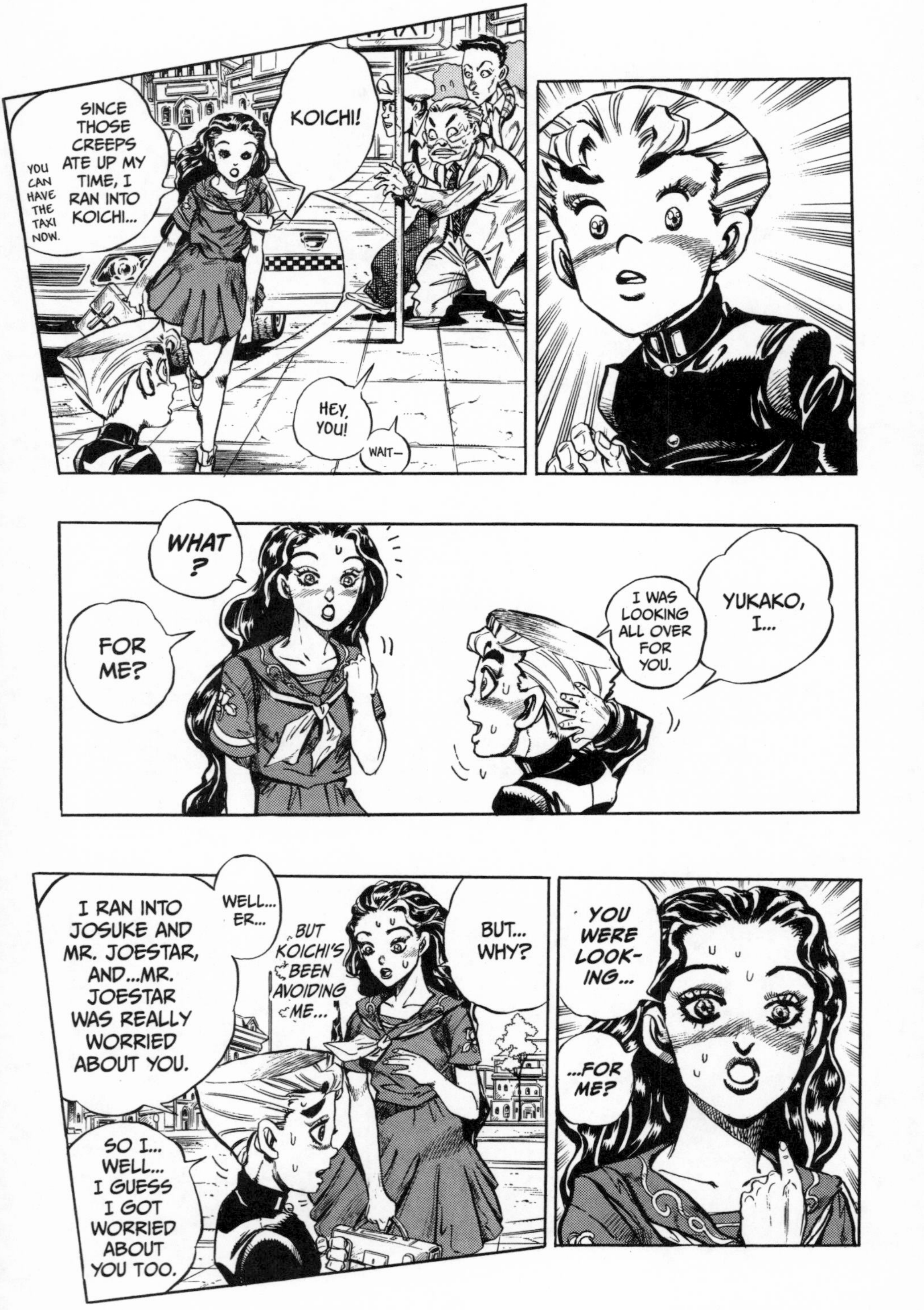
KOICHI!
SINCE THOSE CREEPS ATE UP MY TIME, I RAN INTO KOICHI...
YOU CAN HAVE THE TAXI NOW.
HEY, YOU!
WAIT—
YUKAKO, I...
I WAS LOOKING ALL OVER FOR YOU.
WHAT?
FOR ME?
YOU WERE LOOKING...
...FOR ME?
BUT... WHY?
BUT KOICHI'S BEEN AVOIDING ME...
WELL... ER...
I RAN INTO JOSUKE AND MR. JOESTAR, AND...MR. JOESTAR WAS REALLY WORRIED ABOUT YOU.
SO I... WELL... I GUESS I GOT WORRIED ABOUT YOU TOO.

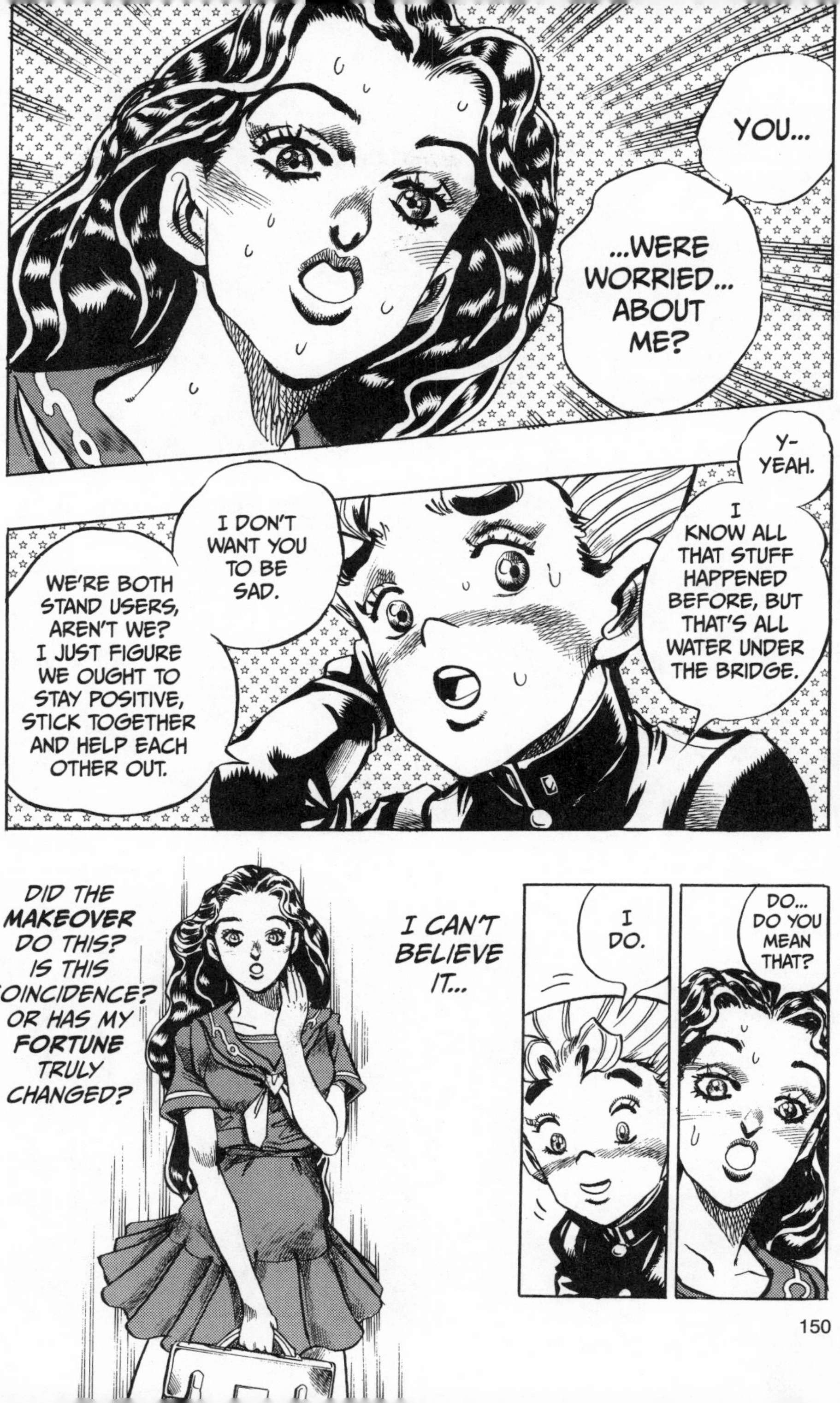
YOU...
...WERE WORRIED... ABOUT ME?
Y- YEAH.
I KNOW ALL THAT STUFF HAPPENED BEFORE, BUT THAT'S ALL WATER UNDER THE BRIDGE.
I DON'T WANT YOU TO BE SAD.
WE'RE BOTH STAND USERS, AREN'T WE? I JUST FIGURE WE OUGHT TO STAY POSITIVE, STICK TOGETHER AND HELP EACH OTHER OUT.
DO... DO YOU MEAN THAT?
I DO.
I CAN'T BELIEVE IT...
DID THE MAKEOVER DO THIS? IS THIS COINCIDENCE? OR HAS MY FORTUNE TRULY CHANGED?

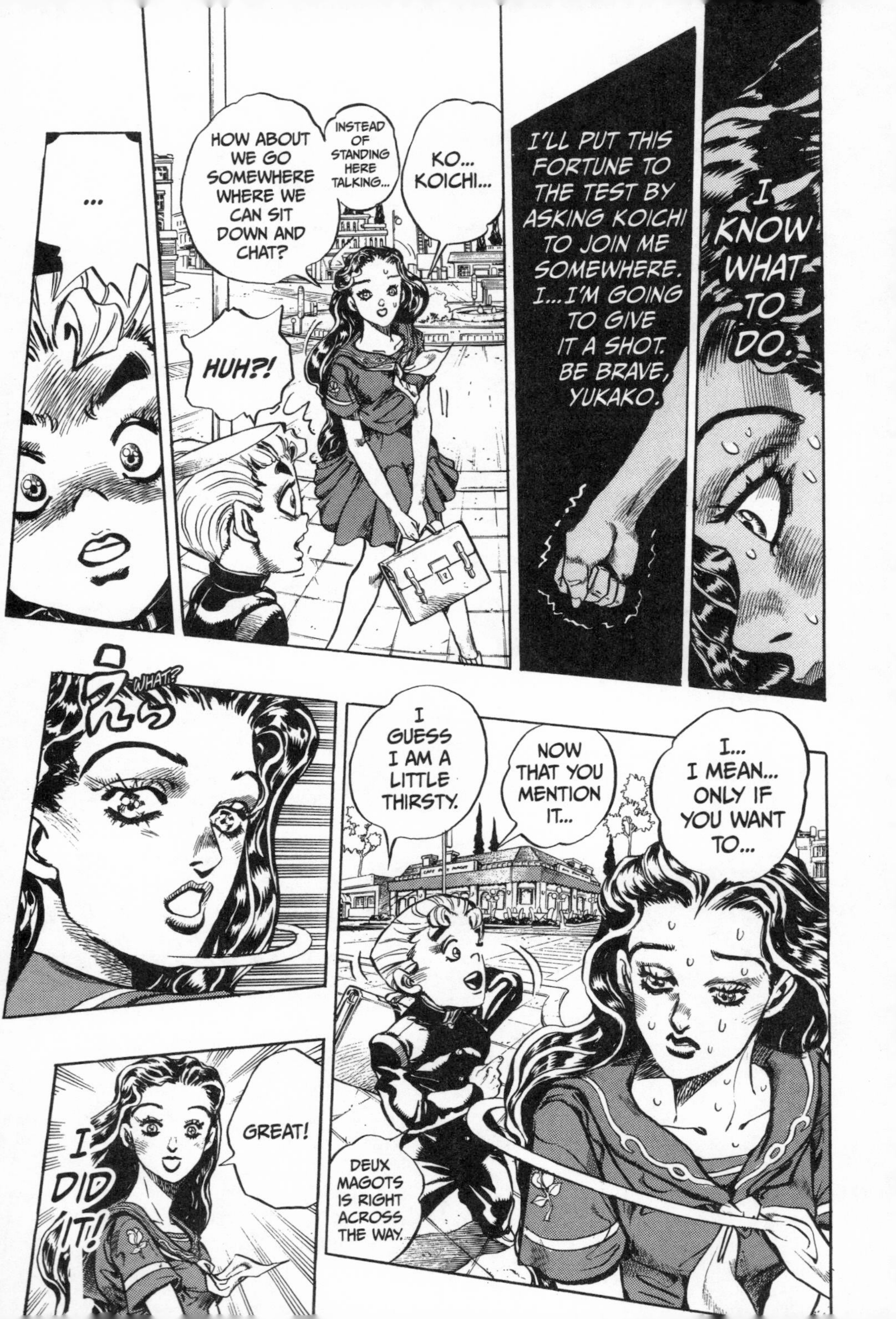
I KNOW WHAT TO DO.
I'LL PUT THIS FORTUNE TO THE TEST BY ASKING KOICHI TO JOIN ME SOMEWHERE. I...I'M GOING TO GIVE IT A SHOT. BE BRAVE, YUKAKO.
KO... KOICHI...
INSTEAD OF STANDING HERE TALKING...
HOW ABOUT WE GO SOMEWHERE WHERE WE CAN SIT DOWN AND CHAT?
HUH?!
...
I... I MEAN... ONLY IF YOU WANT TO...
NOW THAT YOU MENTION IT...
I GUESS I AM A LITTLE THIRSTY.
DEUX MAGOTS IS RIGHT ACROSS THE WAY.
えっ
WHAT?
GREAT!
I DID IT!

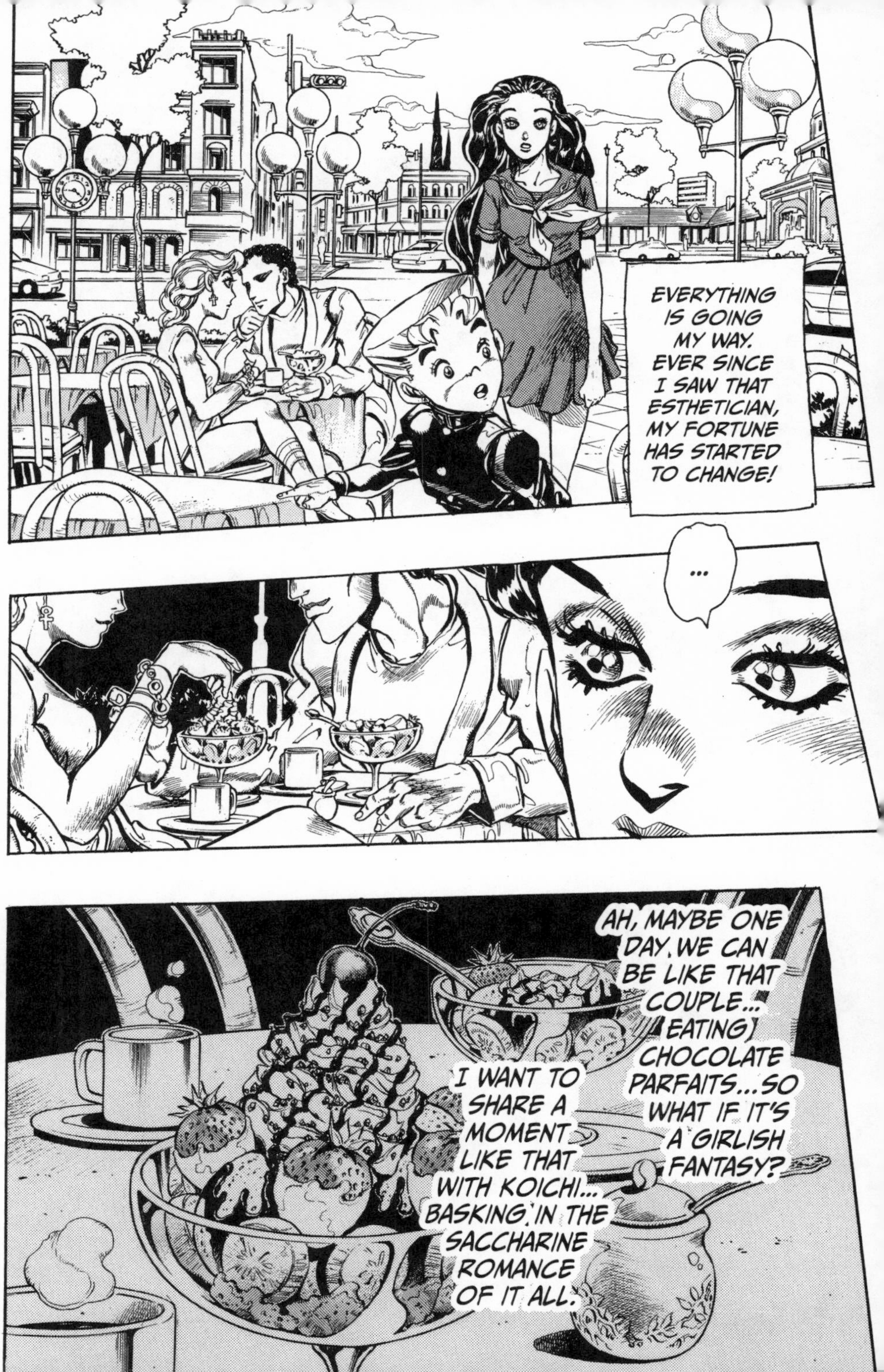
EVERYTHING IS GOING MY WAY. EVER SINCE I SAW THAT ESTHETICIAN, MY FORTUNE HAS STARTED TO CHANGE!
...
AH, MAYBE ONE DAY, WE CAN BE LIKE THAT COUPLE... EATING CHOCOLATE PARFAITS...SO WHAT IF IT'S A GIRLISH FANTASY?
I WANT TO SHARE A MOMENT LIKE THAT WITH KOICHI... BASKING IN THE SACCHARINE ROMANCE OF IT ALL.

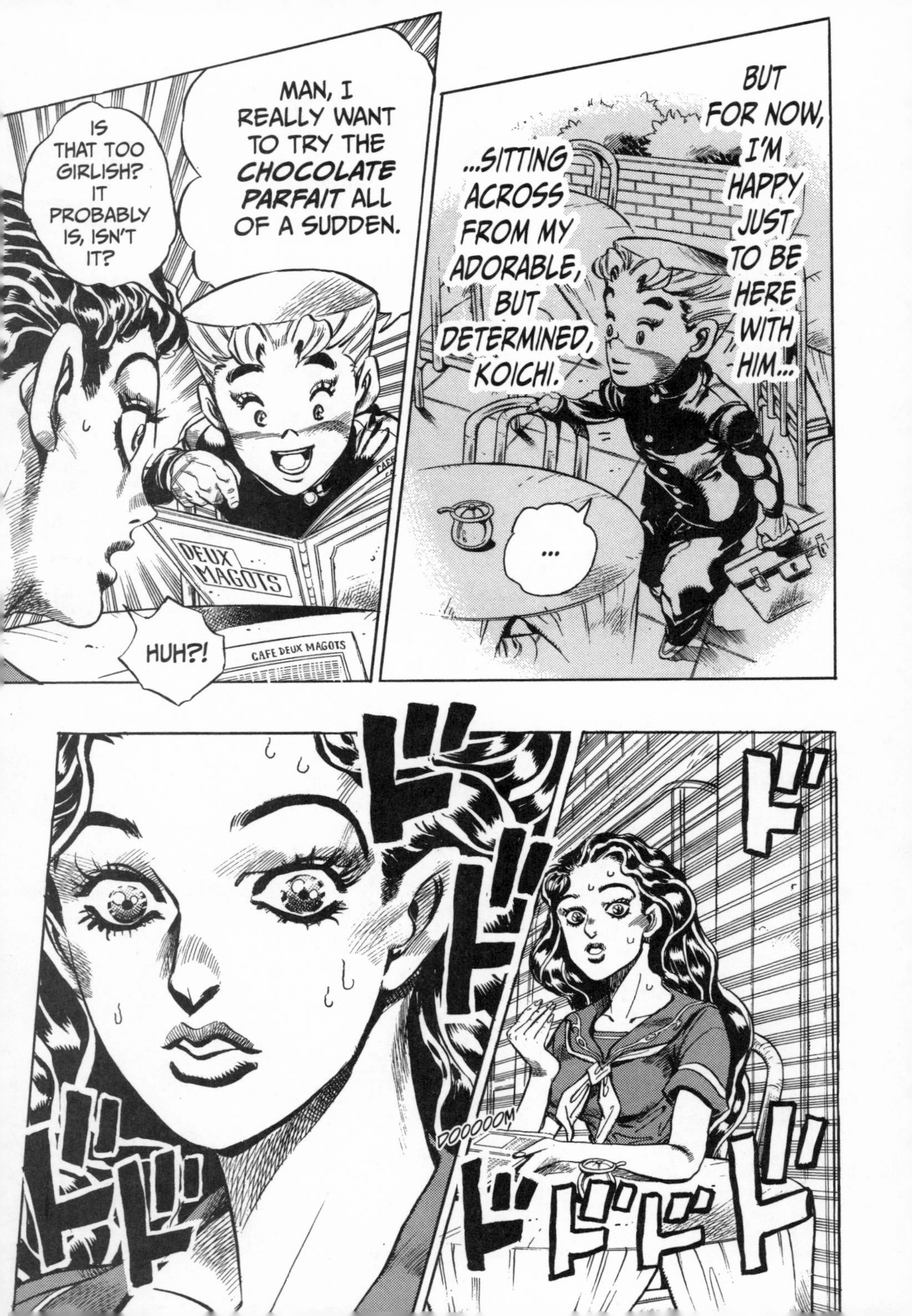
BUT FOR NOW, I'M HAPPY JUST TO BE HERE WITH HIM...
...SITTING ACROSS FROM MY ADORABLE, BUT DETERMINED, KOICHI.
...
MAN, I REALLY WANT TO TRY THE CHOCOLATE PARFAIT ALL OF A SUDDEN.
IS THAT TOO GIRLISH? IT PROBABLY IS, ISN'T IT?
DEUX MAGOTS
CAFE DEUX MAGOTS
HUH?!
DOOOOOM
ドドドドド

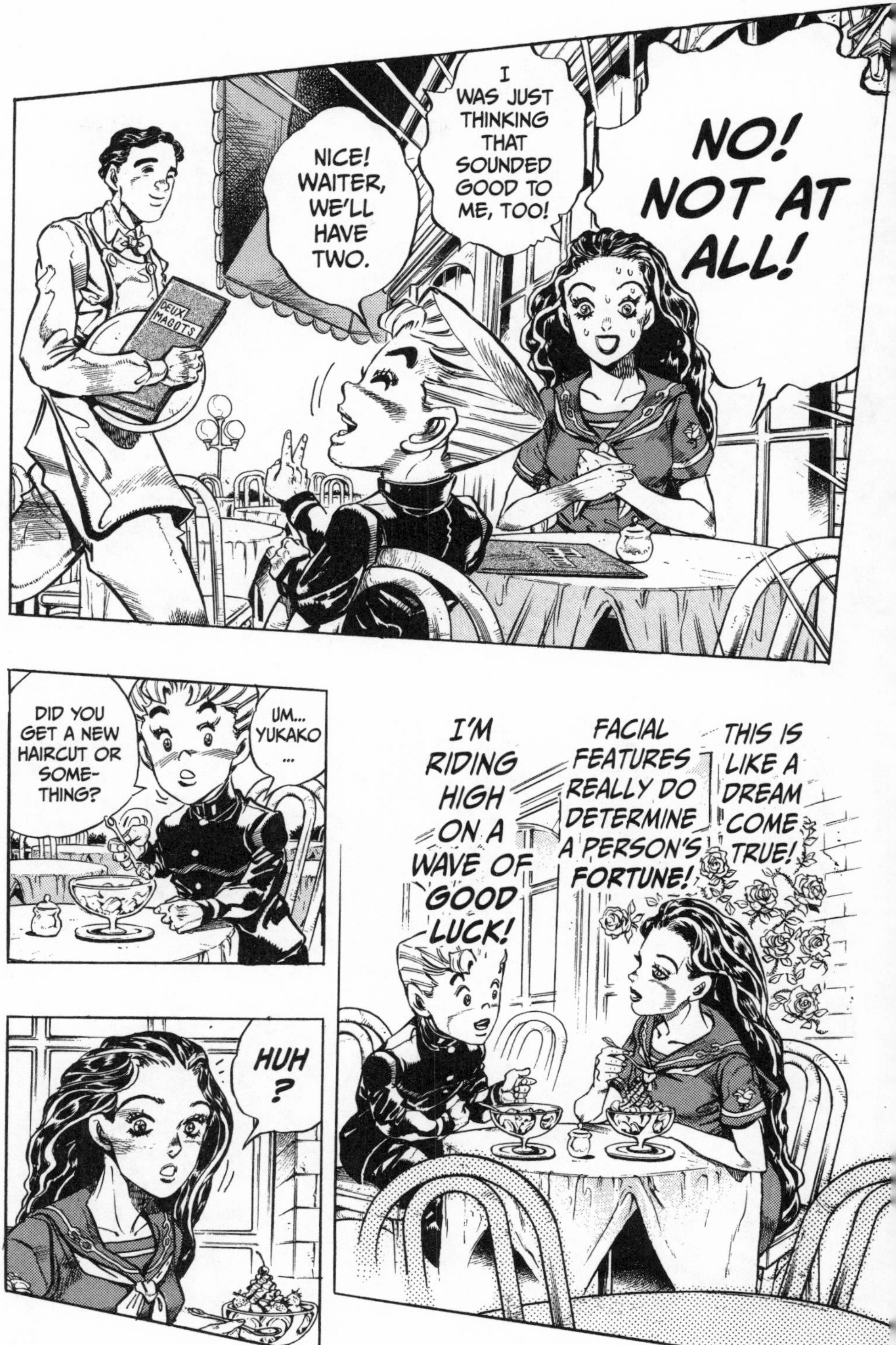
NO! NOT AT ALL!
I WAS JUST THINKING THAT SOUNDED GOOD TO ME, TOO!
NICE! WAITER, WE'LL HAVE TWO.
DEUX MAGOTS
THIS IS LIKE A DREAM COME TRUE!
FACIAL FEATURES REALLY DO DETERMINE A PERSON'S FORTUNE!
I'M RIDING HIGH ON A WAVE OF GOOD LUCK!
UM... YUKAKO ...
DID YOU GET A NEW HAIRCUT OR SOME-THING?
HUH ?

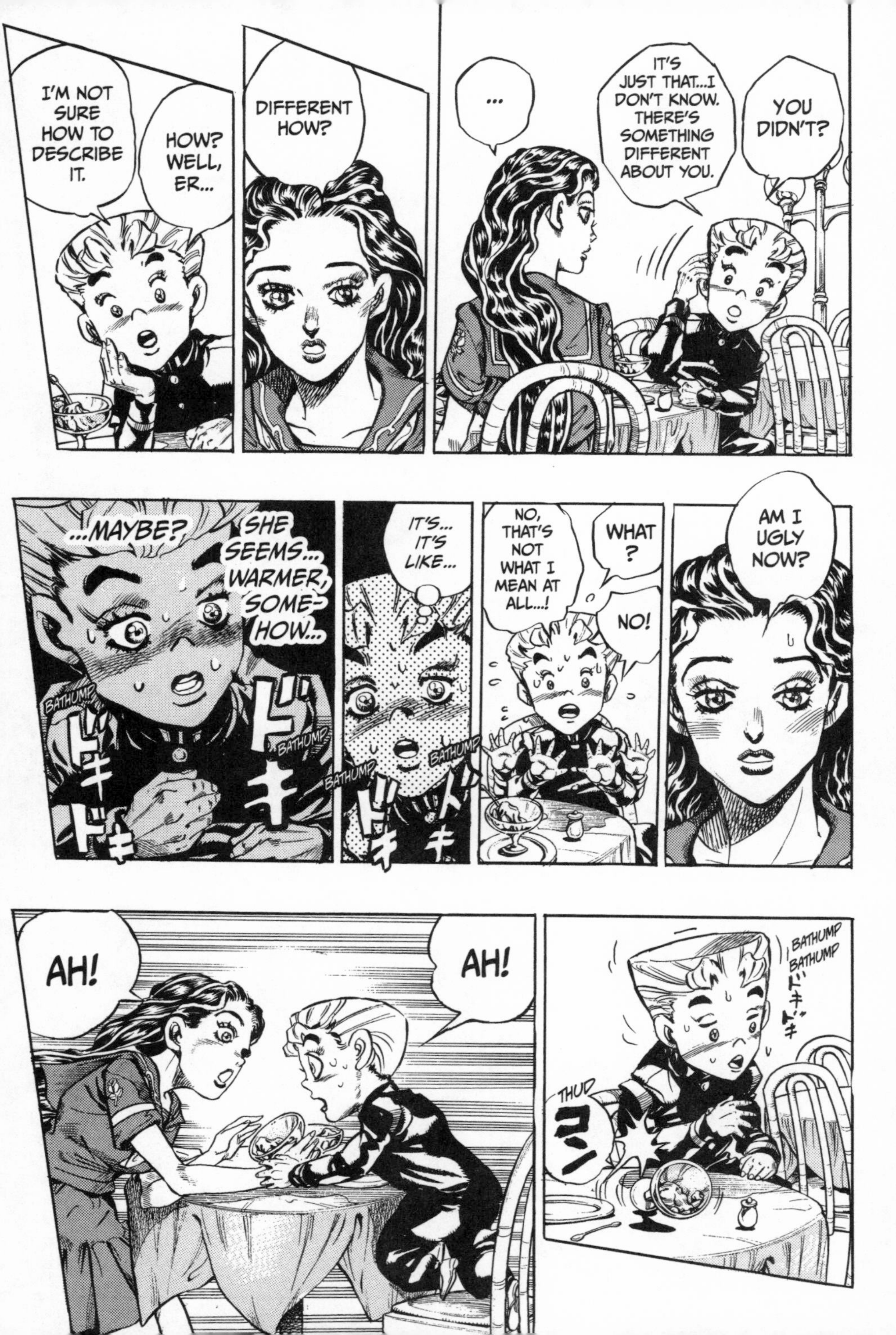
YOU DIDN'T?
IT'S JUST THAT...I DON'T KNOW. THERE'S SOMETHING DIFFERENT ABOUT YOU.
...
DIFFERENT HOW?
HOW? WELL, ER...
I'M NOT SURE HOW TO DESCRIBE IT.
AM I UGLY NOW?
WHAT?
NO!
NO, THAT'S NOT WHAT I MEAN AT ALL...!
IT'S... IT'S LIKE...
BATHUMP
BATHUMP
SHE SEEMS... WARMER, SOME-HOW...
...MAYBE?
BATHUMP
BATHUMP
BATHUMP BATHUMP
THUD
AH!
AH!

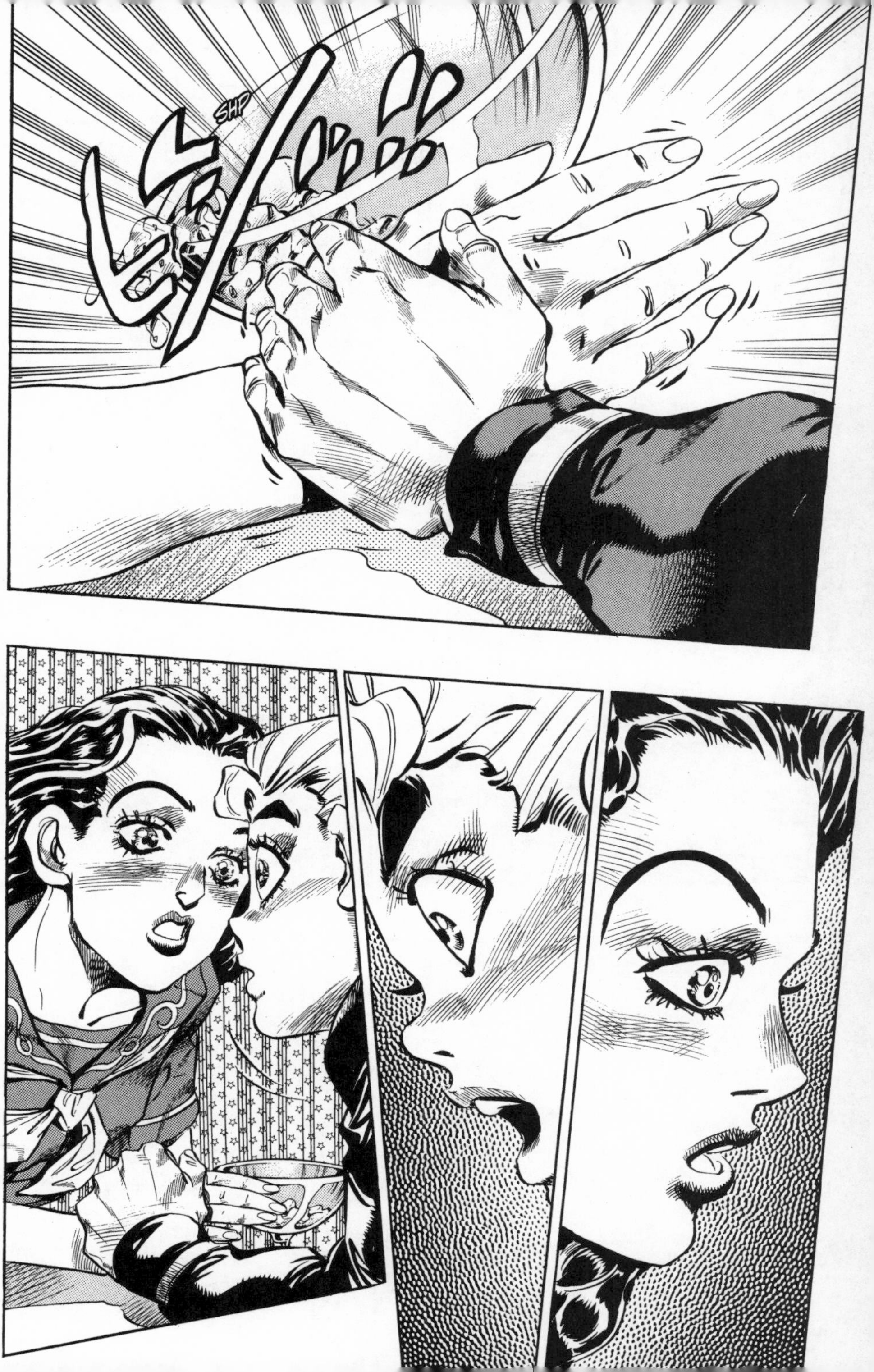
SHP

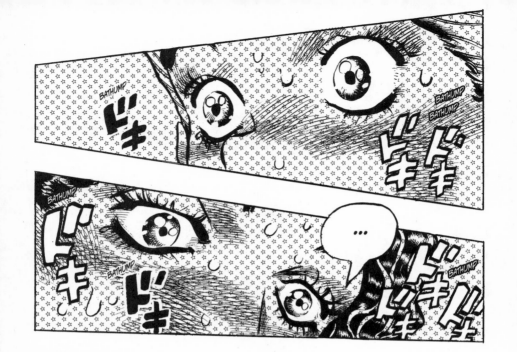

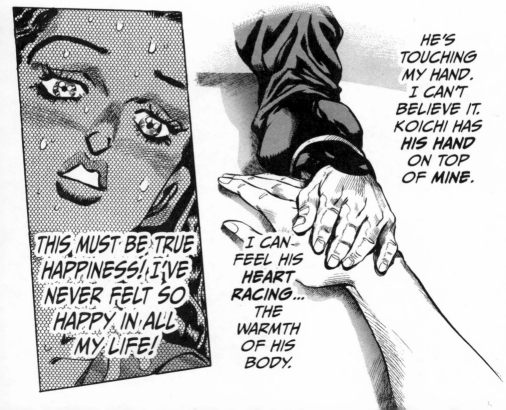

BATHUMP
BATHUMP
ドキドキ
BATHUMP
ドキ
...
BATHUMP
ドキドキ
BATHUMP
ドキ
BATHUMP
ドキ
HE'S TOUCHING MY HAND. I CAN'T BELIEVE IT. KOICHI HAS HIS HAND ON TOP OF MINE.
I CAN FEEL HIS HEART RACING... THE WARMTH OF HIS BODY.
THIS MUST BE TRUE HAPPINESS! I'VE NEVER FELT SO HAPPY IN ALL MY LIFE!

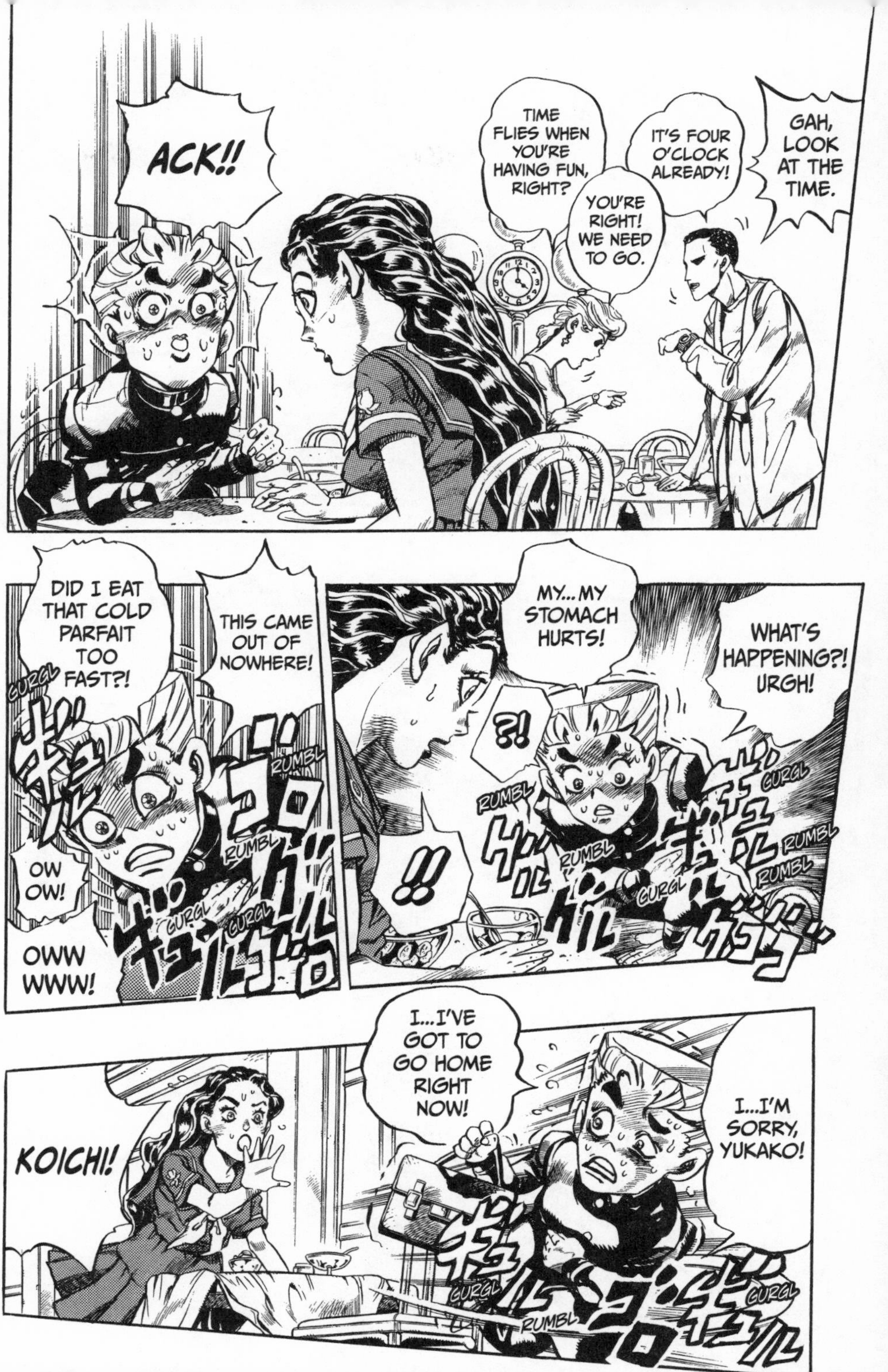
GAH, LOOK AT THE TIME.
IT'S FOUR O'CLOCK ALREADY!
YOU'RE RIGHT! WE NEED TO GO.
TIME FLIES WHEN YOU'RE HAVING FUN, RIGHT?
ACK!!
WHAT'S HAPPENING?! URGH!
MY... MY STOMACH HURTS!
?!
GURGL
RUMBL
RUMBL
RUMBL
GURGL
RUMBL
!!
THIS CAME OUT OF NOWHERE!
DID I EAT THAT COLD PARFAIT TOO FAST?!
GURGL
RUMBL
RUMBL
OW OW!
GURGL
GURGL
OWW WWW!
I...I'M SORRY, YUKAKO!
I...I'VE GOT TO GO HOME RIGHT NOW!
KOICHI!
GURGL
GURGL
RUMBL

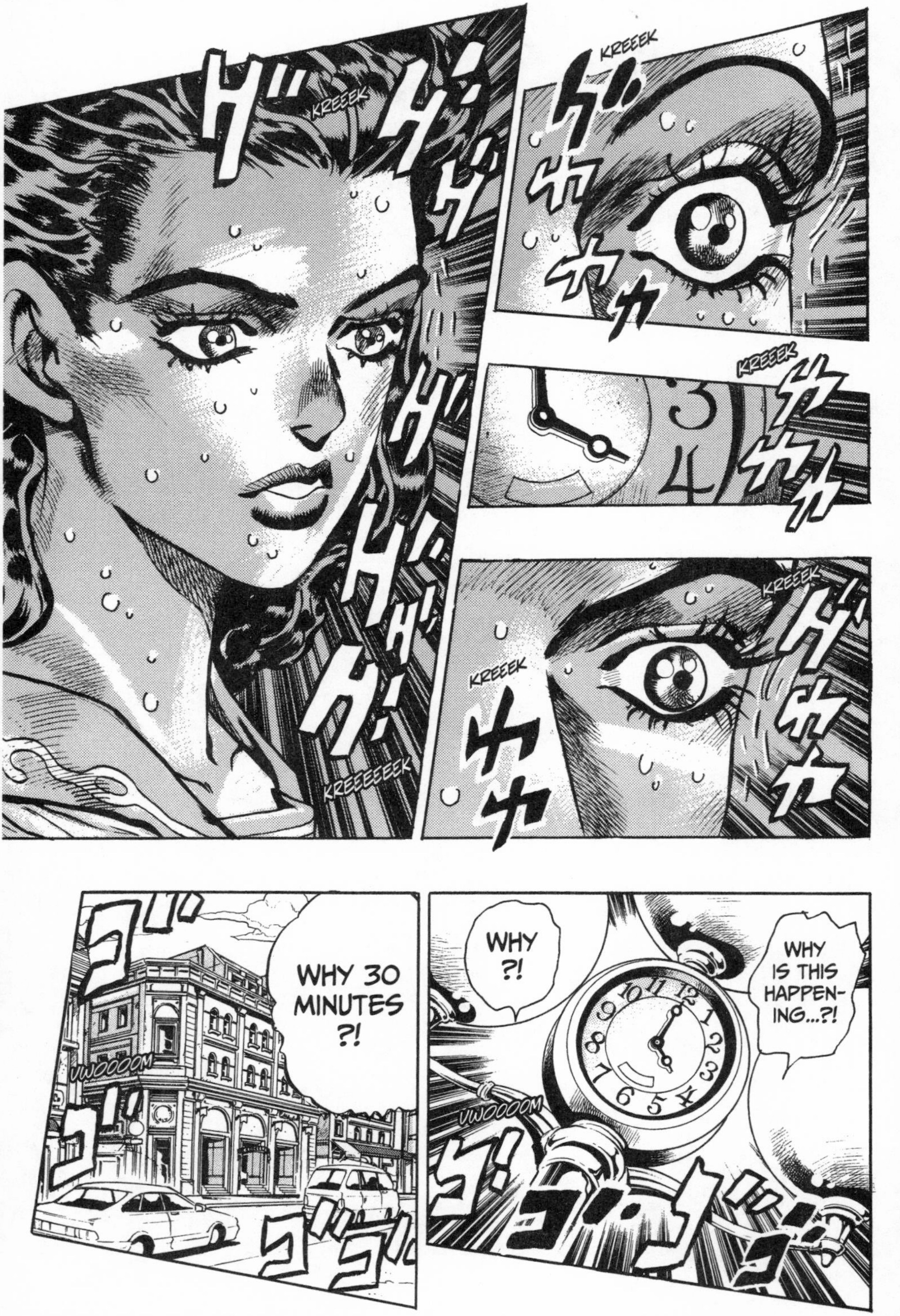
KREEEK
KREEEK
KREEEK
KREEEK
KREEEK
KREEEEEEK
WHY ?!
WHY IS THIS HAPPEN-ING...?!
UWOOOOM
WHY 30 MINUTES ?!
UWOOOOM

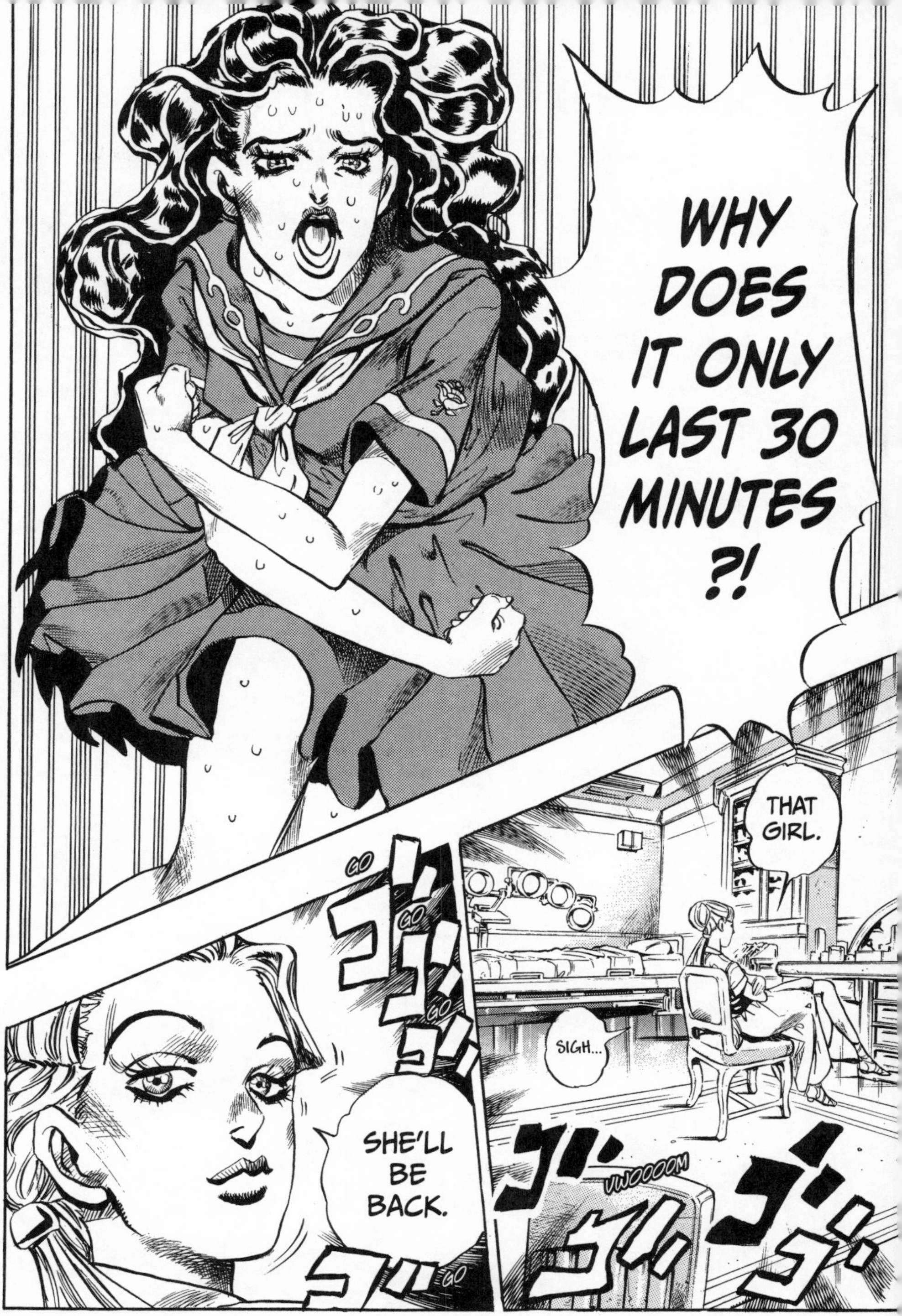
WHY DOES IT ONLY LAST 30 MINUTES ?!
THAT GIRL.
SIGH...
UWOOOOM
GO
GO
GO
SHE'LL BE BACK.
GO

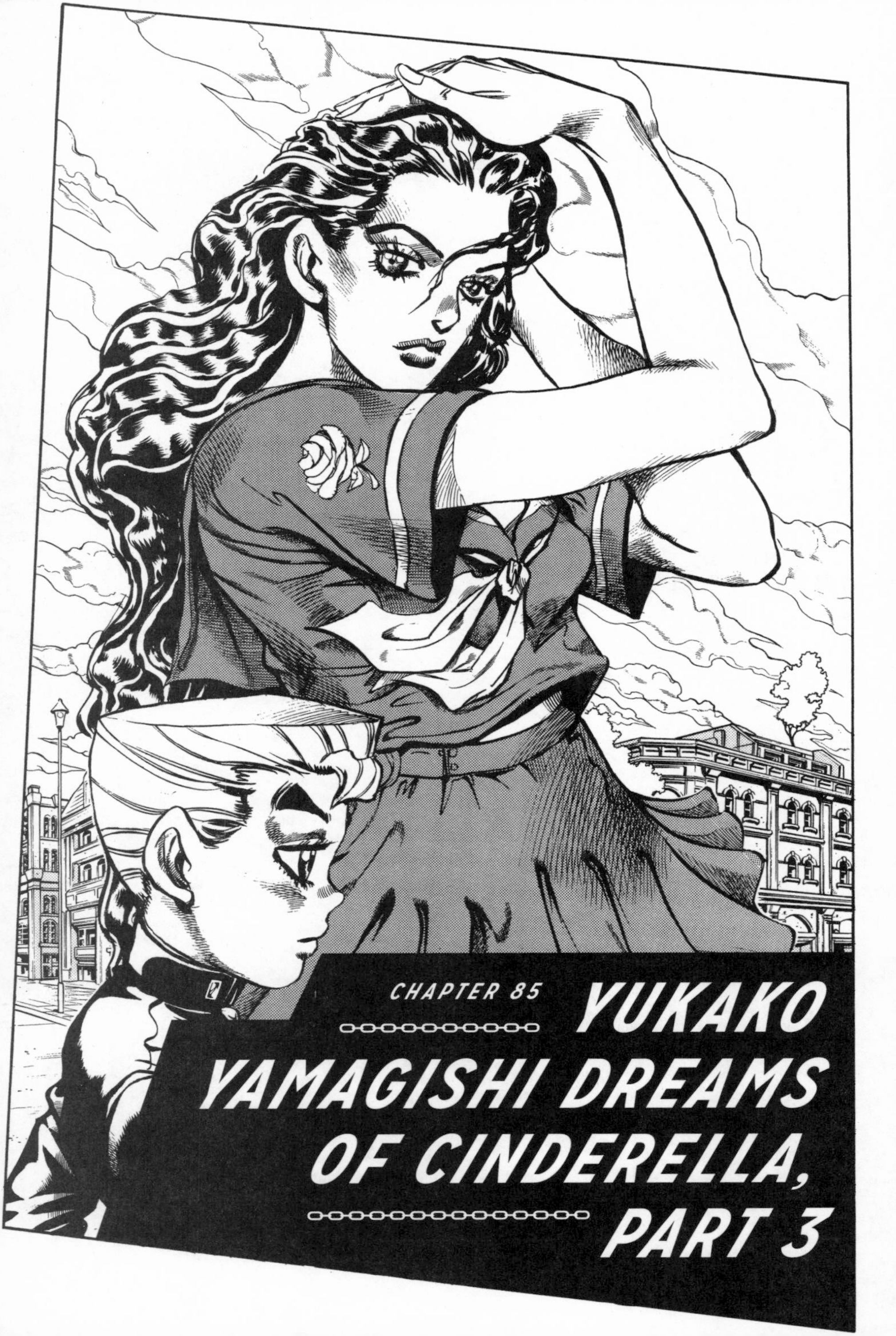
CHAPTER 85
YUKAKO YAMAGISHI DREAMS OF CINDERELLA, PART 3

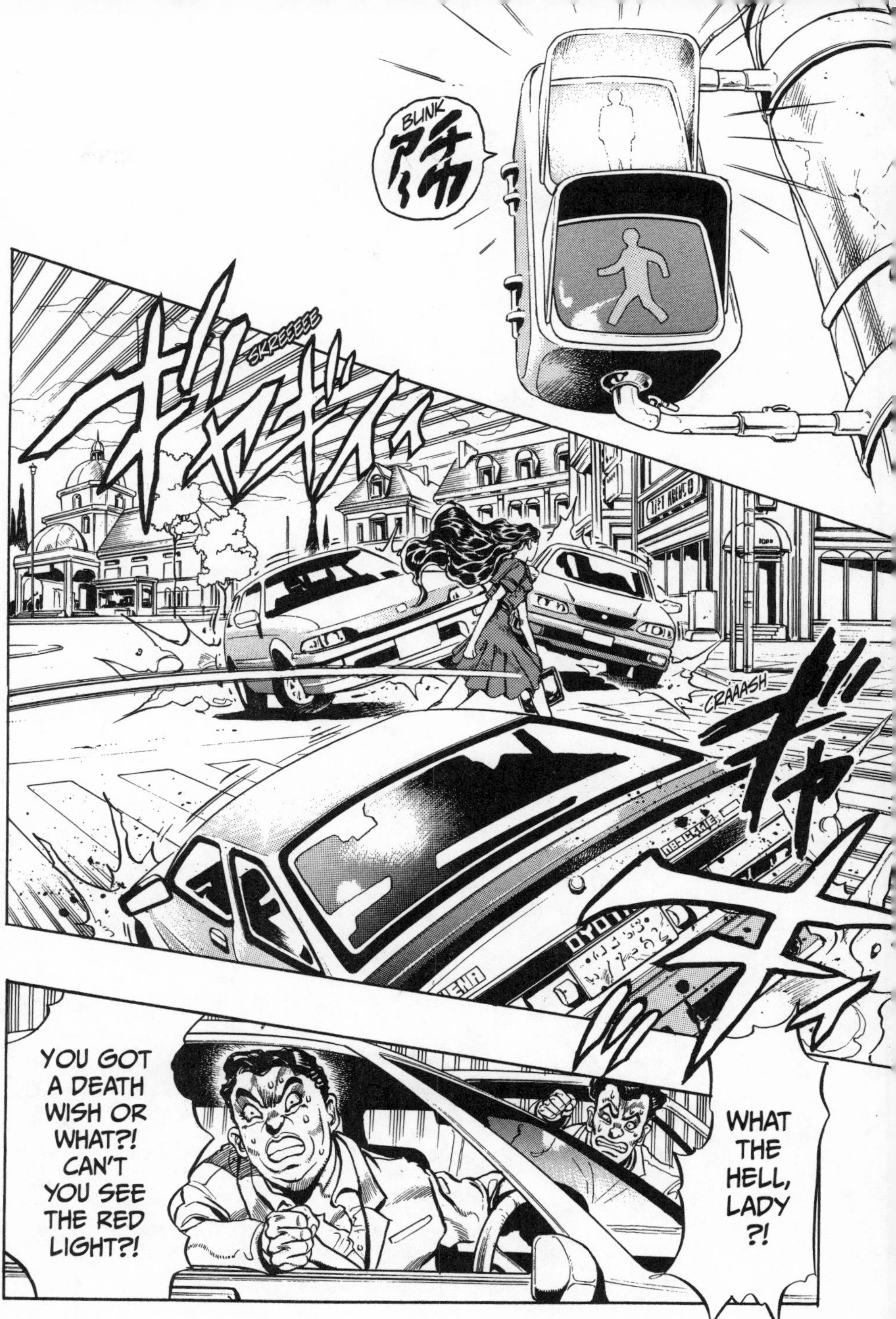
BLINK
CRAAASH
WHAT THE HELL, LADY?!
YOU GOT A DEATH WISH OR WHAT?! CAN'T YOU SEE THE RED LIGHT?!

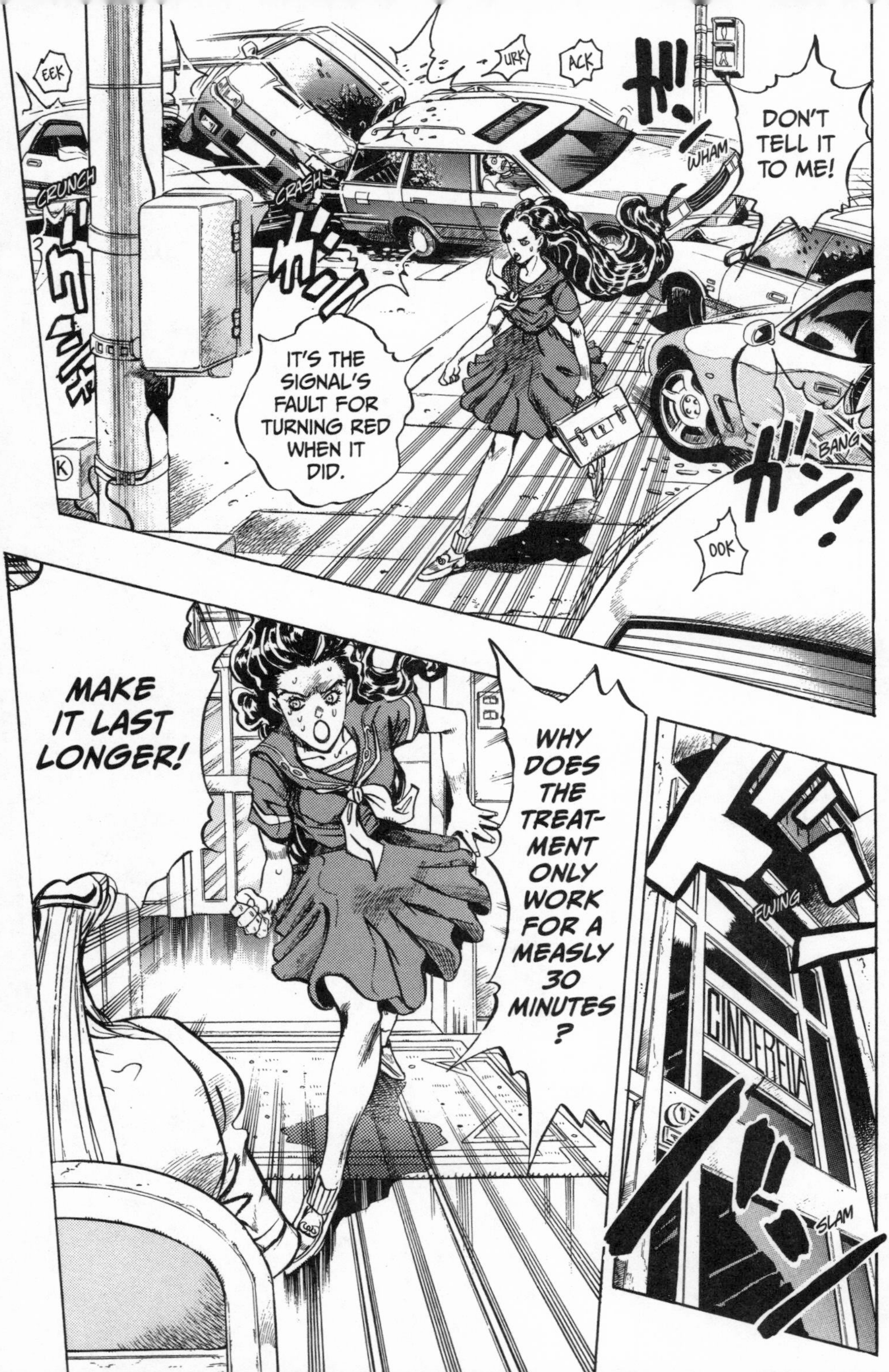
DON'T TELL IT TO ME!
WHAM
ACK
URK
EEK
CRUNCH
CRASH
IT'S THE SIGNAL'S FAULT FOR TURNING RED WHEN IT DID.
BANG
OOK
FWING
CINDERELLA
SLAM
WHY DOES THE TREAT-MENT ONLY WORK FOR A MEASLY 30 MINUTES?
MAKE IT LAST LONGER!

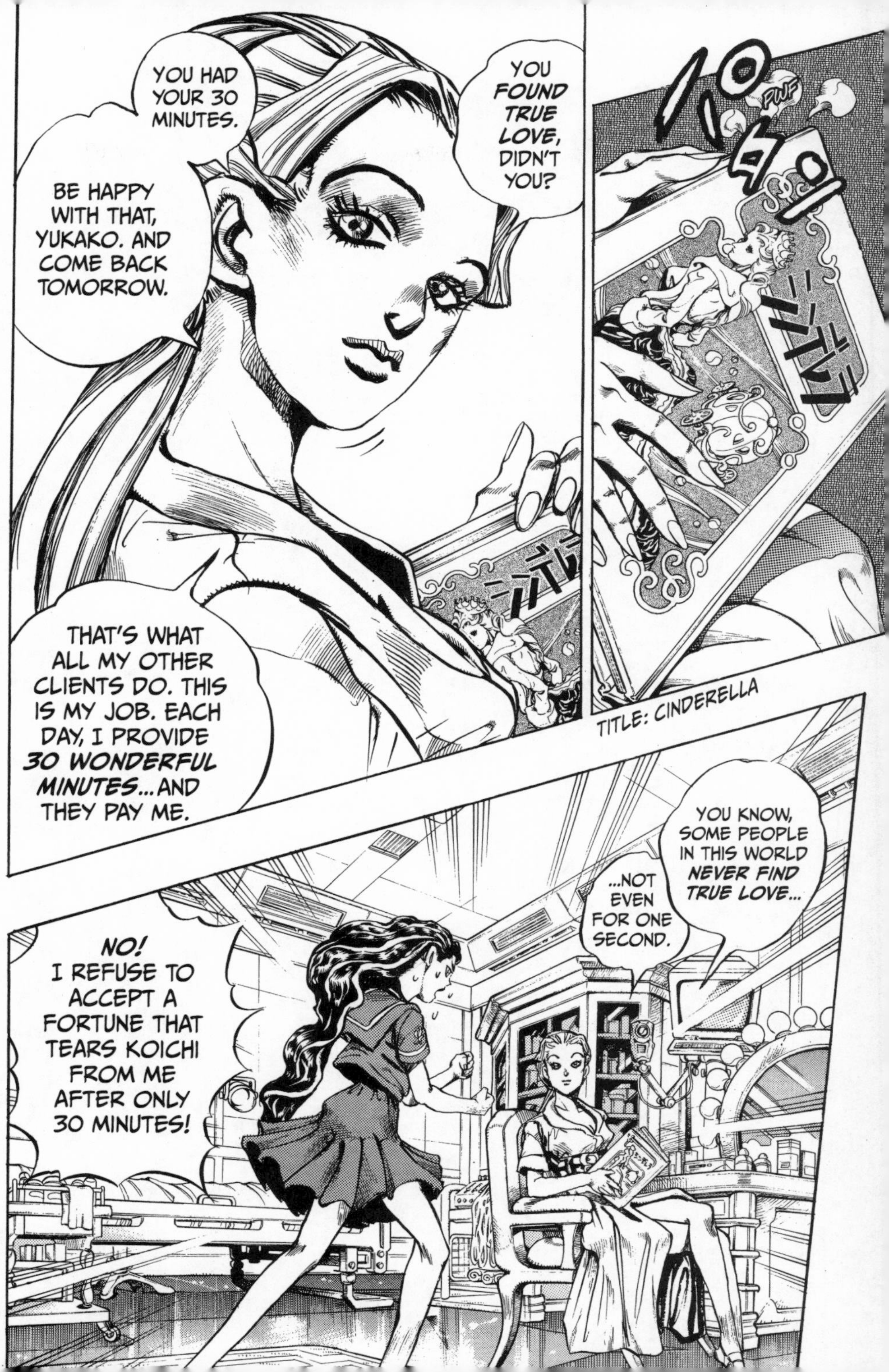
PWF
TITLE: CINDERELLA
YOU FOUND TRUE LOVE, DIDN'T YOU?
YOU HAD YOUR 30 MINUTES.
BE HAPPY WITH THAT, YUKAKO. AND COME BACK TOMORROW.
THAT'S WHAT ALL MY OTHER CLIENTS DO. THIS IS MY JOB. EACH DAY, I PROVIDE 30 WONDERFUL MINUTES...AND THEY PAY ME.
YOU KNOW, SOME PEOPLE IN THIS WORLD NEVER FIND TRUE LOVE...
...NOT EVEN FOR ONE SECOND.
NO! I REFUSE TO ACCEPT A FORTUNE THAT TEARS KOICHI FROM ME AFTER ONLY 30 MINUTES!

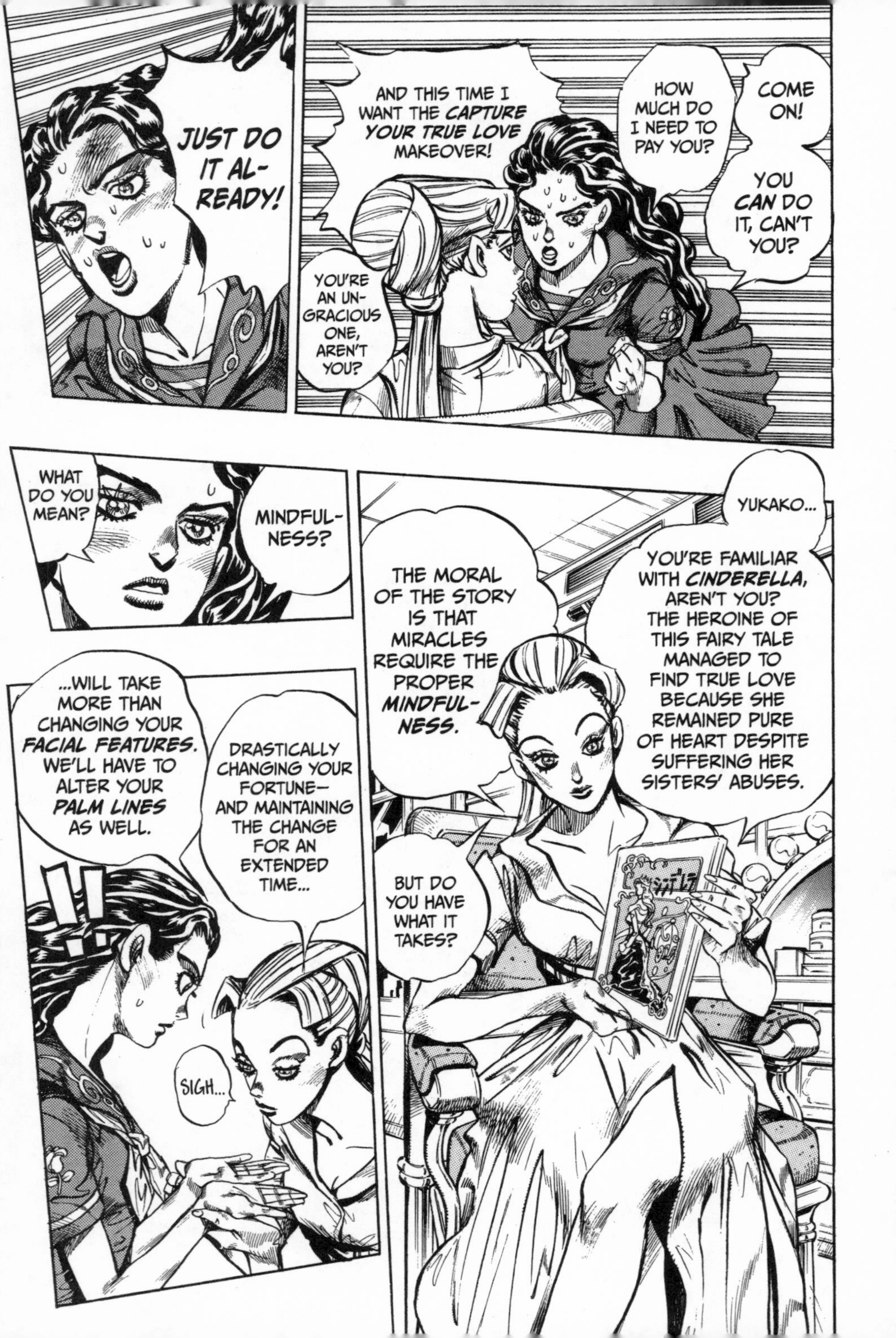
COME ON!
YOU CAN DO IT, CAN'T YOU?
HOW MUCH DO I NEED TO PAY YOU?
AND THIS TIME I WANT THE CAPTURE YOUR TRUE LOVE MAKEOVER!
YOU'RE AN UNGRACIOUS ONE, AREN'T YOU?
JUST DO IT ALREADY!
YUKAKO...
YOU'RE FAMILIAR WITH CINDERELLA, AREN'T YOU? THE HEROINE OF THIS FAIRY TALE MANAGED TO FIND TRUE LOVE BECAUSE SHE REMAINED PURE OF HEART DESPITE SUFFERING HER SISTERS' ABUSES.
THE MORAL OF THE STORY IS THAT MIRACLES REQUIRE THE PROPER MINDFULNESS.
BUT DO YOU HAVE WHAT IT TAKES?
MINDFULNESS?
WHAT DO YOU MEAN?
DRASTICALLY CHANGING YOUR FORTUNE— AND MAINTAINING THE CHANGE FOR AN EXTENDED TIME...
...WILL TAKE MORE THAN CHANGING YOUR FACIAL FEATURES. WE'LL HAVE TO ALTER YOUR PALM LINES AS WELL.
!!
SIGH...

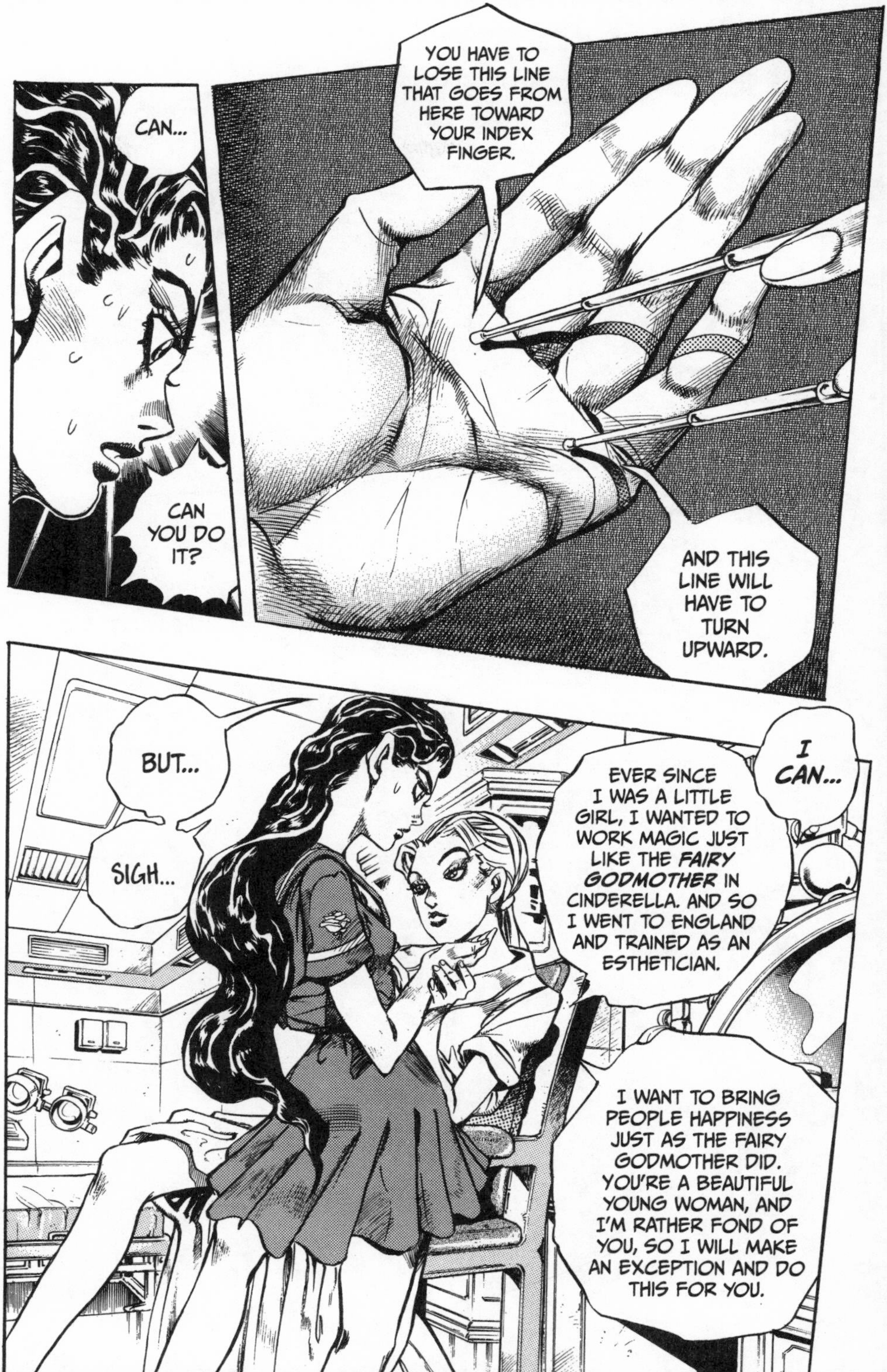
YOU HAVE TO LOSE THIS LINE THAT GOES FROM HERE TOWARD YOUR INDEX FINGER.
AND THIS LINE WILL HAVE TO TURN UPWARD.
CAN...
CAN YOU DO IT?
I CAN...
EVER SINCE I WAS A LITTLE GIRL, I WANTED TO WORK MAGIC JUST LIKE THE *FAIRY GODMOTHER* IN CINDERELLA. AND SO I WENT TO ENGLAND AND TRAINED AS AN ESTHETICIAN.
BUT...
SIGH...
I WANT TO BRING PEOPLE HAPPINESS JUST AS THE FAIRY GODMOTHER DID. YOU'RE A BEAUTIFUL YOUNG WOMAN, AND I'M RATHER FOND OF YOU, SO I WILL MAKE AN EXCEPTION AND DO THIS FOR YOU.

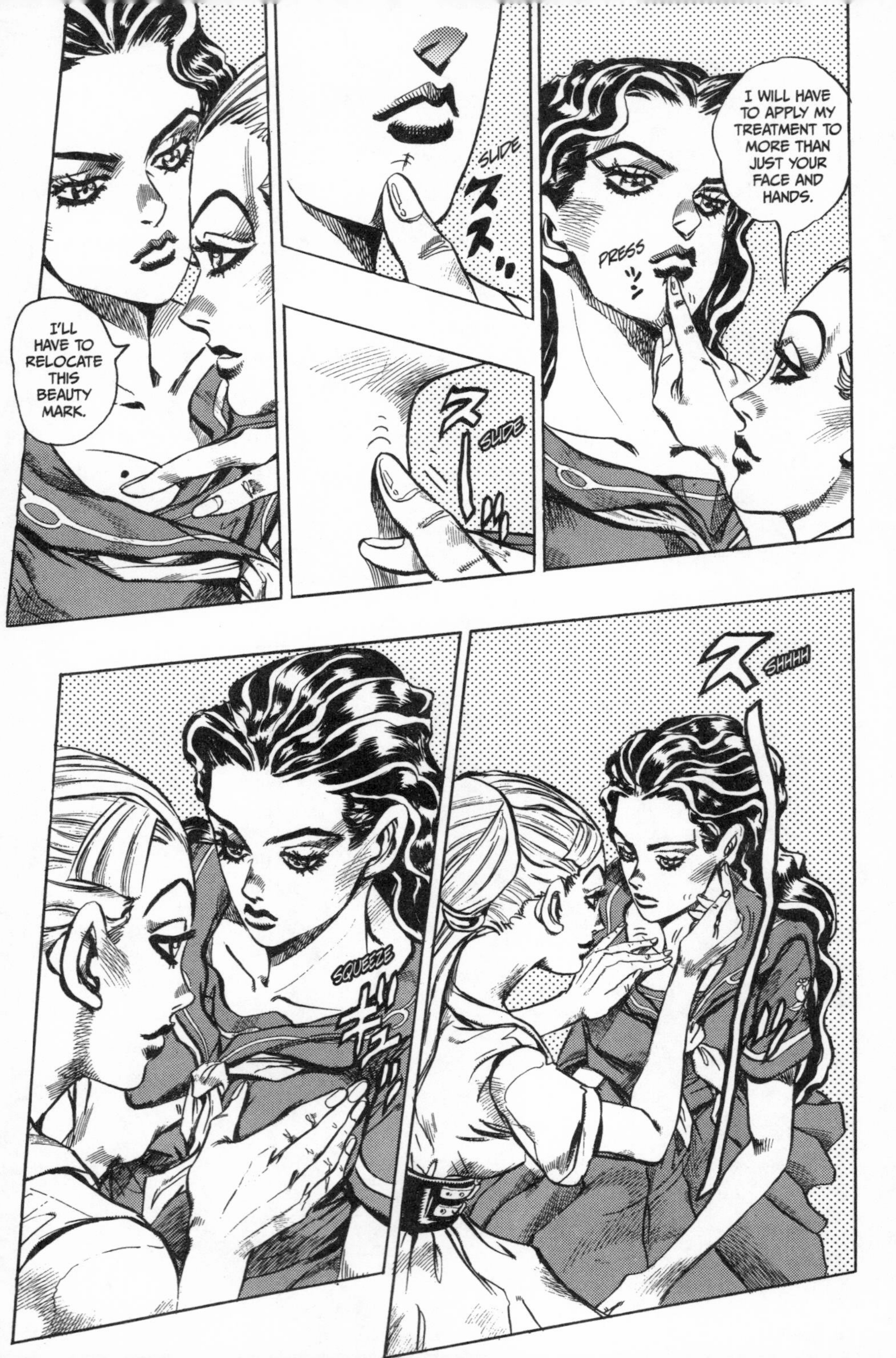
I WILL HAVE TO APPLY MY TREATMENT TO MORE THAN JUST YOUR FACE AND HANDS.
PRESS
SLIDE
SLIDE
I'LL HAVE TO RELOCATE THIS BEAUTY MARK.
SHHHH
SQUEEZE

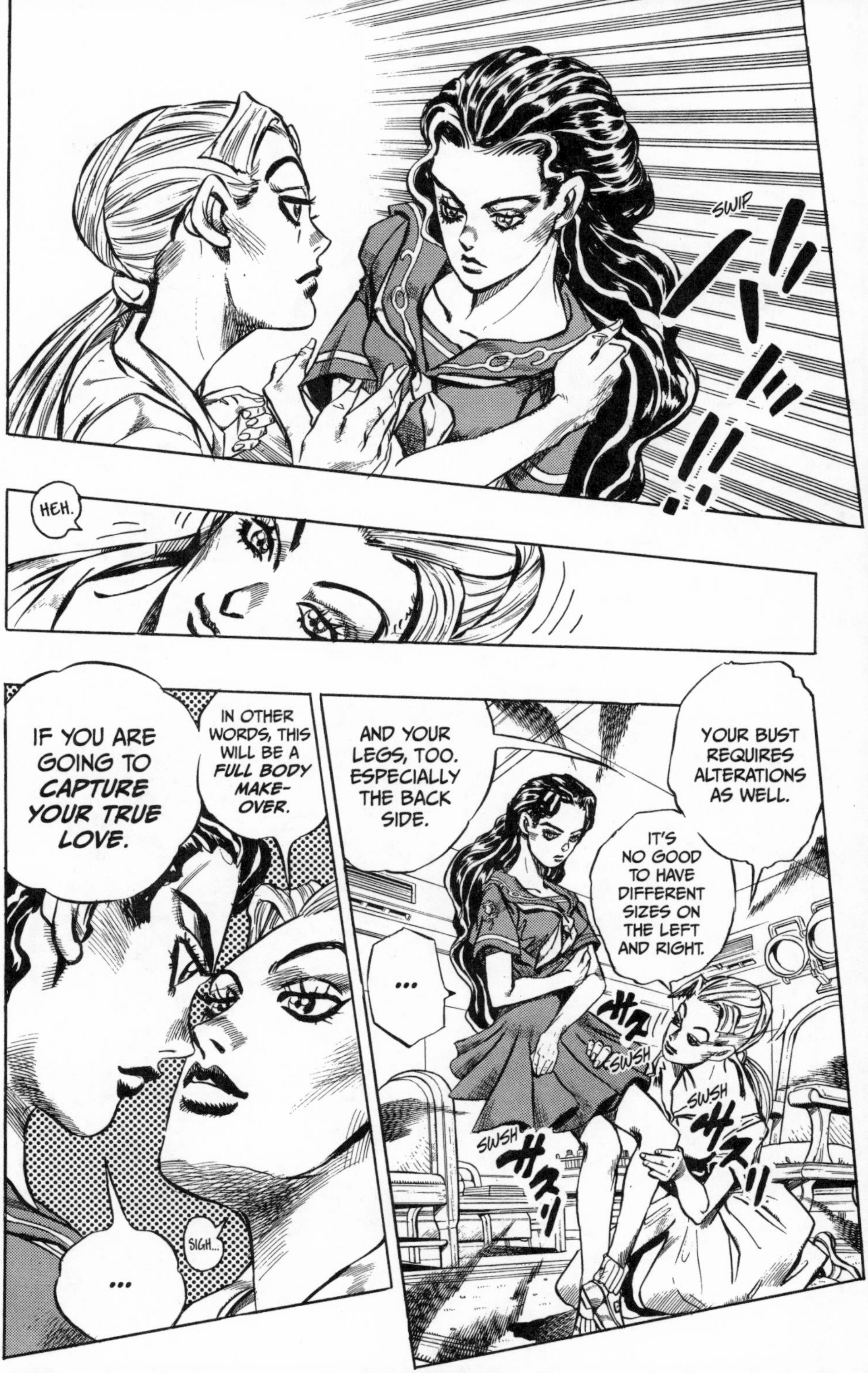
SWIP
HEH.
YOUR BUST REQUIRES ALTERATIONS AS WELL.
AND YOUR LEGS, TOO. ESPECIALLY THE BACK SIDE.
IT'S NO GOOD TO HAVE DIFFERENT SIZES ON THE LEFT AND RIGHT.
...
SWSH
SWSH
SWSH
IN OTHER WORDS, THIS WILL BE A FULL BODY MAKE-OVER.
IF YOU ARE GOING TO CAPTURE YOUR TRUE LOVE.
SIGH...
...

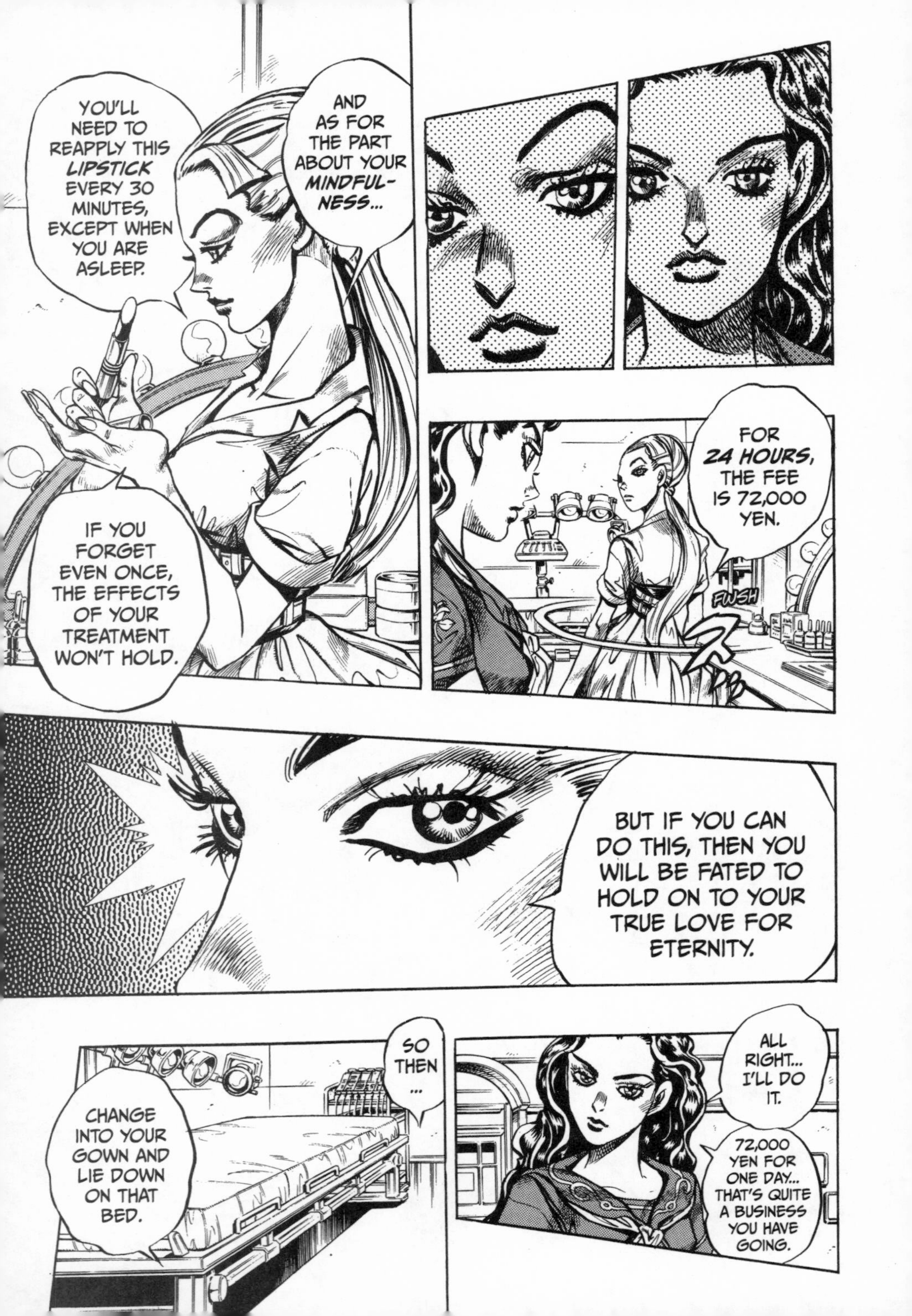
FOR 24 HOURS, THE FEE IS 72,000 YEN.
FWSH
YOU'LL NEED TO REAPPLY THIS LIPSTICK EVERY 30 MINUTES, EXCEPT WHEN YOU ARE ASLEEP.
IF YOU FORGET EVEN ONCE, THE EFFECTS OF YOUR TREATMENT WON'T HOLD.
AND AS FOR THE PART ABOUT YOUR MINDFUL-NESS...
BUT IF YOU CAN DO THIS, THEN YOU WILL BE FATED TO HOLD ON TO YOUR TRUE LOVE FOR ETERNITY.
ALL RIGHT... I'LL DO IT.
72,000 YEN FOR ONE DAY... THAT'S QUITE A BUSINESS YOU HAVE GOING.
SO THEN ...
CHANGE INTO YOUR GOWN AND LIE DOWN ON THAT BED.

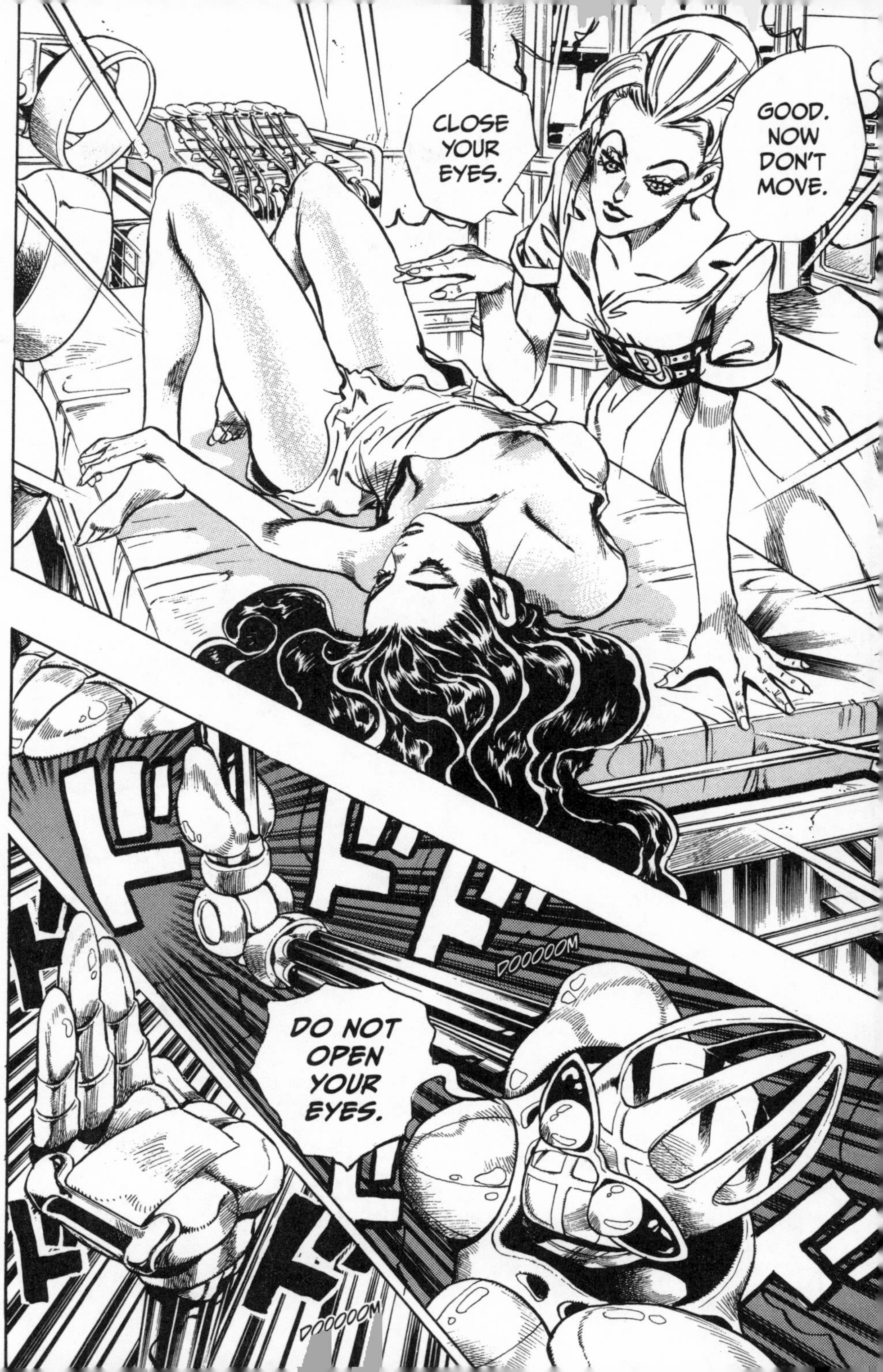
GOOD. NOW DON'T MOVE.
CLOSE YOUR EYES.
DOOOOOM
DO NOT OPEN YOUR EYES.
DOOOOOM

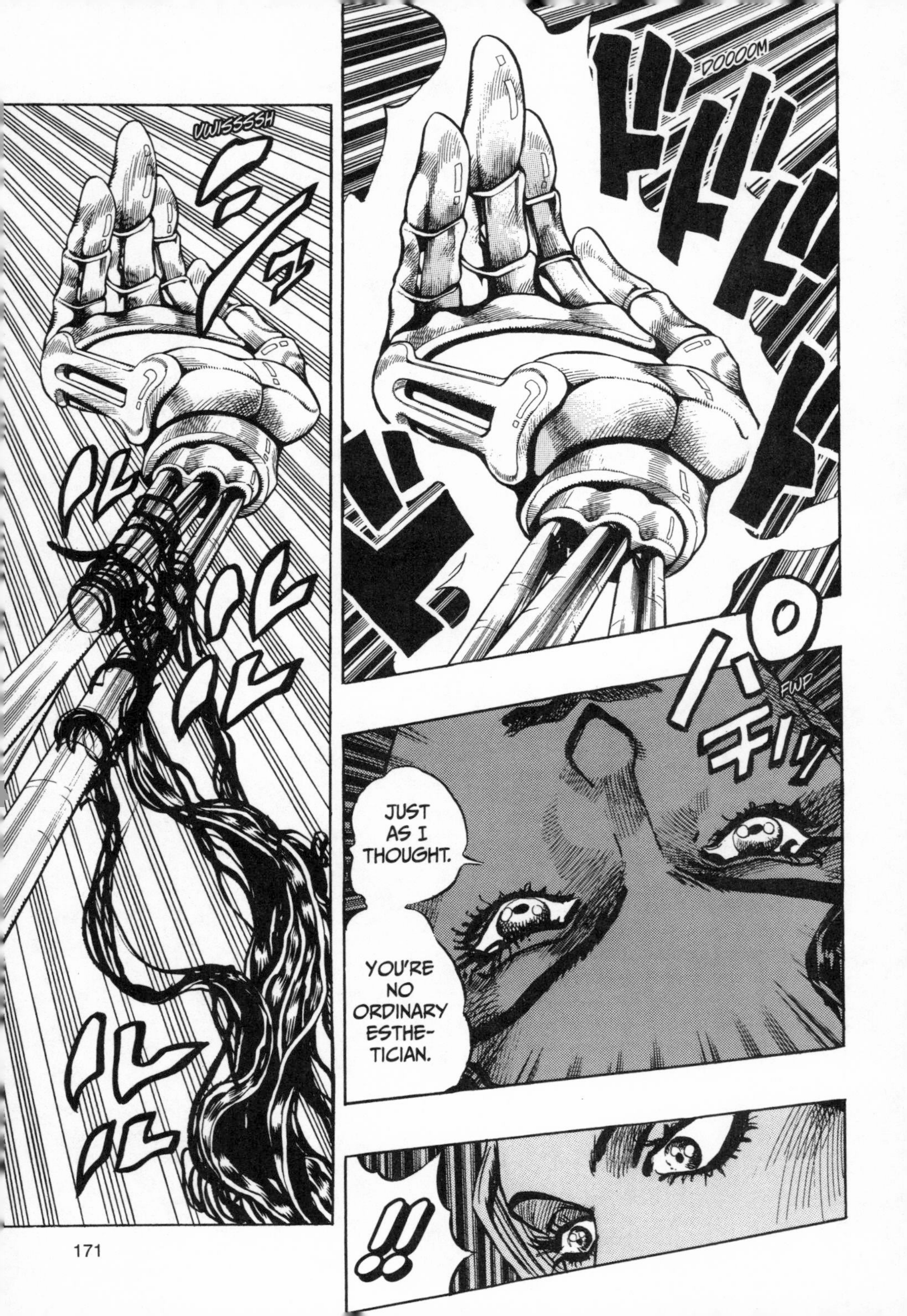
DOOOOM
FWP
JUST AS I THOUGHT.
YOU'RE NO ORDINARY ESTHETICIAN.
VWISSSSH

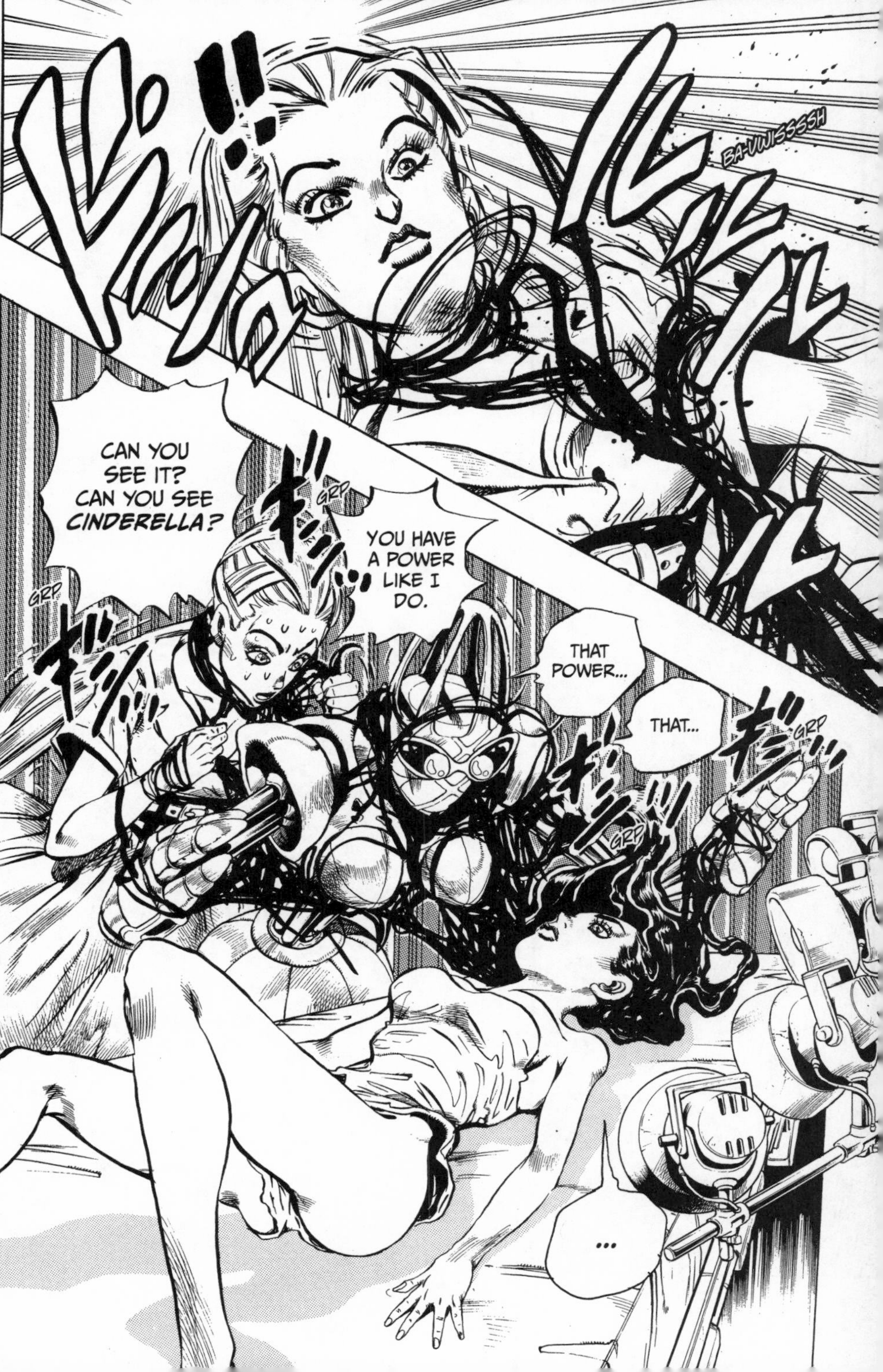
BA-UWISSSSH
CAN YOU SEE IT? CAN YOU SEE CINDERELLA?
GRP
YOU HAVE A POWER LIKE I DO.
GRP
THAT POWER...
THAT...
GRP
GRP
...

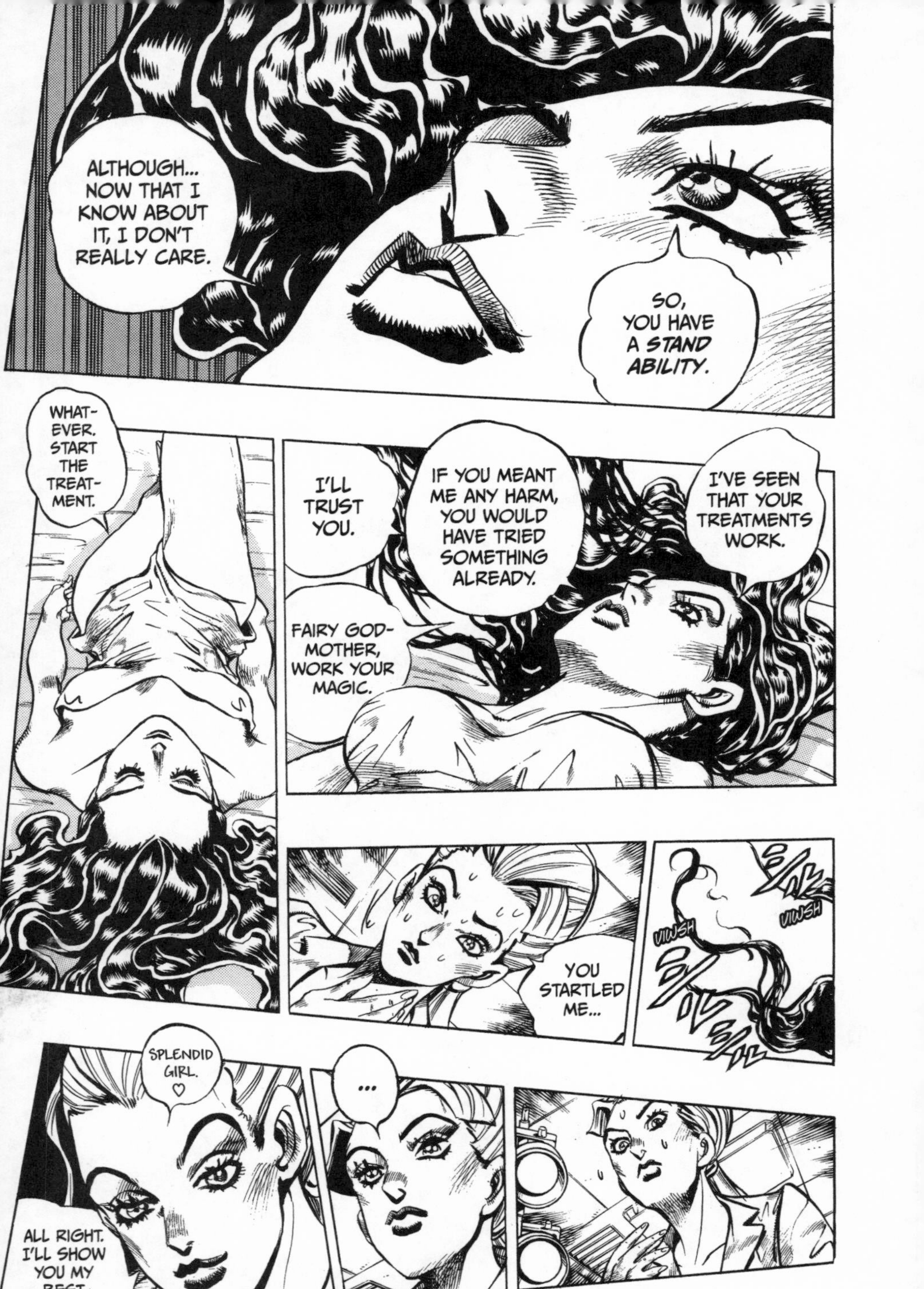
SO, YOU HAVE A *STAND ABILITY.*
ALTHOUGH... NOW THAT I KNOW ABOUT IT, I DON'T REALLY CARE.
I'VE SEEN THAT YOUR TREATMENTS WORK.
IF YOU MEANT ME ANY HARM, YOU WOULD HAVE TRIED SOMETHING ALREADY.
I'LL TRUST YOU.
FAIRY GOD-MOTHER, WORK YOUR MAGIC.
VIWSH
VIWSH
YOU STARTLED ME...
WHAT-EVER. START THE TREAT-MENT.
...
SPLENDID GIRL. ♡
ALL RIGHT. I'LL SHOW YOU MY BEST WORK.

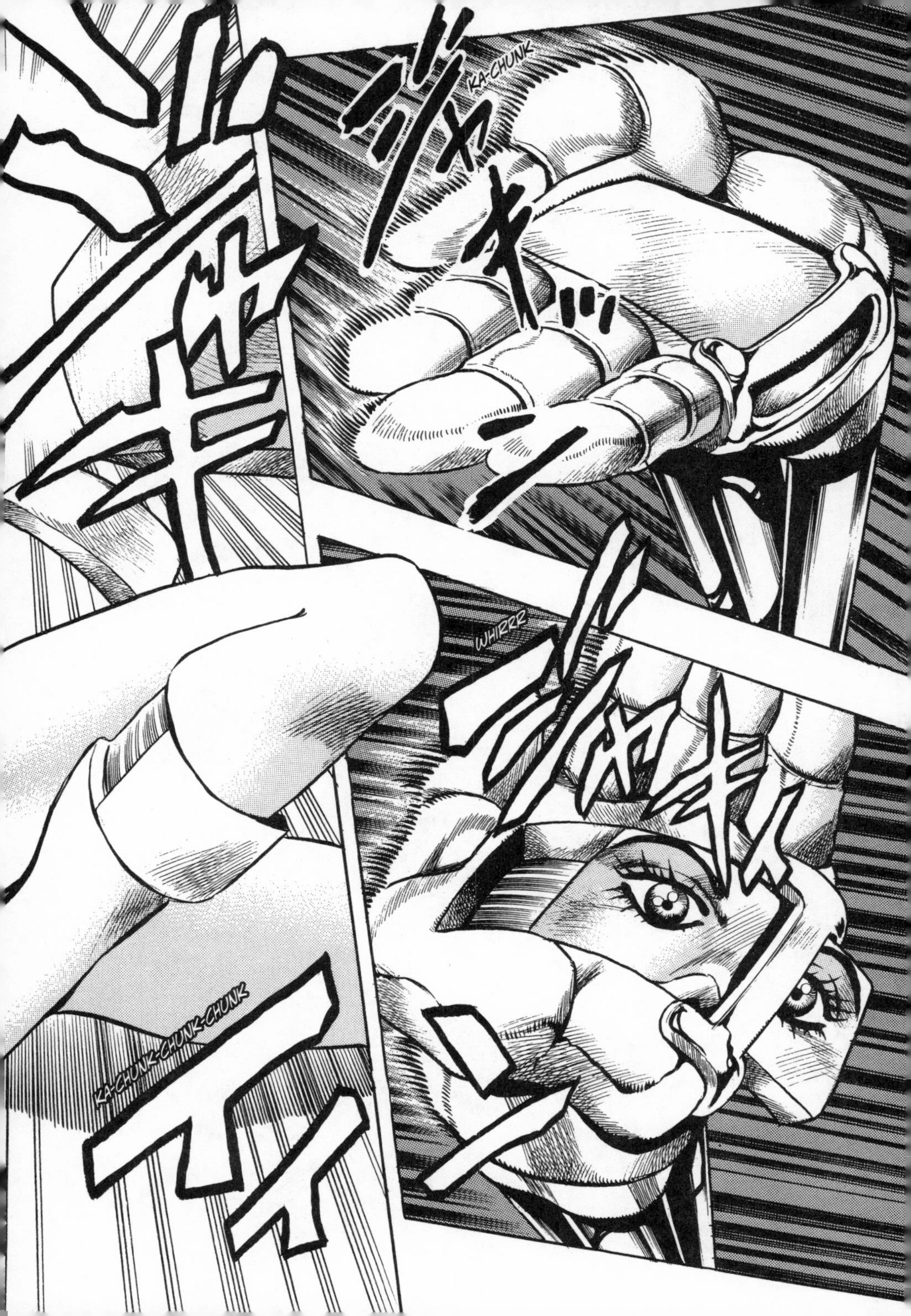
KA-CHUNK
WHIRRR
KA-CHUNK-CHUNK-CHUNK

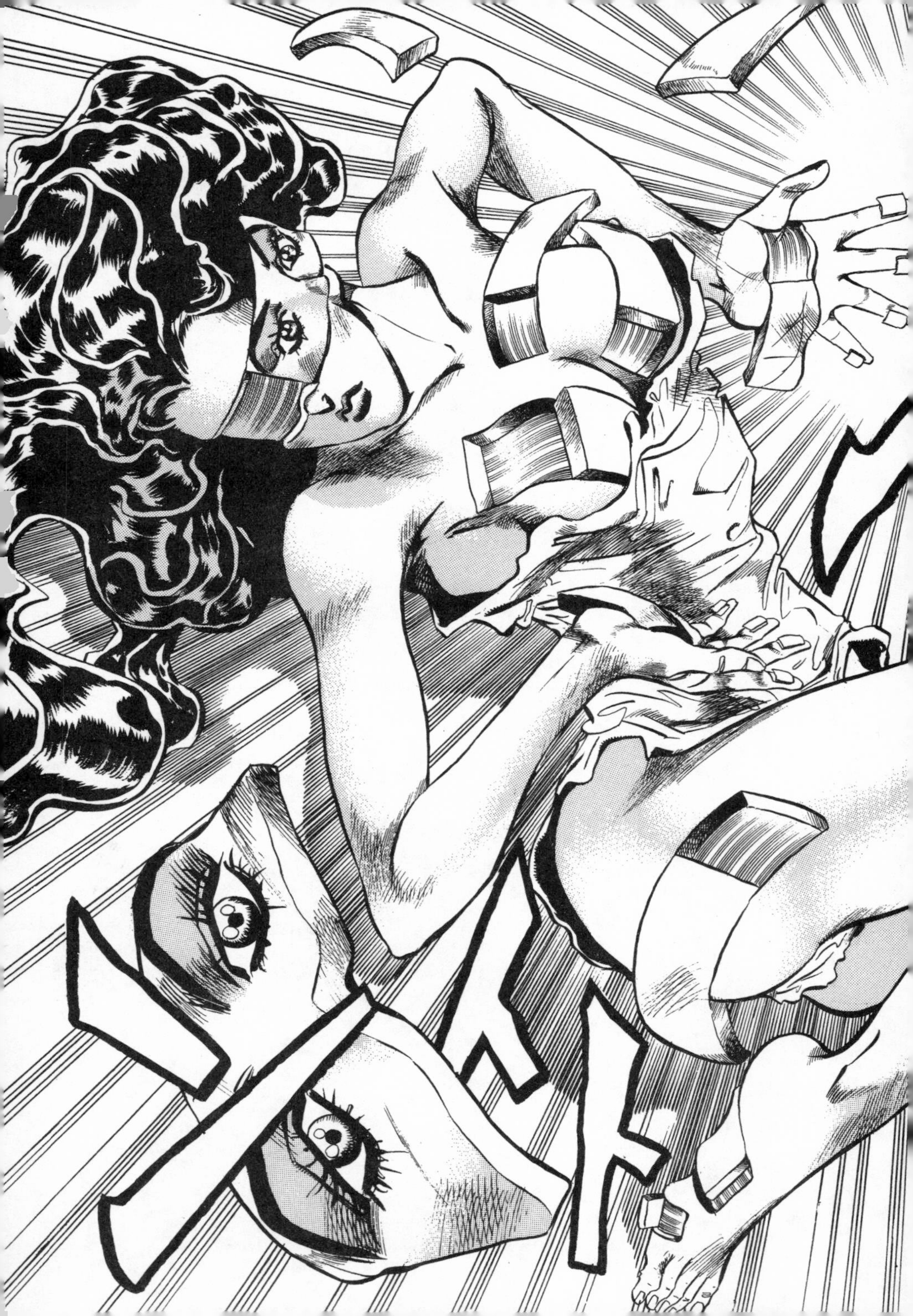

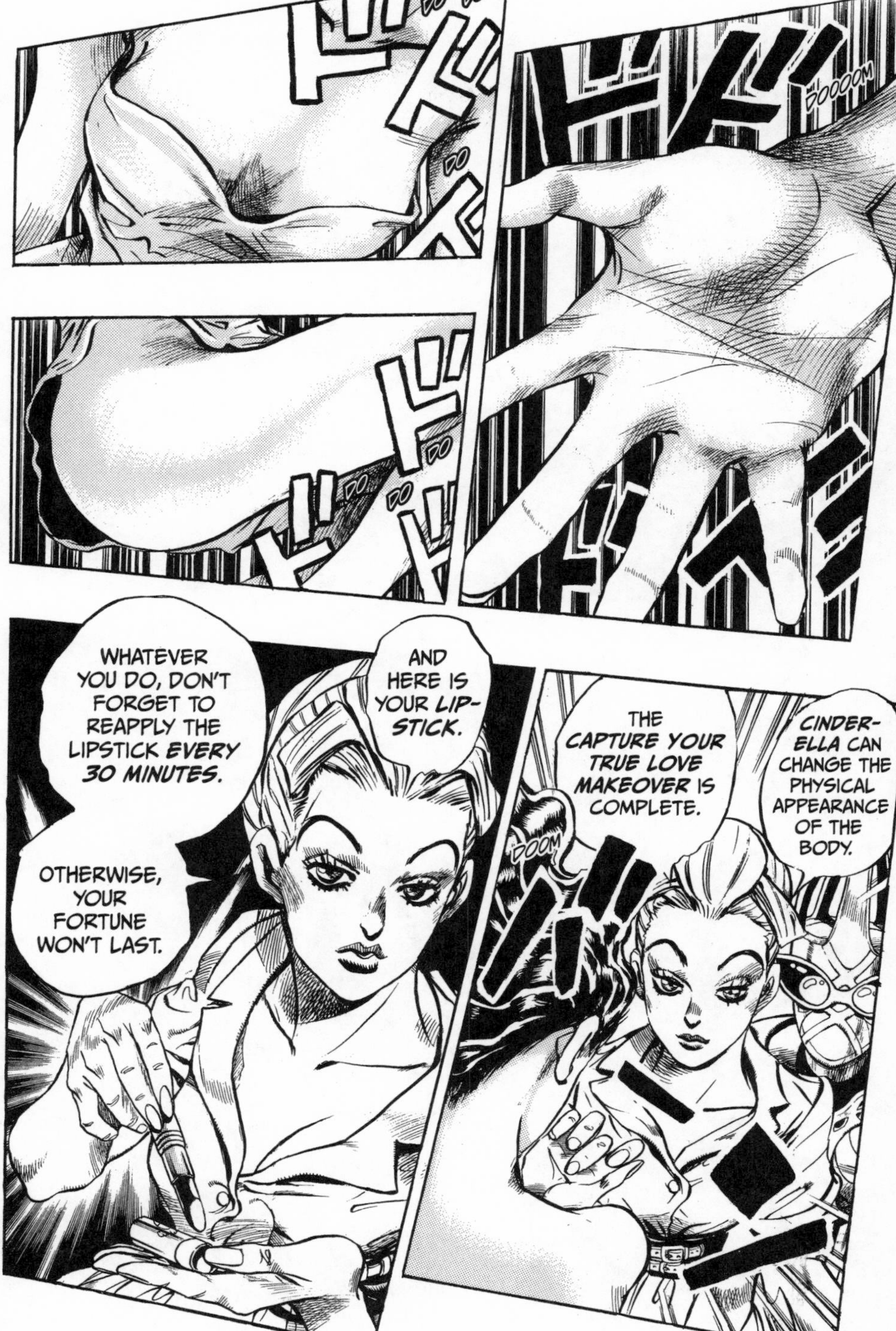
DOOOOM
DO DO
DO
DO
DO
DO
DO
CINDER-ELLA CAN CHANGE THE PHYSICAL APPEARANCE OF THE BODY.
THE CAPTURE YOUR TRUE LOVE MAKEOVER IS COMPLETE.
DOOM
AND HERE IS YOUR LIP-STICK.
WHATEVER YOU DO, DON'T FORGET TO REAPPLY THE LIPSTICK EVERY 30 MINUTES.
OTHERWISE, YOUR FORTUNE WON'T LAST.

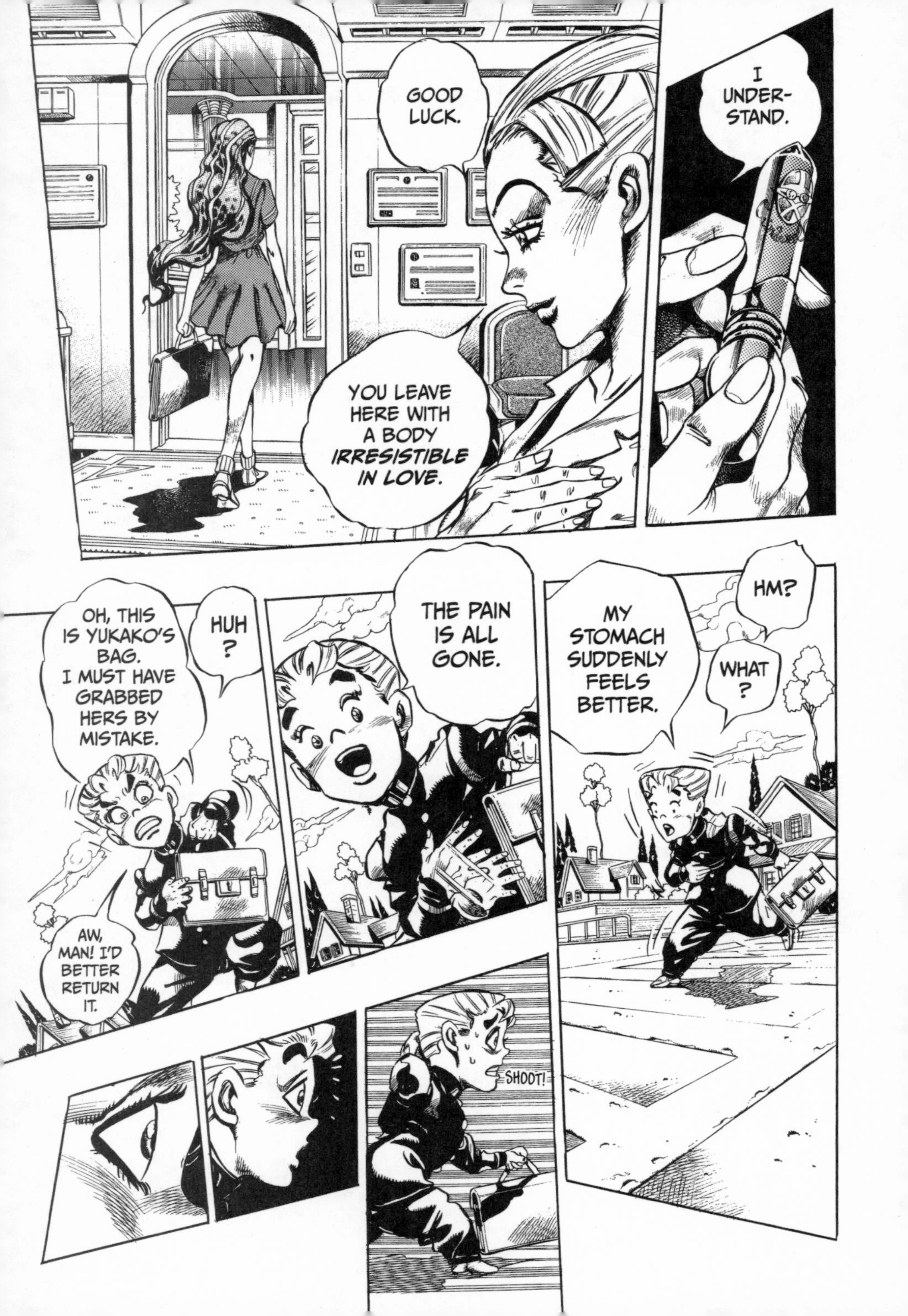
I UNDER-STAND.
GOOD LUCK.
YOU LEAVE HERE WITH A BODY *IRRESISTIBLE IN LOVE*.
HM?
MY STOMACH SUDDENLY FEELS BETTER.
WHAT?
THE PAIN IS ALL GONE.
HUH?
OH, THIS IS YUKAKO'S BAG. I MUST HAVE GRABBED HERS BY MISTAKE.
AW, MAN! I'D BETTER RETURN IT.
SHOOT!

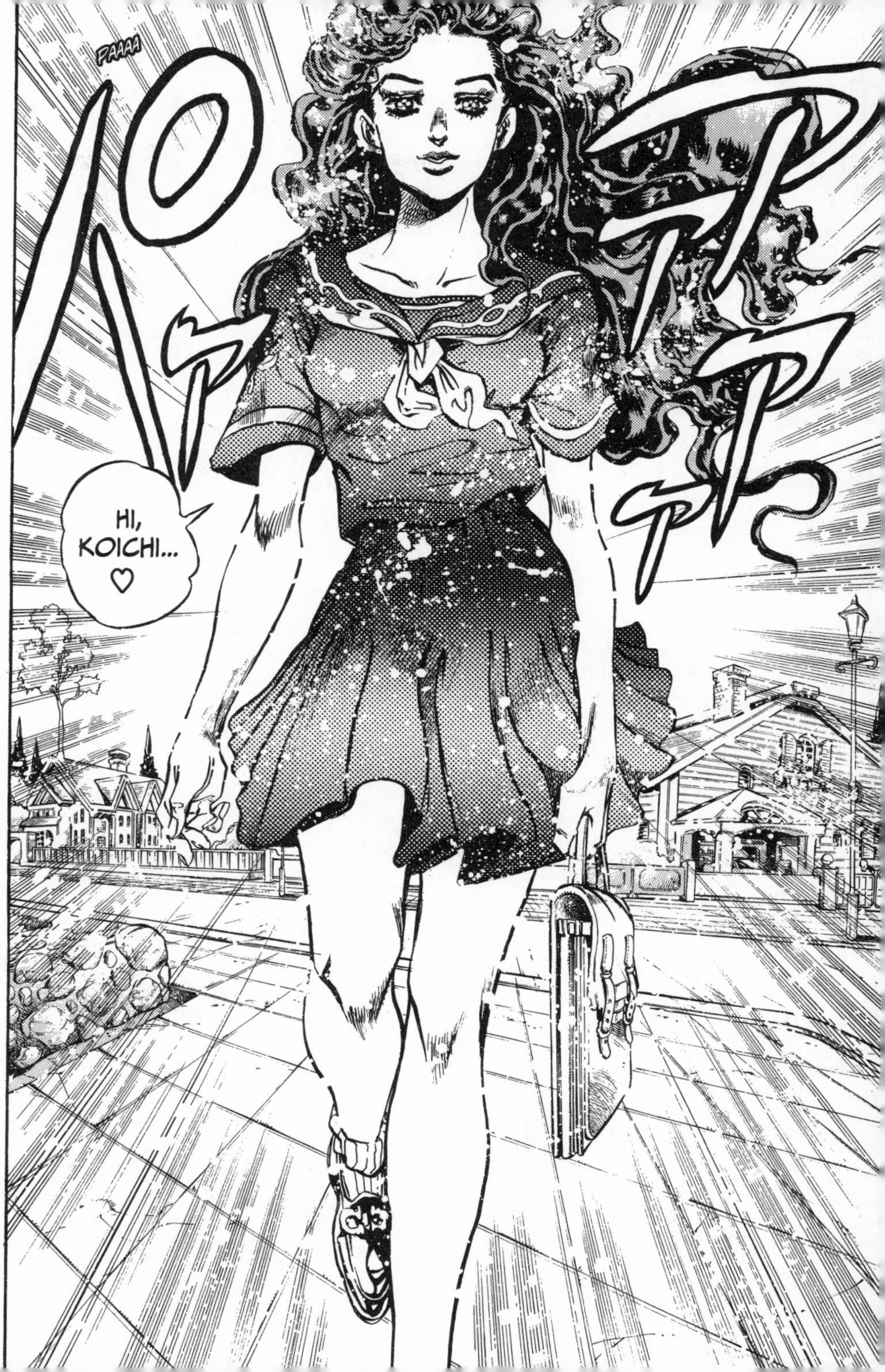
PAAAA
HI, KOICHI... ♡

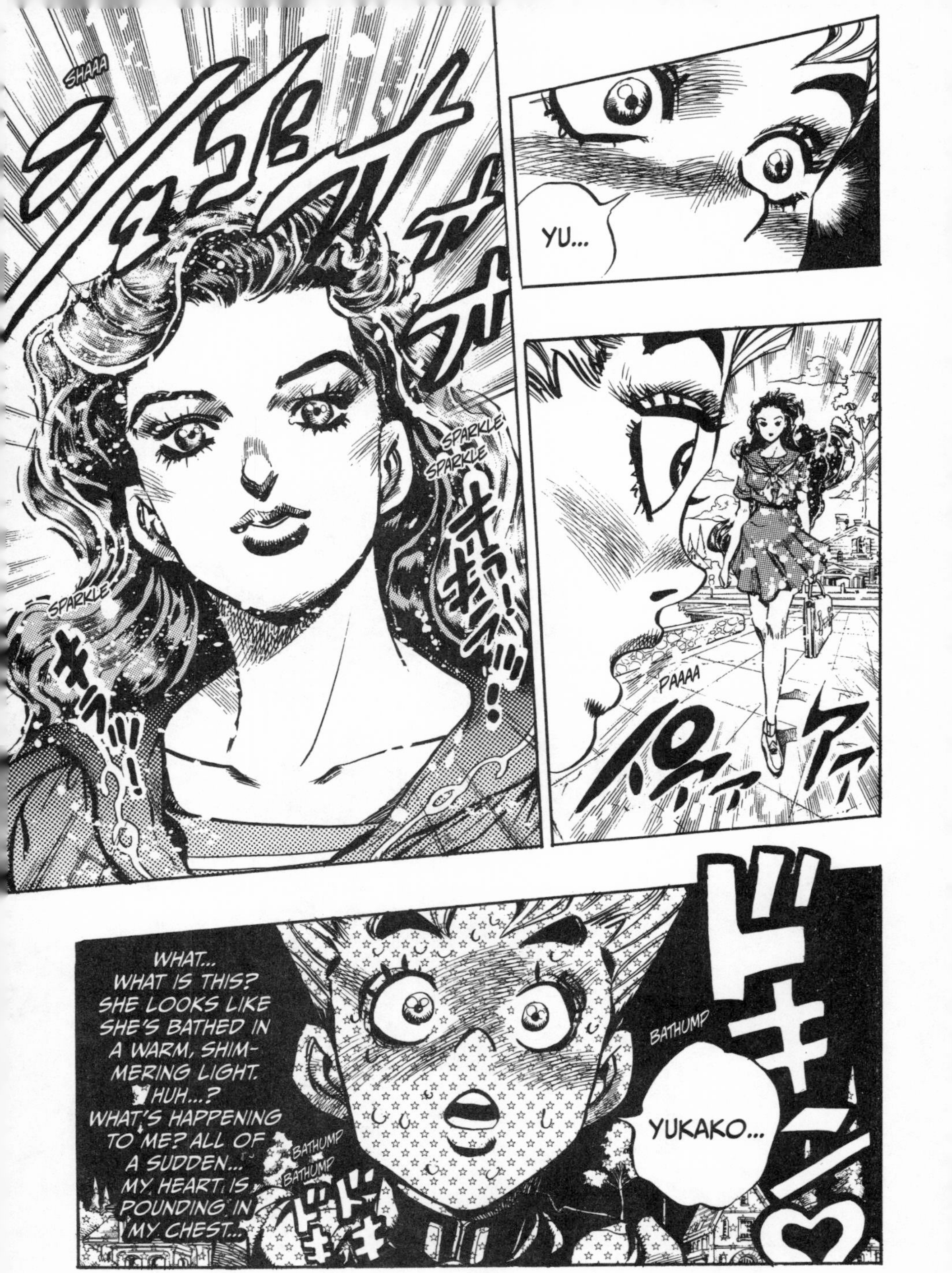
YU...
PAAAA
SHAAA
SPARKLE
SPARKLE
SPARKLE
BATHUMP
YUKAKO...
WHAT... WHAT IS THIS? SHE LOOKS LIKE SHE'S BATHED IN A WARM, SHIM-MERING LIGHT. HUH...? WHAT'S HAPPENING TO ME? ALL OF A SUDDEN... MY HEART IS POUNDING IN MY CHEST...
BATHUMP
BATHUMP

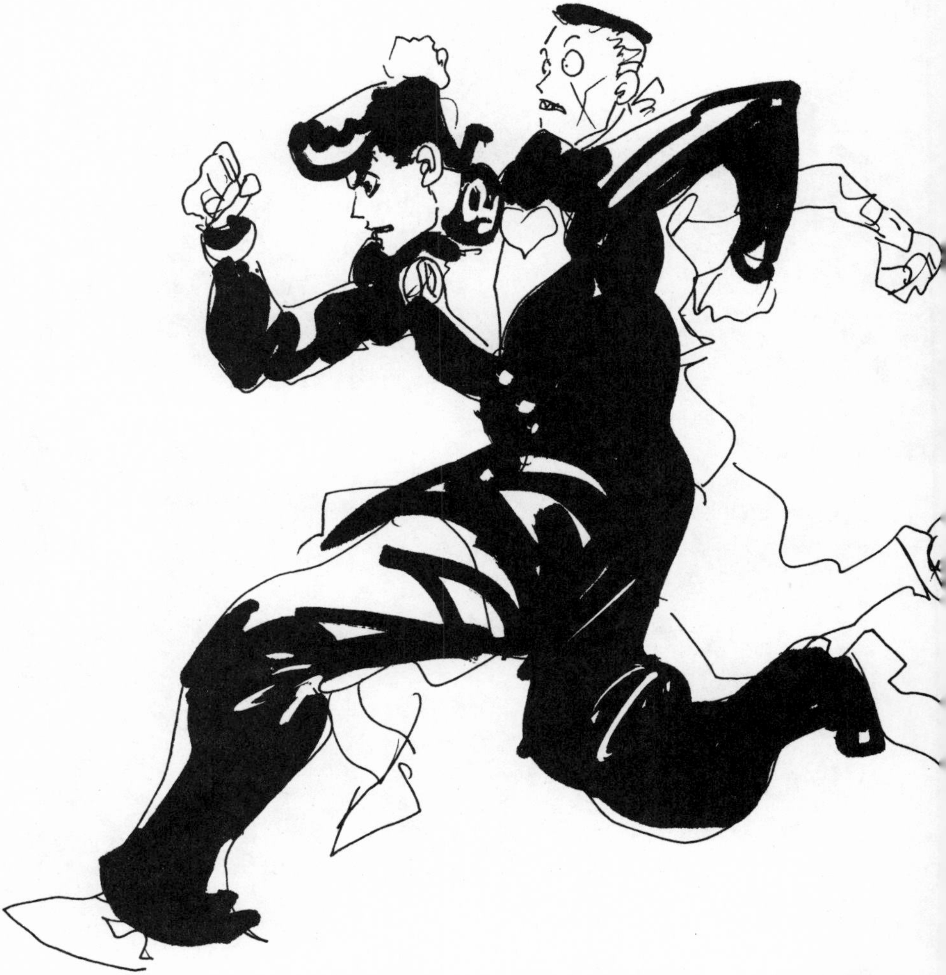

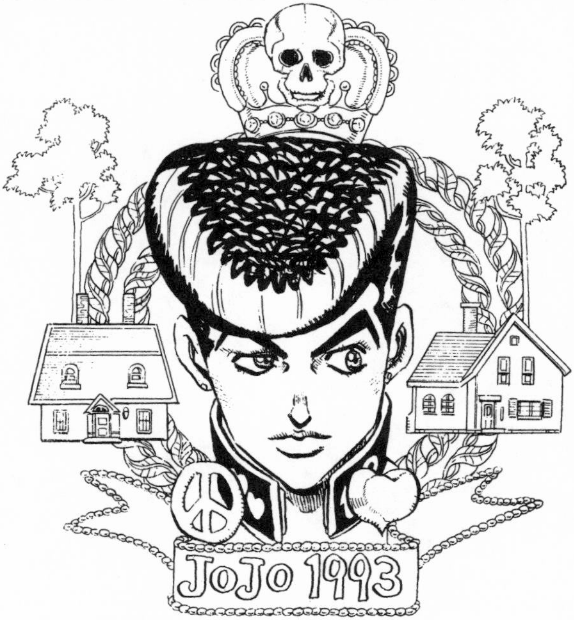
JoJo 1993

1993 Postcard Illustration

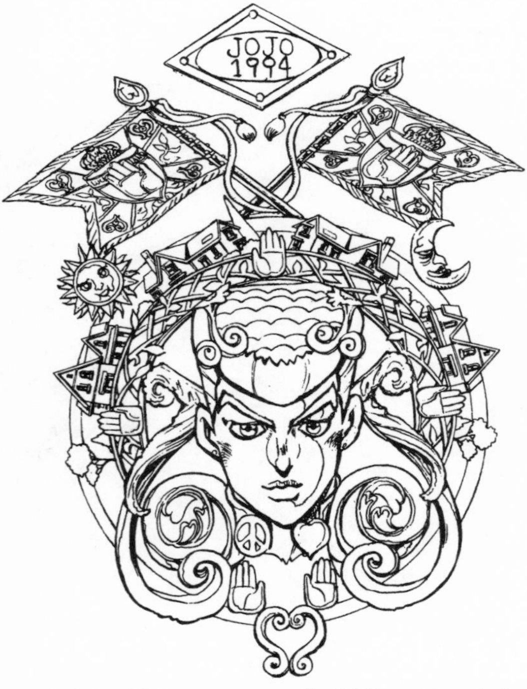
JOJO
1994

1994 Postcard Illustration

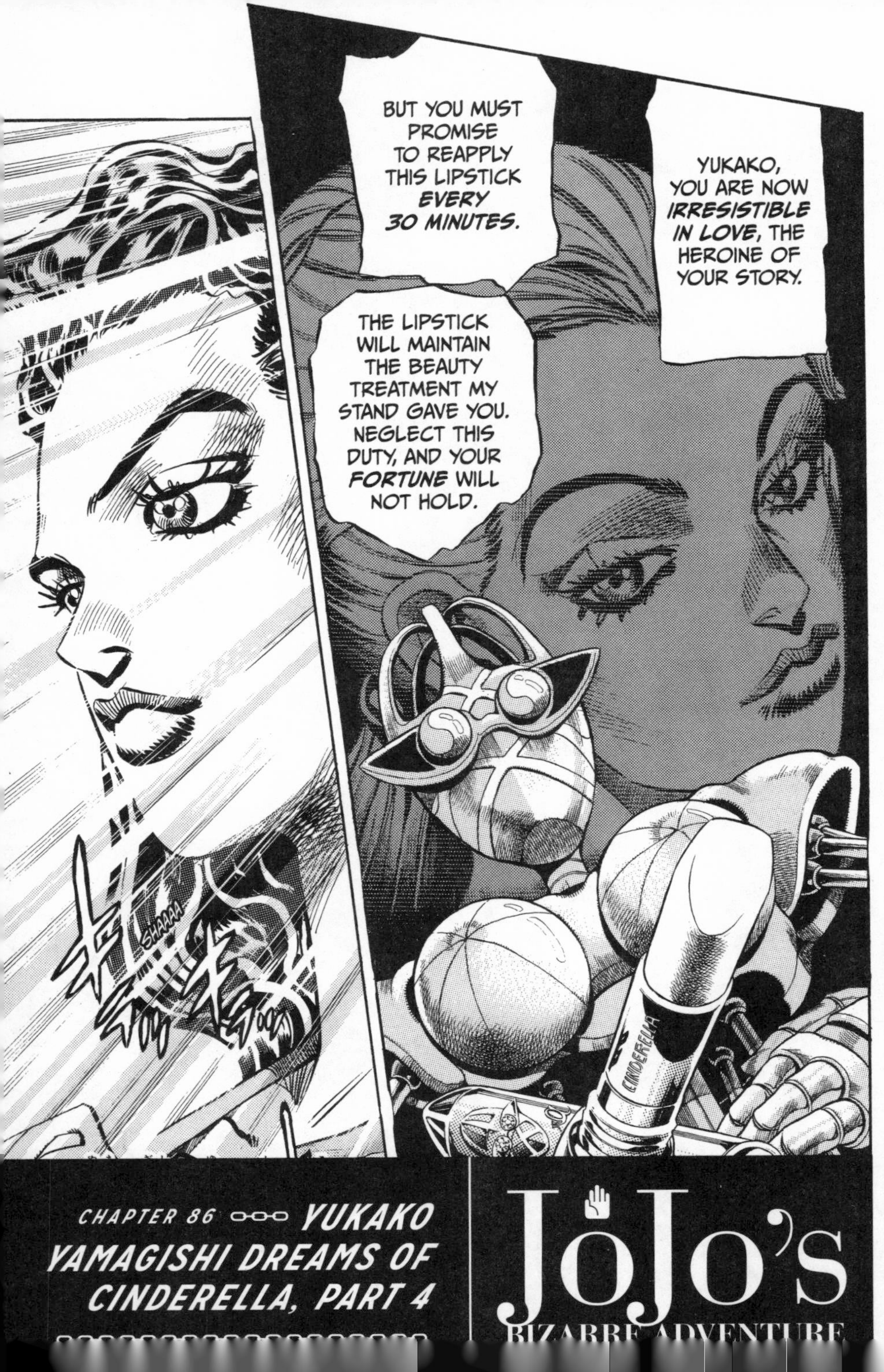
YUKAKO, YOU ARE NOW IRRESISTIBLE IN LOVE, THE HEROINE OF YOUR STORY.
BUT YOU MUST PROMISE TO REAPPLY THIS LIPSTICK EVERY 30 MINUTES.
THE LIPSTICK WILL MAINTAIN THE BEAUTY TREATMENT MY STAND GAVE YOU. NEGLECT THIS DUTY, AND YOUR FORTUNE WILL NOT HOLD.
CINDERELLA
SHAAAA

CHAPTER 86 ○-○-○ YUKAKO YAMAGISHI DREAMS OF CINDERELLA, PART 4

JoJo's BIZARRE ADVENTURE

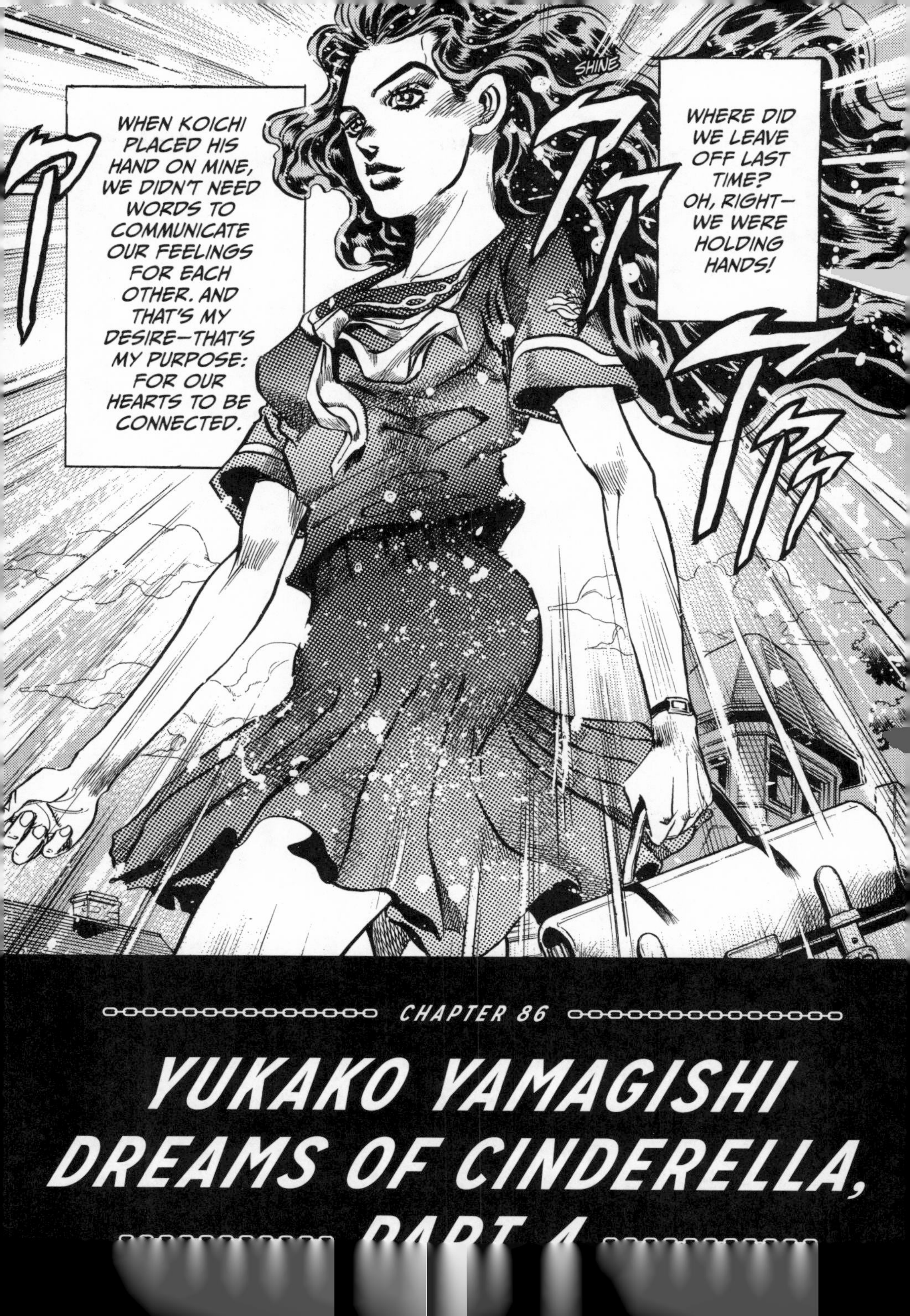
SHINE
WHERE DID WE LEAVE OFF LAST TIME? OH, RIGHT—WE WERE HOLDING HANDS!
WHEN KOICHI PLACED HIS HAND ON MINE, WE DIDN'T NEED WORDS TO COMMUNICATE OUR FEELINGS FOR EACH OTHER. AND THAT'S MY DESIRE—THAT'S MY PURPOSE: FOR OUR HEARTS TO BE CONNECTED.

CHAPTER 86

YUKAKO YAMAGISHI DREAMS OF CINDERELLA, PART 4

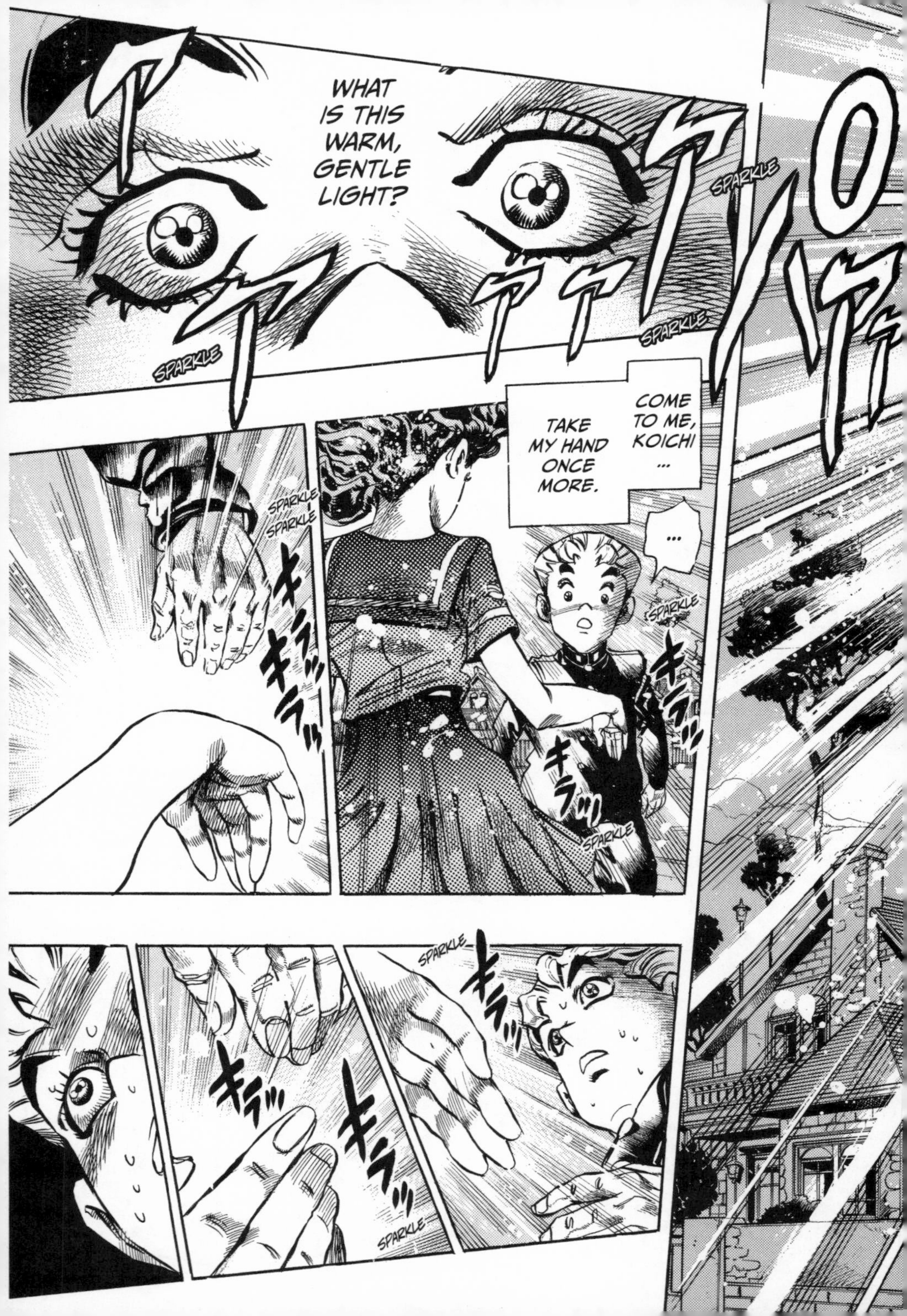
SPARKLE
WHAT IS THIS WARM, GENTLE LIGHT?
SPARKLE
SPARKLE
COME TO ME, KOICHI ...
TAKE MY HAND ONCE MORE.
...
SPARKLE
SPARKLE
SPARKLE
SPARKLE
SPARKLE
SPARKLE

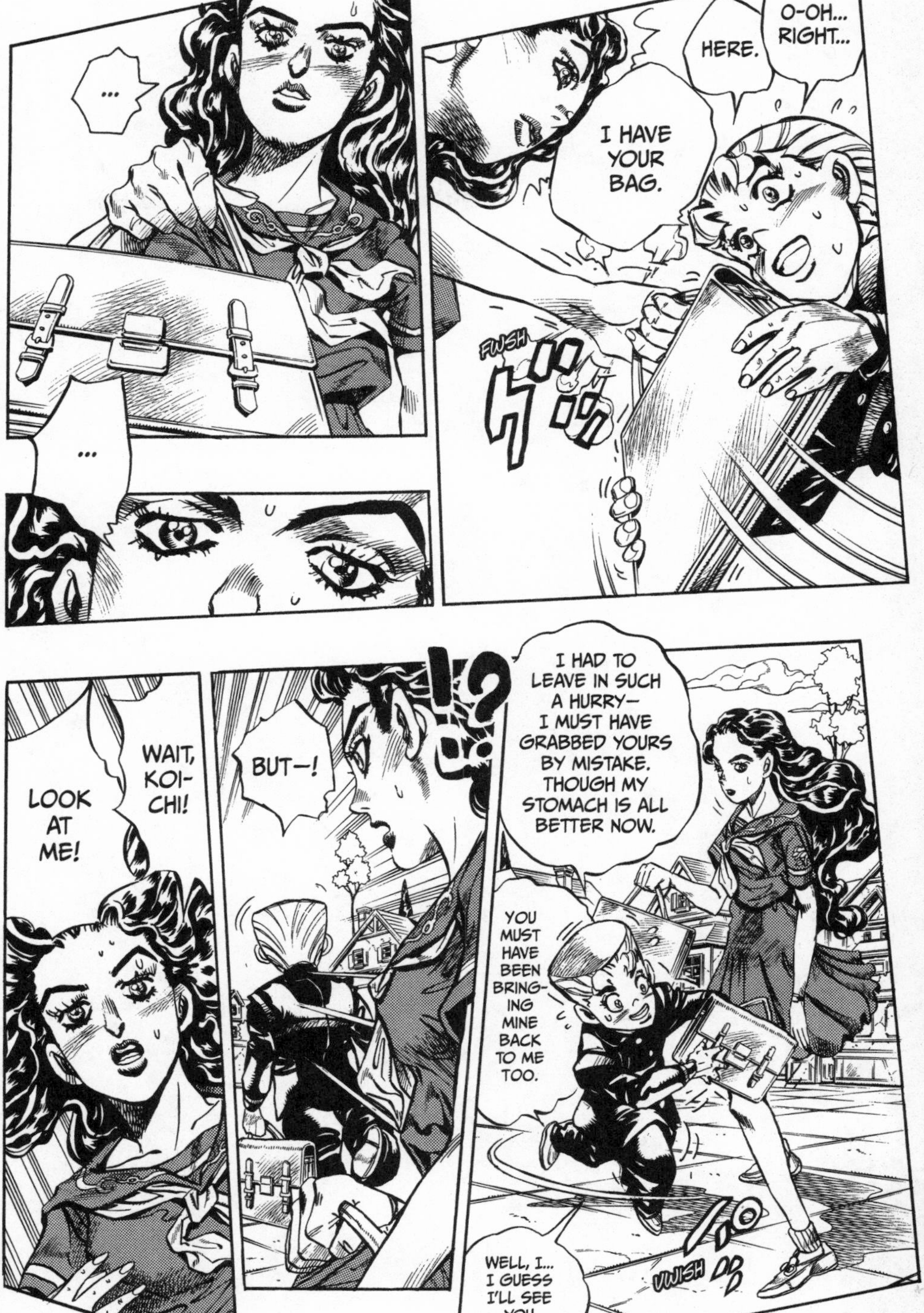
O-OH... RIGHT...
HERE.
I HAVE YOUR BAG.
FWSH
...
...
I HAD TO LEAVE IN SUCH A HURRY— I MUST HAVE GRABBED YOURS BY MISTAKE. THOUGH MY STOMACH IS ALL BETTER NOW.
YOU MUST HAVE BEEN BRING-ING MINE BACK TO ME TOO.
WELL, I... I GUESS I'LL SEE YOU LATER!
VWISH
!?
BUT—!
WAIT, KOI-CHI!
LOOK AT ME!

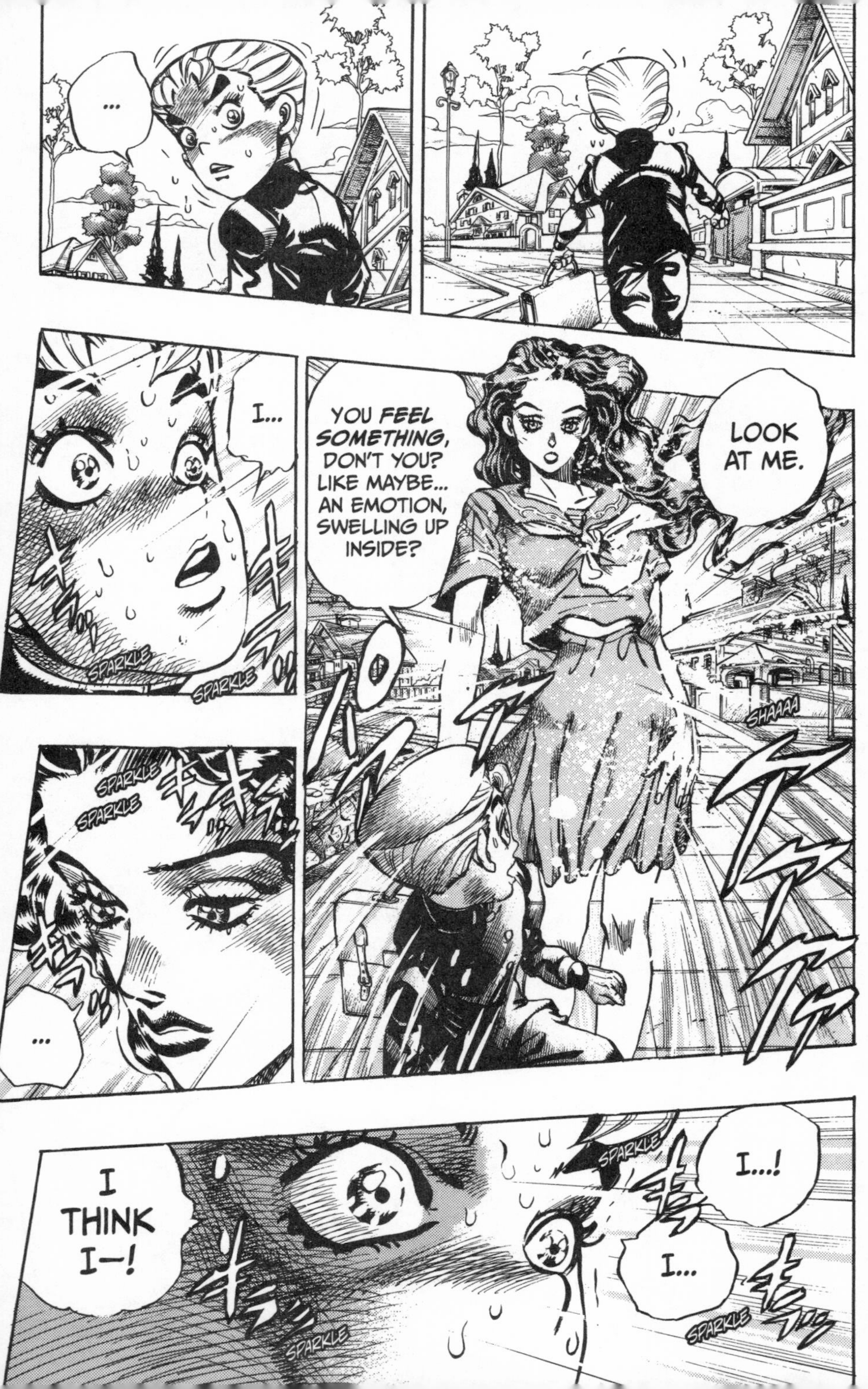
...
LOOK AT ME.
YOU *FEEL SOMETHING*, DON'T YOU? LIKE MAYBE... AN EMOTION, SWELLING UP INSIDE?
SHAAAA
I...
SPARKLE
SPARKLE
SPARKLE
SPARKLE
...
SPARKLE
I...!
I...
SPARKLE
I THINK I—!
SPARKLE

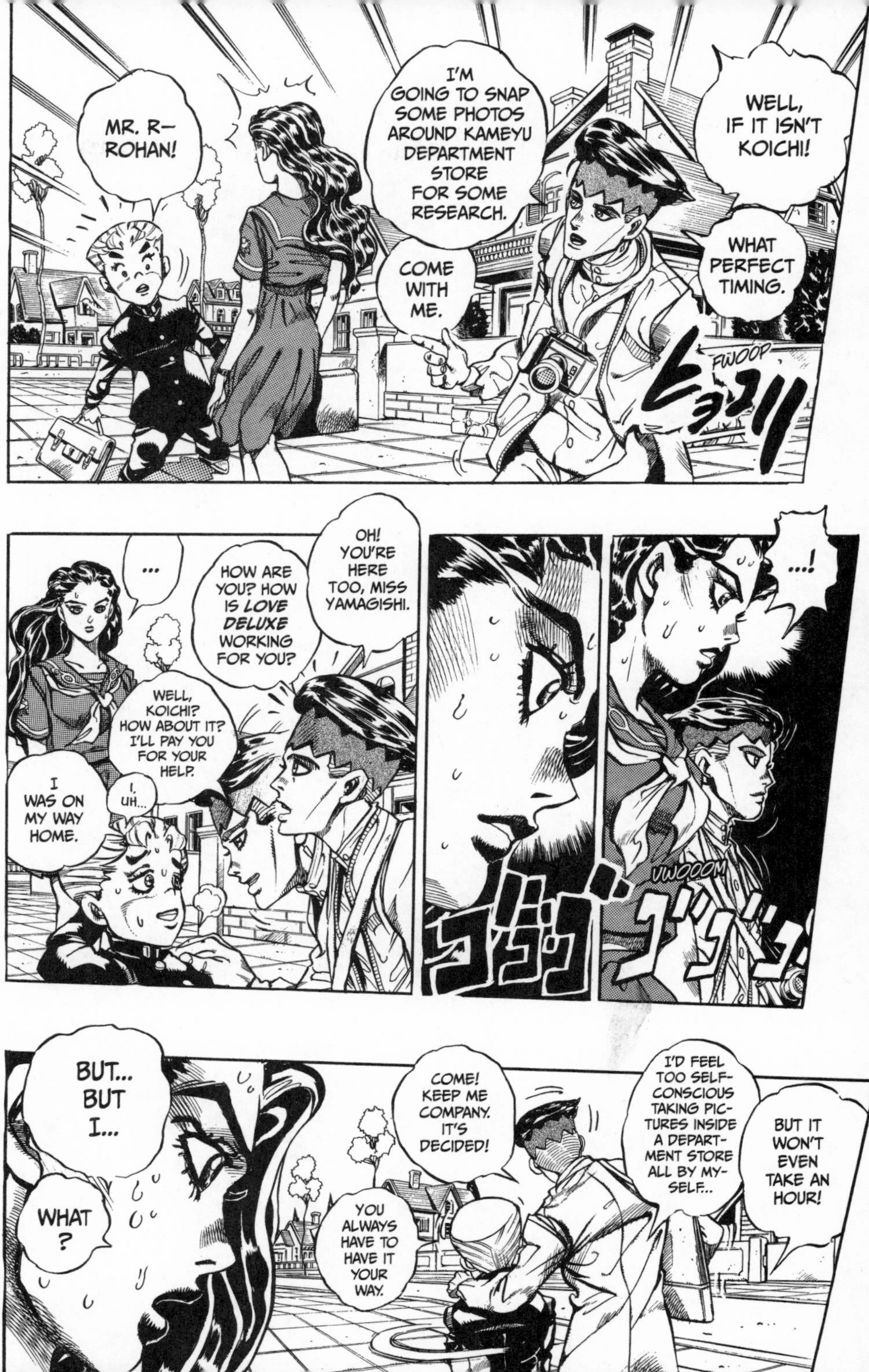
WELL, IF IT ISN'T KOICHI!
WHAT PERFECT TIMING.
FWOOP
I'M GOING TO SNAP SOME PHOTOS AROUND KAMEYU DEPARTMENT STORE FOR SOME RESEARCH.
COME WITH ME.
MR. R— ROHAN!
...!
VWOOOM
OH! YOU'RE HERE TOO, MISS YAMAGISHI.
HOW ARE YOU? HOW IS *LOVE DELUXE* WORKING FOR YOU?
...
WELL, KOICHI? HOW ABOUT IT? I'LL PAY YOU FOR YOUR HELP.
I, UH...
I WAS ON MY WAY HOME.
BUT IT WON'T EVEN TAKE AN HOUR!
I'D FEEL TOO SELF-CONSCIOUS TAKING PICTURES INSIDE A DEPARTMENT STORE ALL BY MYSELF...
COME! KEEP ME COMPANY. IT'S DECIDED!
YOU ALWAYS HAVE TO HAVE IT YOUR WAY.
BUT... BUT I...
WHAT?

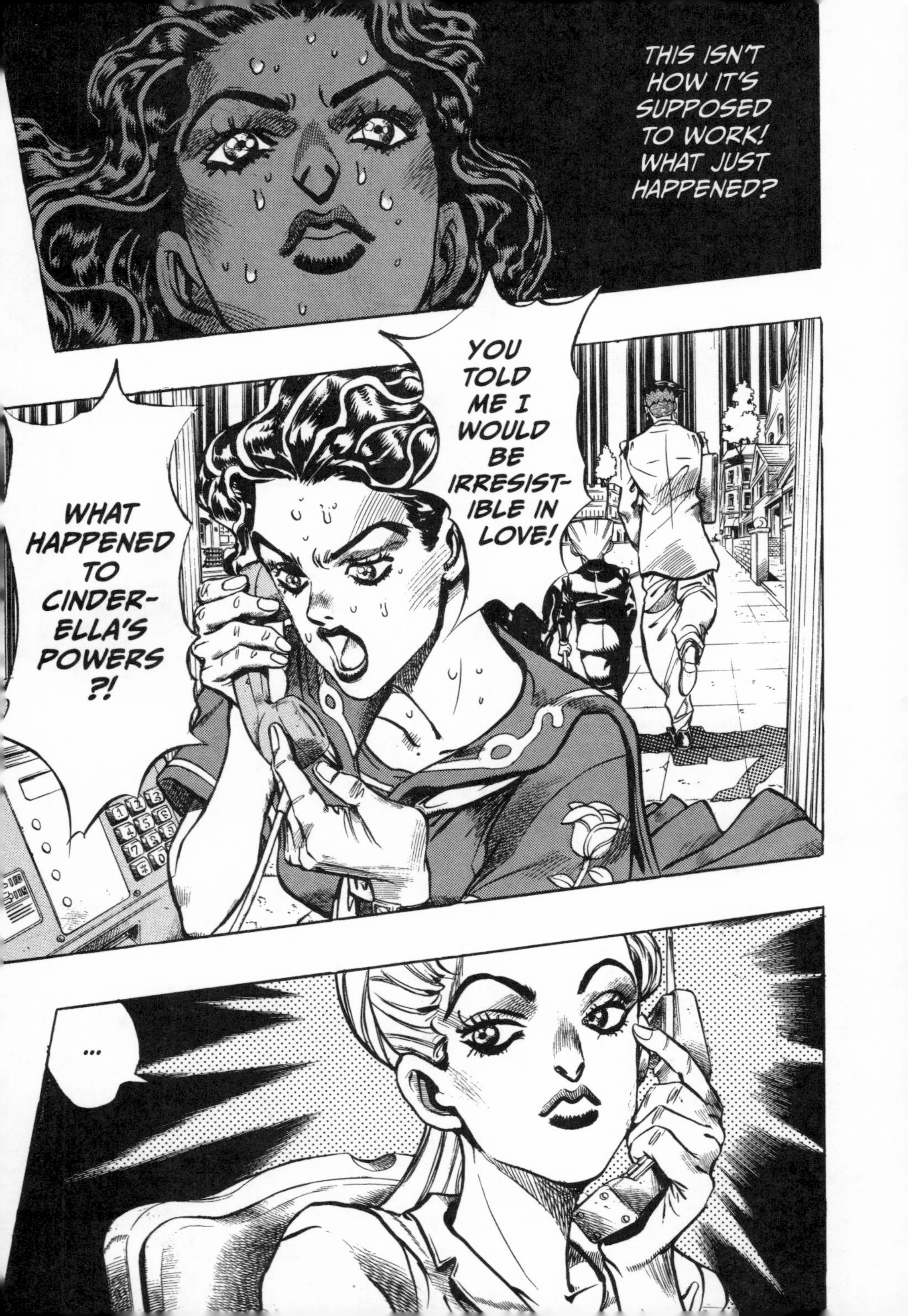
THIS ISN'T HOW IT'S SUPPOSED TO WORK! WHAT JUST HAPPENED?
YOU TOLD ME I WOULD BE IRRESIST-IBLE IN LOVE!
WHAT HAPPENED TO CINDER-ELLA'S POWERS ?!
...

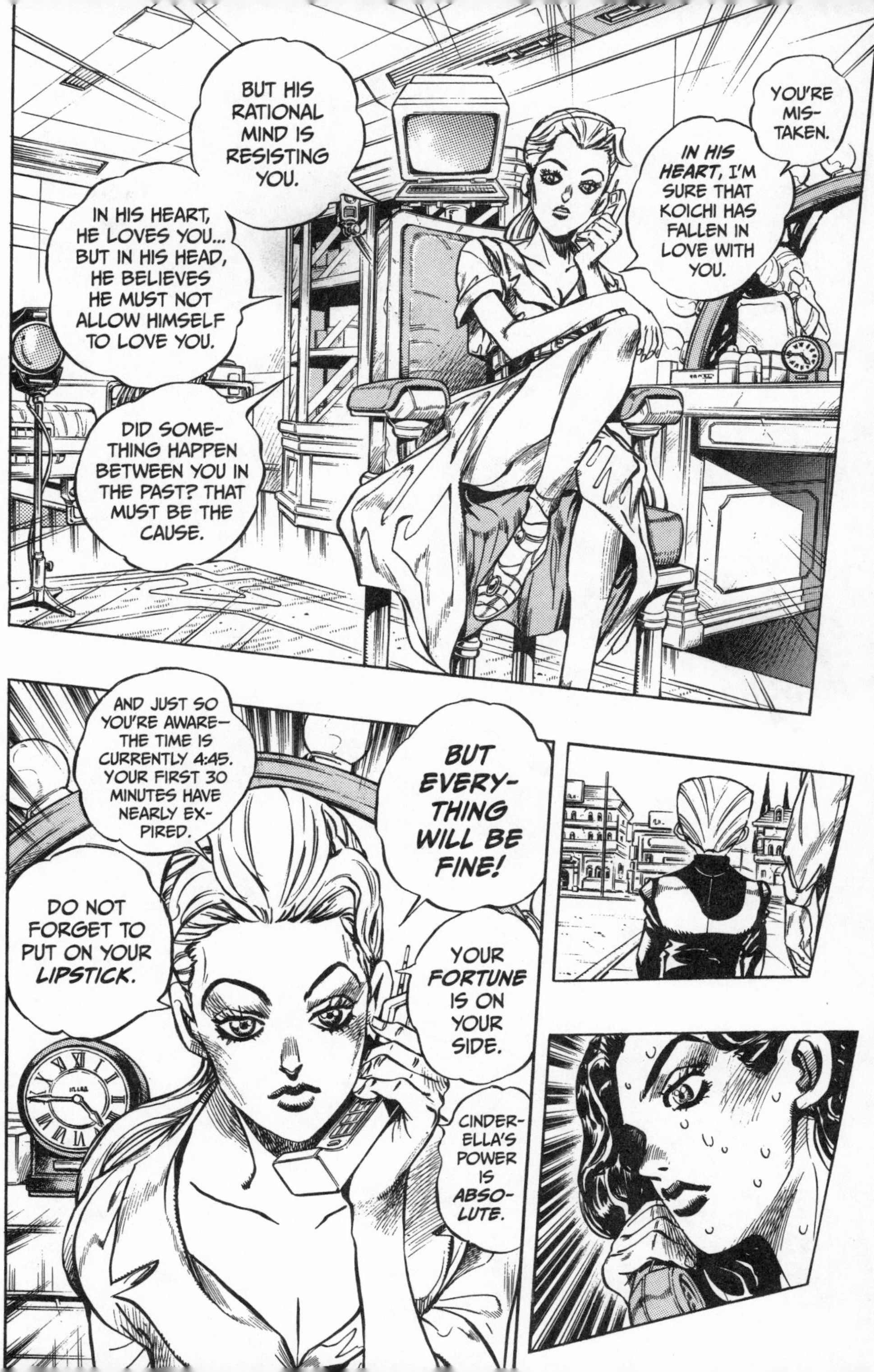
YOU'RE MIS-TAKEN.
IN HIS HEART, I'M SURE THAT KOICHI HAS FALLEN IN LOVE WITH YOU.
BUT HIS RATIONAL MIND IS RESISTING YOU.
IN HIS HEART, HE LOVES YOU... BUT IN HIS HEAD, HE BELIEVES HE MUST NOT ALLOW HIMSELF TO LOVE YOU.
DID SOME-THING HAPPEN BETWEEN YOU IN THE PAST? THAT MUST BE THE CAUSE.
BUT EVERY-THING WILL BE FINE!
YOUR *FORTUNE* IS ON YOUR SIDE.
CINDER-ELLA'S POWER IS *ABSO-LUTE*.
AND JUST SO YOU'RE AWARE— THE TIME IS CURRENTLY 4:45. YOUR FIRST 30 MINUTES HAVE NEARLY EX-PIRED.
DO NOT FORGET TO PUT ON YOUR *LIPSTICK*.

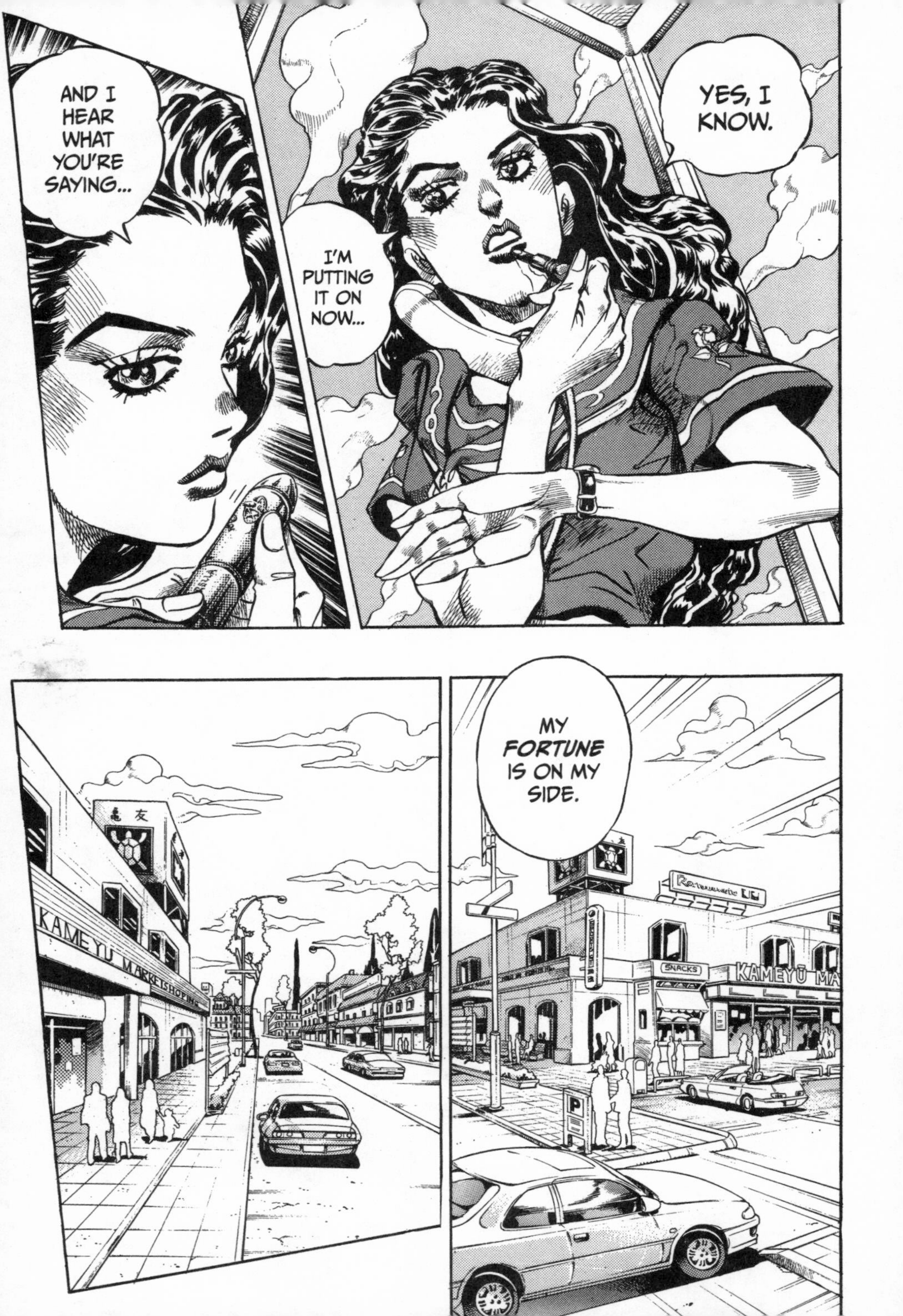
YES, I KNOW.
I'M PUTTING IT ON NOW...
AND I HEAR WHAT YOU'RE SAYING...
MY *FORTUNE* IS ON MY SIDE.
SNACKS
KAMEYU MA
亀友
KAMEYU MARKETSHOPPING

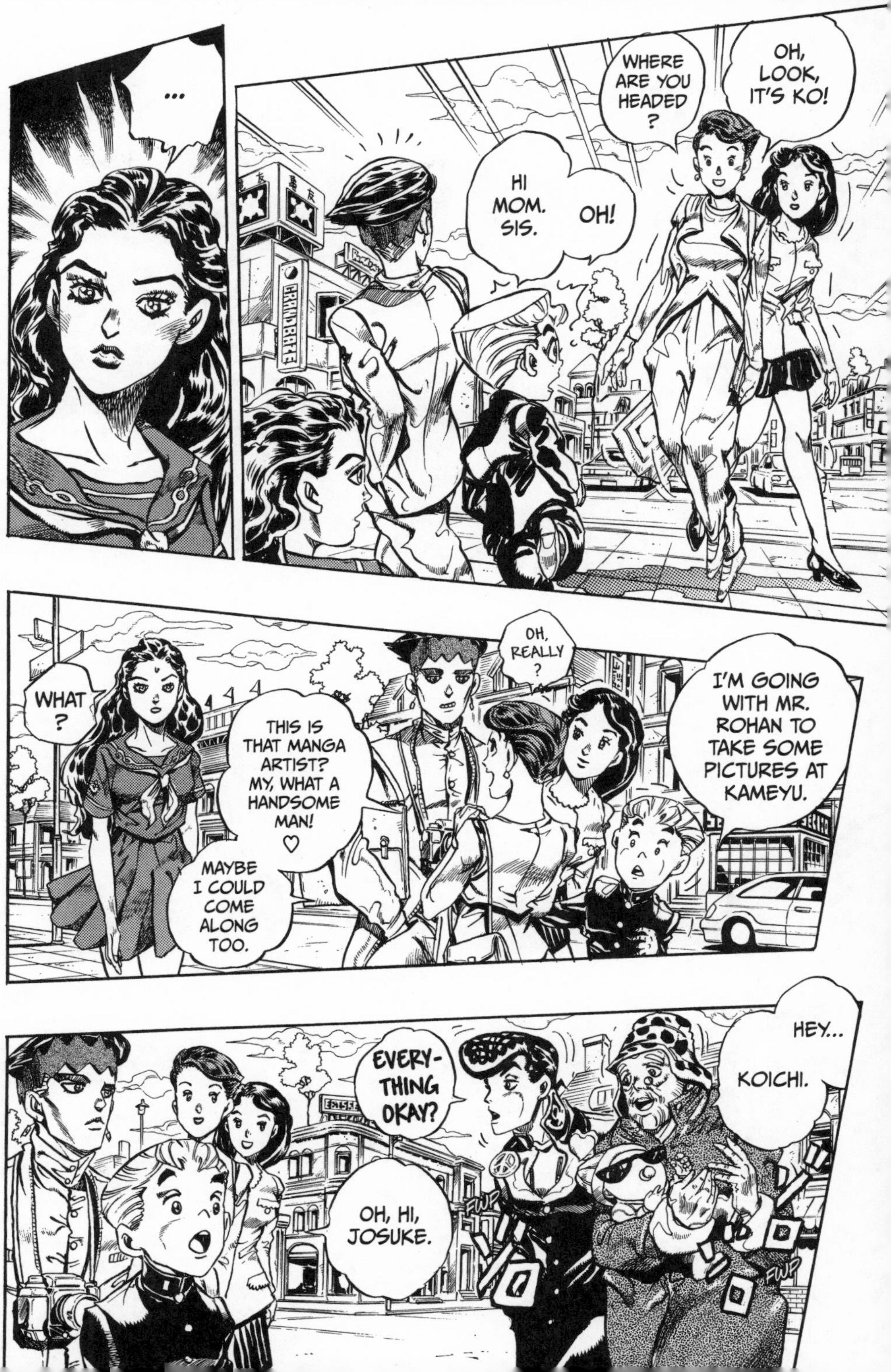
OH, LOOK, IT'S KO!
WHERE ARE YOU HEADED?
OH!
HI MOM. SIS.
...
I'M GOING WITH MR. ROHAN TO TAKE SOME PICTURES AT KAMEYU.
OH, REALLY?
THIS IS THAT MANGA ARTIST? MY, WHAT A HANDSOME MAN! ♡
MAYBE I COULD COME ALONG TOO.
WHAT?
HEY...
KOICHI.
FWUP
EVERY-THING OKAY?
FWUP
OH, HI, JOSUKE.

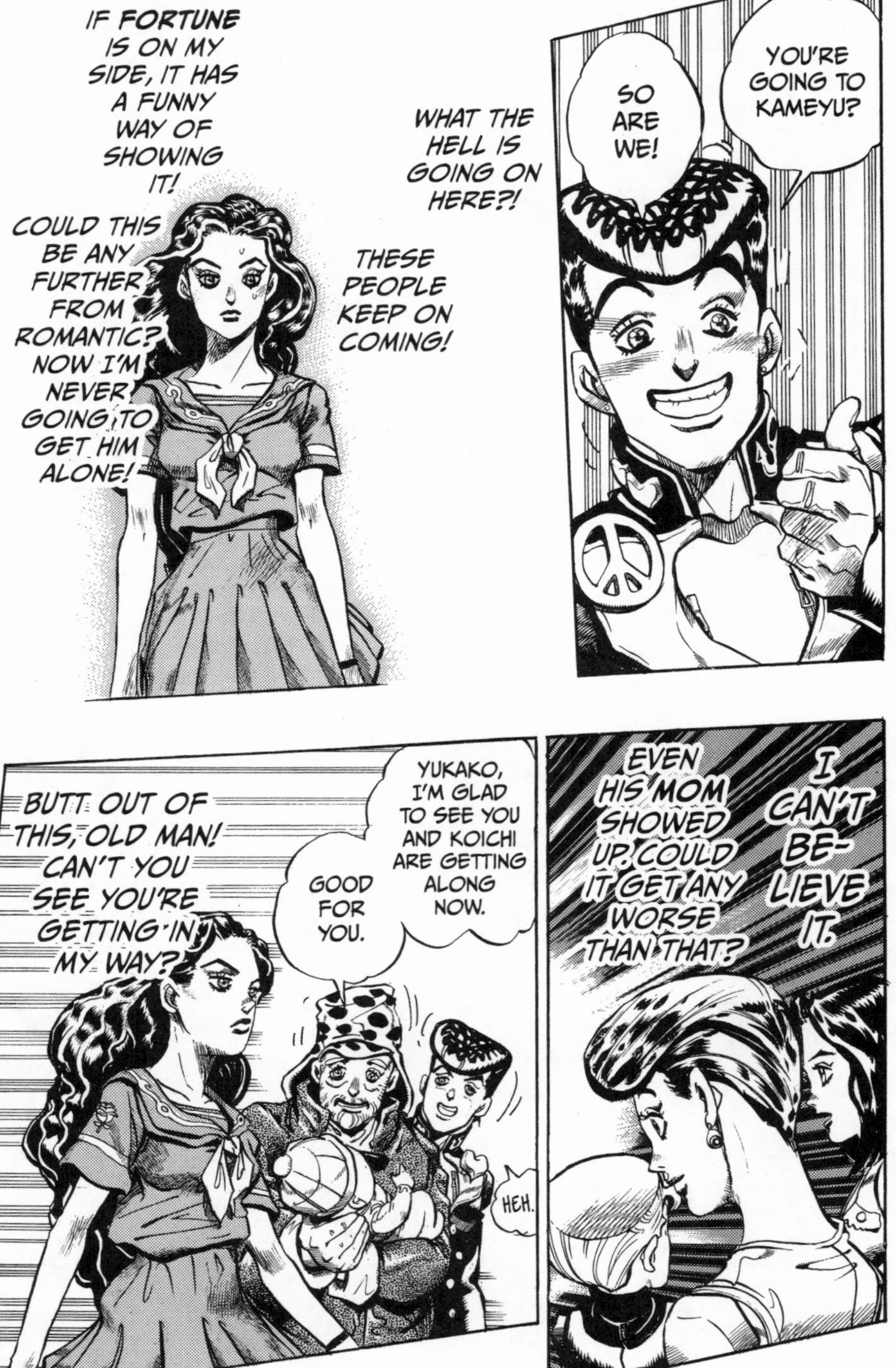
YOU'RE GOING TO KAMEYU?
SO ARE WE!
WHAT THE HELL IS GOING ON HERE?!
IF **FORTUNE** IS ON MY SIDE, IT HAS A FUNNY WAY OF SHOWING IT!
THESE PEOPLE KEEP ON COMING!
COULD THIS BE ANY FURTHER FROM ROMANTIC? NOW I'M NEVER GOING TO GET HIM ALONE!
I CAN'T BE-LIEVE IT.
EVEN HIS MOM SHOWED UP. COULD IT GET ANY WORSE THAN THAT?
YUKAKO, I'M GLAD TO SEE YOU AND KOICHI ARE GETTING ALONG NOW.
GOOD FOR YOU.
BUTT OUT OF THIS, OLD MAN! CAN'T YOU SEE YOU'RE GETTING IN MY WAY?
HEH.

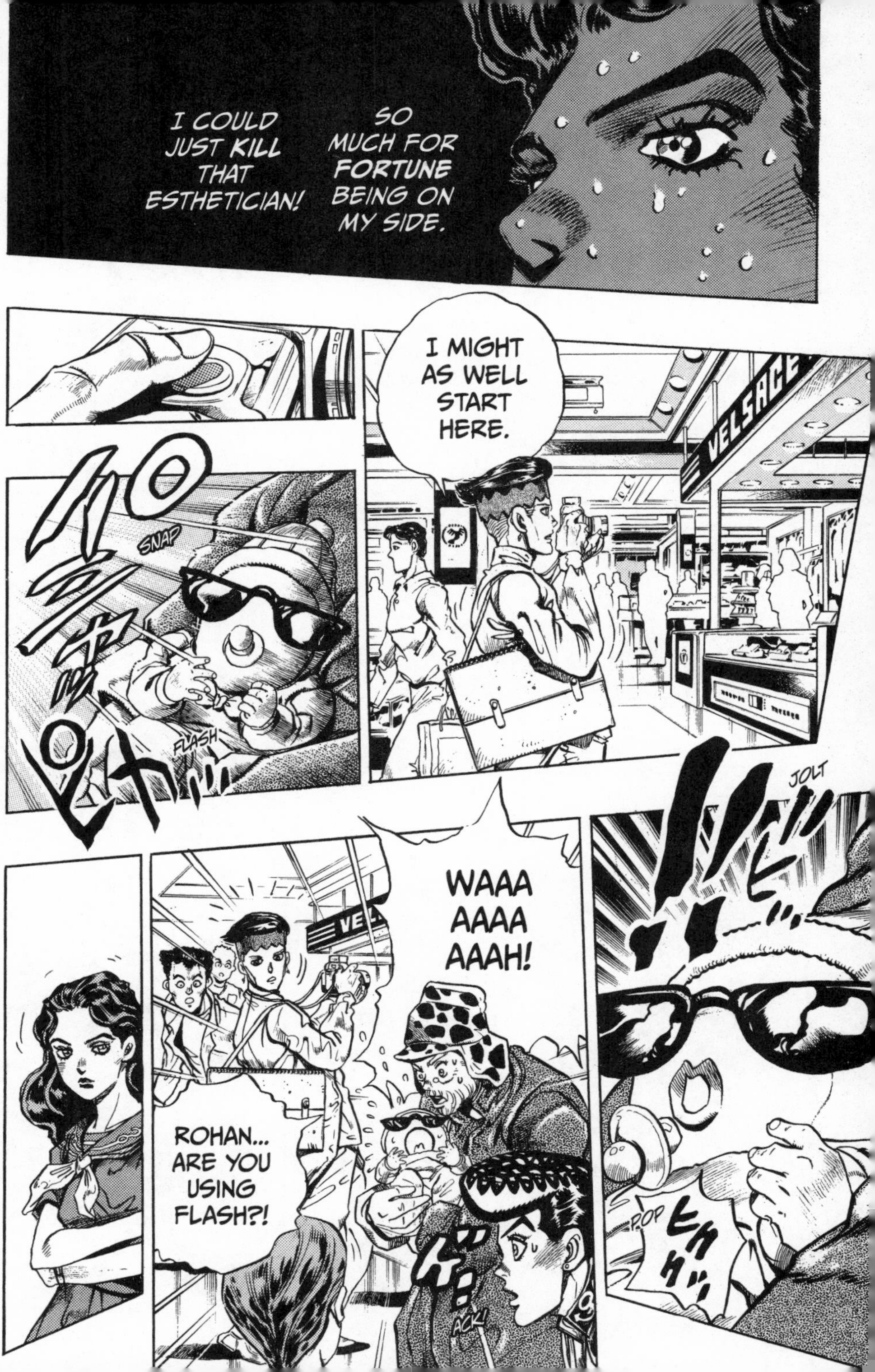
SO MUCH FOR FORTUNE BEING ON MY SIDE.
I COULD JUST KILL THAT ESTHETICIAN!
VELSACE
I MIGHT AS WELL START HERE.
SNAP
FLASH
JOLT
POP
WAAA AAAA AAAH!
ROHAN... ARE YOU USING FLASH?!
ACK!

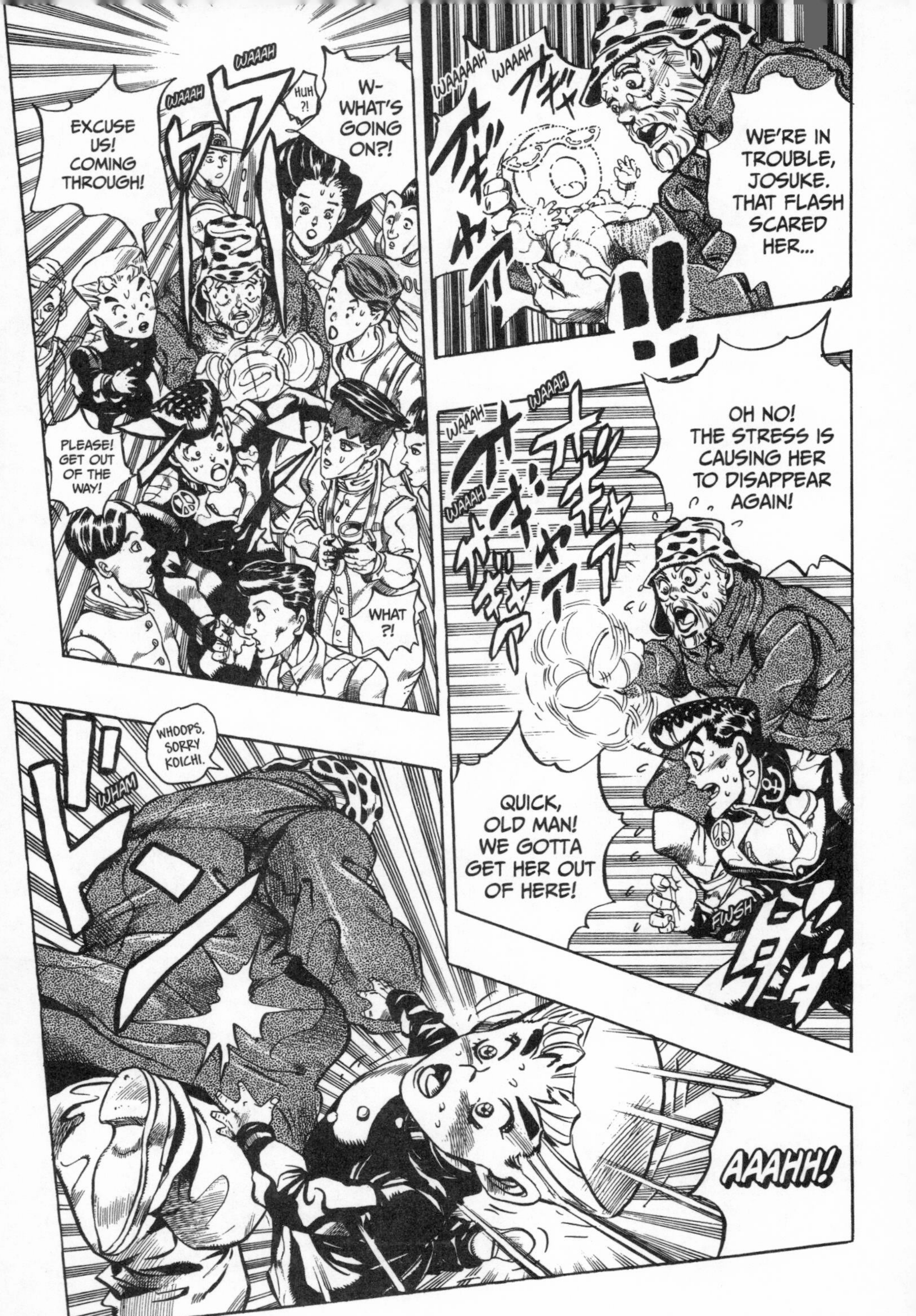
WAAAAAH
WAAAH
WE'RE IN TROUBLE, JOSUKE. THAT FLASH SCARED HER...
WAAAH
WAAAH
WAAAH
OH NO! THE STRESS IS CAUSING HER TO DISAPPEAR AGAIN!
QUICK, OLD MAN! WE GOTTA GET HER OUT OF HERE!
FWSH
W- WHAT'S GOING ON?!
HUH ?!
WAAAH
WAAAH
EXCUSE US! COMING THROUGH!
PLEASE! GET OUT OF THE WAY!
WHAT ?!
WHOOPS, SORRY KOICHI.
WHAM
AAAHH!

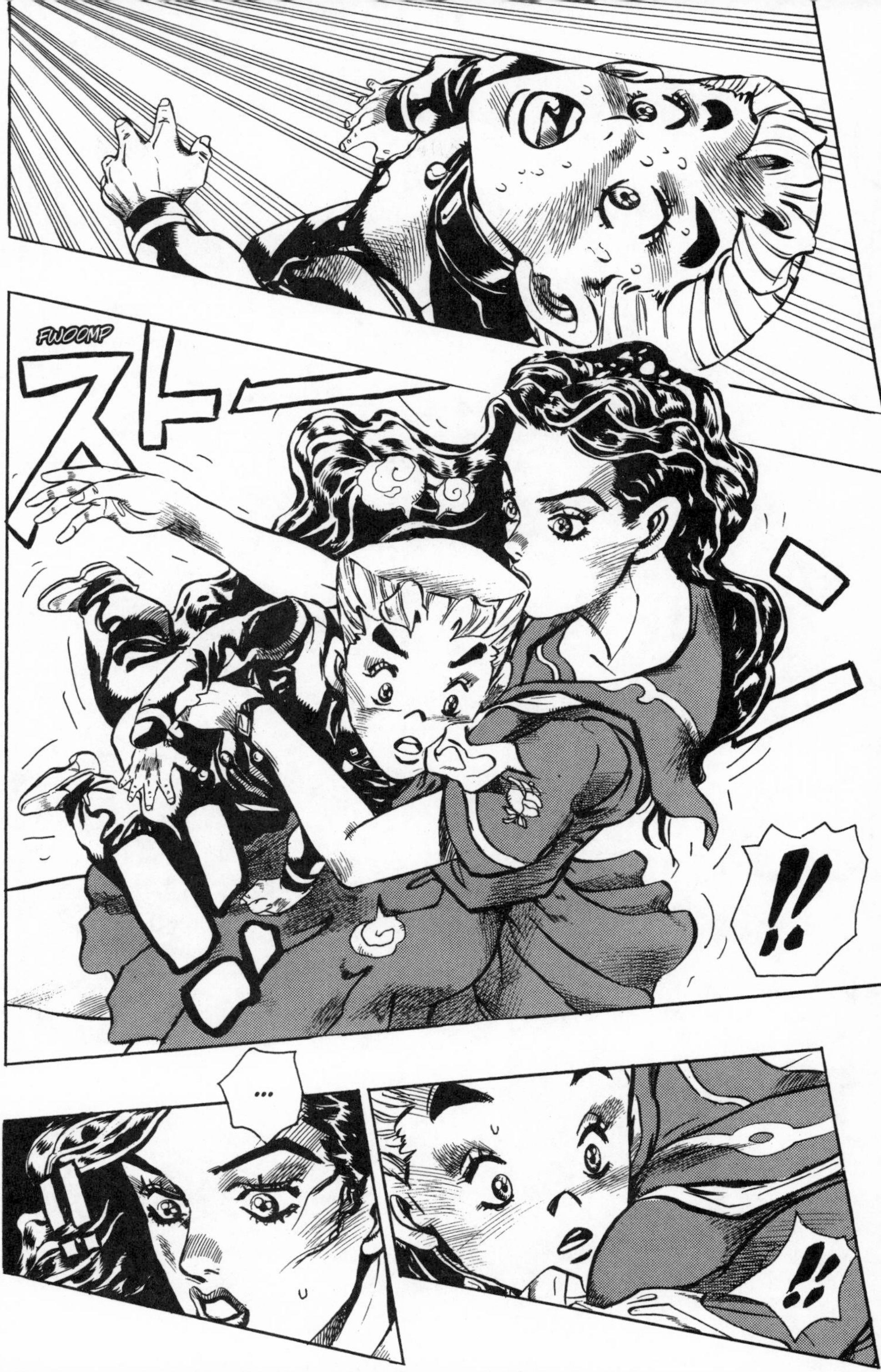
FWOOMP
ストーン
!!
...
!!

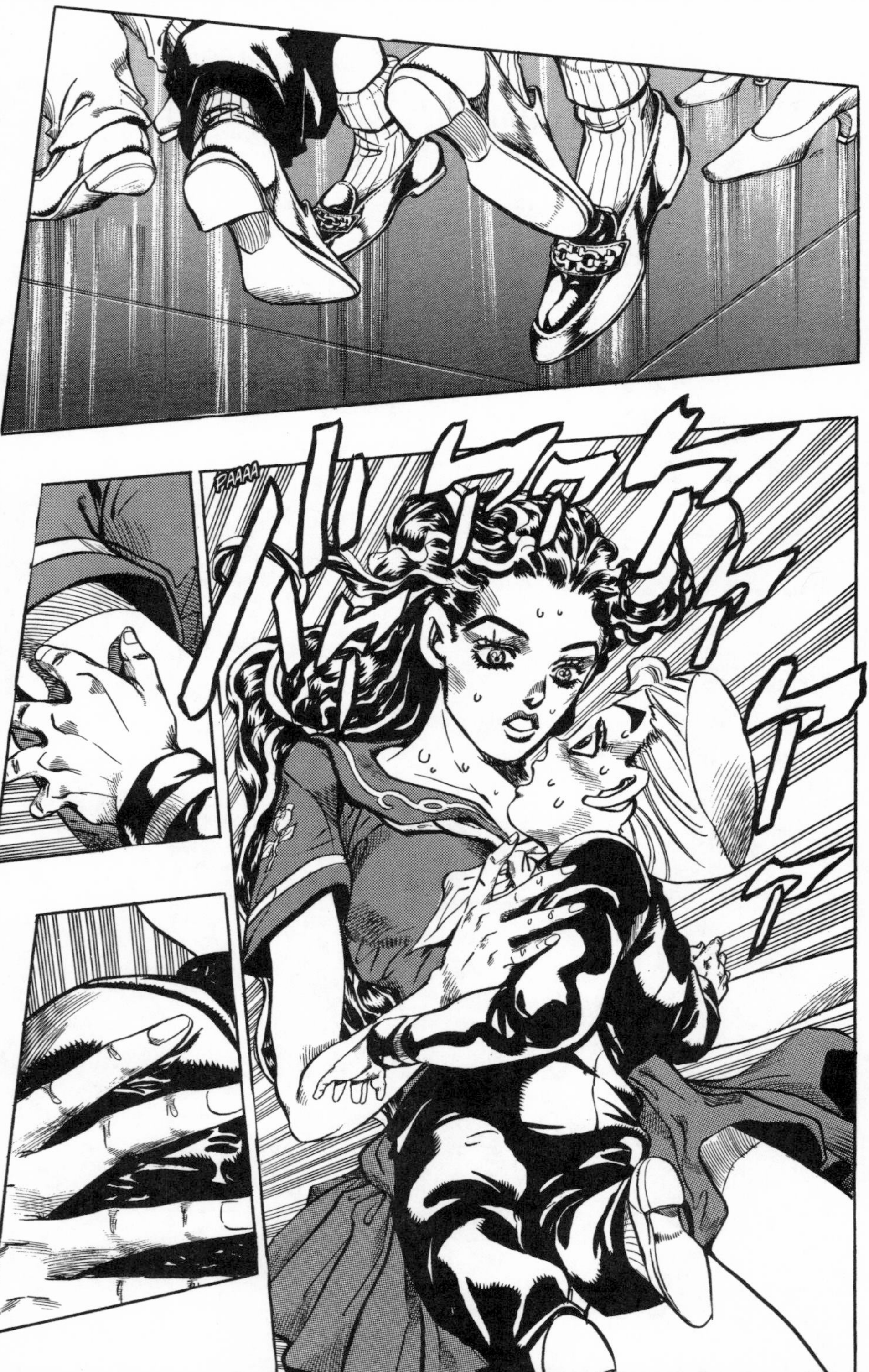
PAAAA

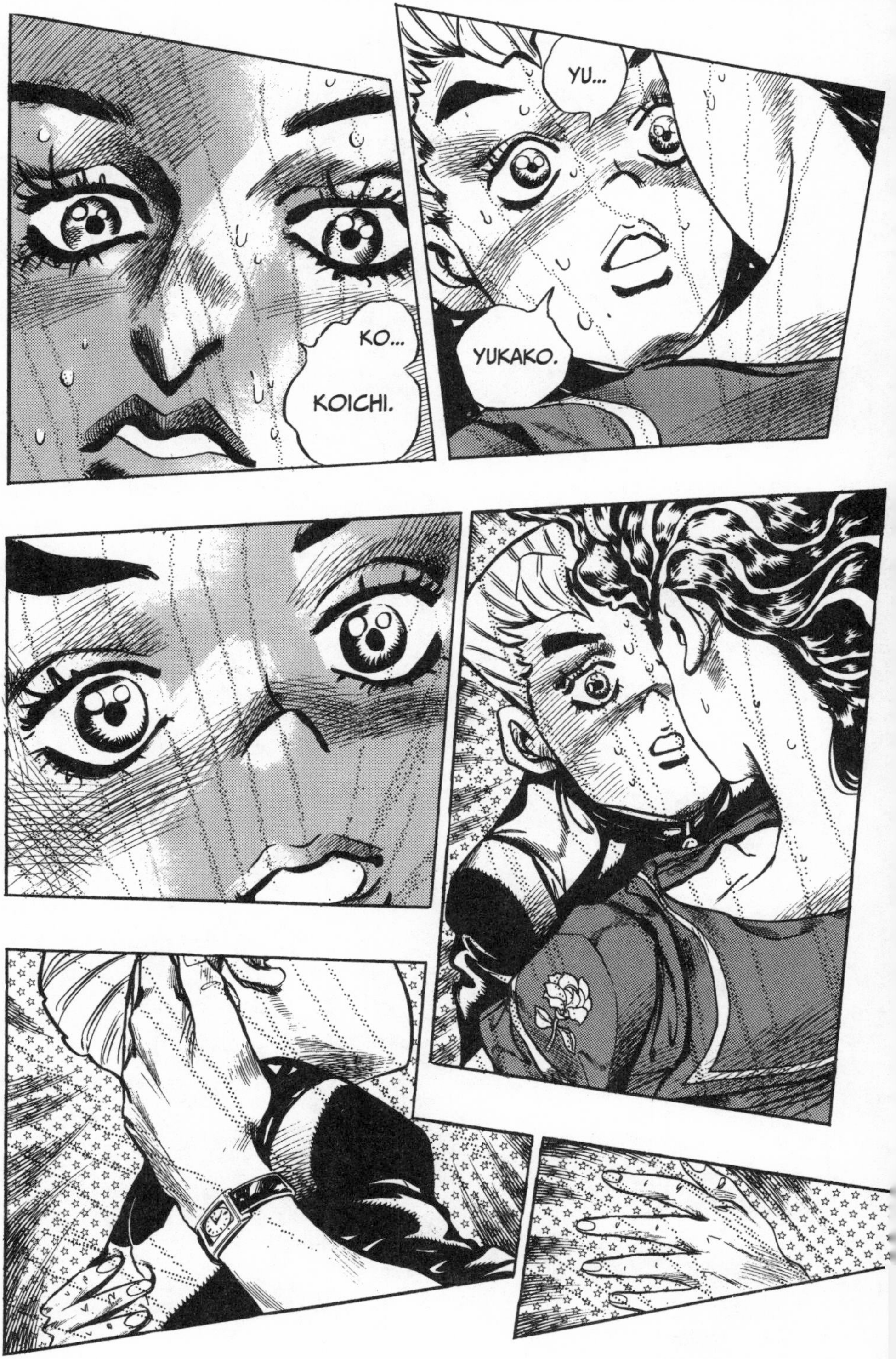
YU...
YUKAKO.
KO...
KOICHI.

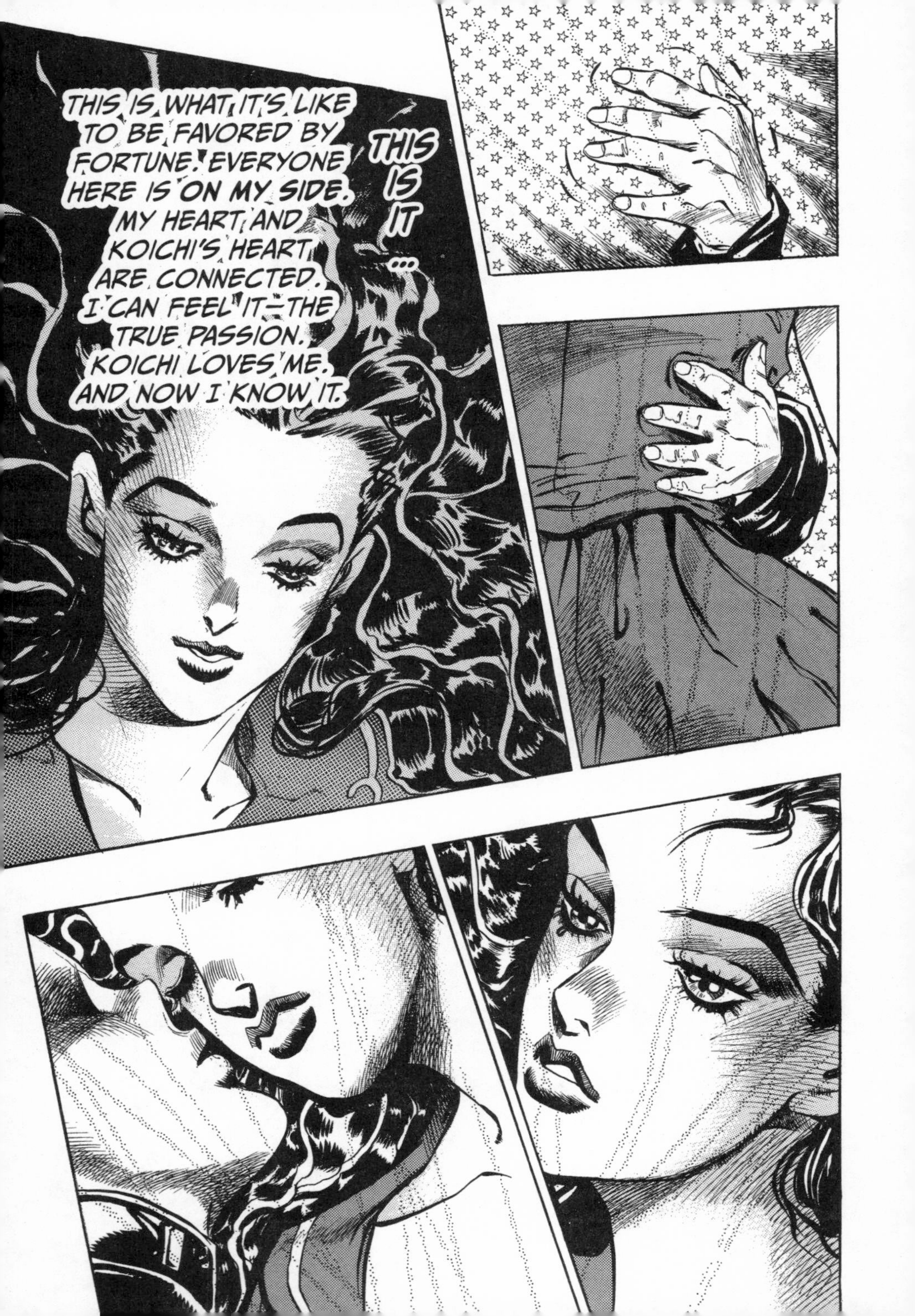
THIS IS IT...
THIS IS WHAT IT'S LIKE TO BE FAVORED BY FORTUNE. EVERYONE HERE IS ON MY SIDE. MY HEART AND KOICHI'S HEART ARE CONNECTED. I CAN FEEL IT—THE TRUE PASSION. KOICHI LOVES ME. AND NOW I KNOW IT.

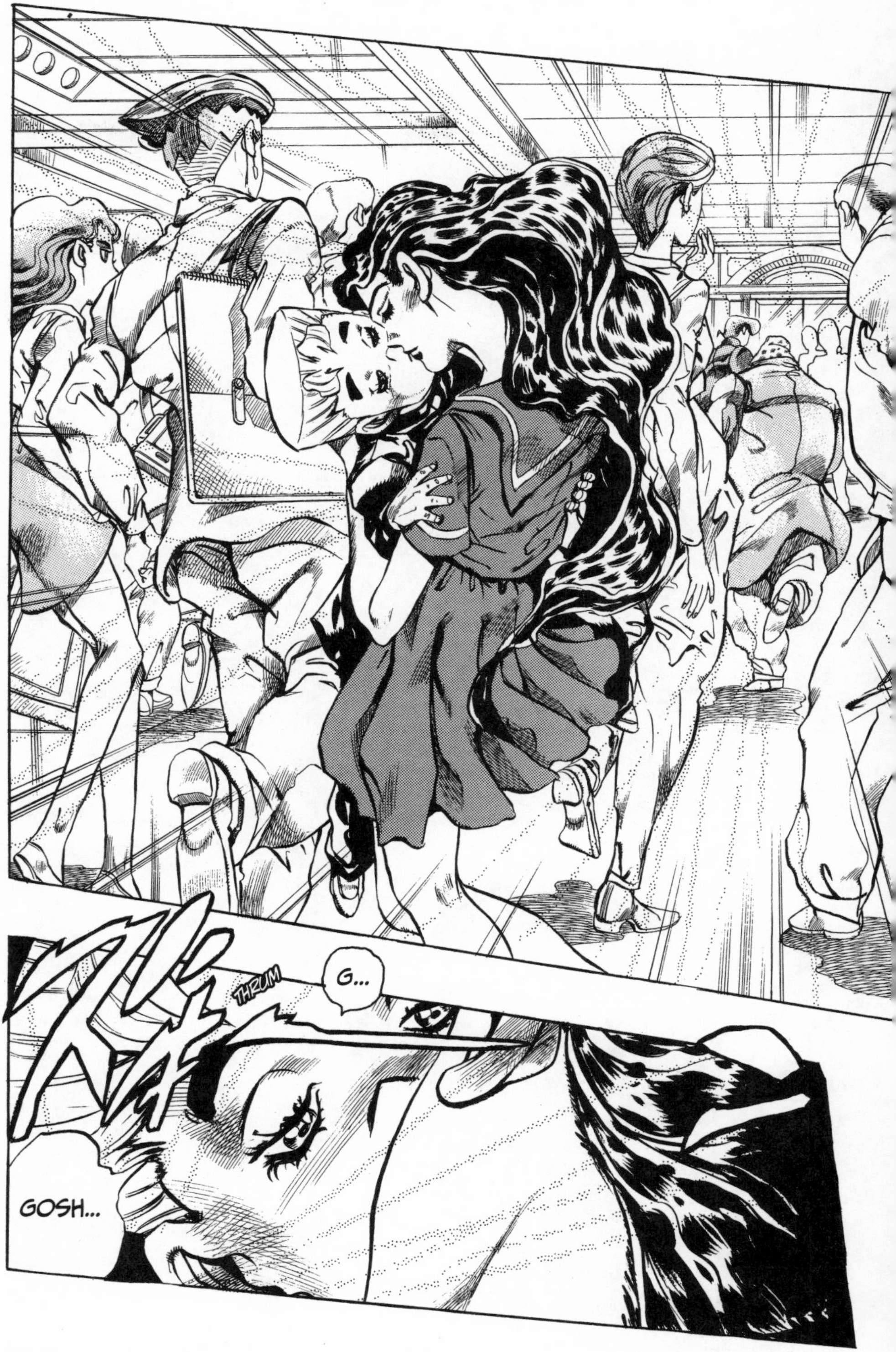
G...
THRUM
GOSH...

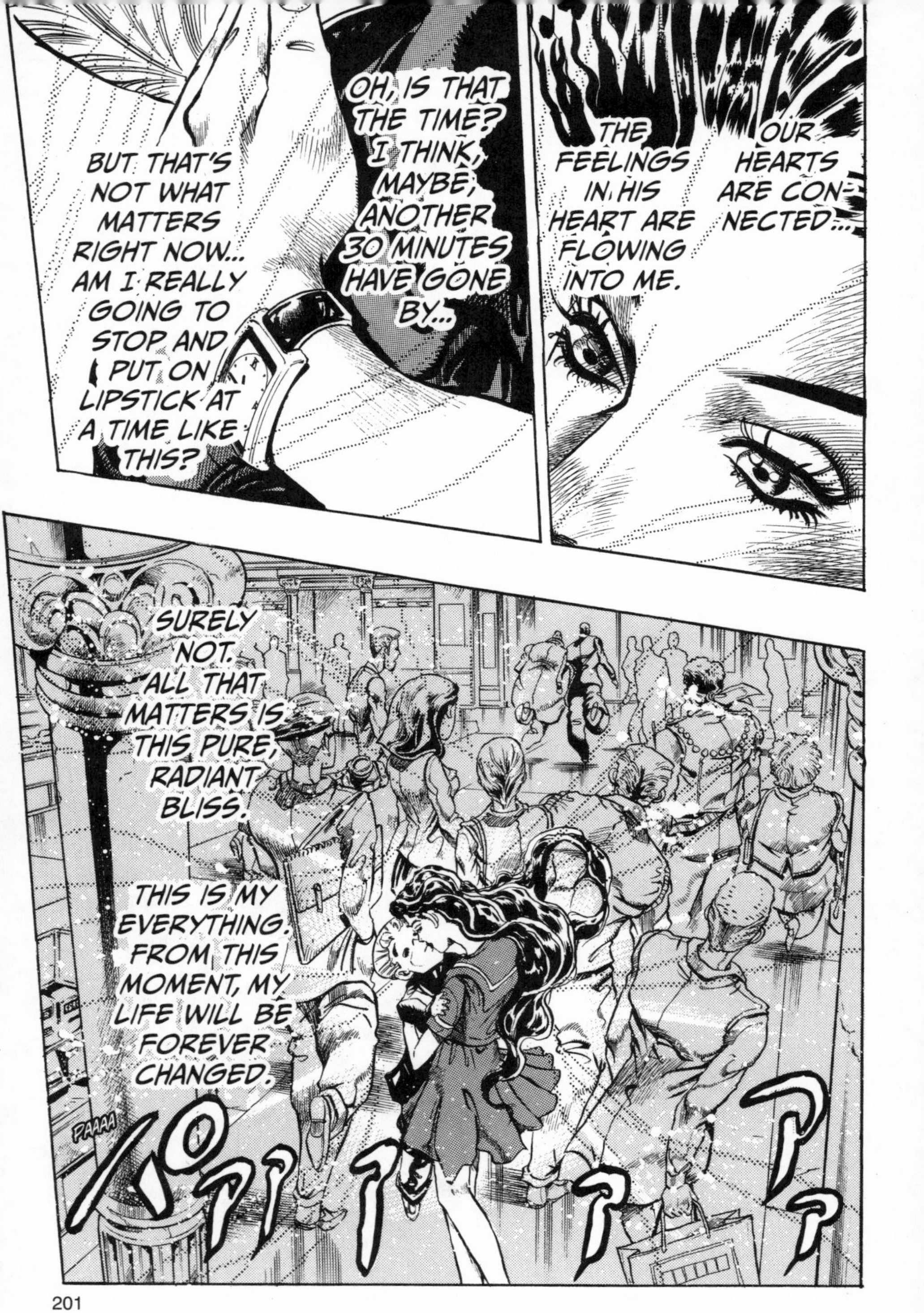
OUR HEARTS ARE CONNECTED...
THE FEELINGS IN HIS HEART ARE FLOWING INTO ME.
OH, IS THAT THE TIME? I THINK, MAYBE, ANOTHER 30 MINUTES HAVE GONE BY...
BUT THAT'S NOT WHAT MATTERS RIGHT NOW... AM I REALLY GOING TO STOP AND PUT ON LIPSTICK AT A TIME LIKE THIS?
SURELY NOT. ALL THAT MATTERS IS THIS PURE, RADIANT BLISS.
THIS IS MY EVERYTHING. FROM THIS MOMENT, MY LIFE WILL BE FOREVER CHANGED.
PAAAA

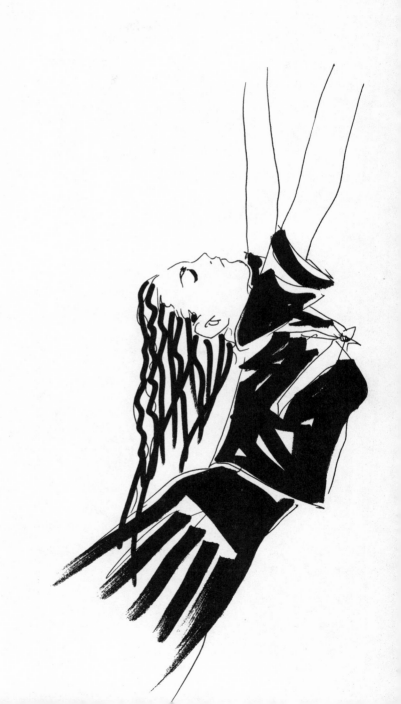

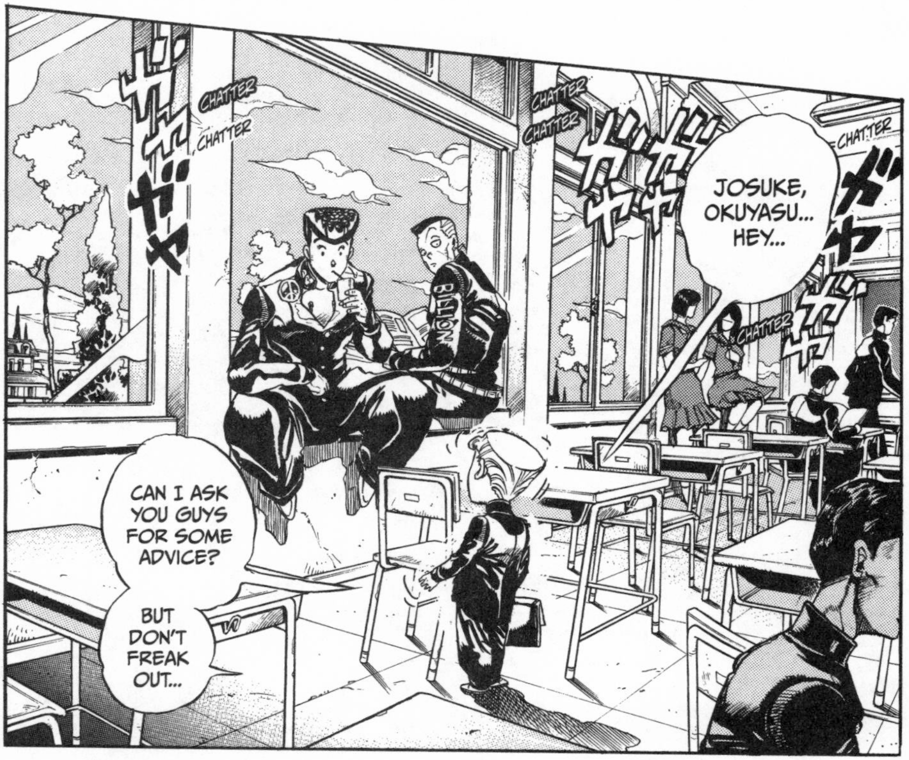
CHATTER
CHATTER
JOSUKE, OKUYASU... HEY...
CHATTER
CHATTER
CHATTER
CHATTER
BILLION
CAN I ASK YOU GUYS FOR SOME ADVICE?
BUT DON'T FREAK OUT...

CHAPTER 87

YUKAKO YAMAGISHI DREAMS OF CINDERELLA, PART 5

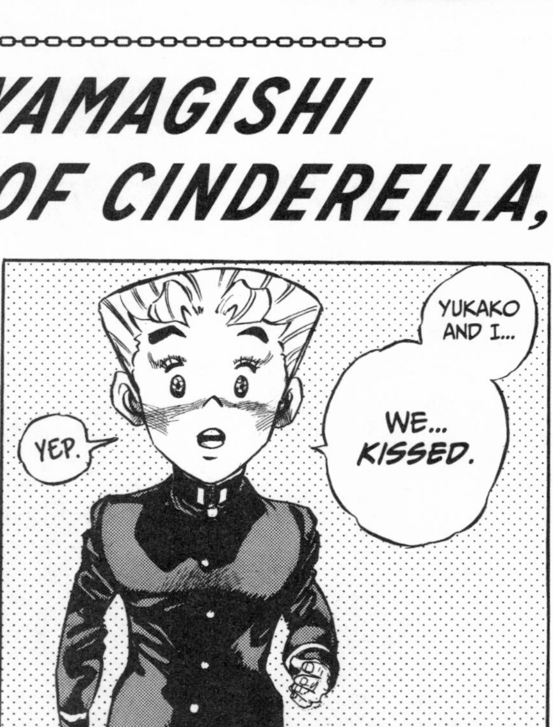
YUKAKO AND I...
WE... KISSED.
YEP.

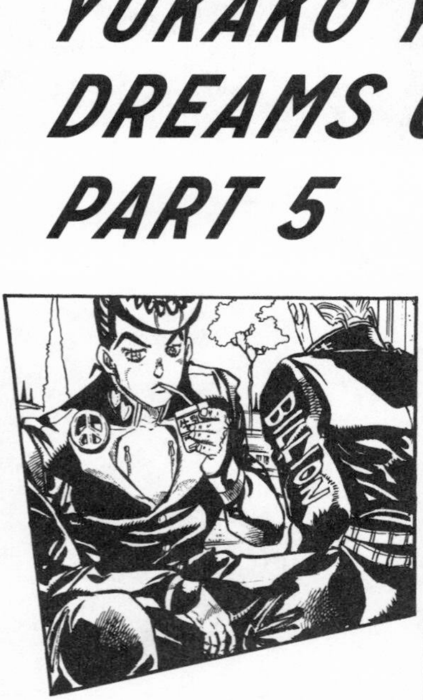
BILLION

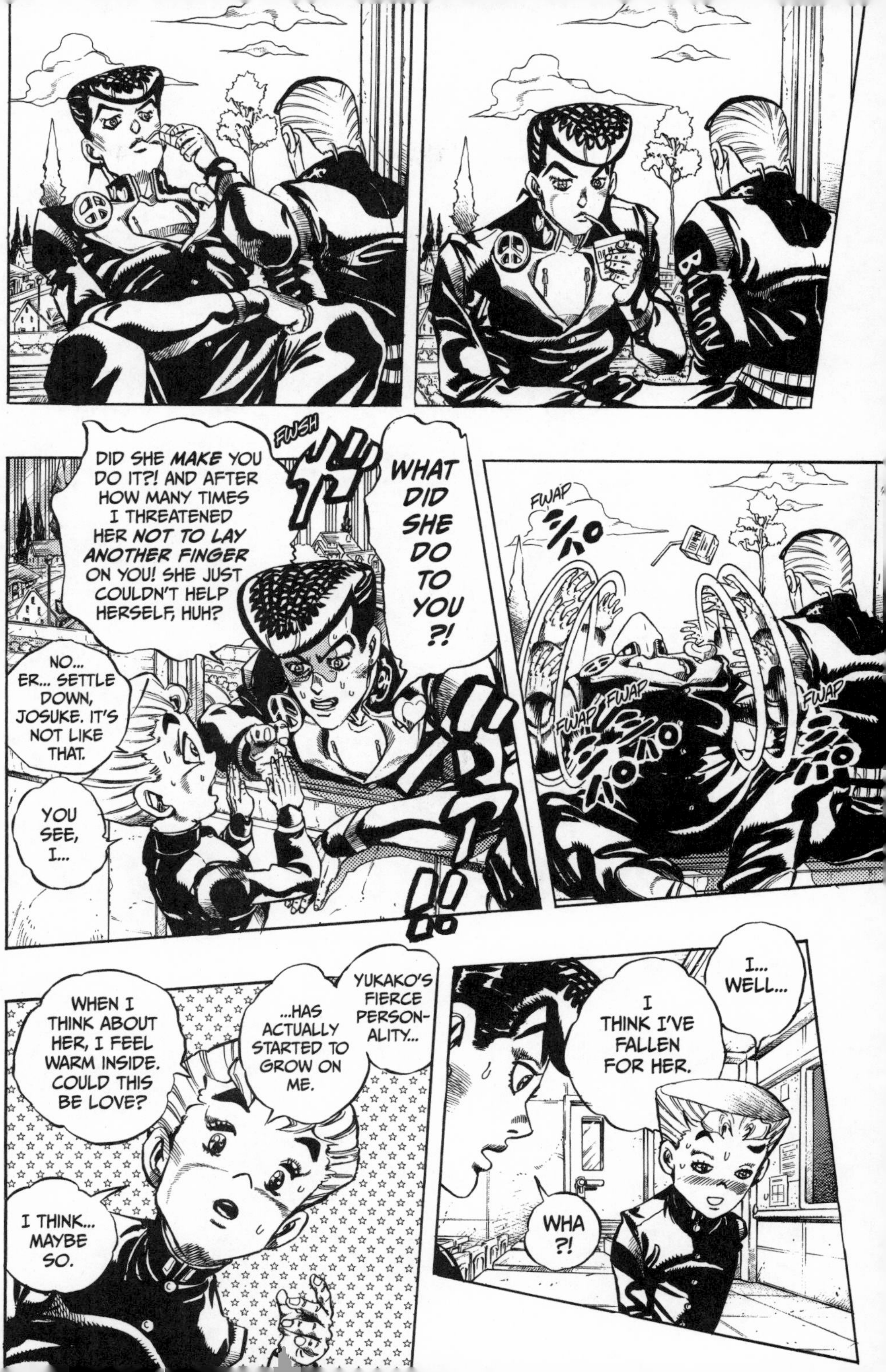
FWAP
FWAP
FWAP
FWAP
FWSH
WHAT DID SHE DO TO YOU?!
DID SHE *MAKE* YOU DO IT?! AND AFTER HOW MANY TIMES I THREATENED HER *NOT TO LAY ANOTHER FINGER* ON YOU! SHE JUST COULDN'T HELP HERSELF, HUH?
NO... ER... SETTLE DOWN, JOSUKE. IT'S NOT LIKE THAT.
YOU SEE, I...
I... WELL...
I THINK I'VE FALLEN FOR HER.
WHA?!
YUKAKO'S FIERCE PERSONALITY...
...HAS ACTUALLY STARTED TO GROW ON ME.
WHEN I THINK ABOUT HER, I FEEL WARM INSIDE. COULD THIS BE LOVE?
I THINK... MAYBE SO.

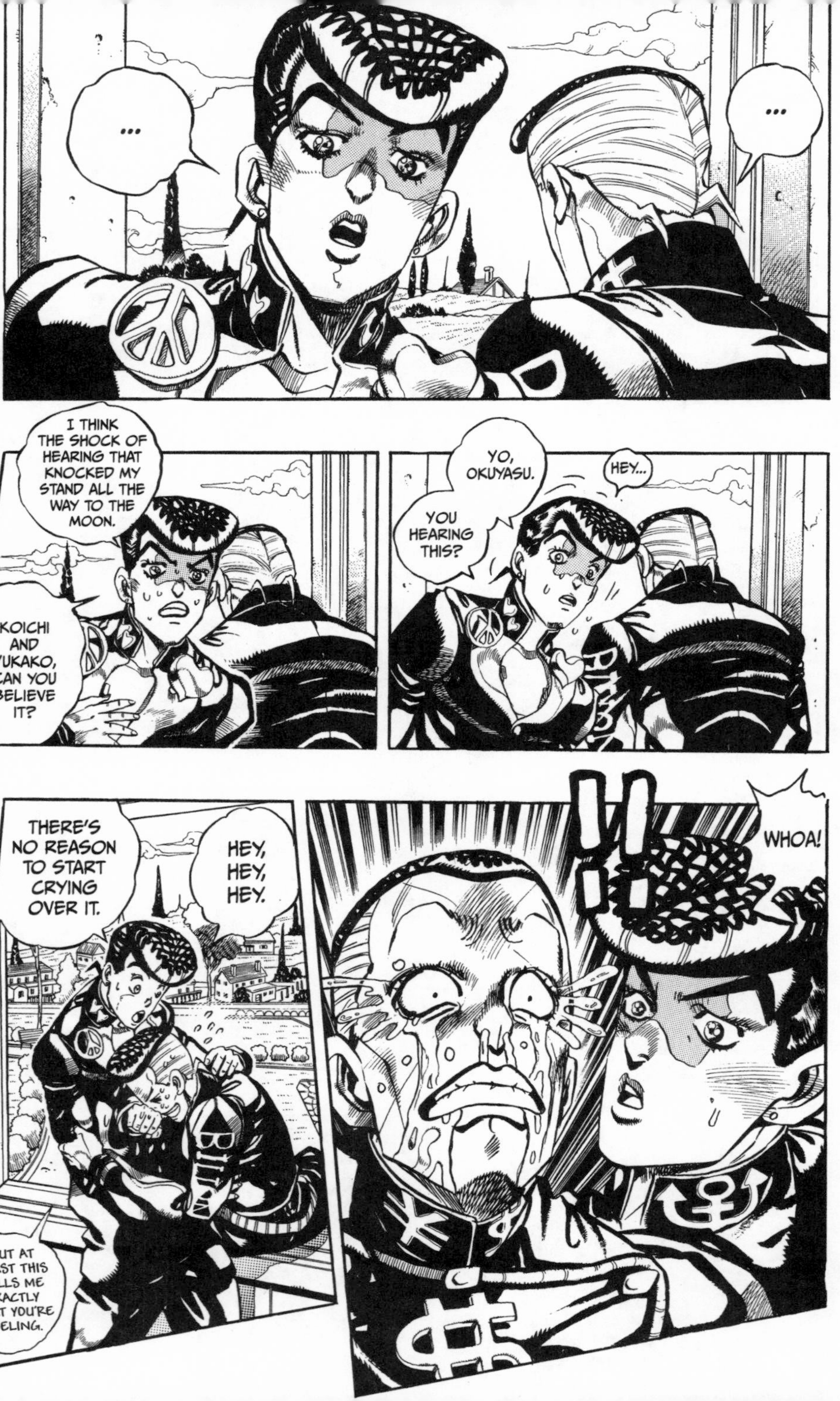
...
...
HEY...
YO, OKUYASU.
YOU HEARING THIS?
I THINK THE SHOCK OF HEARING THAT KNOCKED MY STAND ALL THE WAY TO THE MOON.
KOICHI AND YUKAKO, CAN YOU BELIEVE IT?
!!
WHOA!
HEY, HEY, HEY.
THERE'S NO REASON TO START CRYING OVER IT.
BUT AT LEAST THIS TELLS ME EXACTLY WHAT YOU'RE FEELING.

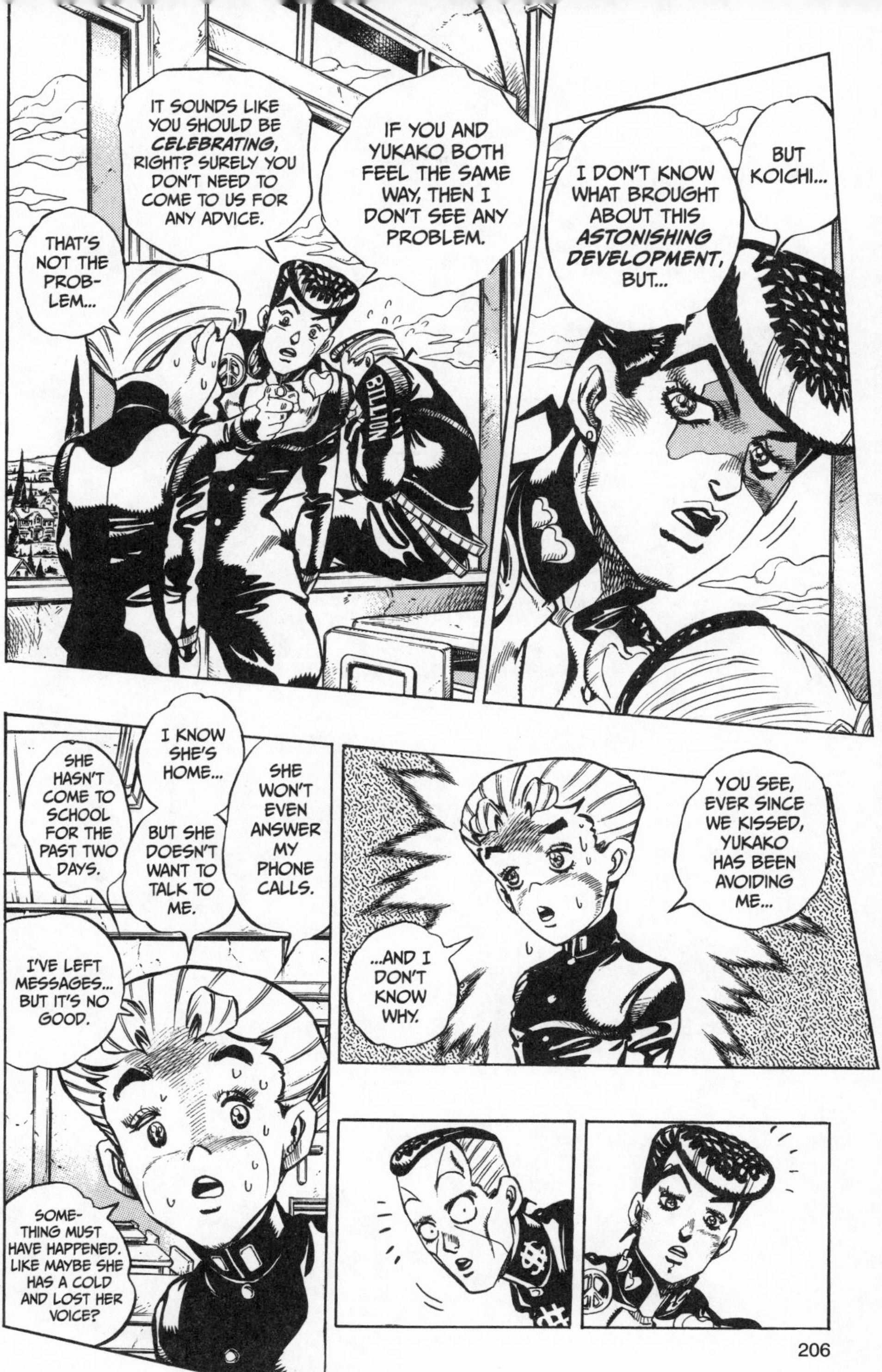
BUT KOICHI...
I DON'T KNOW WHAT BROUGHT ABOUT THIS ASTONISHING DEVELOPMENT, BUT...
IF YOU AND YUKAKO BOTH FEEL THE SAME WAY, THEN I DON'T SEE ANY PROBLEM.
IT SOUNDS LIKE YOU SHOULD BE CELEBRATING, RIGHT? SURELY YOU DON'T NEED TO COME TO US FOR ANY ADVICE.
THAT'S NOT THE PROB-LEM...
BILLION
YOU SEE, EVER SINCE WE KISSED, YUKAKO HAS BEEN AVOIDING ME...
...AND I DON'T KNOW WHY.
SHE WON'T EVEN ANSWER MY PHONE CALLS.
I KNOW SHE'S HOME...
BUT SHE DOESN'T WANT TO TALK TO ME.
SHE HASN'T COME TO SCHOOL FOR THE PAST TWO DAYS.
I'VE LEFT MESSAGES... BUT IT'S NO GOOD.
SOME-THING MUST HAVE HAPPENED. LIKE MAYBE SHE HAS A COLD AND LOST HER VOICE?

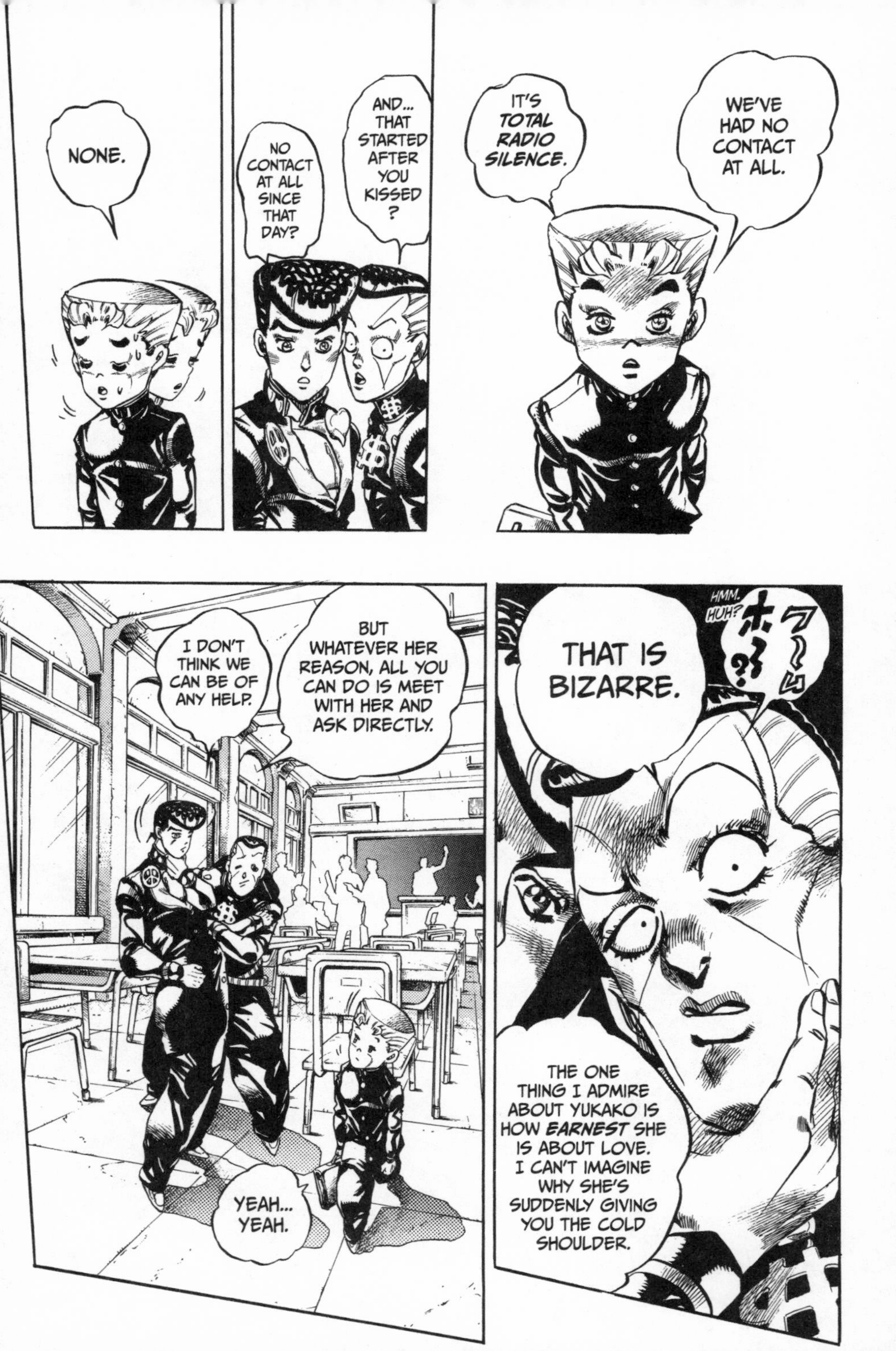
WE'VE HAD NO CONTACT AT ALL.
IT'S *TOTAL RADIO SILENCE*.
AND... THAT STARTED AFTER YOU KISSED?
NO CONTACT AT ALL SINCE THAT DAY?
NONE.
HMM. HUH?
フ〜ム
ホ??
THAT IS BIZARRE.
THE ONE THING I ADMIRE ABOUT YUKAKO IS HOW *EARNEST* SHE IS ABOUT LOVE. I CAN'T IMAGINE WHY SHE'S SUDDENLY GIVING YOU THE COLD SHOULDER.
BUT WHATEVER HER REASON, ALL YOU CAN DO IS MEET WITH HER AND ASK DIRECTLY.
I DON'T THINK WE CAN BE OF ANY HELP.
YEAH... YEAH.

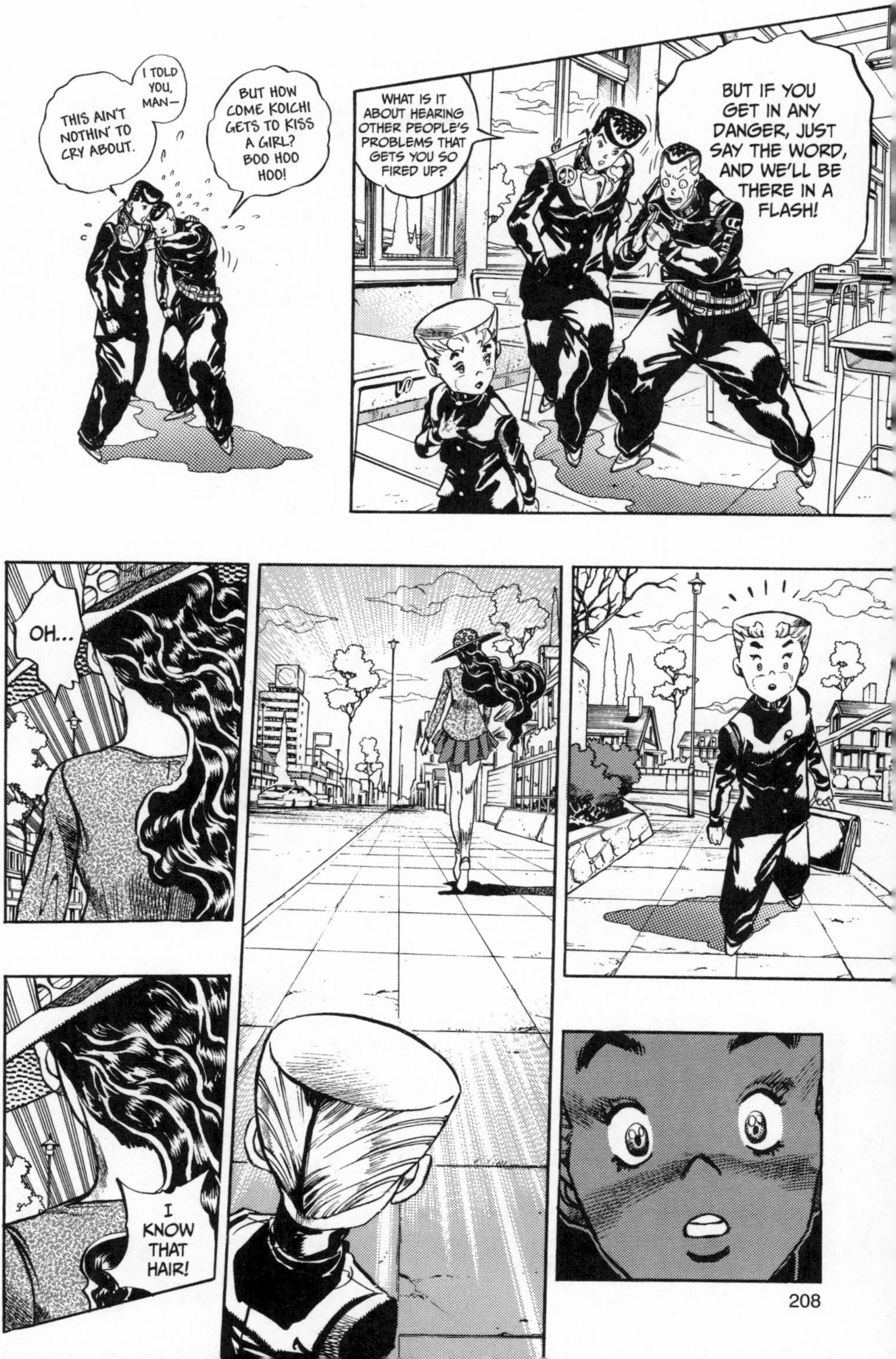
BUT IF YOU GET IN ANY DANGER, JUST SAY THE WORD, AND WE'LL BE THERE IN A FLASH!
WHAT IS IT ABOUT HEARING OTHER PEOPLE'S PROBLEMS THAT GETS YOU SO FIRED UP?
BUT HOW COME KOICHI GETS TO KISS A GIRL? BOO HOO HOO!
I TOLD YOU, MAN—
THIS AIN'T NOTHIN' TO CRY ABOUT.
OH...
I KNOW THAT HAIR!

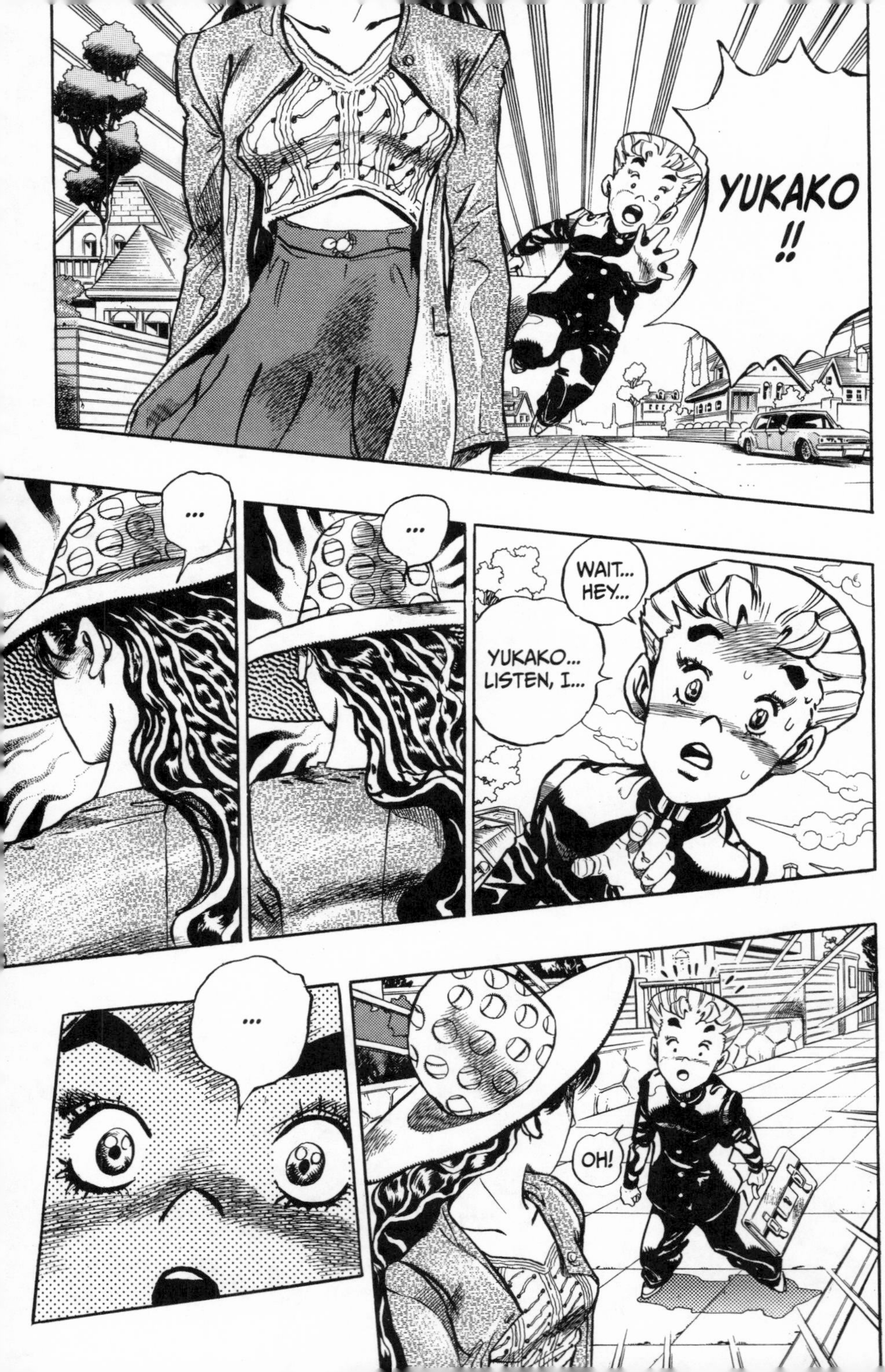
YUKAKO!!
WAIT... HEY...
YUKAKO... LISTEN, I...
...
...
OH!
...

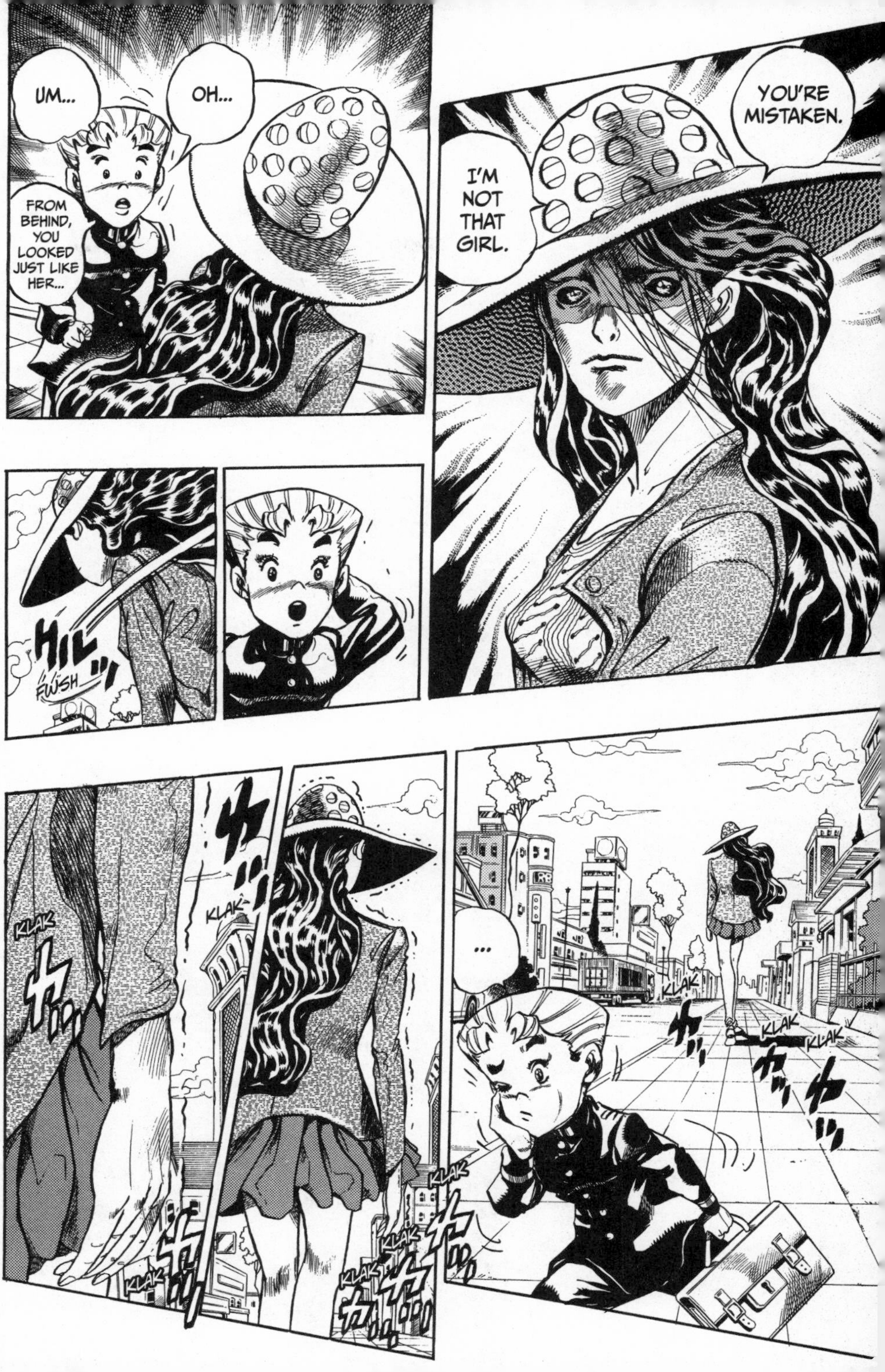
YOU'RE MISTAKEN.
I'M NOT THAT GIRL.
OH...
UM...
FROM BEHIND, YOU LOOKED JUST LIKE HER...
FWISH
...
KLAK
KLAK
KLAK
KLAK
KLAK
KLAK
KLAK
KLAK
KLAK

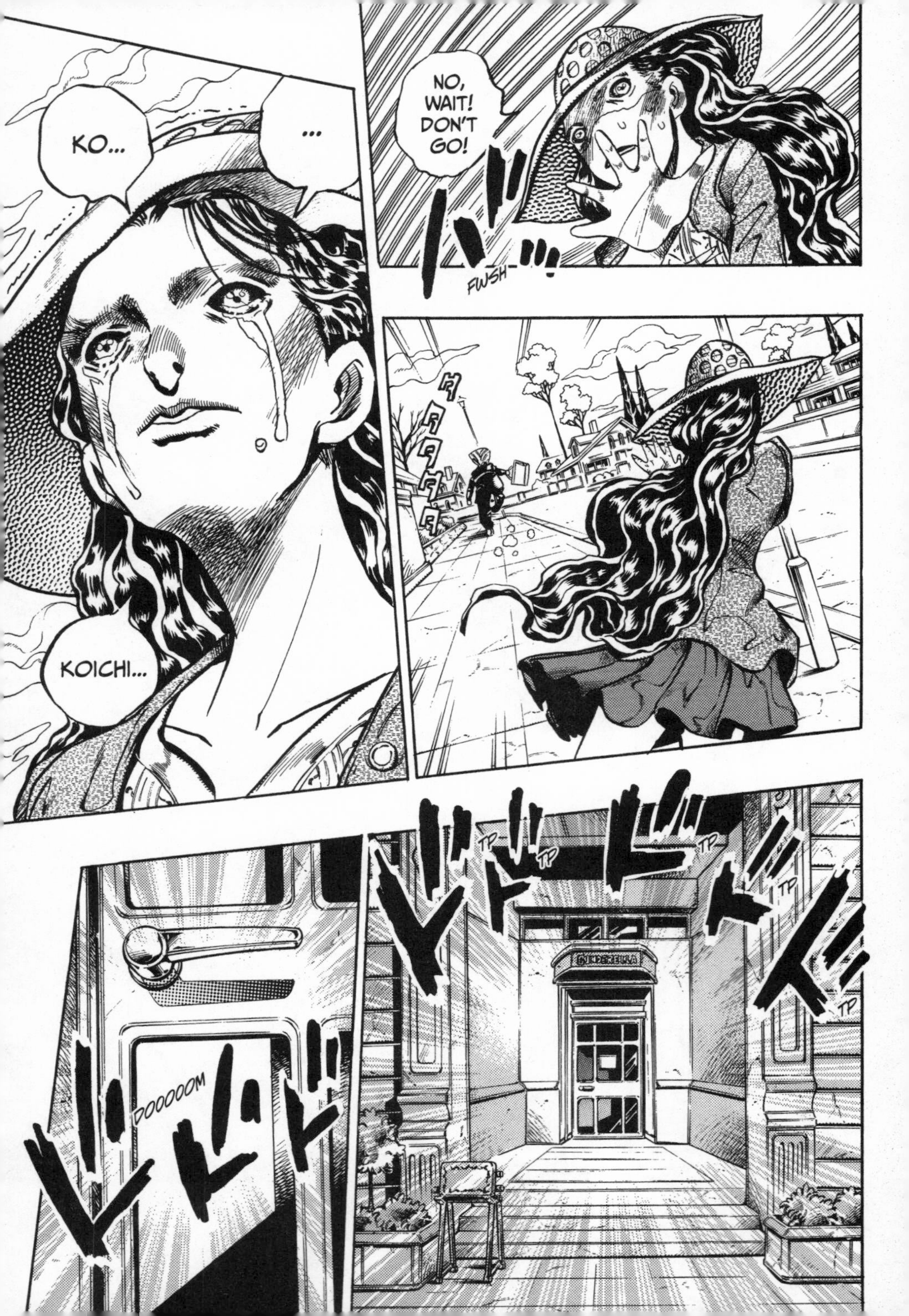
NO, WAIT! DON'T GO!
FWSH
KO...
...
KOICHI...
TP
TP
TP
TP
TP
DOOOOOM

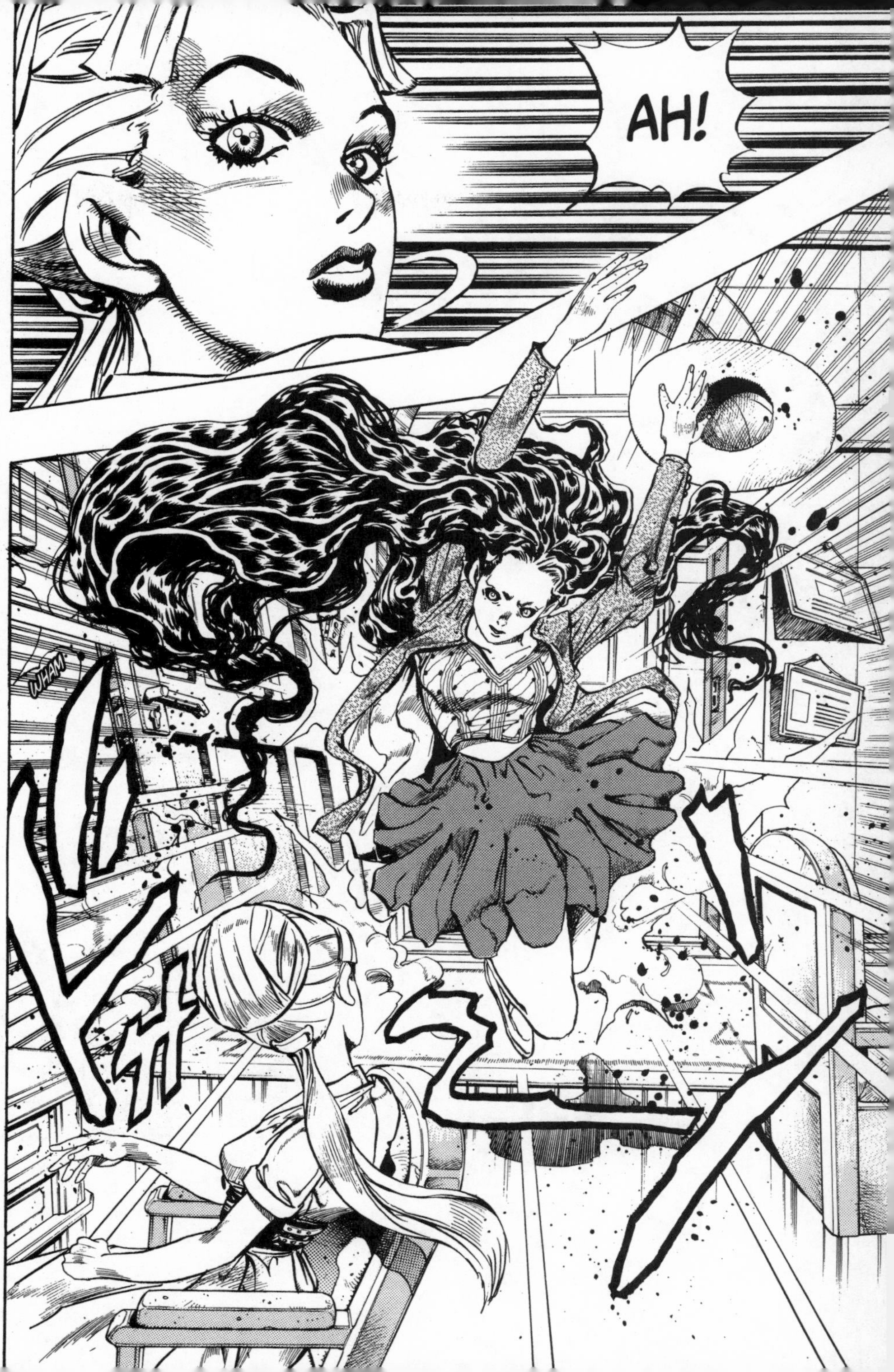
AH!
WHAM

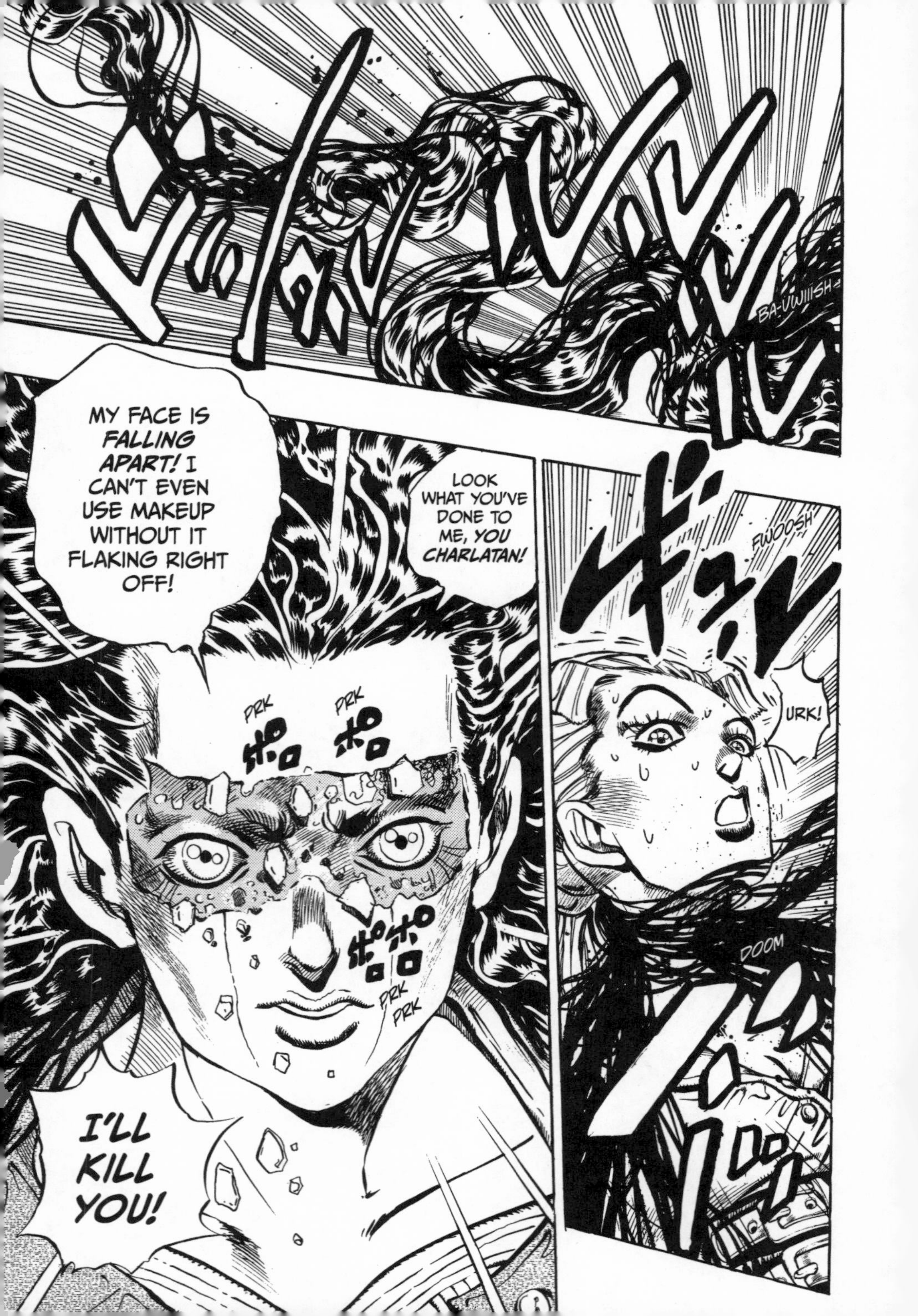
BA-UWIIISH
FWOOSH
URK!
DOOM
MY FACE IS FALLING APART! I CAN'T EVEN USE MAKEUP WITHOUT IT FLAKING RIGHT OFF!
LOOK WHAT YOU'VE DONE TO ME, YOU CHARLATAN!
PRK PRK
PRK PRK
I'LL KILL YOU!

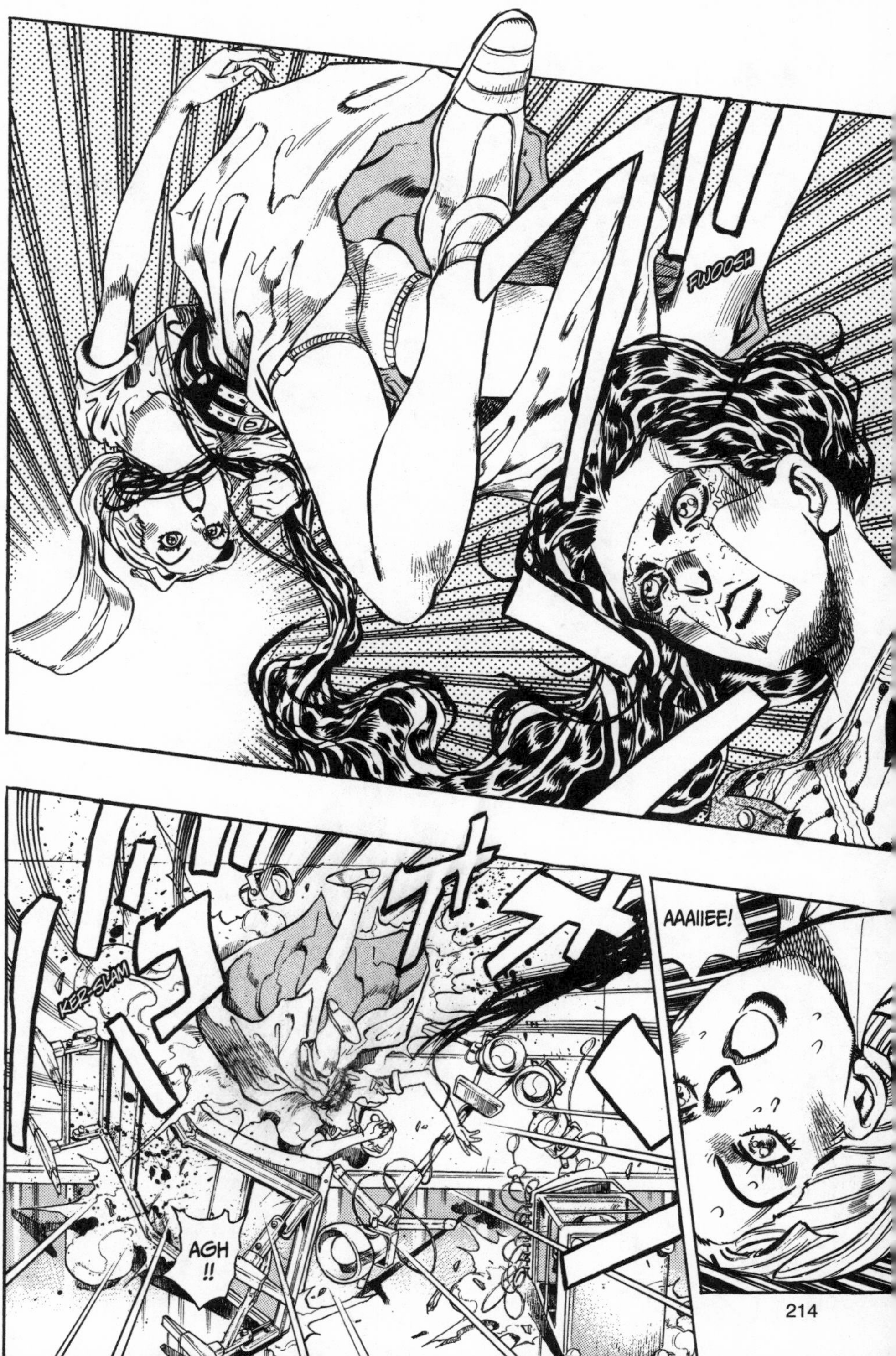
FWOOSH
AAAIIEE!
KER-SLAM
AGH !!

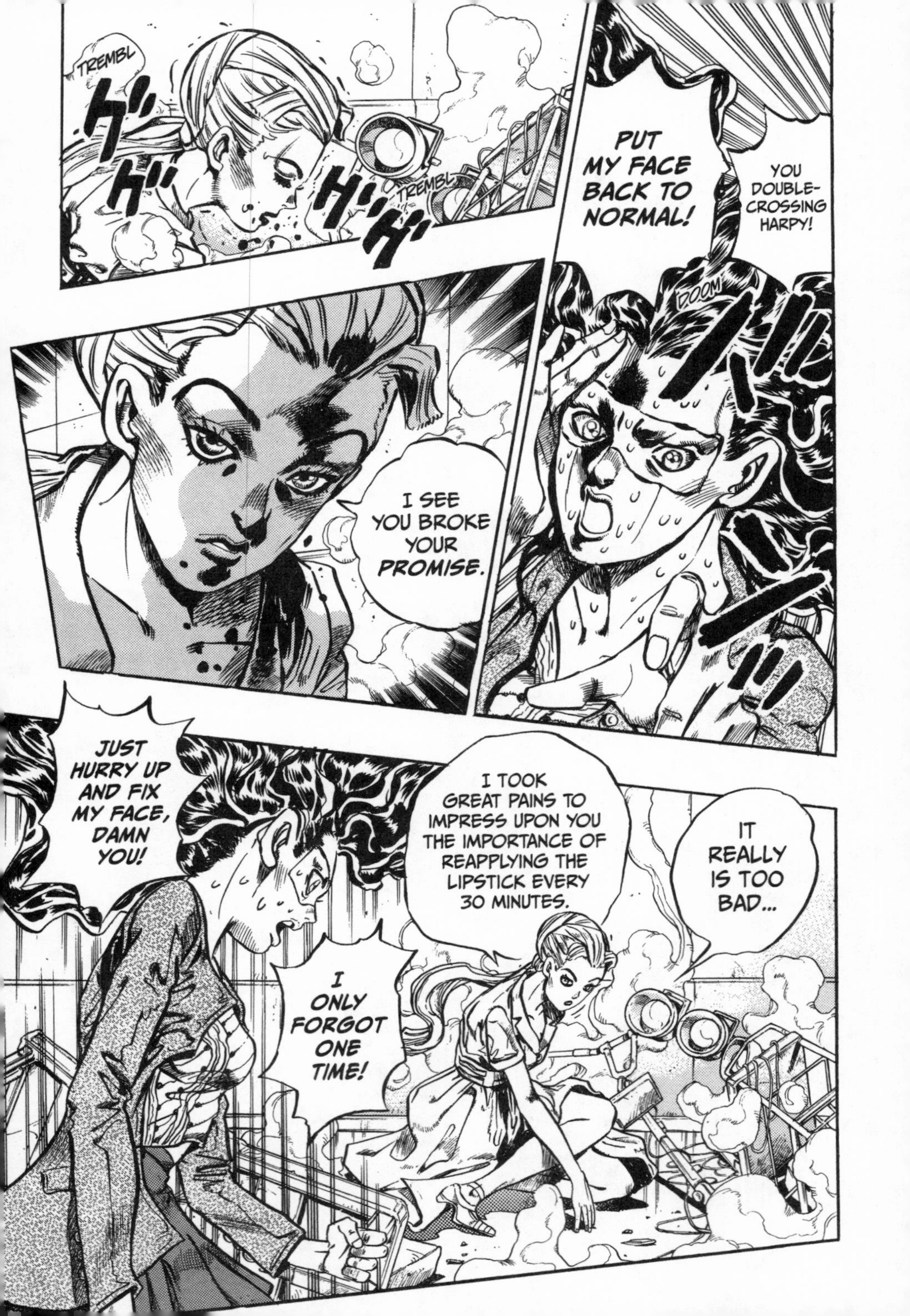
PUT MY FACE BACK TO NORMAL!
YOU DOUBLE-CROSSING HARPY!
DOOM
TREMBL
TREMBL
I SEE YOU BROKE YOUR PROMISE.
IT REALLY IS TOO BAD...
I TOOK GREAT PAINS TO IMPRESS UPON YOU THE IMPORTANCE OF REAPPLYING THE LIPSTICK EVERY 30 MINUTES.
JUST HURRY UP AND FIX MY FACE, DAMN YOU!
I ONLY FORGOT ONE TIME!

AH!
WHAT... WHAT IS THIS?
MY HAND ...
?!
BUBBL BUBBL
PWSH
AAA AHH!

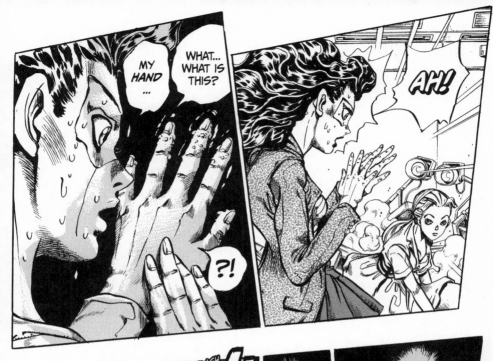

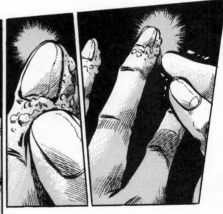

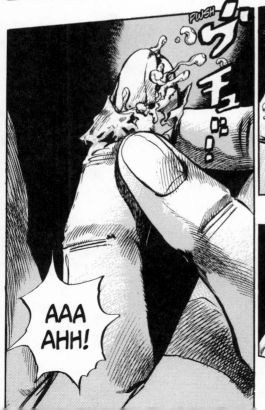

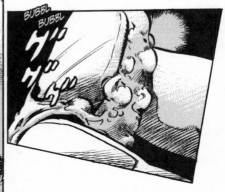

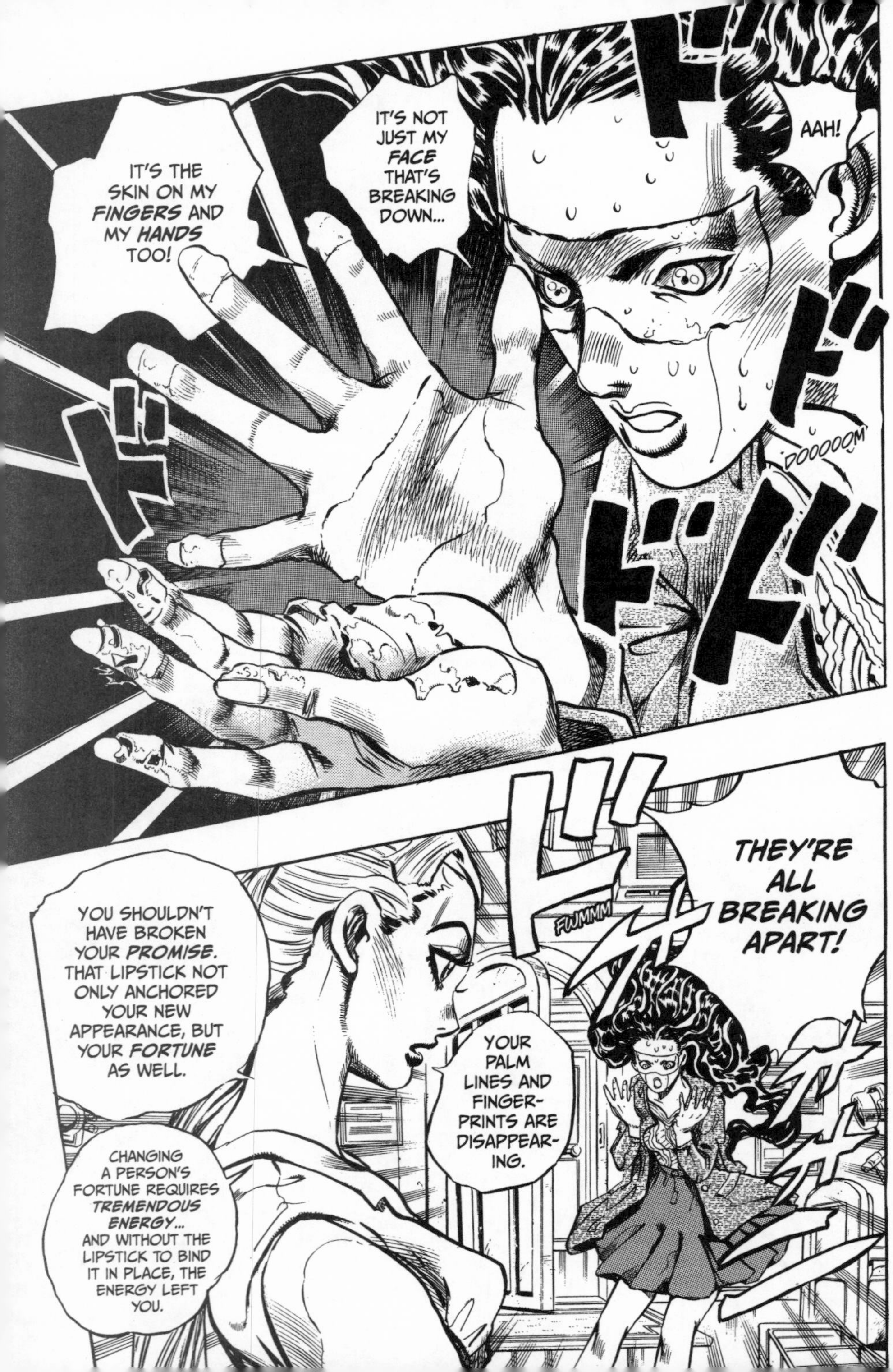
AAH!
IT'S NOT JUST MY FACE THAT'S BREAKING DOWN...
IT'S THE SKIN ON MY FINGERS AND MY HANDS TOO!
DOOOOOM
THEY'RE ALL BREAKING APART!
FWUMMM
YOUR PALM LINES AND FINGER-PRINTS ARE DISAPPEAR-ING.
YOU SHOULDN'T HAVE BROKEN YOUR PROMISE. THAT LIPSTICK NOT ONLY ANCHORED YOUR NEW APPEARANCE, BUT YOUR FORTUNE AS WELL.
CHANGING A PERSON'S FORTUNE REQUIRES TREMENDOUS ENERGY... AND WITHOUT THE LIPSTICK TO BIND IT IN PLACE, THE ENERGY LEFT YOU.

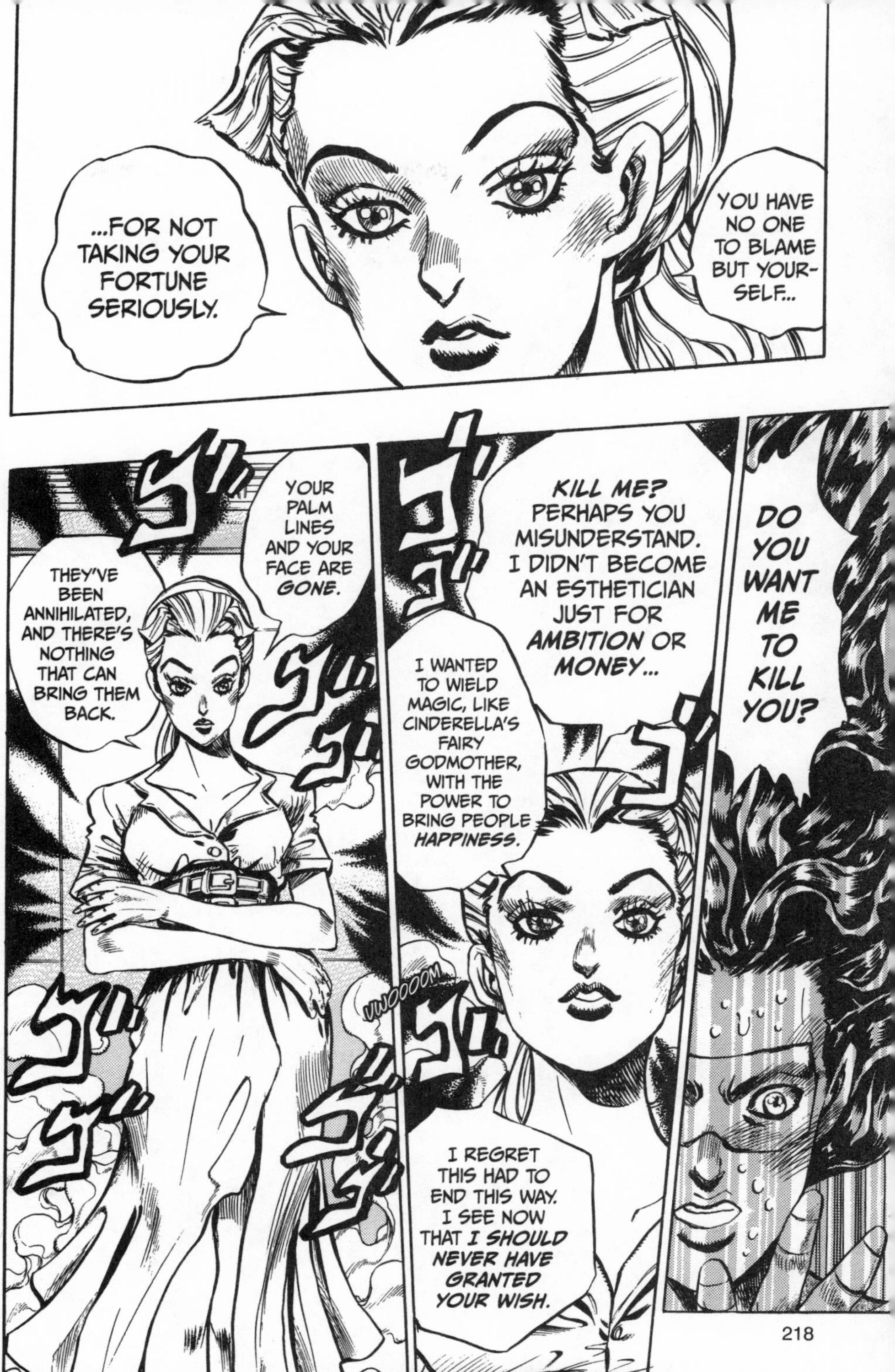
YOU HAVE NO ONE TO BLAME BUT YOUR-SELF...
...FOR NOT TAKING YOUR FORTUNE SERIOUSLY.
DO YOU WANT ME TO KILL YOU?
KILL ME? PERHAPS YOU MISUNDERSTAND. I DIDN'T BECOME AN ESTHETICIAN JUST FOR AMBITION OR MONEY...
I WANTED TO WIELD MAGIC, LIKE CINDERELLA'S FAIRY GODMOTHER, WITH THE POWER TO BRING PEOPLE HAPPINESS.
VWOOOOM
I REGRET THIS HAD TO END THIS WAY. I SEE NOW THAT I SHOULD NEVER HAVE GRANTED YOUR WISH.
YOUR PALM LINES AND YOUR FACE ARE GONE.
THEY'VE BEEN ANNIHILATED, AND THERE'S NOTHING THAT CAN BRING THEM BACK.

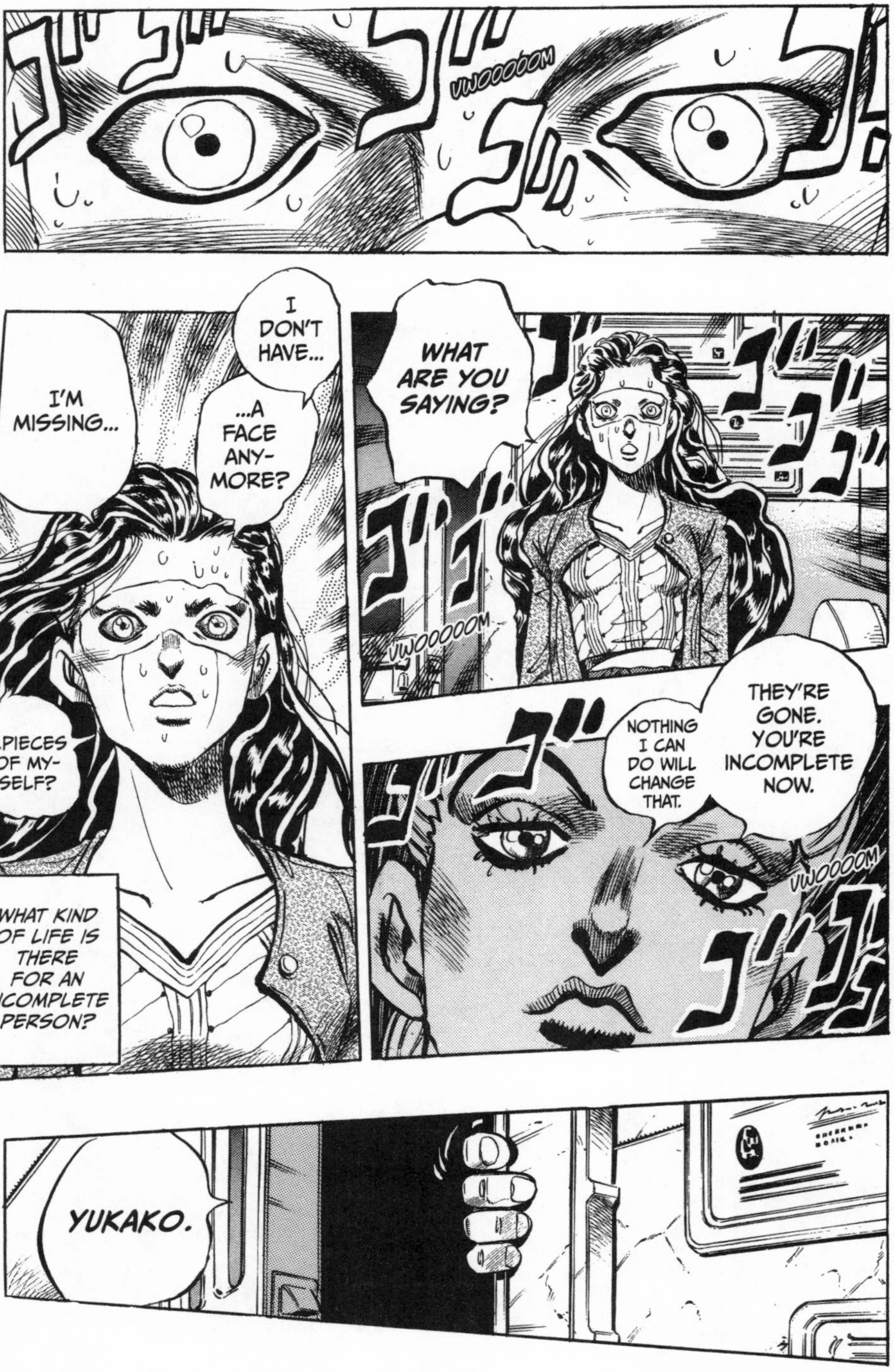
VWOOOOOM
WHAT ARE YOU SAYING?
VWOOOOOM
THEY'RE GONE. YOU'RE INCOMPLETE NOW.
NOTHING I CAN DO WILL CHANGE THAT.
VWOOOOM
I DON'T HAVE...
...A FACE ANYMORE?
I'M MISSING...
...PIECES OF MY-SELF?
WHAT KIND OF LIFE IS THERE FOR AN INCOMPLETE PERSON?
YUKAKO.

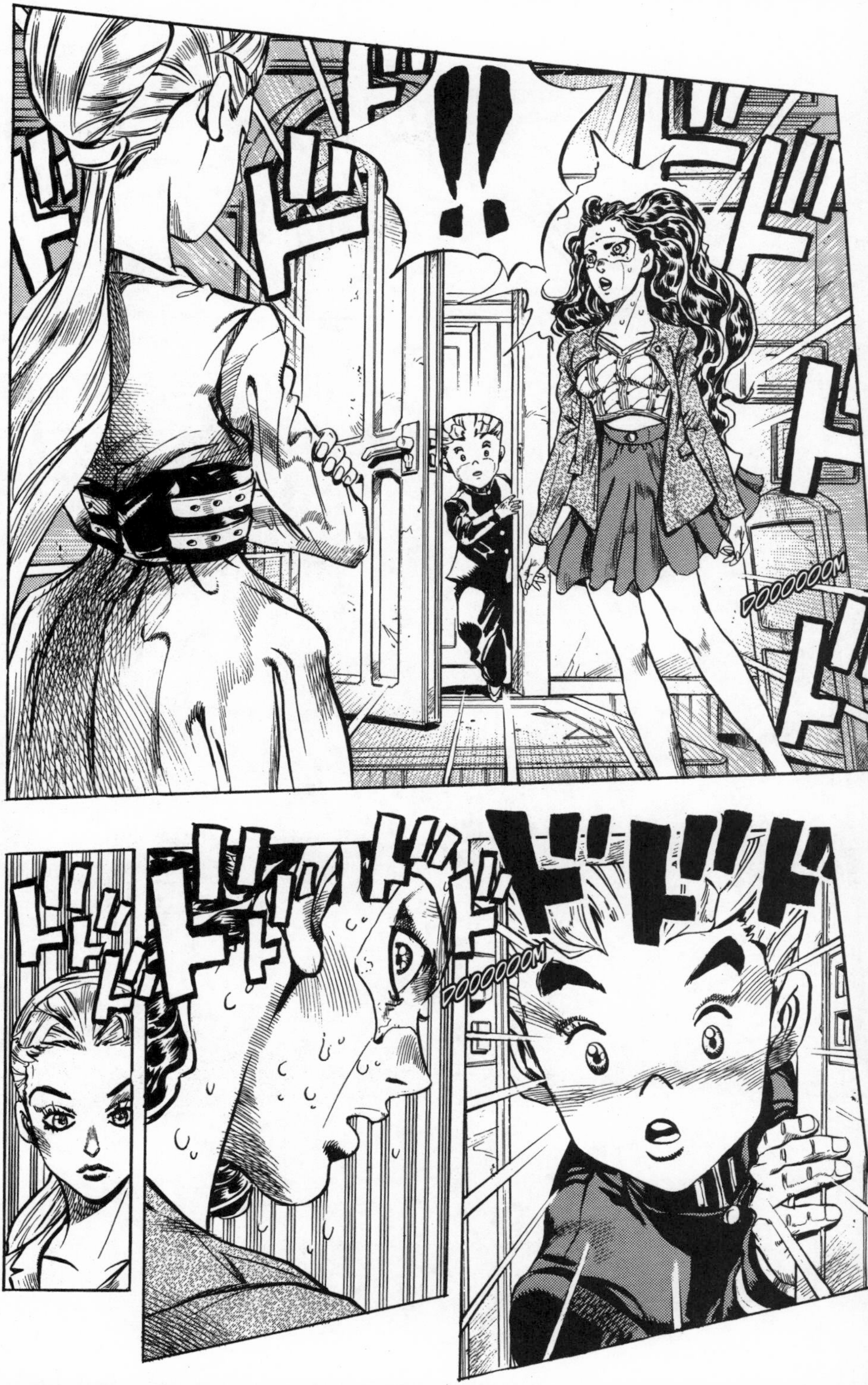
!!
DOOOOOOM
DOOOOOOM

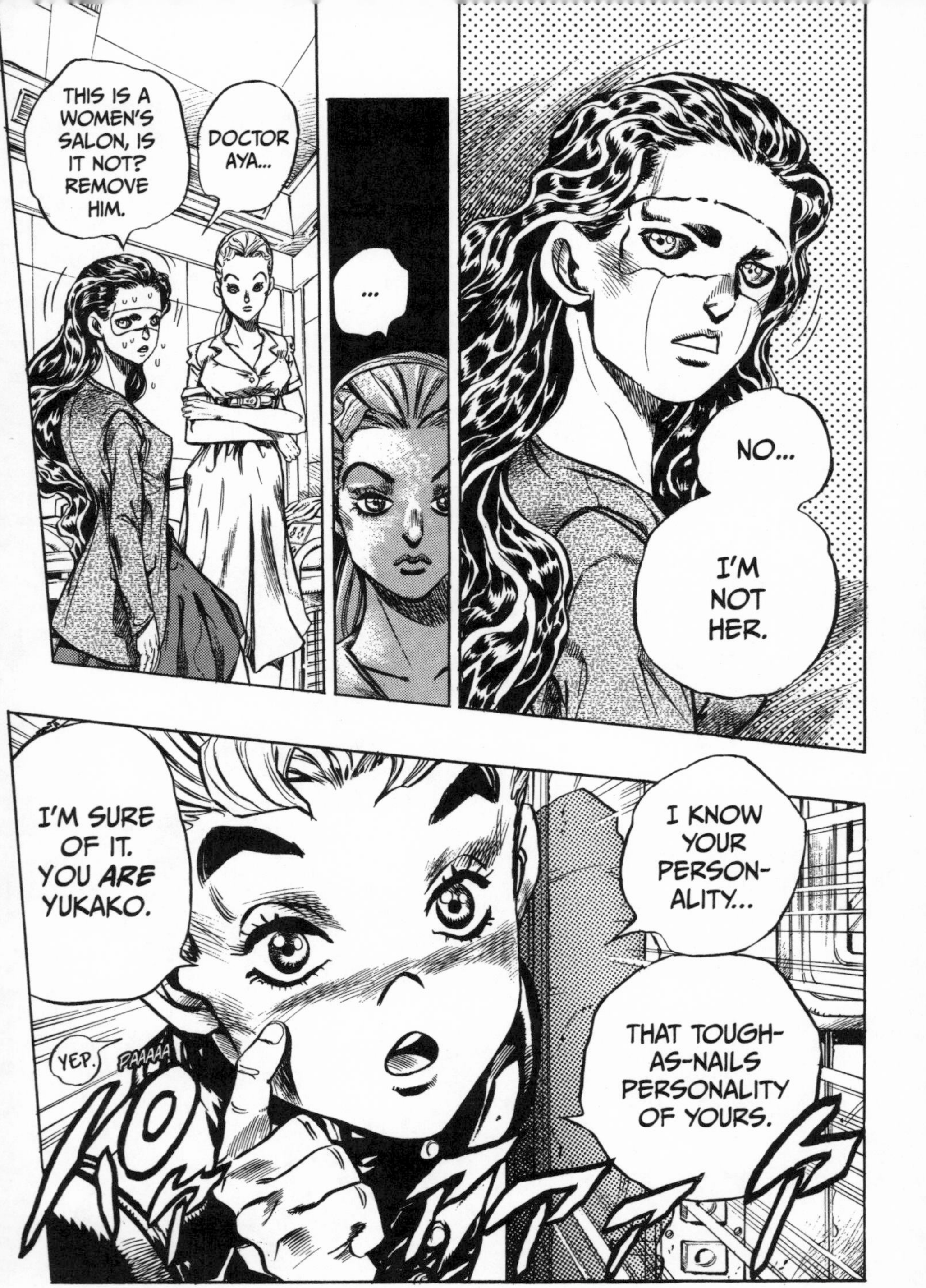
NO...
I'M NOT HER.
...
DOCTOR AYA...
THIS IS A WOMEN'S SALON, IS IT NOT? REMOVE HIM.
I KNOW YOUR PERSON-ALITY...
THAT TOUGH-AS-NAILS PERSONALITY OF YOURS.
I'M SURE OF IT. YOU ARE YUKAKO.
YEP.
PAAAAA

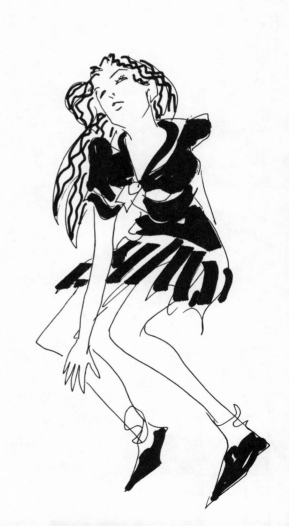

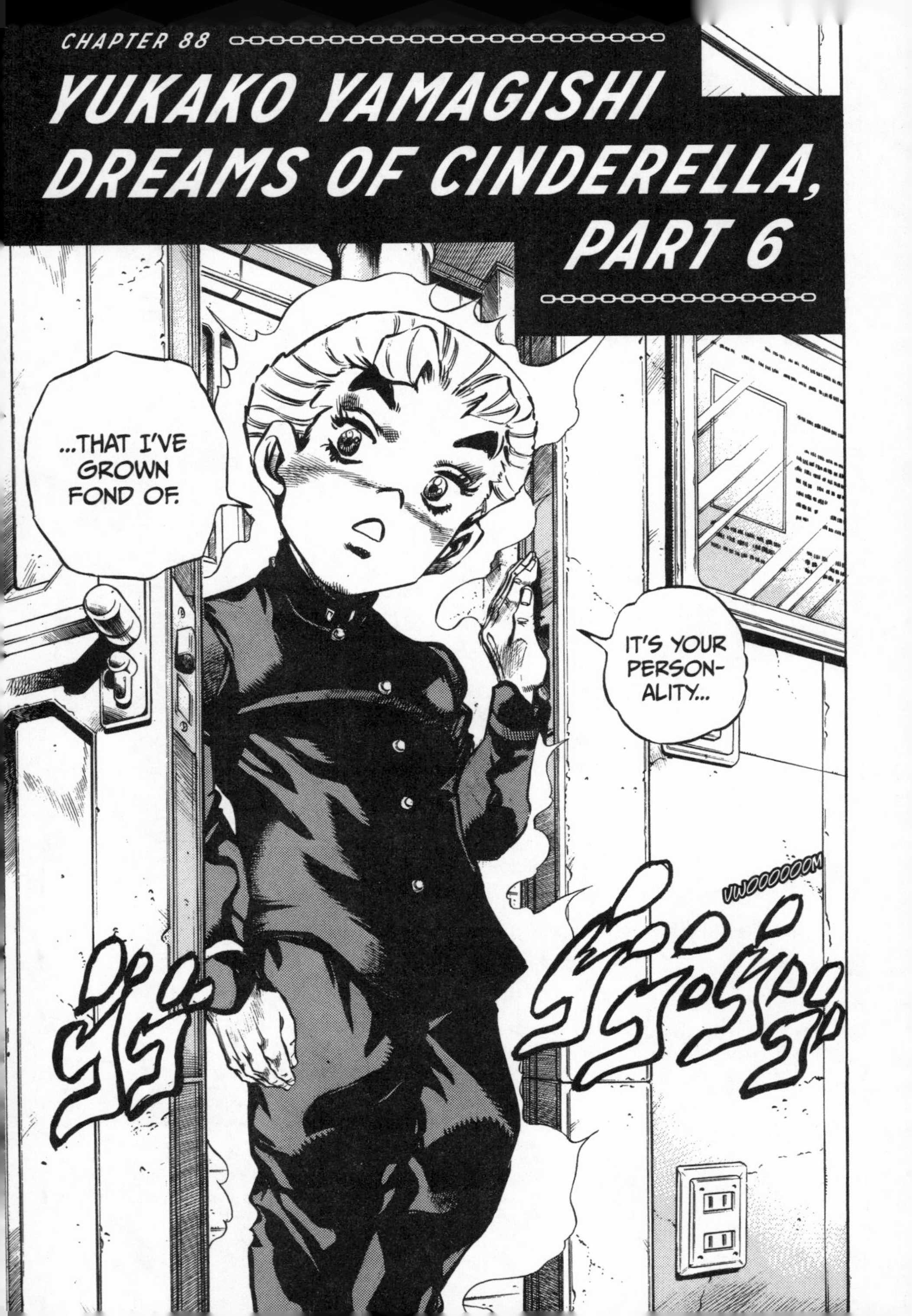
CHAPTER 88
YUKAKO YAMAGISHI DREAMS OF CINDERELLA, PART 6
IT'S YOUR PERSON-ALITY...
...THAT I'VE GROWN FOND OF.
VWOOOOOOM

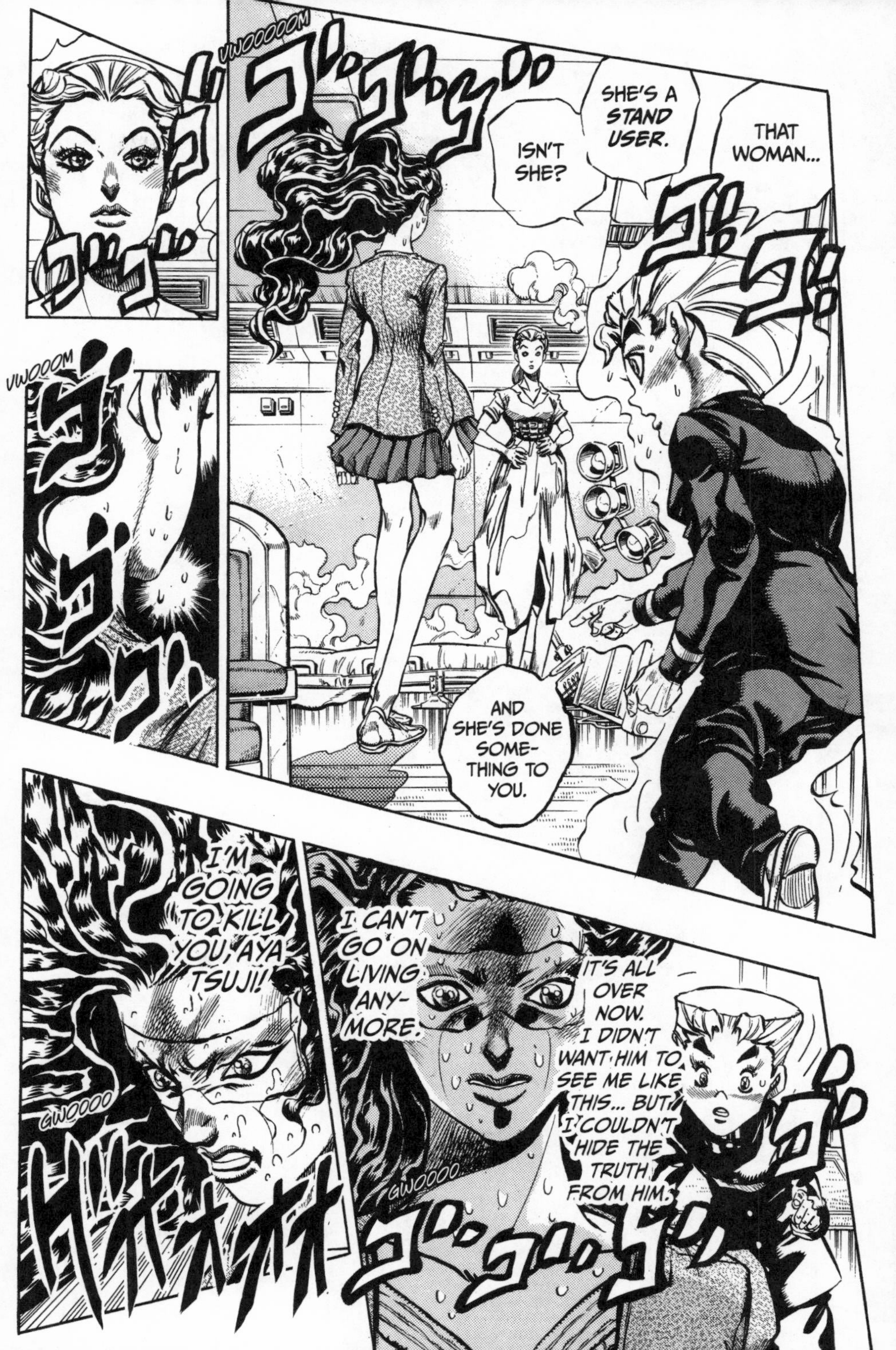
VWOOOOOM
THAT WOMAN...
SHE'S A STAND USER.
ISN'T SHE?
AND SHE'S DONE SOMETHING TO YOU.
VWOOOM
IT'S ALL OVER NOW. I DIDN'T WANT HIM TO SEE ME LIKE THIS... BUT I COULDN'T HIDE THE TRUTH FROM HIM.
I CAN'T GO ON LIVING ANYMORE.
GWOOOO
I'M GOING TO KILL YOU, AYA TSUJI!
GWOOOO

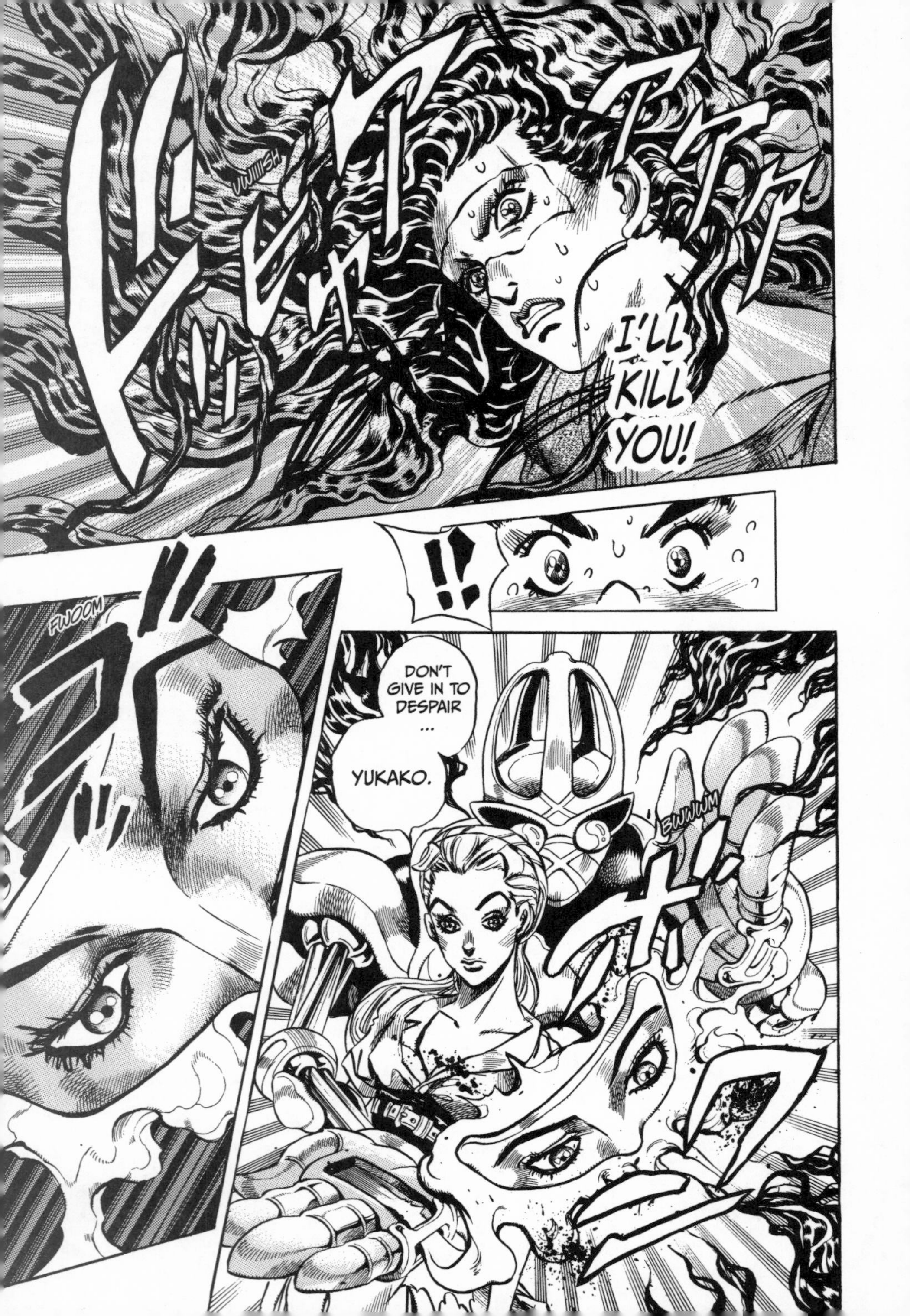
VWIIIISH
I'LL KILL YOU!
!!
DON'T GIVE IN TO DESPAIR ...
YUKAKO.
BWWWM
FWOOM

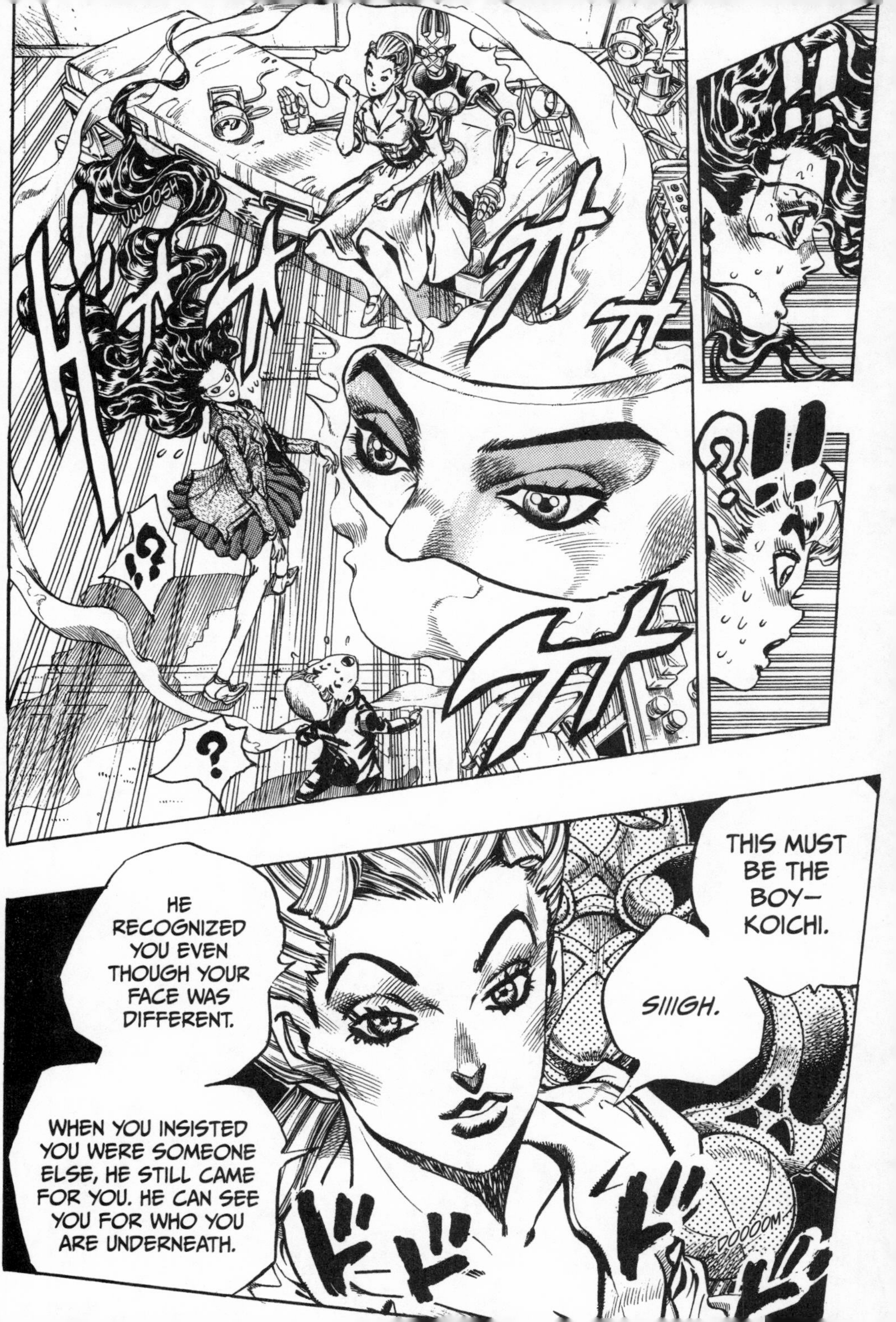
!!?
?!!
VWOOSH
!?
?
THIS MUST BE THE BOY— KOICHI.
SIIIGH.
HE RECOGNIZED YOU EVEN THOUGH YOUR FACE WAS DIFFERENT.
WHEN YOU INSISTED YOU WERE SOMEONE ELSE, HE STILL CAME FOR YOU. HE CAN SEE YOU FOR WHO YOU ARE UNDERNEATH.
DOOOOM

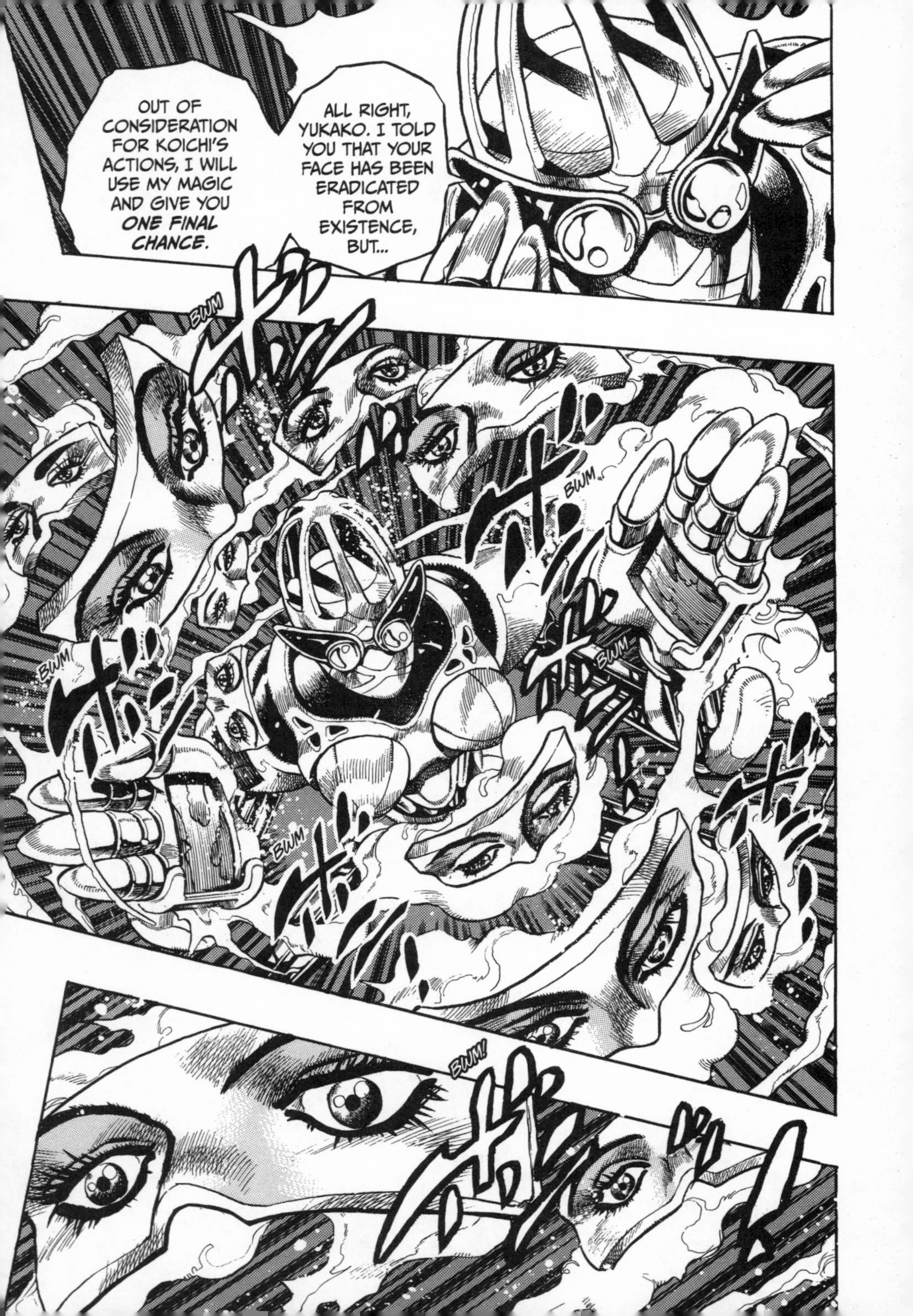
ALL RIGHT, YUKAKO. I TOLD YOU THAT YOUR FACE HAS BEEN ERADICATED FROM EXISTENCE, BUT...
OUT OF CONSIDERATION FOR KOICHI'S ACTIONS, I WILL USE MY MAGIC AND GIVE YOU *ONE FINAL CHANCE*.
BWM
BWM
BWM
BWM
BWM
BWM!

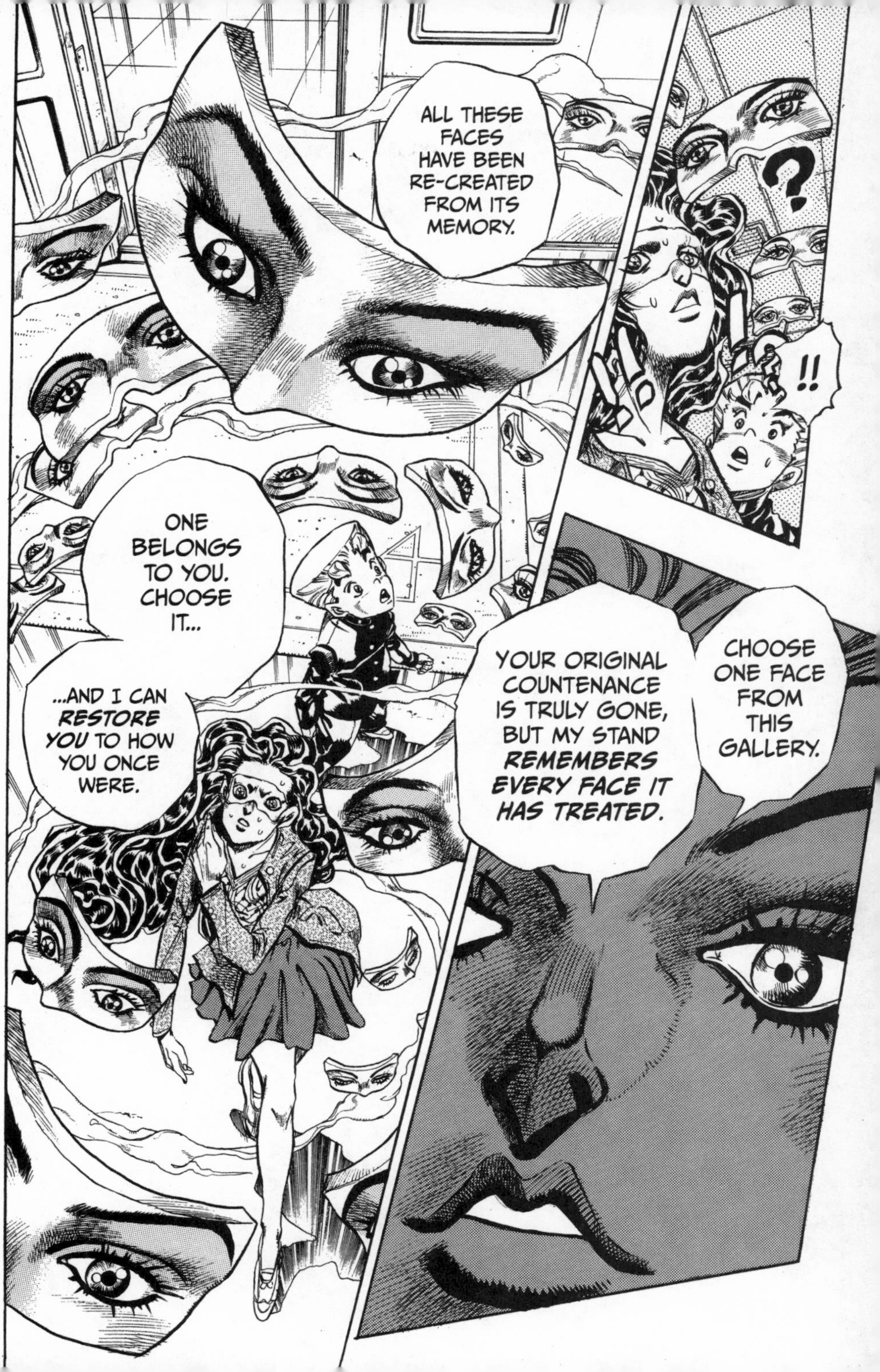
?
!!
CHOOSE ONE FACE FROM THIS GALLERY.
YOUR ORIGINAL COUNTENANCE IS TRULY GONE, BUT MY STAND *REMEMBERS EVERY FACE* IT *HAS TREATED.*
ALL THESE FACES HAVE BEEN RE-CREATED FROM ITS MEMORY.
ONE BELONGS TO YOU. CHOOSE IT...
...AND I CAN *RESTORE YOU* TO HOW YOU ONCE WERE.

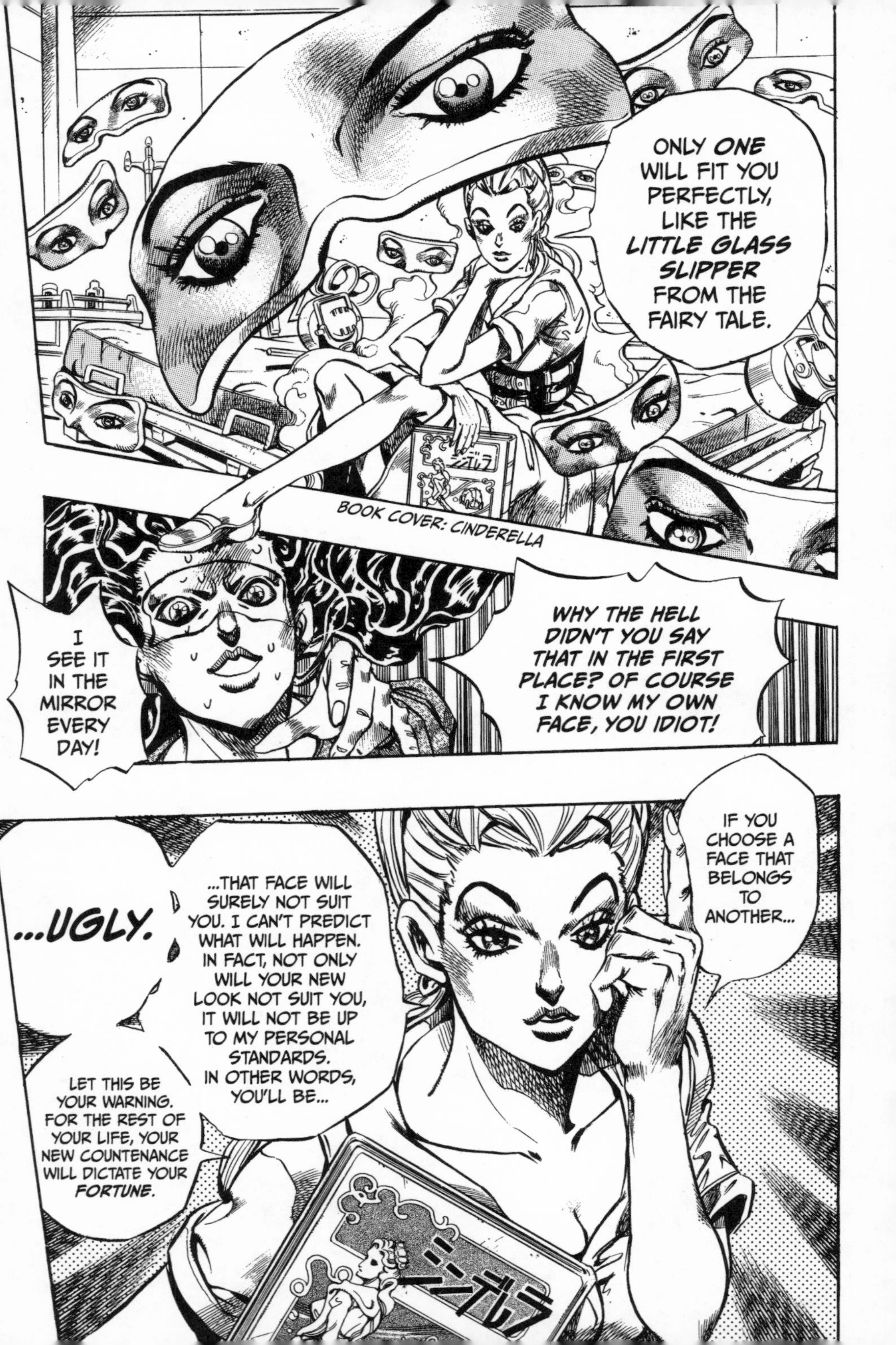
ONLY ONE WILL FIT YOU PERFECTLY, LIKE THE LITTLE GLASS SLIPPER FROM THE FAIRY TALE.
BOOK COVER: CINDERELLA
WHY THE HELL DIDN'T YOU SAY THAT IN THE FIRST PLACE? OF COURSE I KNOW MY OWN FACE, YOU IDIOT!
I SEE IT IN THE MIRROR EVERY DAY!
IF YOU CHOOSE A FACE THAT BELONGS TO ANOTHER...
...THAT FACE WILL SURELY NOT SUIT YOU. I CAN'T PREDICT WHAT WILL HAPPEN. IN FACT, NOT ONLY WILL YOUR NEW LOOK NOT SUIT YOU, IT WILL NOT BE UP TO MY PERSONAL STANDARDS. IN OTHER WORDS, YOU'LL BE...
...UGLY.
LET THIS BE YOUR WARNING. FOR THE REST OF YOUR LIFE, YOUR NEW COUNTENANCE WILL DICTATE YOUR FORTUNE.
シンデレラ

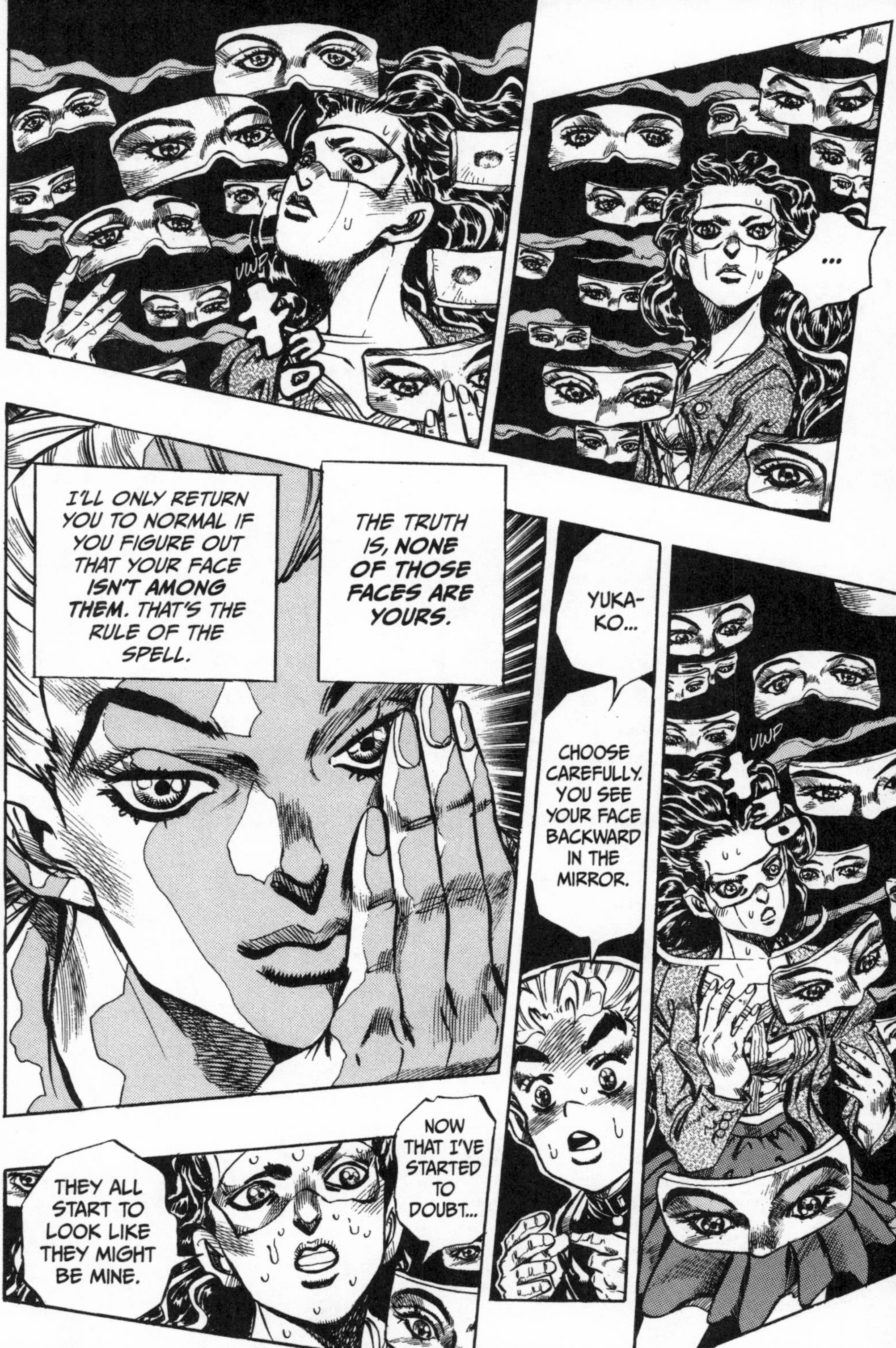
...
VWP
VWP
YUKA-KO...
CHOOSE CAREFULLY. YOU SEE YOUR FACE BACKWARD IN THE MIRROR.
THE TRUTH IS, NONE OF THOSE FACES ARE YOURS.
I'LL ONLY RETURN YOU TO NORMAL IF YOU FIGURE OUT THAT YOUR FACE ISN'T AMONG THEM. THAT'S THE RULE OF THE SPELL.
NOW THAT I'VE STARTED TO DOUBT...
THEY ALL START TO LOOK LIKE THEY MIGHT BE MINE.

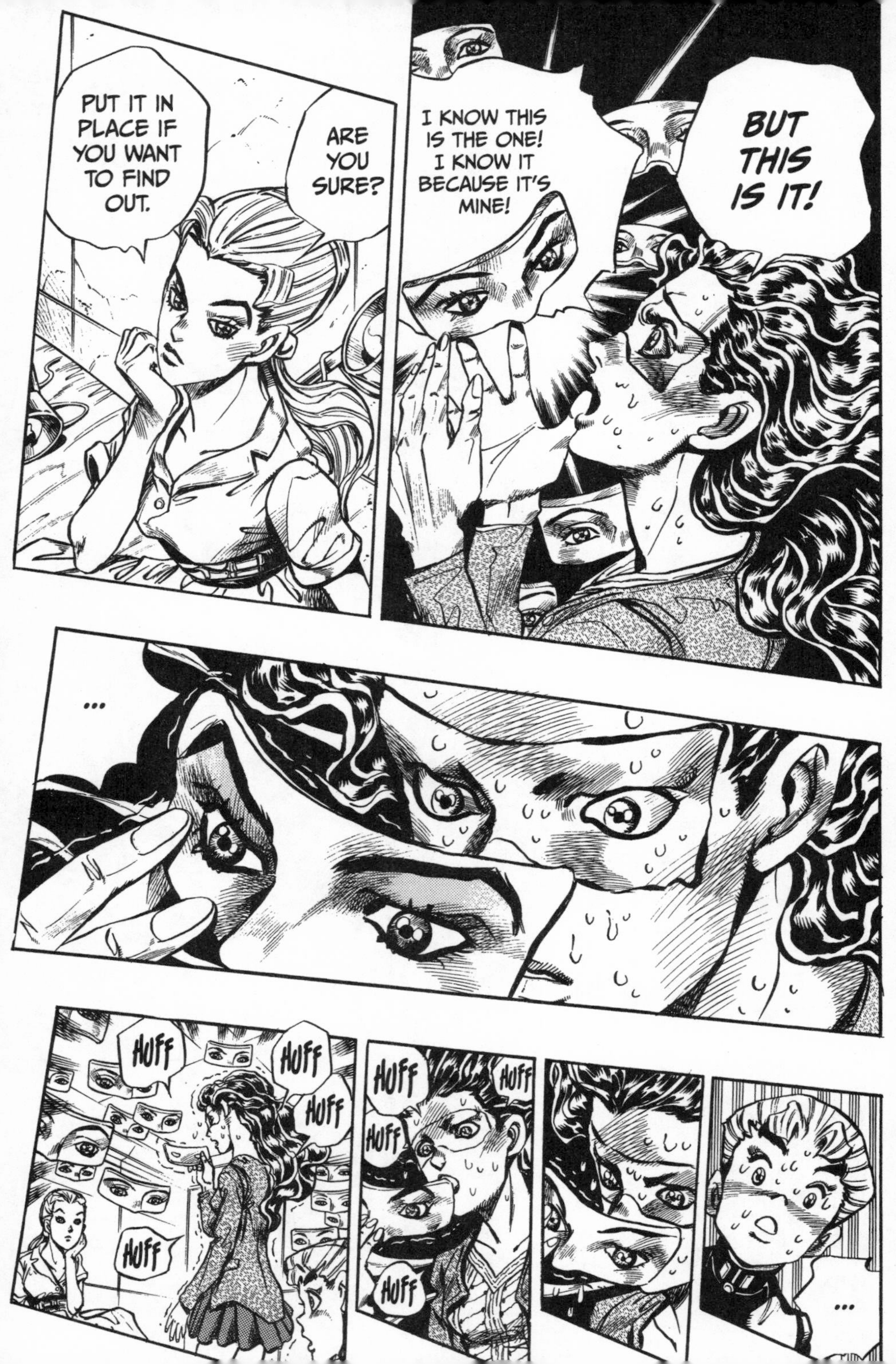
BUT THIS IS IT!
I KNOW THIS IS THE ONE! I KNOW IT BECAUSE IT'S MINE!
ARE YOU SURE?
PUT IT IN PLACE IF YOU WANT TO FIND OUT.
...
...
HUFF
HUFF
HUFF
HUFF
HUFF
HUFF
HUFF
HUFF

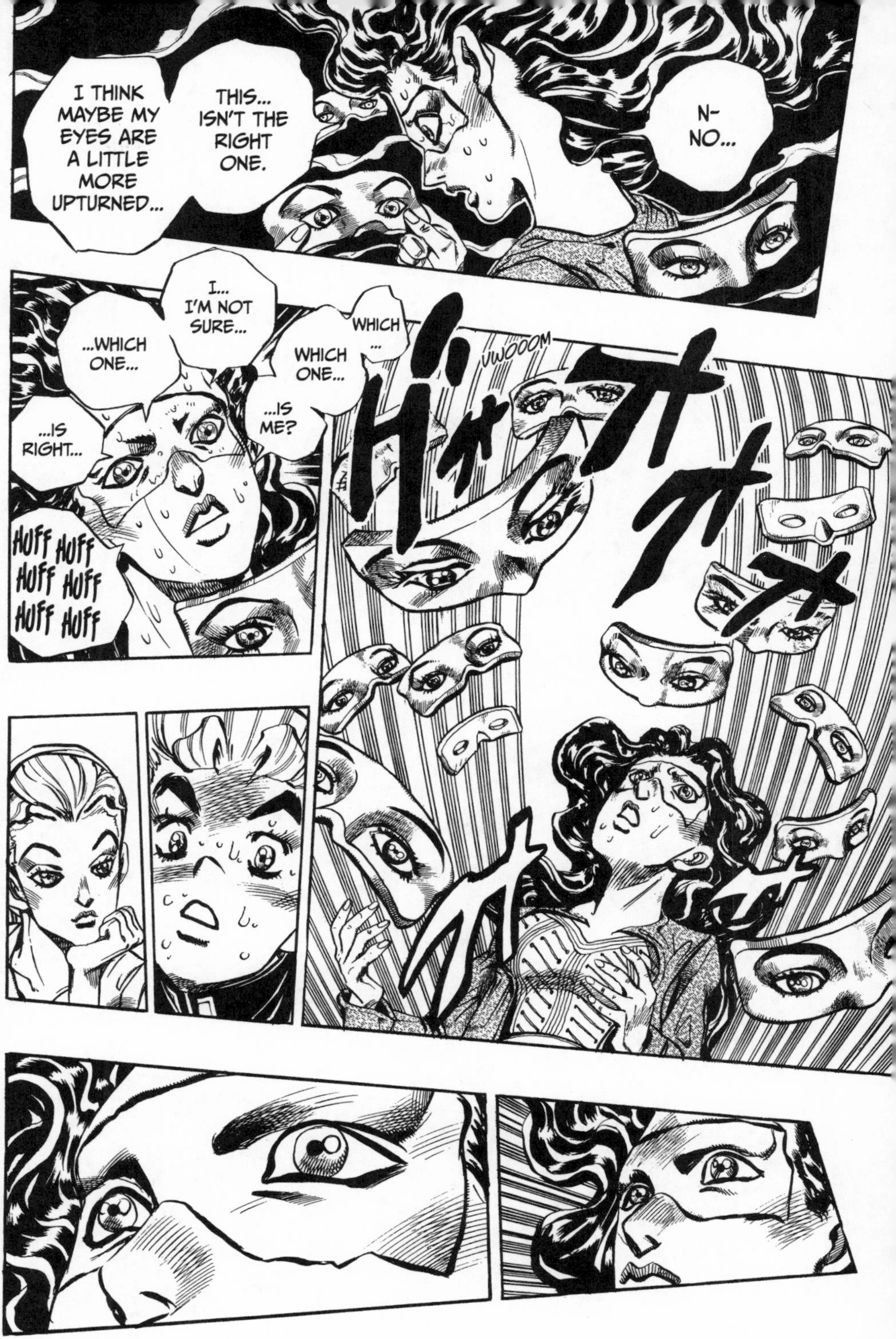
N- NO...
THIS... ISN'T THE RIGHT ONE.
I THINK MAYBE MY EYES ARE A LITTLE MORE UPTURNED...
UWOOOM
WHICH ...
WHICH ONE...
...IS ME?
I... I'M NOT SURE...
...WHICH ONE...
...IS RIGHT...
HUFF HUFF HUFF HUFF HUFF HUFF

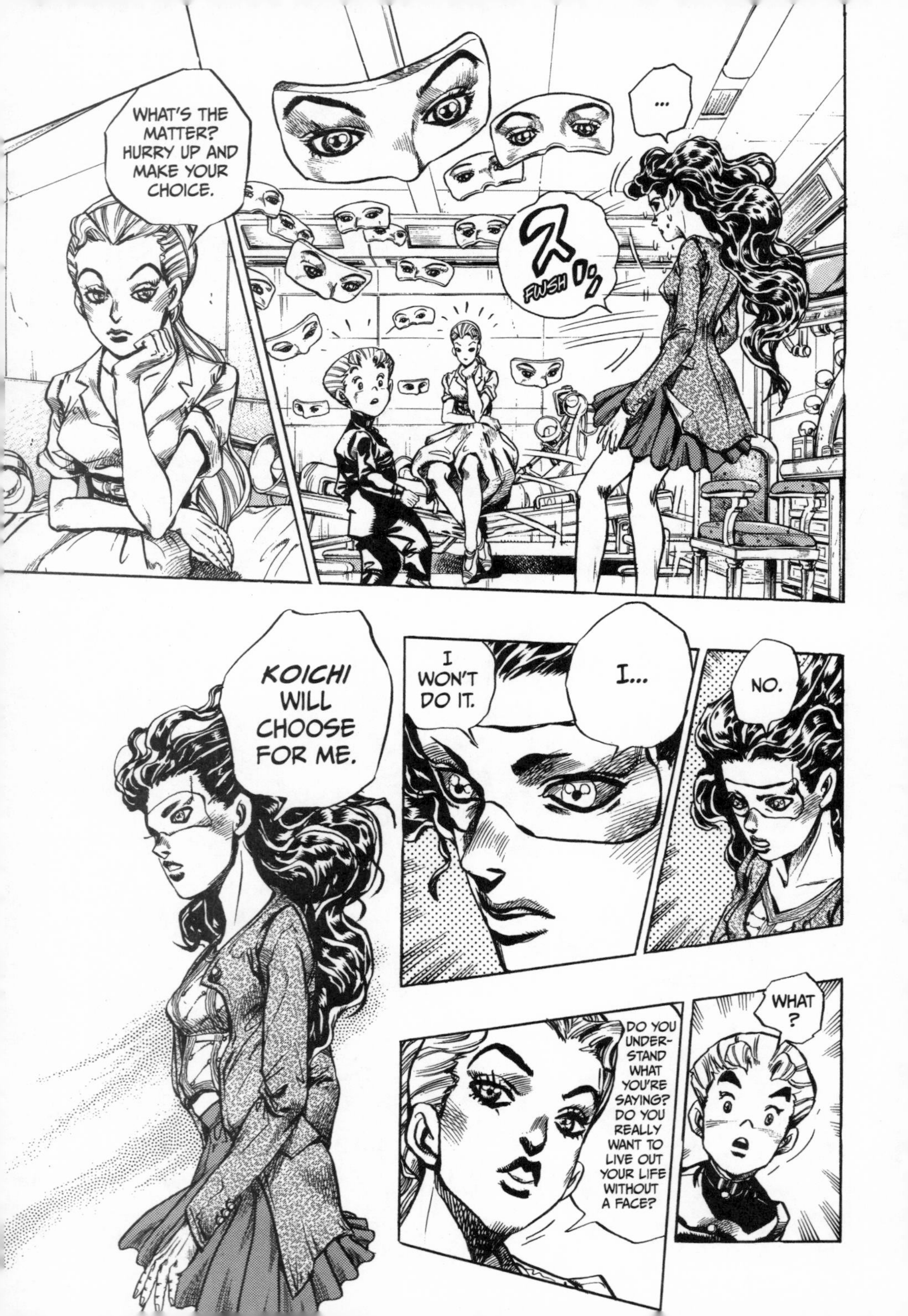
...
スッ
FUSH
WHAT'S THE MATTER? HURRY UP AND MAKE YOUR CHOICE.
NO.
I...
I WON'T DO IT.
WHAT?
DO YOU UNDERSTAND WHAT YOU'RE SAYING? DO YOU REALLY WANT TO LIVE OUT YOUR LIFE WITHOUT A FACE?
KOICHI WILL CHOOSE FOR ME.

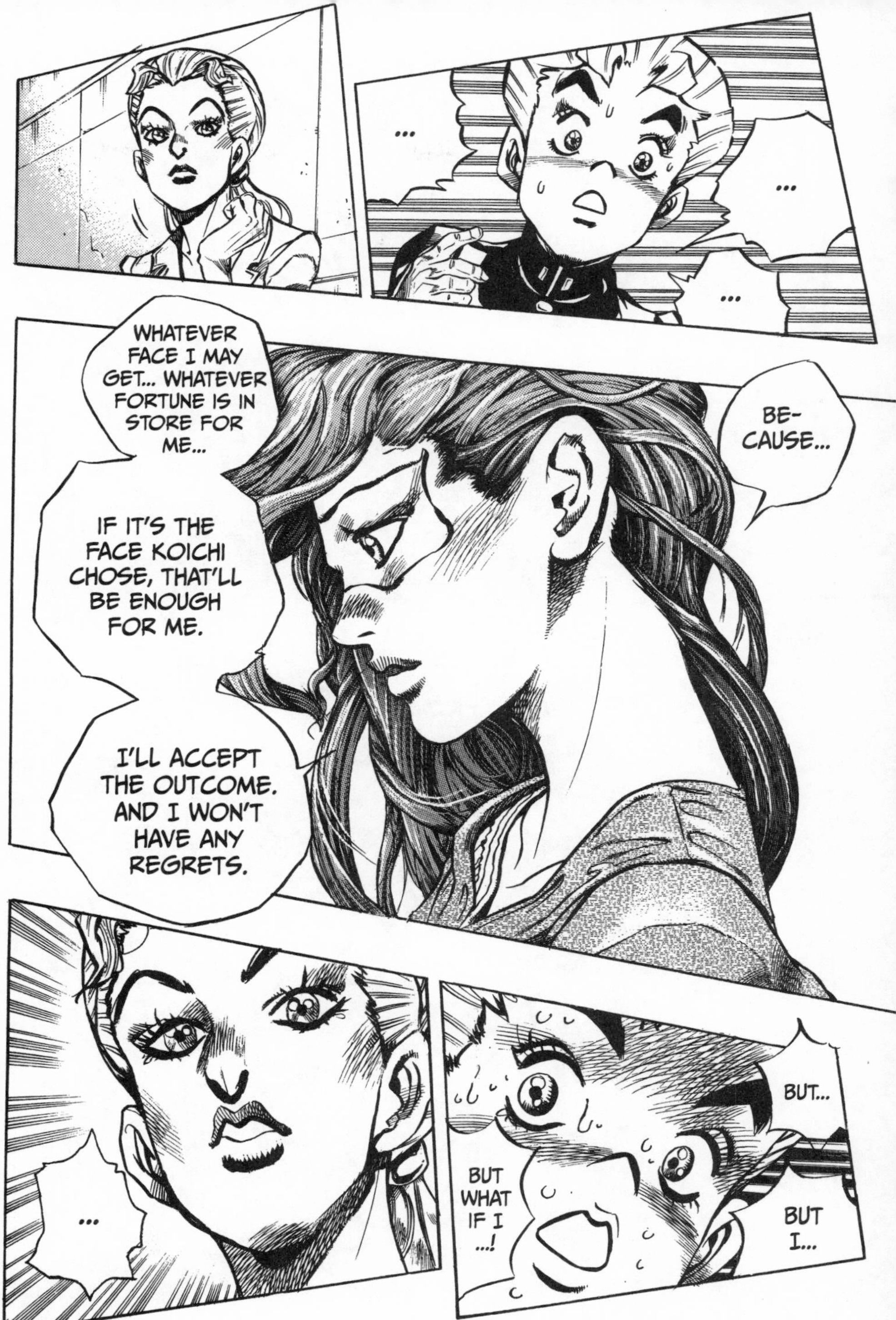
...
...
...
BE-CAUSE...
WHATEVER FACE I MAY GET... WHATEVER FORTUNE IS IN STORE FOR ME...
IF IT'S THE FACE KOICHI CHOSE, THAT'LL BE ENOUGH FOR ME.
I'LL ACCEPT THE OUTCOME. AND I WON'T HAVE ANY REGRETS.
BUT...
BUT I...
BUT WHAT IF I ...!
...

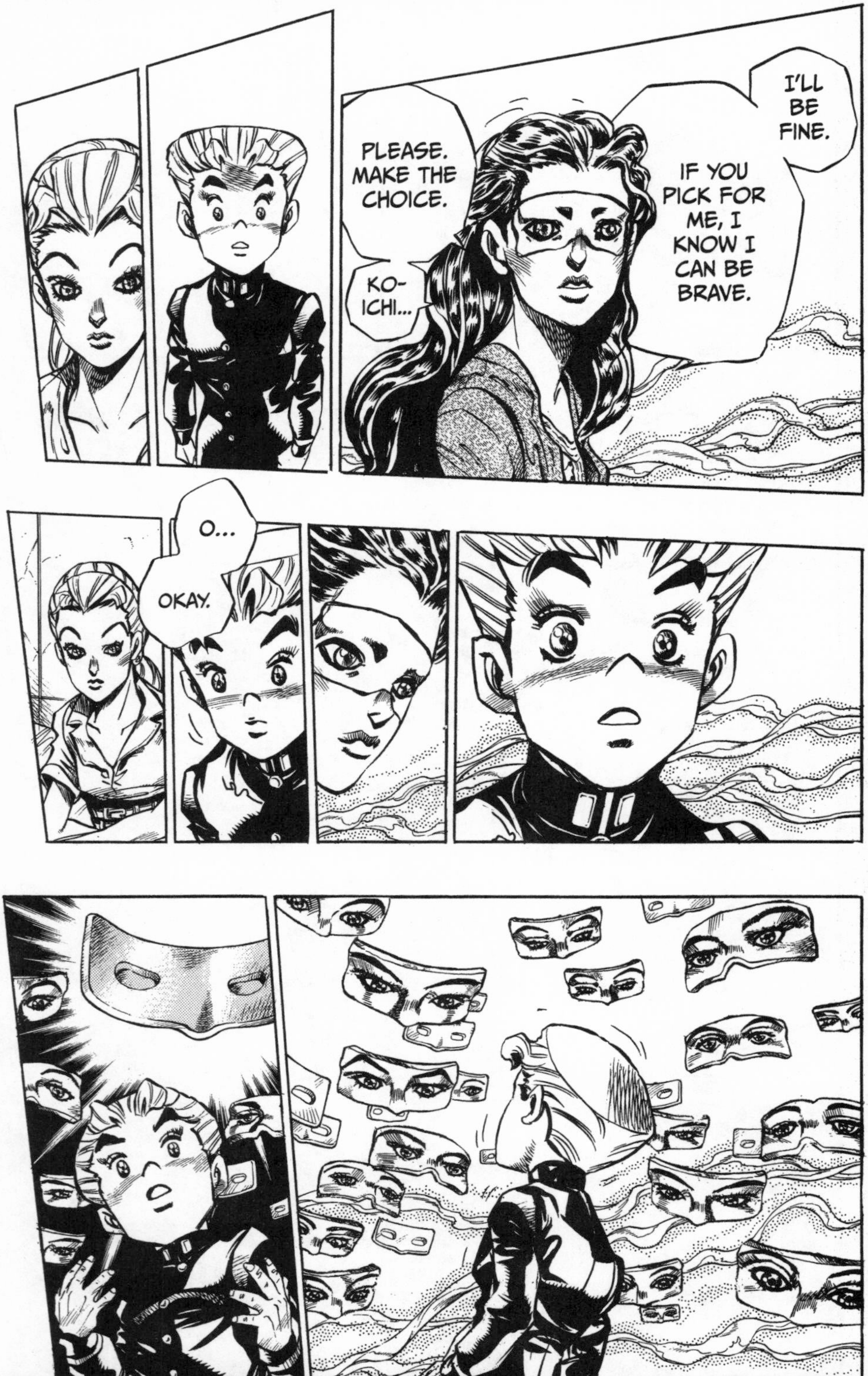
I'LL BE FINE.
IF YOU PICK FOR ME, I KNOW I CAN BE BRAVE.
PLEASE. MAKE THE CHOICE.
KO-ICHI...
O...
OKAY.

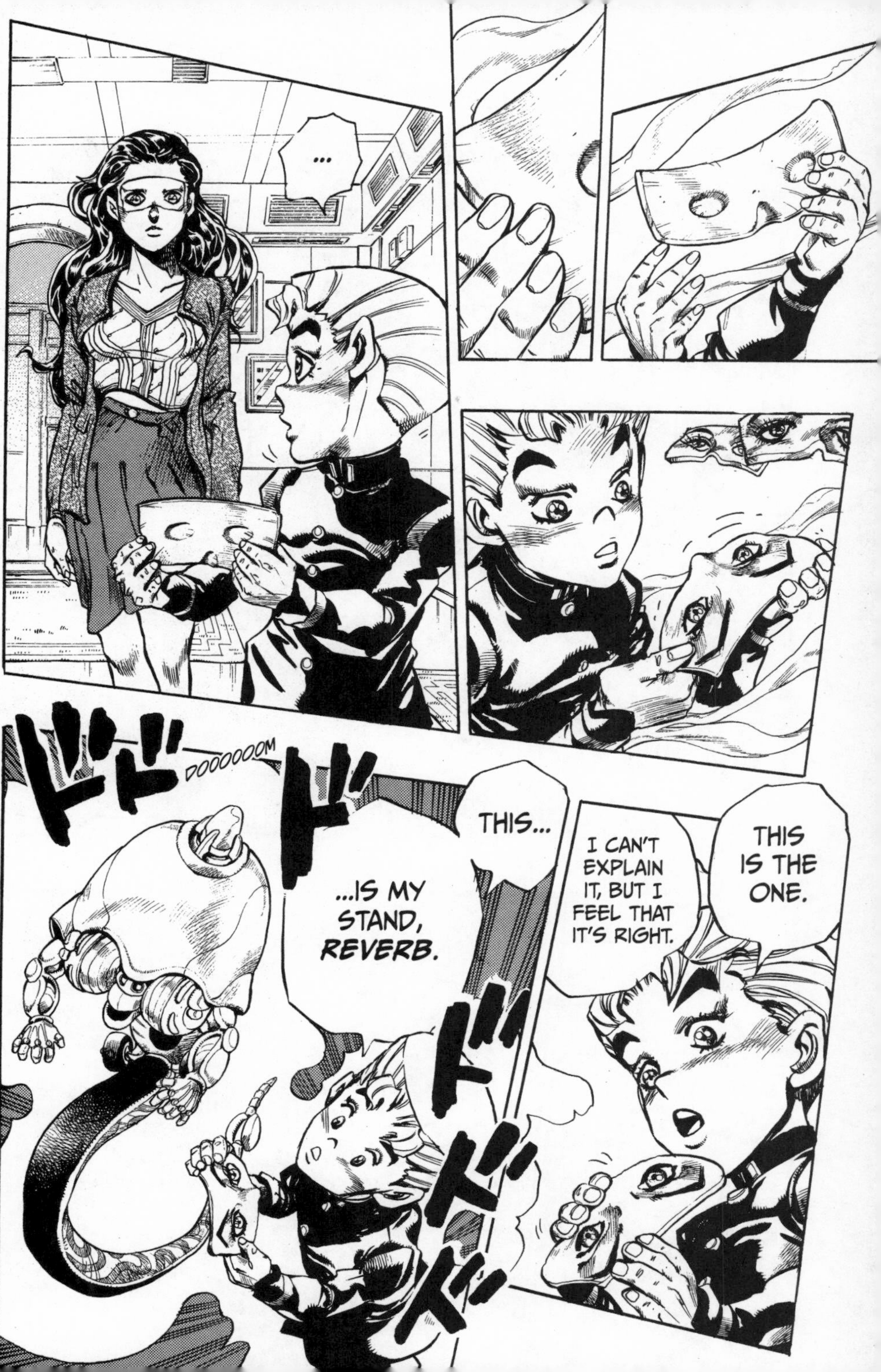
...
THIS IS THE ONE.
I CAN'T EXPLAIN IT, BUT I FEEL THAT IT'S RIGHT.
DOOOOOOM
THIS...
...IS MY STAND, REVERB.

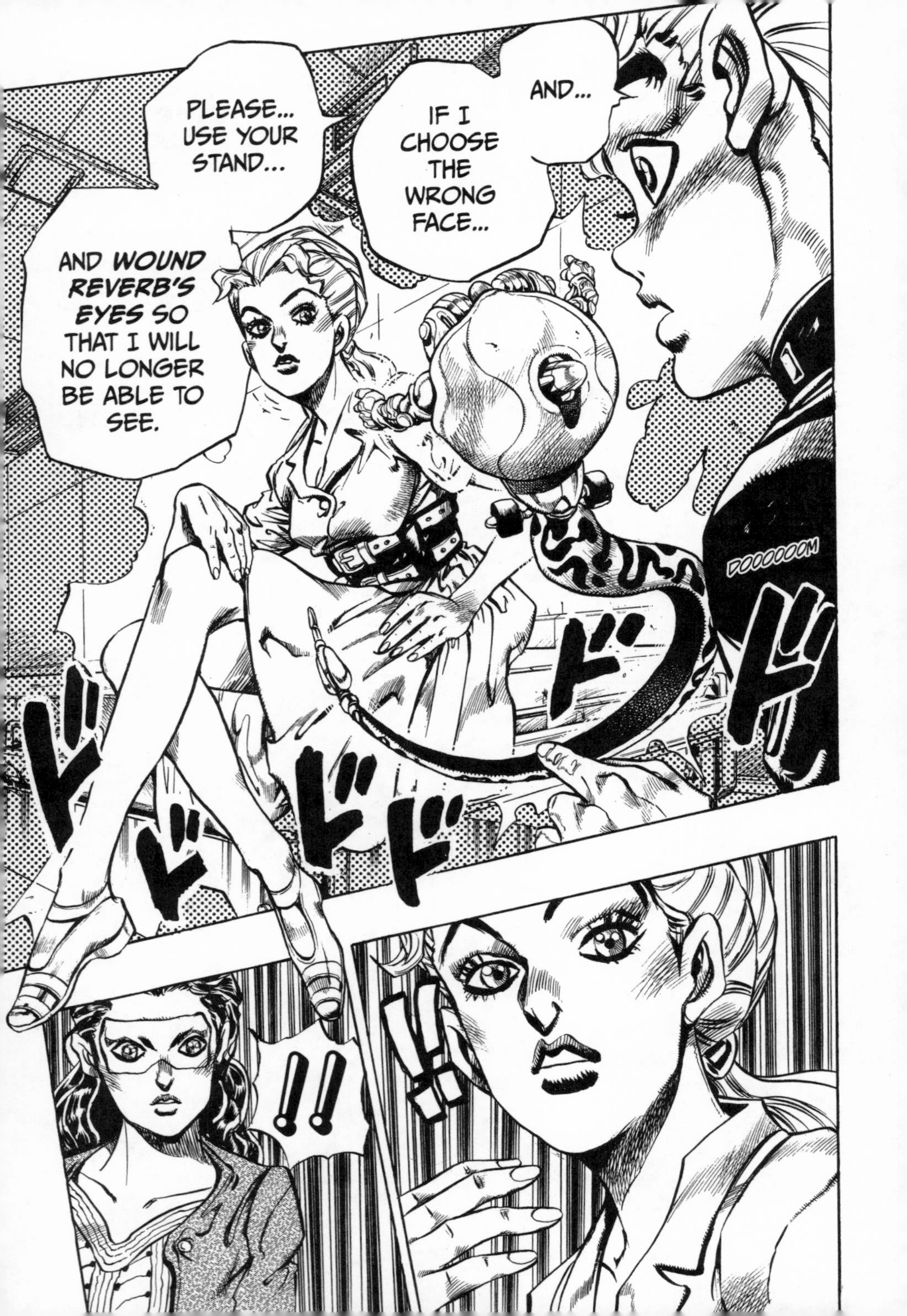
AND...
IF I CHOOSE THE WRONG FACE...
PLEASE... USE YOUR STAND...
AND WOUND REVERB'S EYES SO THAT I WILL NO LONGER BE ABLE TO SEE.
DOOOOOOM
!!

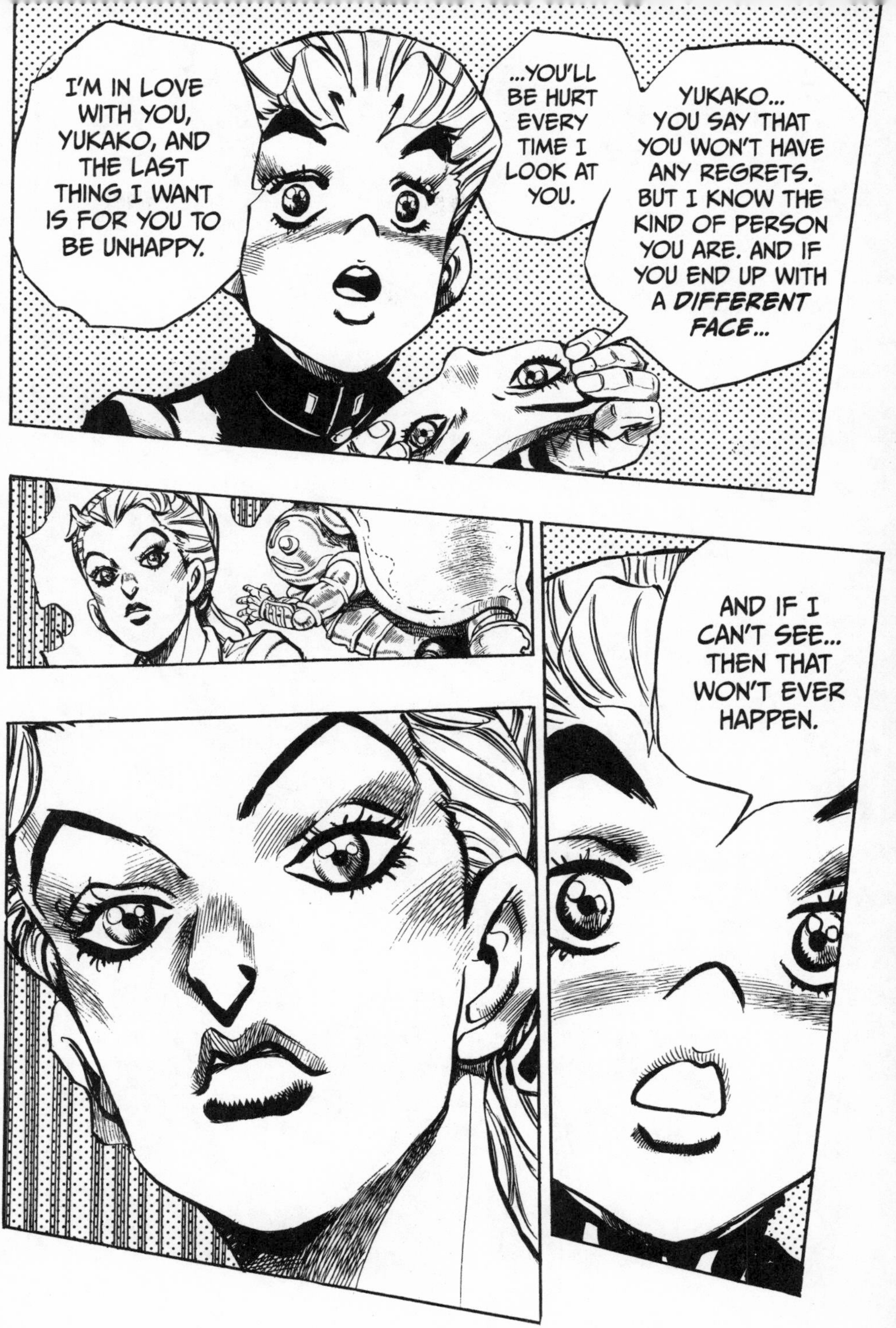
YUKAKO... YOU SAY THAT YOU WON'T HAVE ANY REGRETS. BUT I KNOW THE KIND OF PERSON YOU ARE. AND IF YOU END UP WITH A *DIFFERENT* FACE...
...YOU'LL BE HURT EVERY TIME I LOOK AT YOU.
I'M IN LOVE WITH YOU, YUKAKO, AND THE LAST THING I WANT IS FOR YOU TO BE UNHAPPY.
AND IF I CAN'T SEE... THEN THAT WON'T EVER HAPPEN.

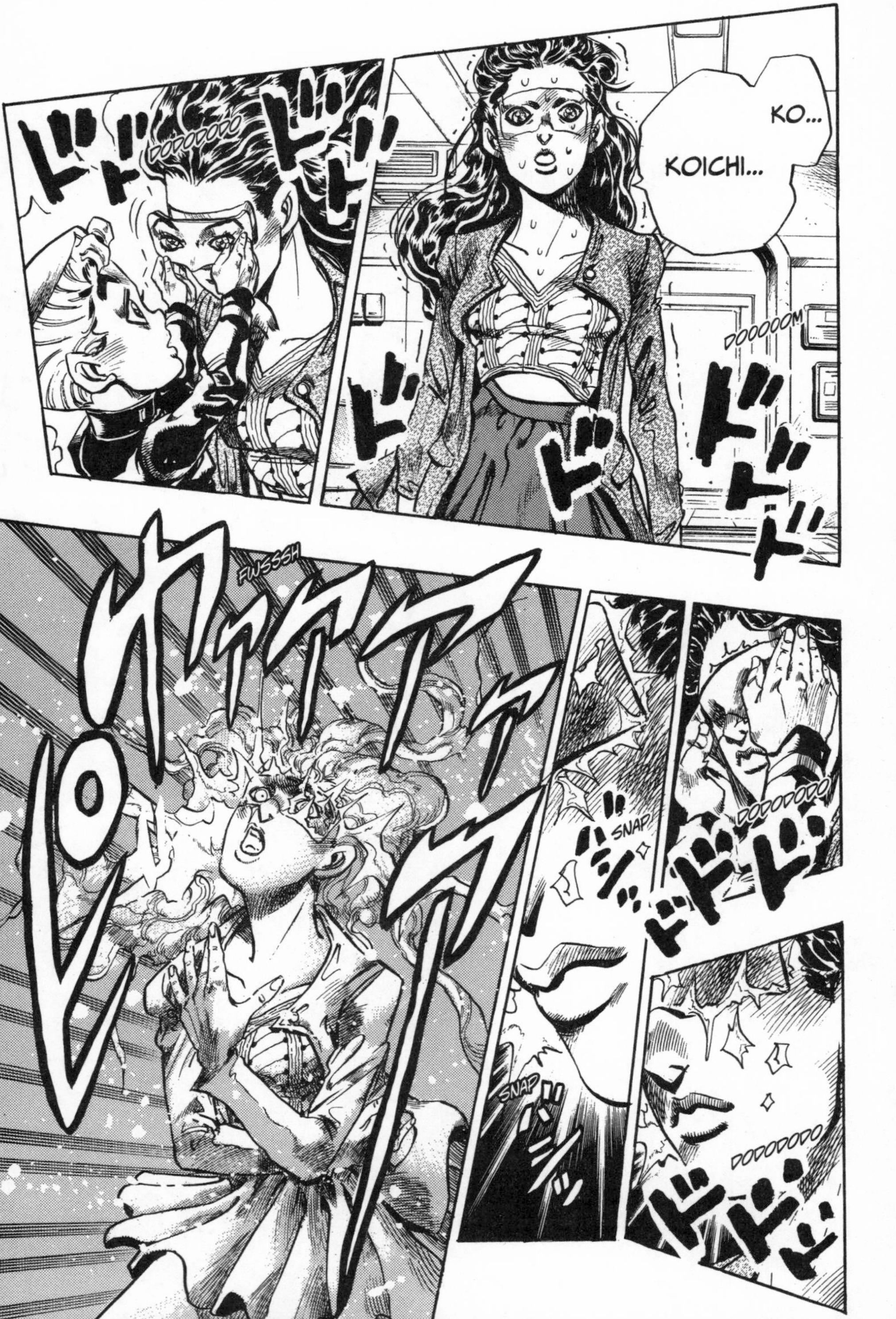
KO...
KOICHI...
DOOOOOM
DODODODO
DODODODO
SNAP
DODODODO
SNAP
FWSSSH

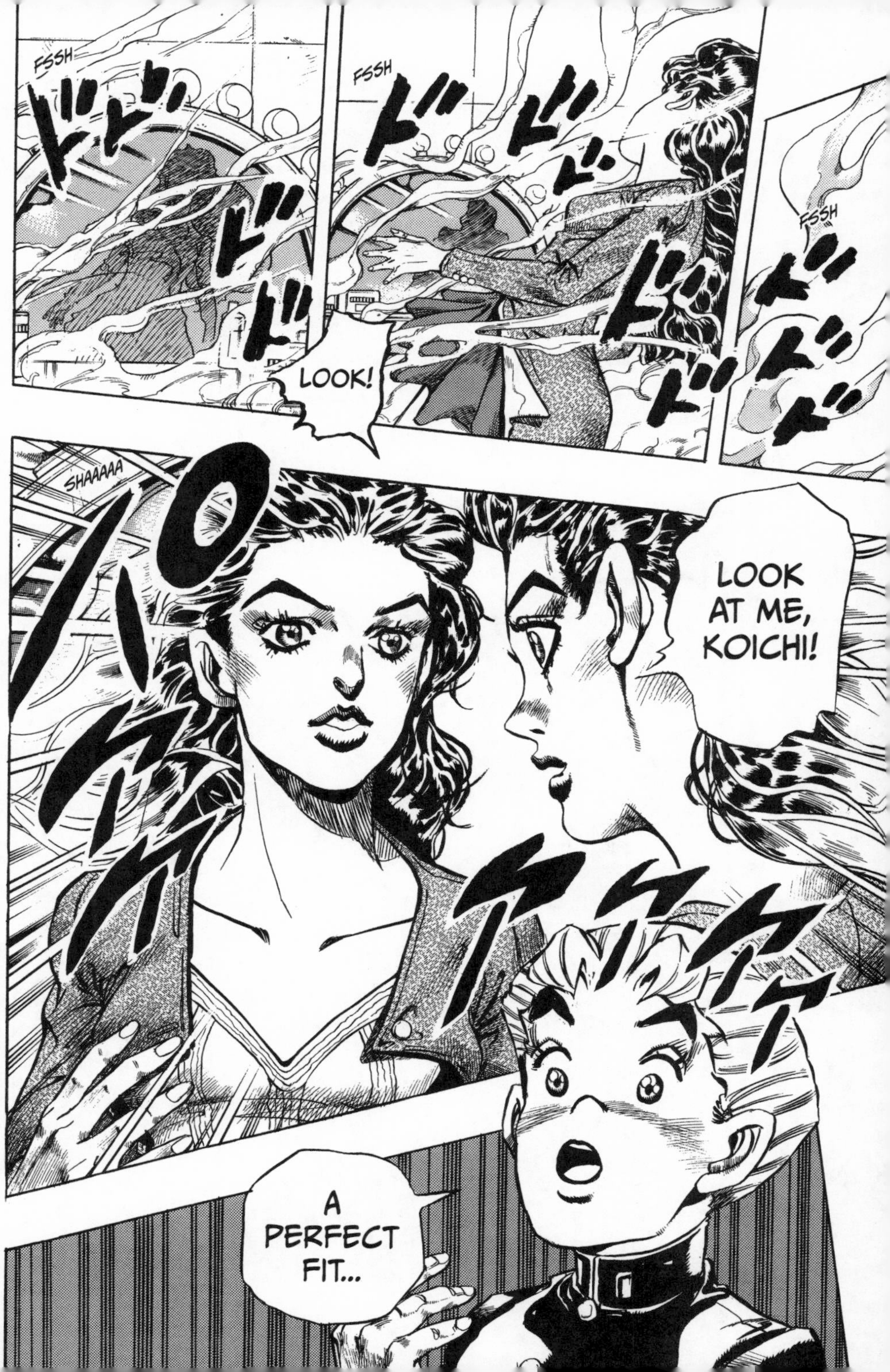
FSSH
FSSH
LOOK!
FSSH
LOOK AT ME, KOICHI!
SHAAAAA
A PERFECT FIT...

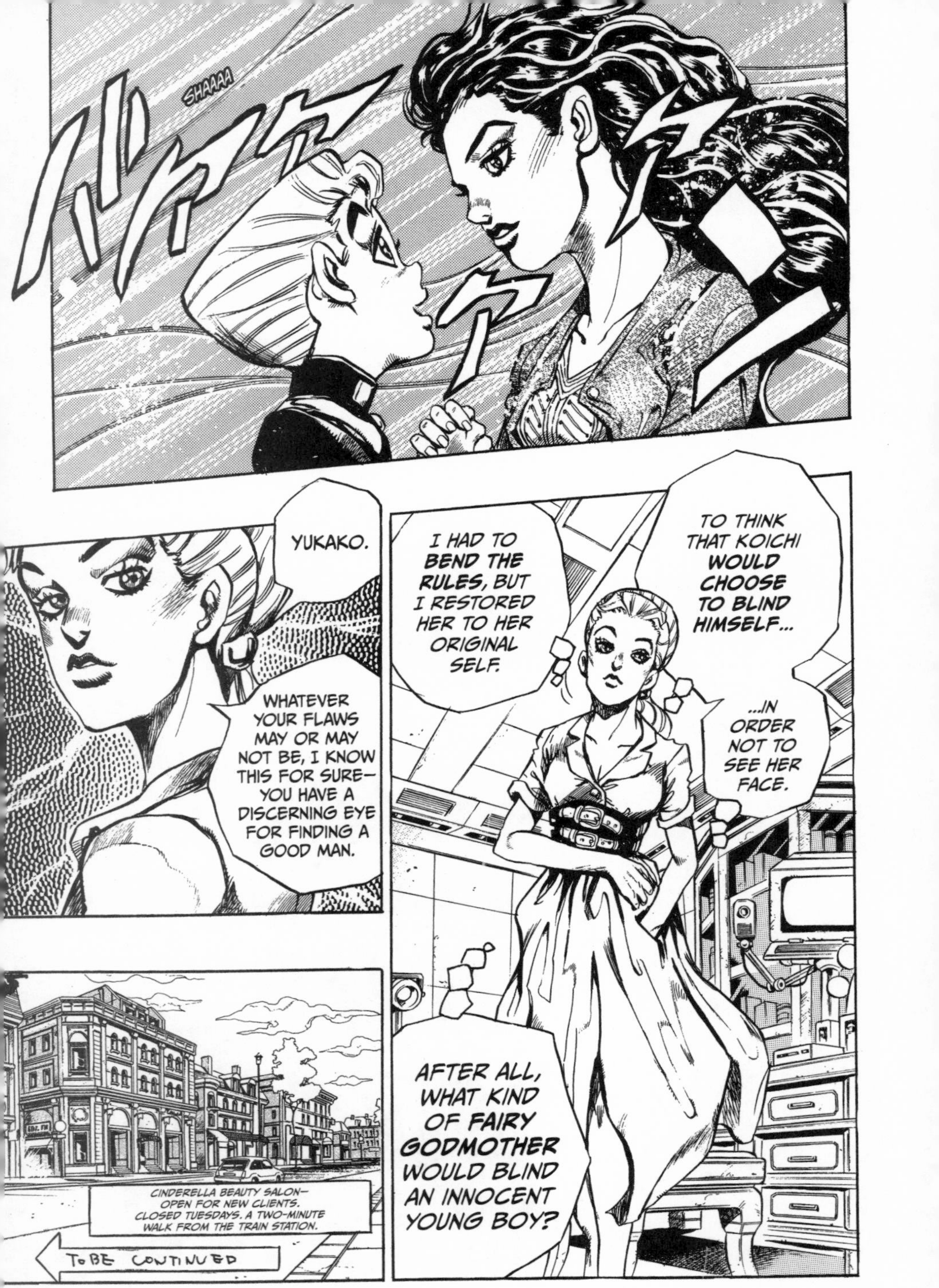
SHAAAA
TO THINK THAT KOICHI WOULD CHOOSE TO BLIND HIMSELF...
...IN ORDER NOT TO SEE HER FACE.
I HAD TO BEND THE RULES, BUT I RESTORED HER TO HER ORIGINAL SELF.
AFTER ALL, WHAT KIND OF FAIRY GODMOTHER WOULD BLIND AN INNOCENT YOUNG BOY?
YUKAKO.
WHATEVER YOUR FLAWS MAY OR MAY NOT BE, I KNOW THIS FOR SURE— YOU HAVE A DISCERNING EYE FOR FINDING A GOOD MAN.
CINDERELLA BEAUTY SALON— OPEN FOR NEW CLIENTS. CLOSED TUESDAYS. A TWO-MINUTE WALK FROM THE TRAIN STATION.
TO BE CONTINUED

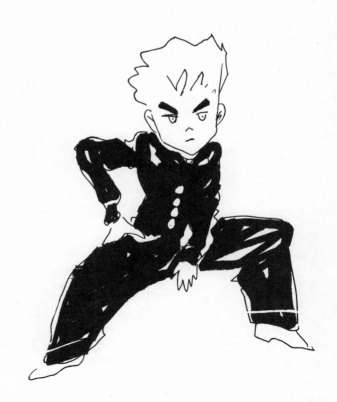

CHAPTER 89

HEART ATTACK, PART 1

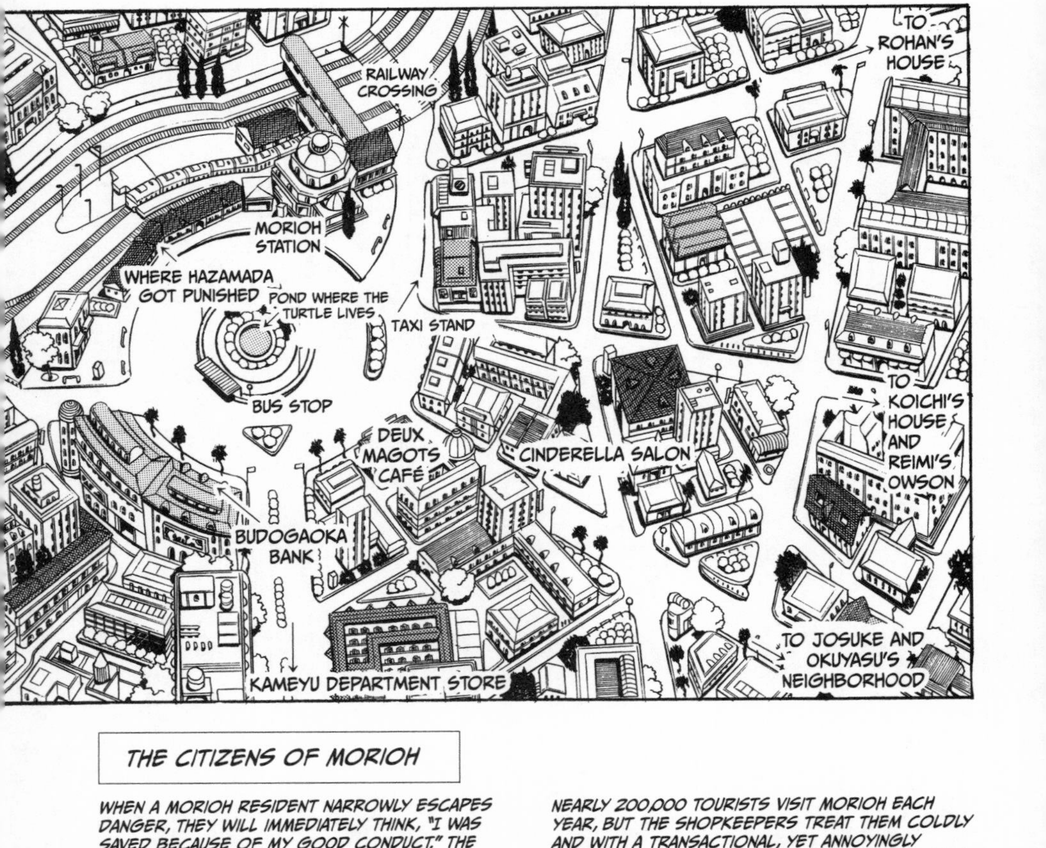

TO ROHAN'S HOUSE
RAILWAY CROSSING
MORIOH STATION
WHERE HAZAMADA GOT PUNISHED
POND WHERE THE TURTLE LIVES
TAXI STAND
BUS STOP
TO KOICHI'S HOUSE AND REIMI'S OWSON
DEUX MAGOTS CAFÉ
CINDERELLA SALON
BUDOGAOKA BANK
TO JOSUKE AND OKUYASU'S NEIGHBORHOOD
KAMEYU DEPARTMENT STORE

THE CITIZENS OF MORIOH

WHEN A MORIOH RESIDENT NARROWLY ESCAPES DANGER, THEY WILL IMMEDIATELY THINK, "I WAS SAVED BECAUSE OF MY GOOD CONDUCT." THE ONES OVER 30 WILL ALSO MUTTER AN OLD SAYING: "WITH FAITH, EVEN A SARDINE'S HEAD CAN BE SACRED." THIS IS NOT TO SUGGEST THAT THE PEOPLE OF MORIOH ARE ESPECIALLY RELIGIOUS, BUT THEY ALL SAY IT JUST THE SAME.

NEARLY 200,000 TOURISTS VISIT MORIOH EACH YEAR, BUT THE SHOPKEEPERS TREAT THEM COLDLY AND WITH A TRANSACTIONAL, YET ANNOYINGLY CONDESCENDING ATTITUDE—AS IF THE MERCHANTS ARE THINKING, "IF YOU WANT TO BUY SOMETHING, THEN FINE, I'LL SELL IT TO YOU." BUT ONCE YOU GET TO KNOW THE LOCALS, THEY'RE ALL ACTUALLY NICE PEOPLE.

*—**TOP 100 TRAVEL DESTINATIONS WITHOUT LEAVING JAPAN**, MINMEI PUBLISHING. PRICE: 1,500 YEN (TAX INCLUSIVE).*

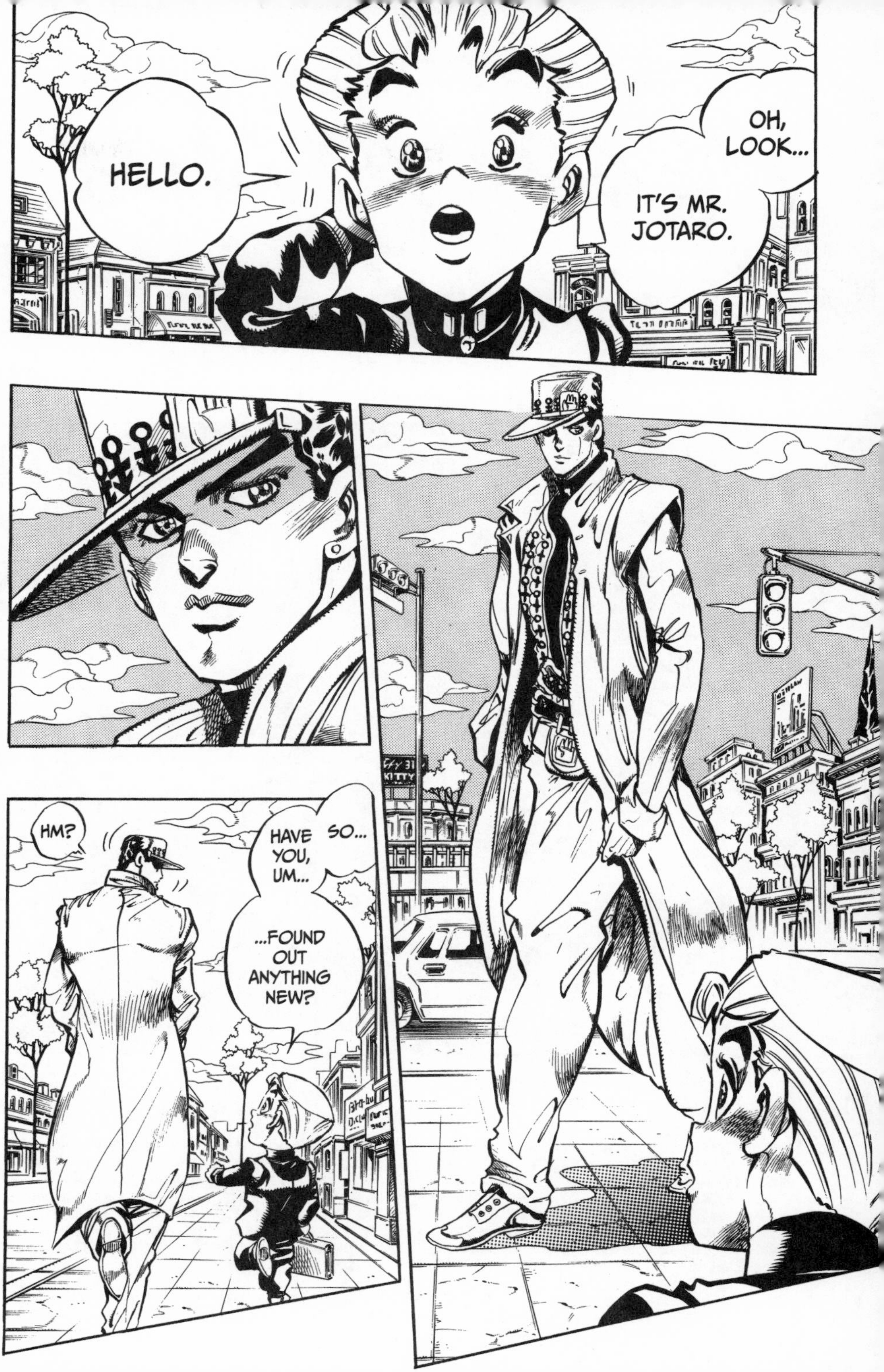
OH, LOOK...
IT'S MR. JOTARO.
HELLO.
SO...
HAVE YOU, UM...
...FOUND OUT ANYTHING NEW?
HM?

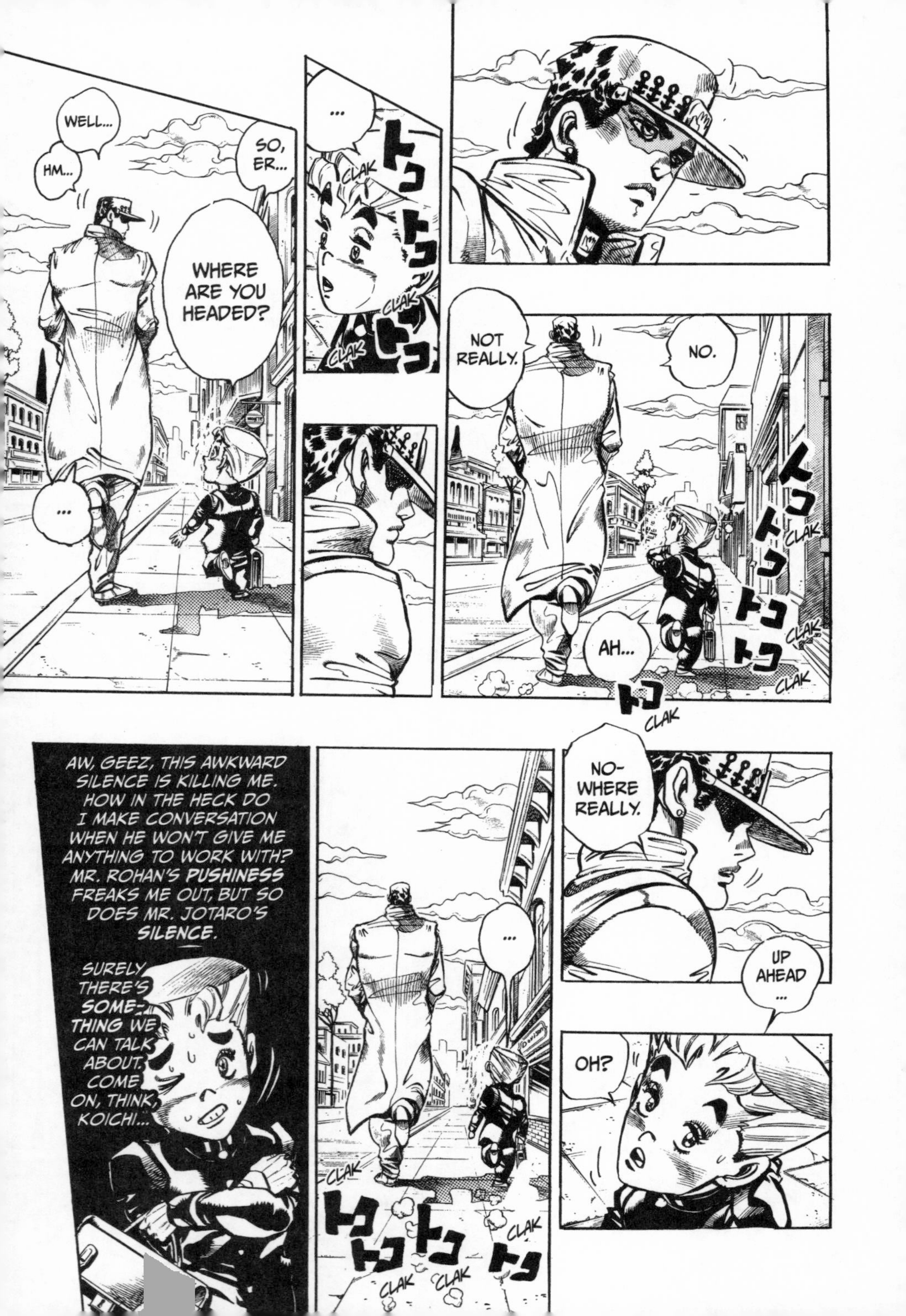
...
トコ
CLAK
トコ
CLAK
トコ
CLAK
SO, ER...
WELL...
HM...
WHERE ARE YOU HEADED?
...
NO.
NOT REALLY.
トコ
CLAK
トコ
トコ
CLAK
トコ
CLAK
AH...
トコ
CLAK
NO-WHERE REALLY.
UP AHEAD...
OH?
...
CLAK
トコ
トコ
トコ
CLAK
CLAK
トコ
CLAK
AW, GEEZ, THIS AWKWARD SILENCE IS KILLING ME. HOW IN THE HECK DO I MAKE CONVERSATION WHEN HE WON'T GIVE ME ANYTHING TO WORK WITH? MR. ROHAN'S PUSHINESS FREAKS ME OUT, BUT SO DOES MR. JOTARO'S SILENCE.
SURELY THERE'S SOME-THING WE CAN TALK ABOUT. COME ON, THINK, KOICHI...

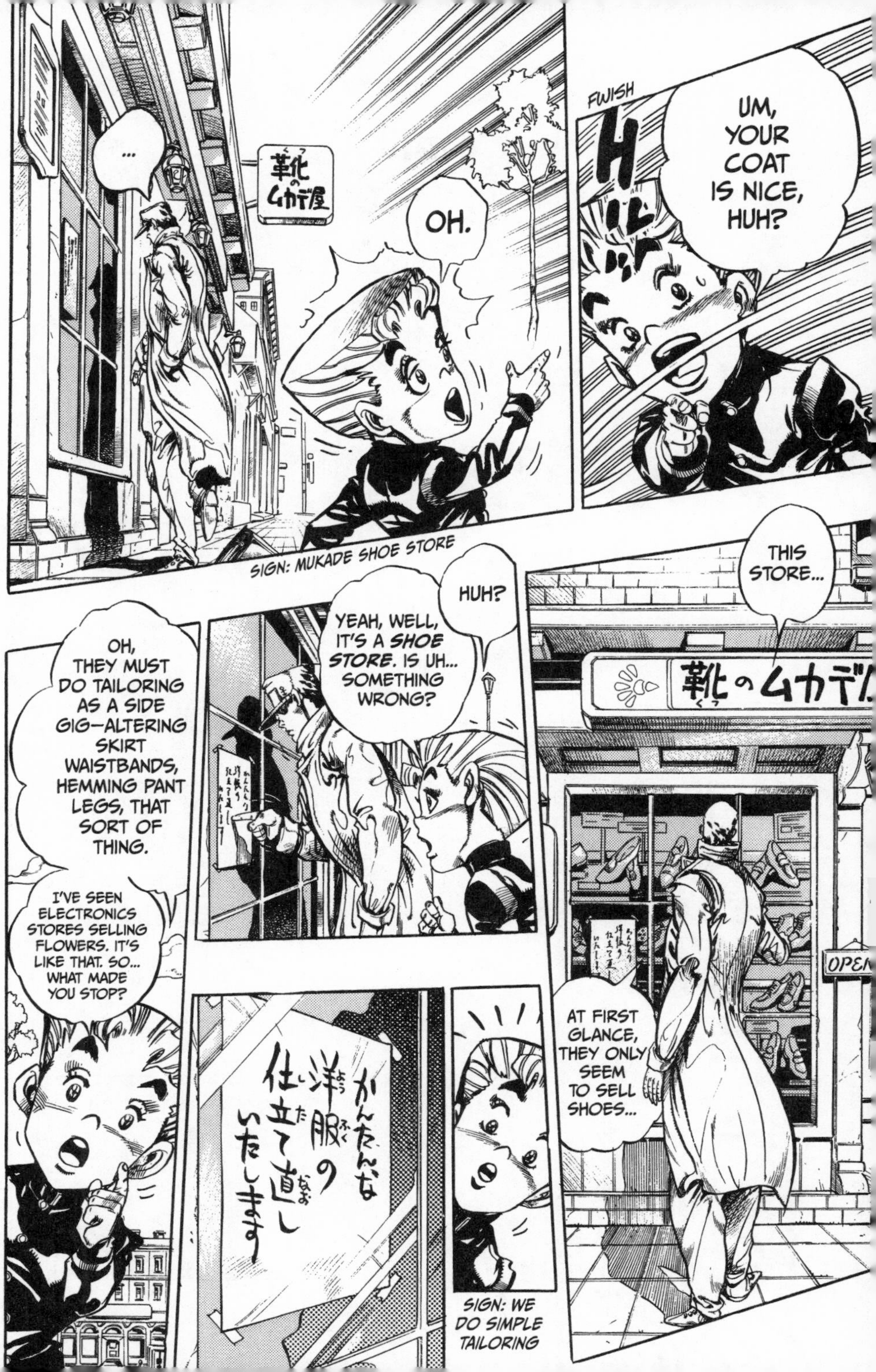
FWISH
UM, YOUR COAT IS NICE, HUH?
OH.
靴のムカデ屋
...
SIGN: MUKADE SHOE STORE
THIS STORE...
靴のムカデ
OPE
AT FIRST GLANCE, THEY ONLY SEEM TO SELL SHOES...
HUH?
YEAH, WELL, IT'S A *SHOE STORE*. IS UH... SOMETHING WRONG?
かんたんな洋服の仕立て直しいたします
SIGN: WE DO SIMPLE TAILORING
OH, THEY MUST DO TAILORING AS A SIDE GIG—ALTERING SKIRT WAISTBANDS, HEMMING PANT LEGS, THAT SORT OF THING.
I'VE SEEN ELECTRONICS STORES SELLING FLOWERS. IT'S LIKE THAT. SO... WHAT MADE YOU STOP?

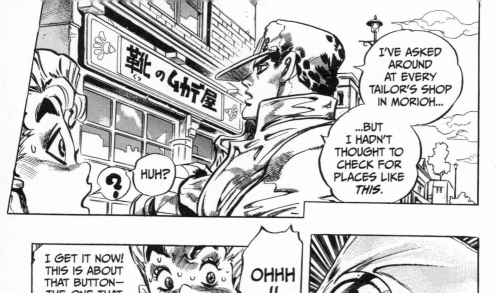

I'VE ASKED AROUND AT EVERY TAILOR'S SHOP IN MORIOH...

...BUT I HADN'T THOUGHT TO CHECK FOR PLACES LIKE *THIS*.

HUH?

?

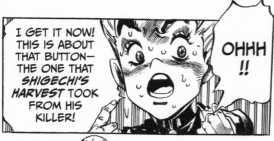

I GET IT NOW! THIS IS ABOUT THAT BUTTON— THE ONE THAT *SHIGECHI'S HARVEST* TOOK FROM HIS KILLER!

OHHH!!

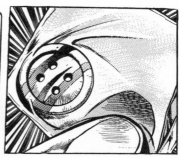

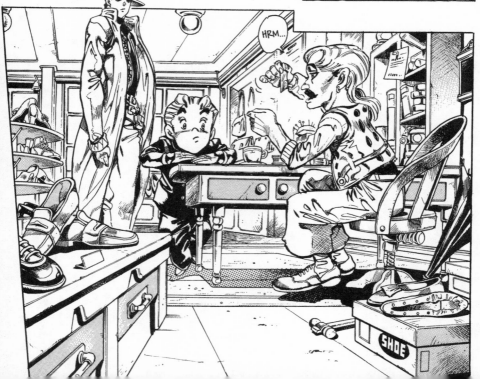

HRM...

SHOE

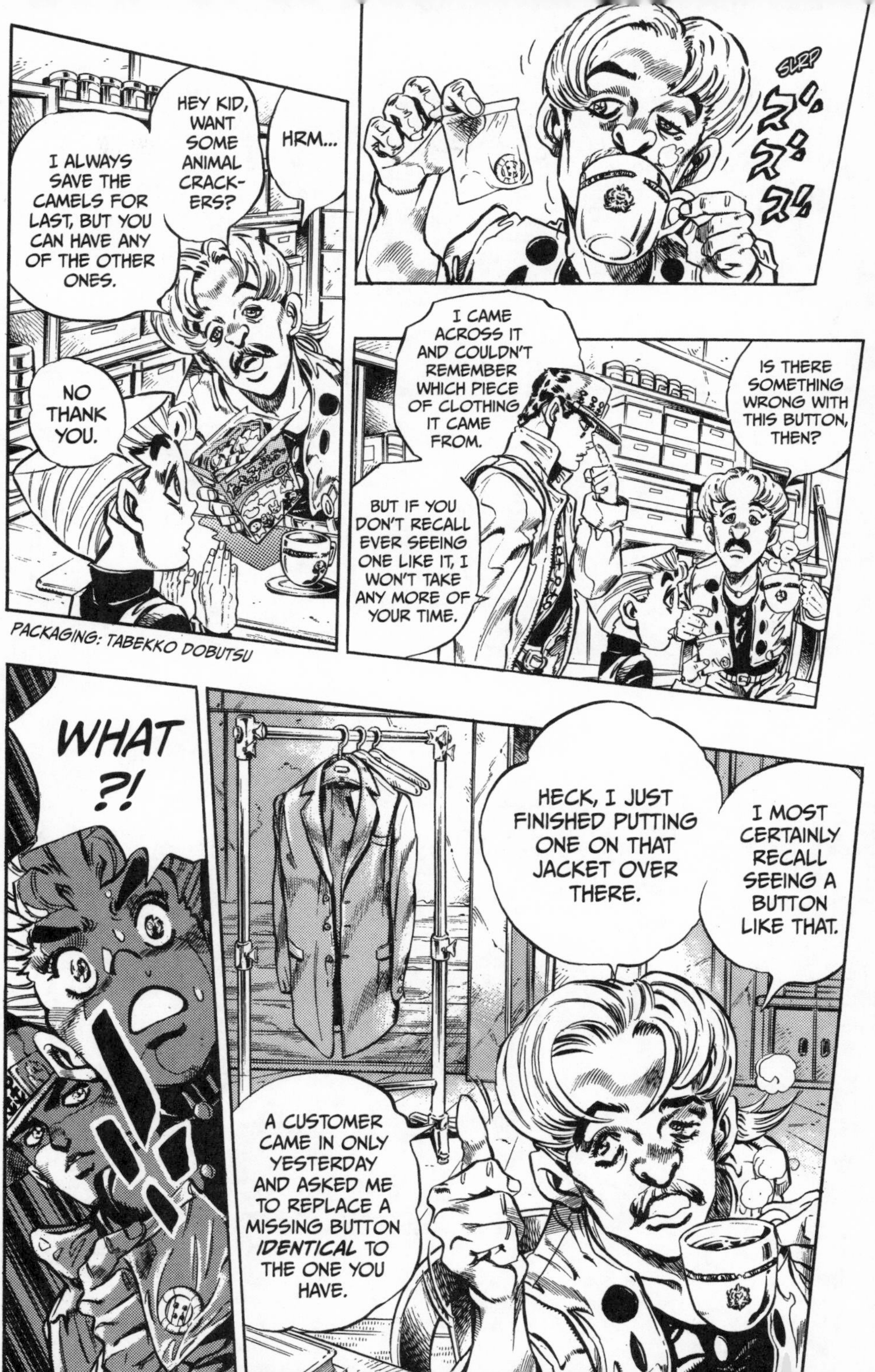
SLURP
IS THERE SOMETHING WRONG WITH THIS BUTTON, THEN?
I CAME ACROSS IT AND COULDN'T REMEMBER WHICH PIECE OF CLOTHING IT CAME FROM.
BUT IF YOU DON'T RECALL EVER SEEING ONE LIKE IT, I WON'T TAKE ANY MORE OF YOUR TIME.
HRM...
HEY KID, WANT SOME ANIMAL CRACK-ERS?
I ALWAYS SAVE THE CAMELS FOR LAST, BUT YOU CAN HAVE ANY OF THE OTHER ONES.
NO THANK YOU.
PACKAGING: TABEKKO DOBUTSU
I MOST CERTAINLY RECALL SEEING A BUTTON LIKE THAT.
HECK, I JUST FINISHED PUTTING ONE ON THAT JACKET OVER THERE.
A CUSTOMER CAME IN ONLY YESTERDAY AND ASKED ME TO REPLACE A MISSING BUTTON IDENTICAL TO THE ONE YOU HAVE.
WHAT ?!

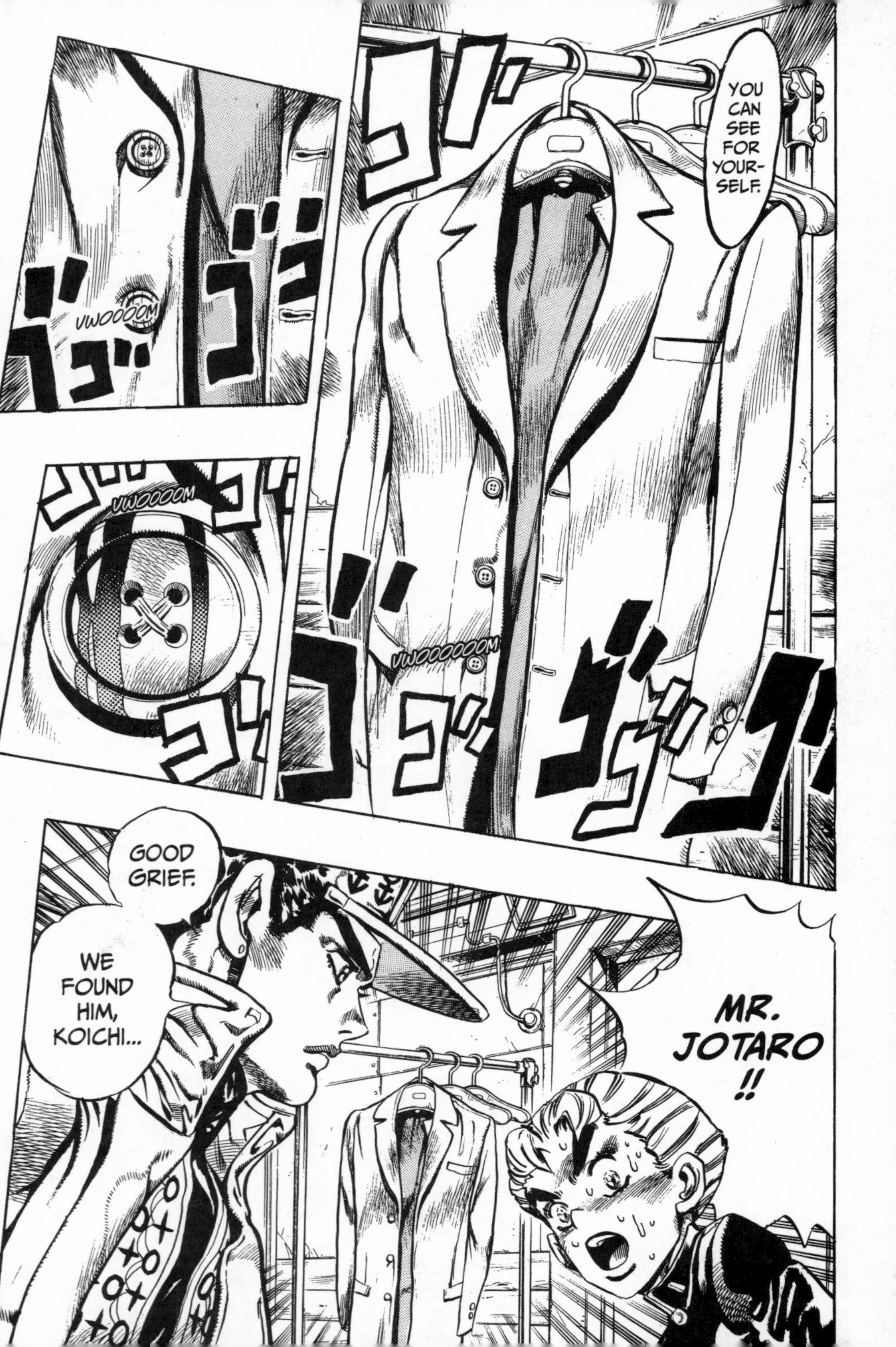
YOU CAN SEE FOR YOURSELF.
VWOOOOOOM
VWOOOOM
VWOOOOM
MR. JOTARO!!
GOOD GRIEF.
WE FOUND HIM, KOICHI...

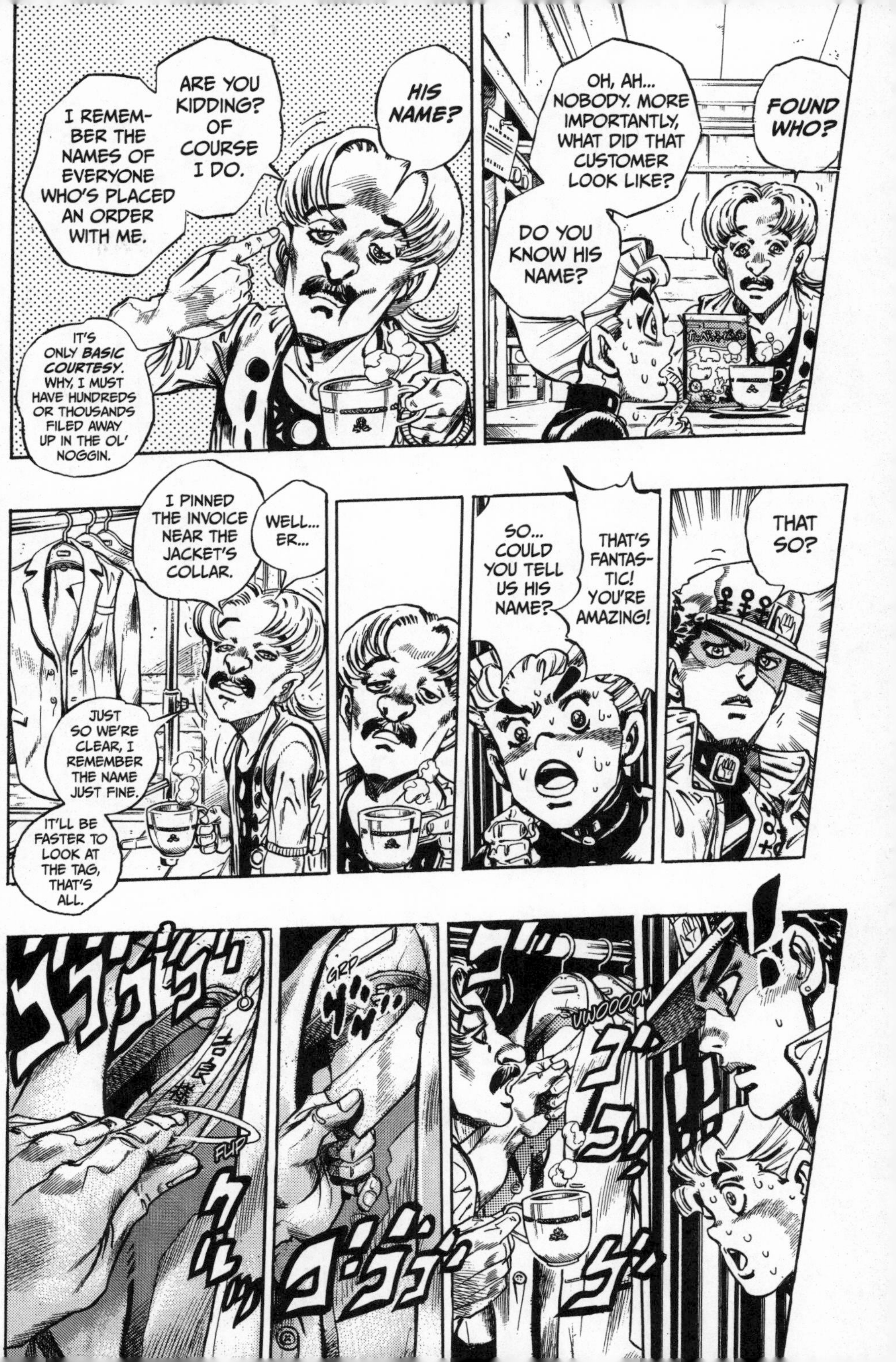
FOUND WHO?
OH, AH... NOBODY. MORE IMPORTANTLY, WHAT DID THAT CUSTOMER LOOK LIKE?
DO YOU KNOW HIS NAME?
HIS NAME?
ARE YOU KIDDING? OF COURSE I DO.
I REMEMBER THE NAMES OF EVERYONE WHO'S PLACED AN ORDER WITH ME.
IT'S ONLY BASIC COURTESY. WHY, I MUST HAVE HUNDREDS OR THOUSANDS FILED AWAY UP IN THE OL' NOGGIN.
THAT SO?
THAT'S FANTASTIC! YOU'RE AMAZING!
SO... COULD YOU TELL US HIS NAME?
WELL... ER...
I PINNED THE INVOICE NEAR THE JACKET'S COLLAR.
JUST SO WE'RE CLEAR, I REMEMBER THE NAME JUST FINE.
IT'LL BE FASTER TO LOOK AT THE TAG, THAT'S ALL.
UWOOOOM
GRP
FLIP

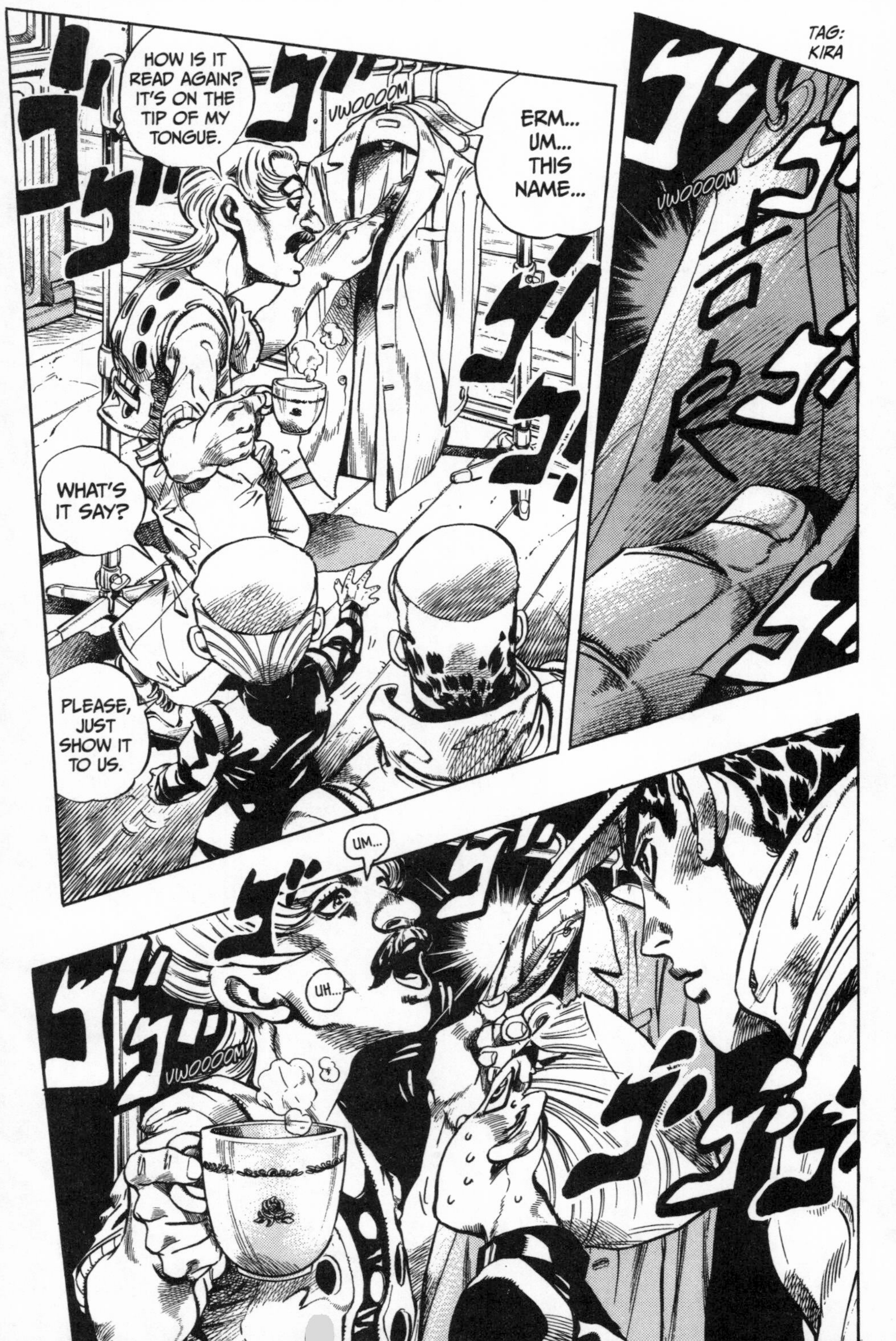
TAG: KIRA
VWOOOOM
ERM... UM... THIS NAME...
VWOOOOM
HOW IS IT READ AGAIN? IT'S ON THE TIP OF MY TONGUE.
WHAT'S IT SAY?
PLEASE, JUST SHOW IT TO US.
UM...
UH...
VWOOOOM

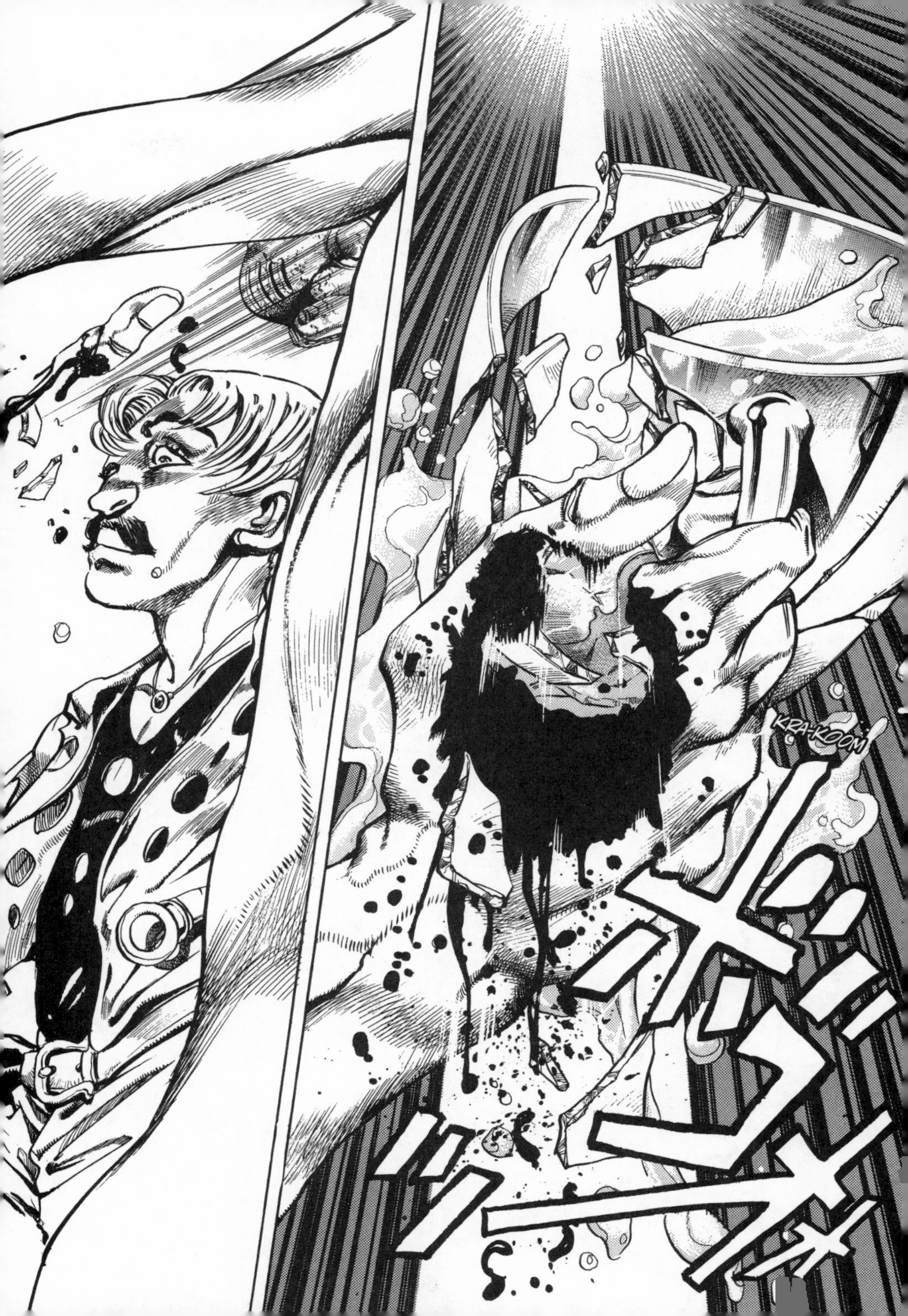
KRA-KOOM

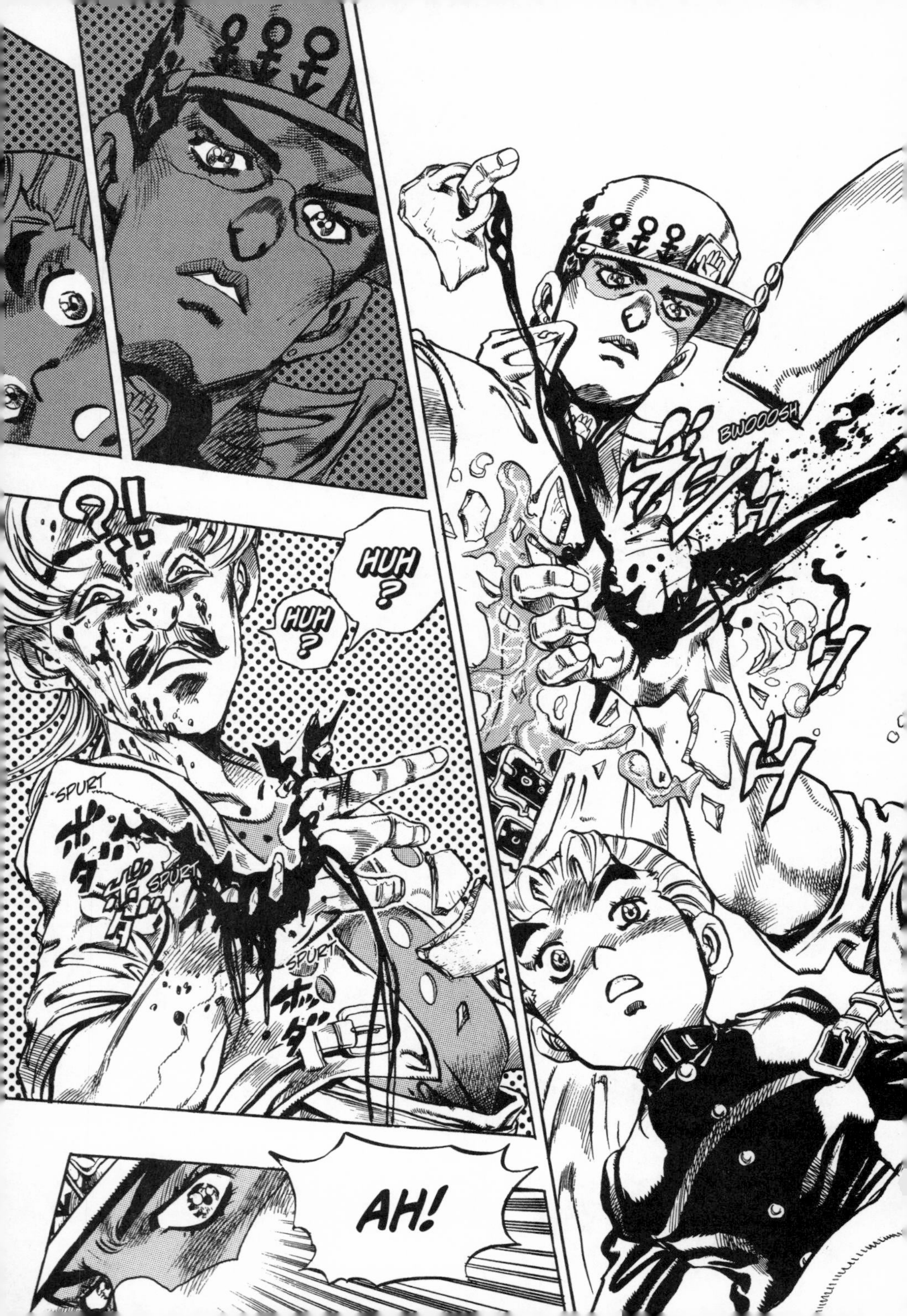

BWOOOSH
HUH?
HUH?
SPURT
SPURT
SPURT
AH!

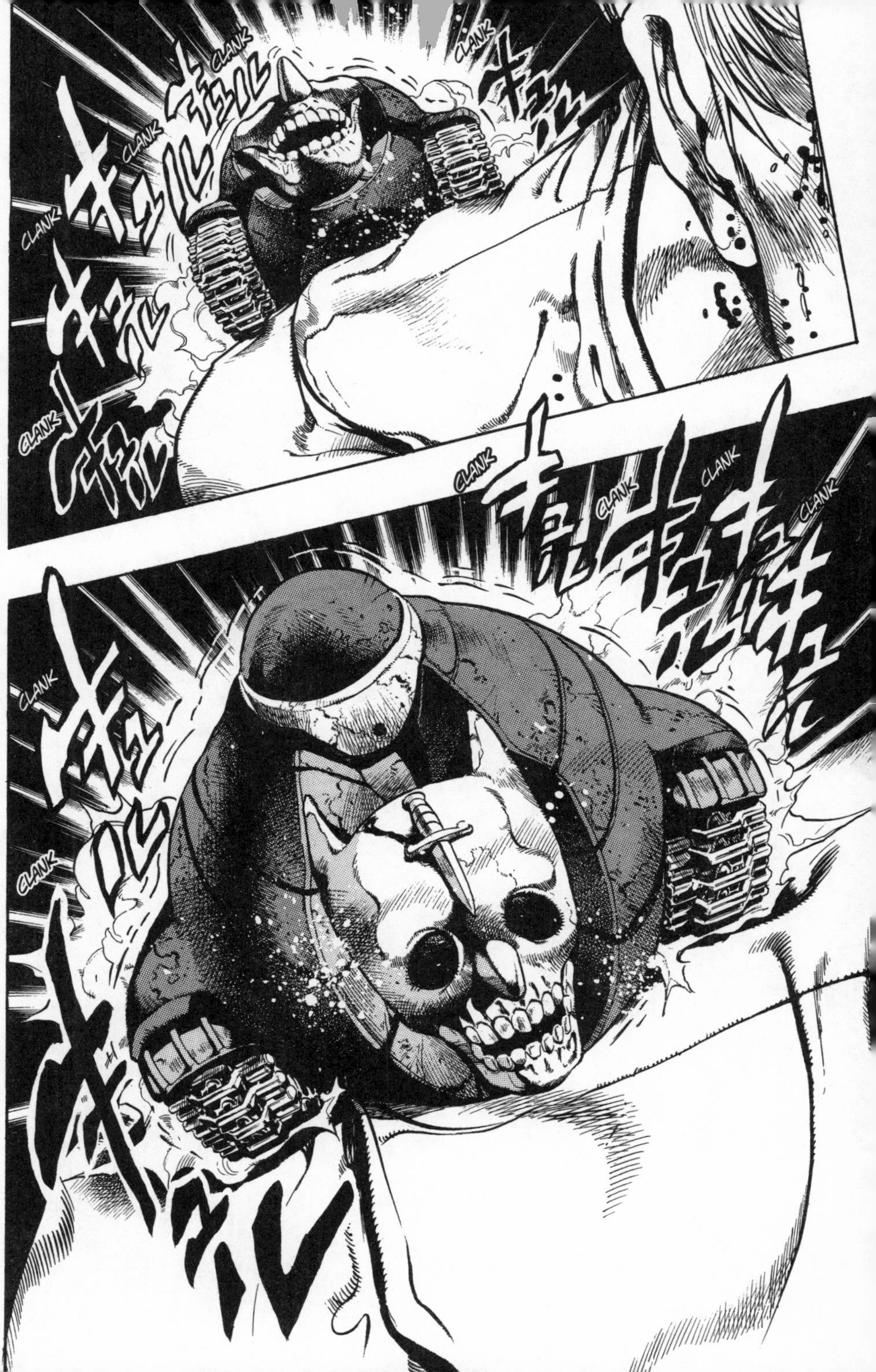
CLANK
CLANK
CLANK
CLANK
CLANK
CLANK
CLANK
CLANK
CLANK
CLANK
CLANK

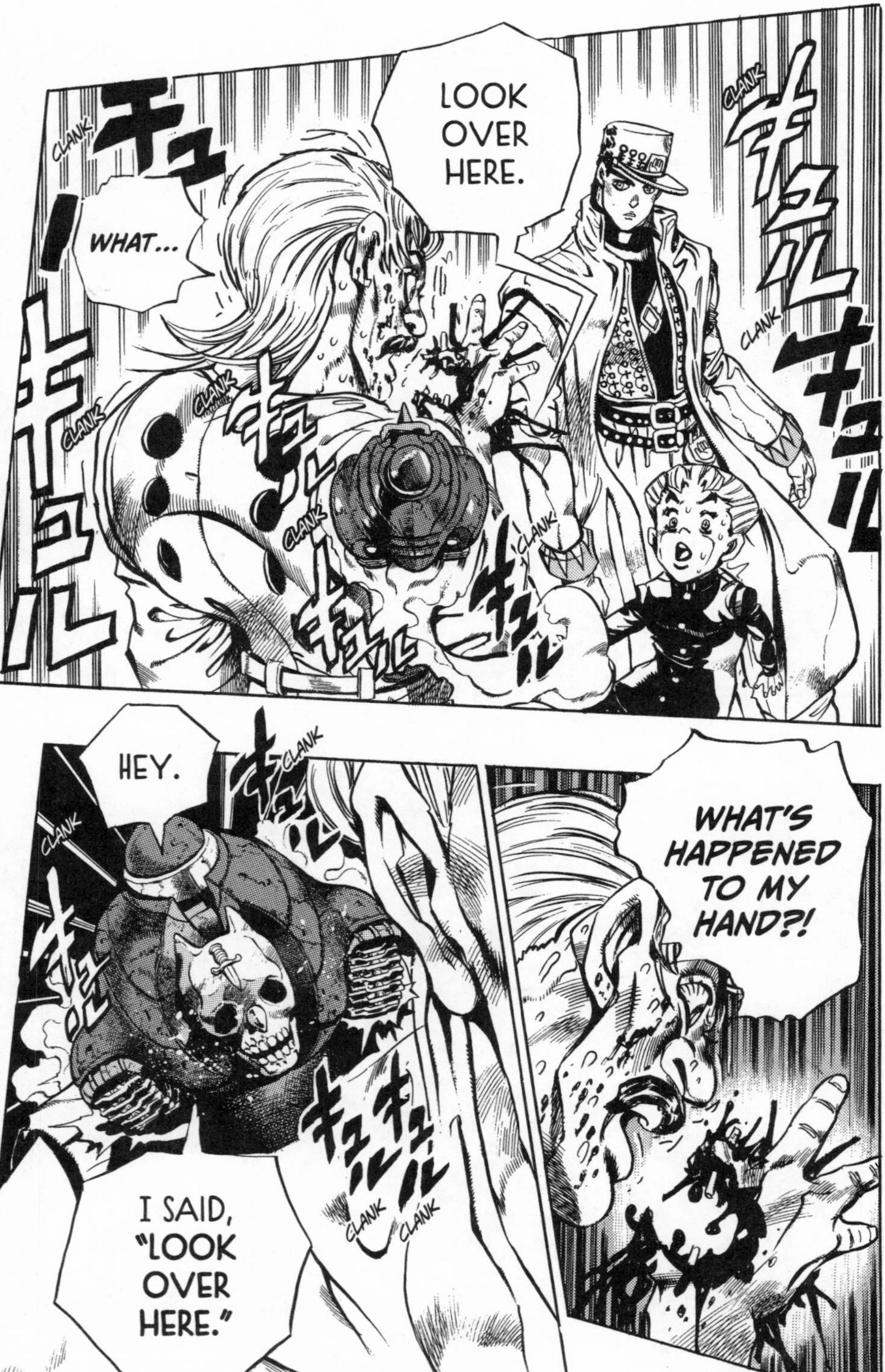
CLANK
LOOK OVER HERE.
CLANK
CLANK
WHAT...
CLANK
CLANK
CLANK
CLANK
WHAT'S HAPPENED TO MY HAND?!
CLANK
HEY.
CLANK
I SAID, "LOOK OVER HERE."
CLANK
CLANK

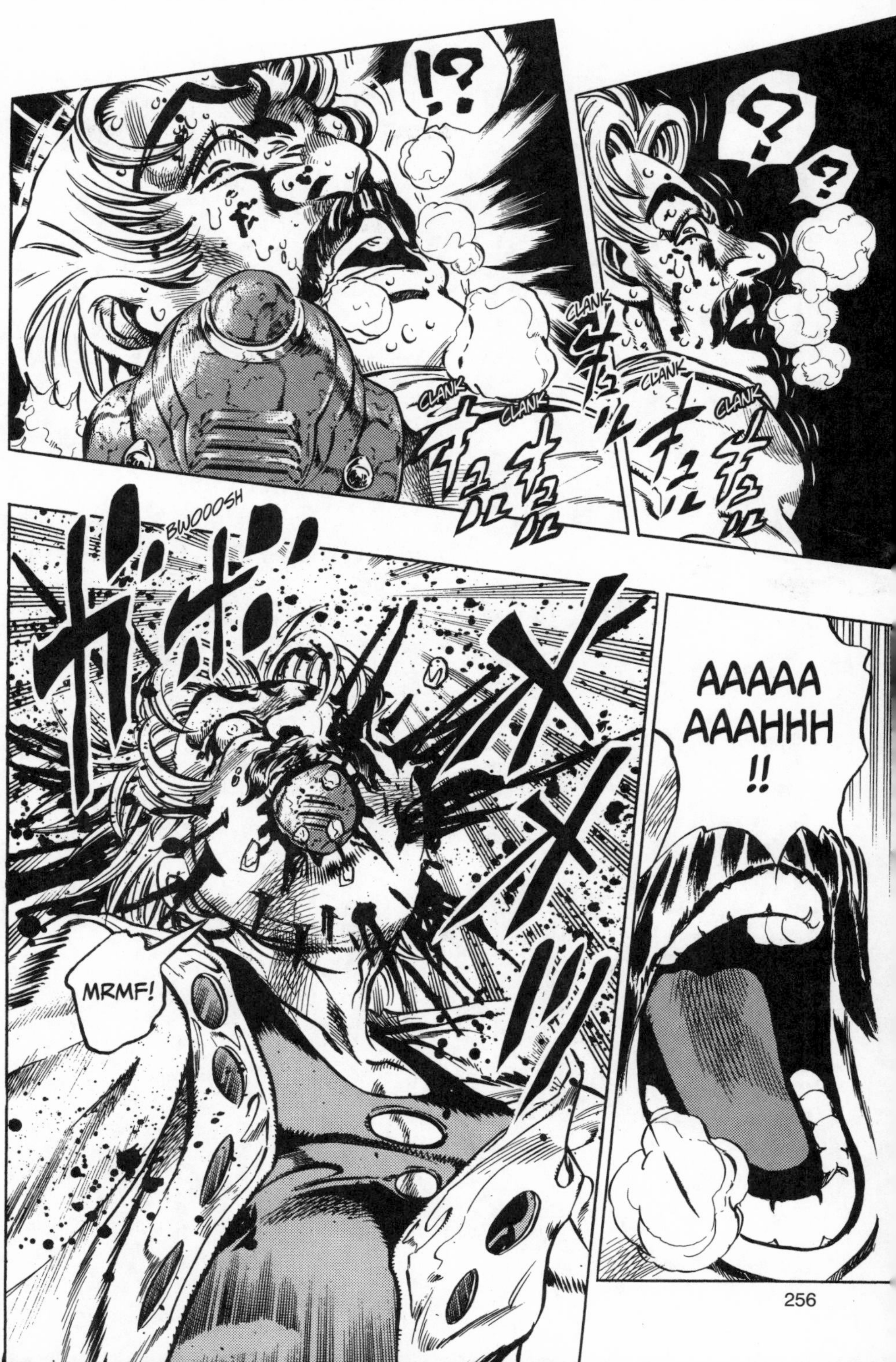
?
?
CLANK
CLANK
CLANK
!?
CLANK
CLANK
AAAAA AAAHHH !!
BWOOOSH
MRMF!

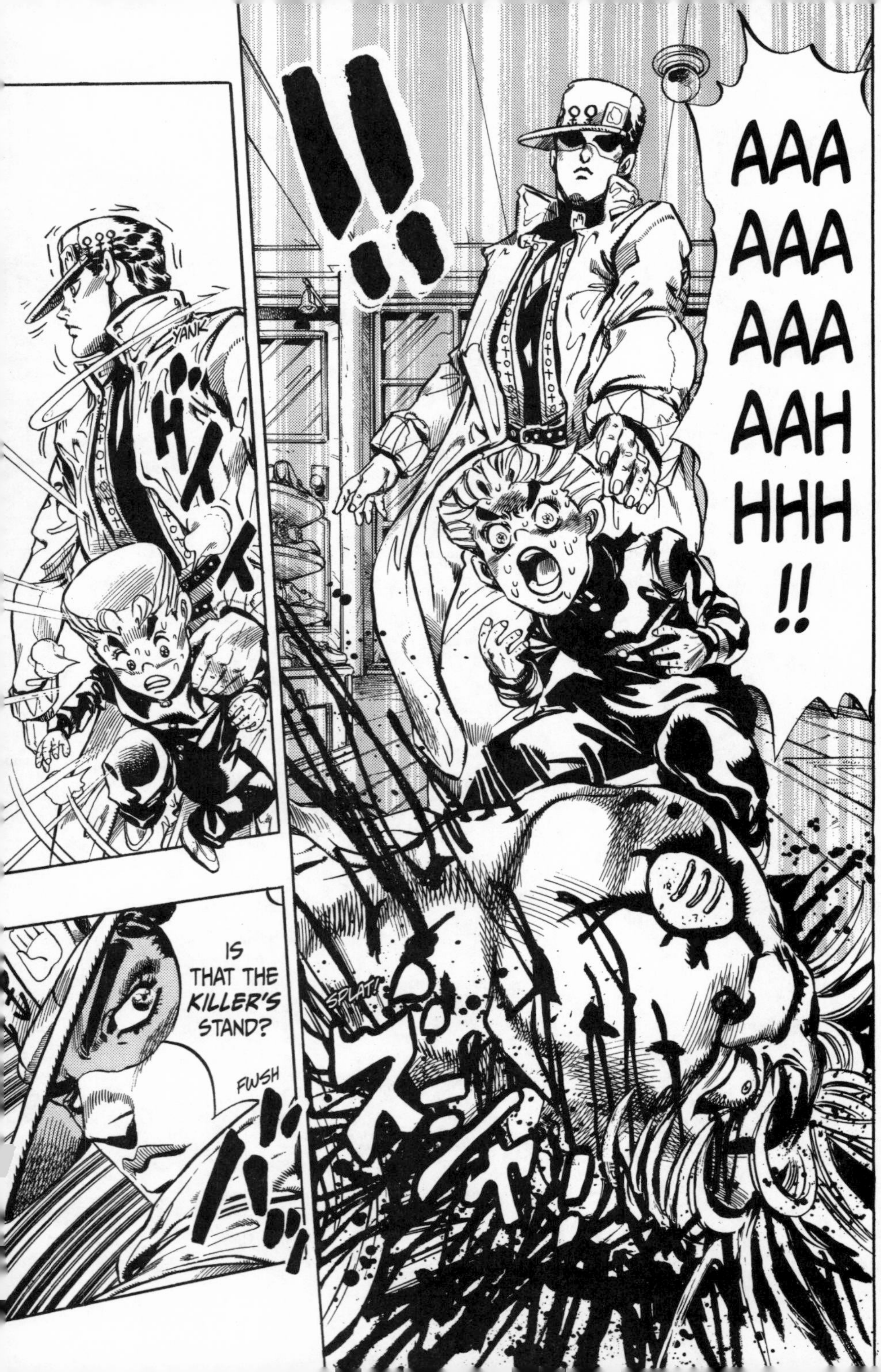
!!
AAAAAAAAAAAAAAHHHH!!
SPLAT!
YANK
IS THAT THE KILLER'S STAND?
FWSH

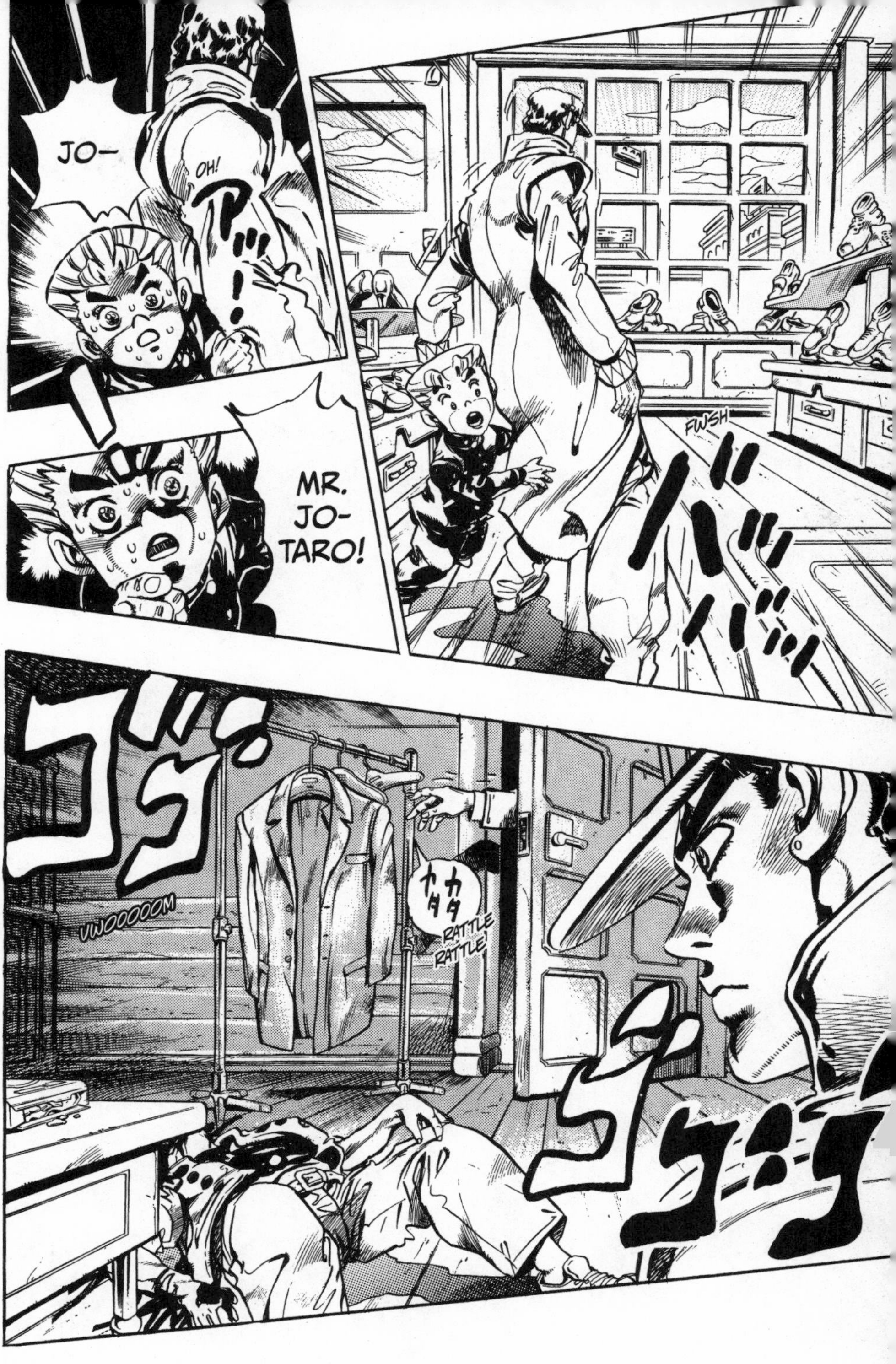
FWSH
JO–
OH!
MR. JO- TARO!
VWOOOOOM
カタカタ
RATTLE RATTLE

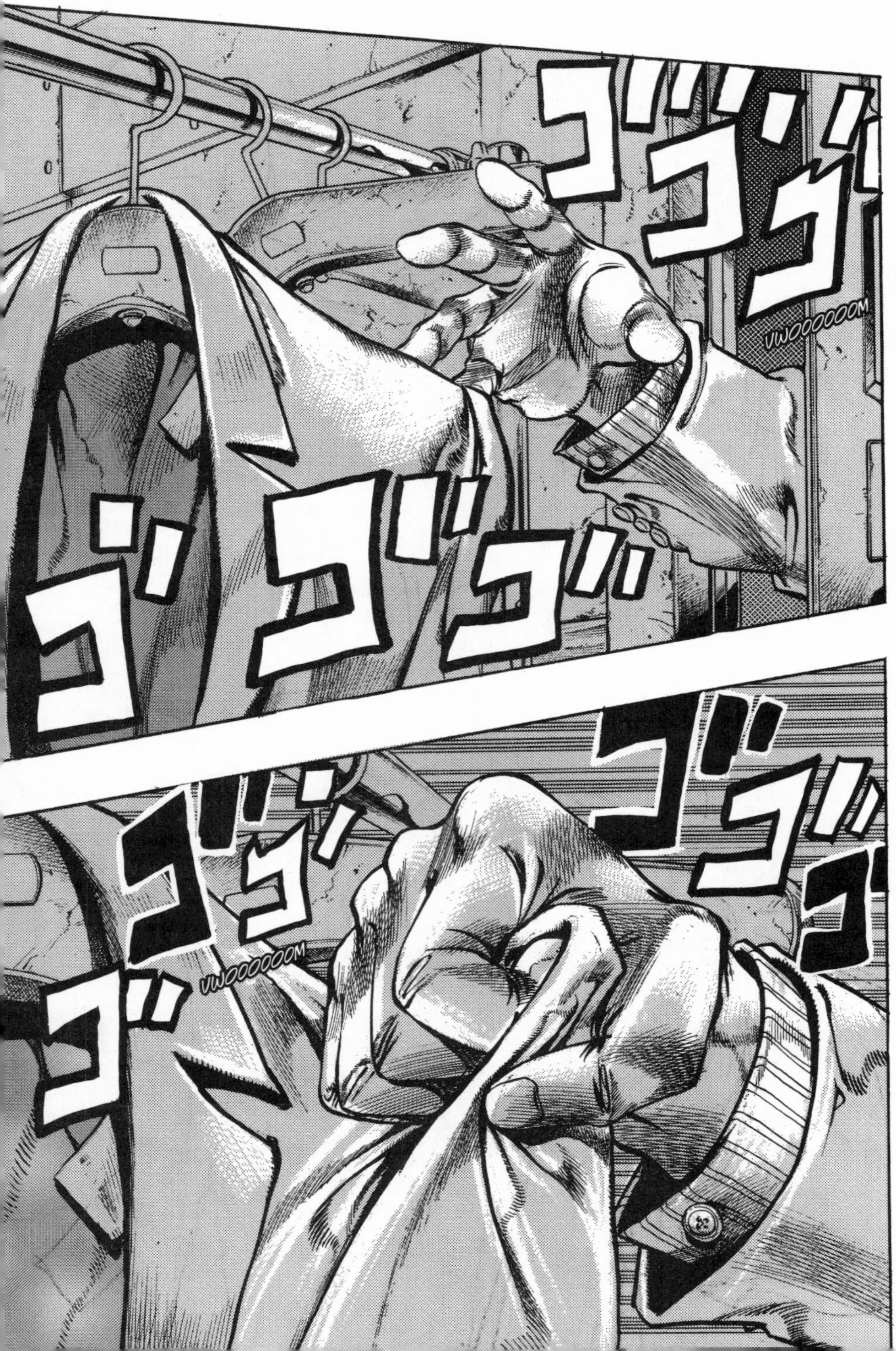
ゴゴゴ
VWOOOOOOM
ゴゴゴ
ゴゴゴ
ゴゴゴ
VWOOOOOOM

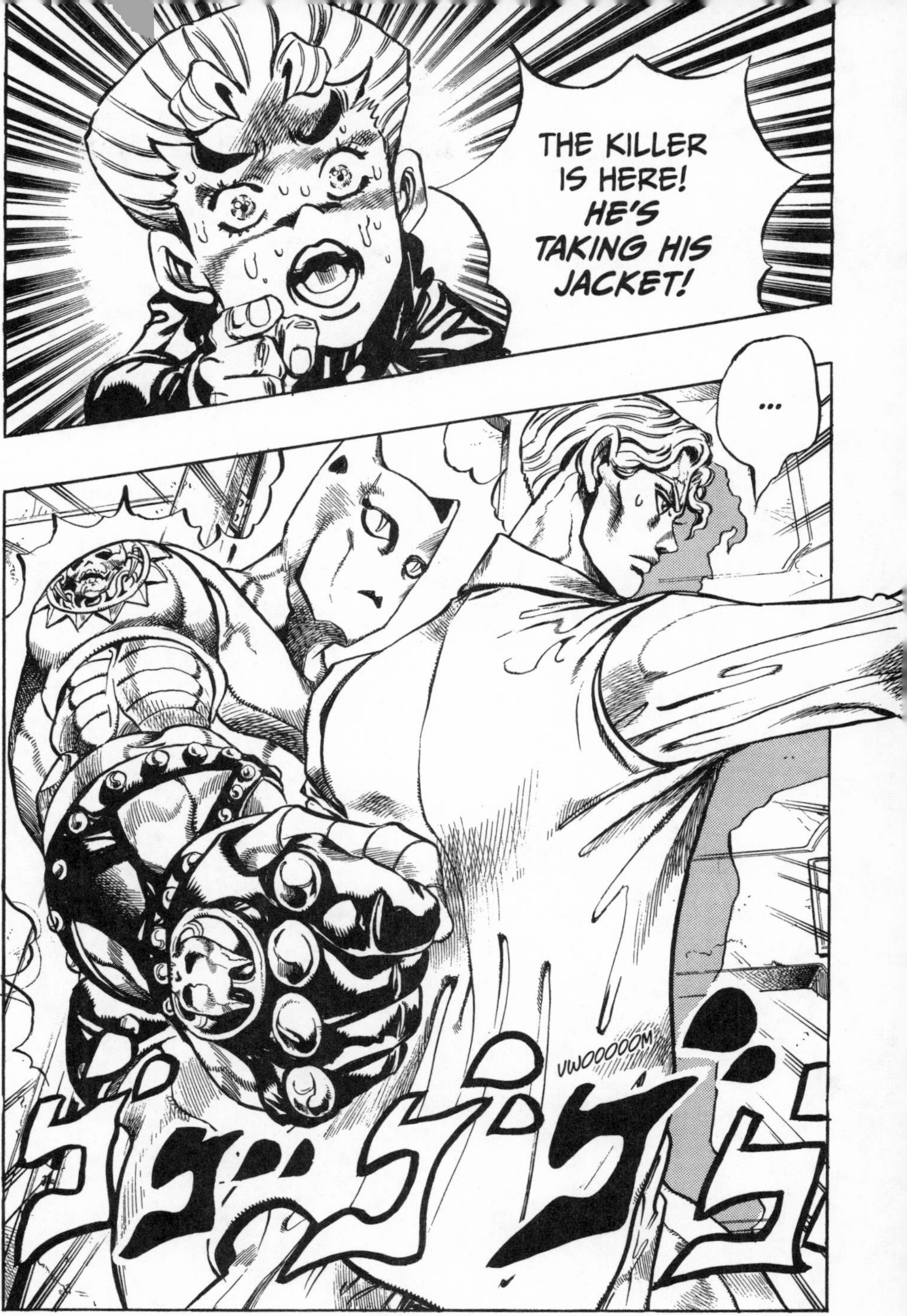
THE KILLER IS HERE! HE'S TAKING HIS JACKET!
...
VWOOOOOM

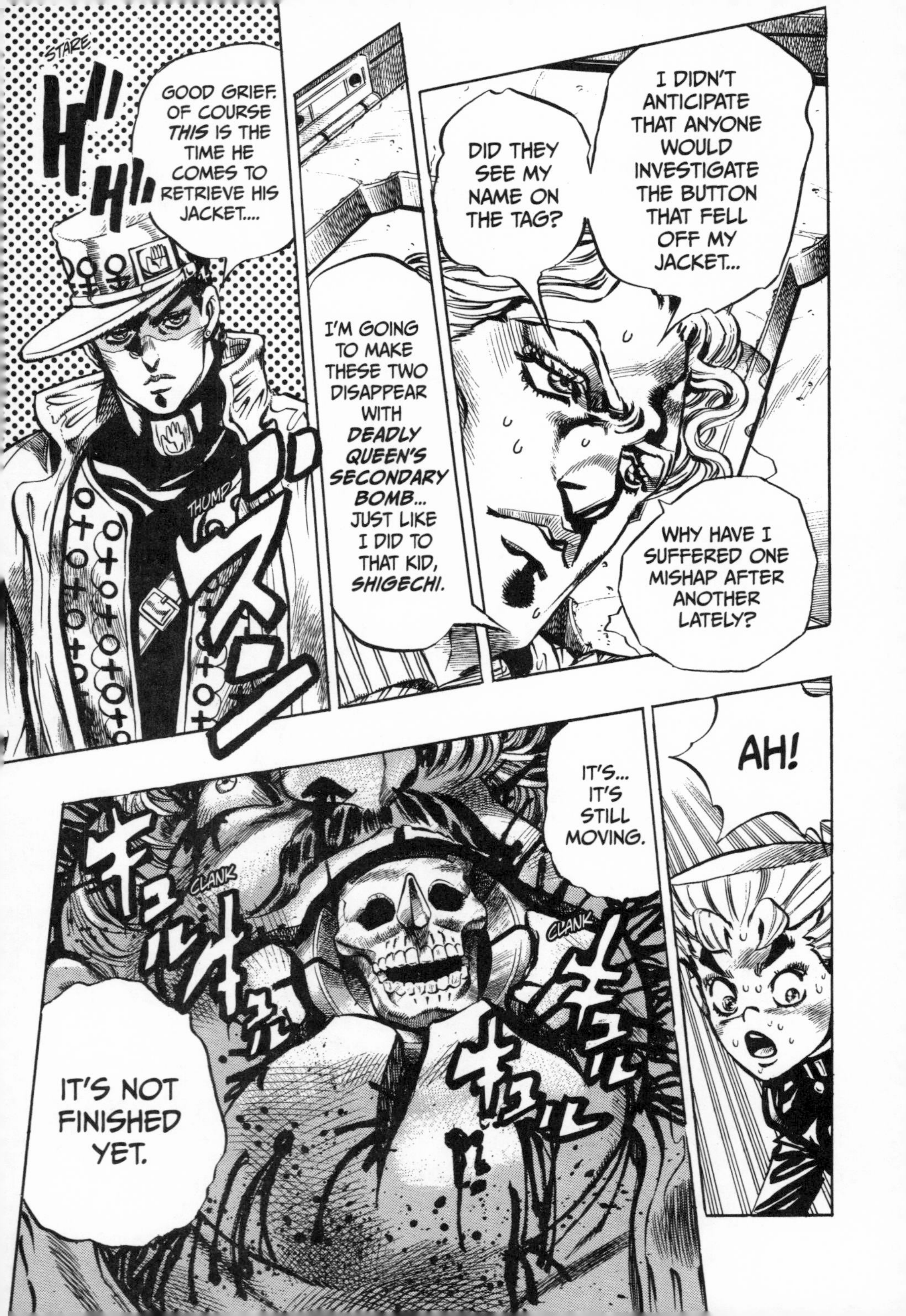
I DIDN'T ANTICIPATE THAT ANYONE WOULD INVESTIGATE THE BUTTON THAT FELL OFF MY JACKET...
DID THEY SEE MY NAME ON THE TAG?
WHY HAVE I SUFFERED ONE MISHAP AFTER ANOTHER LATELY?
I'M GOING TO MAKE THESE TWO DISAPPEAR WITH *DEADLY QUEEN'S SECONDARY BOMB*... JUST LIKE I DID TO THAT KID, *SHIGECHI*.
STARE
GOOD GRIEF. OF COURSE *THIS* IS THE TIME HE COMES TO RETRIEVE HIS JACKET....
THUMP
AH!
IT'S... IT'S STILL MOVING.
CLANK
CLANK
IT'S NOT FINISHED YET.

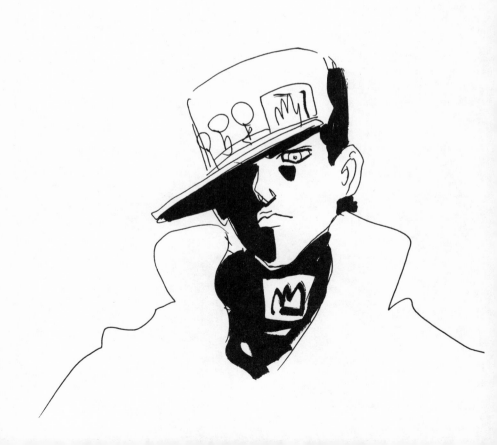

CHAPTER 90

HEART ATTACK, PART 2

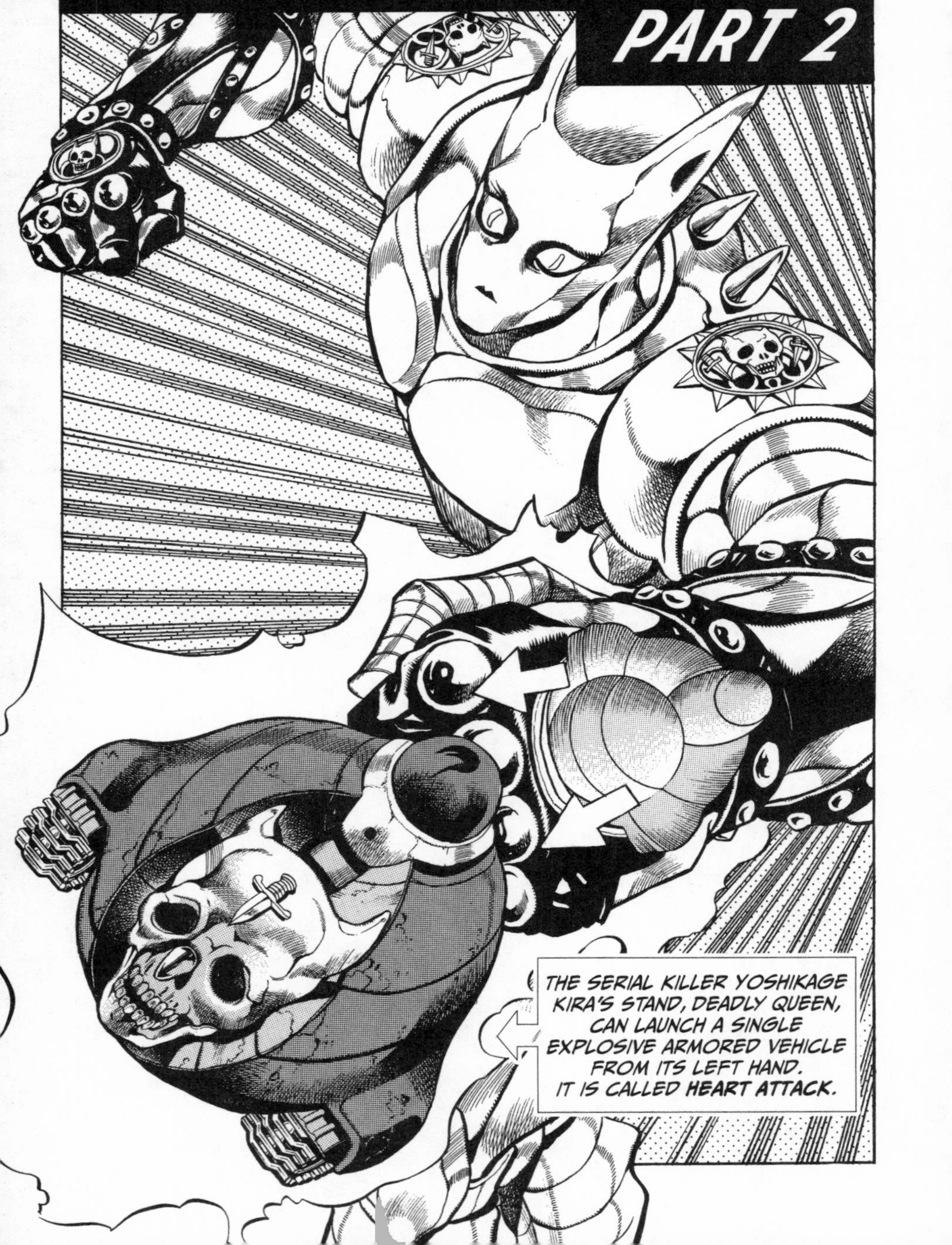
THE SERIAL KILLER YOSHIKAGE KIRA'S STAND, DEADLY QUEEN, CAN LAUNCH A SINGLE EXPLOSIVE ARMORED VEHICLE FROM ITS LEFT HAND. IT IS CALLED HEART ATTACK.

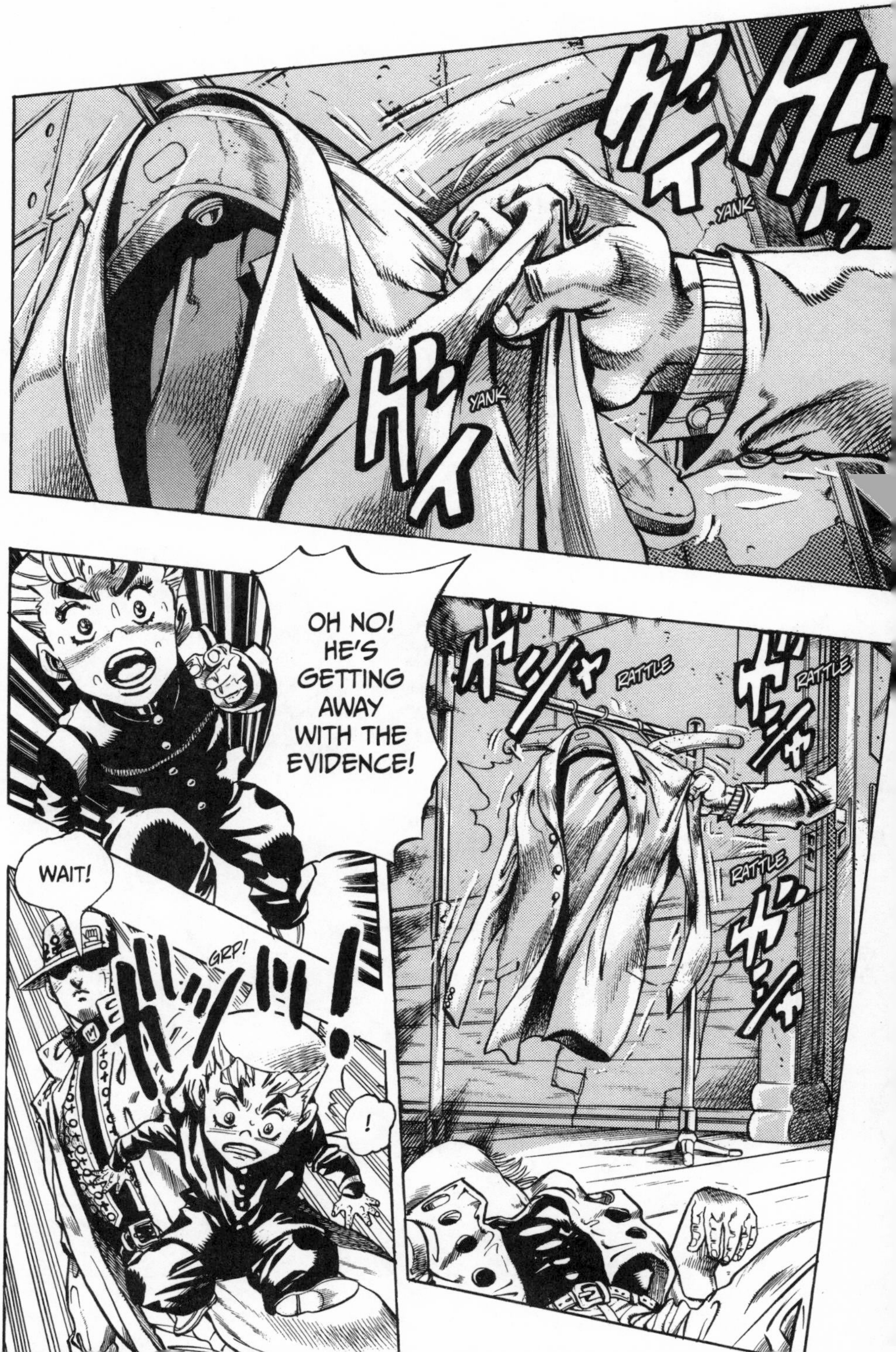
YANK
YANK
RATTLE
RATTLE
RATTLE
OH NO! HE'S GETTING AWAY WITH THE EVIDENCE!
WAIT!
GRP!
!

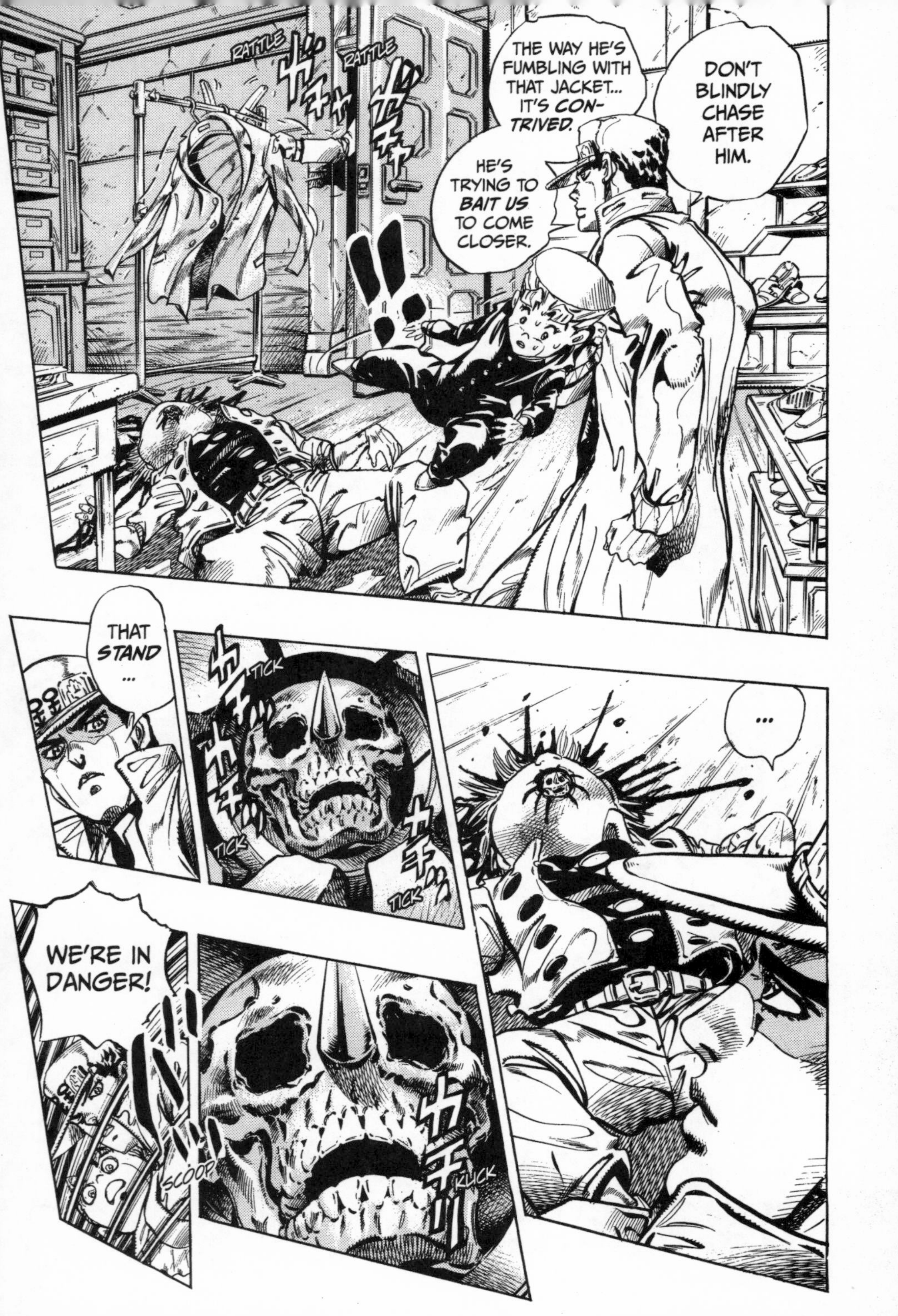
RATTLE
RATTLE
DON'T BLINDLY CHASE AFTER HIM.
THE WAY HE'S FUMBLING WITH THAT JACKET... IT'S CONTRIVED.
HE'S TRYING TO BAIT US TO COME CLOSER.
...
TICK
TICK
TICK
THAT STAND ...
KLICK
WE'RE IN DANGER!
SCOOP

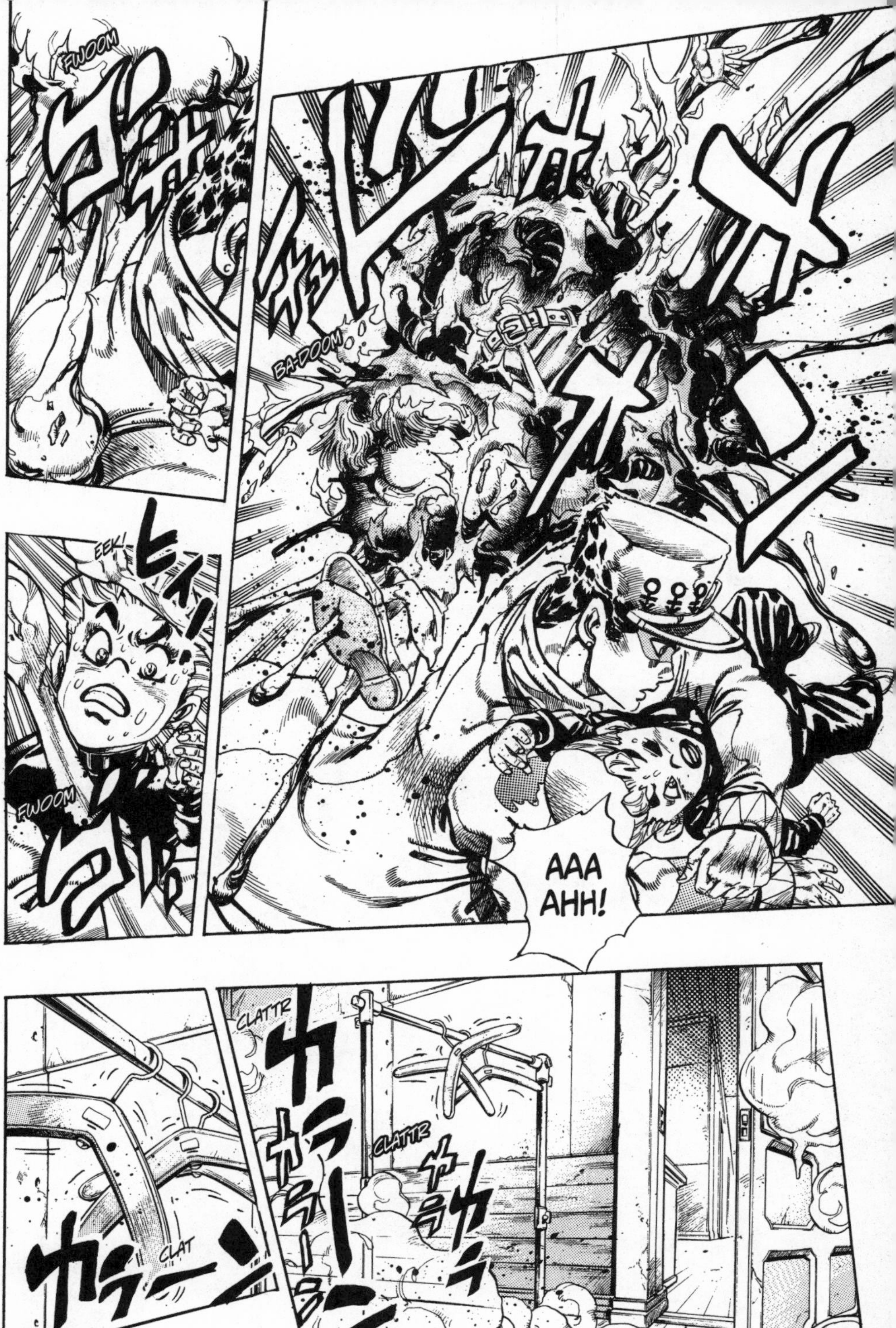
BA-DOOM
AAA AHH!
FWOOM
EEK!
FWOOM
CLATTR
CLATTR
CLAT

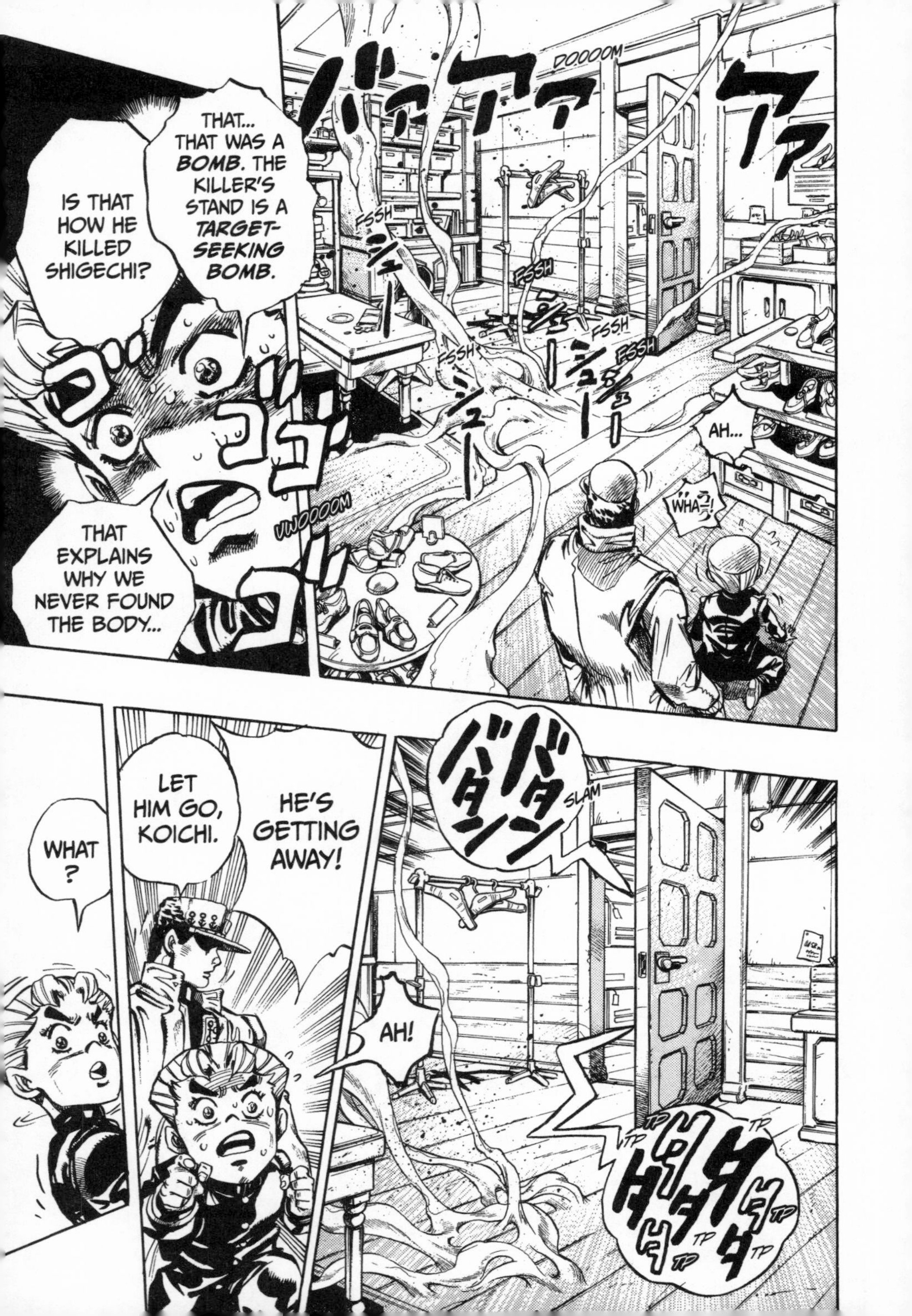
DOOOOM
FSSH
FSSH
FSSH
FSSH
FSSH
AH...
WHA!?
THAT... THAT WAS A BOMB. THE KILLER'S STAND IS A TARGET-SEEKING BOMB.
IS THAT HOW HE KILLED SHIGECHI?
VWOOOOM
THAT EXPLAINS WHY WE NEVER FOUND THE BODY...
SLAM
AH!
TP TP TP TP TP TP TP TP
HE'S GETTING AWAY!
LET HIM GO, KOICHI.
WHAT?

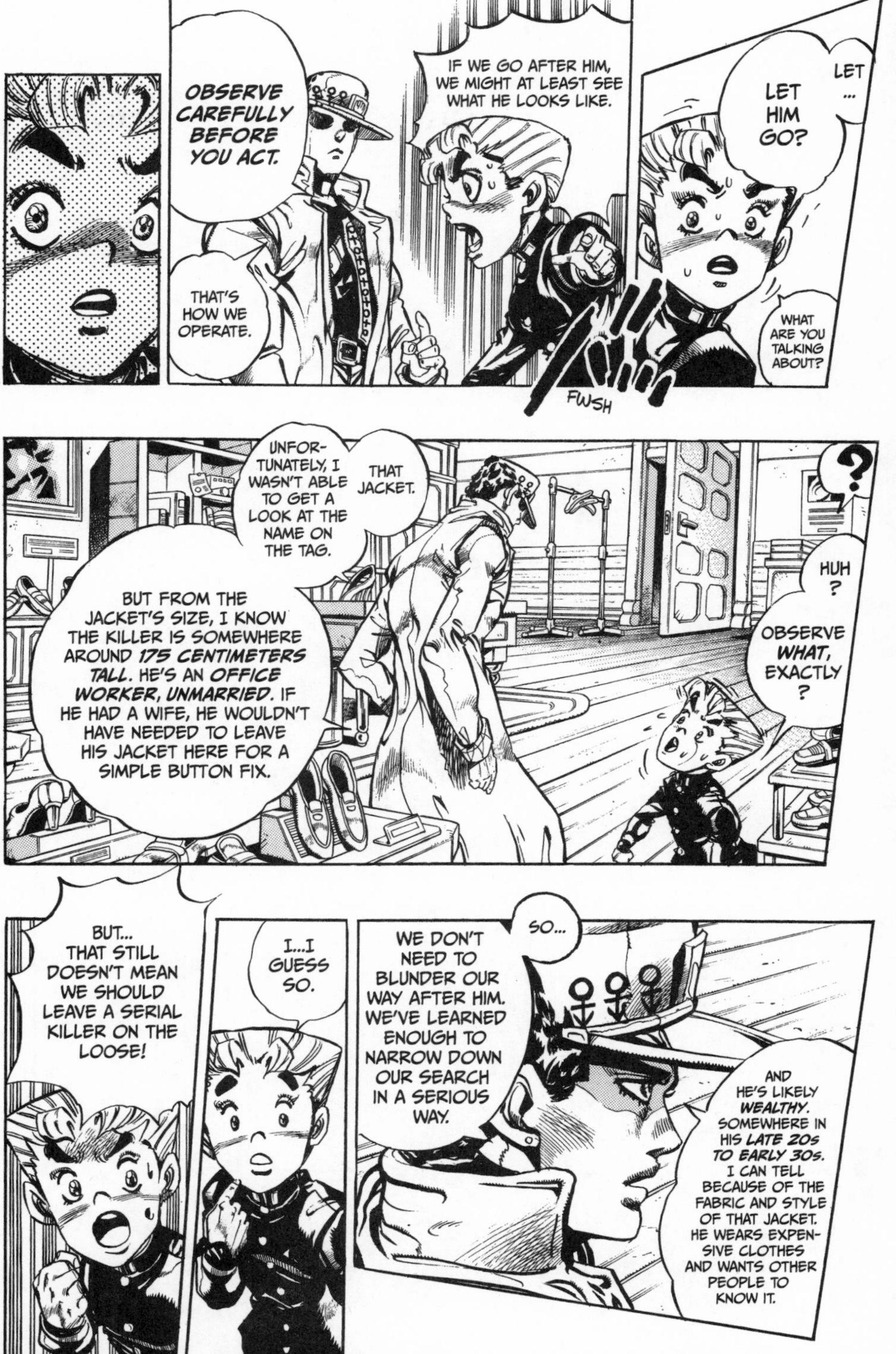
LET ...
LET HIM GO?
WHAT ARE YOU TALKING ABOUT?
FWSH
IF WE GO AFTER HIM, WE MIGHT AT LEAST SEE WHAT HE LOOKS LIKE.
OBSERVE CAREFULLY BEFORE YOU ACT.
THAT'S HOW WE OPERATE.
?
HUH?
OBSERVE WHAT, EXACTLY?
THAT JACKET.
UNFORTUNATELY, I WASN'T ABLE TO GET A LOOK AT THE NAME ON THE TAG.
BUT FROM THE JACKET'S SIZE, I KNOW THE KILLER IS SOMEWHERE AROUND 175 CENTIMETERS TALL. HE'S AN OFFICE WORKER, UNMARRIED. IF HE HAD A WIFE, HE WOULDN'T HAVE NEEDED TO LEAVE HIS JACKET HERE FOR A SIMPLE BUTTON FIX.
SO...
WE DON'T NEED TO BLUNDER OUR WAY AFTER HIM. WE'VE LEARNED ENOUGH TO NARROW DOWN OUR SEARCH IN A SERIOUS WAY.
AND HE'S LIKELY WEALTHY. SOMEWHERE IN HIS LATE 20s TO EARLY 30s. I CAN TELL BECAUSE OF THE FABRIC AND STYLE OF THAT JACKET. HE WEARS EXPENSIVE CLOTHES AND WANTS OTHER PEOPLE TO KNOW IT.
I...I GUESS SO.
BUT... THAT STILL DOESN'T MEAN WE SHOULD LEAVE A SERIAL KILLER ON THE LOOSE!

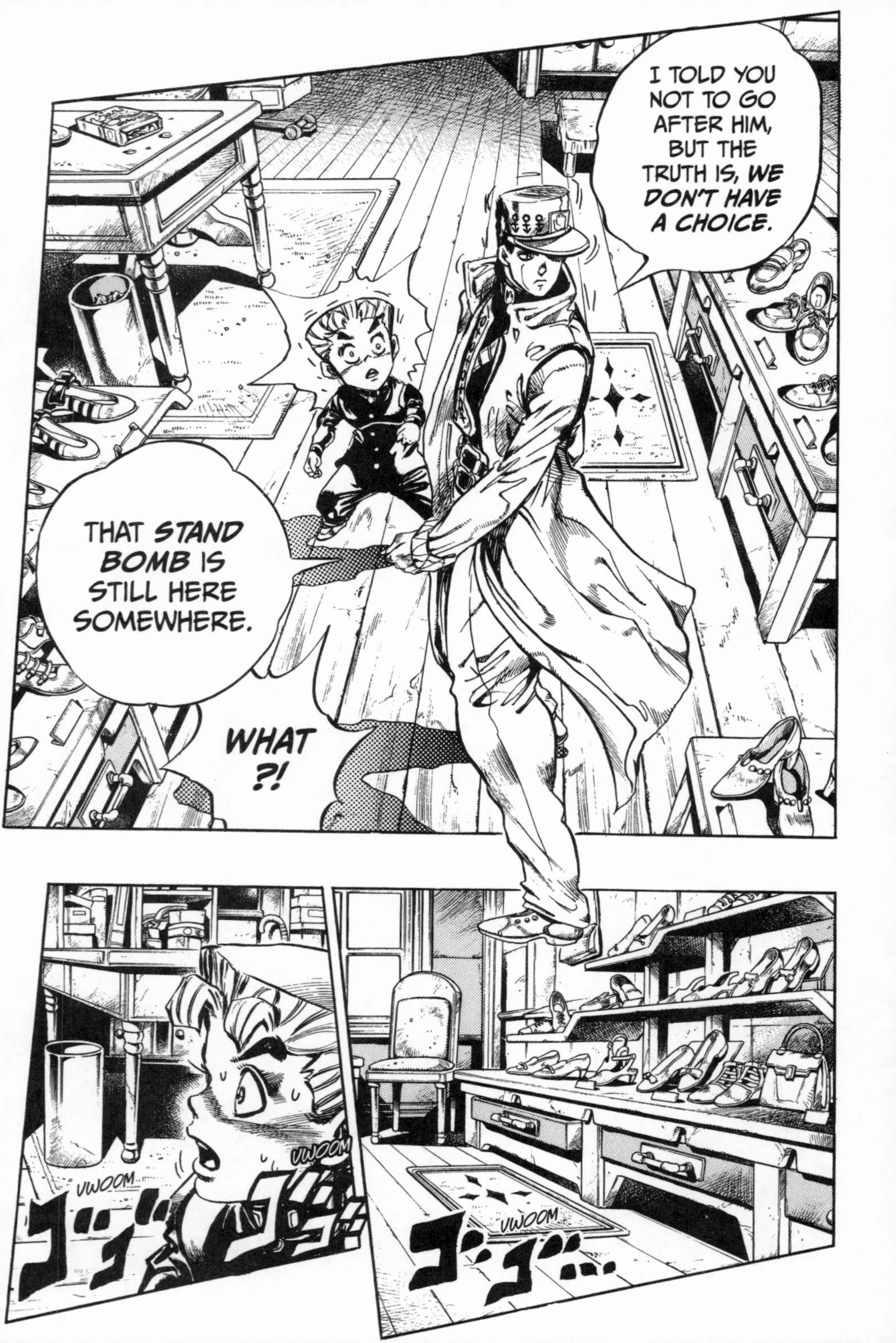

I TOLD YOU NOT TO GO AFTER HIM, BUT THE TRUTH IS, WE DON'T HAVE A CHOICE.
THAT STAND BOMB IS STILL HERE SOMEWHERE.
WHAT?!
VWOOM
UWOOM
VWOOM

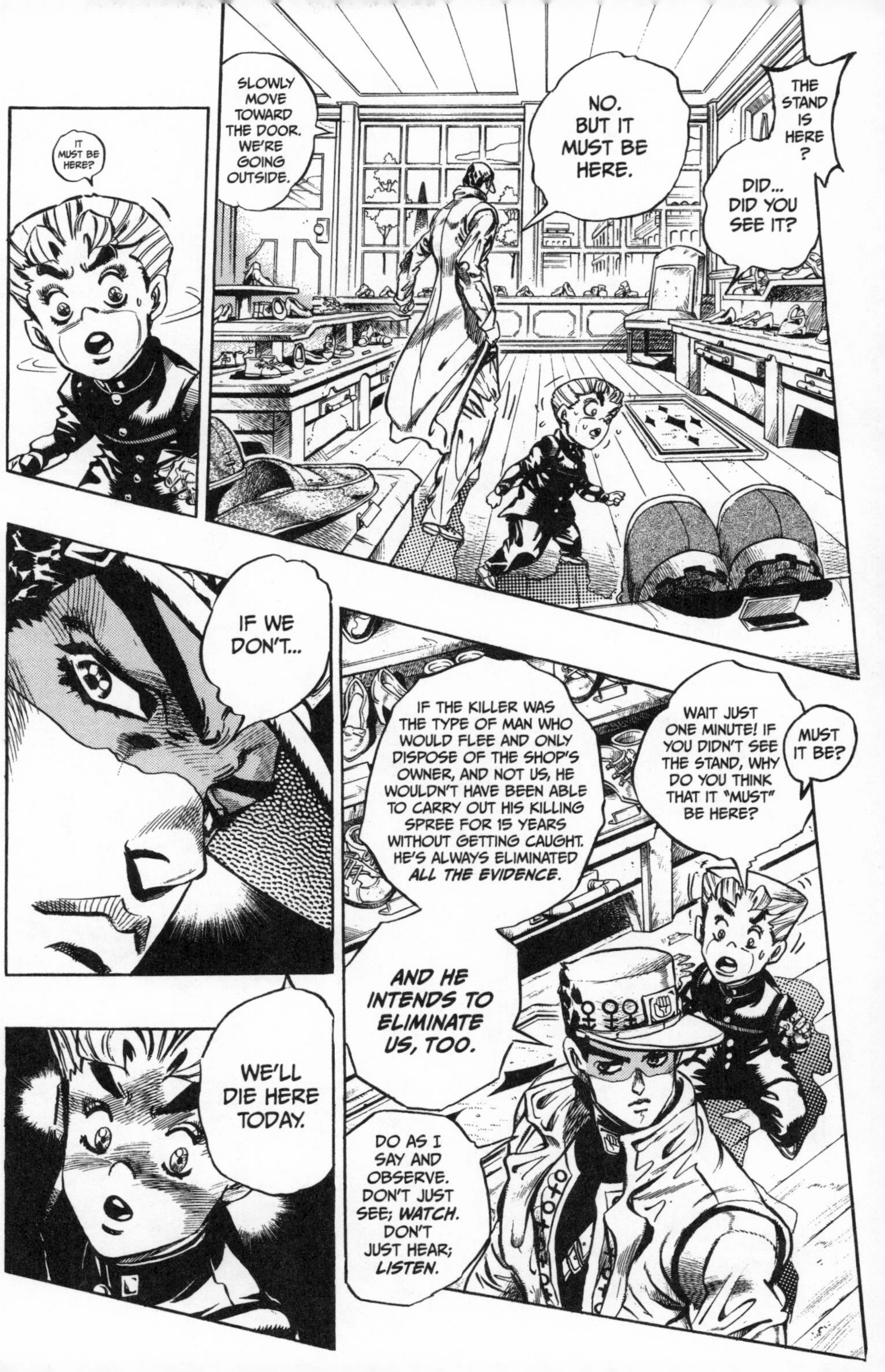
THE STAND IS HERE?
DID... DID YOU SEE IT?
NO. BUT IT MUST BE HERE.
SLOWLY MOVE TOWARD THE DOOR. WE'RE GOING OUTSIDE.
IT MUST BE HERE?
MUST IT BE?
WAIT JUST ONE MINUTE! IF YOU DIDN'T SEE THE STAND, WHY DO YOU THINK THAT IT "MUST" BE HERE?
IF THE KILLER WAS THE TYPE OF MAN WHO WOULD FLEE AND ONLY DISPOSE OF THE SHOP'S OWNER, AND NOT US, HE WOULDN'T HAVE BEEN ABLE TO CARRY OUT HIS KILLING SPREE FOR 15 YEARS WITHOUT GETTING CAUGHT. HE'S ALWAYS ELIMINATED *ALL THE EVIDENCE*.
AND HE INTENDS TO ELIMINATE US, TOO.
DO AS I SAY AND OBSERVE. DON'T JUST SEE; *WATCH*. DON'T JUST HEAR; *LISTEN*.
IF WE DON'T...
WE'LL DIE HERE TODAY.

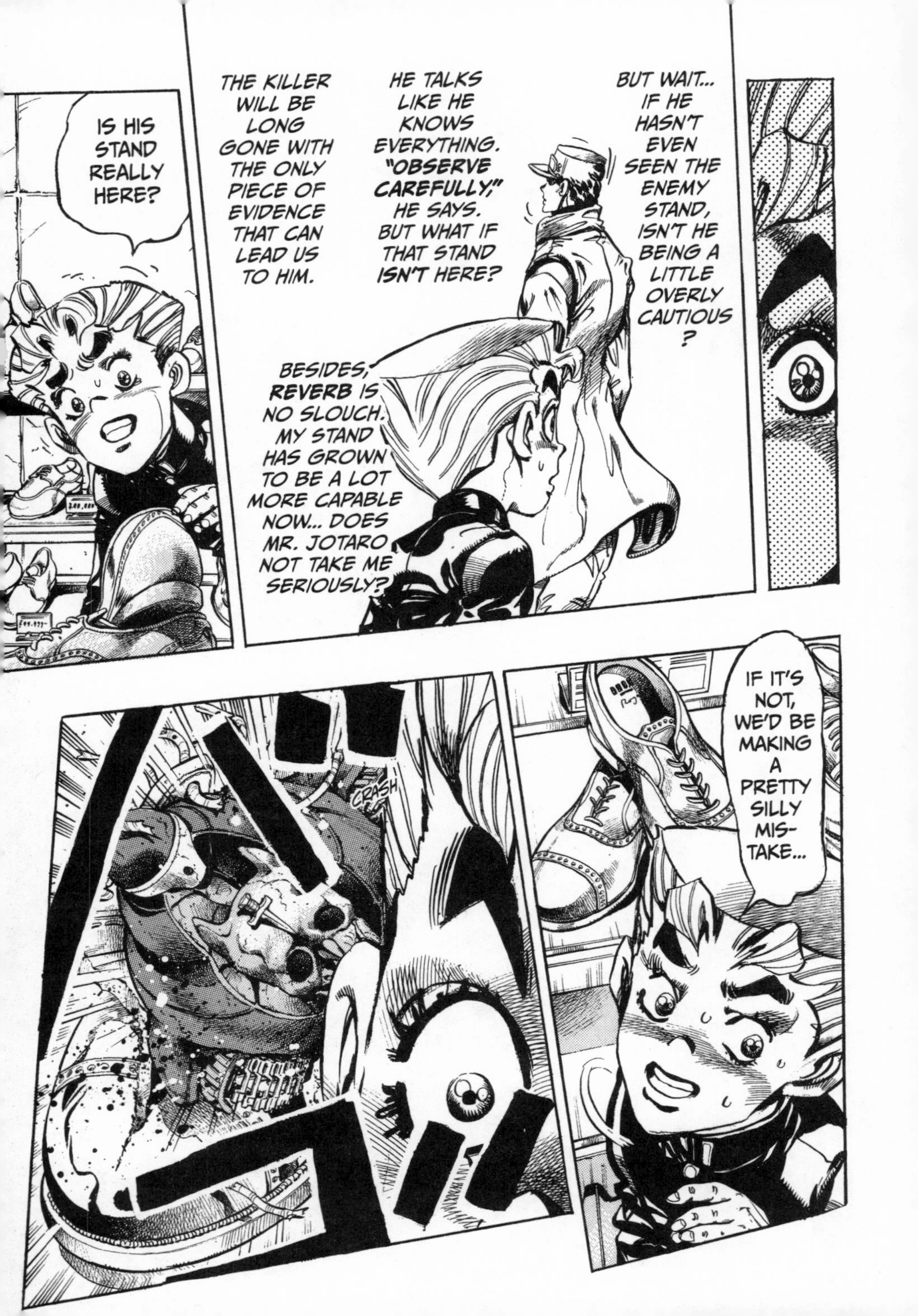
BUT WAIT... IF HE HASN'T EVEN SEEN THE ENEMY STAND, ISN'T HE BEING A LITTLE OVERLY CAUTIOUS?
HE TALKS LIKE HE KNOWS EVERYTHING. **"OBSERVE CAREFULLY,"** HE SAYS. BUT WHAT IF THAT STAND ***ISN'T*** HERE?
THE KILLER WILL BE LONG GONE WITH THE ONLY PIECE OF EVIDENCE THAT CAN LEAD US TO HIM.
BESIDES, **REVERB** IS NO SLOUCH. MY STAND HAS GROWN TO BE A LOT MORE CAPABLE NOW... DOES MR. JOTARO NOT TAKE ME SERIOUSLY?
IS HIS STAND REALLY HERE?
IF IT'S NOT, WE'D BE MAKING A PRETTY SILLY MIS-TAKE...
CRASH

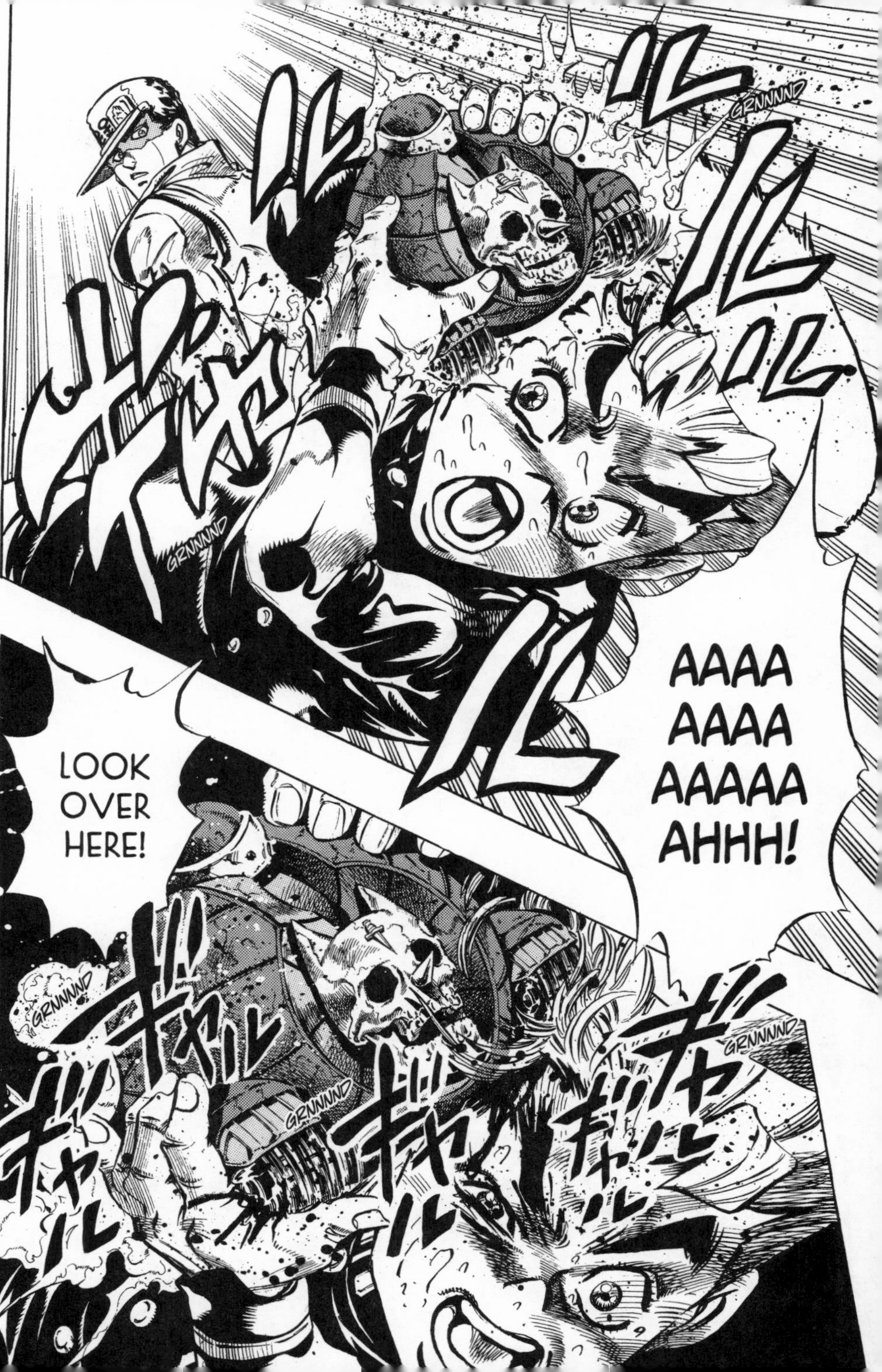

GRNNNND
GRNNNND
AAAA
AAAA
AAAAA
AHHH!
LOOK
OVER
HERE!
GRNNNND
GRNNNND
GRNNNND

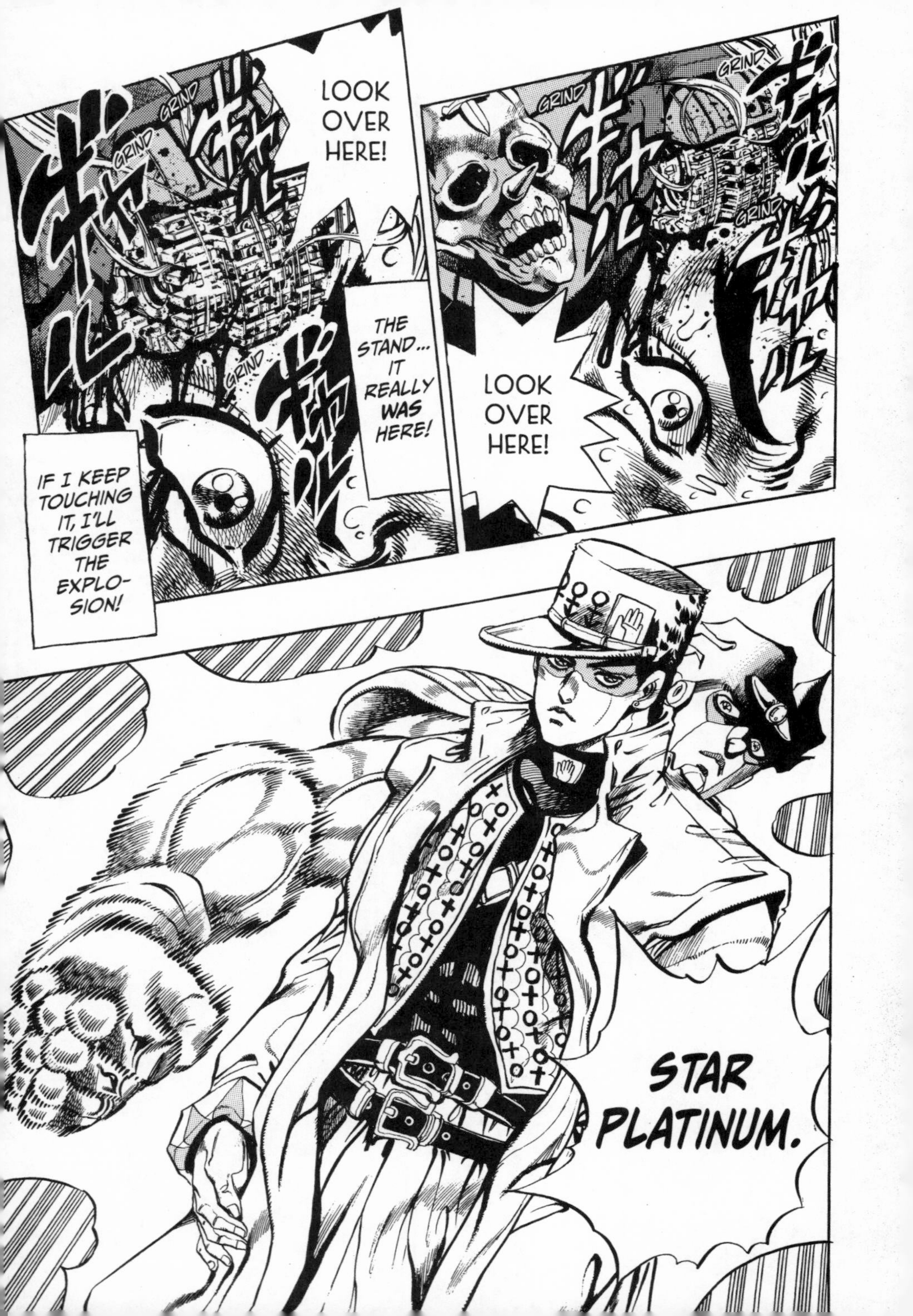
GRIND
GRIND
GRIND
LOOK OVER HERE!
GRIND
GRIND
GRIND
LOOK OVER HERE!
THE STAND... IT REALLY WAS HERE!
IF I KEEP TOUCHING IT, I'LL TRIGGER THE EXPLOSION!
STAR PLATINUM.

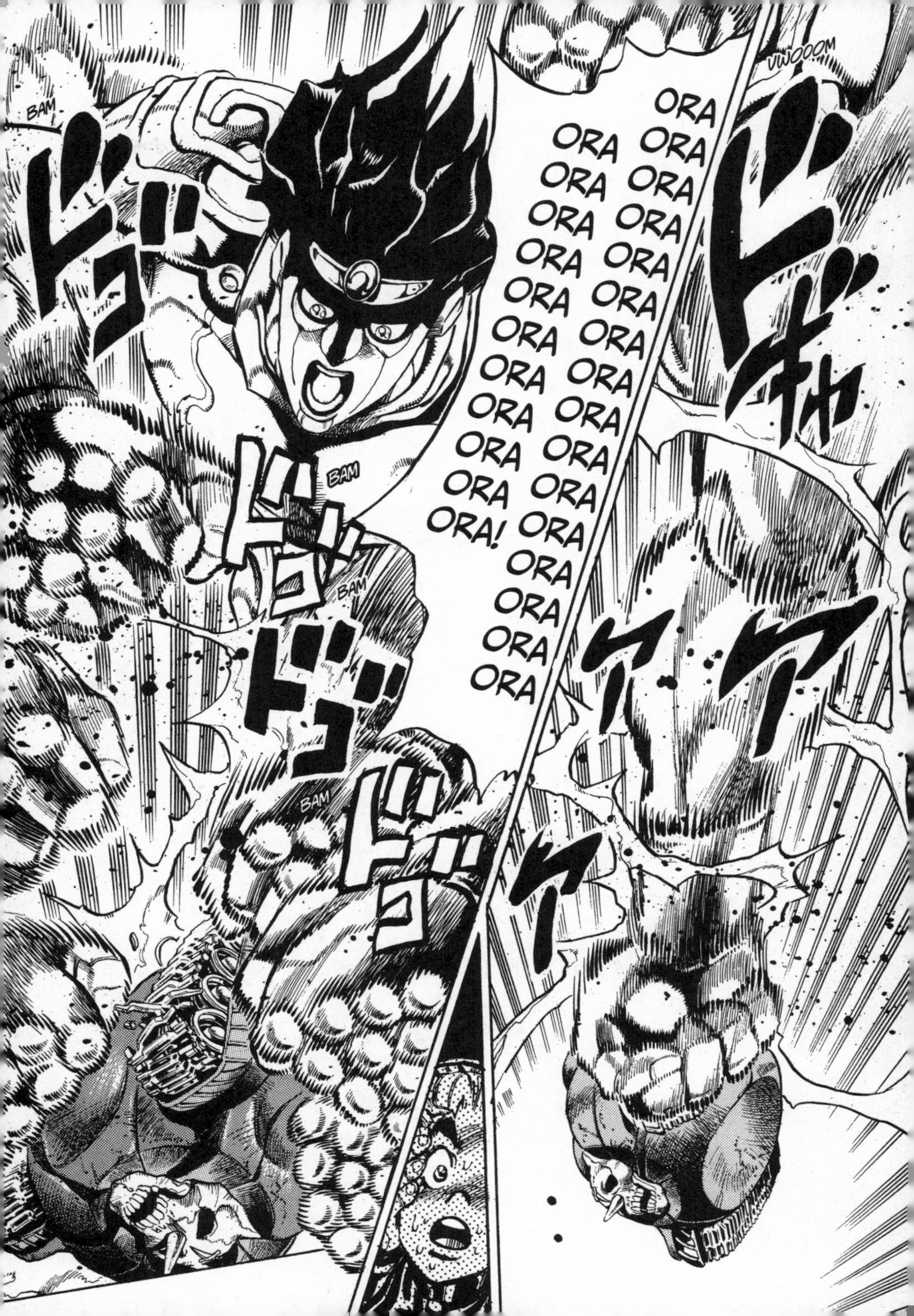
VWOOOM
ORA
ORA ORA
ORA ORA
ORA ORA
ORA ORA
ORA ORA
ORA ORA
ORA ORA
ORA ORA
ORA ORA
ORA ORA
ORA! ORA
ORA
ORA
ORA
ORA
BAM
BAM
BAM
BAM

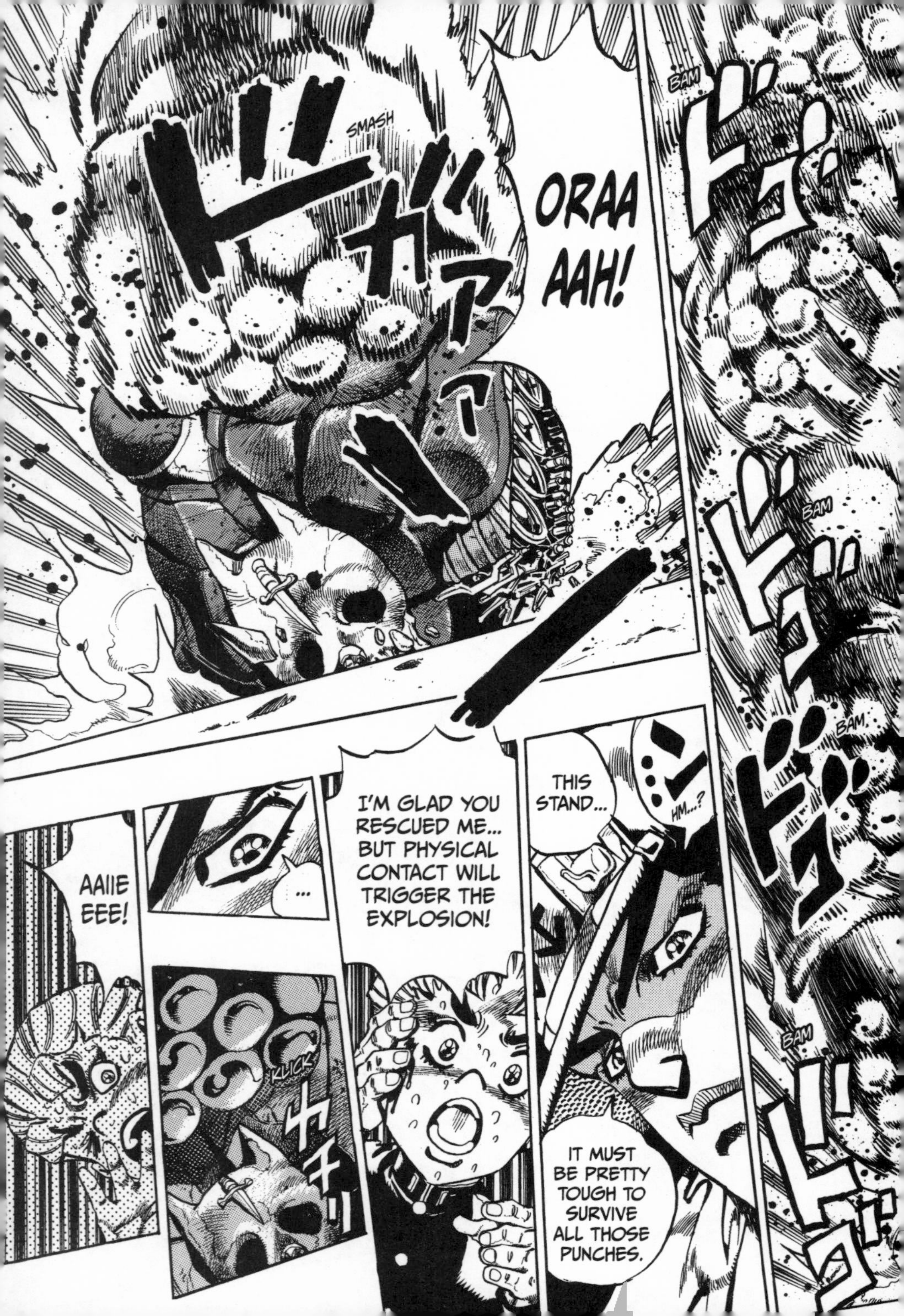
BAM
BAM
BAM
BAM
SMASH
ORAAA AAH!
HM...?
THIS STAND...
IT MUST BE PRETTY TOUGH TO SURVIVE ALL THOSE PUNCHES.
I'M GLAD YOU RESCUED ME... BUT PHYSICAL CONTACT WILL TRIGGER THE EXPLOSION!
...
KLICK
AAIIE EEE!

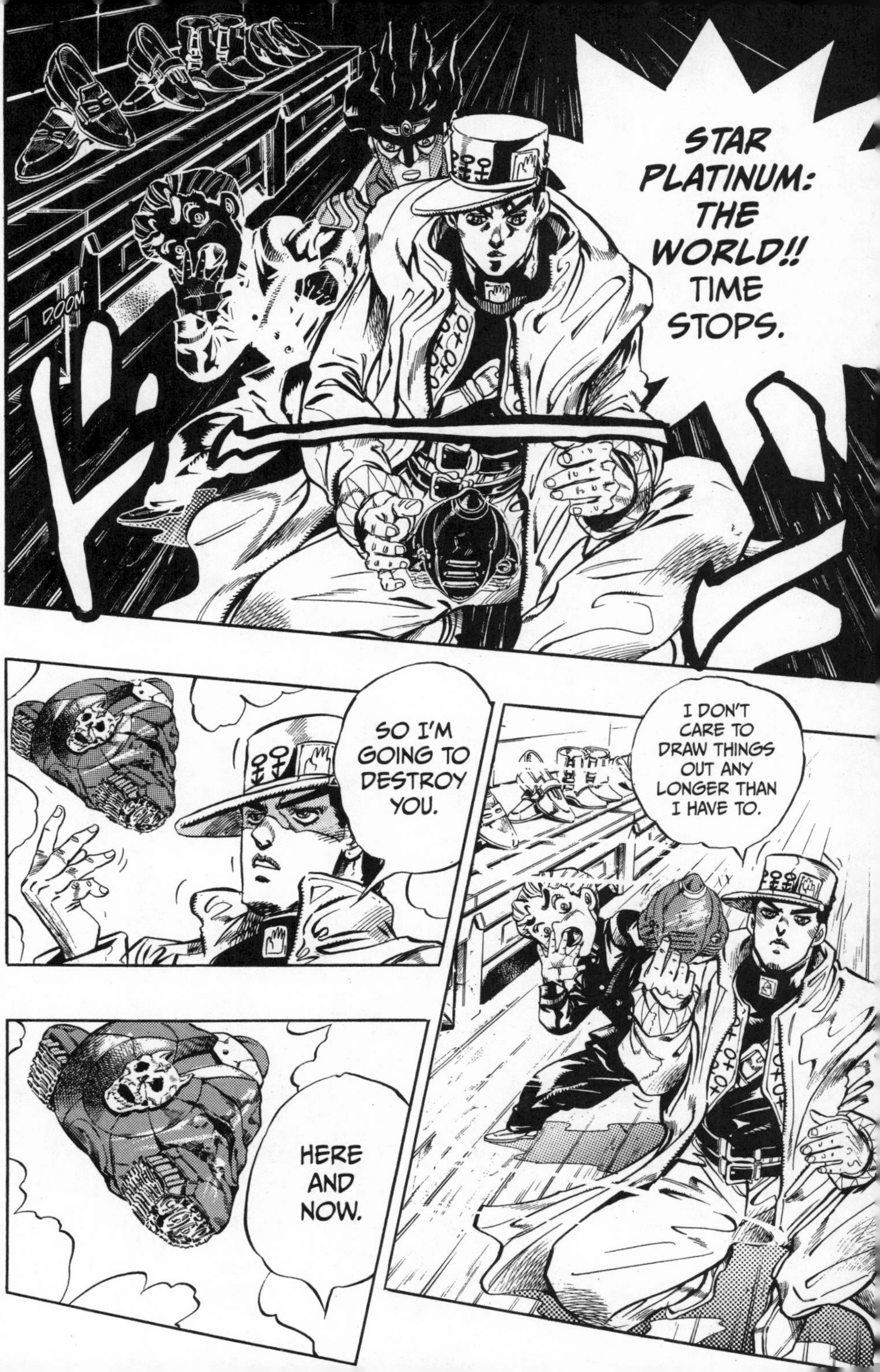
STAR PLATINUM: THE WORLD!! TIME STOPS.
DOOM
I DON'T CARE TO DRAW THINGS OUT ANY LONGER THAN I HAVE TO.
SO I'M GOING TO DESTROY YOU.
HERE AND NOW.

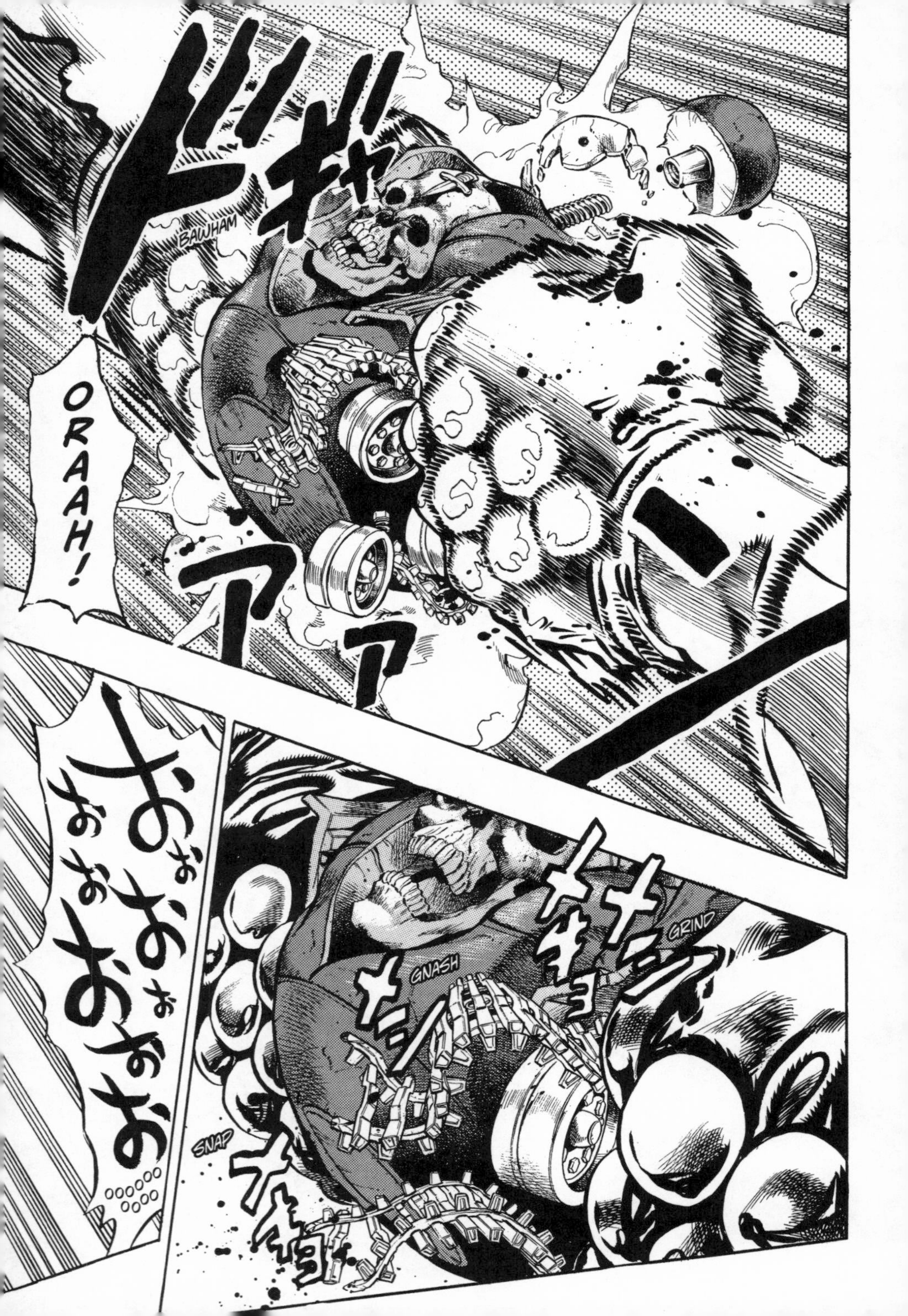
BAWHAM
ORAAH!
GRIND
GNASH
SNAP

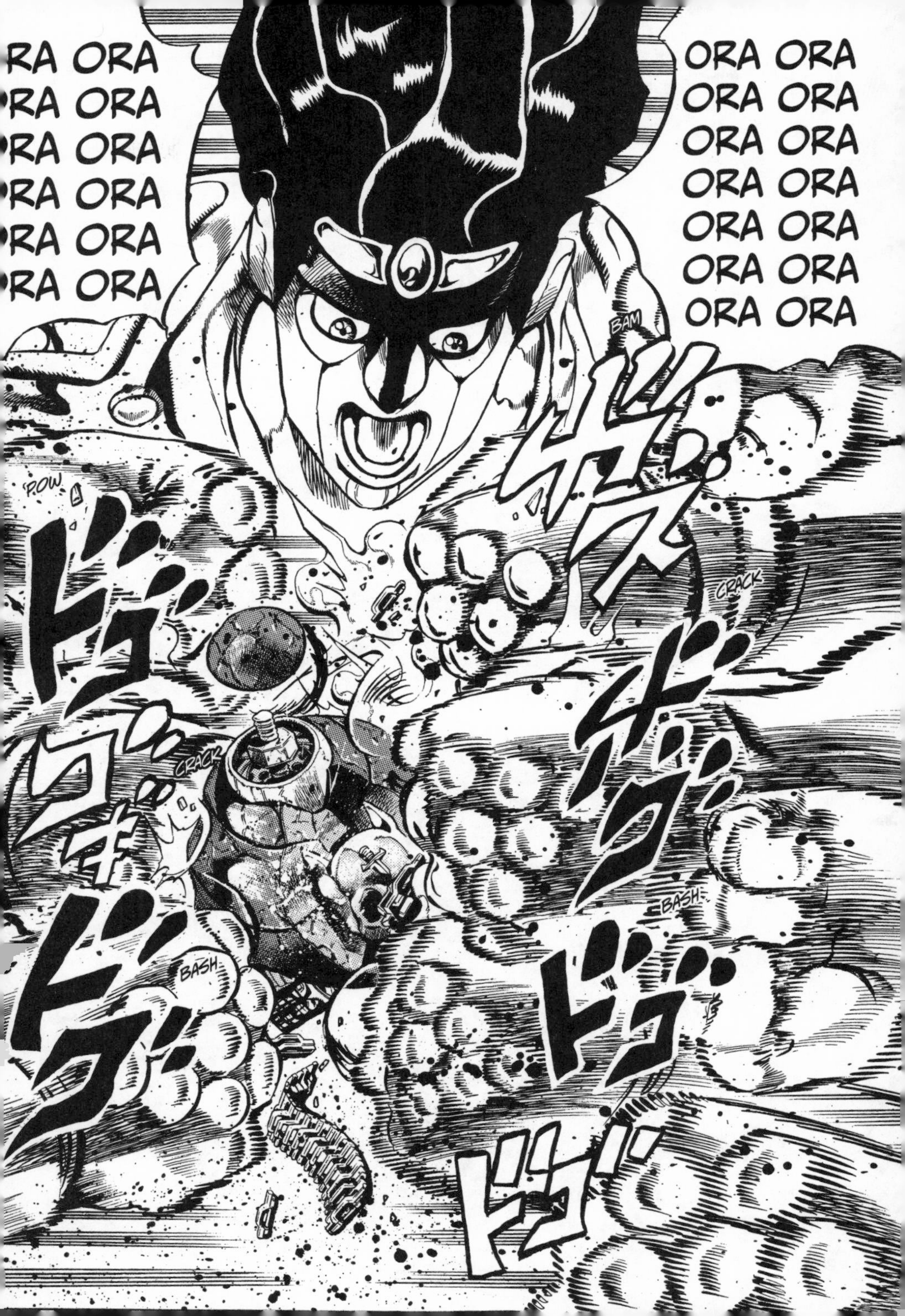
ORA ORA
ORA ORA
ORA ORA
ORA ORA
ORA ORA
ORA ORA
ORA ORA
RA ORA
RA ORA
RA ORA
RA ORA
RA ORA
RA ORA
BAM
CRACK
POW
CRACK
BASH
BASH

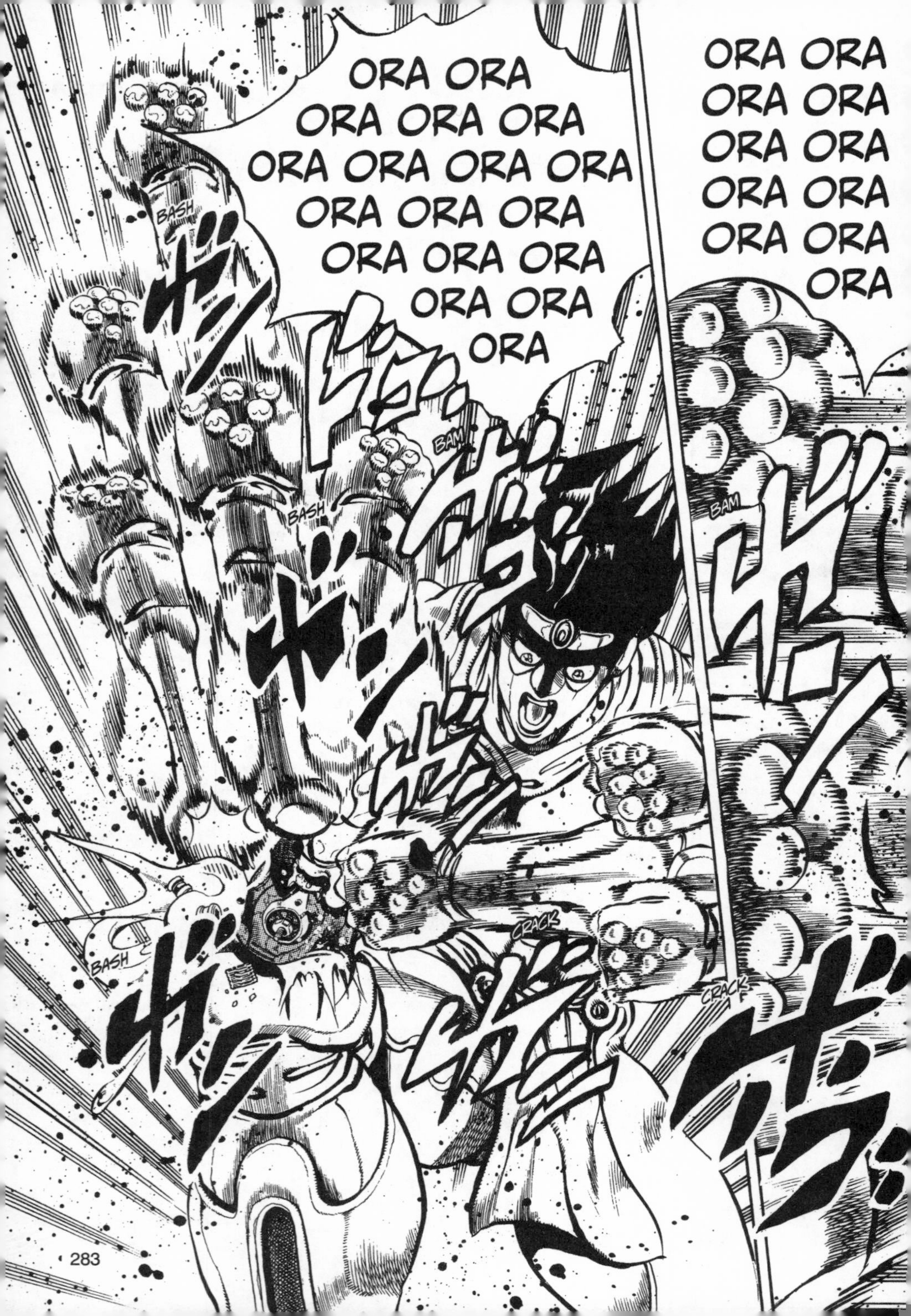
ORA ORA
ORA ORA
ORA ORA
ORA ORA
ORA ORA
ORA
BAM
CRACK
ORA ORA
ORA ORA ORA
ORA ORA ORA ORA
ORA ORA ORA
ORA ORA ORA
ORA ORA
ORA
BASH
BAM
BASH
CRACK
BASH

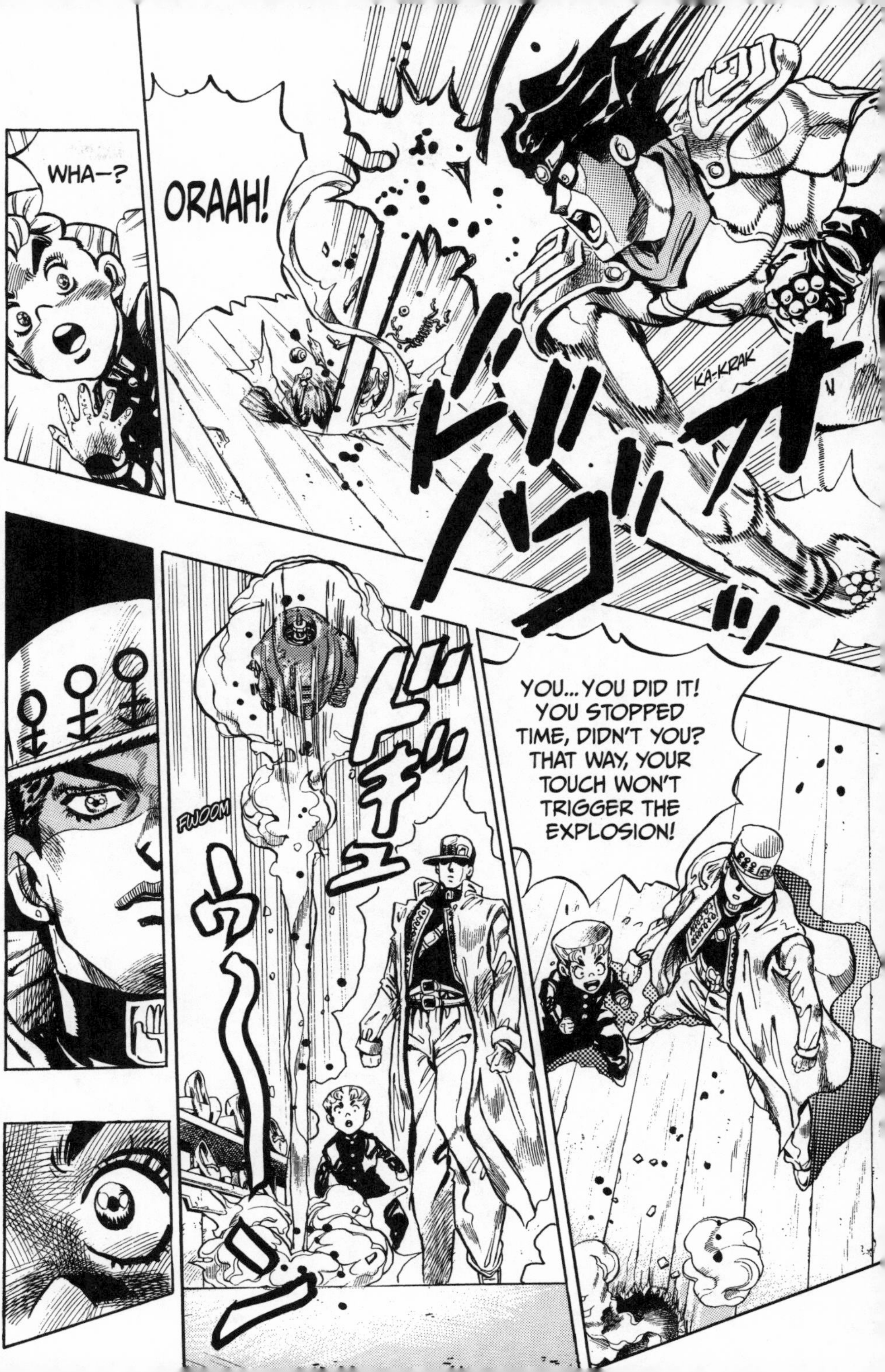
ORAAH!
KA-KRAK
WHA–?
YOU...YOU DID IT! YOU STOPPED TIME, DIDN'T YOU? THAT WAY, YOUR TOUCH WON'T TRIGGER THE EXPLOSION!
FWOOM

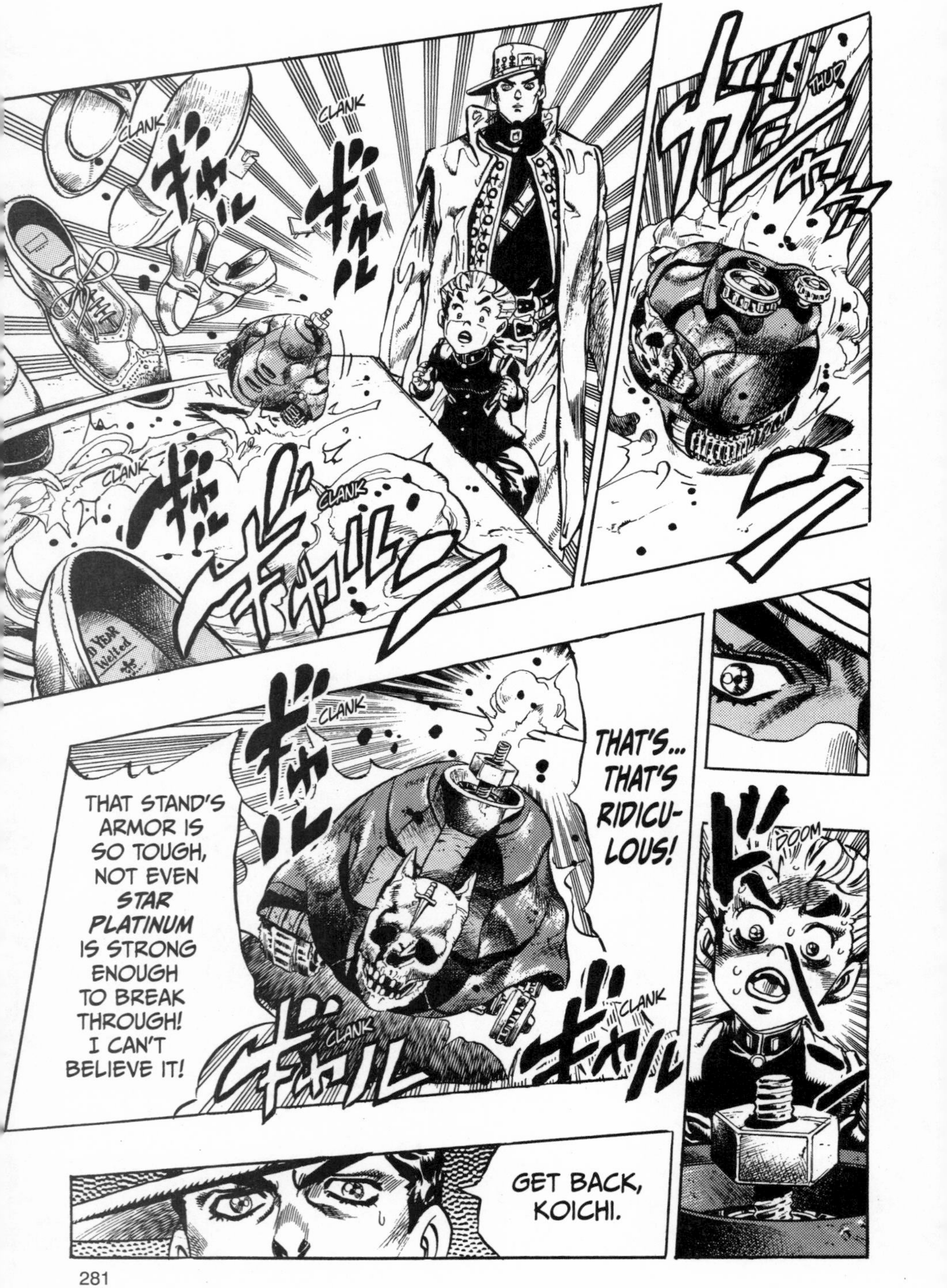
THUD
CLANK
CLANK
CLANK
CLANK
DOOM
CLANK
THAT'S... THAT'S RIDICULOUS!
THAT STAND'S ARMOR IS SO TOUGH, NOT EVEN *STAR PLATINUM* IS STRONG ENOUGH TO BREAK THROUGH! I CAN'T BELIEVE IT!
CLANK
CLANK
GET BACK, KOICHI.

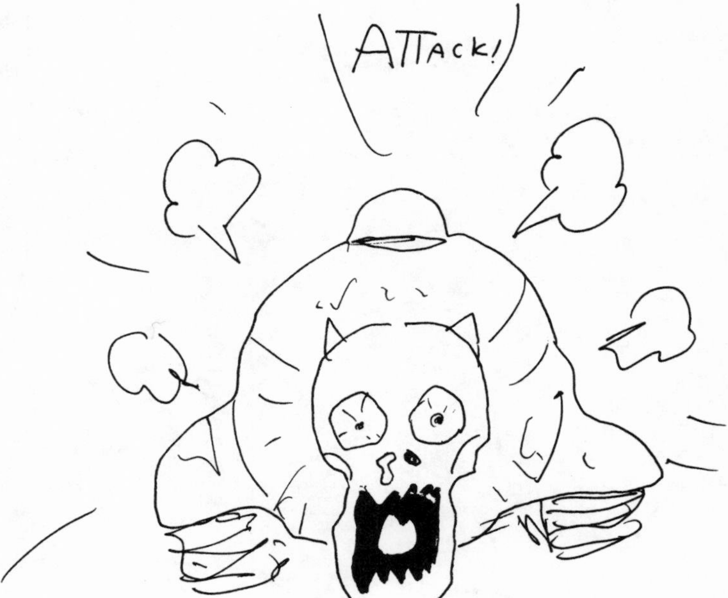
ATTACK!

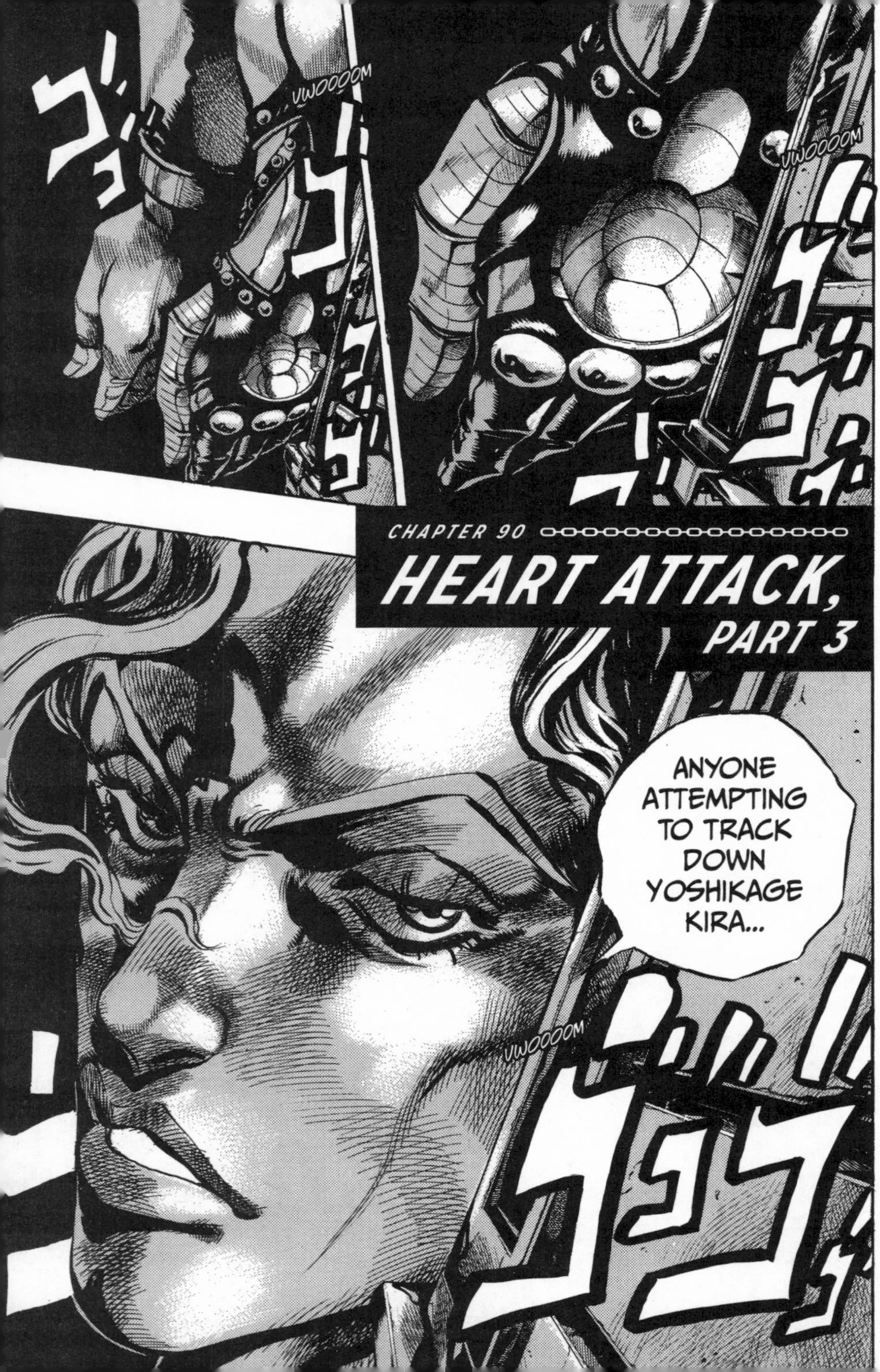
VWOOOOM
VWOOOOM
CHAPTER 90
HEART ATTACK, PART 3
ANYONE ATTEMPTING TO TRACK DOWN YOSHIKAGE KIRA...
VWOOOOM

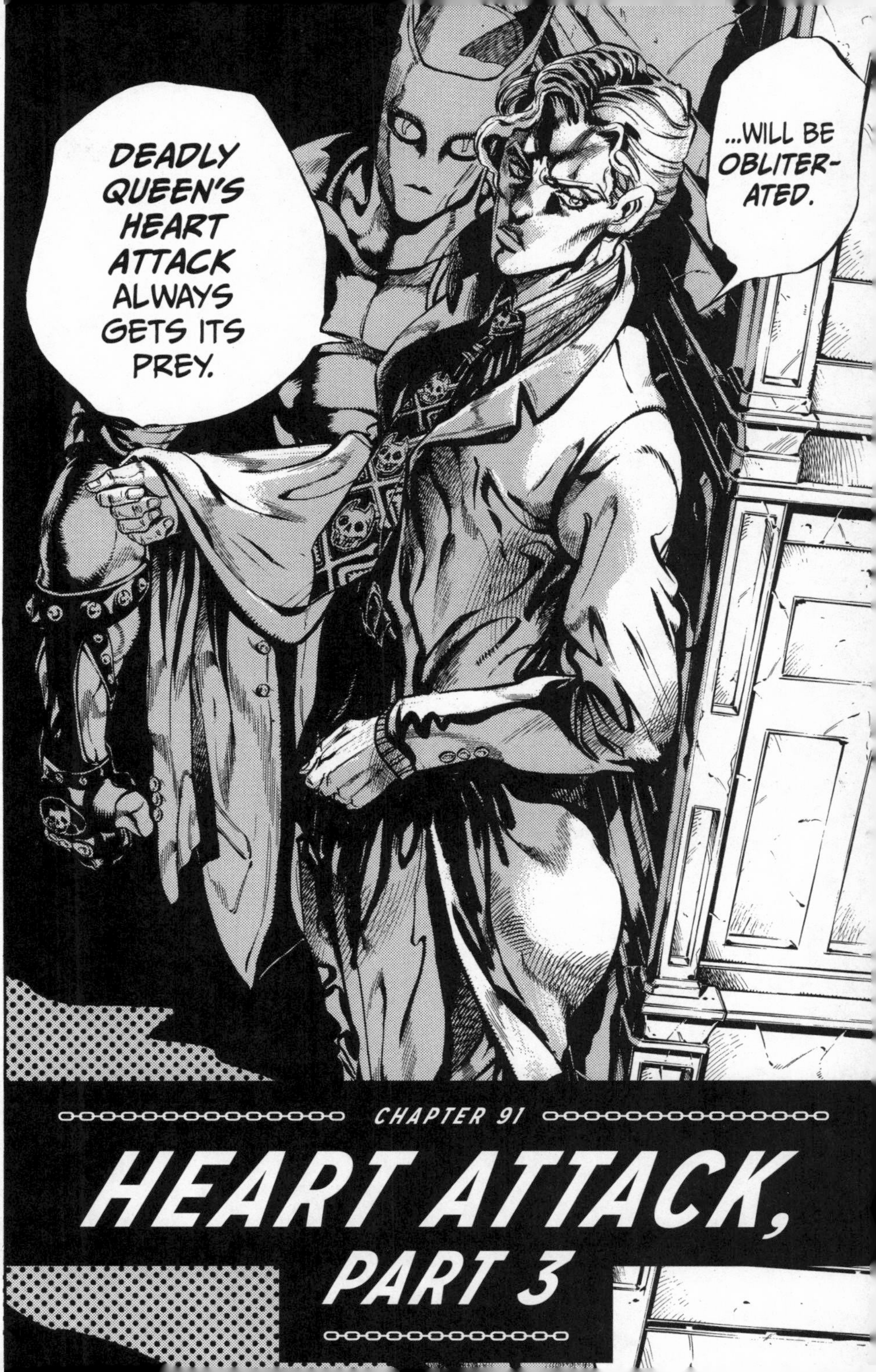
...WILL BE OBLITERATED.
DEADLY QUEEN'S HEART ATTACK ALWAYS GETS ITS PREY.
CHAPTER 91
HEART ATTACK, PART 3

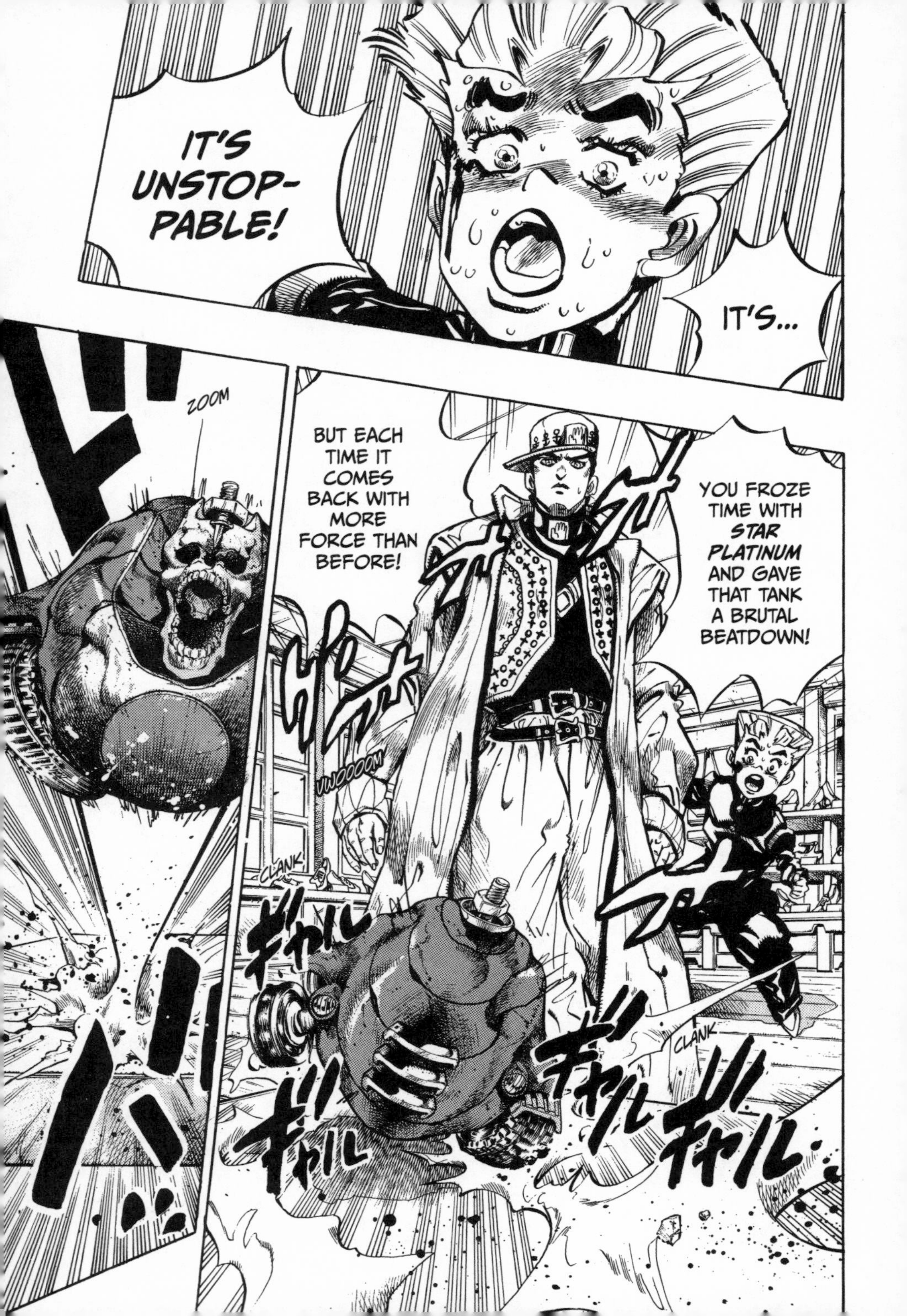
IT'S...
IT'S UNSTOPPABLE!
YOU FROZE TIME WITH STAR PLATINUM AND GAVE THAT TANK A BRUTAL BEATDOWN!
BUT EACH TIME IT COMES BACK WITH MORE FORCE THAN BEFORE!
VWOOOOM
CLANK
CLANK
ZOOM

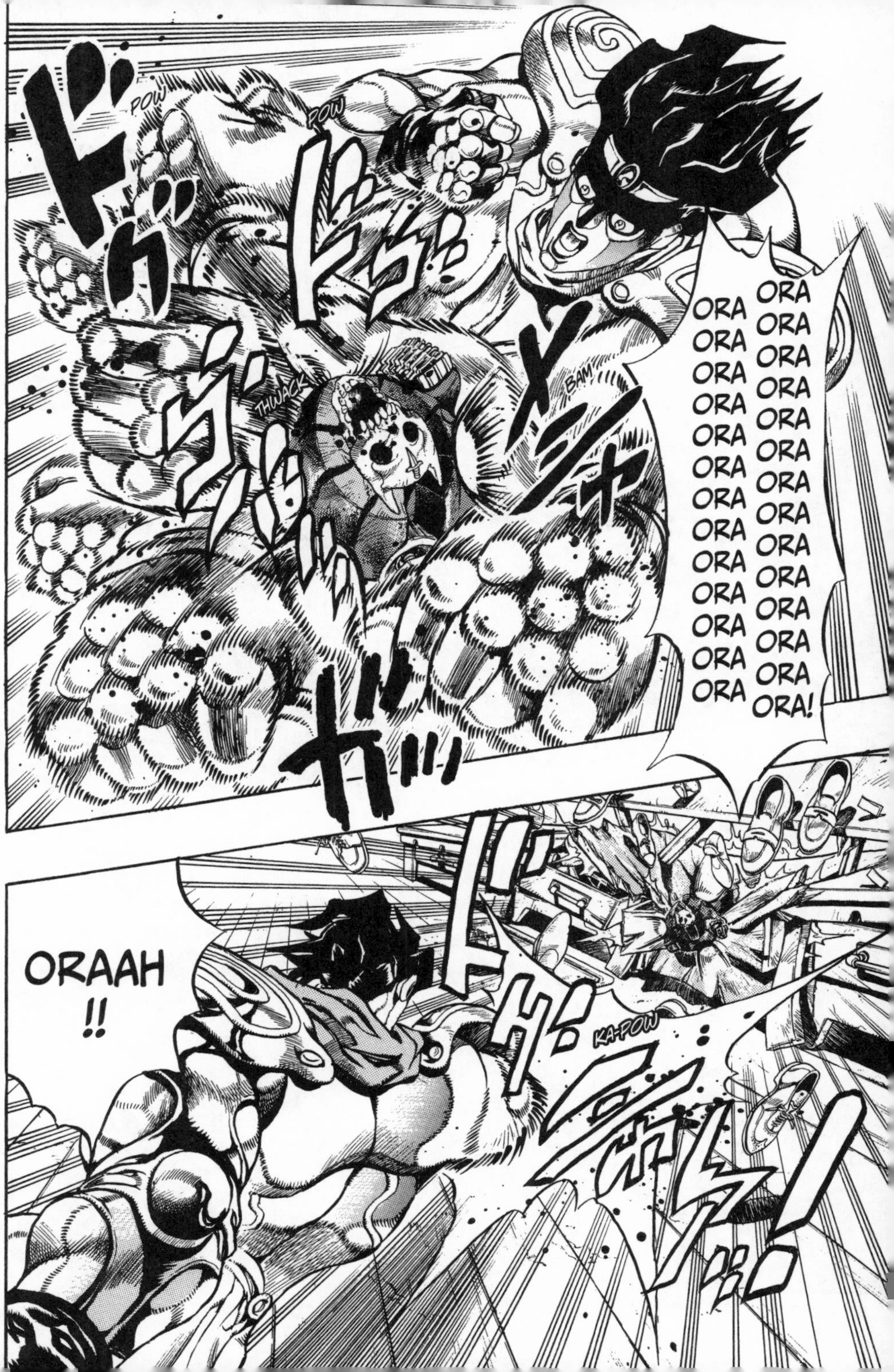

ORA ORA ORA ORA ORA ORA ORA ORA ORA ORA ORA ORA ORA ORA ORA ORA ORA ORA ORA ORA ORA ORA ORA ORA ORA ORA ORA ORA ORA!
BAM
POW
POW
THWACK
KA-POW
ORAAH !!

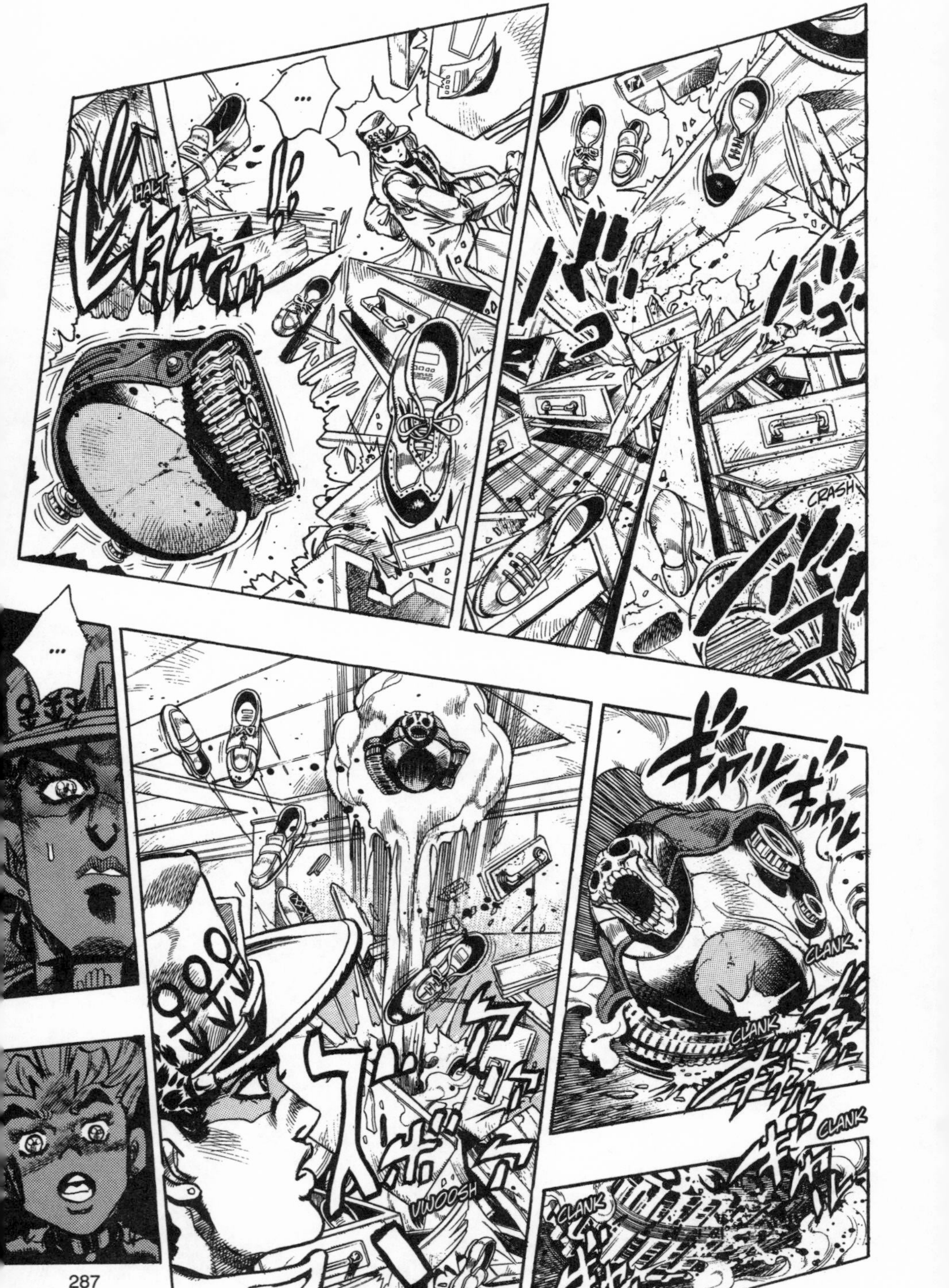
CRASH
...
!?
HALT
CLANK
CLANK
CLANK
CLANK
VWOOSH
...

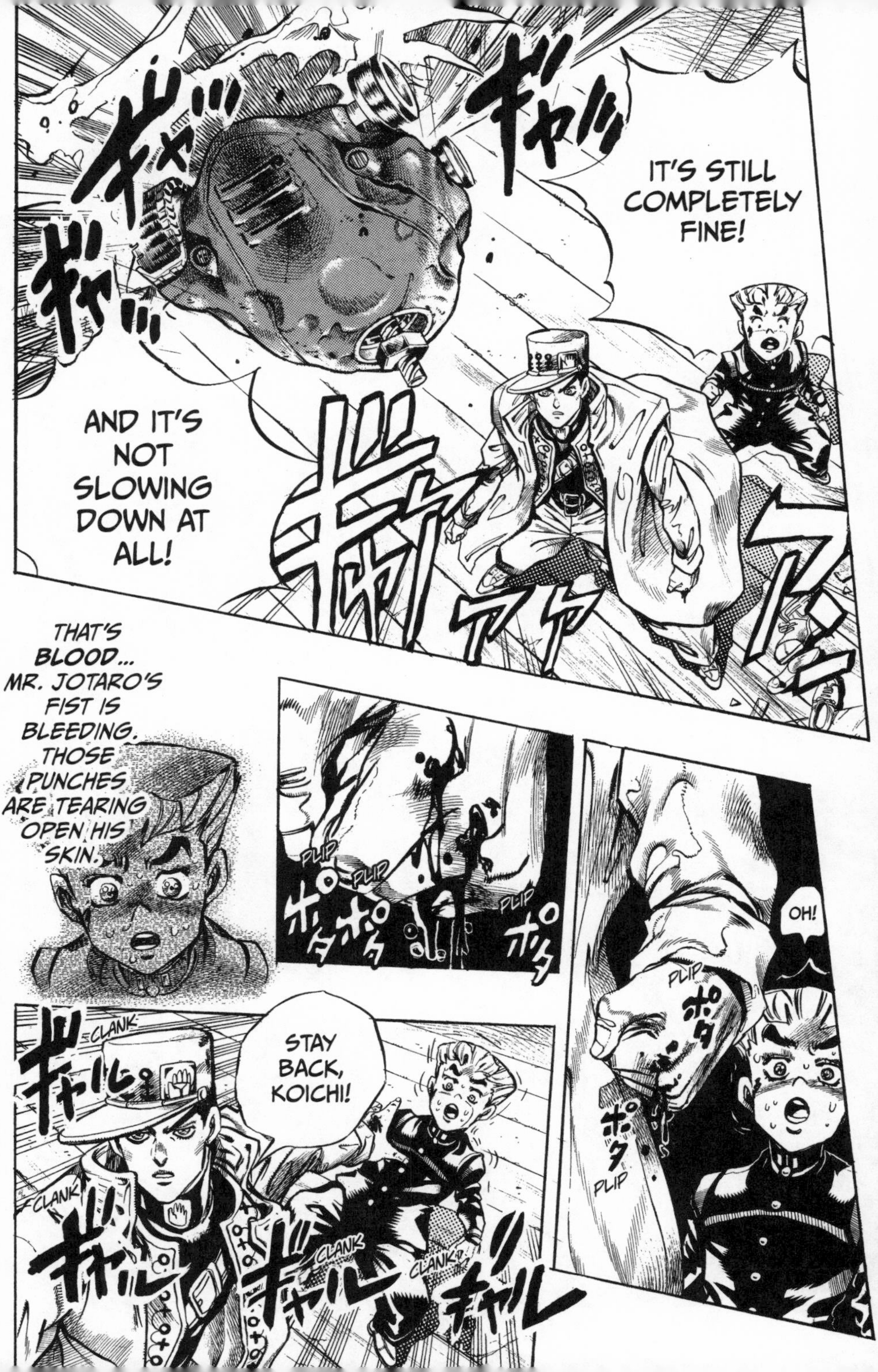
IT'S STILL COMPLETELY FINE!
AND IT'S NOT SLOWING DOWN AT ALL!
OH!
PLIP
PLIP
PLIP
PLIP
PLIP
THAT'S BLOOD... MR. JOTARO'S FIST IS BLEEDING. THOSE PUNCHES ARE TEARING OPEN HIS SKIN.
CLANK
STAY BACK, KOICHI!
CLANK
CLANK
CLANK

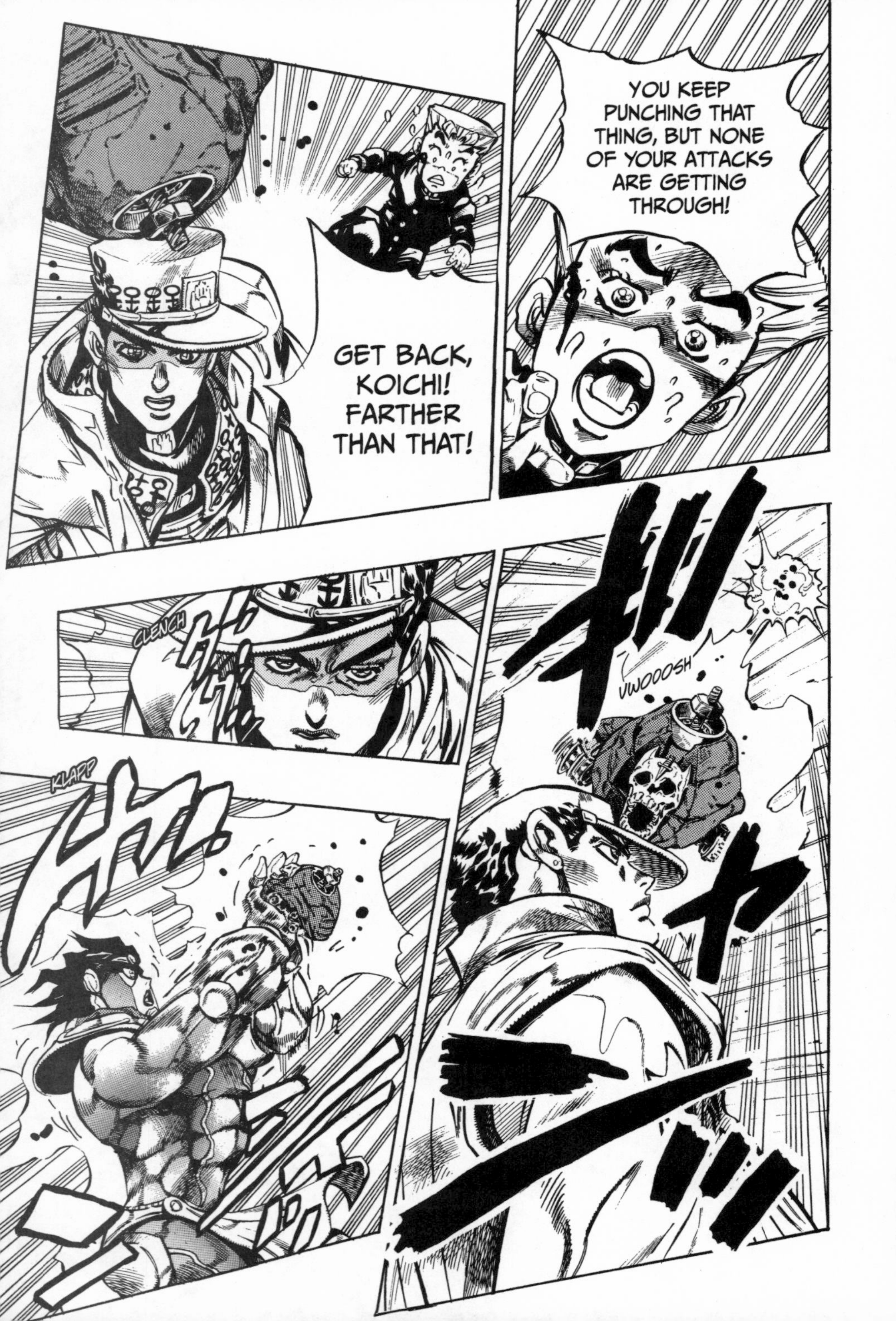
YOU KEEP PUNCHING THAT THING, BUT NONE OF YOUR ATTACKS ARE GETTING THROUGH!
GET BACK, KOICHI! FARTHER THAN THAT!
VWOOOSH
CLENCH
KLAPP

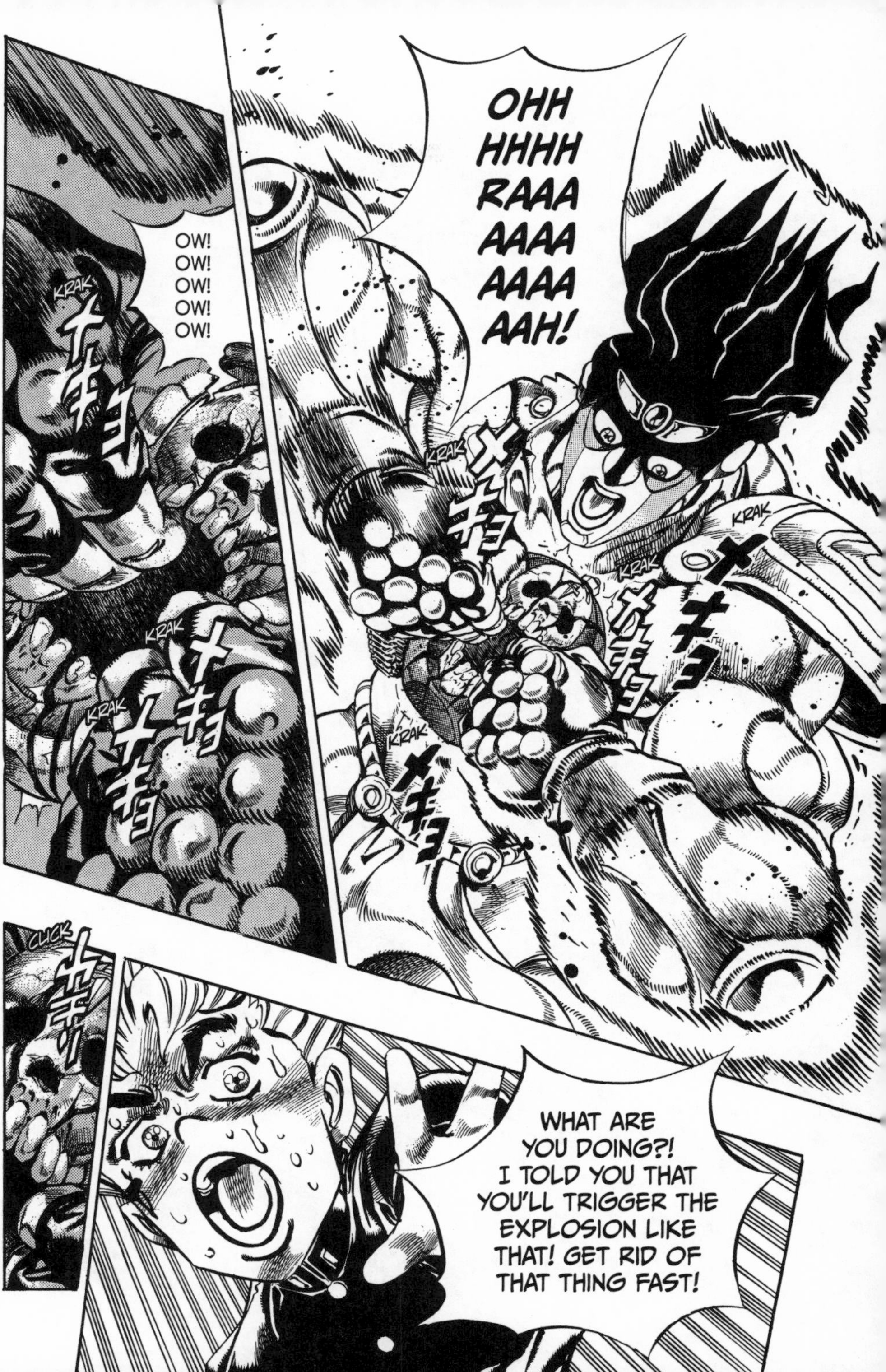
OHH
HHHH
RAAA
AAAA
AAAA
AAH!
KRAK
KRAK
KRAK
KRAK
OW!
OW!
OW!
OW!
OW!
KRAK
KRAK
KRAK
CLICK
WHAT ARE
YOU DOING?!
I TOLD YOU THAT
YOU'LL TRIGGER THE
EXPLOSION LIKE
THAT! GET RID OF
THAT THING FAST!

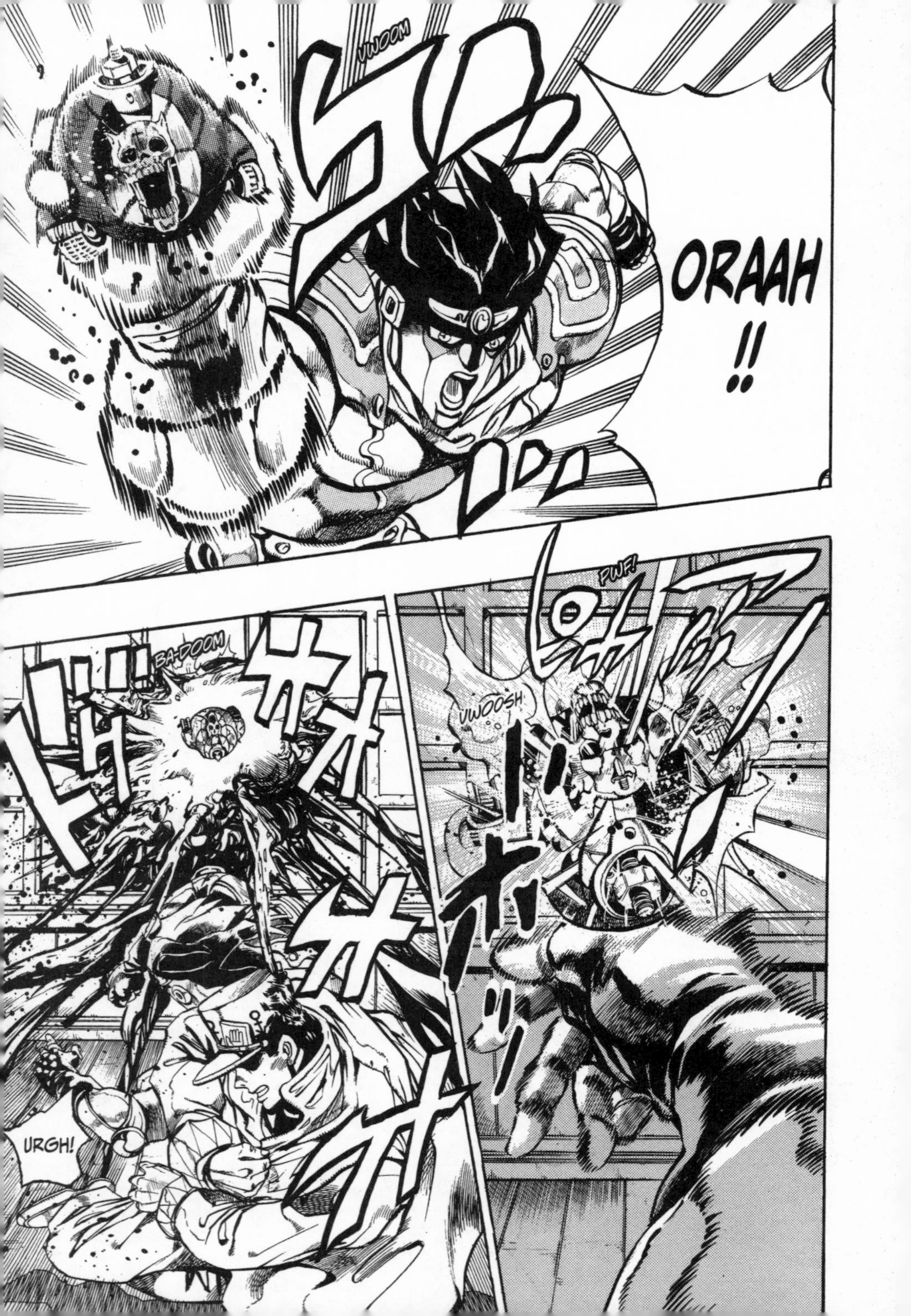
VWOOM
ORAAH
!!
PWF!
VWOOSH
BA-DOOM
URGH!

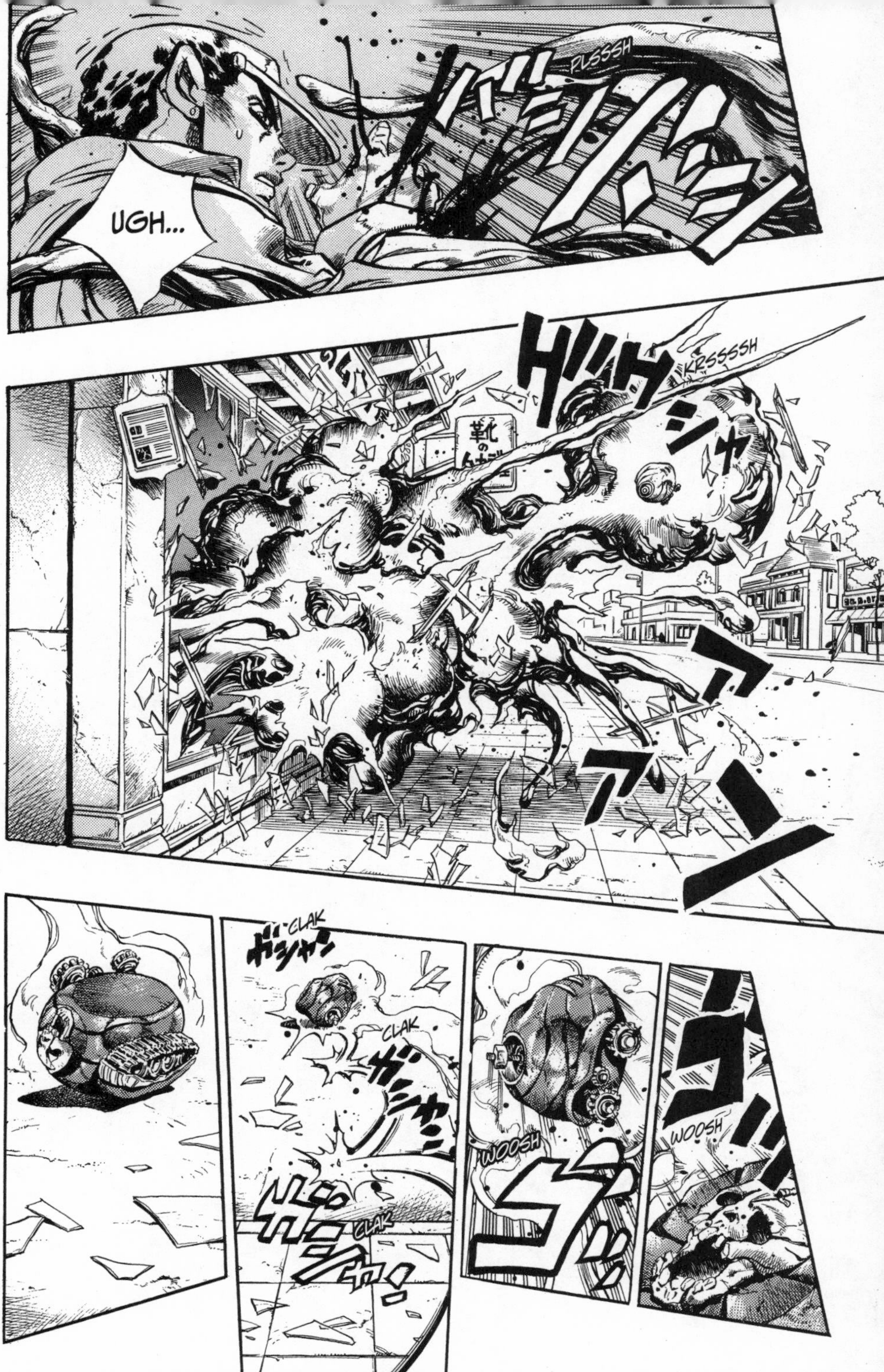
PLSSSH
UGH...
KRSSSSH
WOOSH
WOOSH
CLAK
CLAK
CLAK

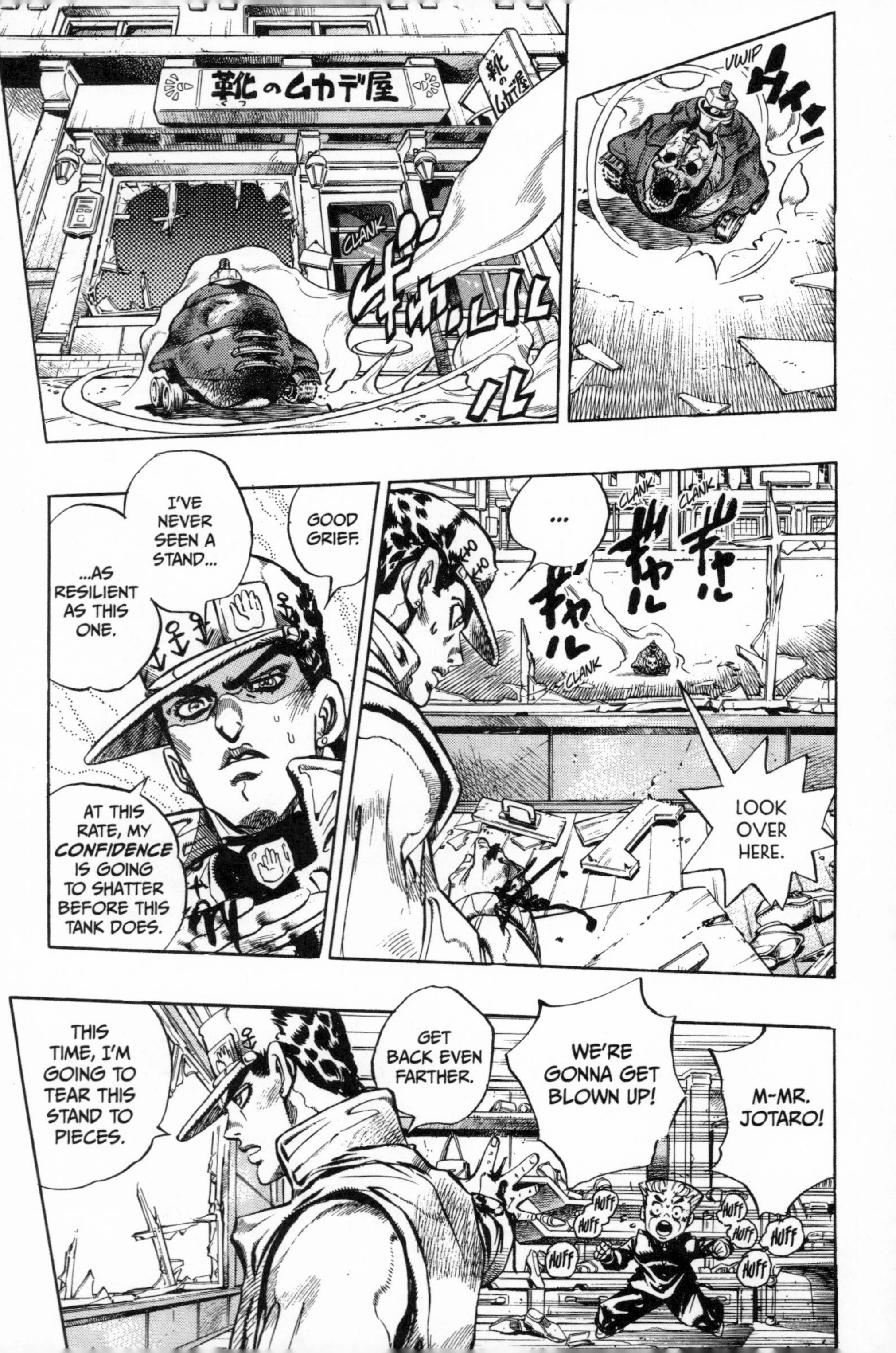
VWIP
靴のムカデ屋
CLANK
...
CLANK
CLANK
CLANK
LOOK OVER HERE.
GOOD GRIEF.
I'VE NEVER SEEN A STAND...
...AS RESILIENT AS THIS ONE.
AT THIS RATE, MY CONFIDENCE IS GOING TO SHATTER BEFORE THIS TANK DOES.
M-MR. JOTARO!
WE'RE GONNA GET BLOWN UP!
HUFF HUFF HUFF HUFF HUFF HUFF
GET BACK EVEN FARTHER.
THIS TIME, I'M GOING TO TEAR THIS STAND TO PIECES.

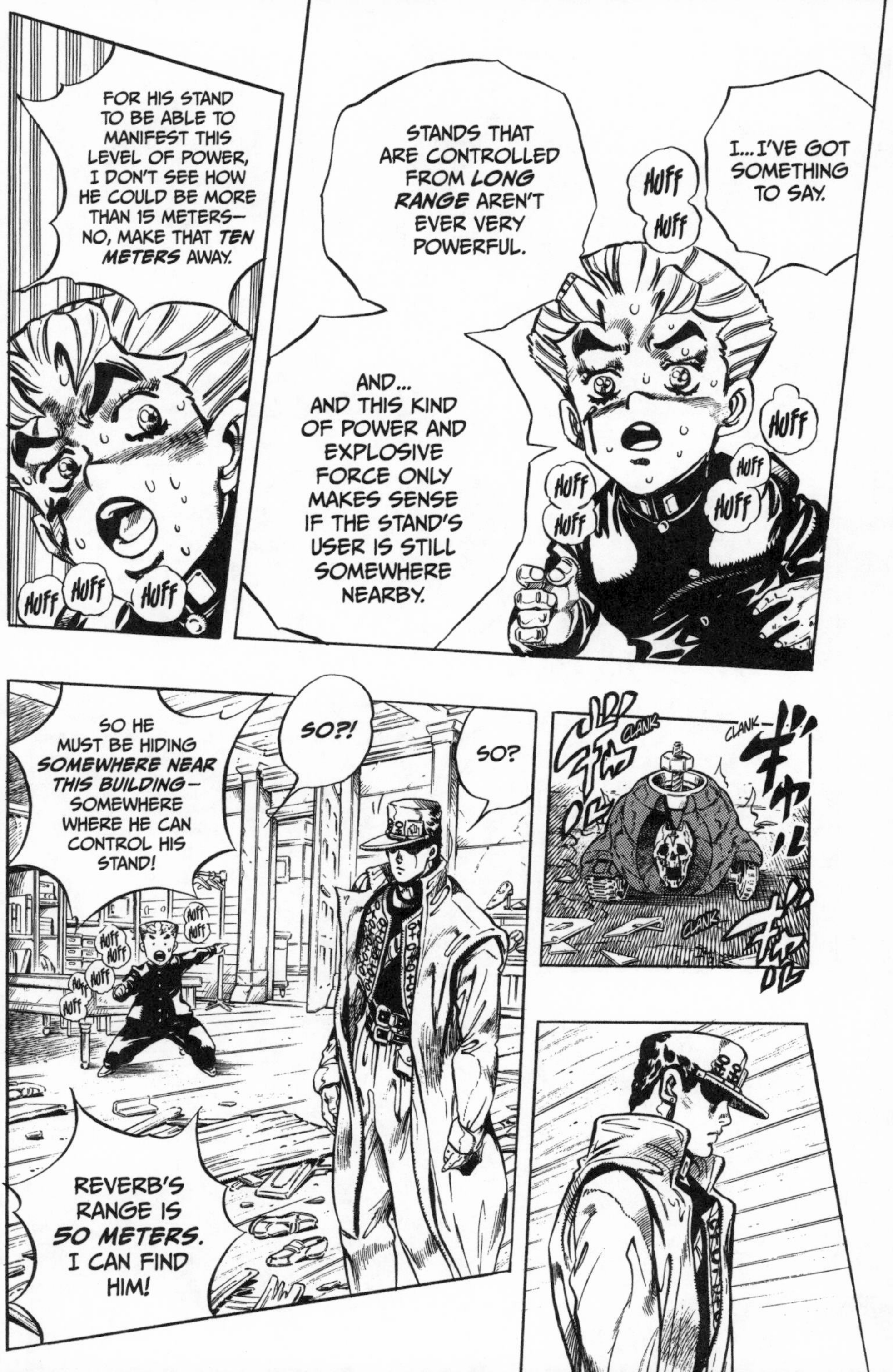
I...I'VE GOT SOMETHING TO SAY.
HUFF
HUFF
STANDS THAT ARE CONTROLLED FROM LONG RANGE AREN'T EVER VERY POWERFUL.
AND... AND THIS KIND OF POWER AND EXPLOSIVE FORCE ONLY MAKES SENSE IF THE STAND'S USER IS STILL SOMEWHERE NEARBY.
HUFF
HUFF
HUFF
HUFF
HUFF
FOR HIS STAND TO BE ABLE TO MANIFEST THIS LEVEL OF POWER, I DON'T SEE HOW HE COULD BE MORE THAN 15 METERS—NO, MAKE THAT TEN METERS AWAY.
HUFF
HUFF
HUFF
CLANK
CLANK
CLANK
SO?
SO?!
SO HE MUST BE HIDING SOMEWHERE NEAR THIS BUILDING—SOMEWHERE WHERE HE CAN CONTROL HIS STAND!
HUFF HUFF
HUFF HUFF
HUFF
HUFF
HUFF
REVERB'S RANGE IS 50 METERS. I CAN FIND HIM!

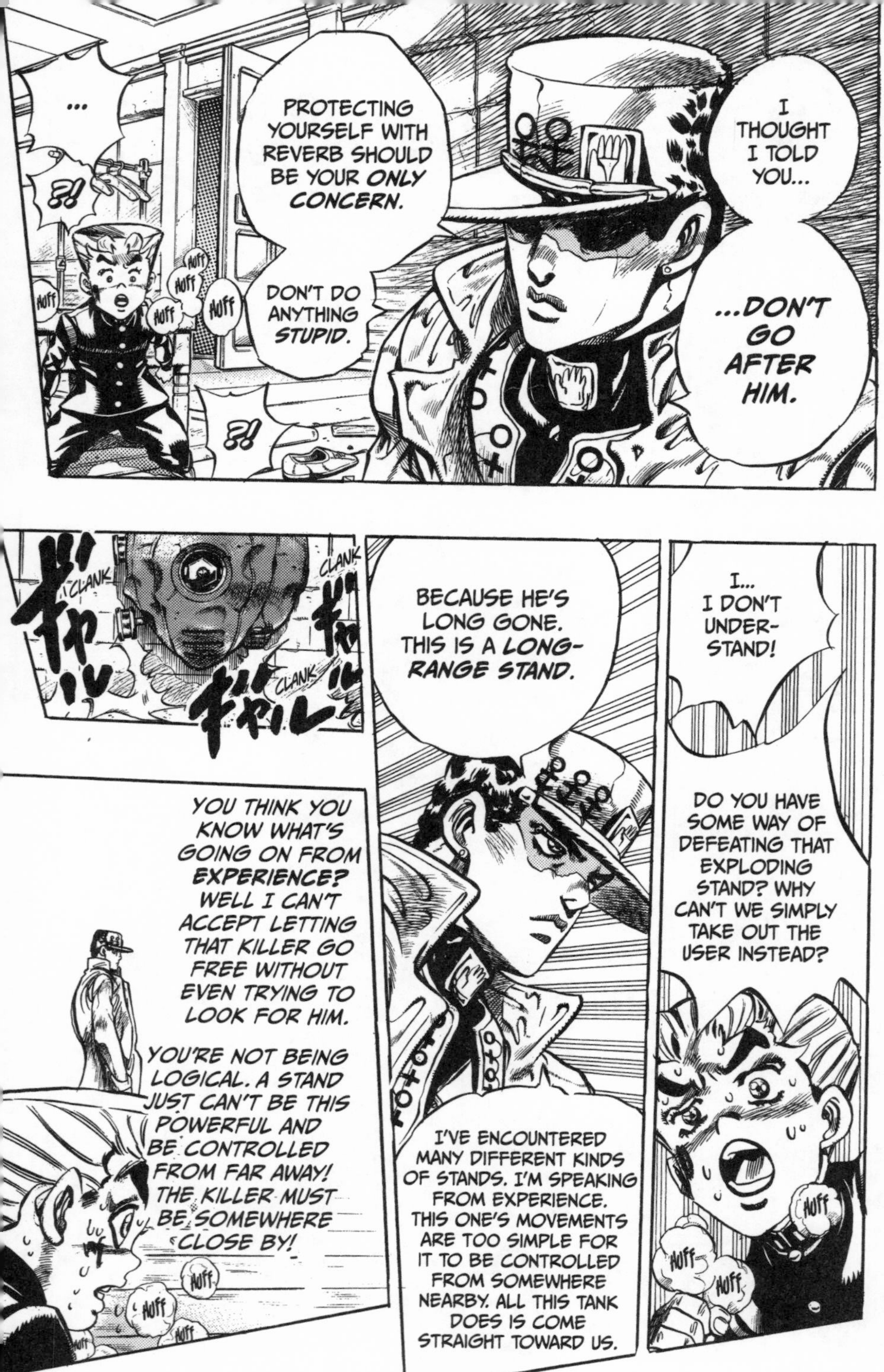
I THOUGHT I TOLD YOU...
...DON'T GO AFTER HIM.
PROTECTING YOURSELF WITH REVERB SHOULD BE YOUR ONLY CONCERN.
DON'T DO ANYTHING STUPID.
...
?!
HUFF
HUFF
HUFF
HUFF
HUFF
?!
I... I DON'T UNDER-STAND!
DO YOU HAVE SOME WAY OF DEFEATING THAT EXPLODING STAND? WHY CAN'T WE SIMPLY TAKE OUT THE USER INSTEAD?
HUFF
HUFF
HUFF
BECAUSE HE'S LONG GONE. THIS IS A LONG-RANGE STAND.
I'VE ENCOUNTERED MANY DIFFERENT KINDS OF STANDS. I'M SPEAKING FROM EXPERIENCE. THIS ONE'S MOVEMENTS ARE TOO SIMPLE FOR IT TO BE CONTROLLED FROM SOMEWHERE NEARBY. ALL THIS TANK DOES IS COME STRAIGHT TOWARD US.
CLANK
CLANK
CLANK
YOU THINK YOU KNOW WHAT'S GOING ON FROM EXPERIENCE? WELL I CAN'T ACCEPT LETTING THAT KILLER GO FREE WITHOUT EVEN TRYING TO LOOK FOR HIM.
YOU'RE NOT BEING LOGICAL. A STAND JUST CAN'T BE THIS POWERFUL AND BE CONTROLLED FROM FAR AWAY! THE KILLER MUST BE SOMEWHERE CLOSE BY!
HUFF
HUFF
HUFF

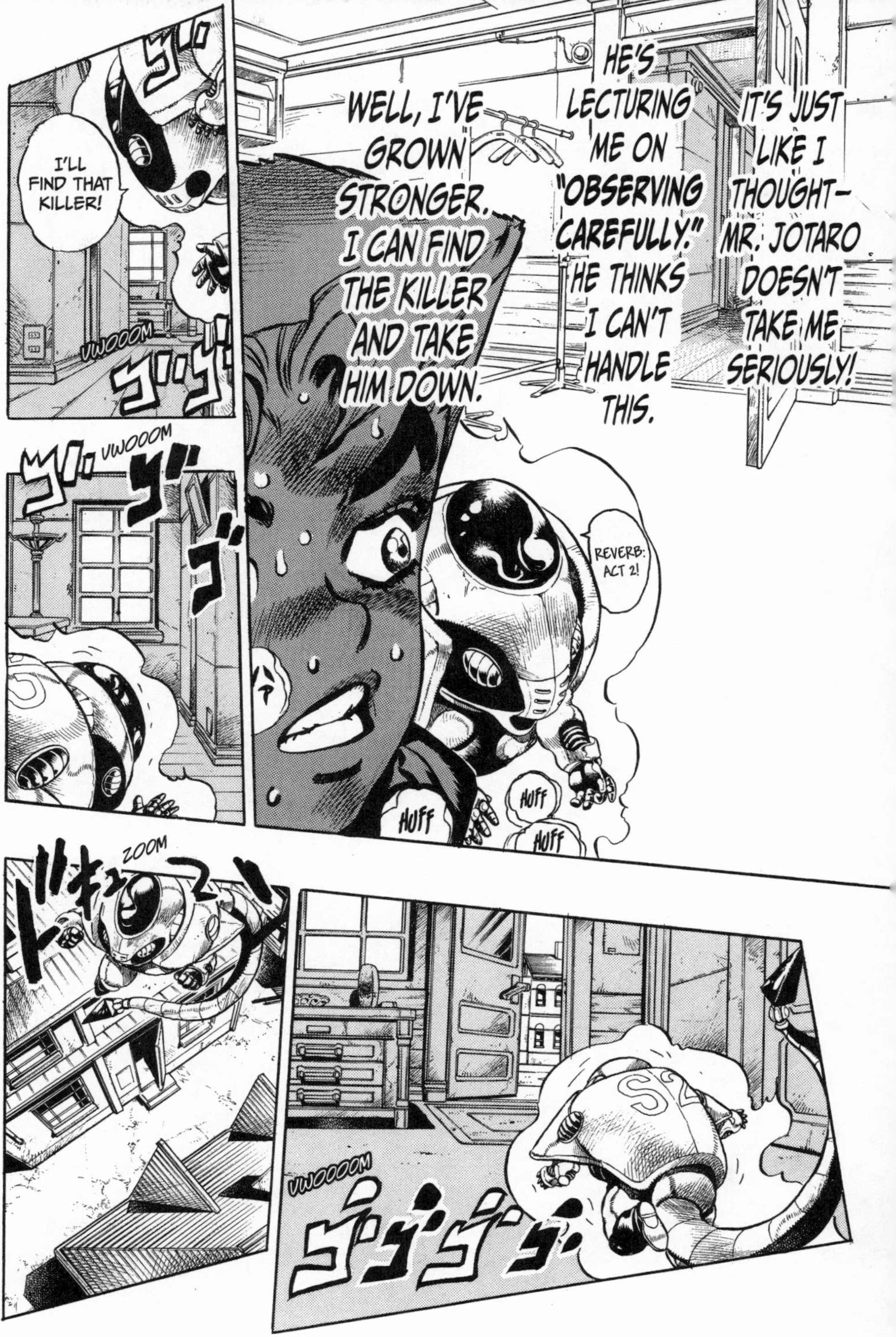
IT'S JUST LIKE I THOUGHT— MR. JOTARO DOESN'T TAKE ME SERIOUSLY!
HE'S LECTURING ME ON "OBSERVING CAREFULLY." HE THINKS I CAN'T HANDLE THIS.
WELL, I'VE GROWN STRONGER. I CAN FIND THE KILLER AND TAKE HIM DOWN.
I'LL FIND THAT KILLER!
VWOOOM
REVERB: ACT 2!
HUFF
HUFF
HUFF
VWOOOM
VWOOOOM
ZOOM

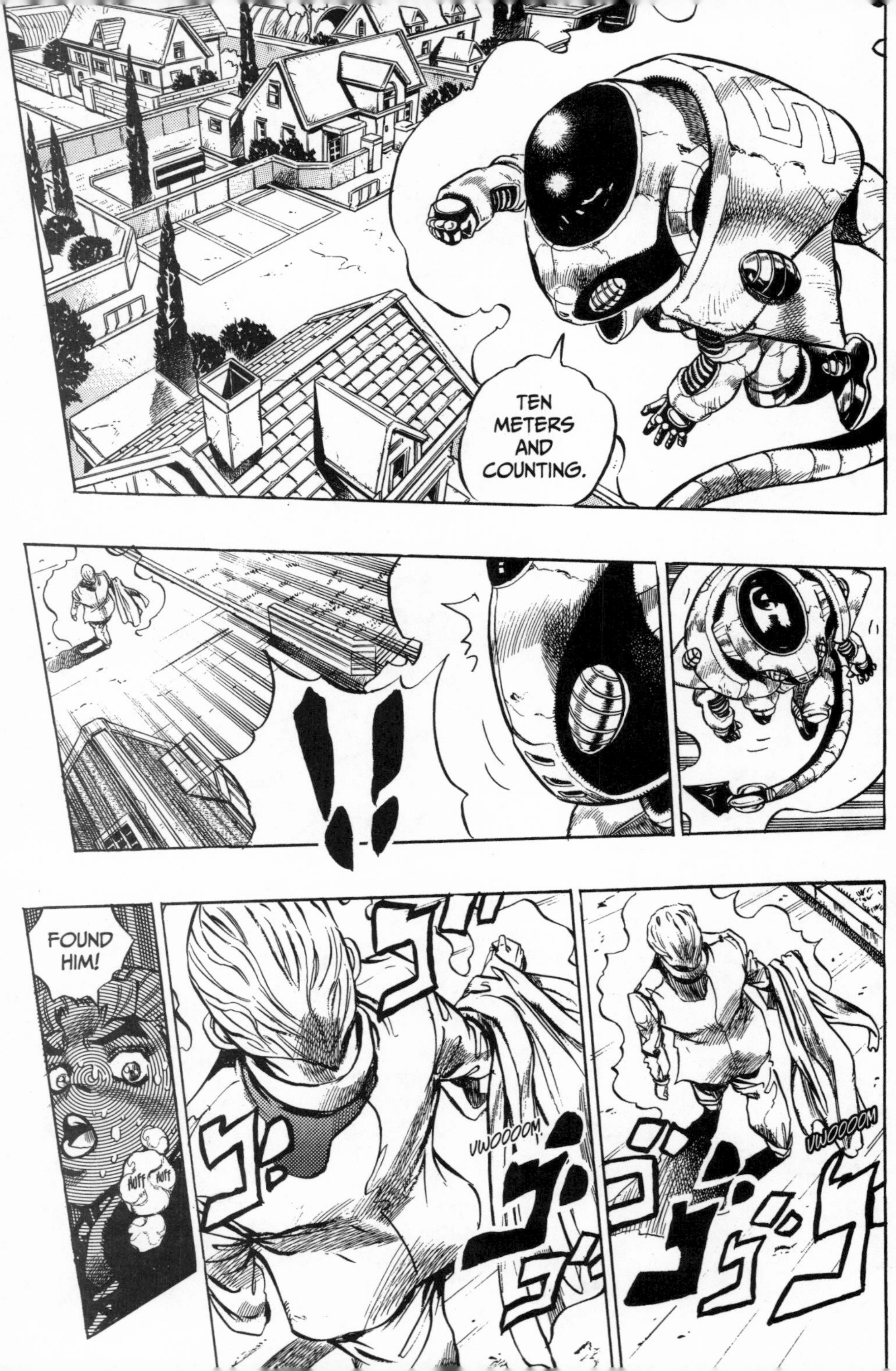

TEN METERS AND COUNTING.
VWOOOOM
VWOOOOM
FOUND HIM!
HUFF HUFF

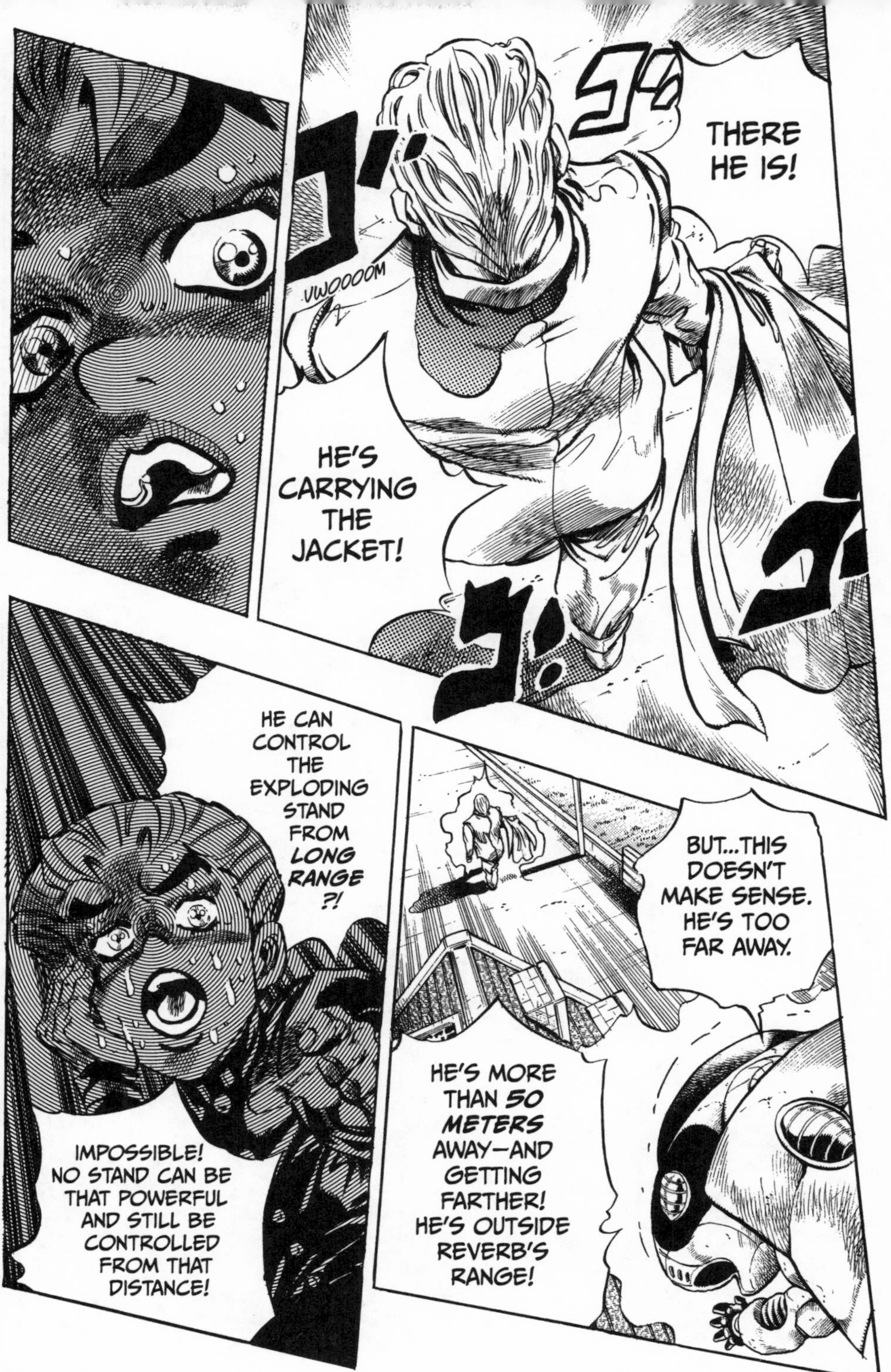

THERE HE IS!
VWOOOOM
HE'S CARRYING THE JACKET!
BUT...THIS DOESN'T MAKE SENSE. HE'S TOO FAR AWAY.
HE'S MORE THAN 50 METERS AWAY—AND GETTING FARTHER! HE'S OUTSIDE REVERB'S RANGE!
HE CAN CONTROL THE EXPLODING STAND FROM LONG RANGE ?!
IMPOSSIBLE! NO STAND CAN BE THAT POWERFUL AND STILL BE CONTROLLED FROM THAT DISTANCE!

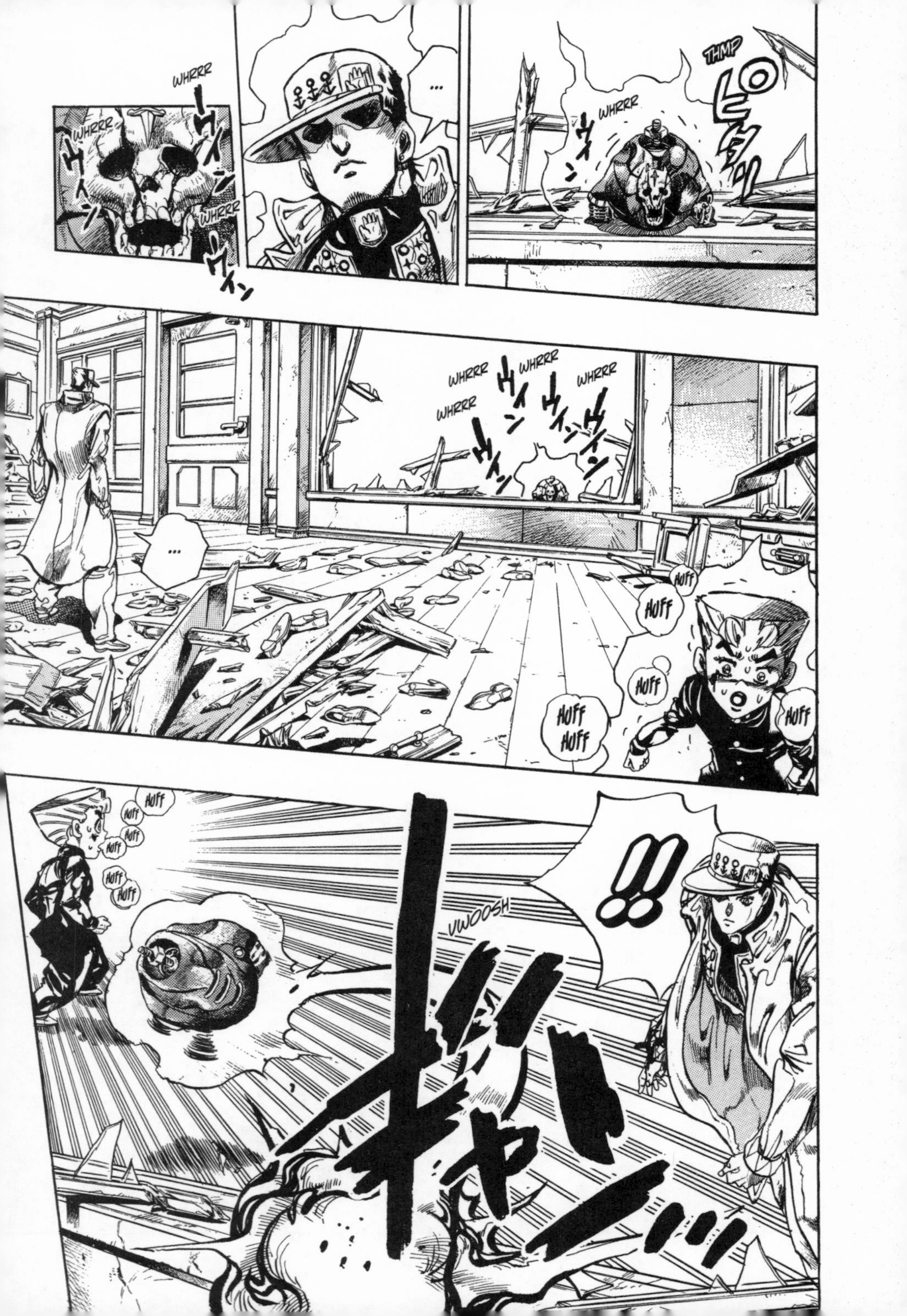

THMP
WHRRR
ウィン
...
WHRRR
WHRRR
WHRRR
WHRRR
WHRRR
WHRRR
HUFF
HUFF
HUFF
HUFF HUFF
HUFF
...
!!
VWOOSH
HUFF
HUFF
HUFF
HUFF
HUFF
HUFF

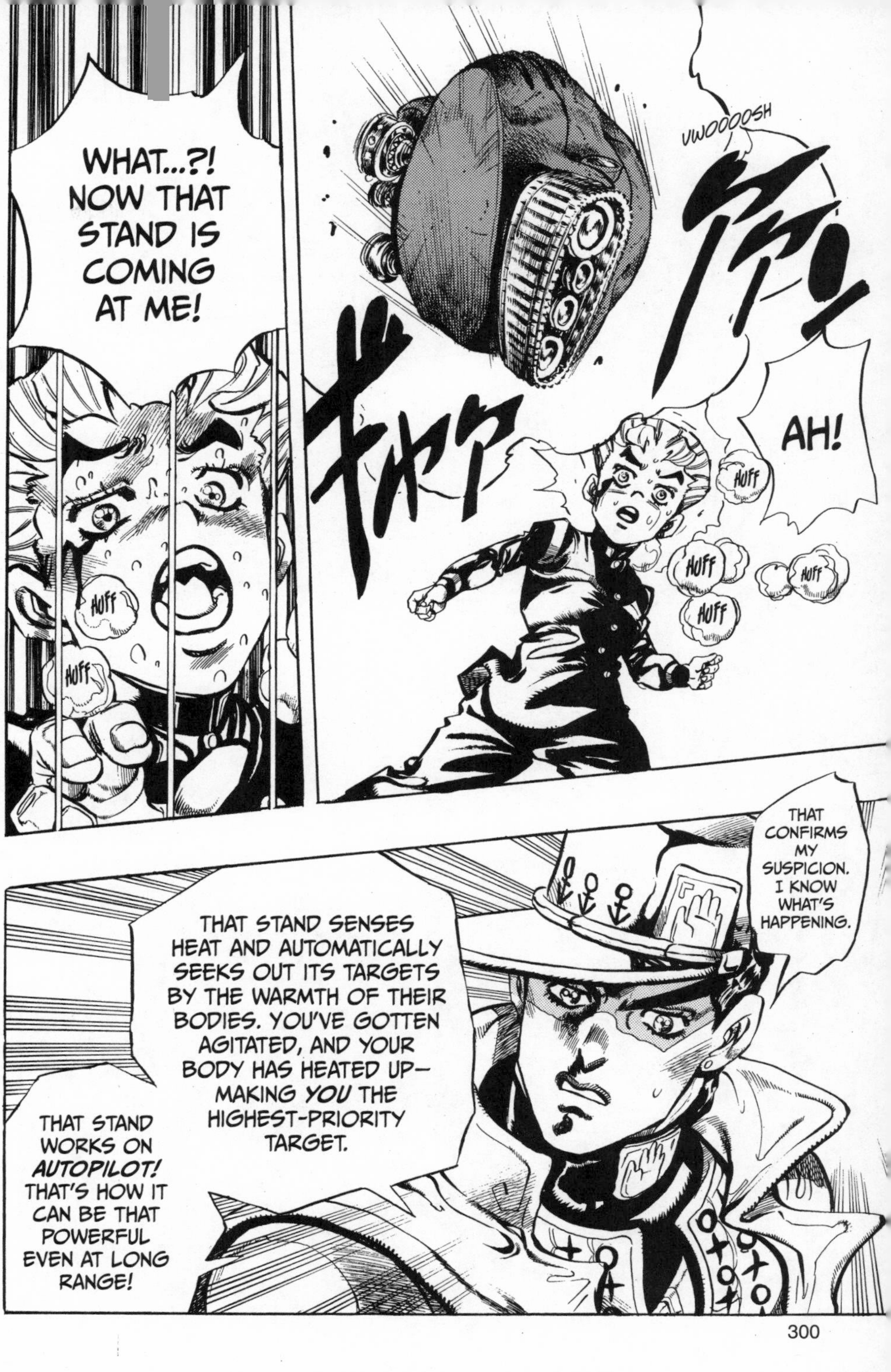
VWOOOOSH
AH!
HUFF
HUFF
HUFF
HUFF
WHAT...?! NOW THAT STAND IS COMING AT ME!
HUFF
HUFF
THAT CONFIRMS MY SUSPICION. I KNOW WHAT'S HAPPENING.
THAT STAND SENSES HEAT AND AUTOMATICALLY SEEKS OUT ITS TARGETS BY THE WARMTH OF THEIR BODIES. YOU'VE GOTTEN AGITATED, AND YOUR BODY HAS HEATED UP—MAKING *YOU* THE HIGHEST-PRIORITY TARGET.
THAT STAND WORKS ON *AUTOPILOT!* THAT'S HOW IT CAN BE THAT POWERFUL EVEN AT LONG RANGE!

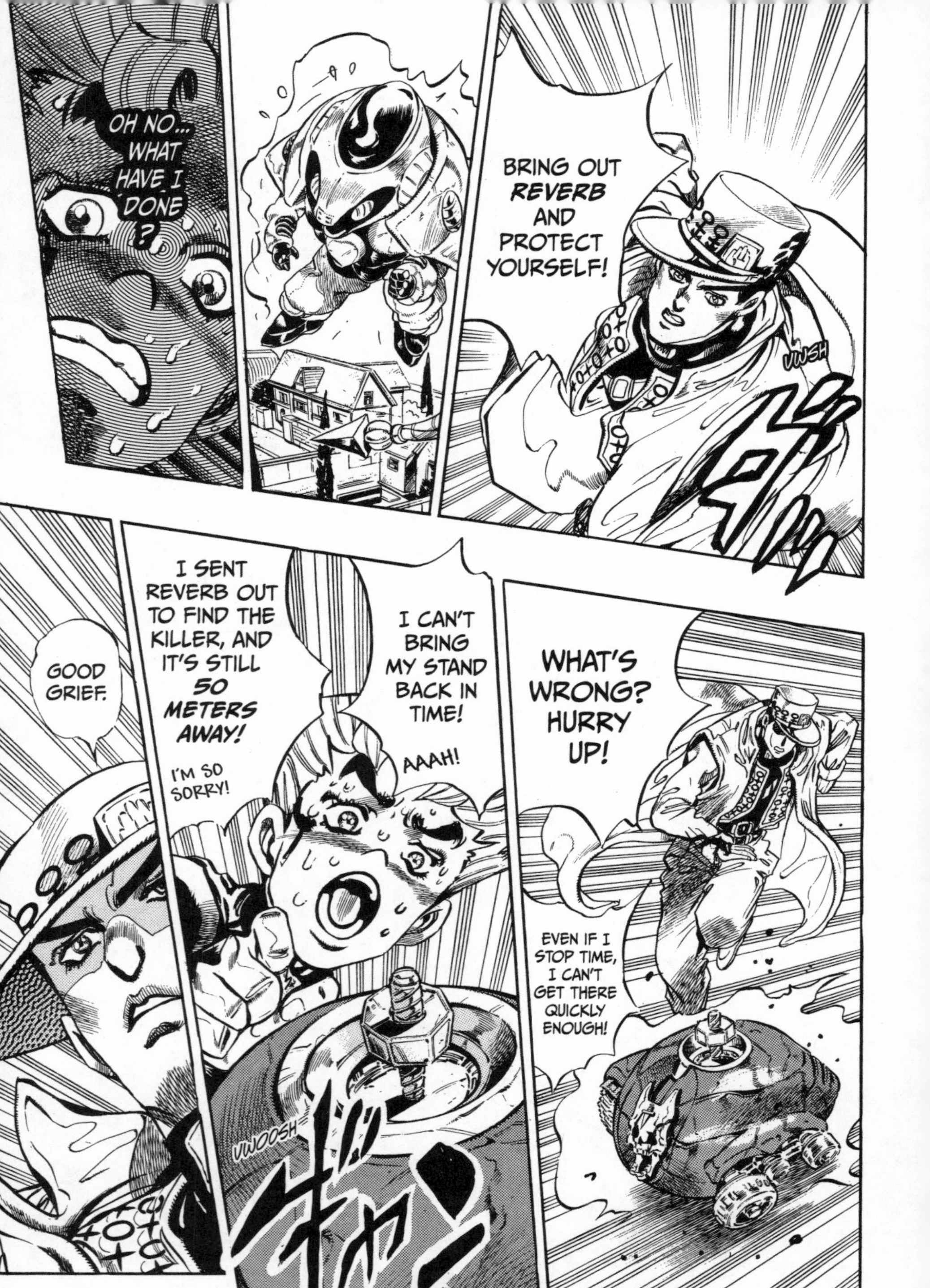
BRING OUT REVERB AND PROTECT YOURSELF!
UWSH
OH NO... WHAT HAVE I DONE?
WHAT'S WRONG? HURRY UP!
EVEN IF I STOP TIME, I CAN'T GET THERE QUICKLY ENOUGH!
I SENT REVERB OUT TO FIND THE KILLER, AND IT'S STILL 50 METERS AWAY!
I CAN'T BRING MY STAND BACK IN TIME!
AAAH!
I'M SO SORRY!
VWOOSH
GOOD GRIEF.

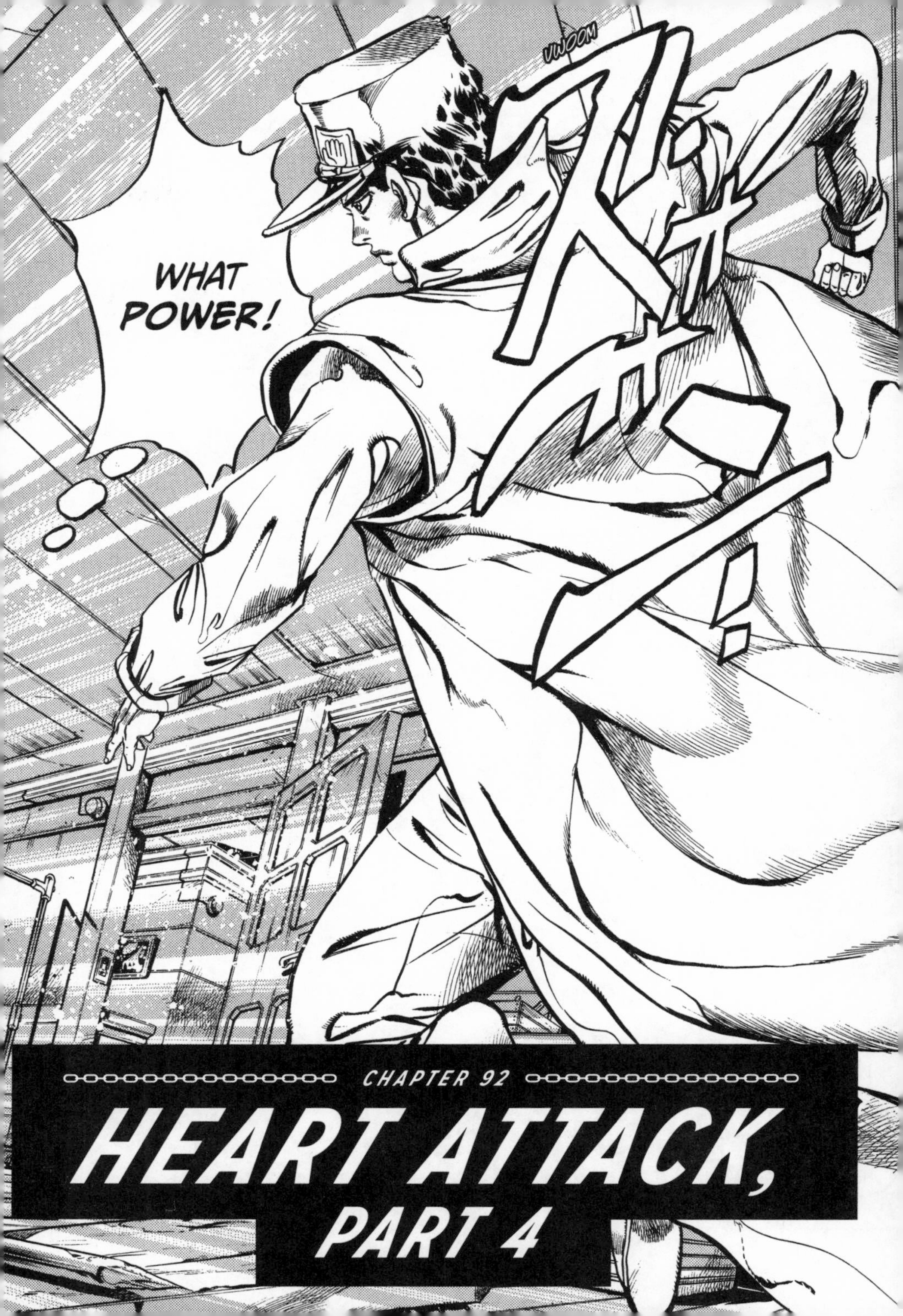
VWOOM
WHAT POWER!

CHAPTER 92

HEART ATTACK, PART 4

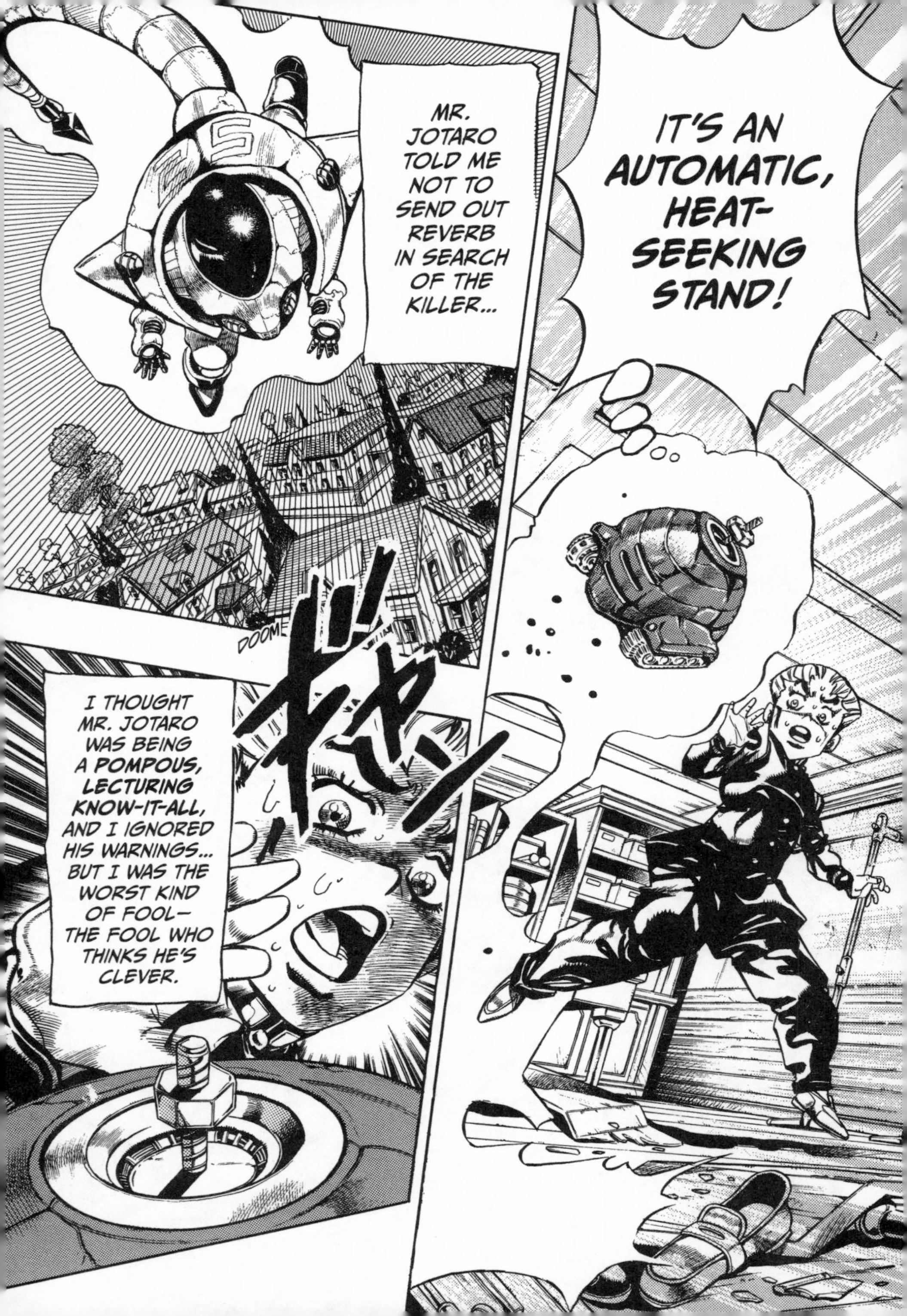
IT'S AN AUTOMATIC, HEAT-SEEKING STAND!
MR. JOTARO TOLD ME NOT TO SEND OUT REVERB IN SEARCH OF THE KILLER...
DOOM
I THOUGHT MR. JOTARO WAS BEING A POMPOUS, LECTURING KNOW-IT-ALL, AND I IGNORED HIS WARNINGS... BUT I WAS THE WORST KIND OF FOOL—THE FOOL WHO THINKS HE'S CLEVER.

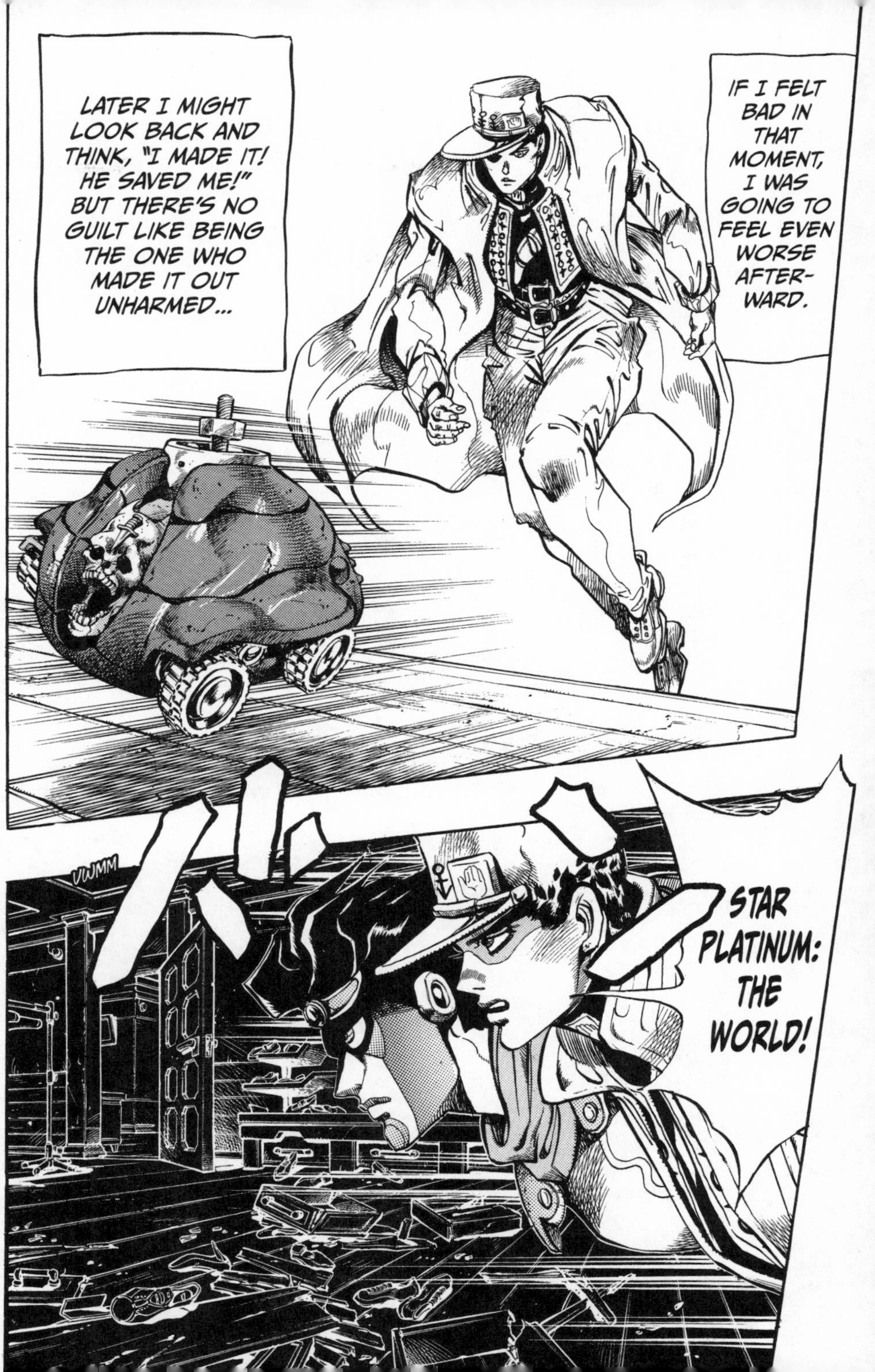
IF I FELT BAD IN THAT MOMENT, I WAS GOING TO FEEL EVEN WORSE AFTER-WARD.
LATER I MIGHT LOOK BACK AND THINK, "I MADE IT! HE SAVED ME!" BUT THERE'S NO GUILT LIKE BEING THE ONE WHO MADE IT OUT UNHARMED...
STAR PLATINUM: THE WORLD!
VWMM

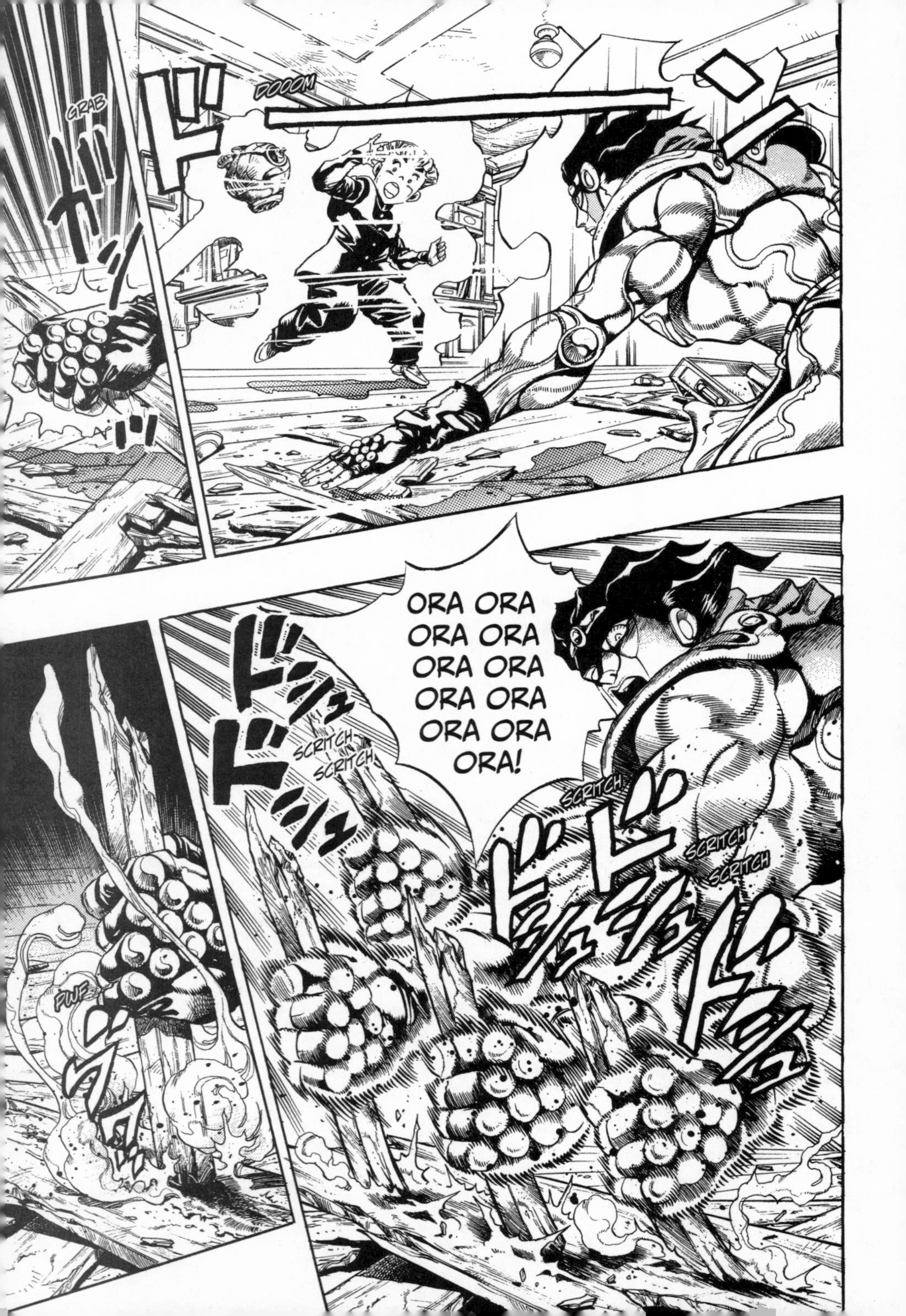
DOOOM
GRAB
ORA ORA ORA ORA ORA ORA ORA ORA ORA ORA ORA!
SCRITCH SCRITCH
SCRITCH
SCRITCH SCRITCH
PWF

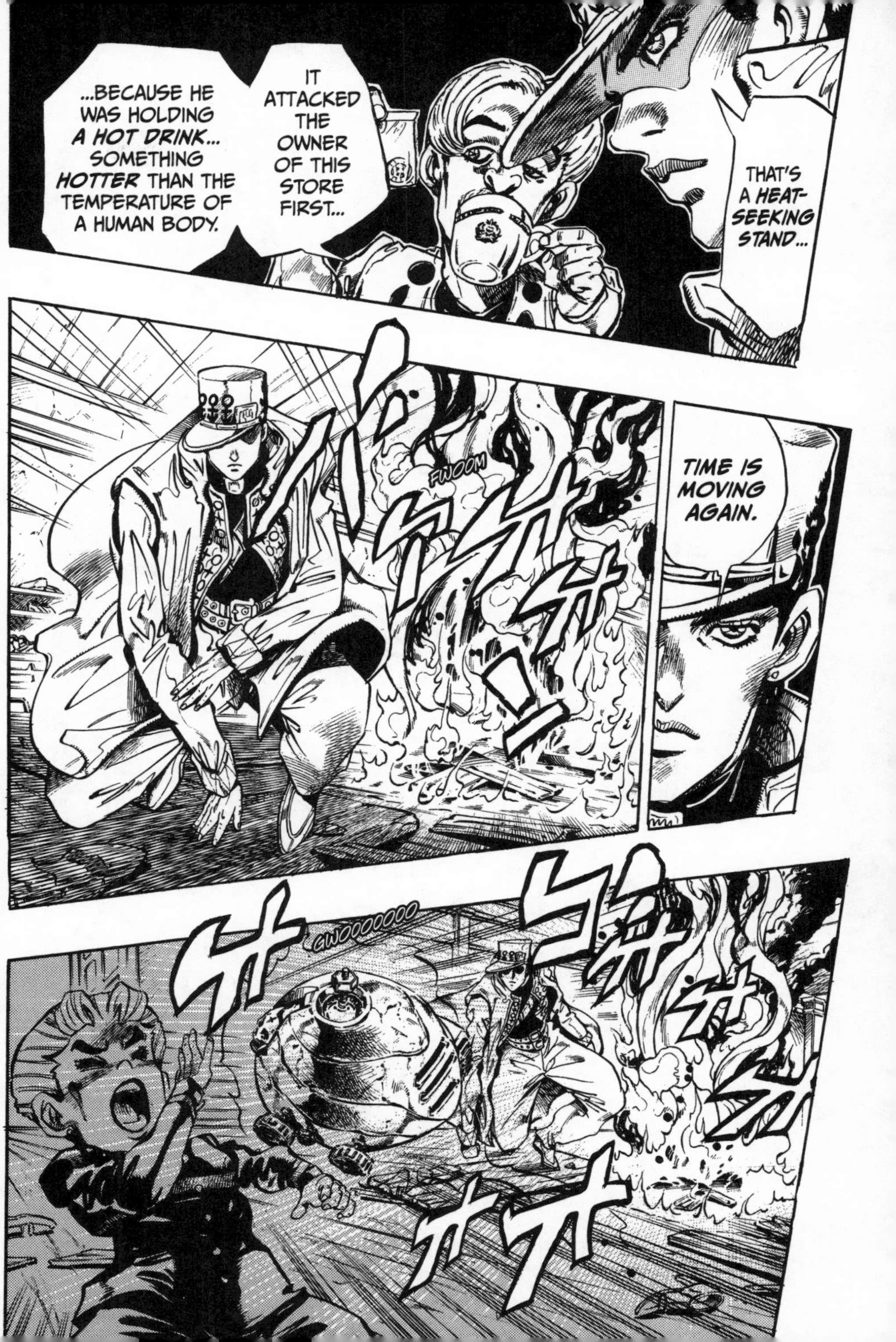
THAT'S A HEAT-SEEKING STAND...
IT ATTACKED THE OWNER OF THIS STORE FIRST...
...BECAUSE HE WAS HOLDING *A HOT DRINK*... SOMETHING *HOTTER* THAN THE TEMPERATURE OF A HUMAN BODY.
TIME IS MOVING AGAIN.
FWOOM
GWOOOOOOO

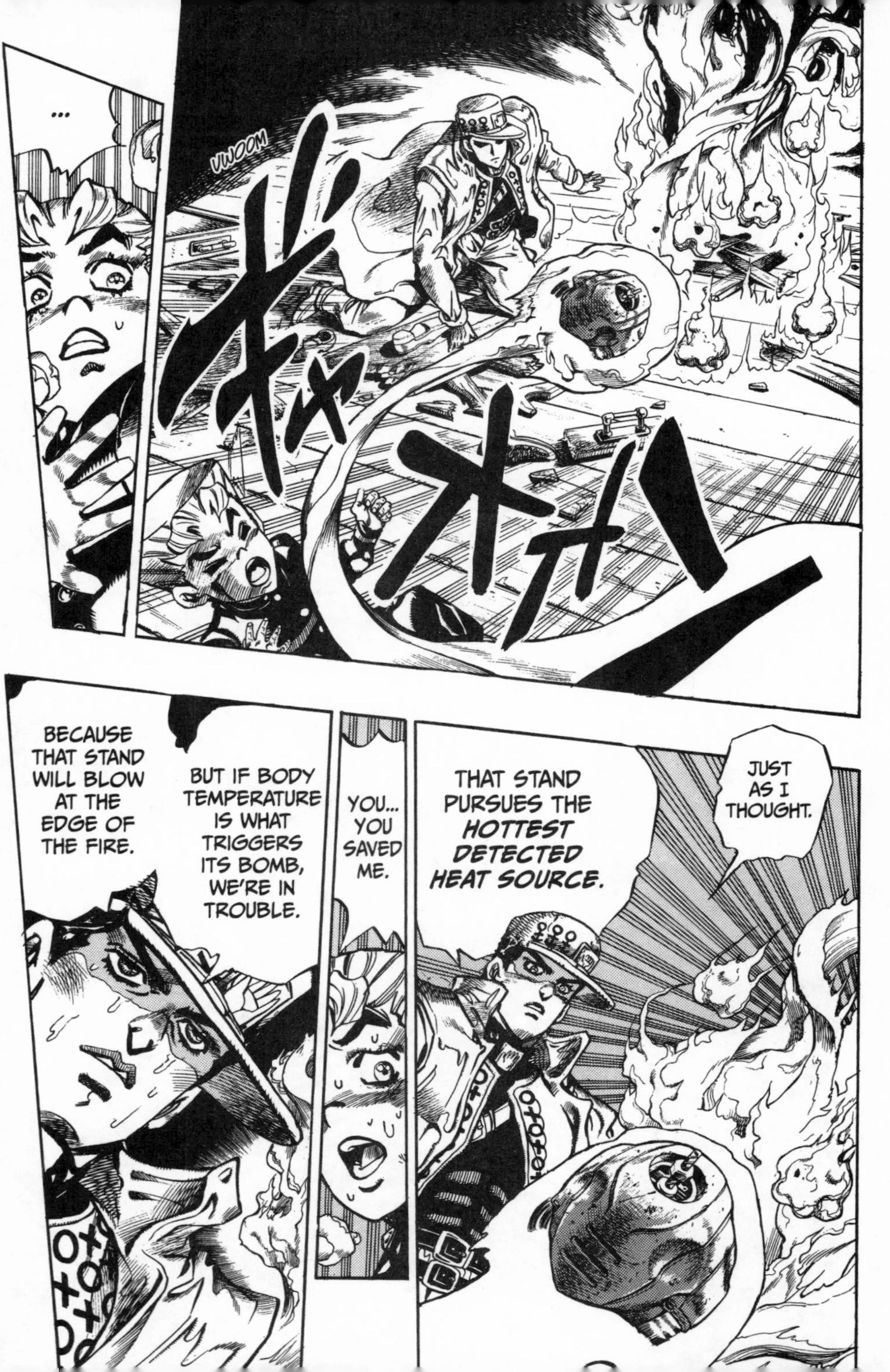

UWOOM
...
JUST AS I THOUGHT.
THAT STAND PURSUES THE HOTTEST DETECTED HEAT SOURCE.
YOU... YOU SAVED ME.
BUT IF BODY TEMPERATURE IS WHAT TRIGGERS ITS BOMB, WE'RE IN TROUBLE.
BECAUSE THAT STAND WILL BLOW AT THE EDGE OF THE FIRE.

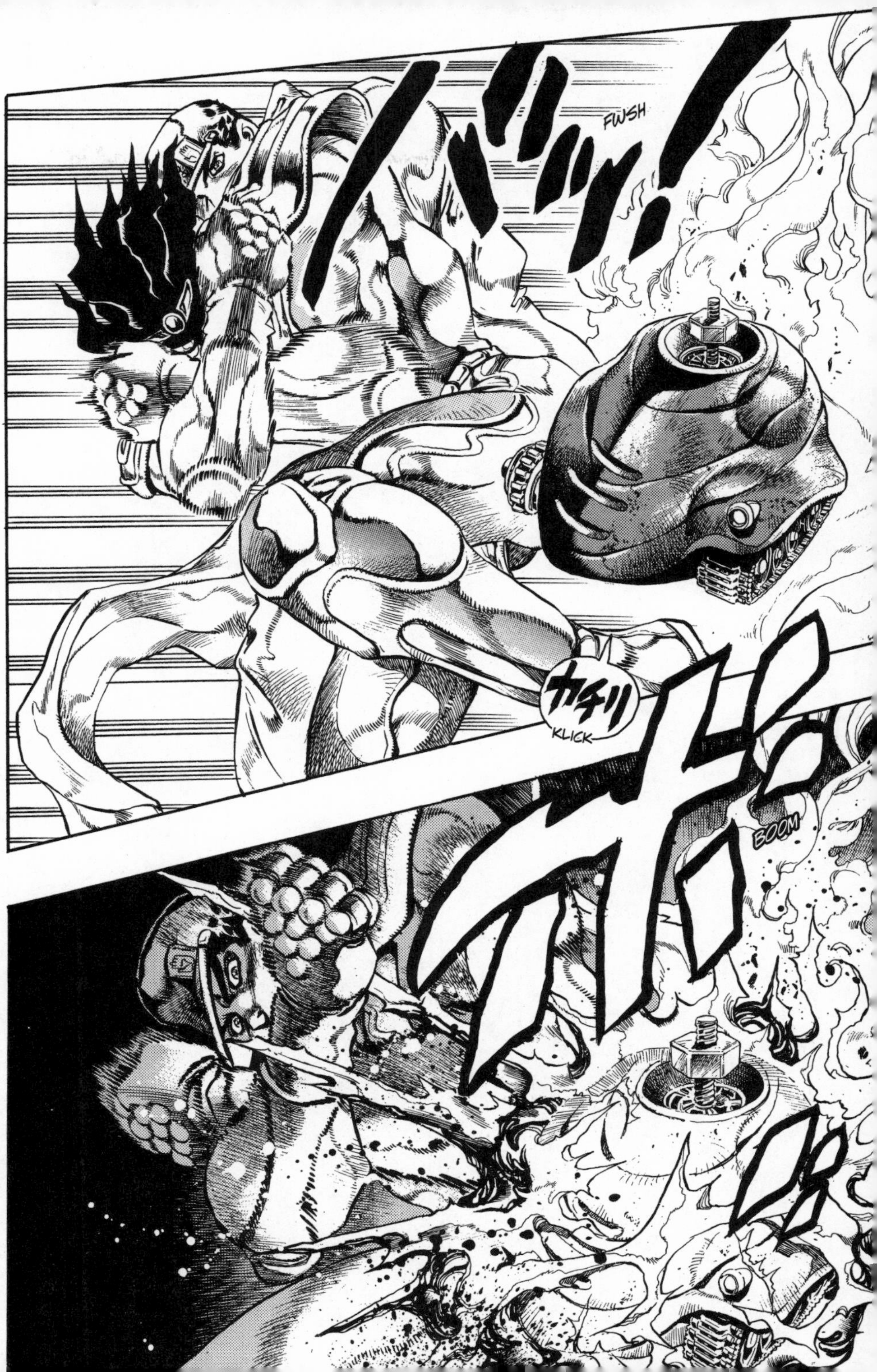
FWSH
カチリ
KLICK
BOOM

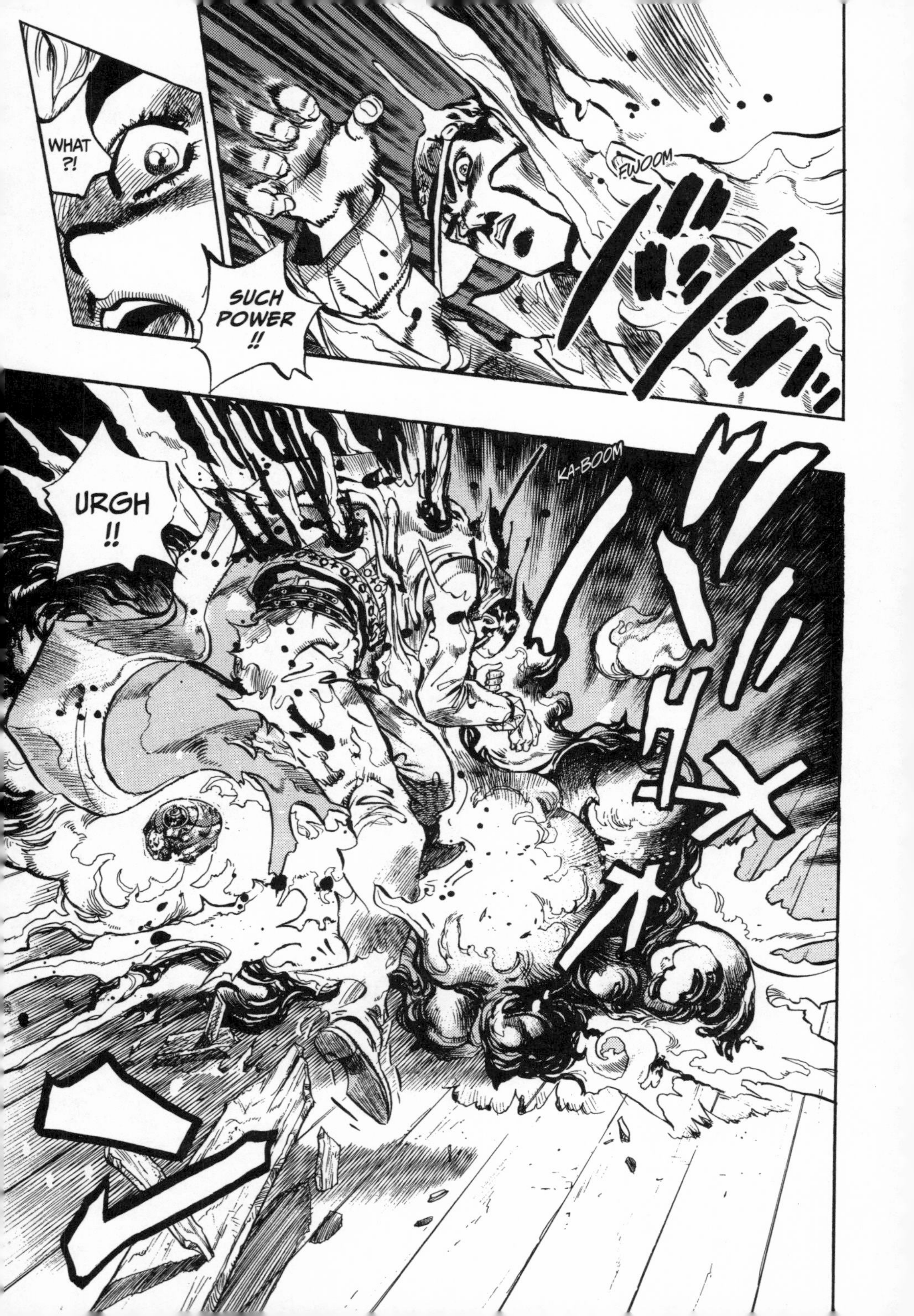
FWOOM
WHAT ?!
SUCH POWER !!
KA-BOOM
URGH !!

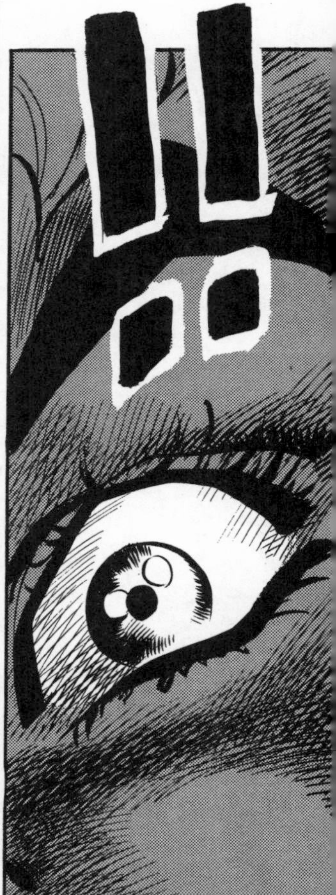
!!

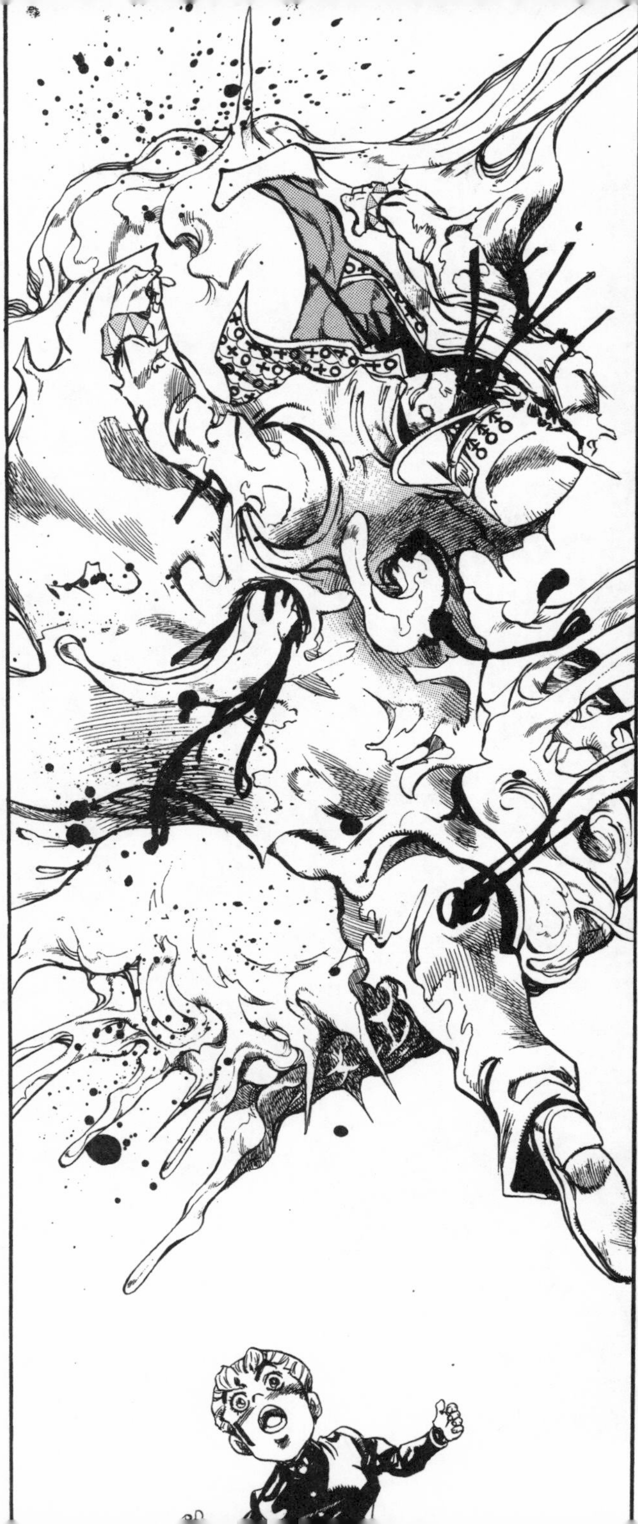

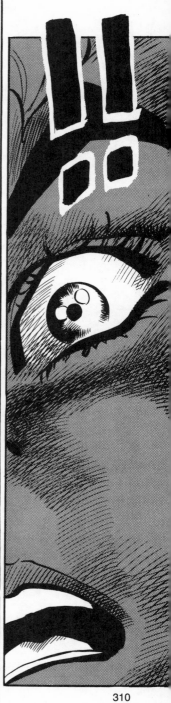

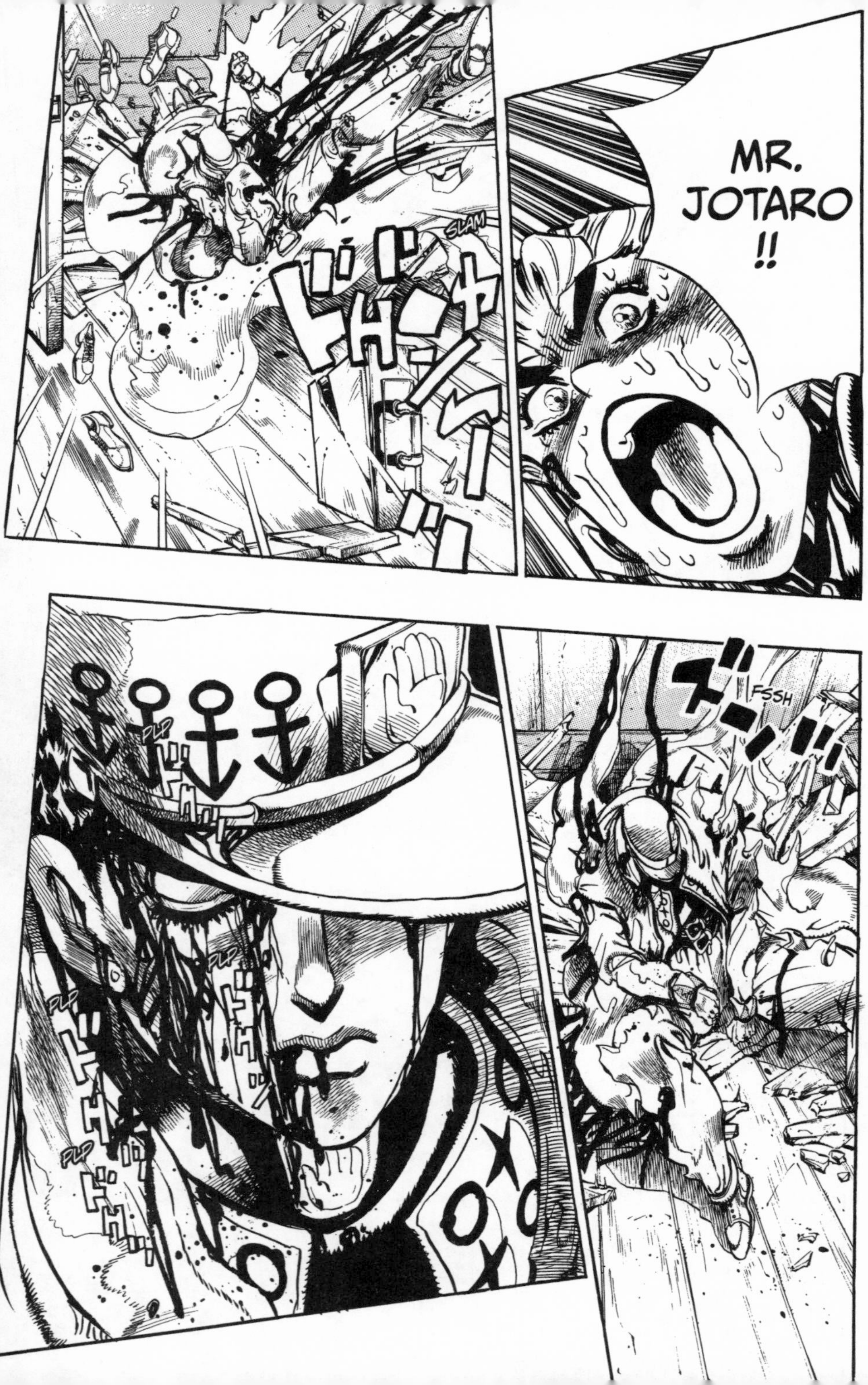
MR. JOTARO !!
SLAM
FSSH
PLP
PLP
PLP
PLP

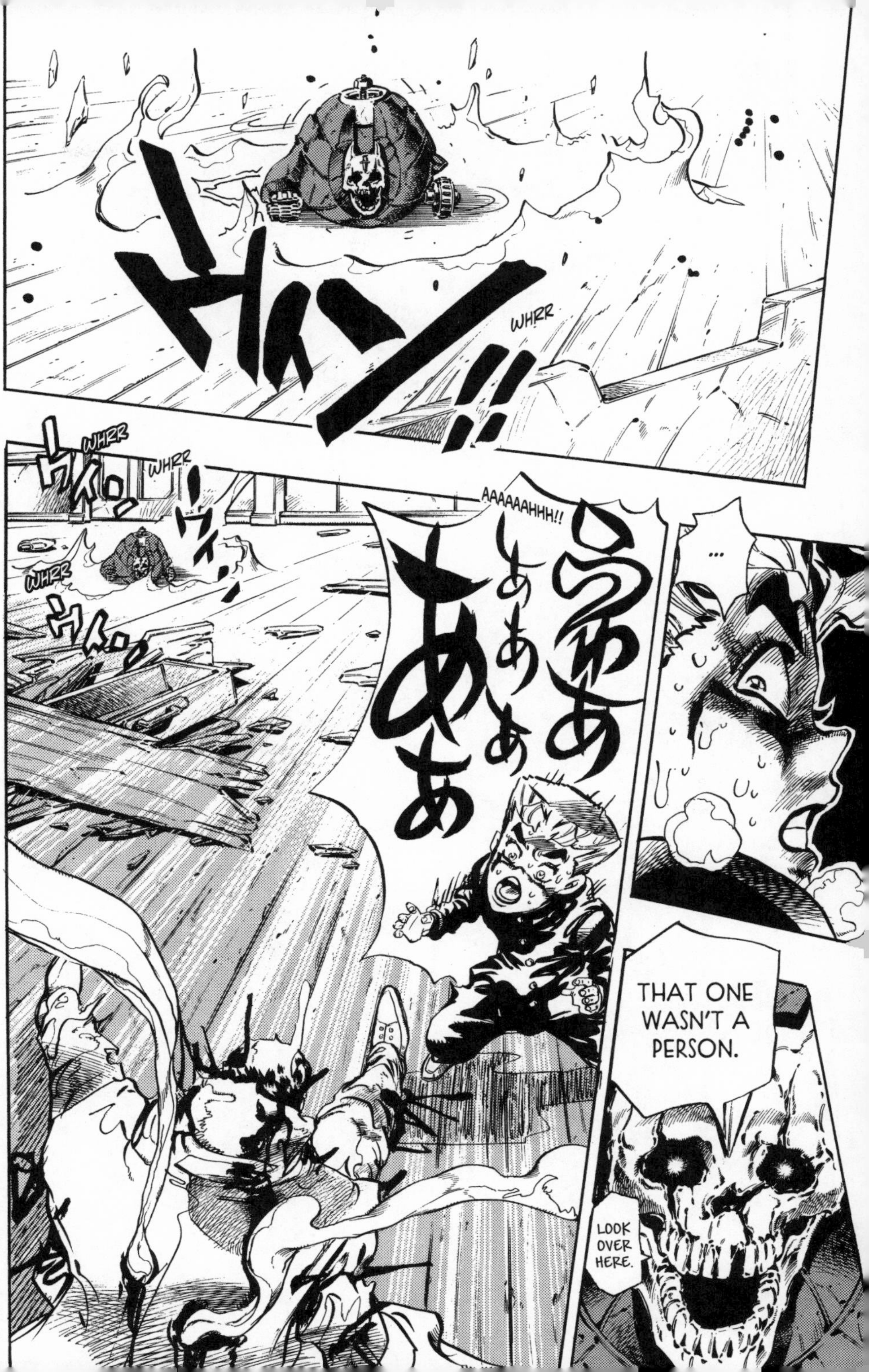

WHRR
...
THAT ONE WASN'T A PERSON.
LOOK OVER HERE.
WHRR
WHRR
WHRR
AAAAAAAHHH!!

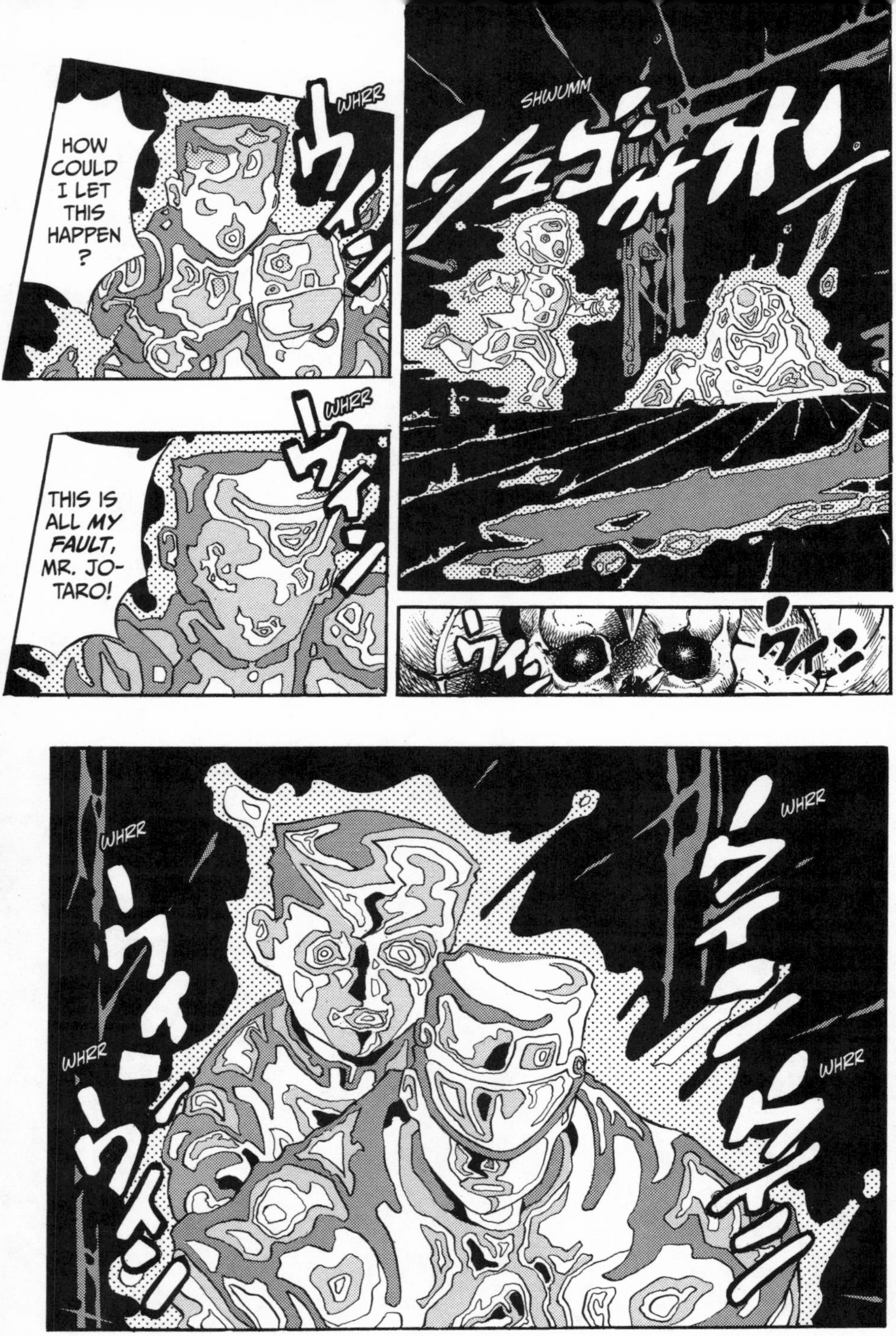
SHWUMM
WHRR
HOW COULD I LET THIS HAPPEN?
WHRR
THIS IS ALL *MY FAULT*, MR. JOTARO!
WHRR
WHRR
WHRR
WHRR

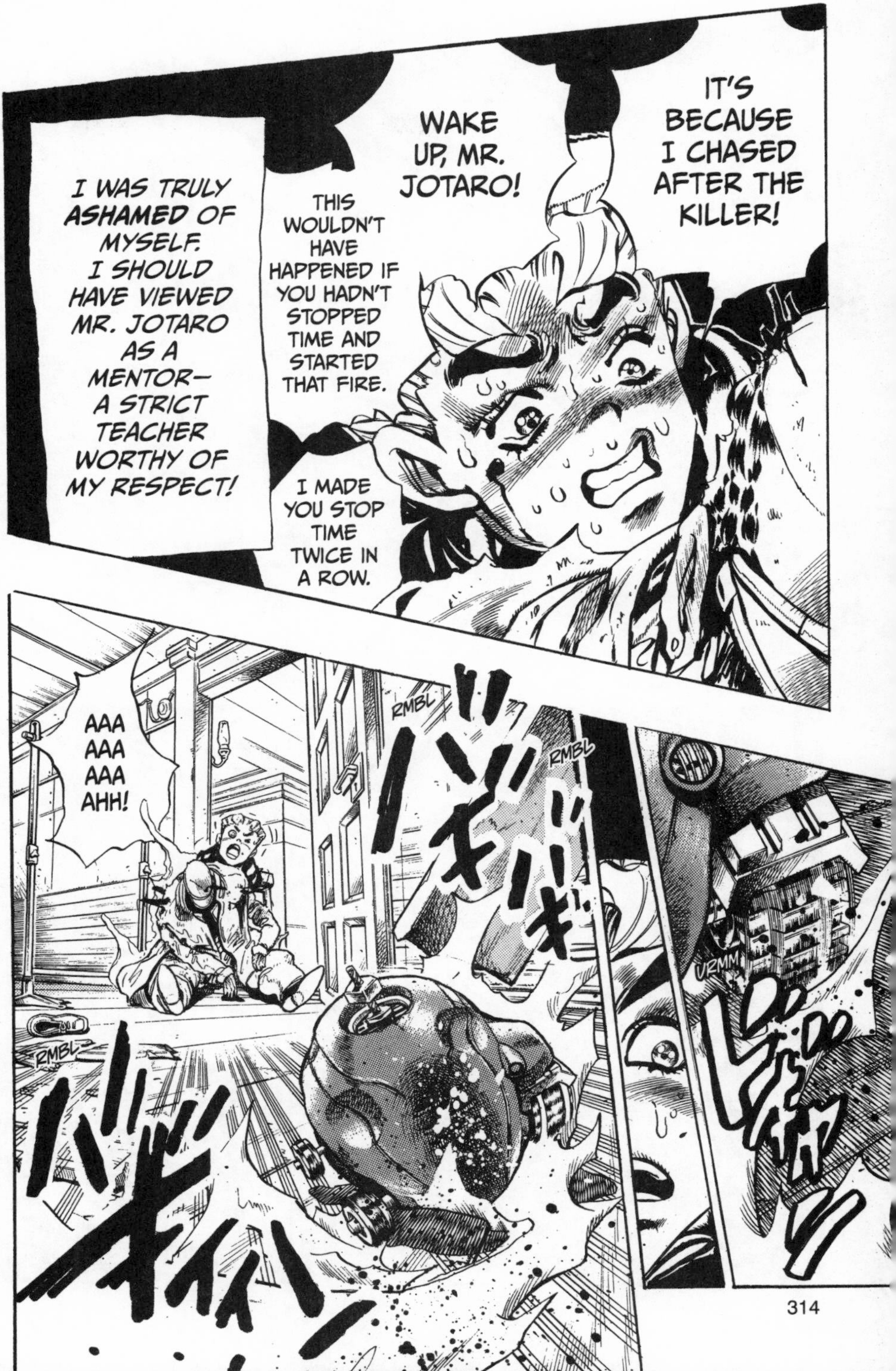
IT'S BECAUSE I CHASED AFTER THE KILLER!
WAKE UP, MR. JOTARO!
THIS WOULDN'T HAVE HAPPENED IF YOU HADN'T STOPPED TIME AND STARTED THAT FIRE.
I MADE YOU STOP TIME TWICE IN A ROW.
I WAS TRULY ASHAMED OF MYSELF. I SHOULD HAVE VIEWED MR. JOTARO AS A MENTOR—A STRICT TEACHER WORTHY OF MY RESPECT!
URMM
RMBL
RMBL
AAA AAA AAA AHH!
RMBL

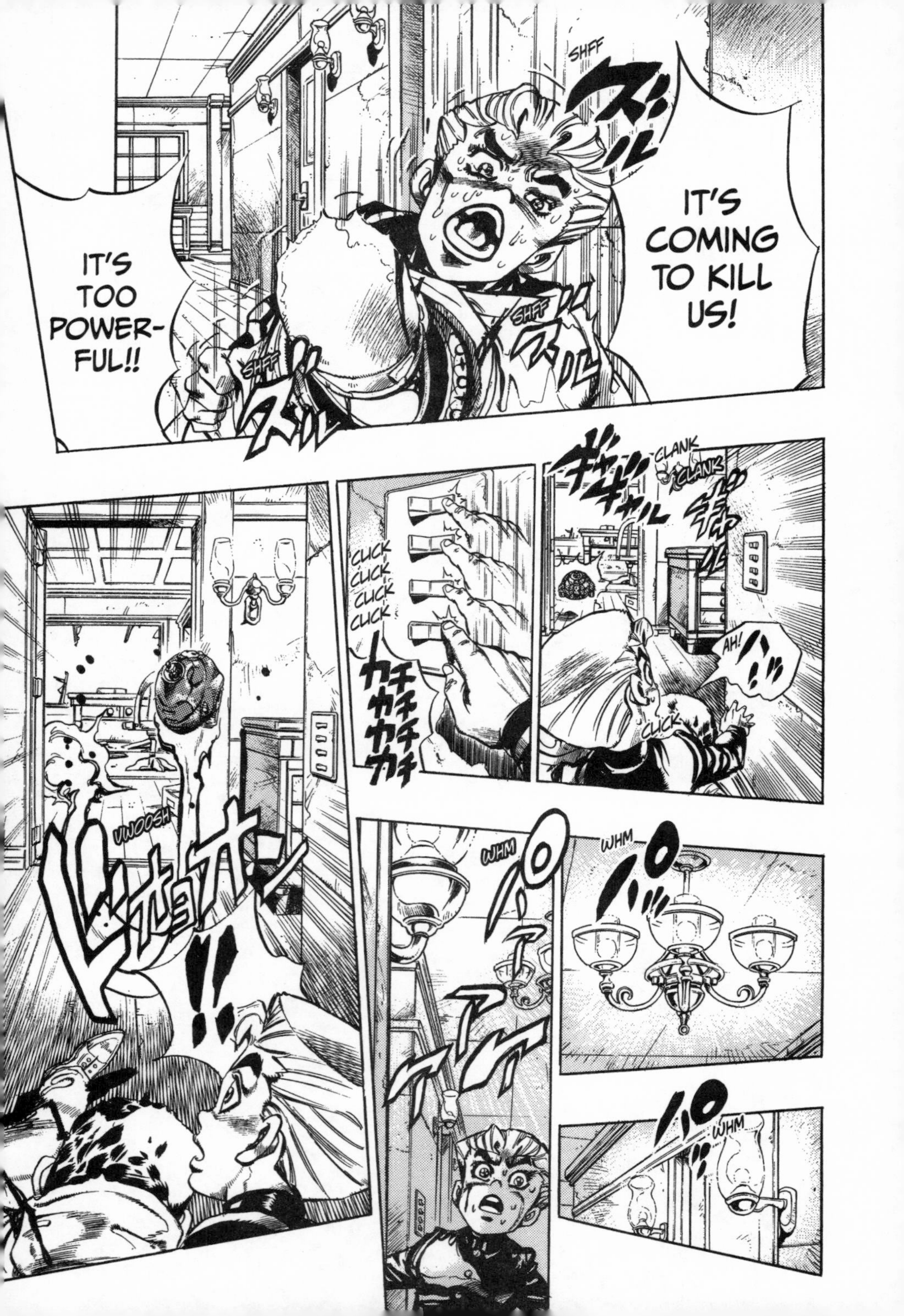
SHFF
IT'S COMING TO KILL US!
SHFF
IT'S TOO POWER-FUL!!
SHFF
CLANK
CLANK
AH!
CLICK
CLICK
CLICK
CLICK
CLICK
WHM
WHM
WHM
UWOOSH

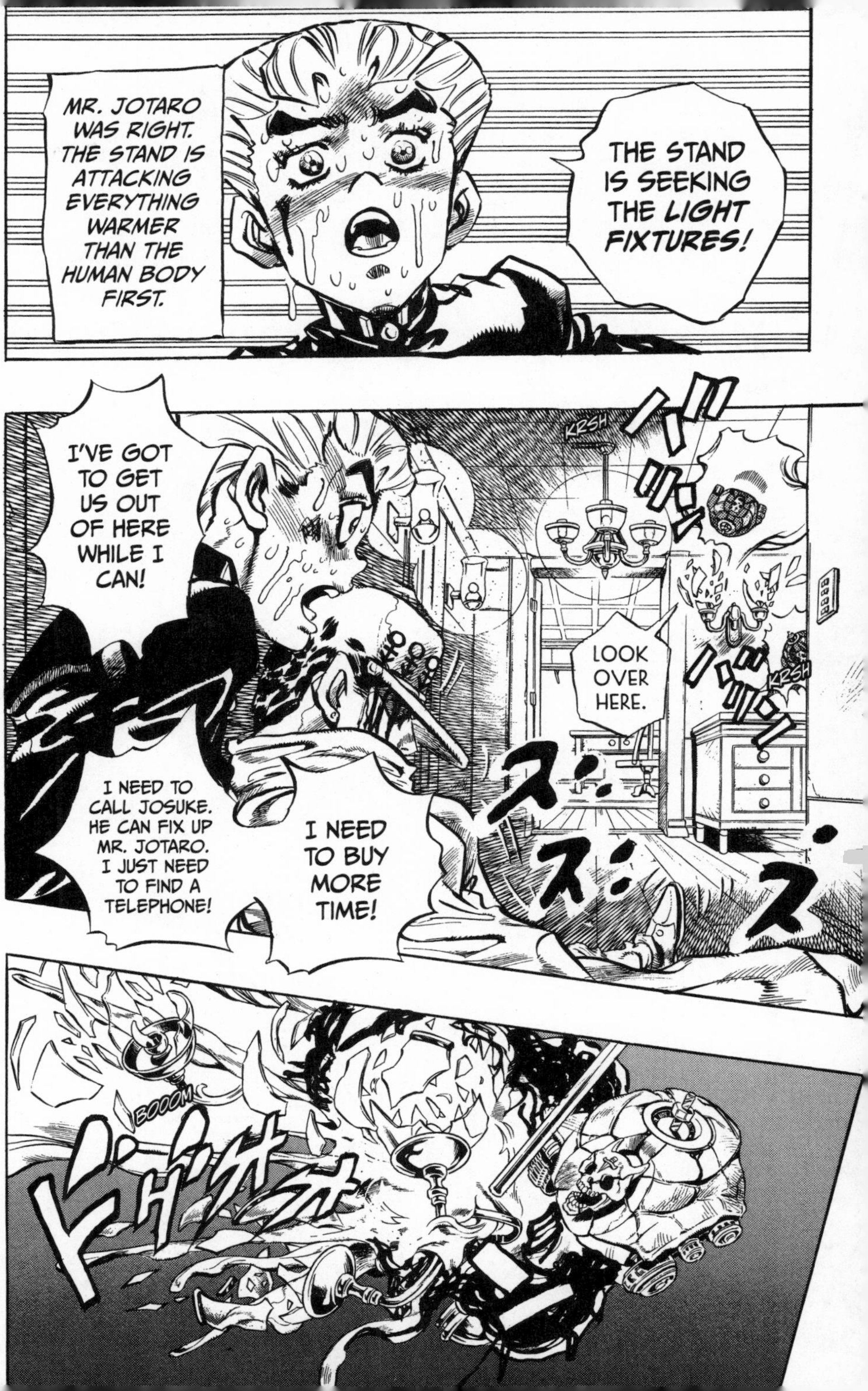
THE STAND IS SEEKING THE LIGHT FIXTURES!
MR. JOTARO WAS RIGHT. THE STAND IS ATTACKING EVERYTHING WARMER THAN THE HUMAN BODY FIRST.
KRSH
LOOK OVER HERE.
KRSH
I'VE GOT TO GET US OUT OF HERE WHILE I CAN!
I NEED TO BUY MORE TIME!
I NEED TO CALL JOSUKE. HE CAN FIX UP MR. JOTARO. I JUST NEED TO FIND A TELEPHONE!
BOOOM

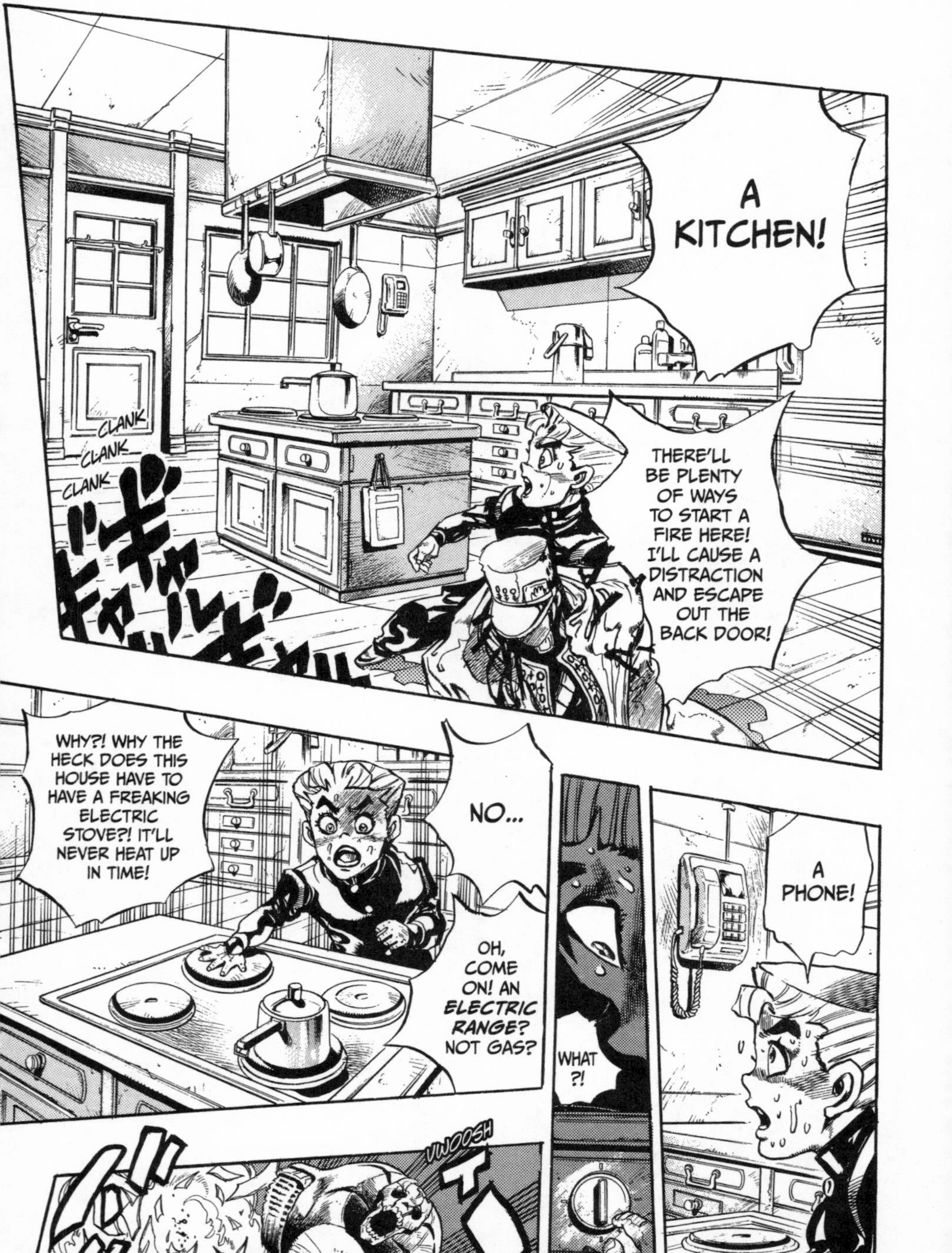
A KITCHEN!
THERE'LL BE PLENTY OF WAYS TO START A FIRE HERE! I'LL CAUSE A DISTRACTION AND ESCAPE OUT THE BACK DOOR!
CLANK
CLANK
CLANK
A PHONE!
WHAT ?!
NO...
OH, COME ON! AN ELECTRIC RANGE? NOT GAS?
WHY?! WHY THE HECK DOES THIS HOUSE HAVE TO HAVE A FREAKING ELECTRIC STOVE?! IT'LL NEVER HEAT UP IN TIME!
VWOOSH

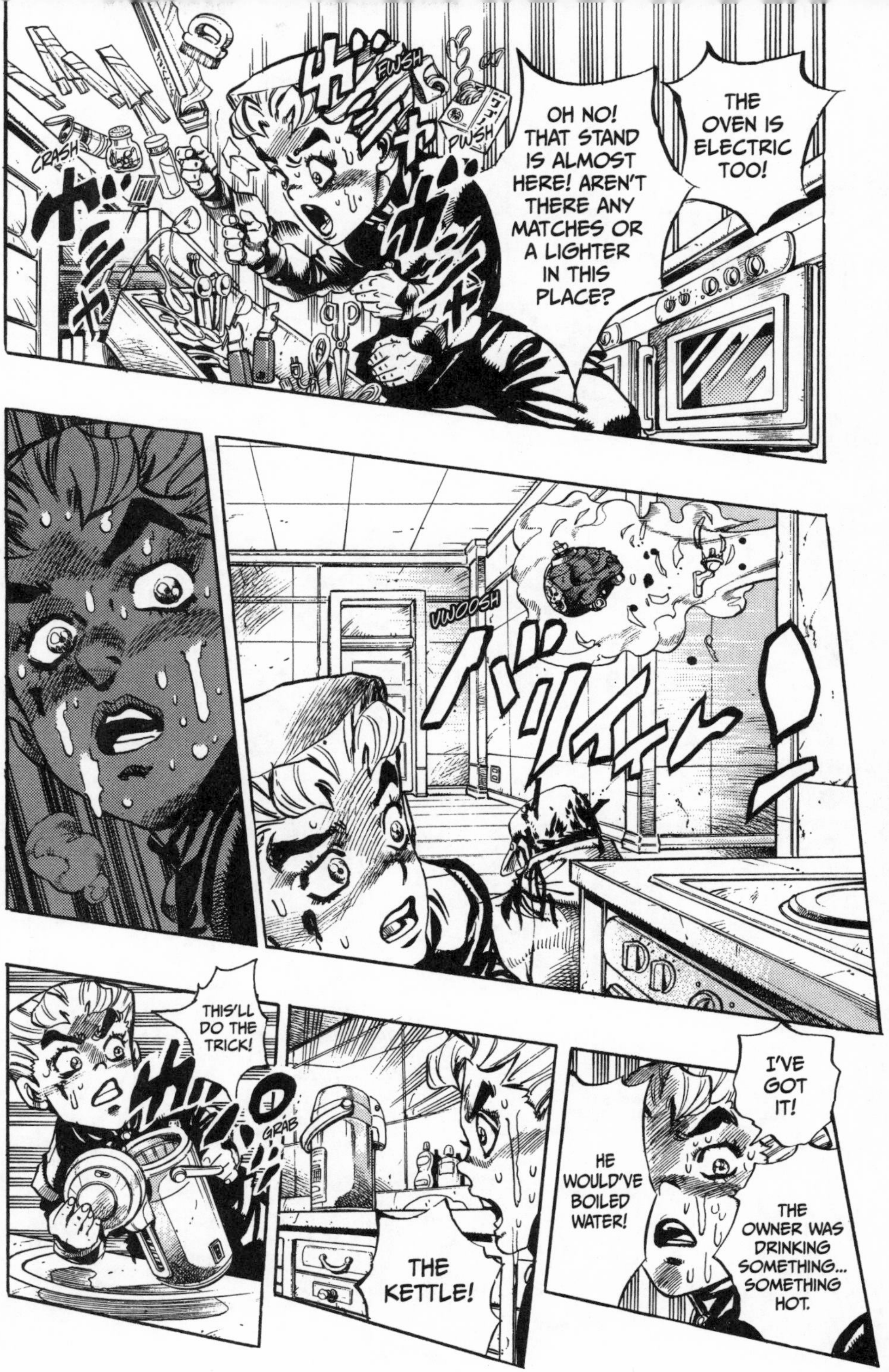
THE OVEN IS ELECTRIC TOO!
OH NO! THAT STAND IS ALMOST HERE! AREN'T THERE ANY MATCHES OR A LIGHTER IN THIS PLACE?
FWSH
PWSH
CRASH
VWOOSH
I'VE GOT IT!
THE OWNER WAS DRINKING SOMETHING... SOMETHING HOT.
HE WOULD'VE BOILED WATER!
THE KETTLE!
THIS'LL DO THE TRICK!
GRAB

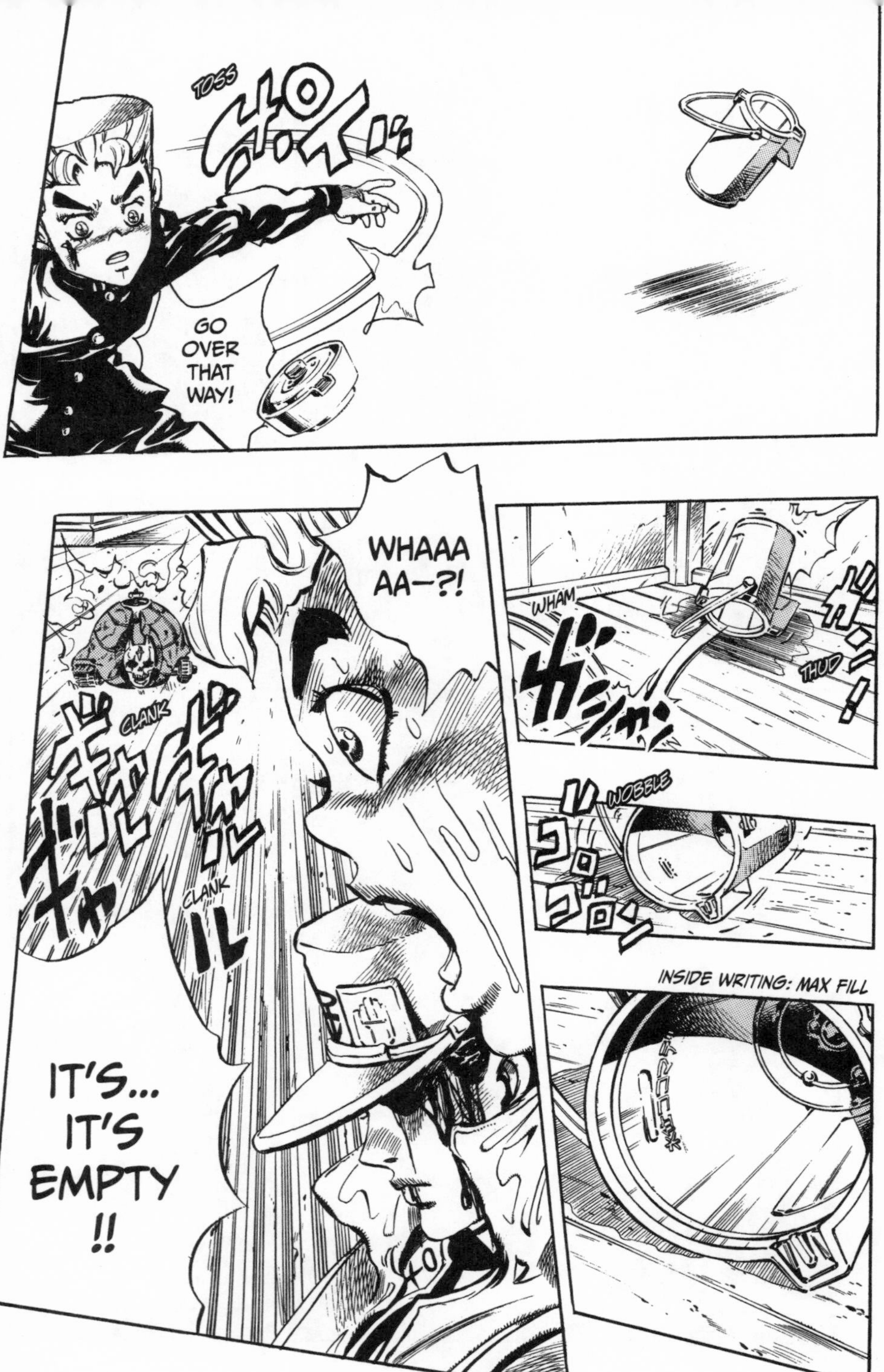
TOSS
GO OVER THAT WAY!
WHAM
THUD
WOBBLE
INSIDE WRITING: MAX FILL
WHAAA AA—?!
CLANK
CLANK
IT'S... IT'S EMPTY!!

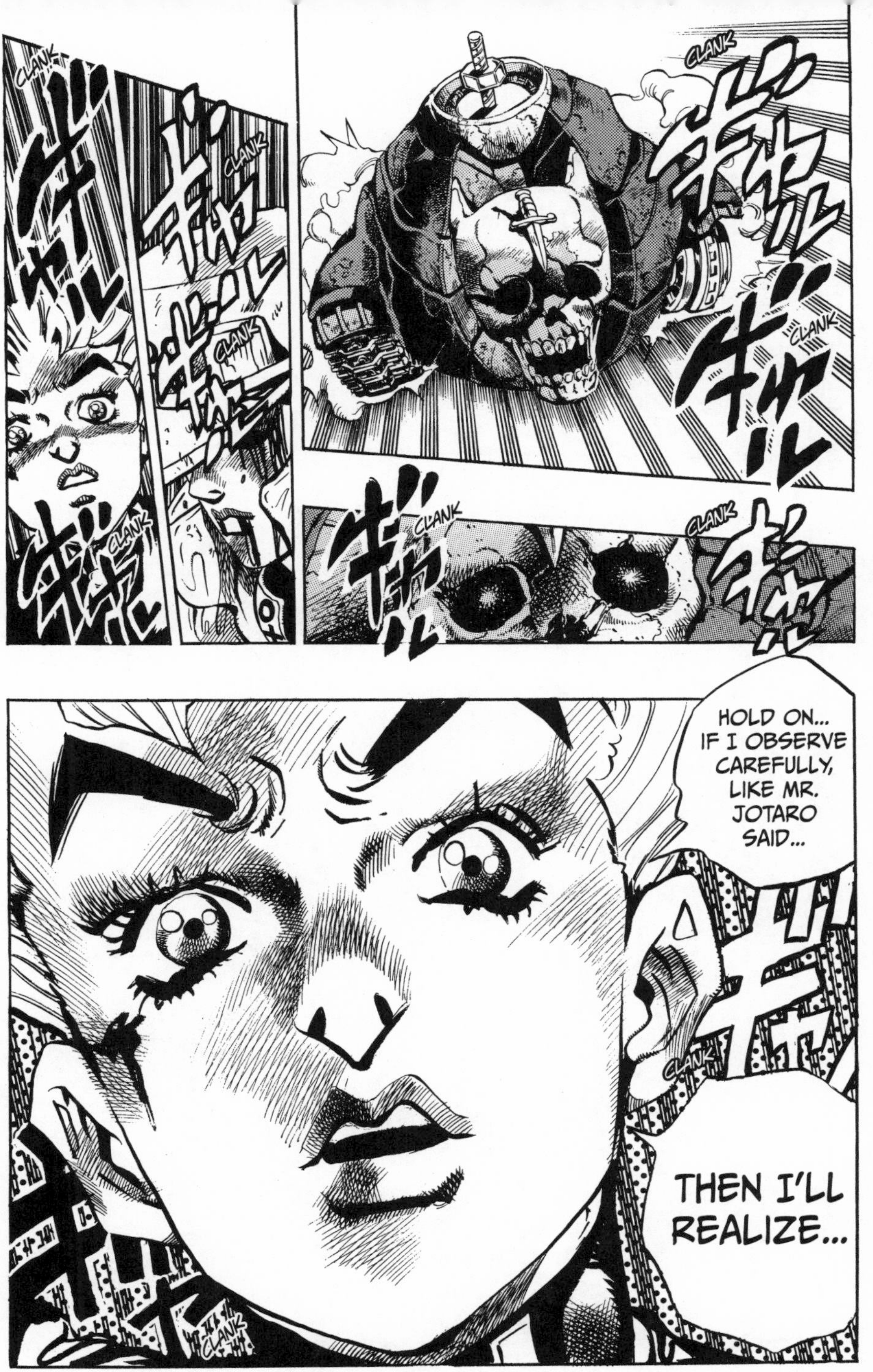
CLANK
CLANK
CLANK
CLANK
CLANK
CLANK
CLANK
CLANK
CLANK
HOLD ON... IF I OBSERVE CAREFULLY, LIKE MR. JOTARO SAID...
CLANK
THEN I'LL REALIZE...
CLANK

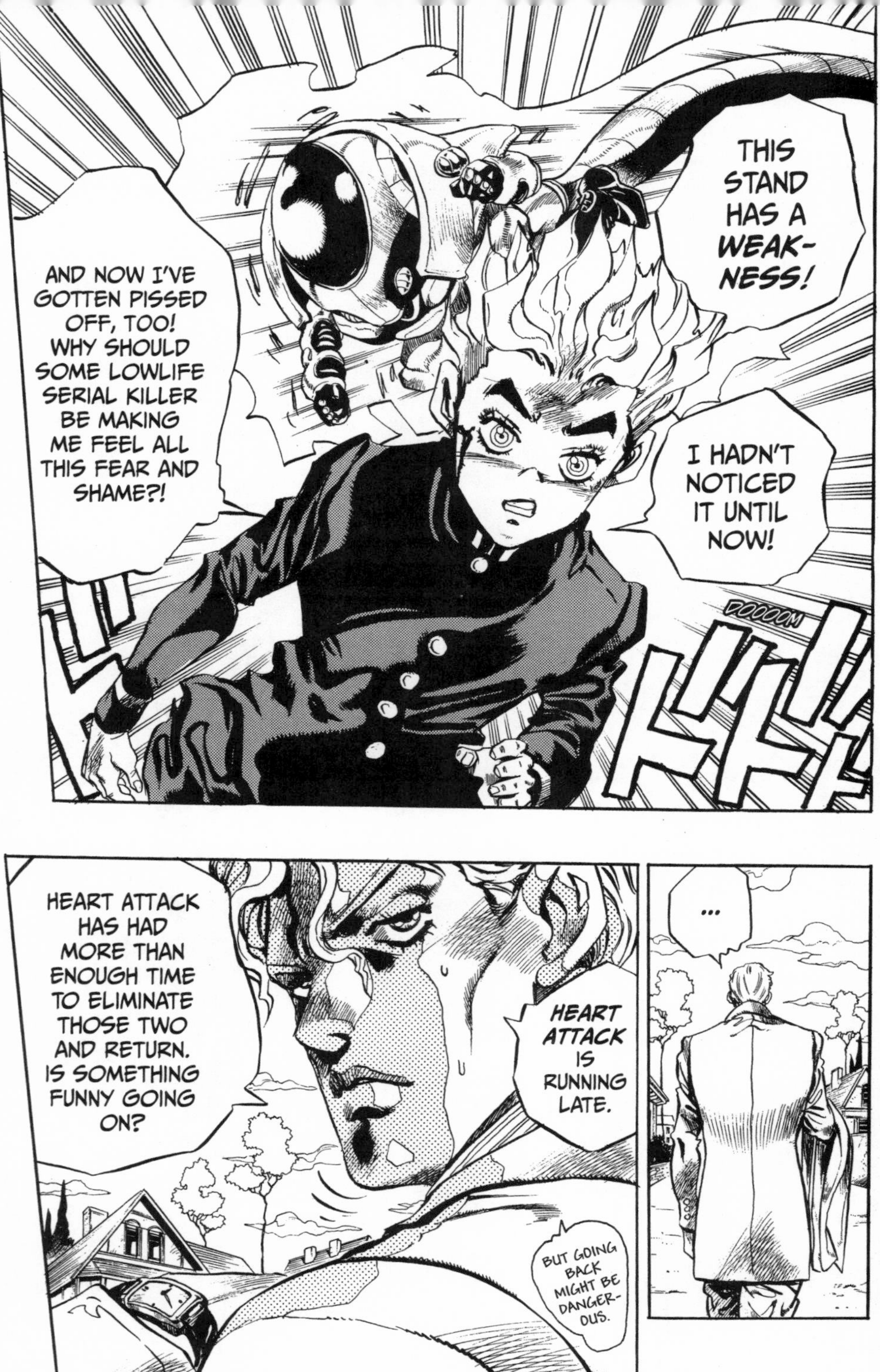
THIS STAND HAS A WEAK-NESS!
AND NOW I'VE GOTTEN PISSED OFF, TOO! WHY SHOULD SOME LOWLIFE SERIAL KILLER BE MAKING ME FEEL ALL THIS FEAR AND SHAME?!
I HADN'T NOTICED IT UNTIL NOW!
DOOOOM
...
HEART ATTACK IS RUNNING LATE.
HEART ATTACK HAS HAD MORE THAN ENOUGH TIME TO ELIMINATE THOSE TWO AND RETURN. IS SOMETHING FUNNY GOING ON?
BUT GOING BACK MIGHT BE DANGER-OUS.

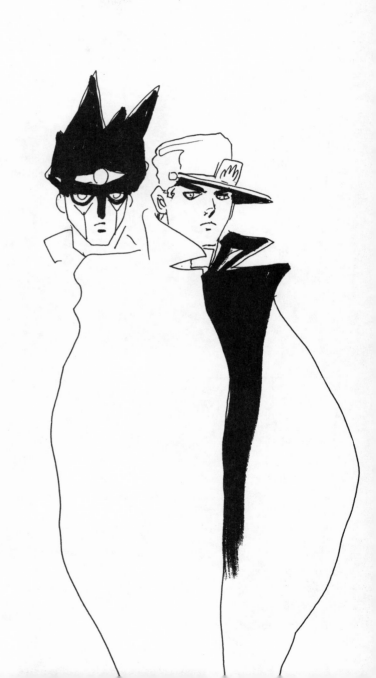

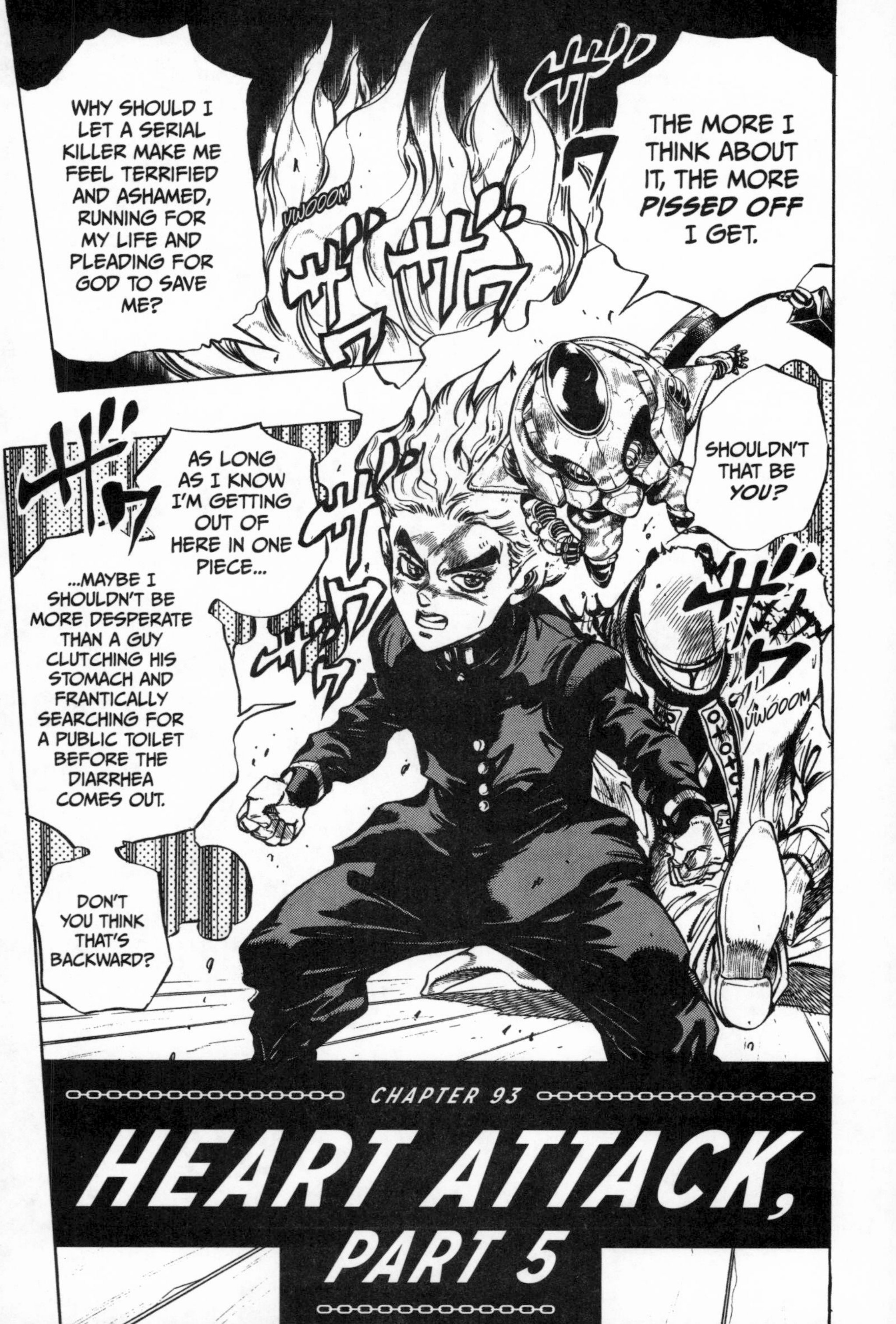
THE MORE I THINK ABOUT IT, THE MORE *PISSED OFF* I GET.
WHY SHOULD I LET A SERIAL KILLER MAKE ME FEEL TERRIFIED AND ASHAMED, RUNNING FOR MY LIFE AND PLEADING FOR GOD TO SAVE ME?
VWOOOM
SHOULDN'T THAT BE *YOU?*
VWOOOM
AS LONG AS I KNOW I'M GETTING OUT OF HERE IN ONE PIECE...
...MAYBE I SHOULDN'T BE MORE DESPERATE THAN A GUY CLUTCHING HIS STOMACH AND FRANTICALLY SEARCHING FOR A PUBLIC TOILET BEFORE THE DIARRHEA COMES OUT.
DON'T YOU THINK THAT'S BACKWARD?

CHAPTER 93

HEART ATTACK, PART 5

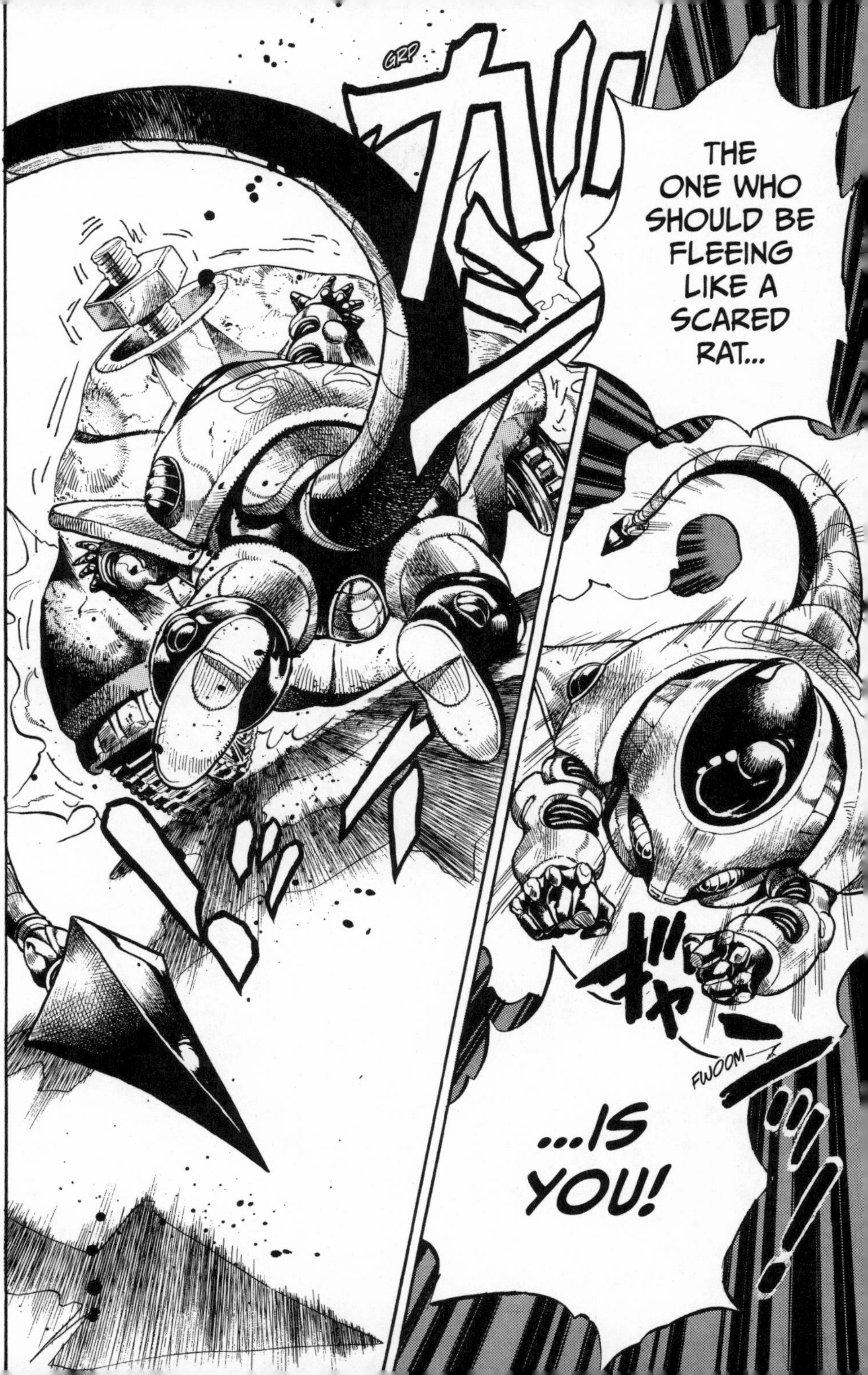
THE ONE WHO SHOULD BE FLEEING LIKE A SCARED RAT...
FWOOM
...IS YOU!
GRP

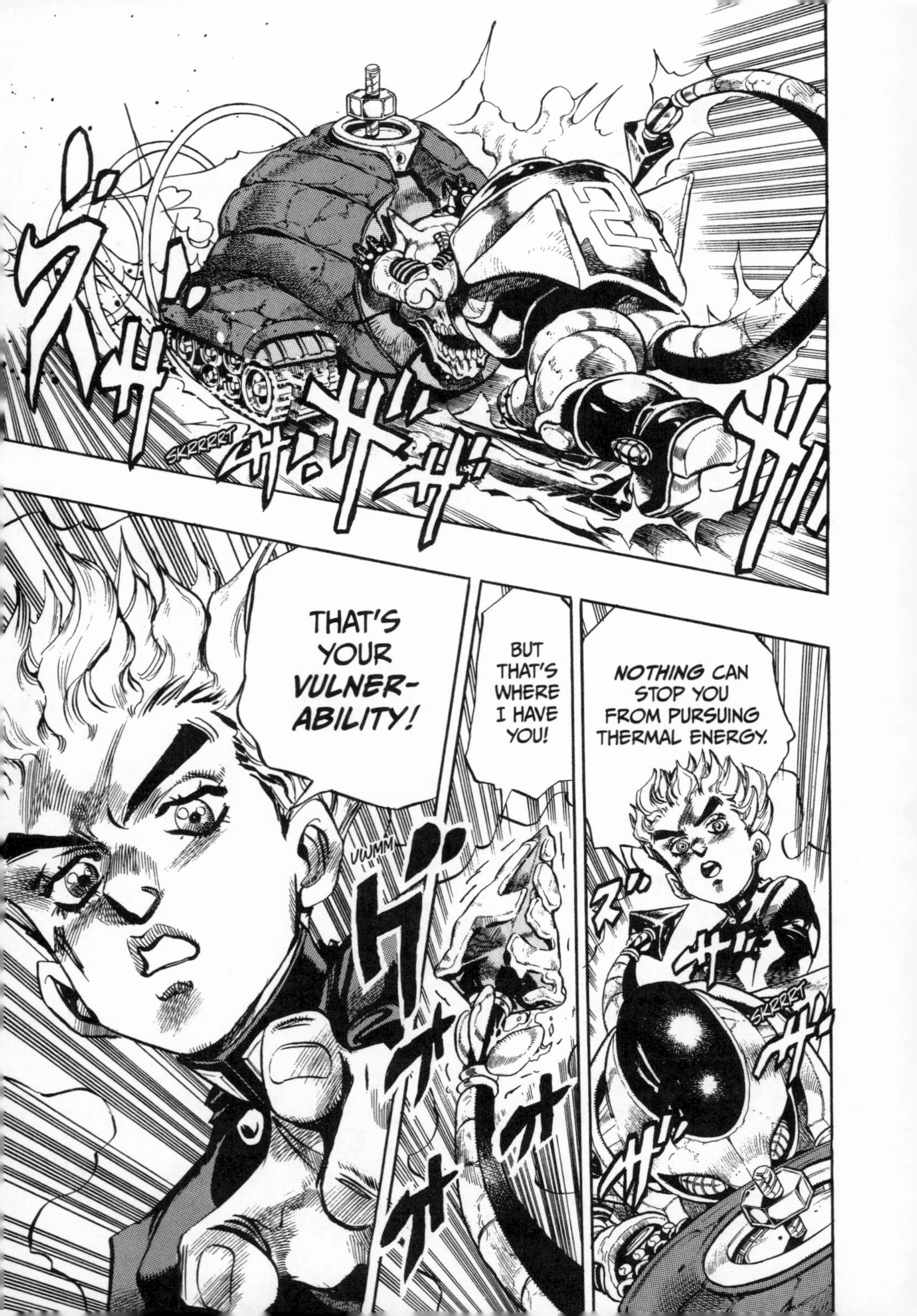
SKRRRRT
NOTHING CAN STOP YOU FROM PURSUING THERMAL ENERGY.
SKRRRT
BUT THAT'S WHERE I HAVE YOU!
THAT'S YOUR VULNER-ABILITY!
VWMM

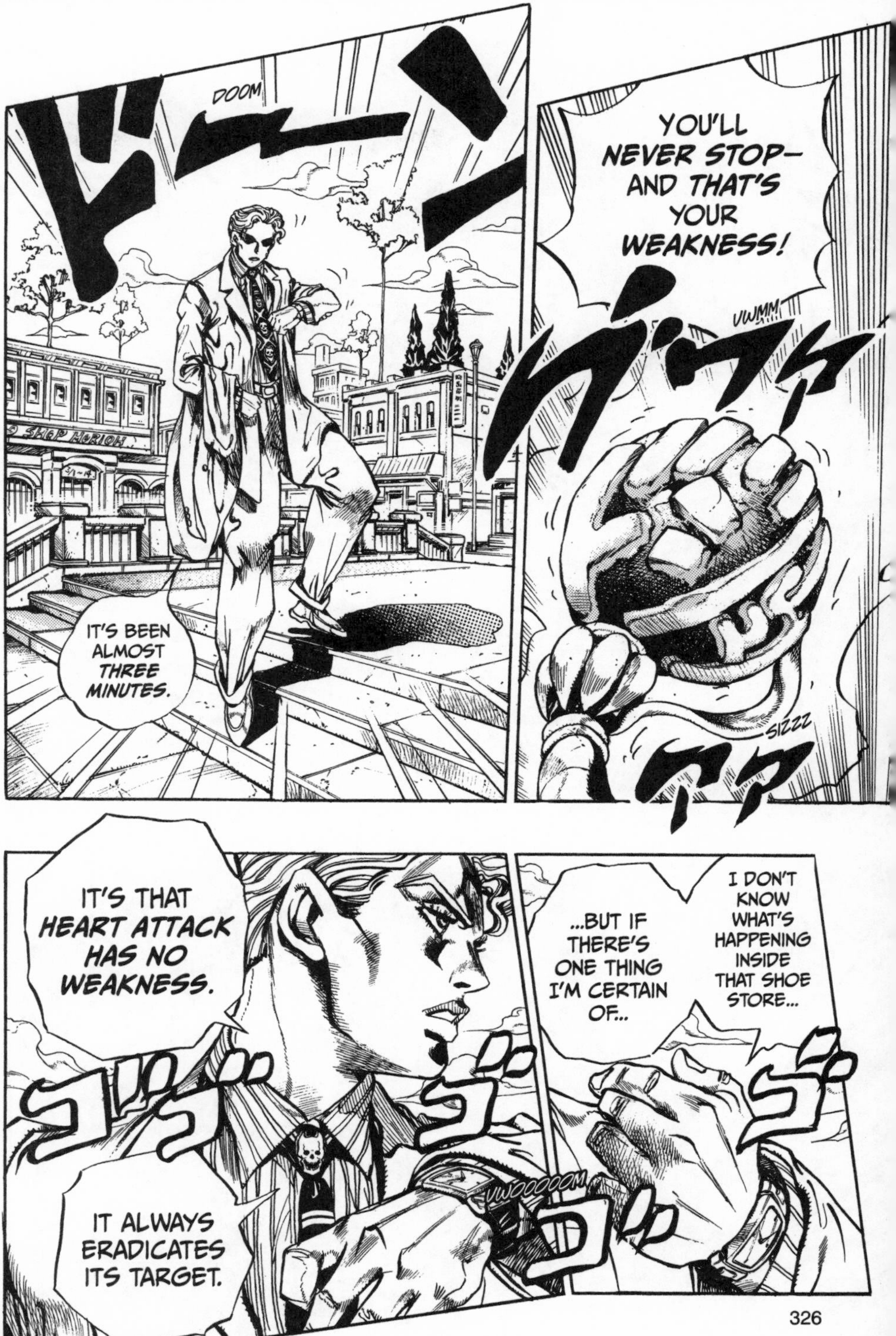
YOU'LL NEVER STOP— AND THAT'S YOUR WEAKNESS!
UWMM
SIZZZ
DOOM
IT'S BEEN ALMOST THREE MINUTES.
I DON'T KNOW WHAT'S HAPPENING INSIDE THAT SHOE STORE...
...BUT IF THERE'S ONE THING I'M CERTAIN OF...
VWOOOOOM
IT'S THAT HEART ATTACK HAS NO WEAKNESS.
IT ALWAYS ERADICATES ITS TARGET.

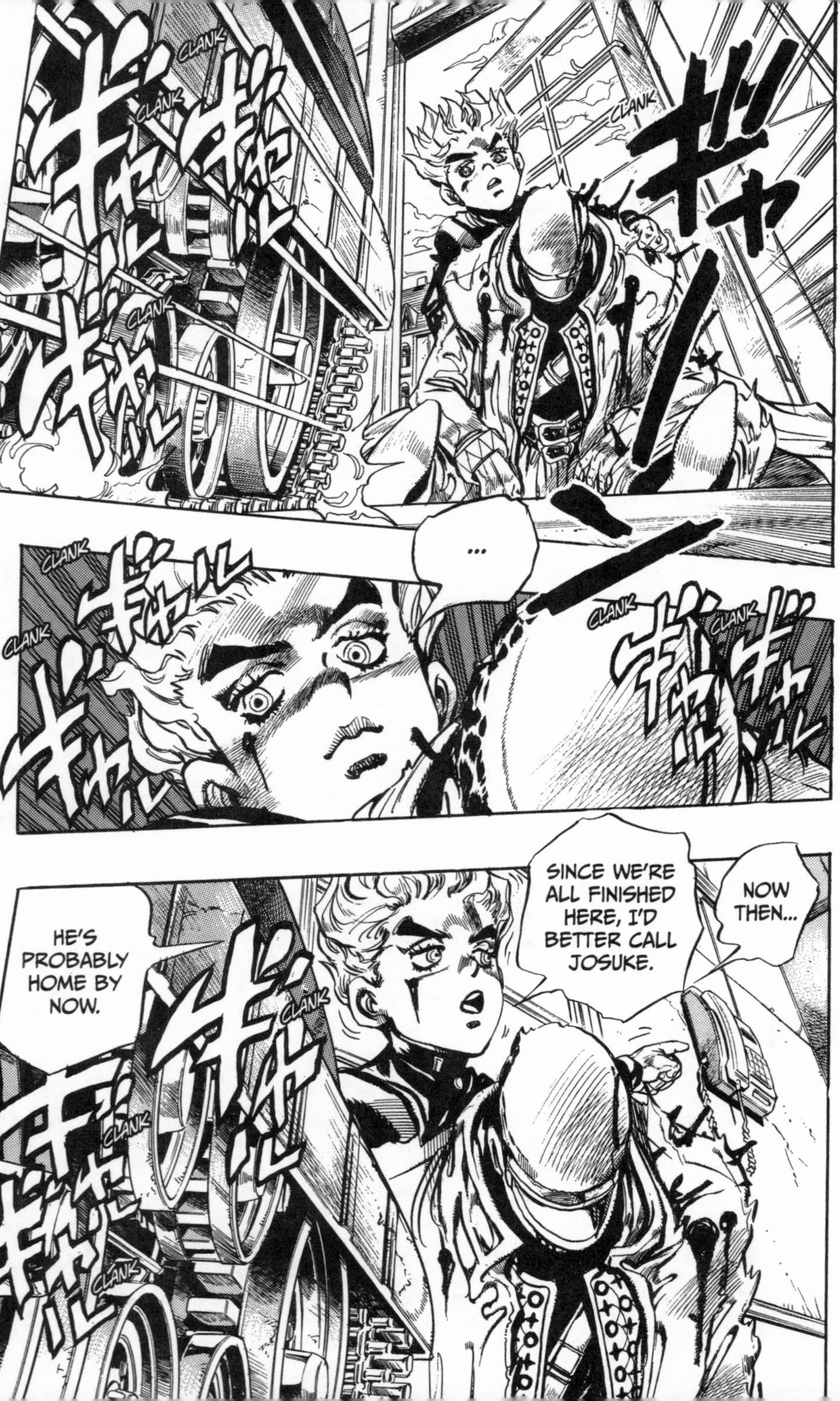
CLANK
CLANK
CLANK
CLANK
...
CLANK
CLANK
CLANK
CLANK
NOW THEN...
SINCE WE'RE ALL FINISHED HERE, I'D BETTER CALL JOSUKE.
HE'S PROBABLY HOME BY NOW.
CLANK
CLANK
CLANK

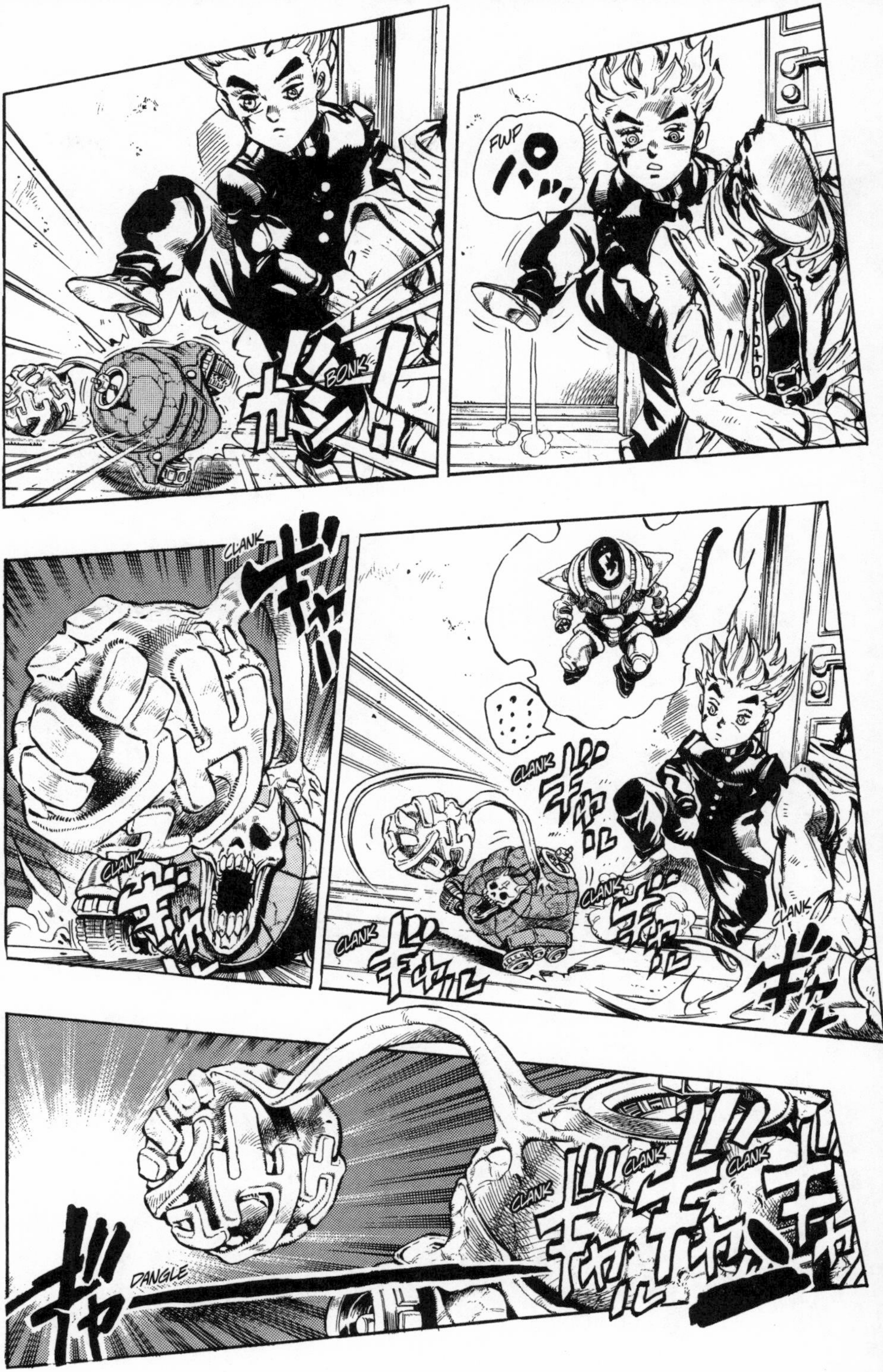
FWUP
パッ
BONK
CLANK
CLANK
CLANK
CLANK
CLANK
CLANK
CLANK
CLANK
CLANK
DANGLE

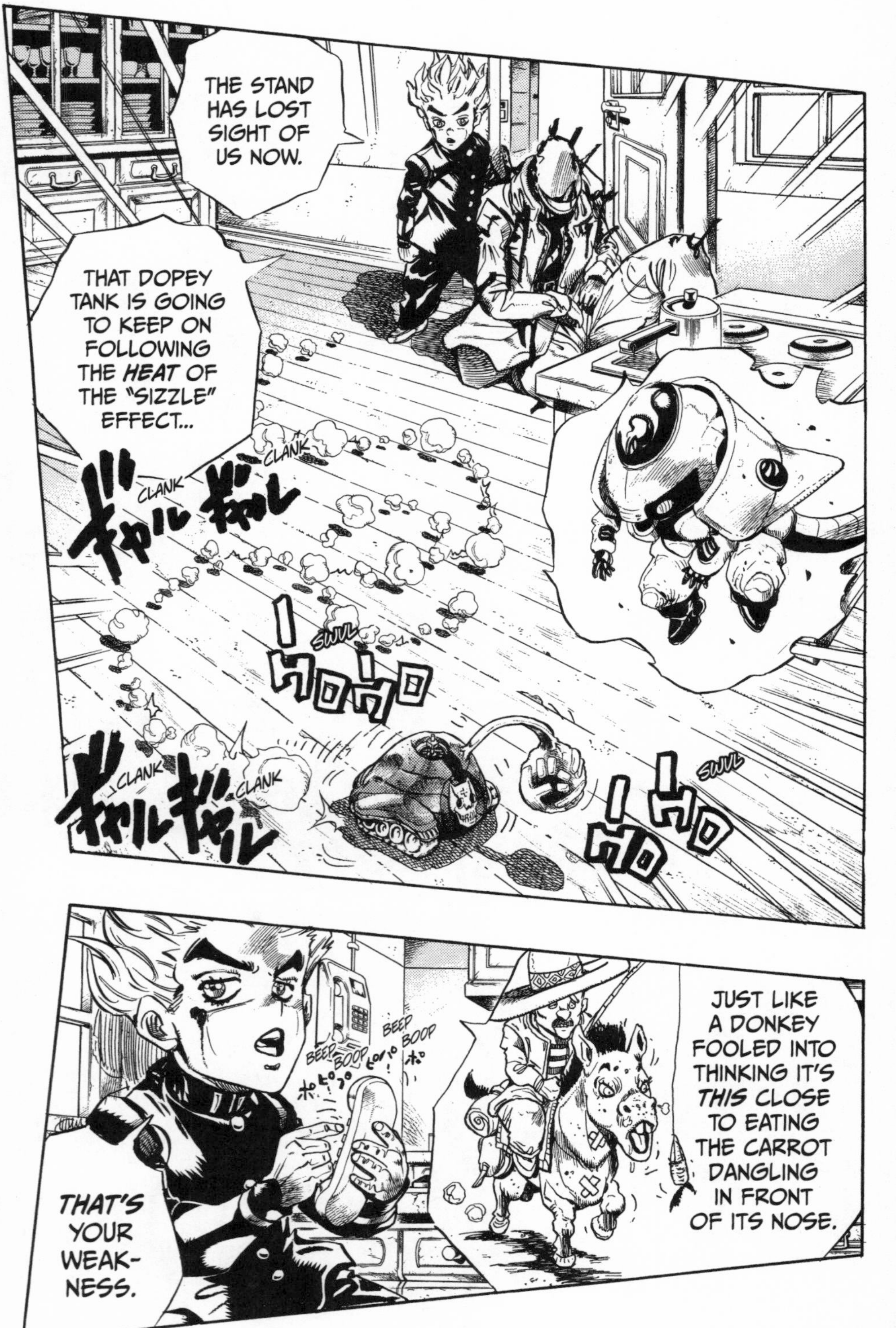
THE STAND HAS LOST SIGHT OF US NOW.
THAT DOPEY TANK IS GOING TO KEEP ON FOLLOWING THE *HEAT* OF THE "SIZZLE" EFFECT...
CLANK CLANK
SWUL
CLANK CLANK
SWUL
JUST LIKE A DONKEY FOOLED INTO THINKING IT'S *THIS* CLOSE TO EATING THE CARROT DANGLING IN FRONT OF ITS NOSE.
BEEP BOOP BEEP BOOP
THAT'S YOUR WEAKNESS.

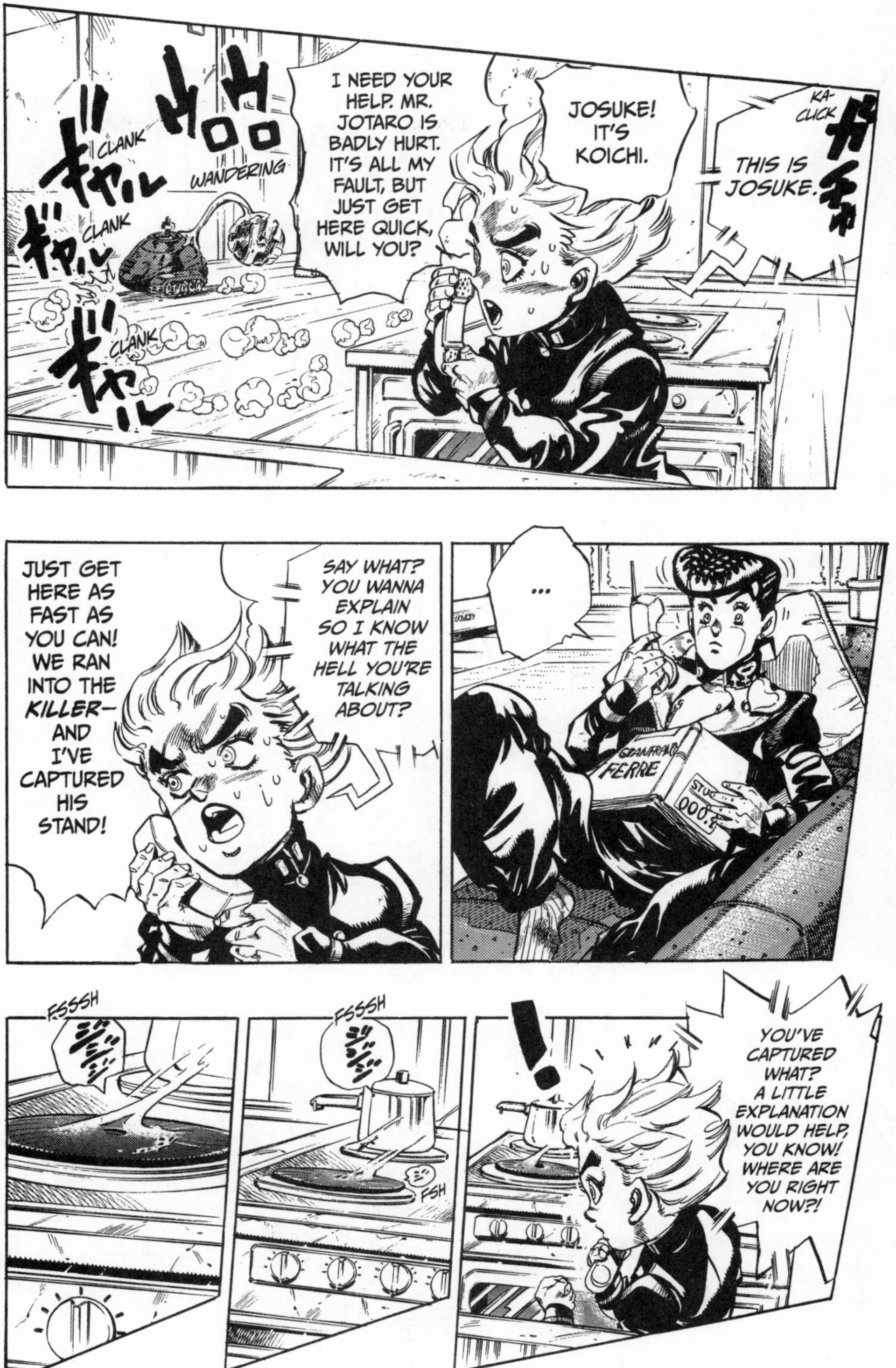
KA-CLICK
THIS IS JOSUKE.
JOSUKE! IT'S KOICHI.
I NEED YOUR HELP. MR. JOTARO IS BADLY HURT. IT'S ALL MY FAULT, BUT JUST GET HERE QUICK, WILL YOU?
WANDERING
CLANK
CLANK
CLANK
...
SAY WHAT? YOU WANNA EXPLAIN SO I KNOW WHAT THE HELL YOU'RE TALKING ABOUT?
JUST GET HERE AS FAST AS YOU CAN! WE RAN INTO THE KILLER— AND I'VE CAPTURED HIS STAND!
YOU'VE CAPTURED WHAT? A LITTLE EXPLANATION WOULD HELP, YOU KNOW! WHERE ARE YOU RIGHT NOW?!
FSSSH
FSH
FSSSH

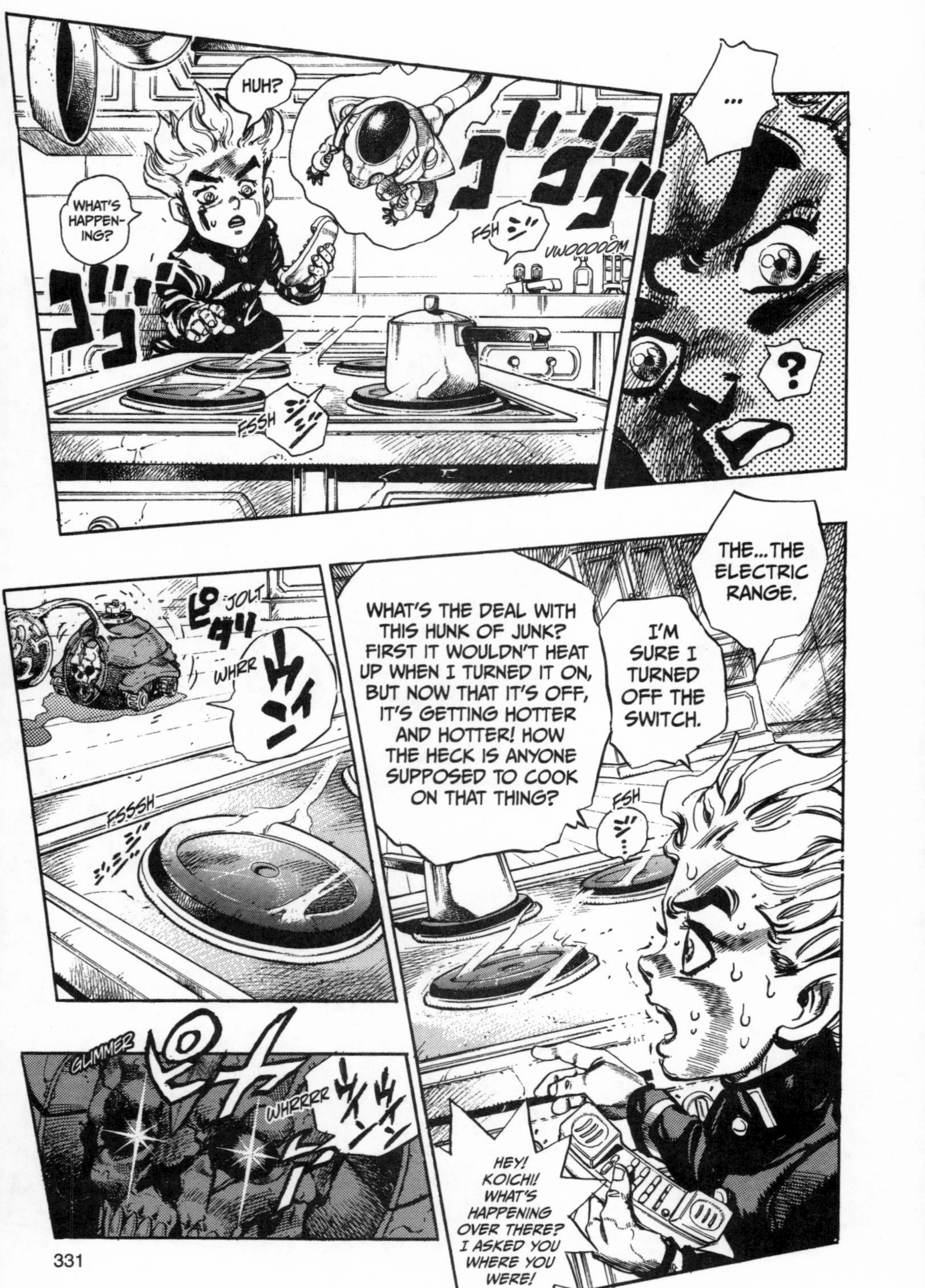
...
?
HUH?
FSH
VWOOOOOM
WHAT'S HAPPEN-ING?
FSSH
THE...THE ELECTRIC RANGE.
I'M SURE I TURNED OFF THE SWITCH.
WHAT'S THE DEAL WITH THIS HUNK OF JUNK? FIRST IT WOULDN'T HEAT UP WHEN I TURNED IT ON, BUT NOW THAT IT'S OFF, IT'S GETTING HOTTER AND HOTTER! HOW THE HECK IS ANYONE SUPPOSED TO COOK ON THAT THING?
FSH
HEY! KOICHI! WHAT'S HAPPENING OVER THERE? I ASKED YOU WHERE YOU WERE!
JOLT
WHRR
FSSSH
GLIMMER
WHRRR

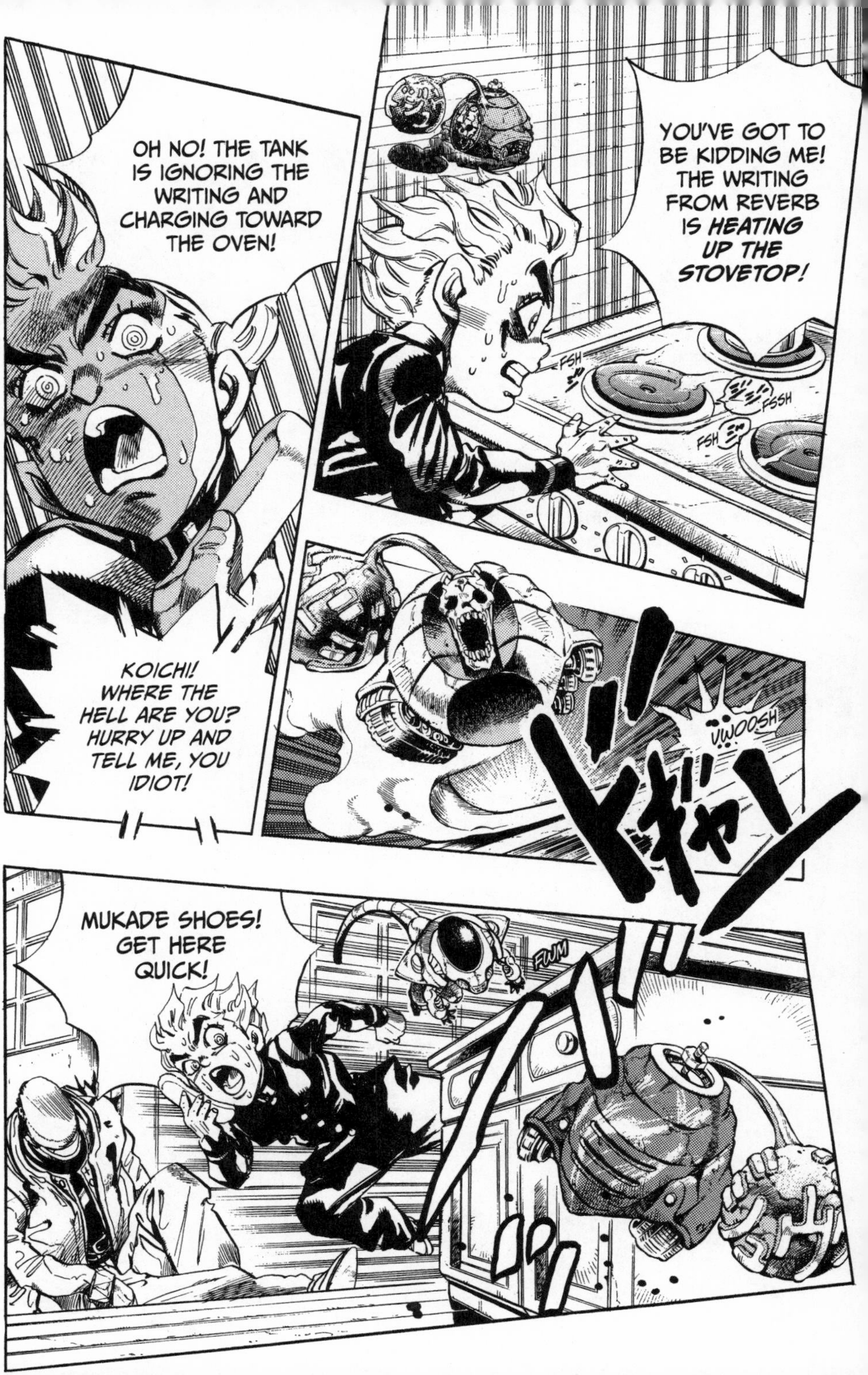
YOU'VE GOT TO BE KIDDING ME! THE WRITING FROM REVERB IS *HEATING UP THE STOVETOP!*
FSH
FSSH
FSH
VWOOSH
OH NO! THE TANK IS IGNORING THE WRITING AND CHARGING TOWARD THE OVEN!
KOICHI! WHERE THE HELL ARE YOU? HURRY UP AND TELL ME, YOU IDIOT!
MUKADE SHOES! GET HERE QUICK!
FUM

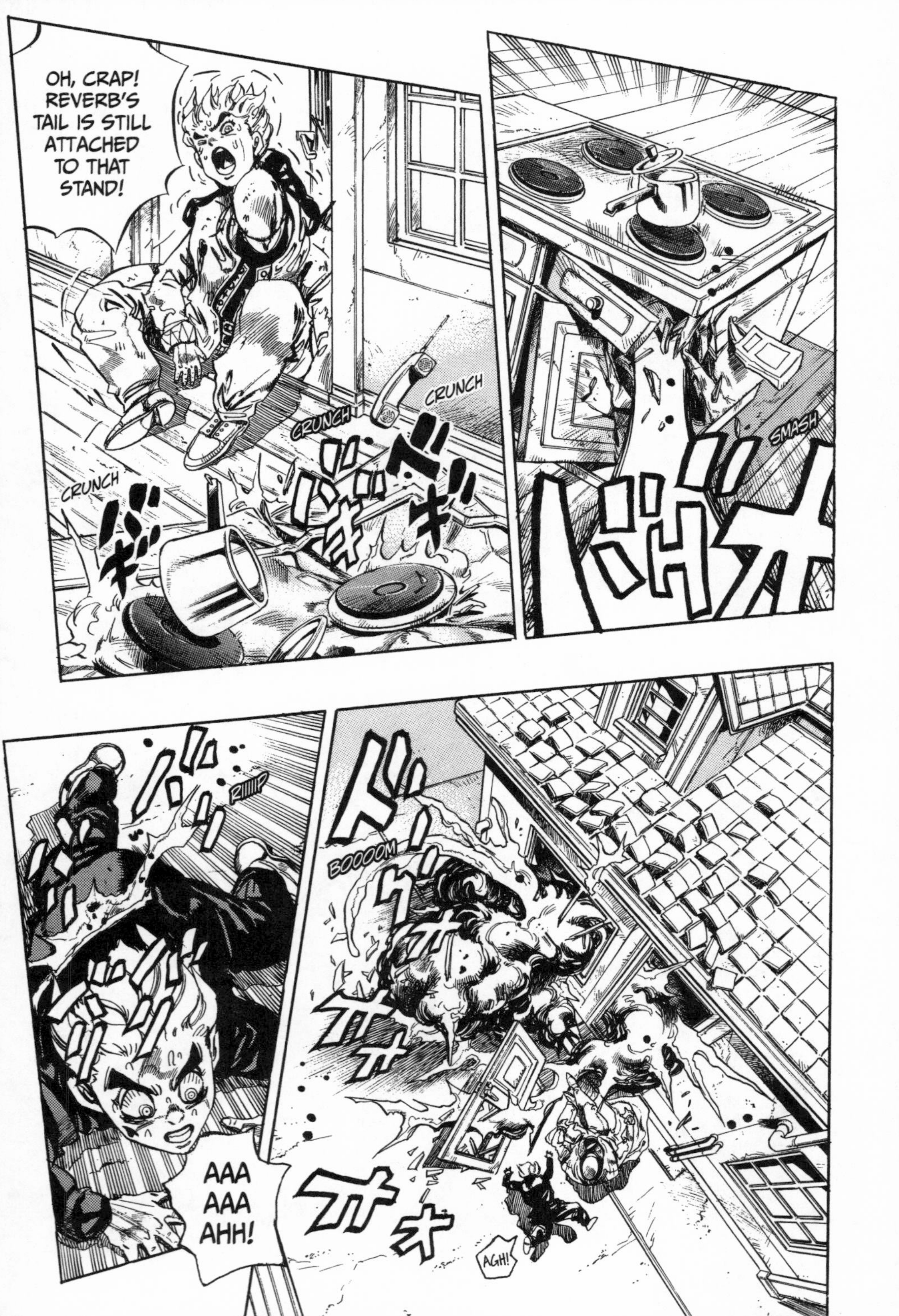
SMASH
OH, CRAP! REVERB'S TAIL IS STILL ATTACHED TO THAT STAND!
CRUNCH
CRUNCH
CRUNCH
BOOOOM
AGH!
RIIIIP
AAA AAA AHH!

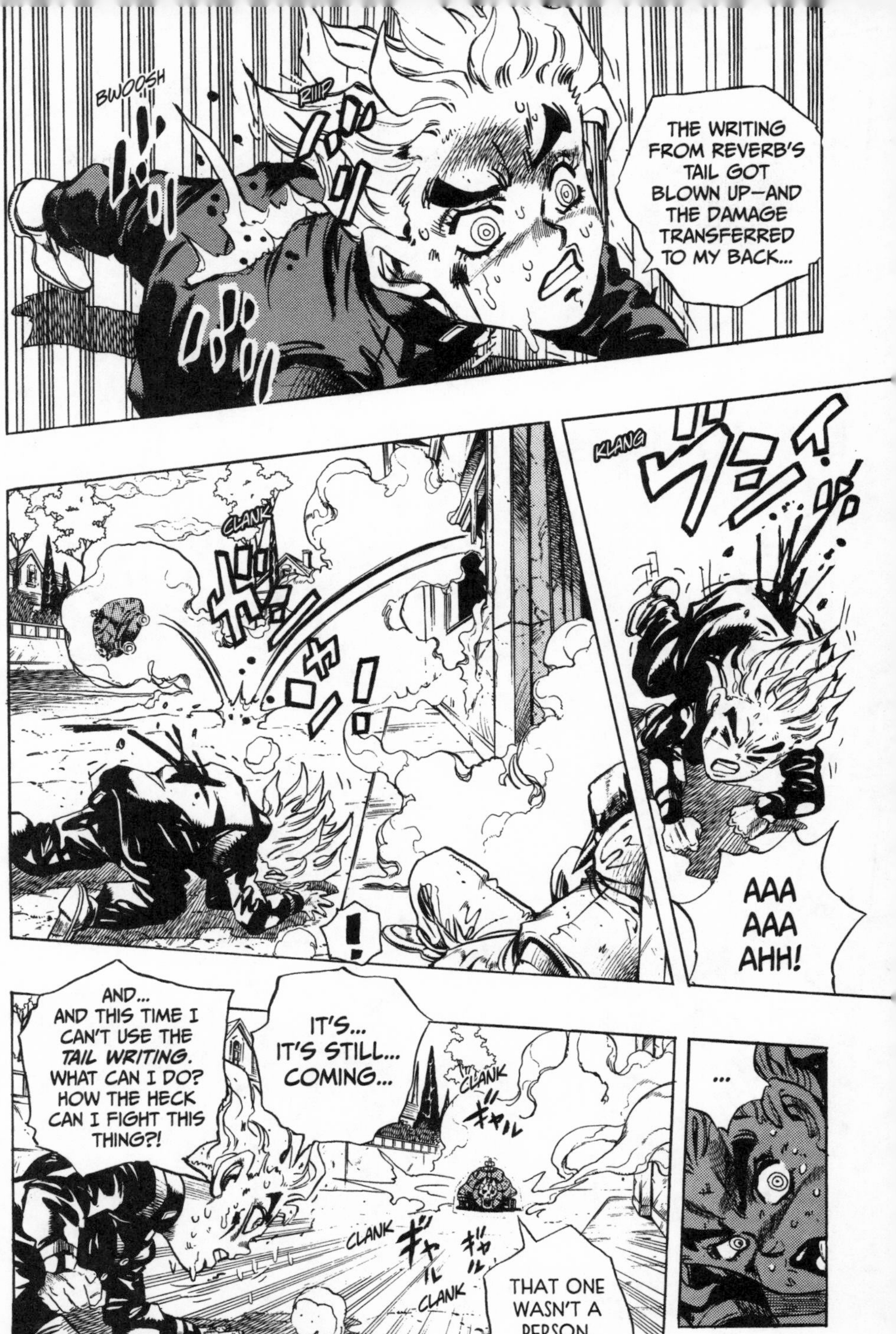
BWOOSH
RIIP
THE WRITING FROM REVERB'S TAIL GOT BLOWN UP—AND THE DAMAGE TRANSFERRED TO MY BACK...
KLANG
AAA AAA AHH!
CLANK
...
CLANK
IT'S... IT'S STILL... COMING...
AND... AND THIS TIME I CAN'T USE THE *TAIL WRITING*. WHAT CAN I DO? HOW THE HECK CAN I FIGHT THIS THING?!
CLANK
CLANK
THAT ONE WASN'T A PERSON.

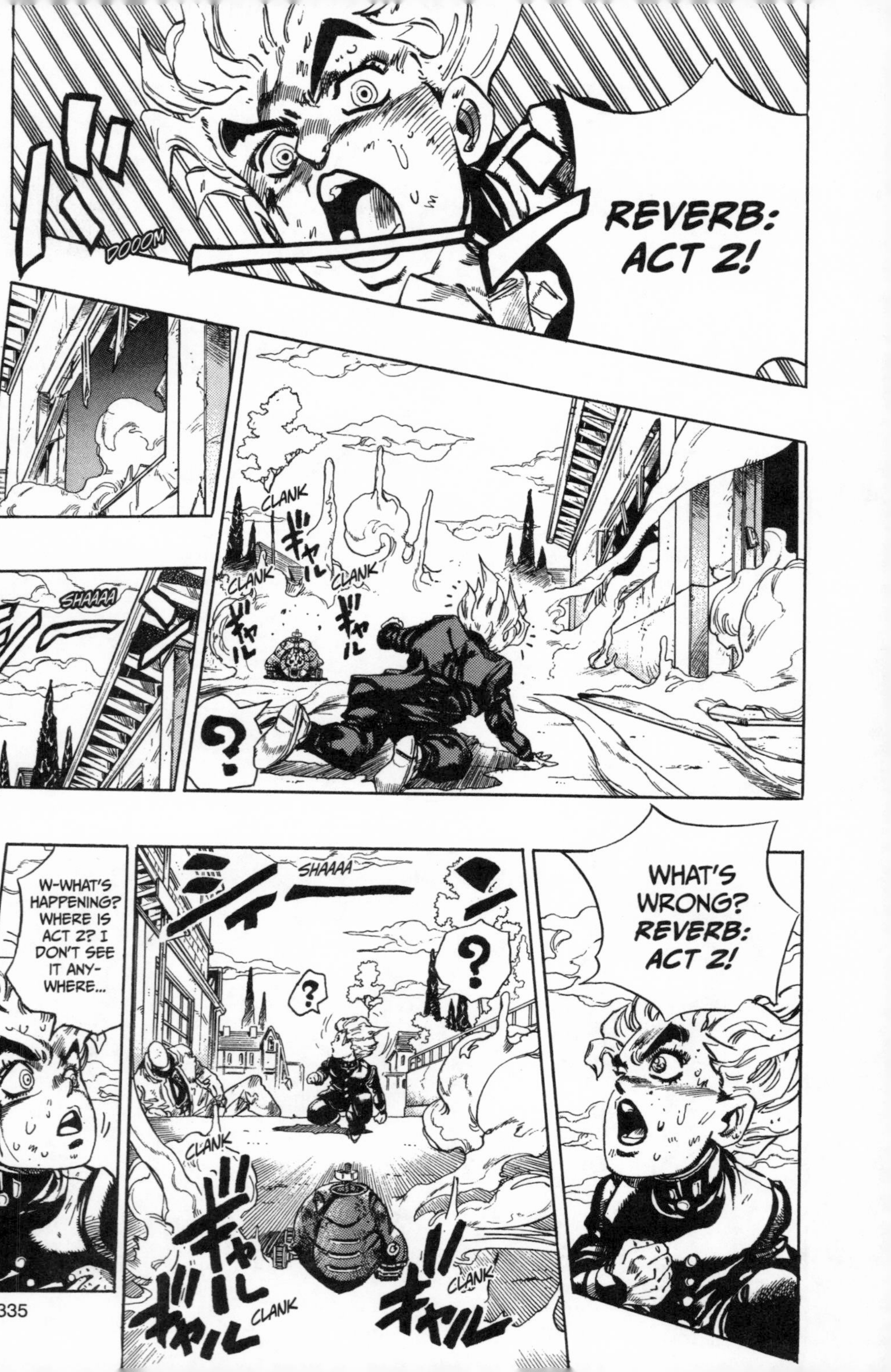
DOOOM
REVERB: ACT 2!
CLANK
CLANK
CLANK
?
SHAAAA
WHAT'S WRONG? REVERB: ACT 2!
SHAAAA
?
?
CLANK
CLANK
CLANK
W-WHAT'S HAPPENING? WHERE IS ACT 2? I DON'T SEE IT ANY-WHERE...

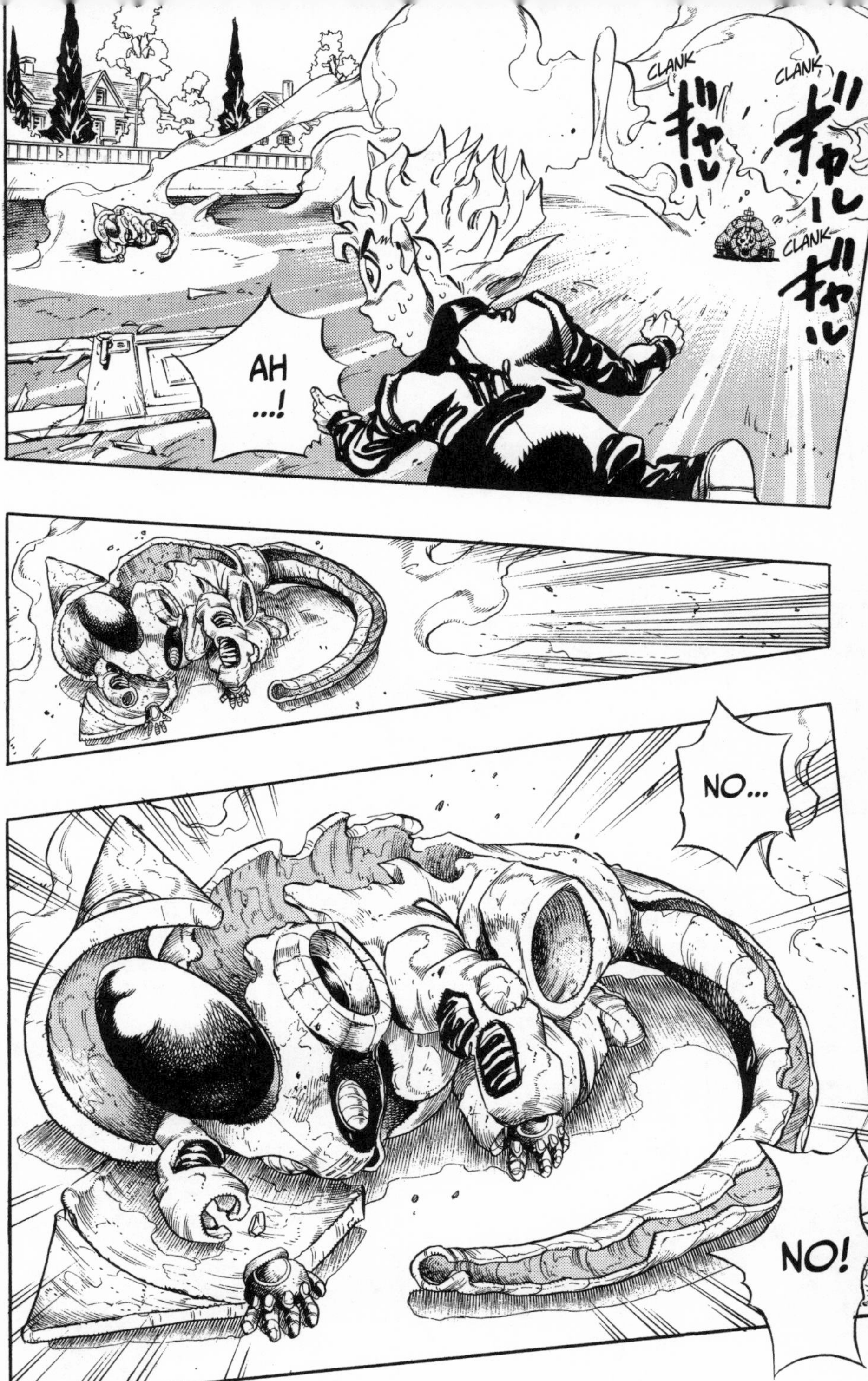
CLANK
CLANK
CLANK
AH ...!
NO...
NO!

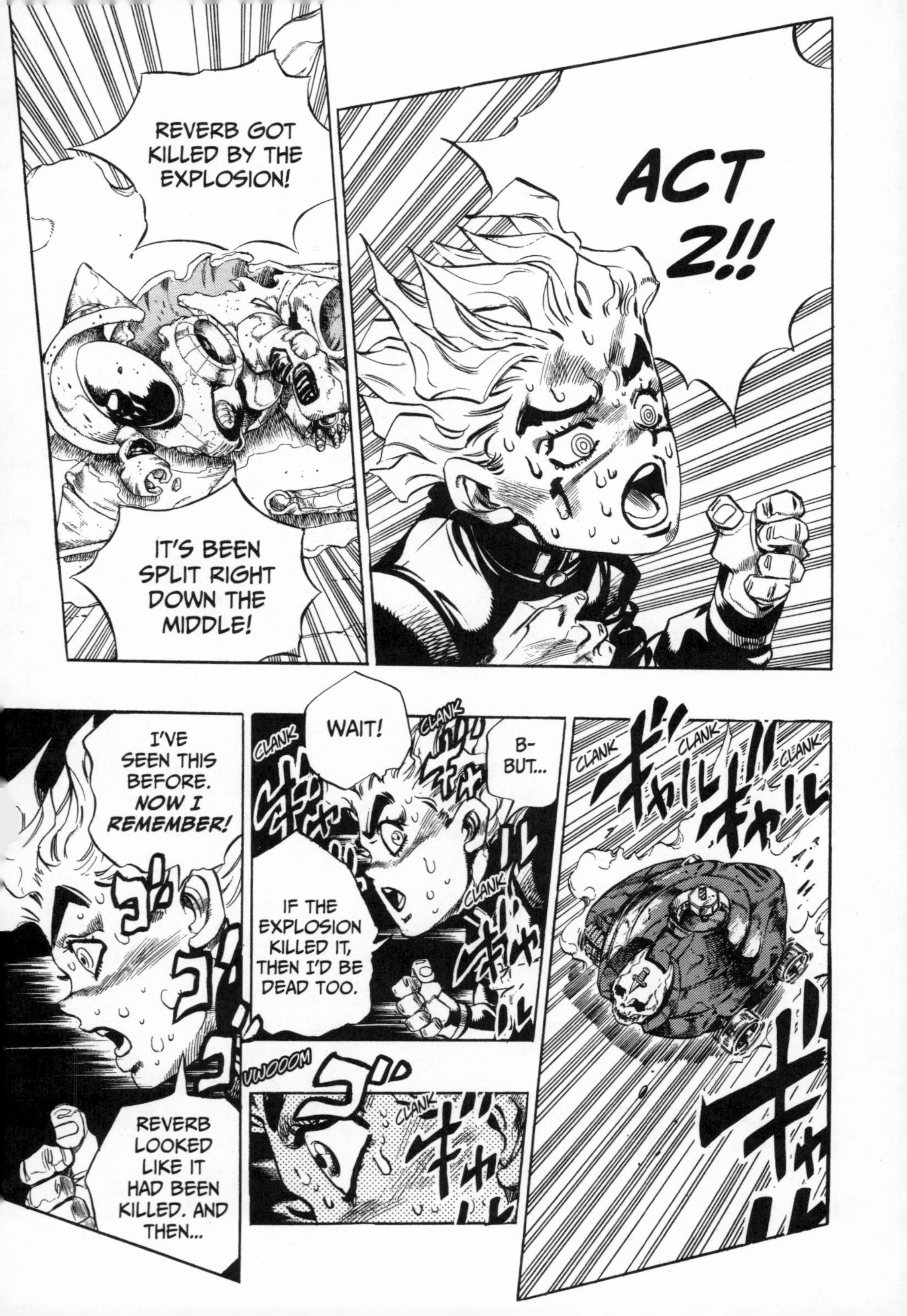
ACT 2!!
REVERB GOT KILLED BY THE EXPLOSION!
IT'S BEEN SPLIT RIGHT DOWN THE MIDDLE!
CLANK
CLANK
CLANK
B- BUT...
WAIT!
CLANK
CLANK
CLANK
IF THE EXPLOSION KILLED IT, THEN I'D BE DEAD TOO.
UWOOOM
CLANK
I'VE SEEN THIS BEFORE. *NOW I REMEMBER!*
REVERB LOOKED LIKE IT HAD BEEN KILLED. AND THEN...

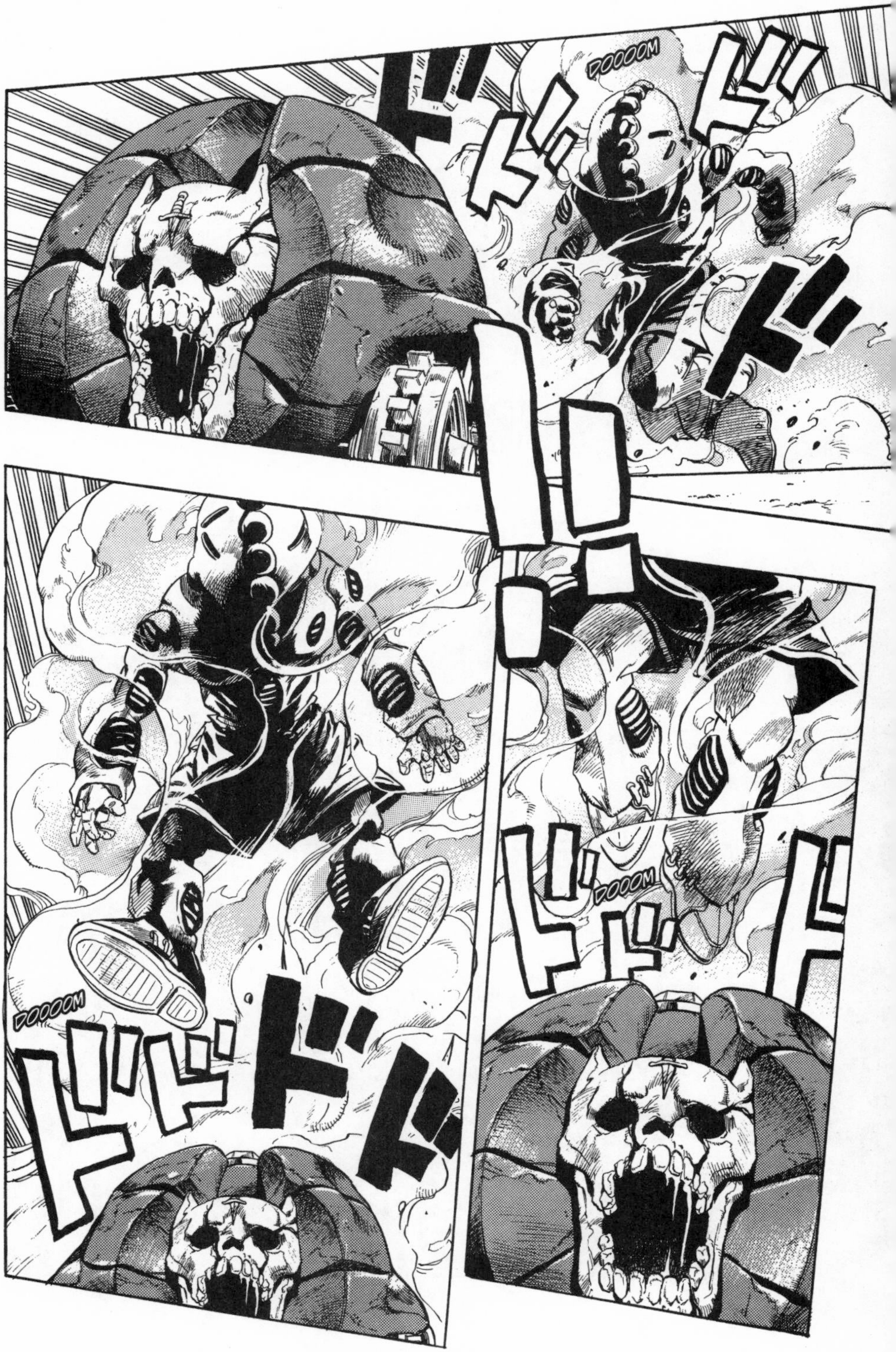
DOOOOM
!!
DOOOM
DOOOOM

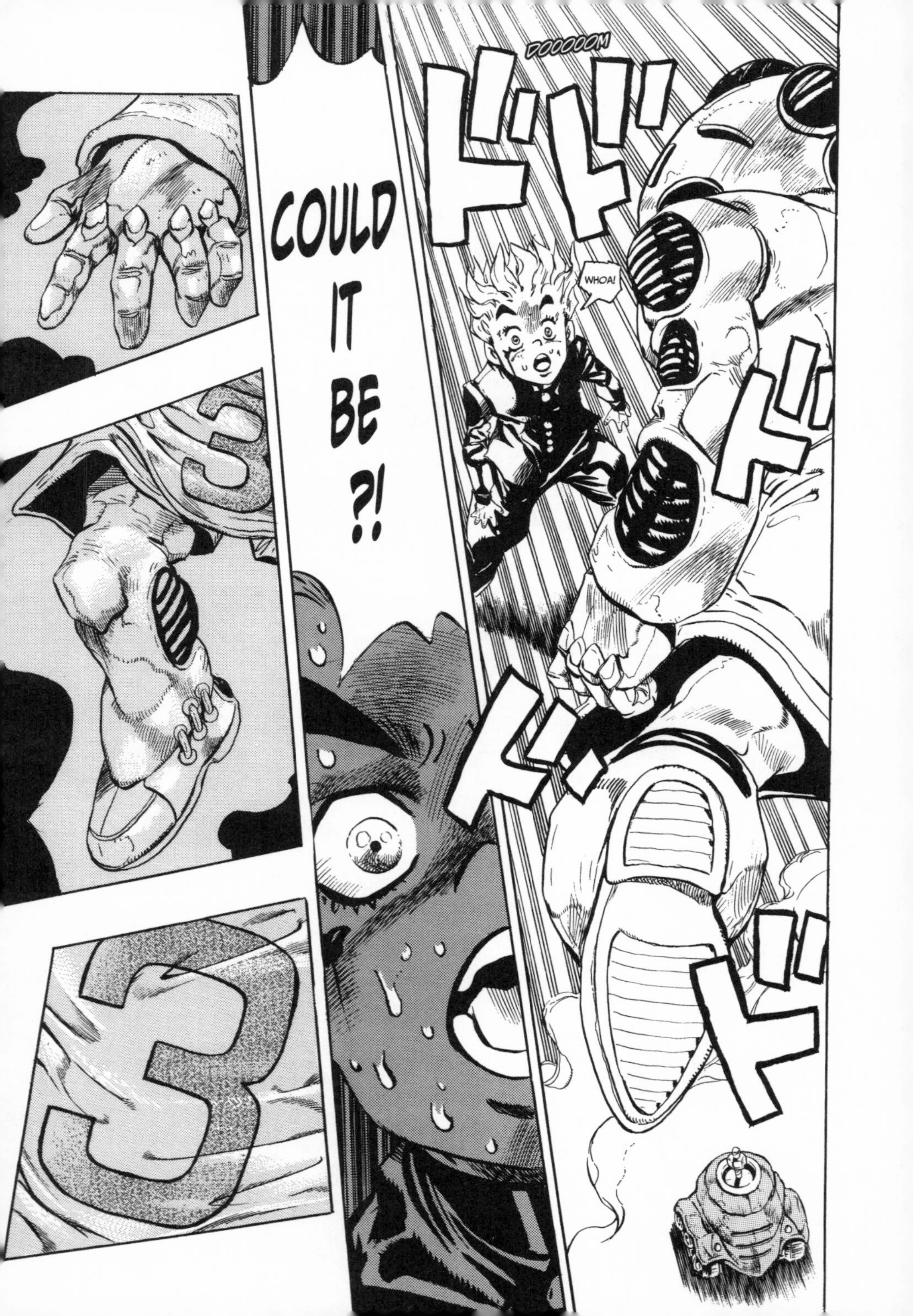
DOOOOOM
WHOA!
COULD IT BE ?!

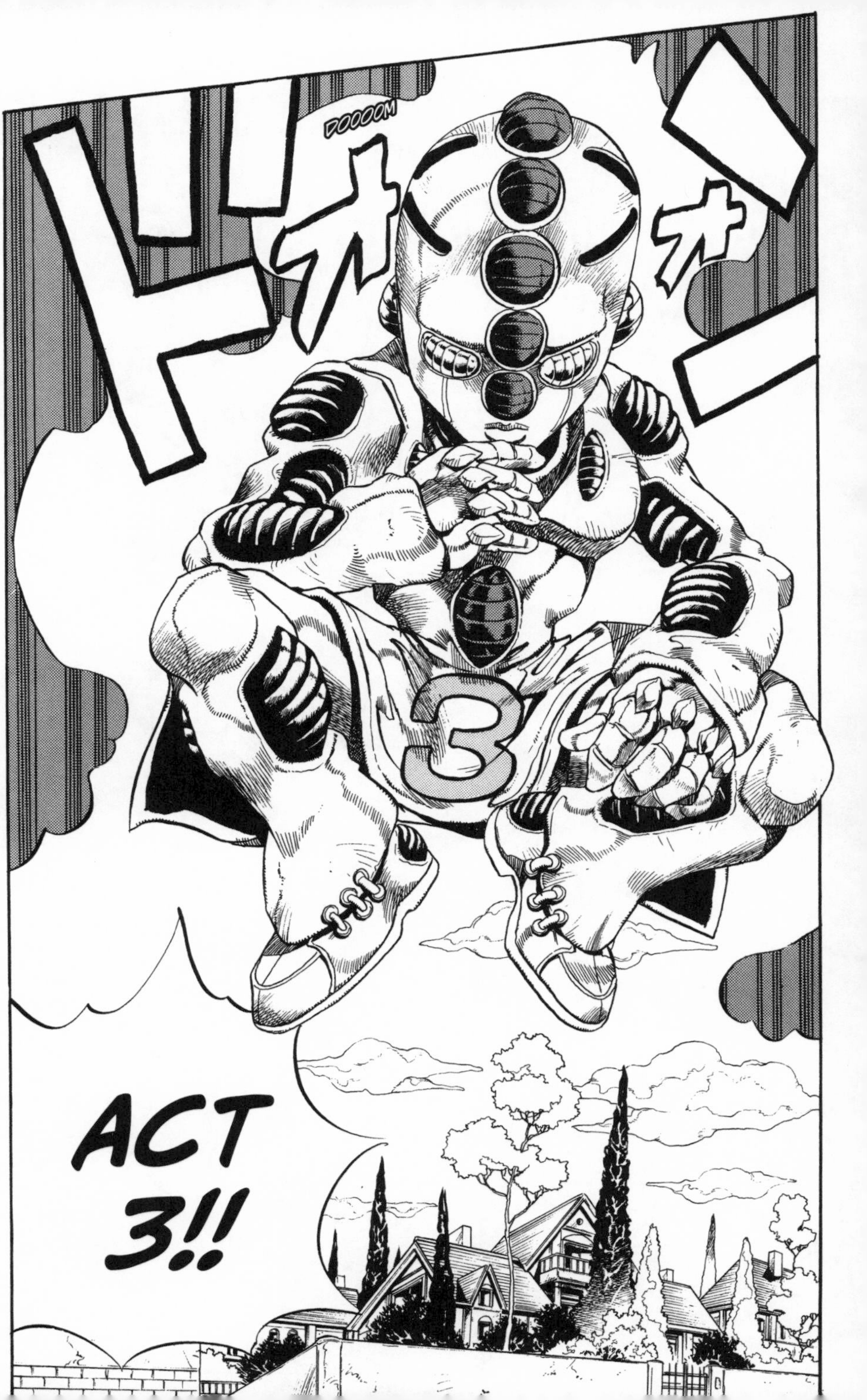
ドーオーオーン
DOOOOM
ACT 3!!

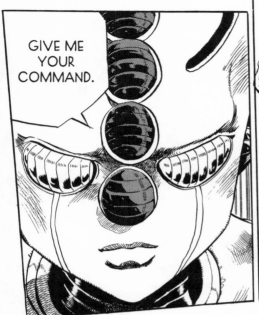

GIVE ME YOUR COMMAND.

YOU'RE NUMBER THREE, AREN'T YOU?

...

I MEAN... YOU ARE MY STAND... AREN'T YOU?

MAYBE?

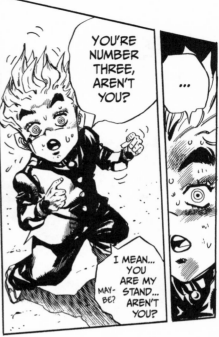

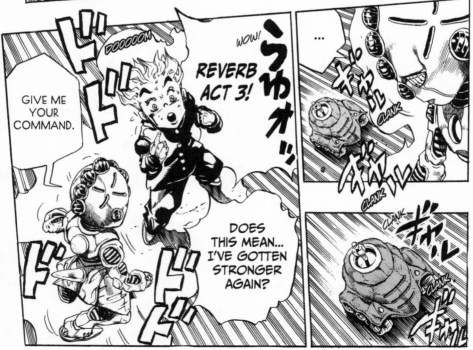

GIVE ME YOUR COMMAND.

DOOOOOM

ドッ
ドッ

WOW!

REVERB ACT 3!

らゆオッ

DOES THIS MEAN... I'VE GOTTEN STRONGER AGAIN?

ド゛

ド゛

...

CLANK

CLANK

CLANK

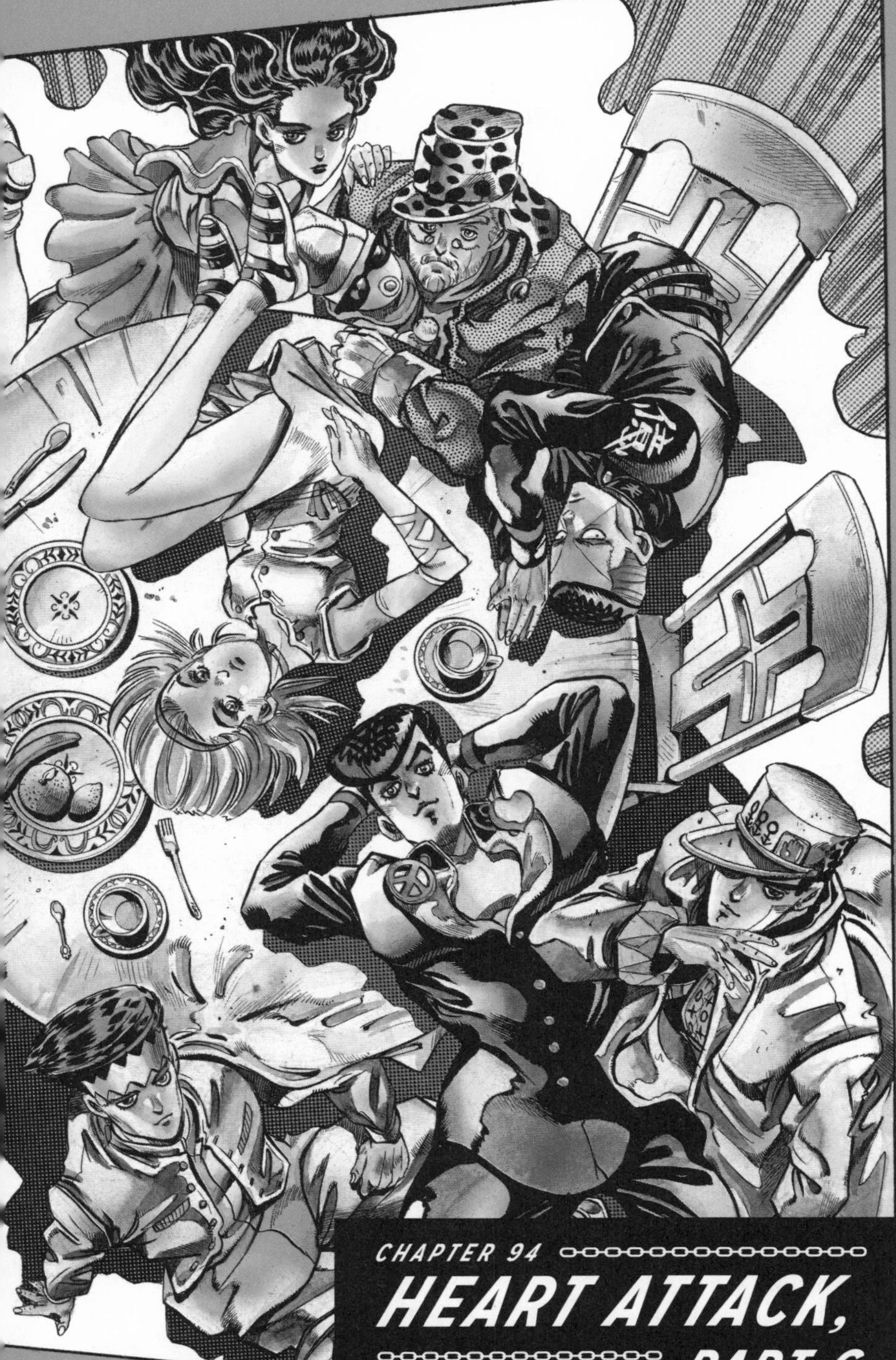

CHAPTER 94

HEART ATTACK, PART 6

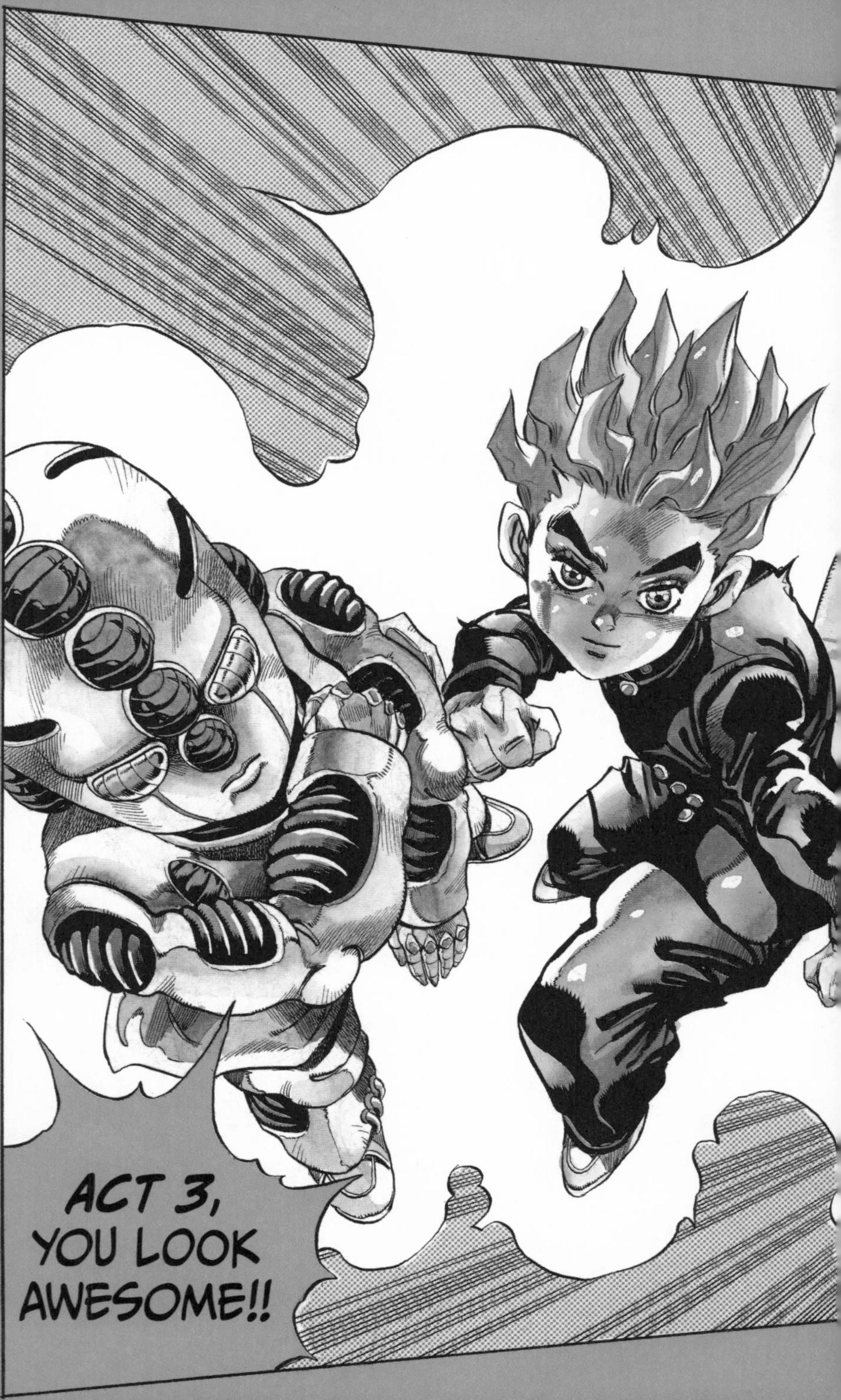
ACT 3,
YOU LOOK
AWESOME!!

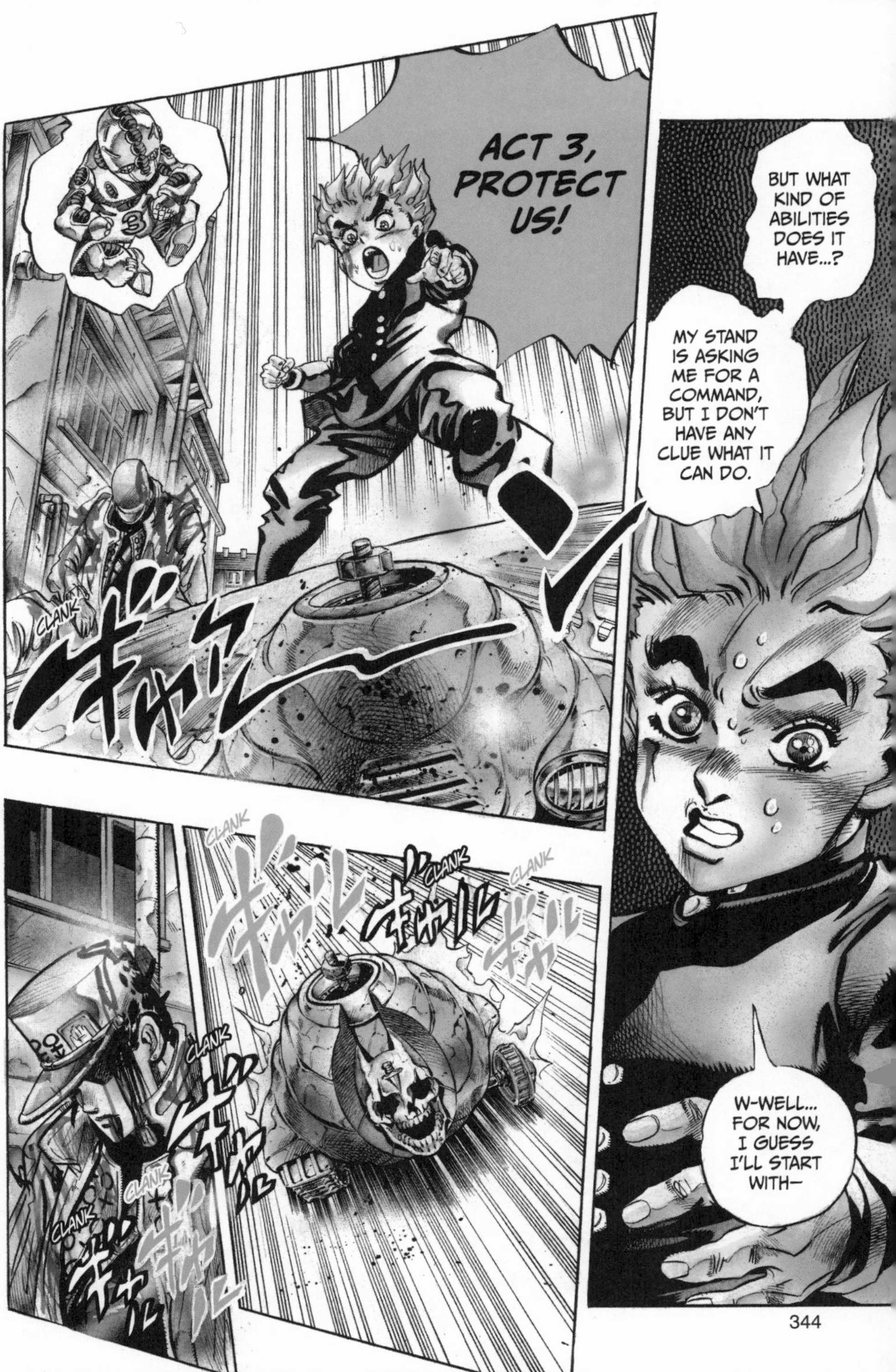
BUT WHAT KIND OF ABILITIES DOES IT HAVE...?
MY STAND IS ASKING ME FOR A COMMAND, BUT I DON'T HAVE ANY CLUE WHAT IT CAN DO.
W-WELL... FOR NOW, I GUESS I'LL START WITH—
ACT 3, PROTECT US!
CLANK
CLANK
CLANK
CLANK
CLANK
CLANK
CLANK

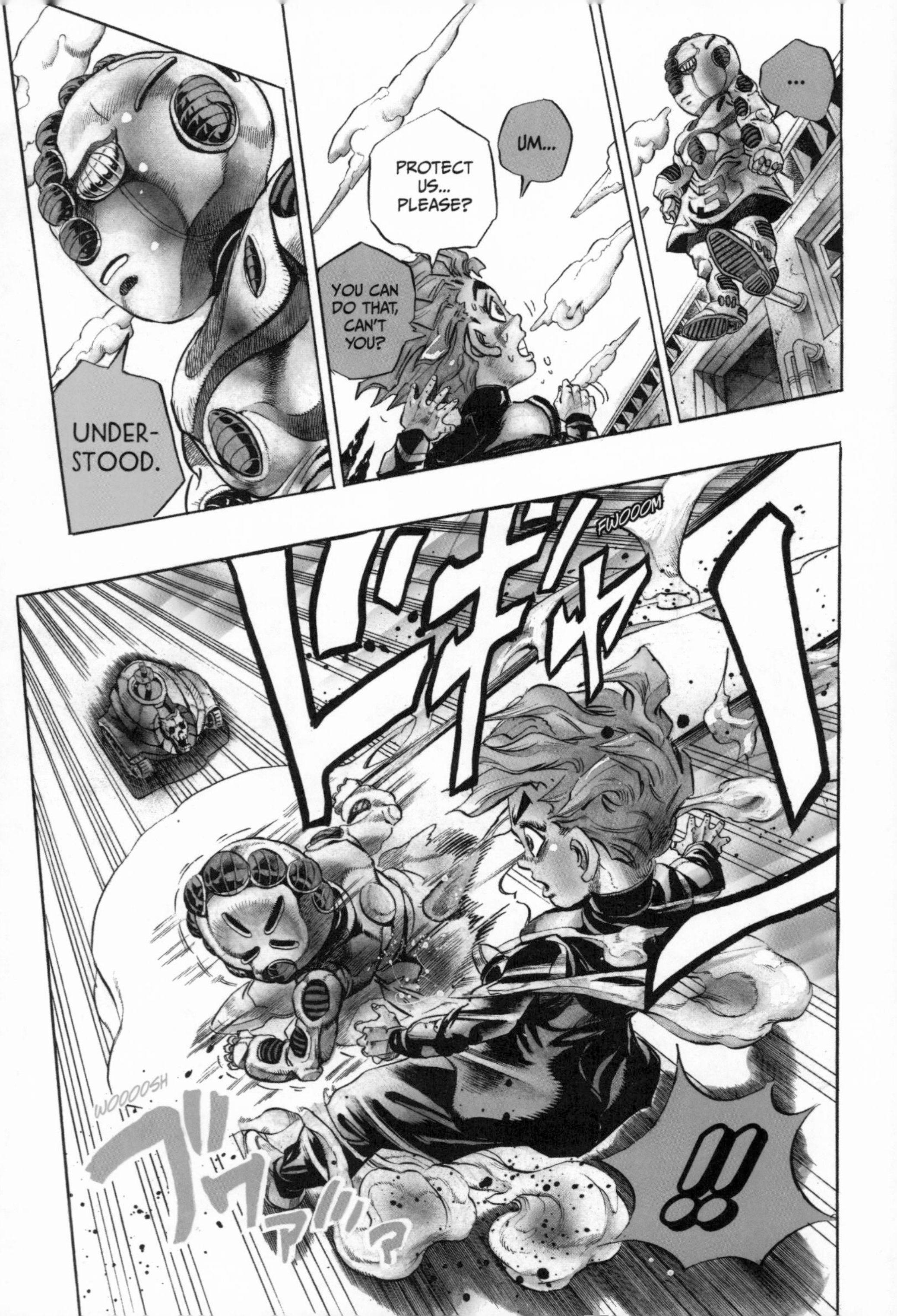
...
UM...
PROTECT US... PLEASE?
YOU CAN DO THAT, CAN'T YOU?
UNDER-STOOD.
FWOOOM
!!
WOOOOSH

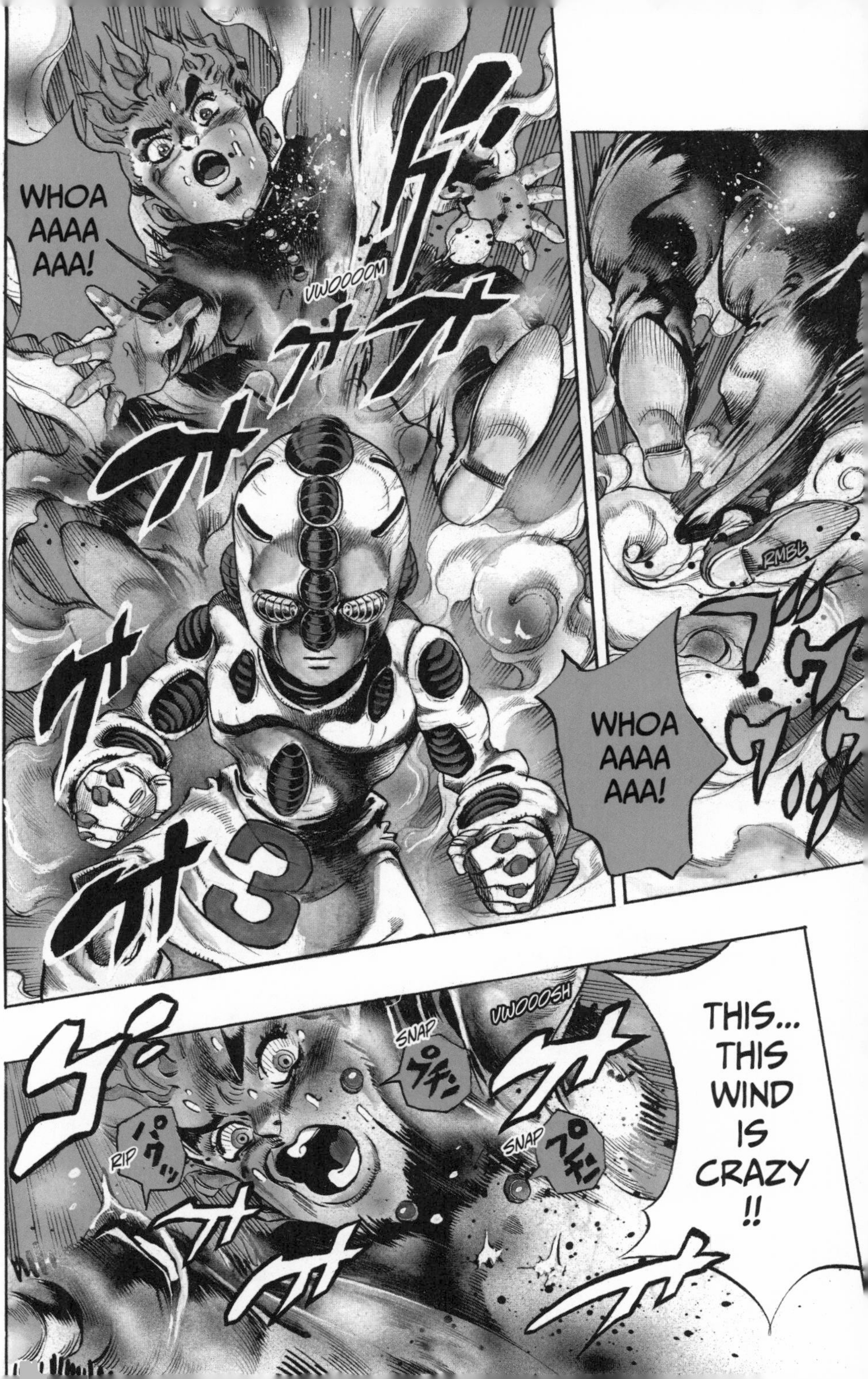
RMBL
WHOA AAAA AAA!
WHOA AAAA AAA!
VWOOOOM
THIS... THIS WIND IS CRAZY!!
VWOOOSH
SNAP
SNAP
RIP

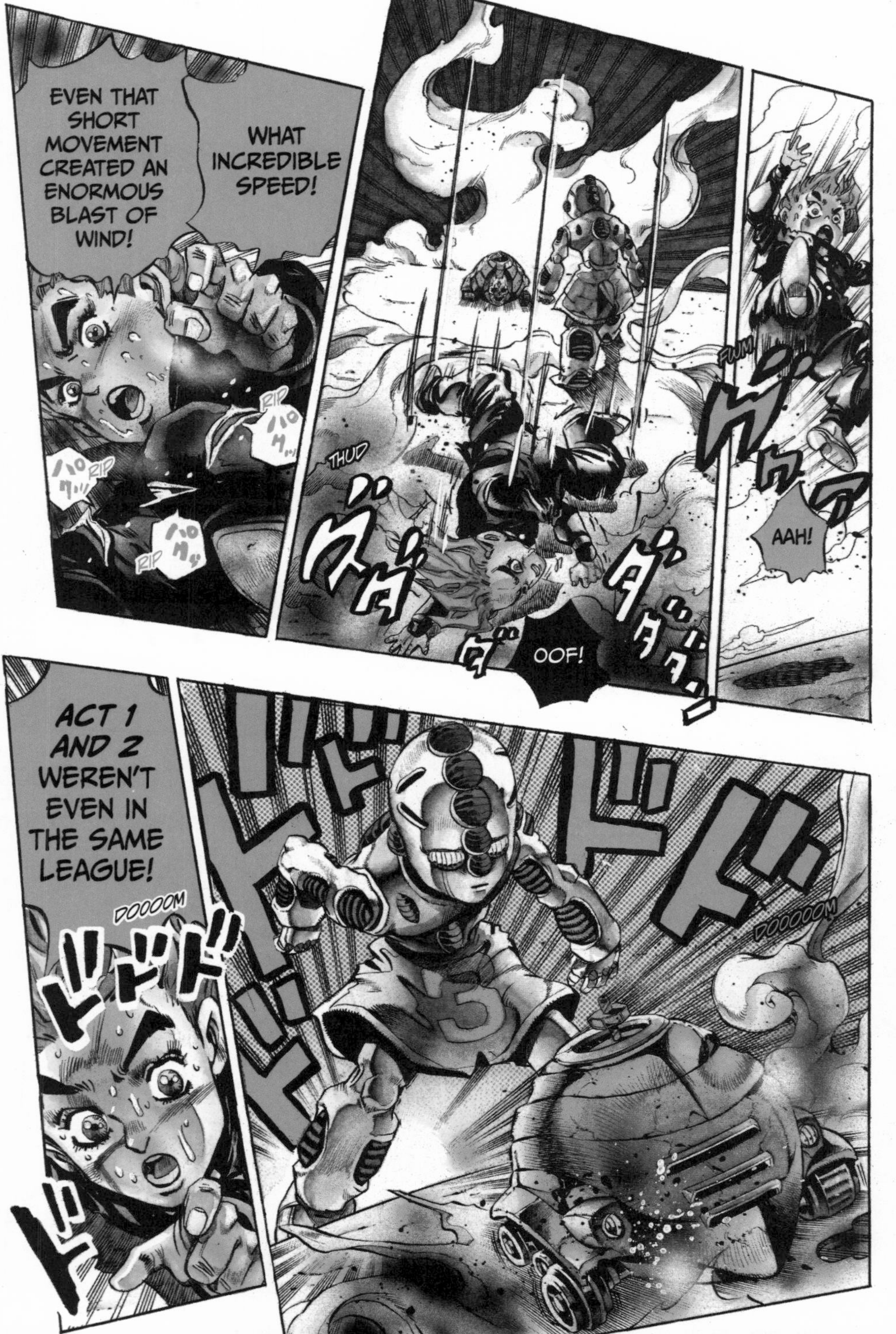
FWUM
AAH!
THUD
OOF!
WHAT INCREDIBLE SPEED!
EVEN THAT SHORT MOVEMENT CREATED AN ENORMOUS BLAST OF WIND!
RIP
RIP
RIP
DOOOOOM
ACT 1 AND 2 WEREN'T EVEN IN THE SAME LEAGUE!
DOOOOM

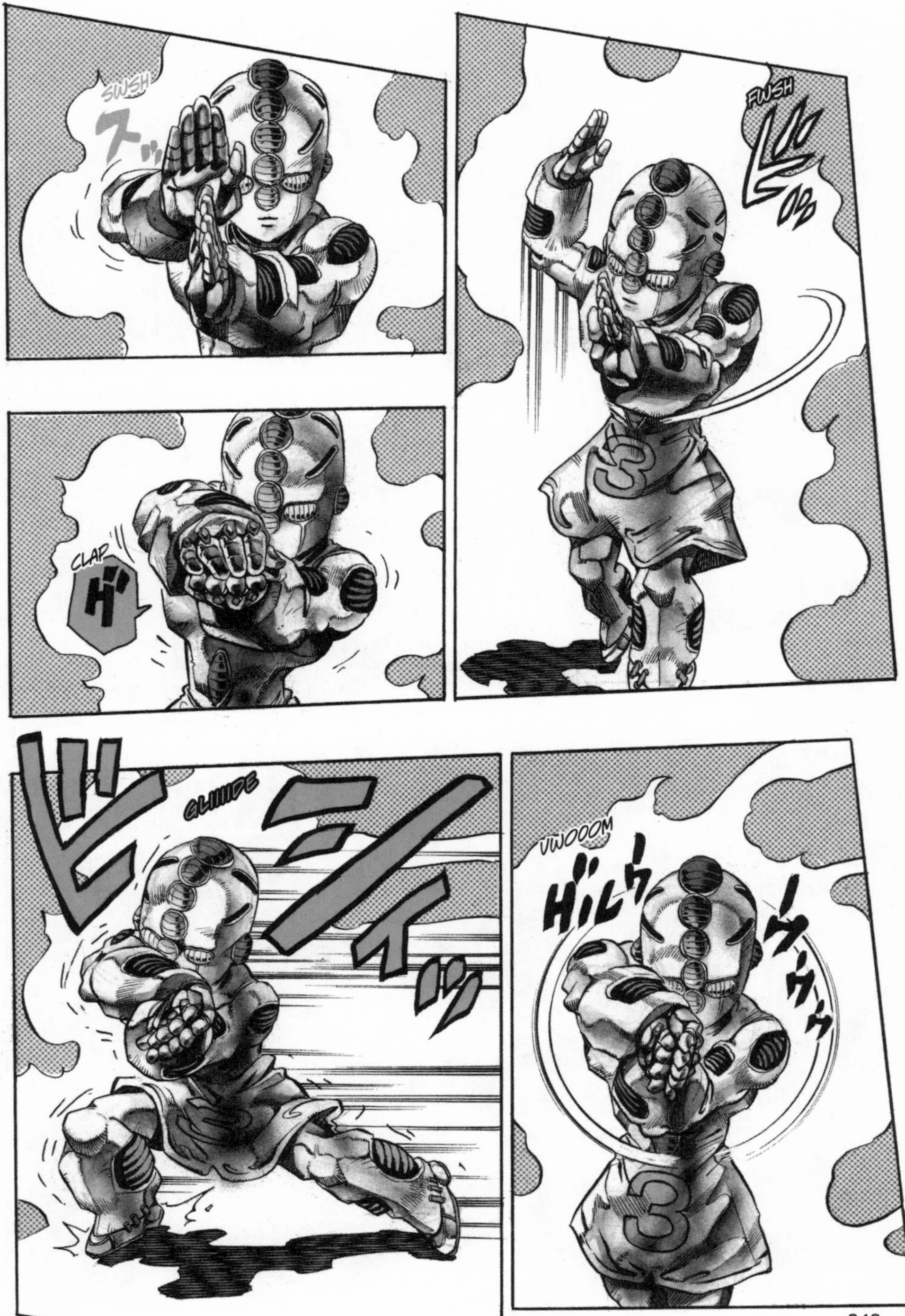
FWSH
SWSH
スッ
CLAP
VWOOOM
GLIIIIDE

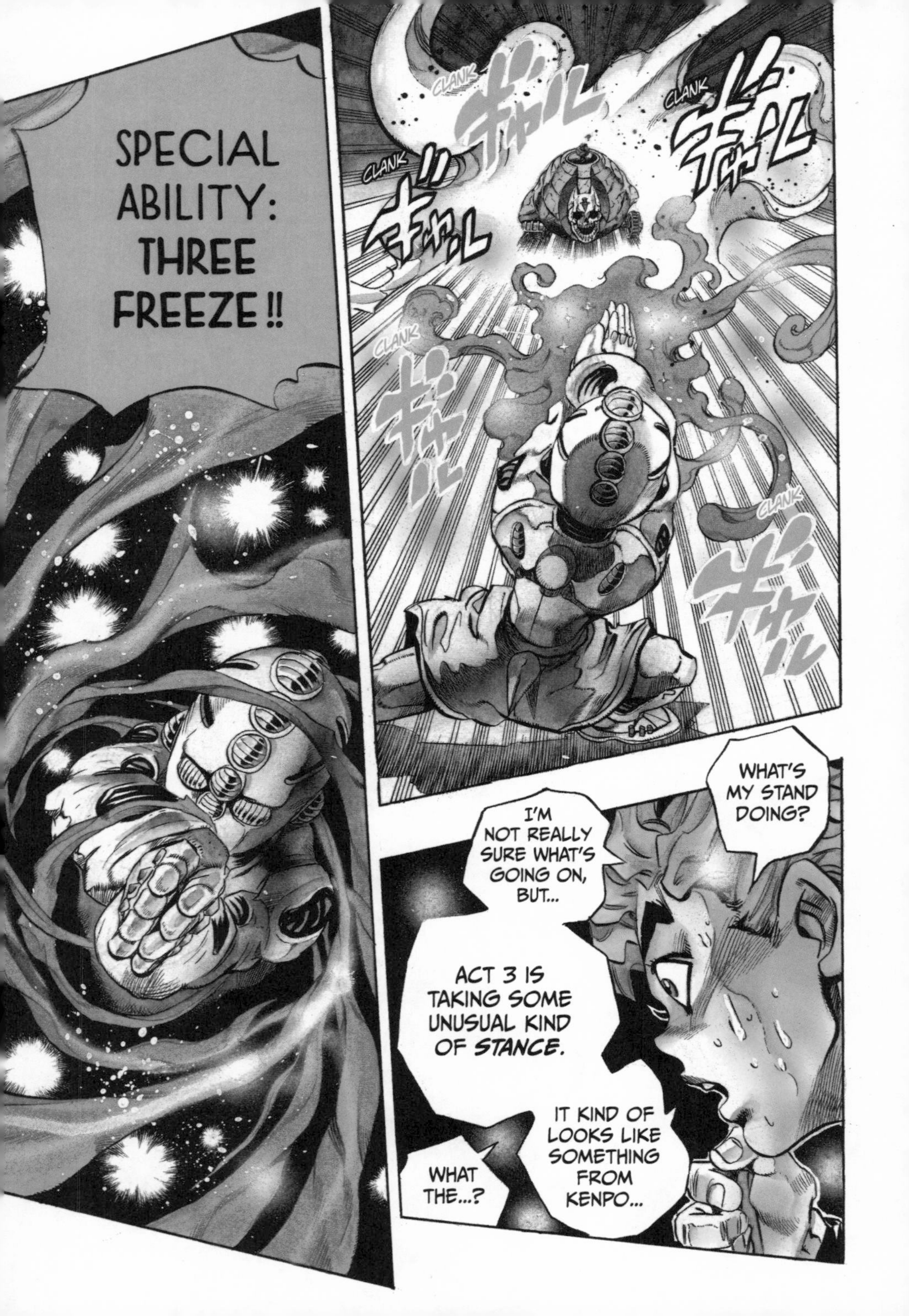
CLANK
CLANK
CLANK
CLANK
CLANK
WHAT'S MY STAND DOING?
I'M NOT REALLY SURE WHAT'S GOING ON, BUT...
ACT 3 IS TAKING SOME UNUSUAL KIND OF STANCE.
IT KIND OF LOOKS LIKE SOMETHING FROM KENPO...
WHAT THE...?
SPECIAL ABILITY: THREE FREEZE!!

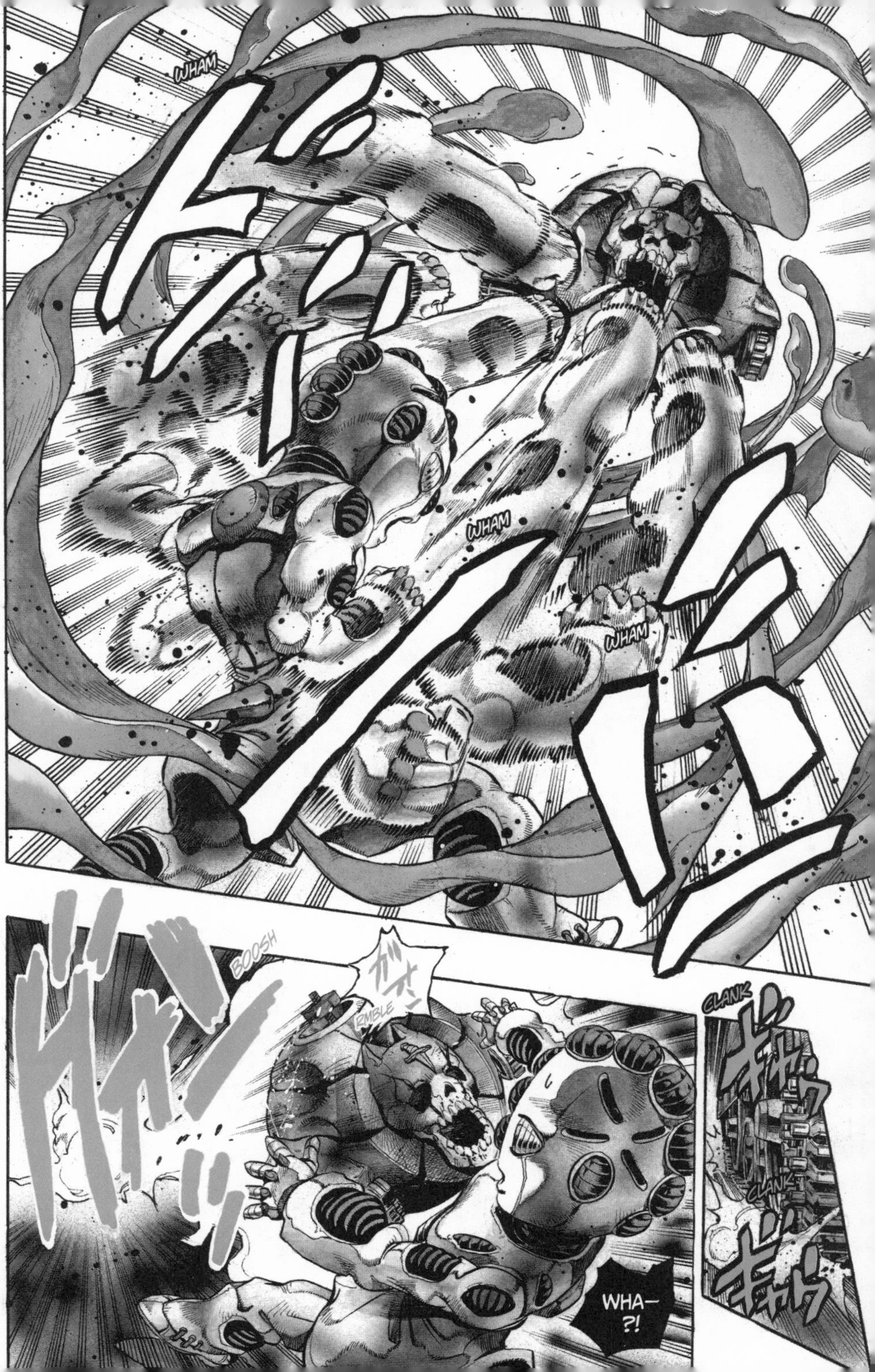
WHAM
WHAM
WHAM
CLANK
CLANK
BOOSH
RMBLE
WHA—?!

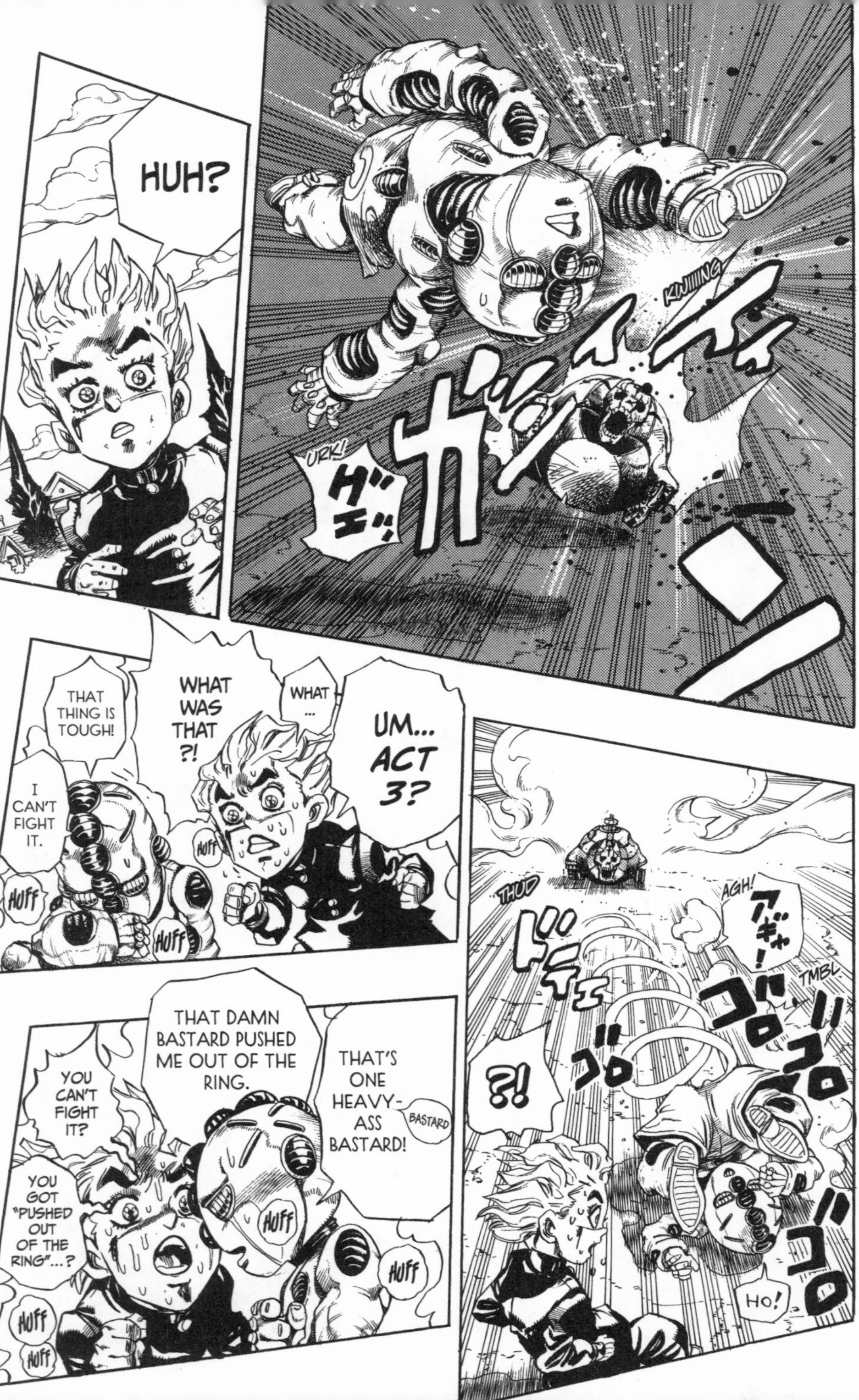
KWIIING
URK!
HUH?
THUD
AGH!
アギャ!
TMBL
?!
HO!
UM... ACT 3?
WHAT ...
WHAT WAS THAT ?!
THAT THING IS TOUGH!
I CAN'T FIGHT IT.
HUFF
HUFF
HUFF
THAT'S ONE HEAVY-ASS BASTARD!
BASTARD
THAT DAMN BASTARD PUSHED ME OUT OF THE RING.
YOU CAN'T FIGHT IT?
YOU GOT "PUSHED OUT OF THE RING"...?
HUFF
HUFF
HUFF
HUFF

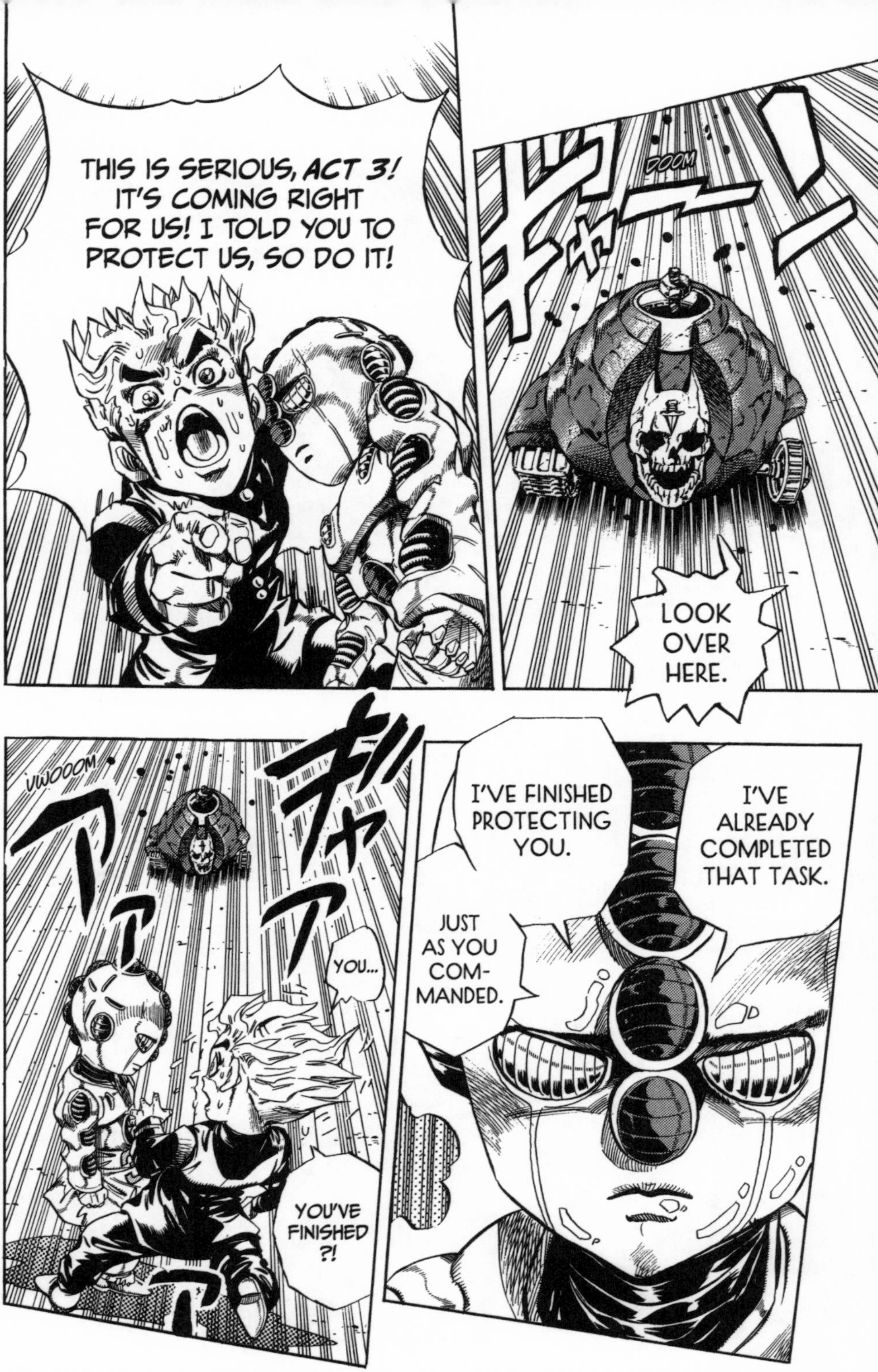
DOOM
LOOK OVER HERE.
THIS IS SERIOUS, ACT 3! IT'S COMING RIGHT FOR US! I TOLD YOU TO PROTECT US, SO DO IT!
I'VE ALREADY COMPLETED THAT TASK.
I'VE FINISHED PROTECTING YOU.
JUST AS YOU COM-MANDED.
VWOOOM
YOU...
YOU'VE FINISHED?!

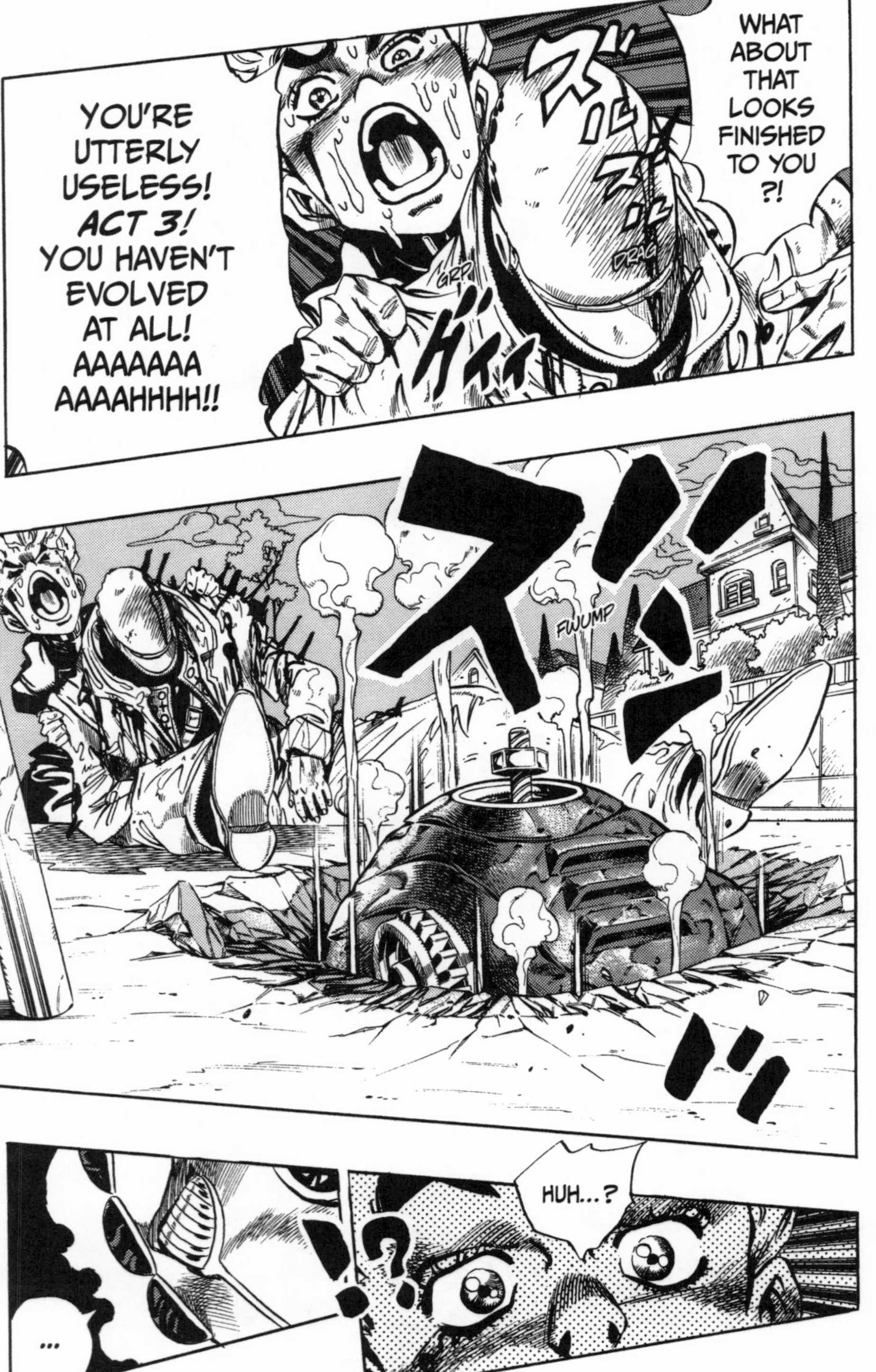
WHAT ABOUT THAT LOOKS FINISHED TO YOU ?!
DRAG
GRP
YOU'RE UTTERLY USELESS! ACT 3! YOU HAVEN'T EVOLVED AT ALL! AAAAAAA AAAAHHHH!!
FWUMP
HUH...?
...

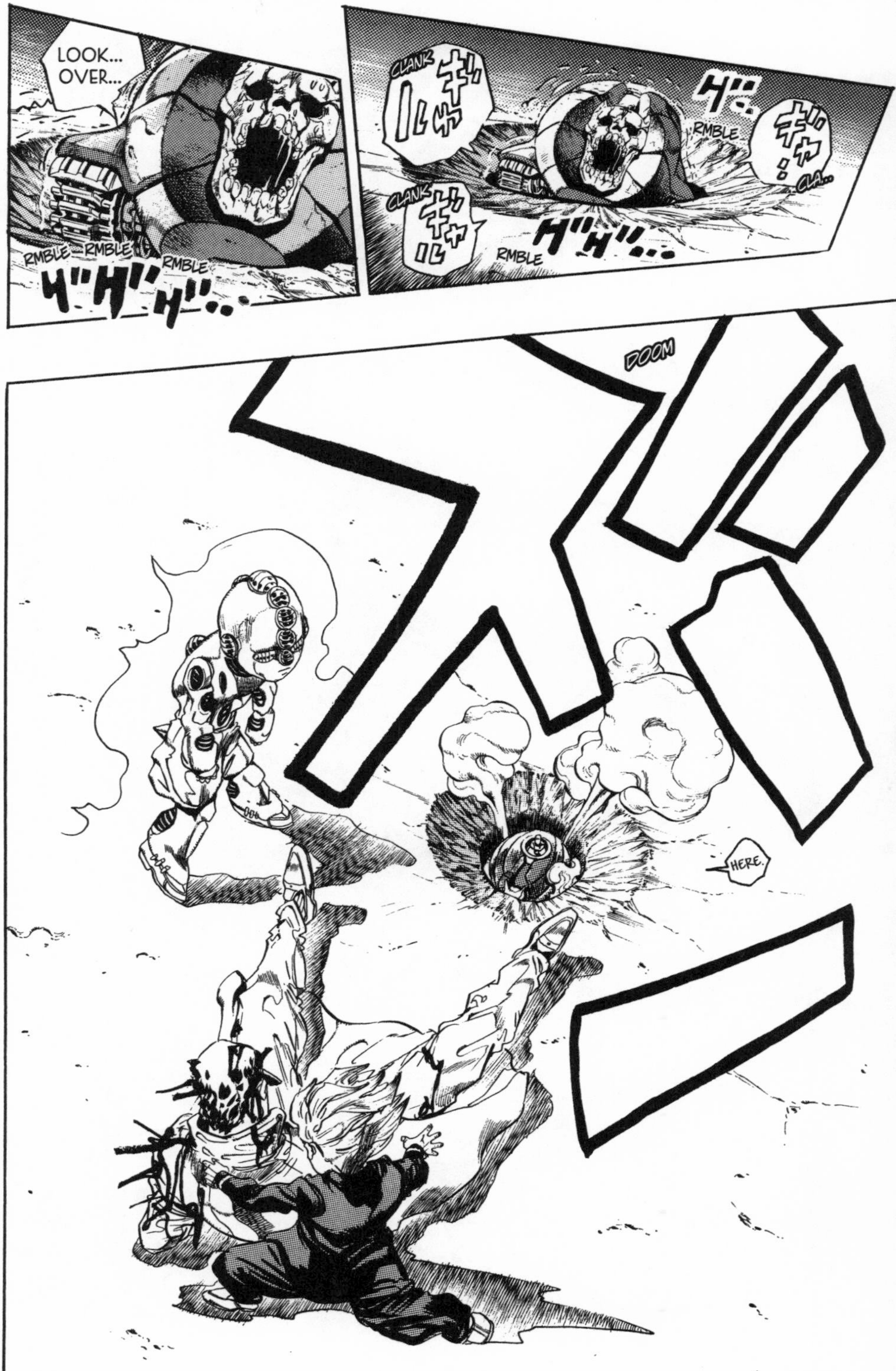
CLANK
RMBLE
CLA...
CLANK
RMBLE
LOOK... OVER...
RMBLE RMBLE
RMBLE
DOOM
HERE.

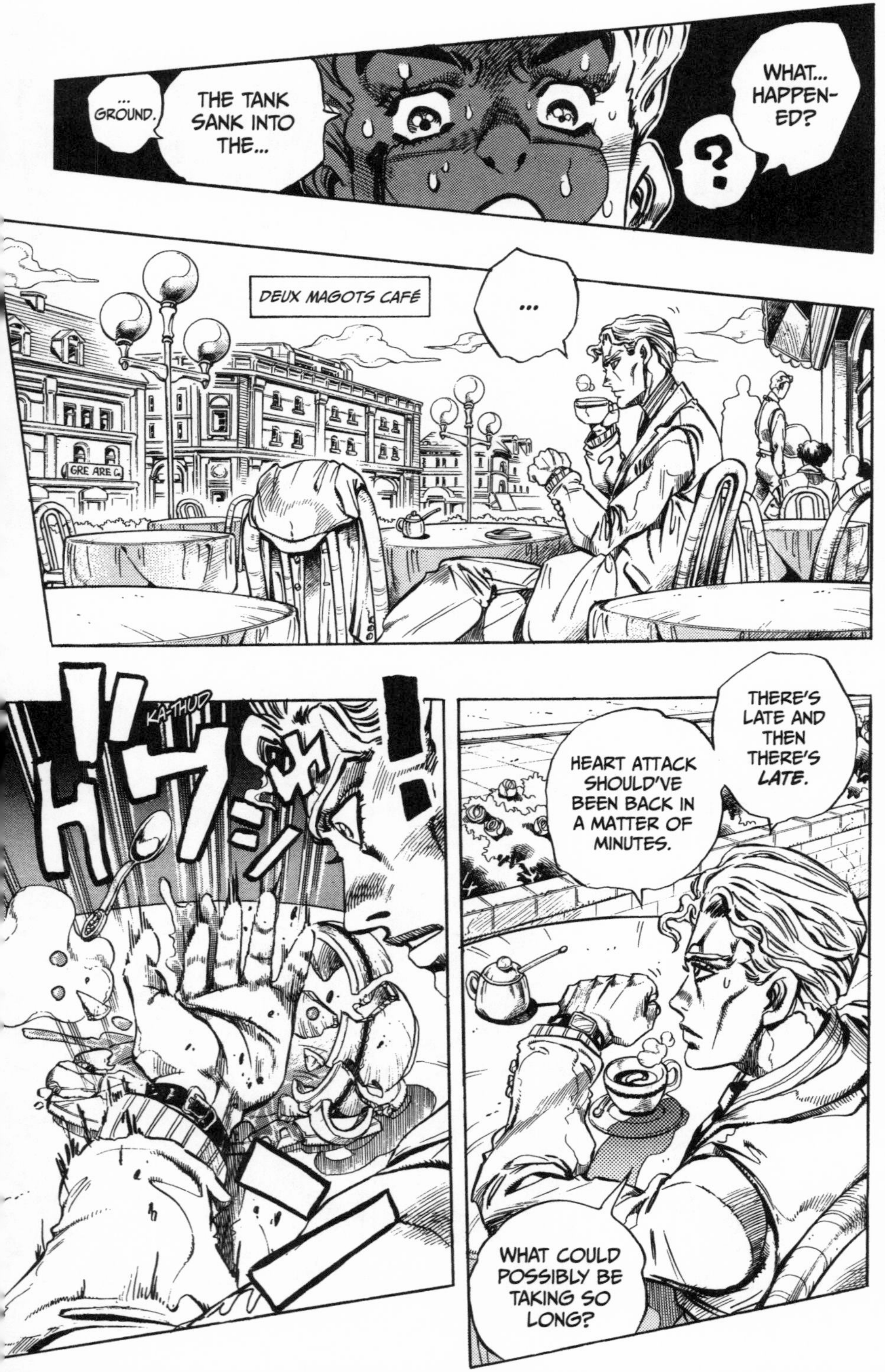
WHAT... HAPPEN-ED?
?
THE TANK SANK INTO THE...
... GROUND.
DEUX MAGOTS CAFÉ
...
THERE'S LATE AND THEN THERE'S *LATE*.
HEART ATTACK SHOULD'VE BEEN BACK IN A MATTER OF MINUTES.
WHAT COULD POSSIBLY BE TAKING SO LONG?
KA-THUD

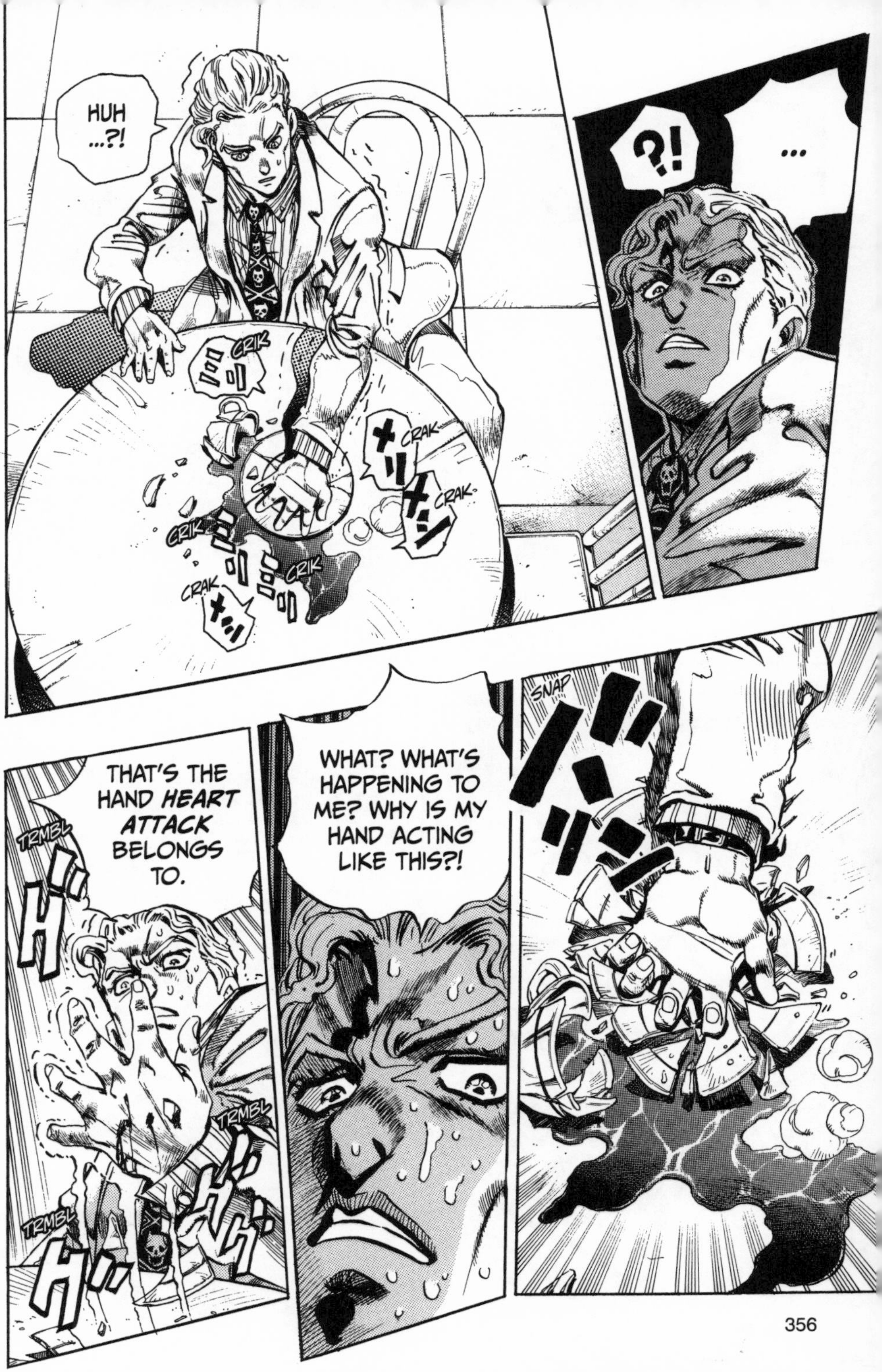
?!
...
HUH ...?!
CRIK
CRAK
CRAK
CRIK
CRIK
CRAK
SNAP
WHAT? WHAT'S HAPPENING TO ME? WHY IS MY HAND ACTING LIKE THIS?!
THAT'S THE HAND HEART ATTACK BELONGS TO.
TRMBL
TRMBL
TRMBL

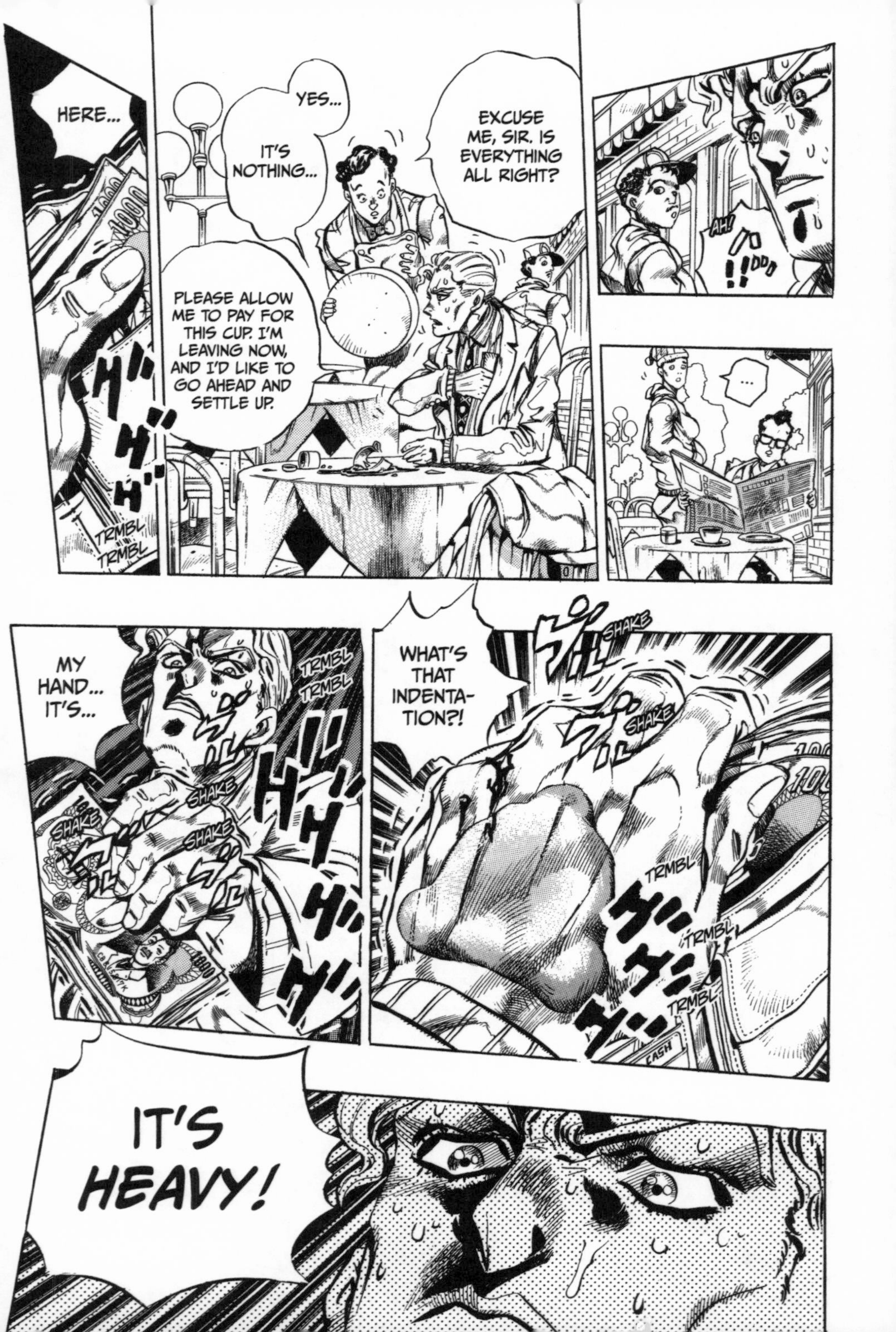
AH!
...
EXCUSE ME, SIR. IS EVERYTHING ALL RIGHT?
YES... IT'S NOTHING...
PLEASE ALLOW ME TO PAY FOR THIS CUP. I'M LEAVING NOW, AND I'D LIKE TO GO AHEAD AND SETTLE UP.
HERE...
TRMBL TRMBL
WHAT'S THAT INDENTATION?!
SHAKE
SHAKE
TRMBL
TRMBL
TRMBL
CASH
MY HAND... IT'S...
TRMBL TRMBL
SHAKE
SHAKE
SHAKE
IT'S HEAVY!

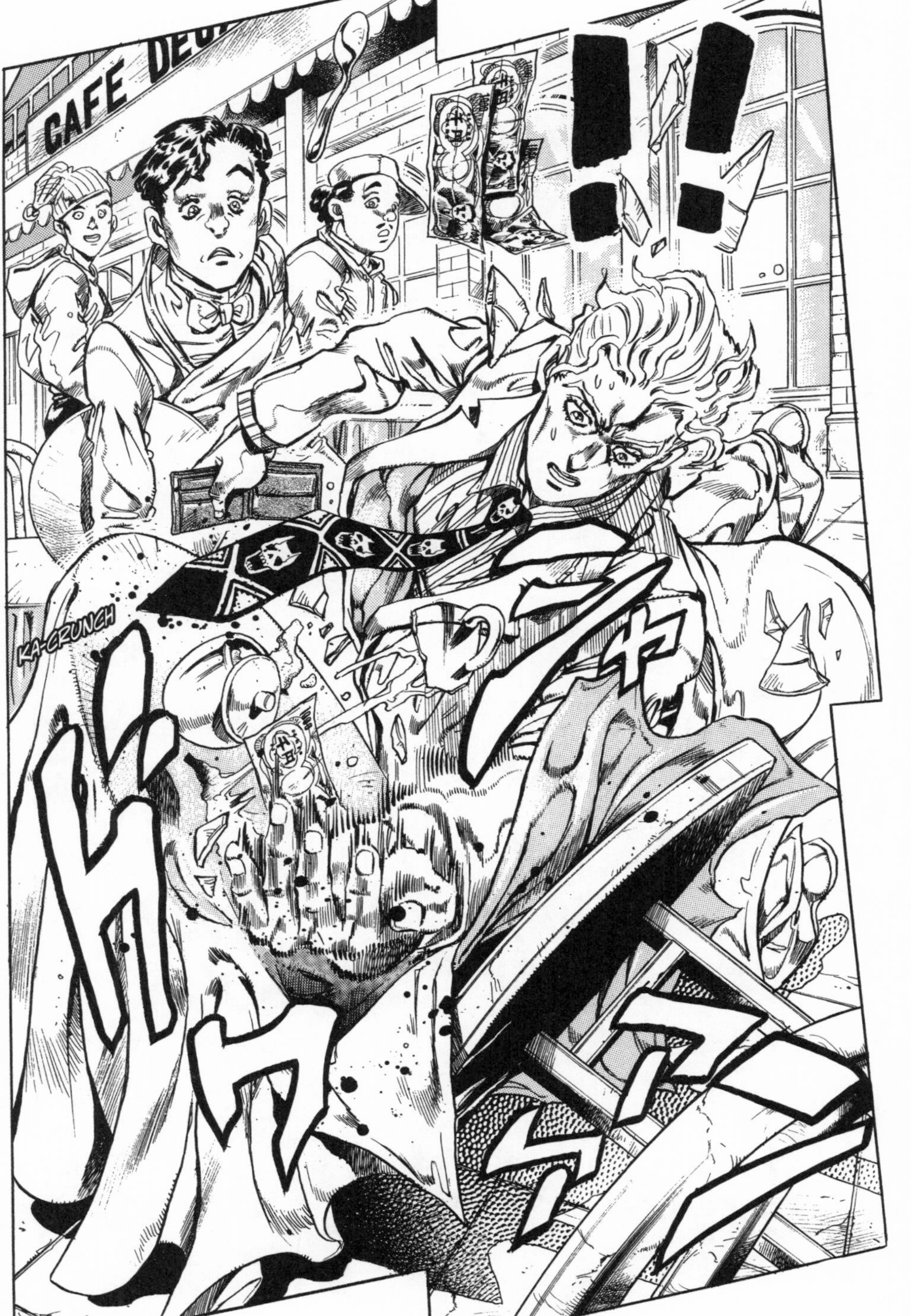
!!
KA-CRUNCH

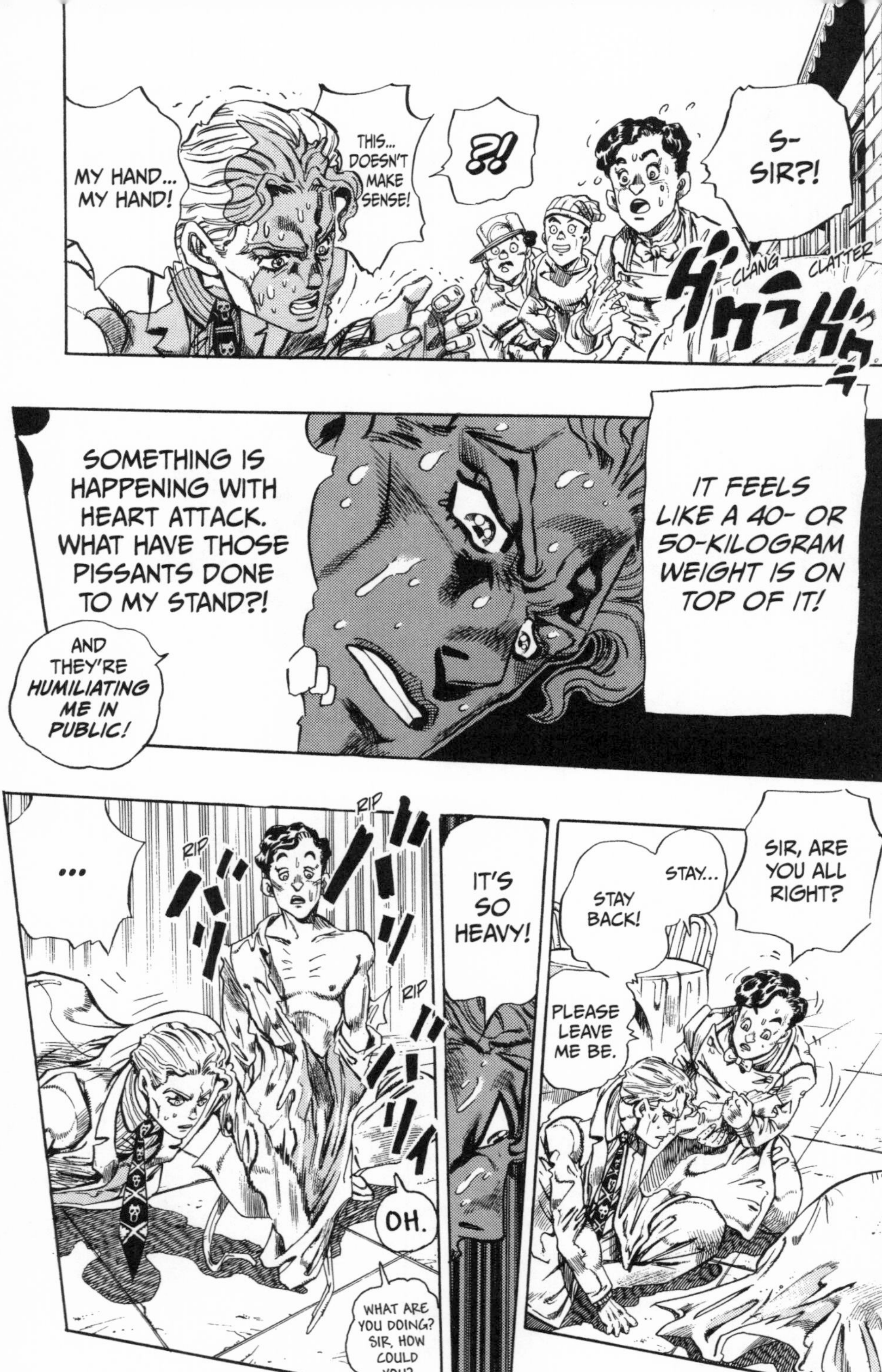
S- SIR?!
CLANG
CLATTER
?!
THIS... DOESN'T MAKE SENSE!
MY HAND... MY HAND!
IT FEELS LIKE A 40- OR 50-KILOGRAM WEIGHT IS ON TOP OF IT!
SOMETHING IS HAPPENING WITH HEART ATTACK. WHAT HAVE THOSE PISSANTS DONE TO MY STAND?!
AND THEY'RE *HUMILIATING* ME IN PUBLIC!
SIR, ARE YOU ALL RIGHT?
STAY...
STAY BACK!
PLEASE LEAVE ME BE.
IT'S SO HEAVY!
RIP
RIP
...
RIP
OH.
WHAT ARE YOU DOING? SIR, HOW COULD YOU?

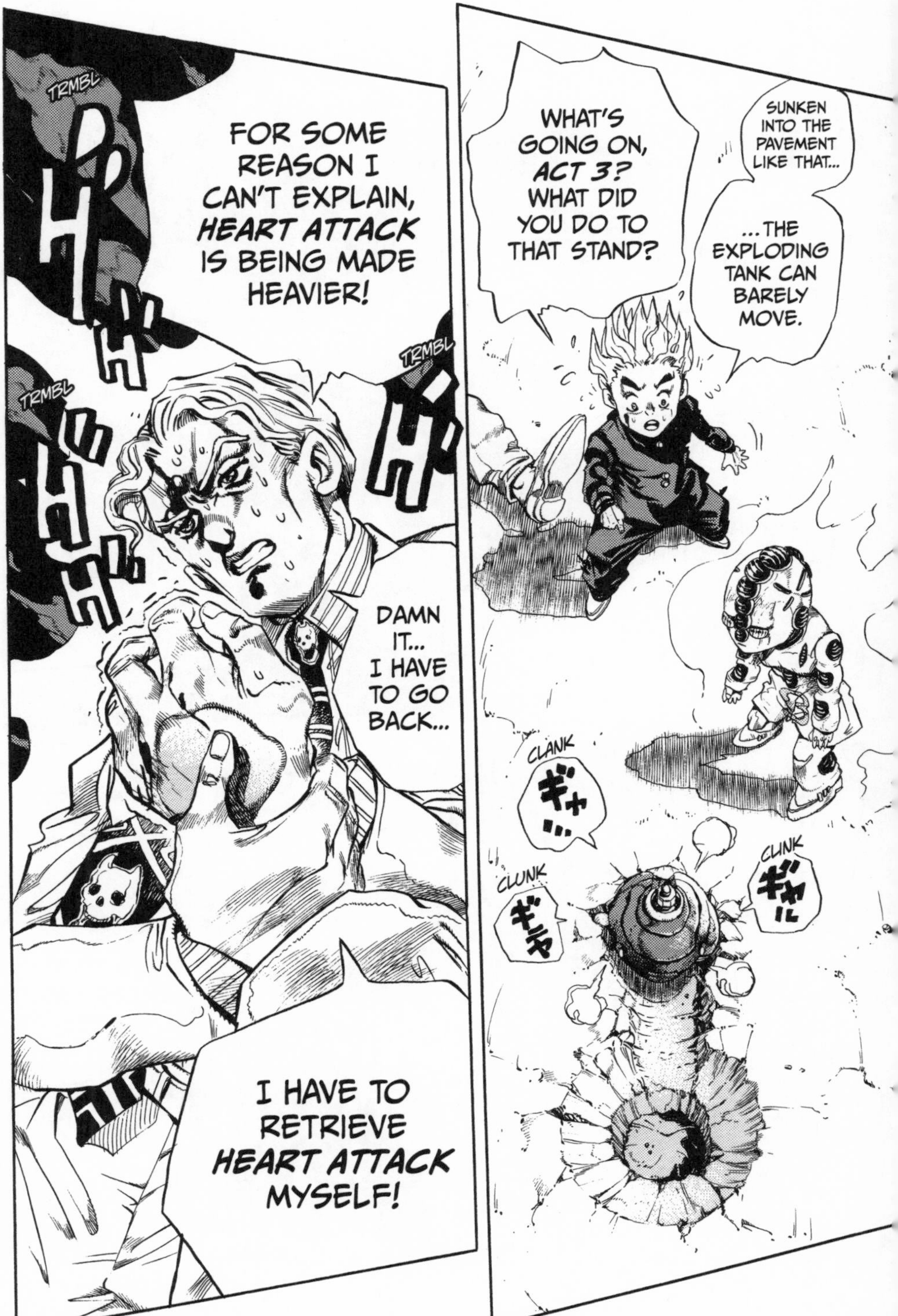
SUNKEN INTO THE PAVEMENT LIKE THAT...
...THE EXPLODING TANK CAN BARELY MOVE.
WHAT'S GOING ON, *ACT 3?* WHAT DID YOU DO TO THAT STAND?
CLANK
CLINK
CLUNK
TRMBL
TRMBL
TRMBL
FOR SOME REASON I CAN'T EXPLAIN, *HEART ATTACK* IS BEING MADE HEAVIER!
DAMN IT... I HAVE TO GO BACK...
I HAVE TO RETRIEVE *HEART ATTACK* MYSELF!

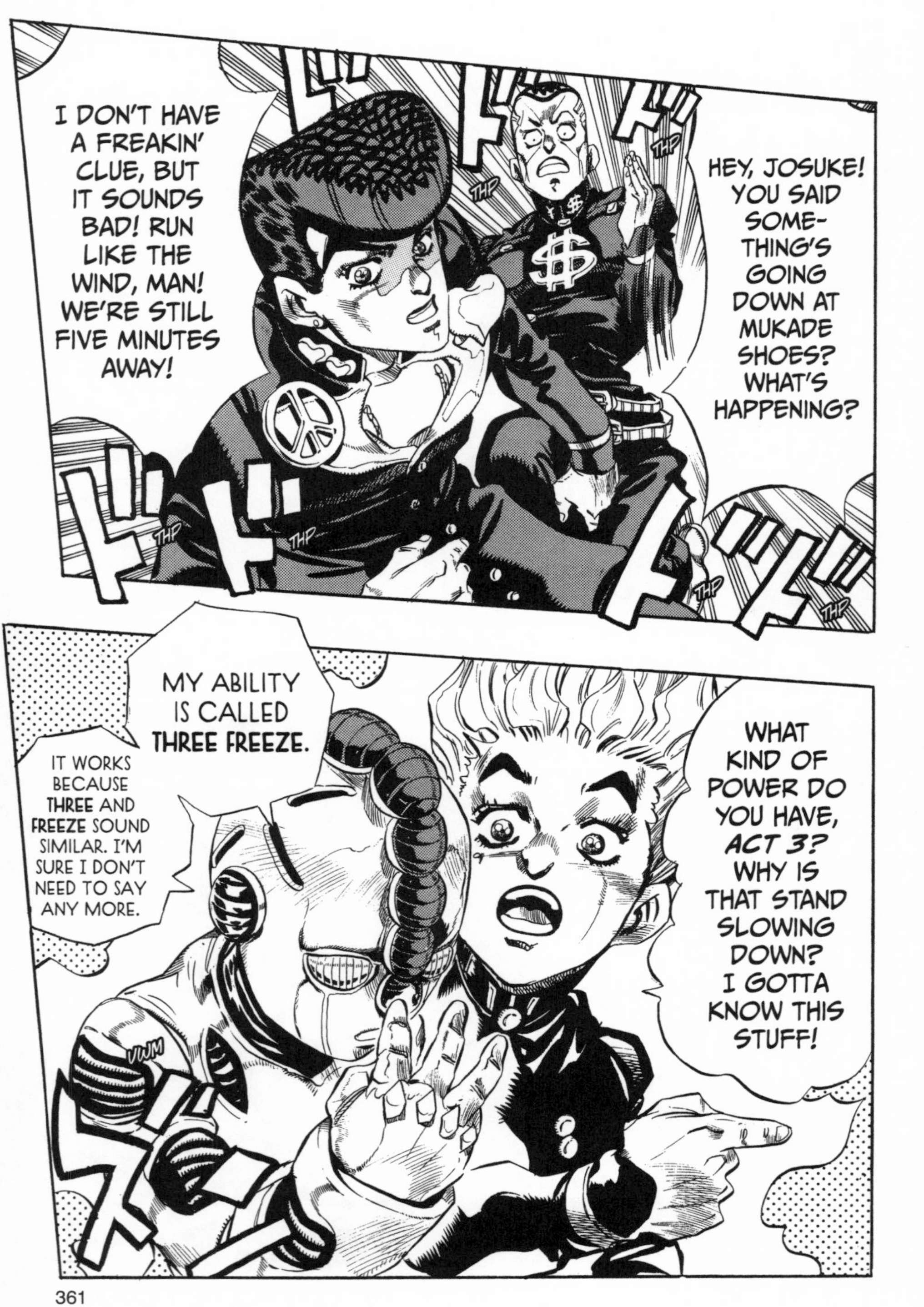
HEY, JOSUKE! YOU SAID SOME-THING'S GOING DOWN AT MUKADE SHOES? WHAT'S HAPPENING?
THP
THP
THP
I DON'T HAVE A FREAKIN' CLUE, BUT IT SOUNDS BAD! RUN LIKE THE WIND, MAN! WE'RE STILL FIVE MINUTES AWAY!
THP
THP
THP
THP
WHAT KIND OF POWER DO YOU HAVE, *ACT 3?* WHY IS THAT STAND SLOWING DOWN? I GOTTA KNOW THIS STUFF!
MY ABILITY IS CALLED **THREE FREEZE.**
IT WORKS BECAUSE **THREE** AND **FREEZE** SOUND SIMILAR. I'M SURE I DON'T NEED TO SAY ANY MORE.
VWM

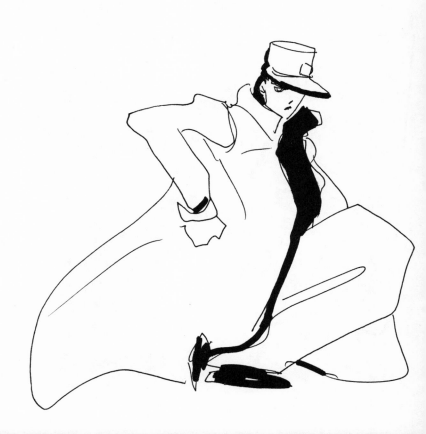

AUTHOR'S COMMENTS

There is a mystery in my life. Every night, at precisely 9 and 11 p.m., the occupant of the unit beneath my studio opens the window to their balcony and hits the outside wall twice with some kind of wooden object. *WHACK! WHACK!* They do this always two times (never three). And then *SLAM!* the window slides shut. What is that sound that echoes through the night sky? What could they possibly be doing? And I mean every night.

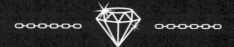

There is another mystery in my life. I know this woman who has a boyfriend who, without fail, leaves their dates at 6 p.m. to go home. What is so important and so urgent that he needs to be home that early?

He's 27, and she'll ask him, "Don't you like me?" And he'll say, "Yeah, I like you." And she'll say, "Don't you think this is too early to go home?" and he goes quiet.

Well, why does he go home? Is he watching anime?

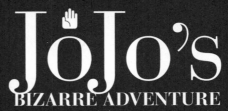

JoJo's
BIZARRE ADVENTURE

PART 4: DIAMOND IS UNBREAKABLE
VOLUME 5
BY HIROHIKO ARAKI

DELUXE HARDCOVER EDITION
Translation: Nathan A Collins
Touch-Up Art & Lettering: Mark McMurray
Design: Adam Grano
Editor: David Brothers

Printed in the U.S.A.

Published by VIZ Media, LLC
P.O. Box 77010
San Francisco, CA 94107

10 9 8 7 6 5 4 3 2 1
First printing, May 2020

VIZ MEDIA
viz.com

SHONEN JUMP
shonenjump.com

THIS IS THE LAST PAGE

JoJo's BIZARRE ADVENTURE

has been printed in the original Japanese format in order to preserve the orientation of the original artwork.

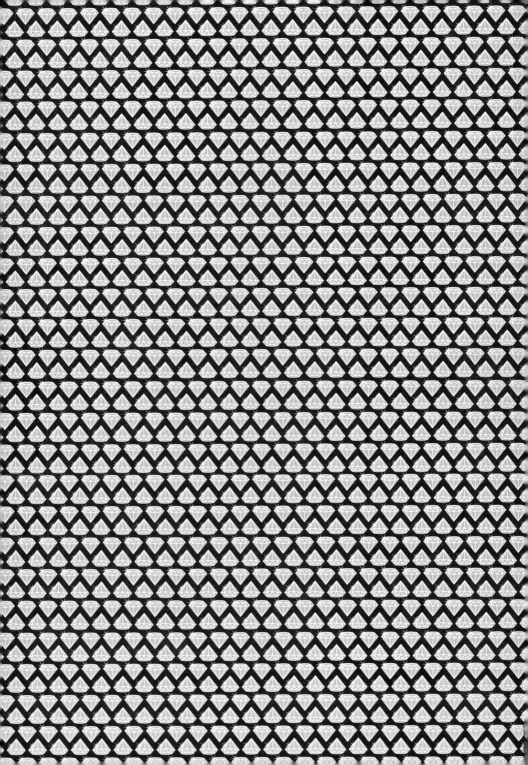

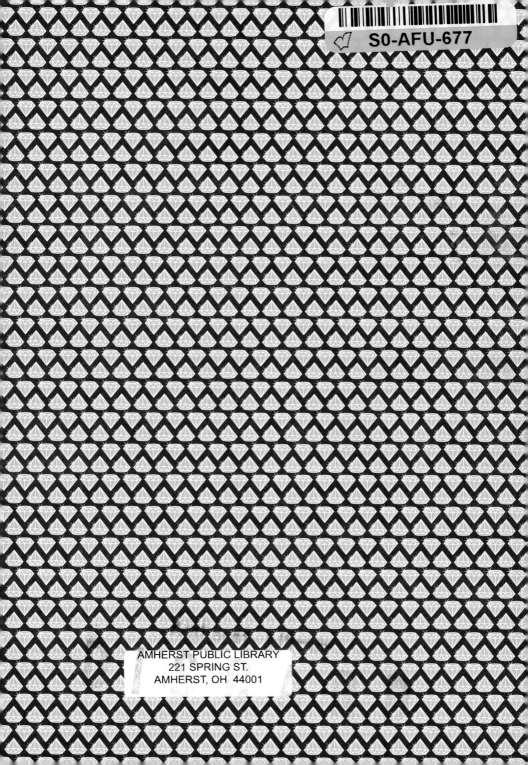